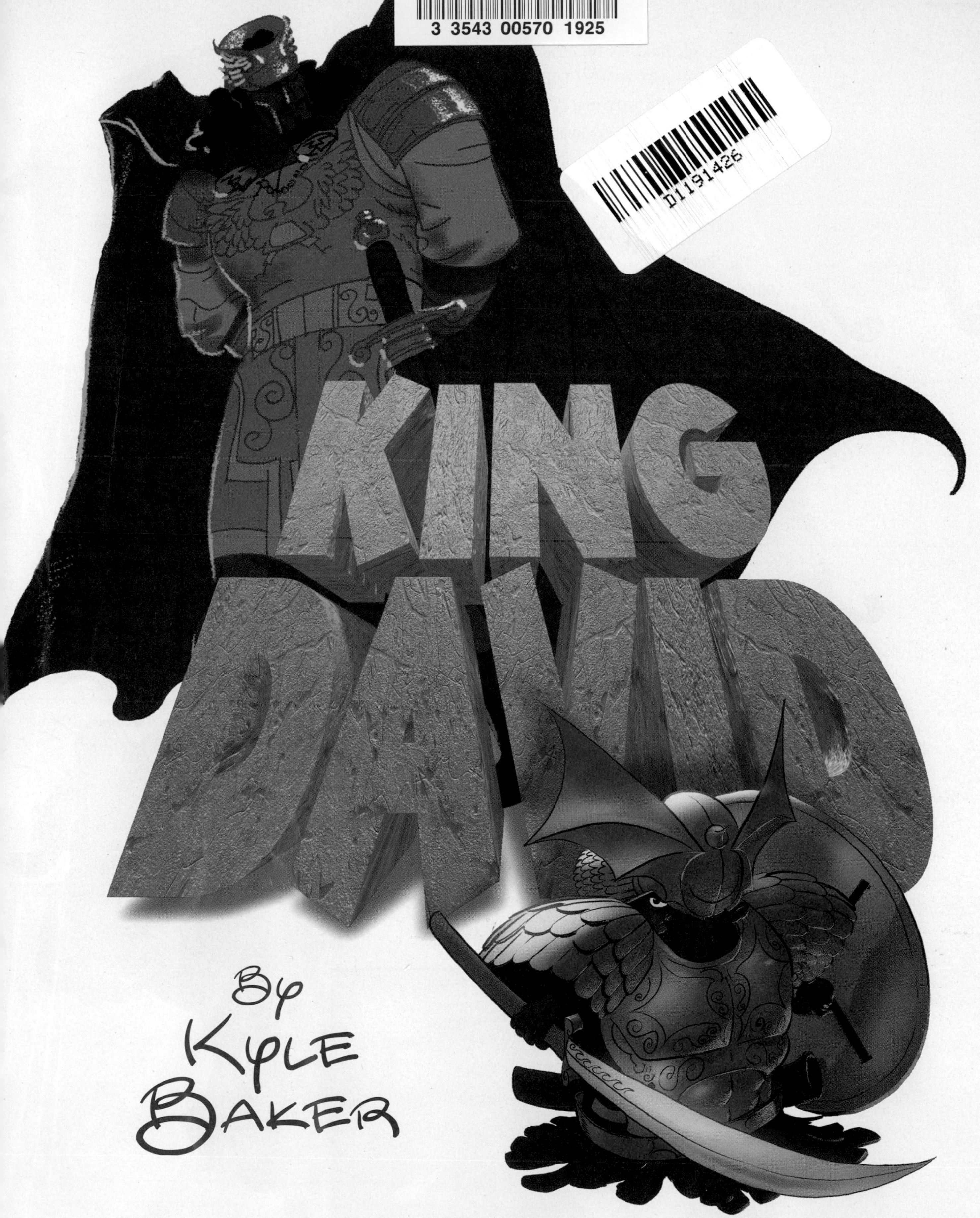

KING DAVID

By
Kyle
Baker

VERTIGO · DC COMICS
NEW YORK, NEW YORK

Kyle Baker is the creator of WHY I HATE SATURN,
YOU ARE HERE, I DIE AT MIDNIGHT,
THE COWBOY WALLY SHOW and
the book you are about to read.

Kyle would like to thank God, his family and
his ancestors, also Zach Baker, Michelley
Cartaya, Carrie Fink, and Brian Rubio.

This book is dedicated to the memory of
Kyle's grandma, Mildred Carter Smith.

DC COMICS

KING DAVID. Published by DC Comics, 1700 Broadway,
New York, NY 10019. Copyright © 2002 Kyle Baker.
All Rights Reserved. All characters featured
in this issue, distinctive likenesses thereof,
and all related indicia are trademarks of Kyle Baker.
VERTIGO is a trademark of DC Comics.
DC Comics does not read or accept unsolicited
submissions of ideas, stories or artwork.
Printed in Canada.
DC Comics. A division of Warner Bros.–An
AOL Time Warner Company

Cover by Kyle Baker

"He's here! The harpist is here!" Shouts a man in armor.

The boy David imagines it must be very hot in one of those helmets.

"We'll take your things. Come! Hurry!" urges another.

"Those are not mine, my father sent them for King Saul," says David. His voice is hoarse, throat dry from hours under the blazing sun on donkeyback.

"Yeah, yeah, quickly. The king needs you now!" retorts the first man.

"Please," says David, "My mother says I must never visit anyone empty-handed."

Saul's attendant speaks. "See? Didn't I tell you? David's a good boy!"

"Somebody bring the donkey."

"Taken care of. We're right behind you. Come on, boy! Faster!"

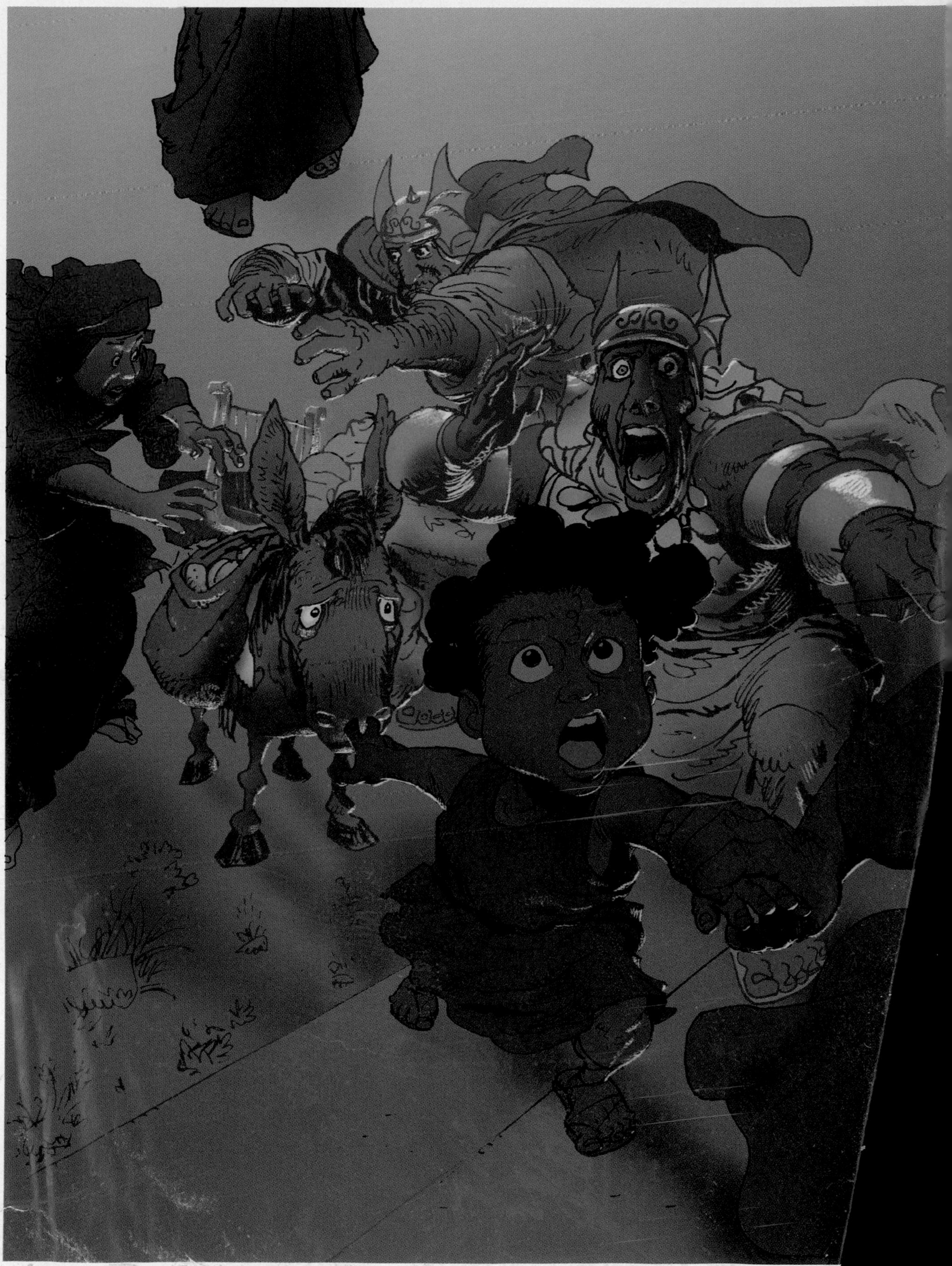

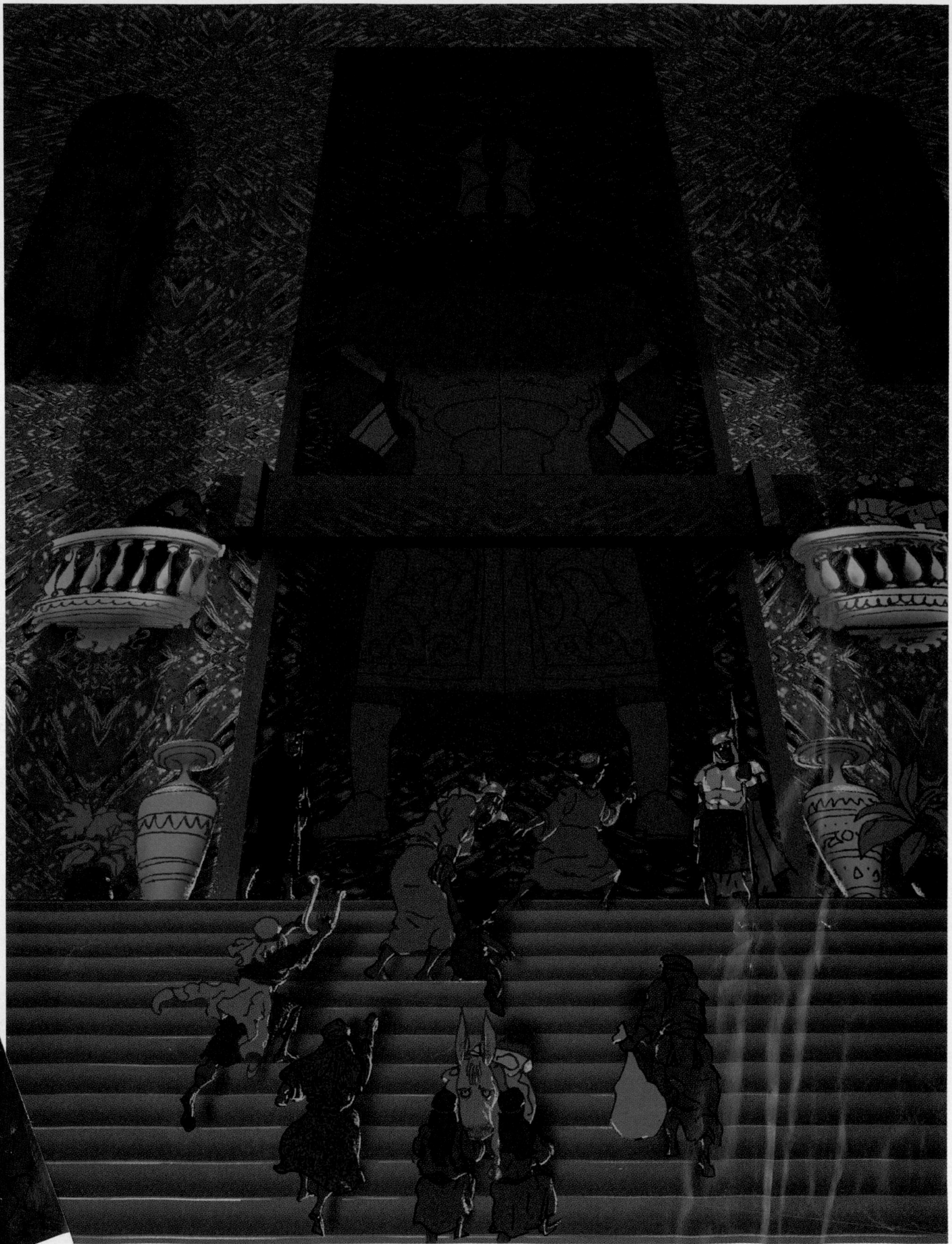

e rush?" asks David. "Your messengers told me only that they needed a harpist. Am I late for a ceremony or--?"

lling screams are heard even through the massive door.

" protests the guard.

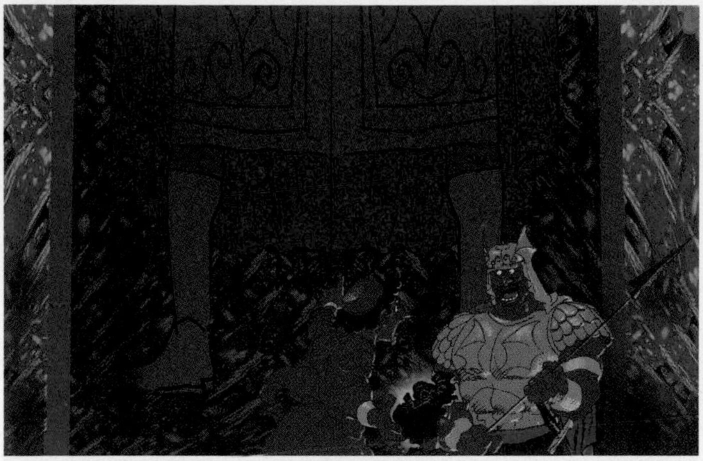

"No wonder they made you a guard. You don't miss a thing," says the attendant. "Get that door open, fast."

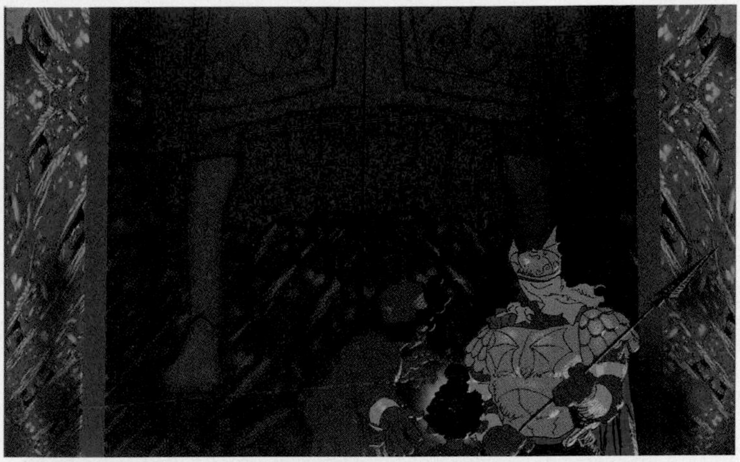

The horrible screams in the next chamber are punctuated with violent crashing sounds, as if heavy furniture and pottery were being smashed. The door vibrates with each blow, straining against the hinges. The bolt bends and splinters, threatening to give way.

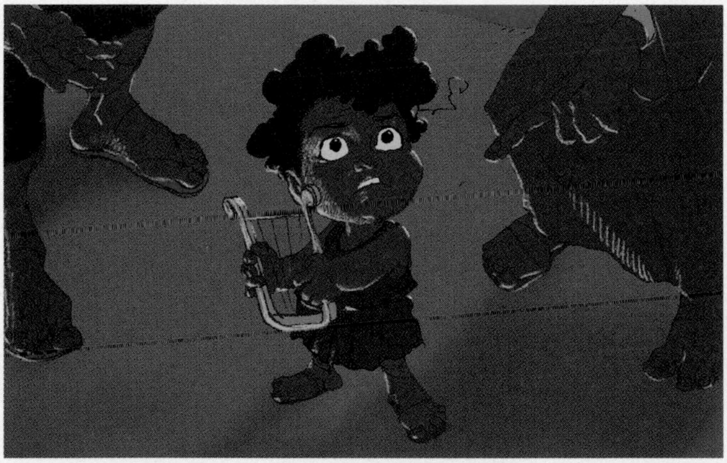

"We can't send a kid in there!" says the guard, "I wouldn't even go in there myself!

"It'll be okay soon as he plays the harp! Open the door!"

"How's the kid gonna play harp with his arms torn off?" asks the guard. "Remember the Kenite?"

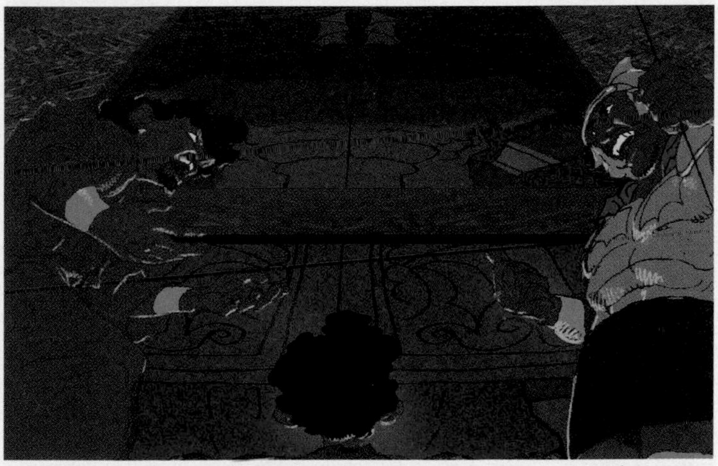

"The Kenite was a lousy harp player! I almost killed him myself! I'm telling you, this kid's great! He played my cousin Rose's wedding. Open that door!"

"What are you, his agent?"

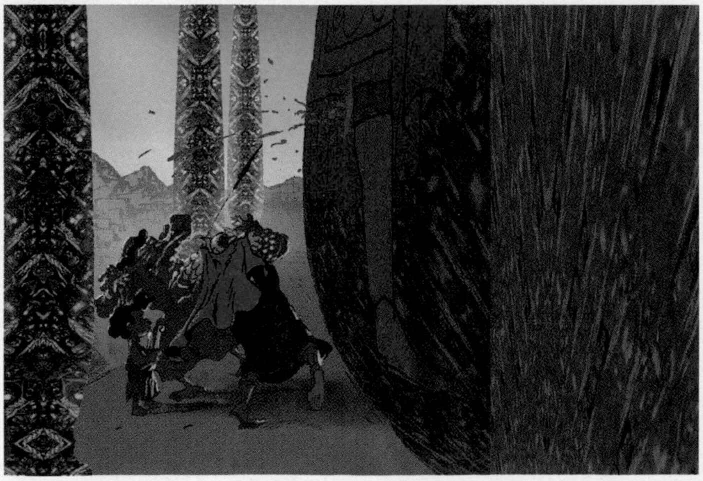

"When you say 'killed'..." asks David, "that is figurative, correct?"

Something splinters loudly against the door, as hot red blood shoots through the crack in the weakening boards. A demonic laugh quickly transforms into a wolflike howl.

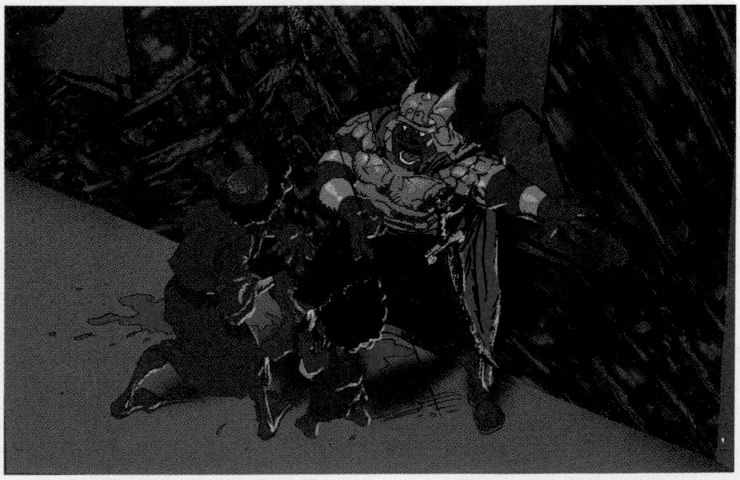

"That's literal, kid!" snaps the guard, "The king'll bite your face off! You really wanna bring that cute face of yours home in a sack?"

"There goes the last eunuch," says the attendant, observing the growing puddle of blood at his feet.

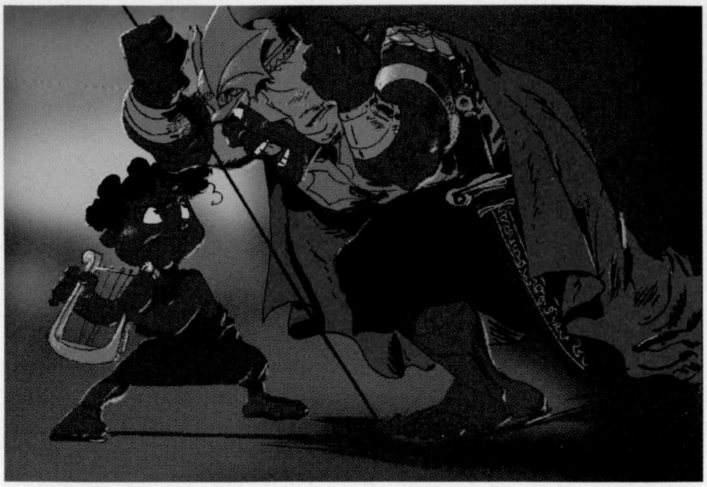

"You're telling me that King Saul is on the other side of that door?"

"Yes, and we got guys on this side with no faces to prove it!"

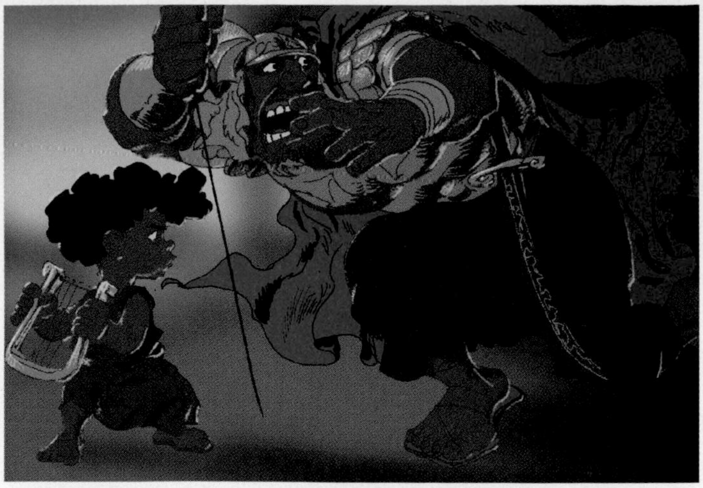

Heavy furniture splinters against the other side of the door. Something roughly the weight of an elephant from the sound of it.

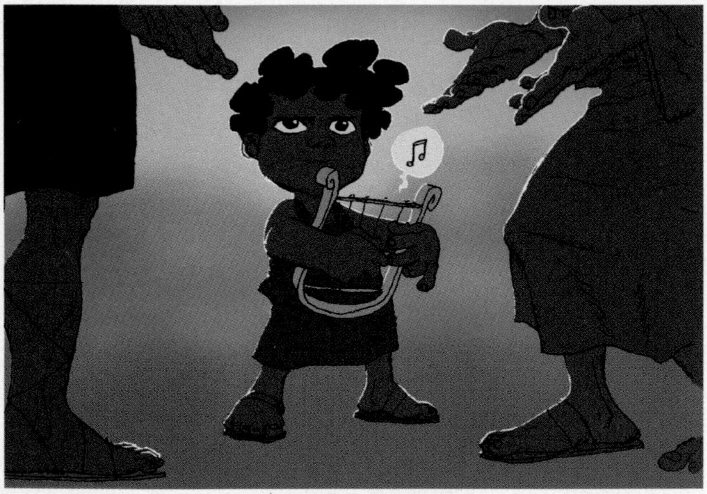

"I thought this was a crummy idea when you first came up with it. And it's still crummy!" says the guard.

"The king agreed to it."

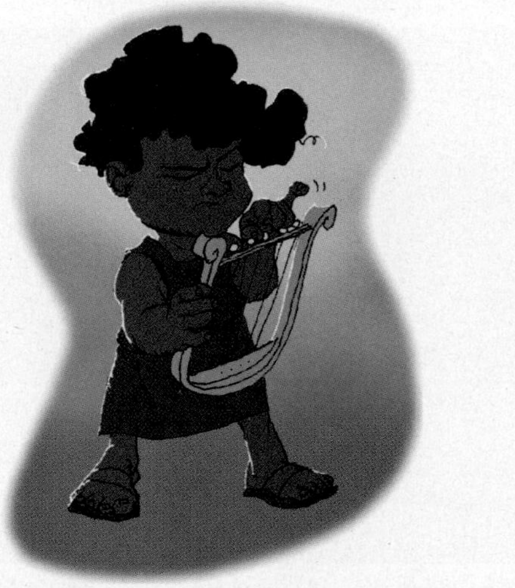

The guard screams, "Well, I guess if the gibbering psychopath who's demolishing the throne room says it's a good idea, then it's okay!"

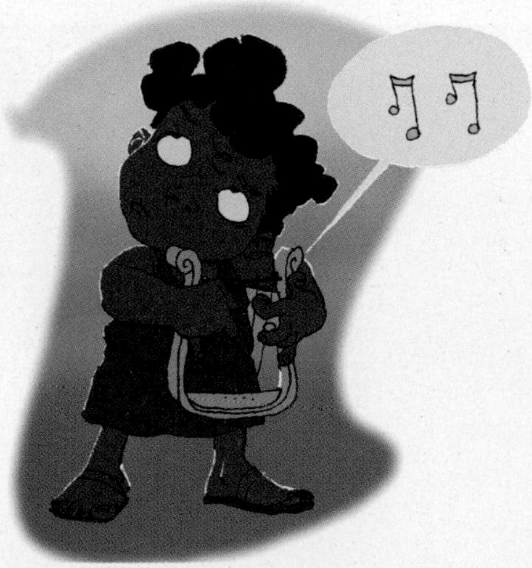

"Listen, genius," the guard continues, "the king's not just a little melancholy, he's not having a 'bad day,' he's being tormented by an evil spirit! And you want to send in a kid with a harp. That's like trying to cure a beheading with chicken soup!"

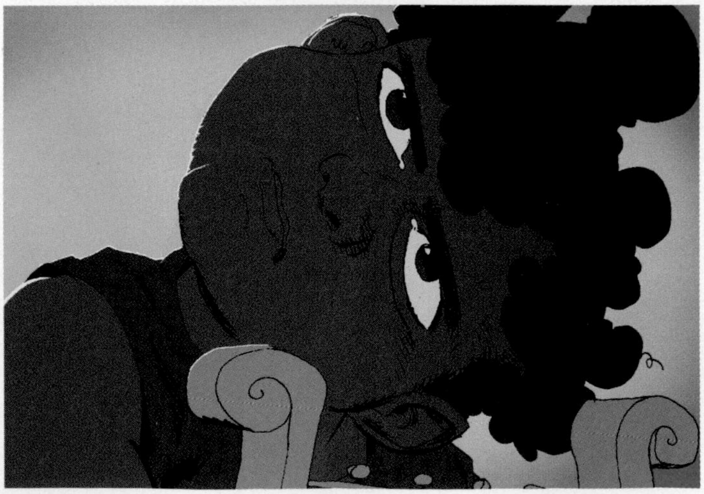

"You want to see a tough audience, try my cousin's wedding!" insists the attendant. "Bride six months' pregnant, looking like eight months, a seventeen-year-old groom with no job. Compared to that crowd, king face-eater's a day in spring! Let me tell you about David--"

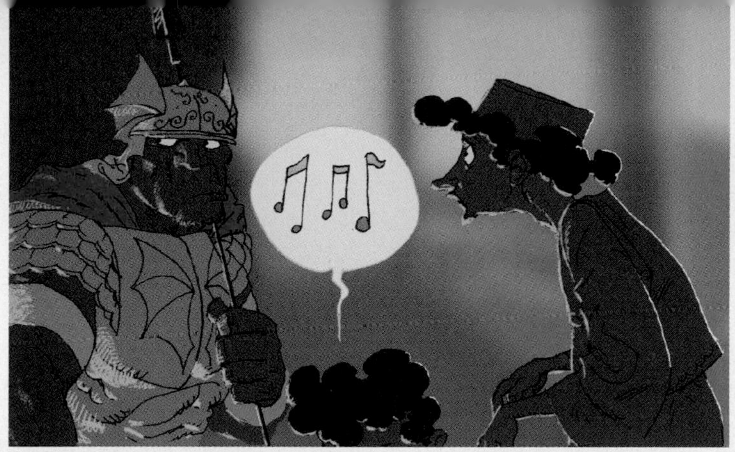

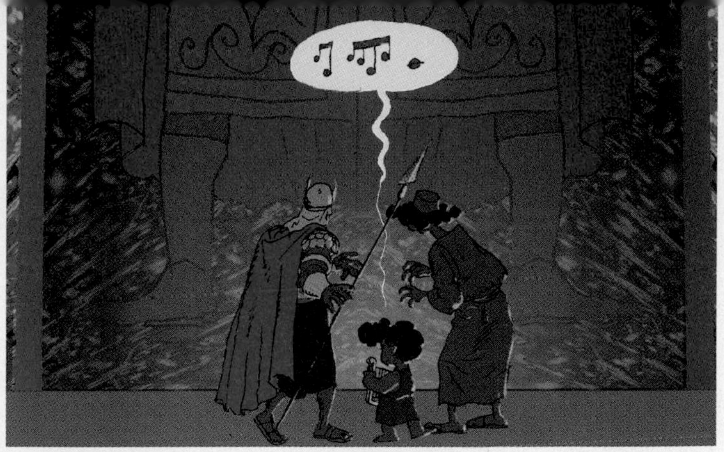

They notice the quiet behind the door.

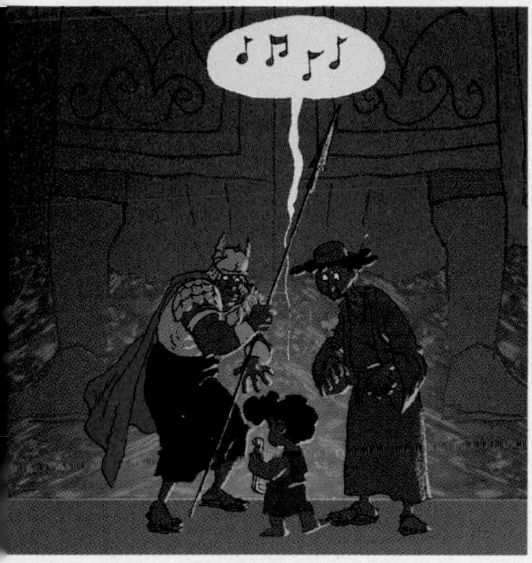

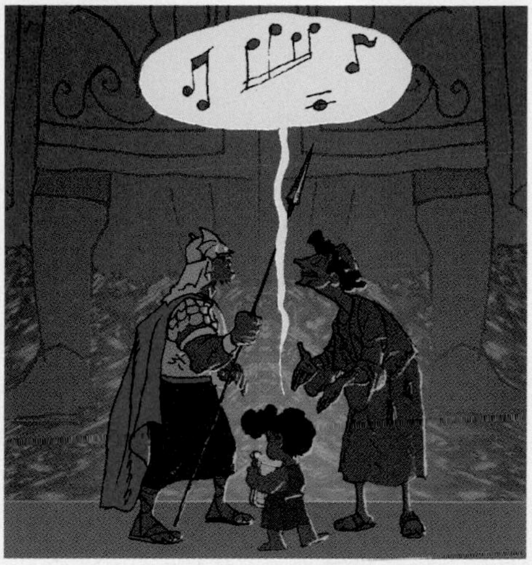

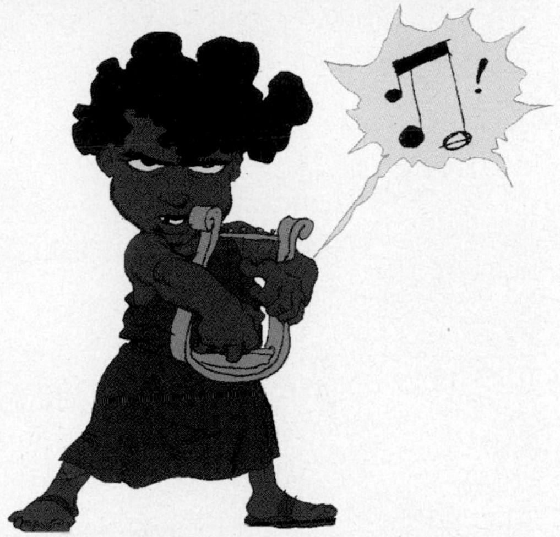

"See? The harp works!"

"You don't think the king heard that 'gibbering psychopath' crack, do you?" asks the guard.

"Please open the door," says David.

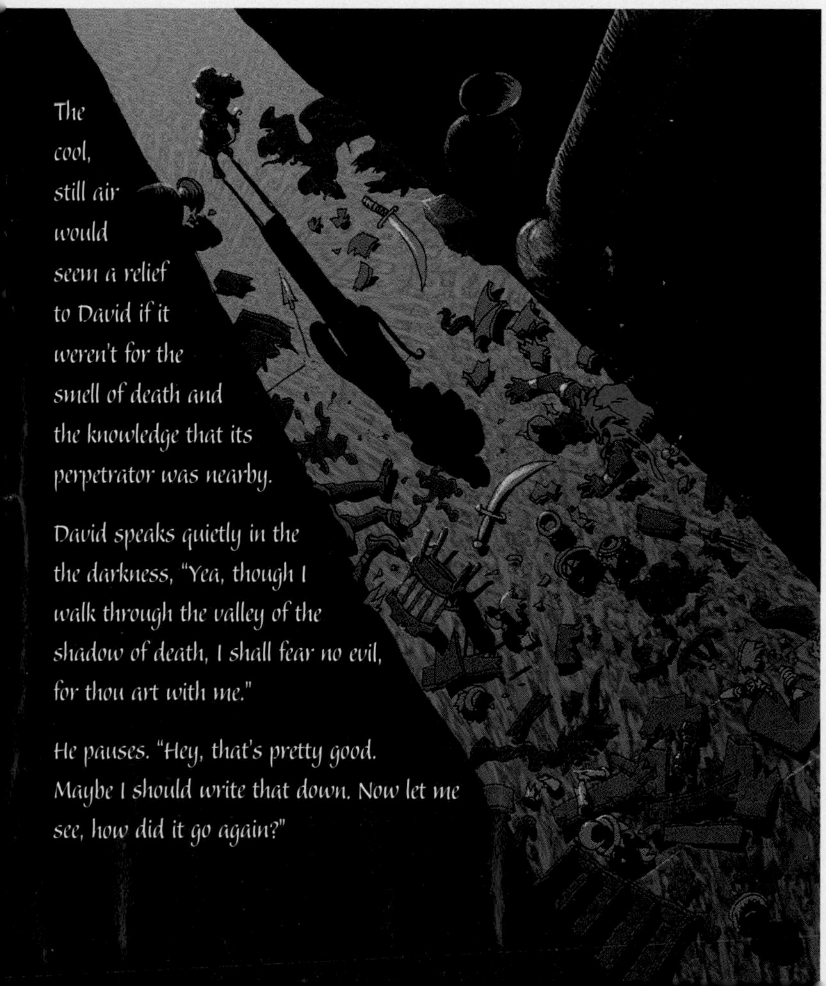

The cool, still air would seem a relief to David if it weren't for the smell of death and the knowledge that its perpetrator was nearby.

David speaks quietly in the the darkness, "Yea, though I walk through the valley of the shadow of death, I shall fear no evil, for thou art with me."

He pauses. "Hey, that's pretty good. Maybe I should write that down. Now let me see, how did it go again?"

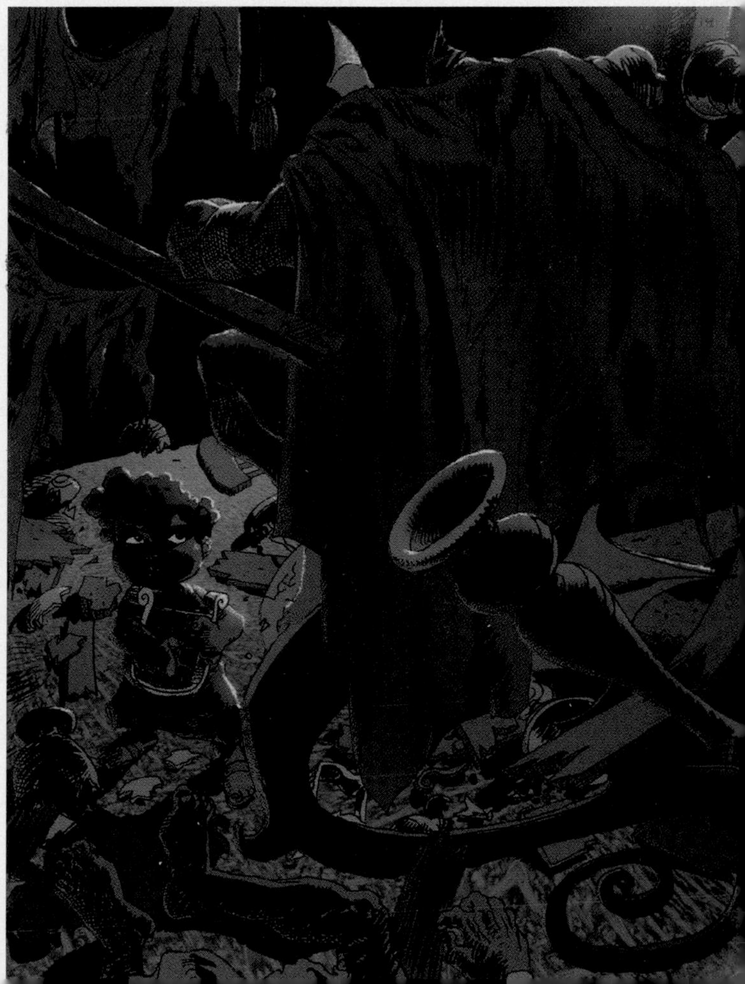

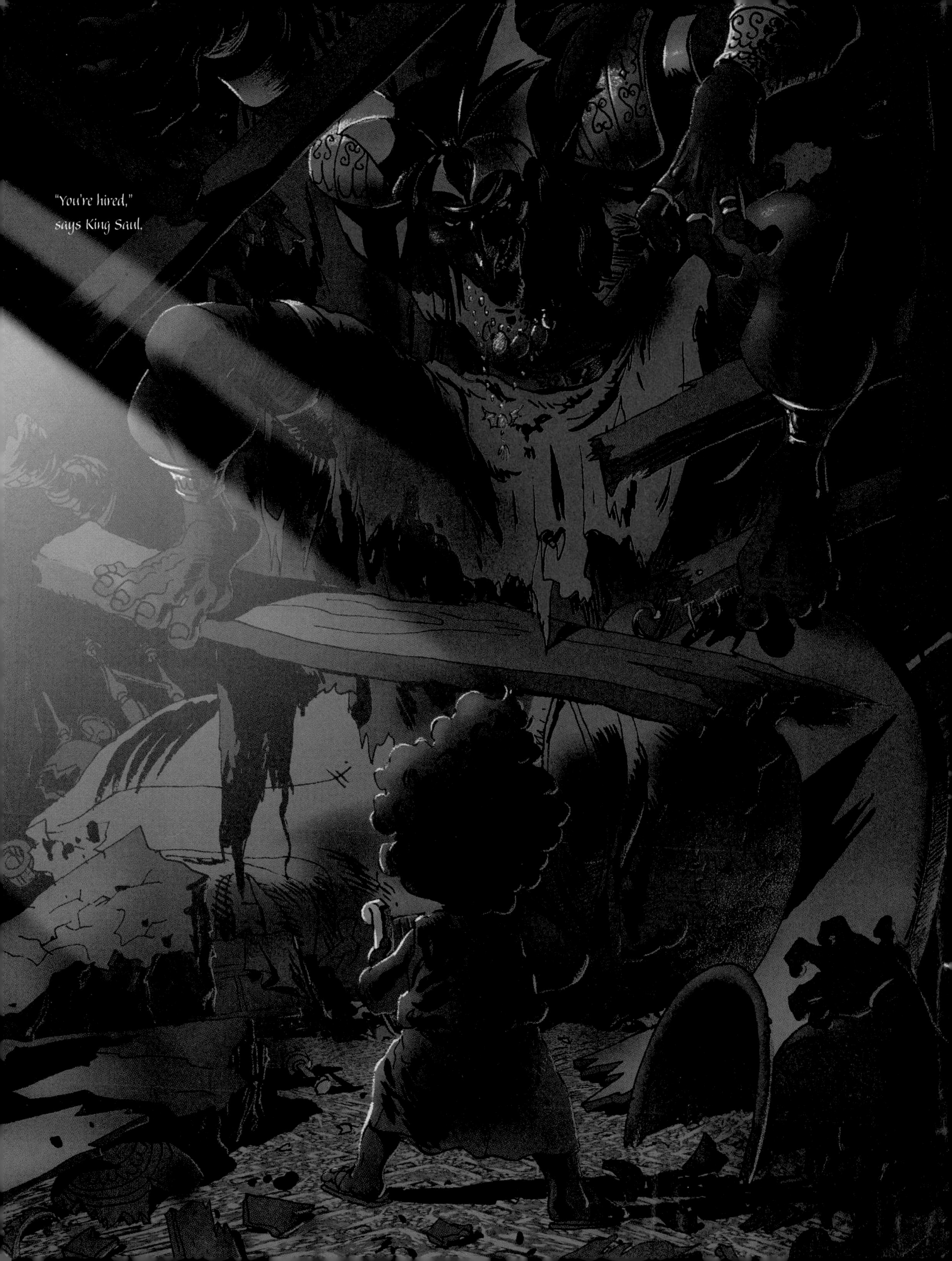
"You're hired," says King Saul.

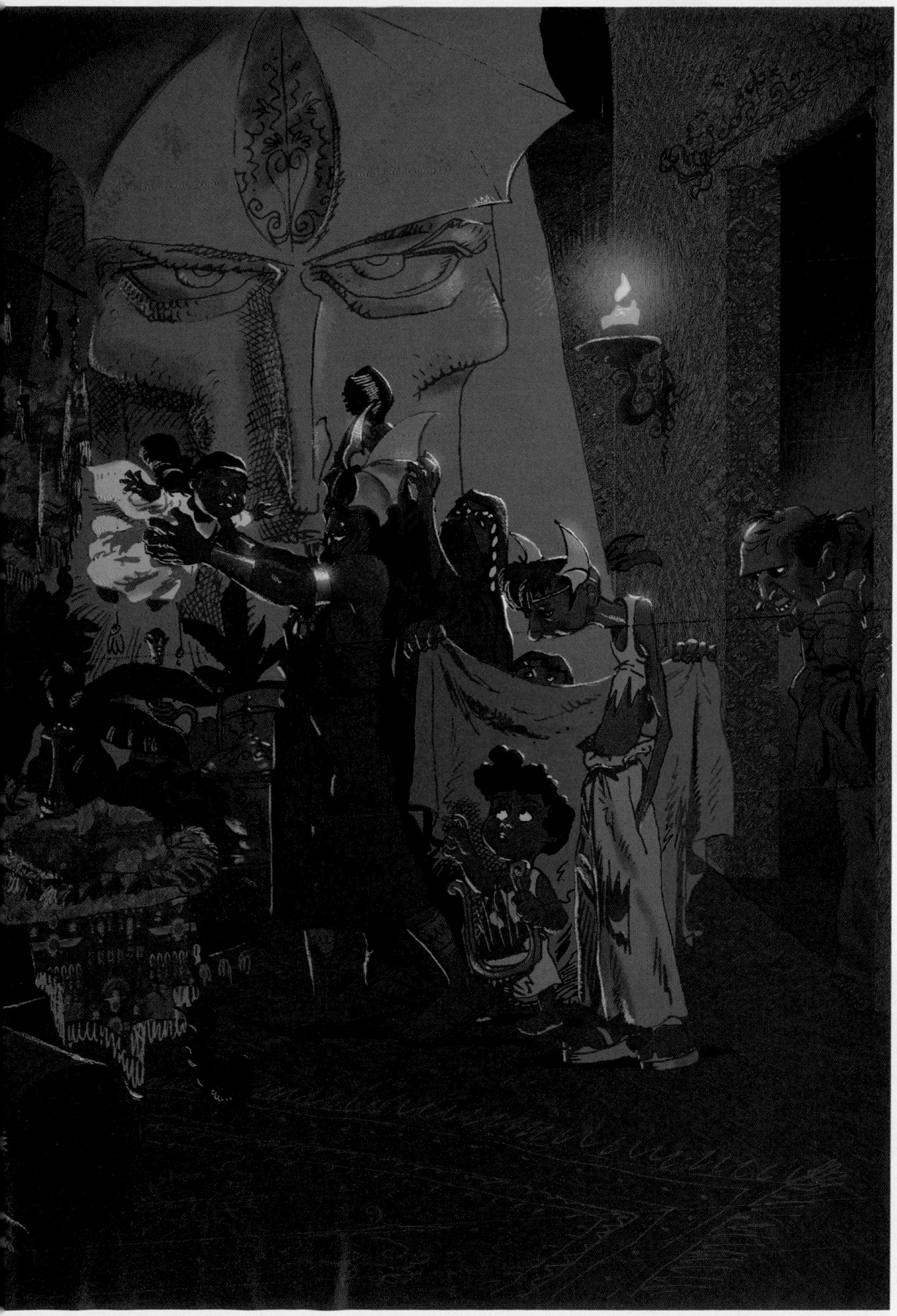

"Your crown, highness," says David.

A servant stands in the doorway. "David, your donkey's loaded at the gate and ready to go."

"In a moment, thank you. Your majesty, I hate to bring this up, but nobody else in the palace has been able to help me. And I was told to come to you."

"To me?" asks Saul.

"Daddy? Can I have some honey?" asks five-year-old Michal.

"Of course you can, sweetheart. You can have as much as you want."

Jonathan, Saul's teenaged son says, "Dad, I need the big chariot. Where is it?"

"Where are you going, Jonathan?"

"Out."

David remains as polite as possible. "Your majesty, I've been an armor bearer here for three months, and I have not yet been paid."

"Well, that's not right. Go to accounting and tell them I said pay you," says Saul. "Out where, Jon? When will you be home?"

"I don't know."

"Accounting said I could not be paid without an invoice," says David.

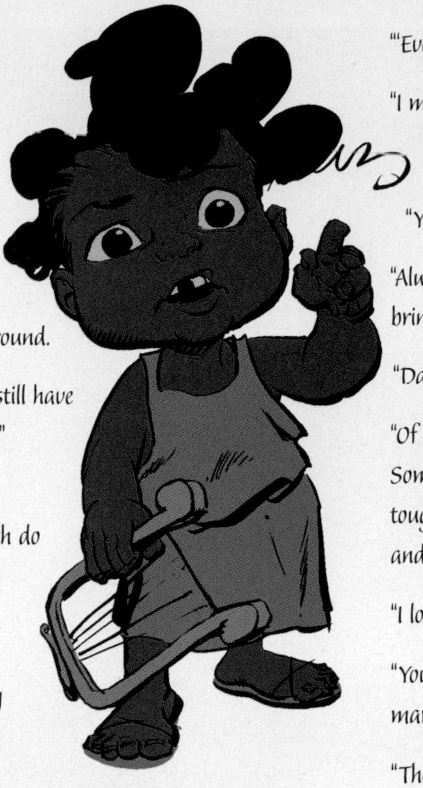

"I don't know anything about invoices," says Saul.

"Daddy, spin me around!" says Michal.

Saul picks Michal up and spins her around.

"I cannot submit an invoice because I still have not been told how much my salary is," explains David.

"I don't know salaries either. How much do the others get?" Saul asks.

"Dad, the chariot?"

"It depends," says David. "The armory says I'm not in their budget because technically I'm entertainment, but the entertainment department says I'm an armor bearer. Neither department head wants to pay me out of their budget because neither of them hired me."

"Who hired you?" asks Saul, wishing this were over by now.

"You did."

"Okay. I'll take care of it. Remind me later. Jon, what did you do to your hair?"

"Everybody wears it like this now."

The guy in the doorway reappears. "You can't leave your donkey parked at the gate, David. It's a yellow zone."

"I'll be right down."

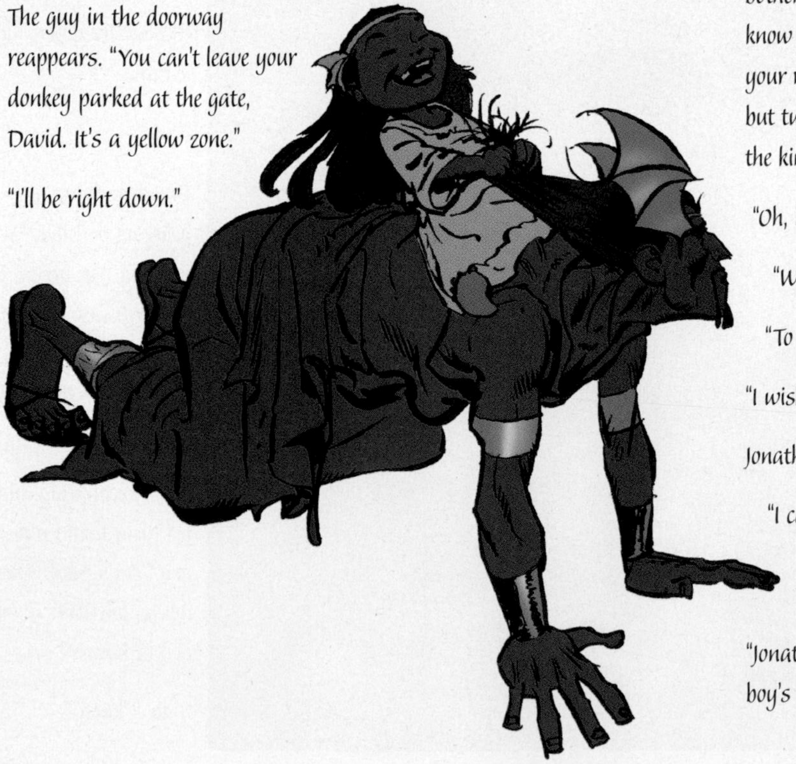

"'Everybody wears it'--I don't wear it like that," says Saul.

"I meant everybody cool."

"What did I ever do to you, Jonathan? What was my terrible crime?"

"You mean besides the time you tried to kill me for eating honey?"

"Always the honey! That was a long time ago. Are you just going to keep bringing that up forever?"

"Daddy, are you going to kill me for eating honey?"

"Of course not, dear. Your brother's taking it completely out of context. Someday, when Jonathan's a king and father himself he'll understand that tough decisions have to be made and everything isn't black and white, right and wrong. Sometimes there's no right answer."

"I love you, daddy. I'm going to marry you."

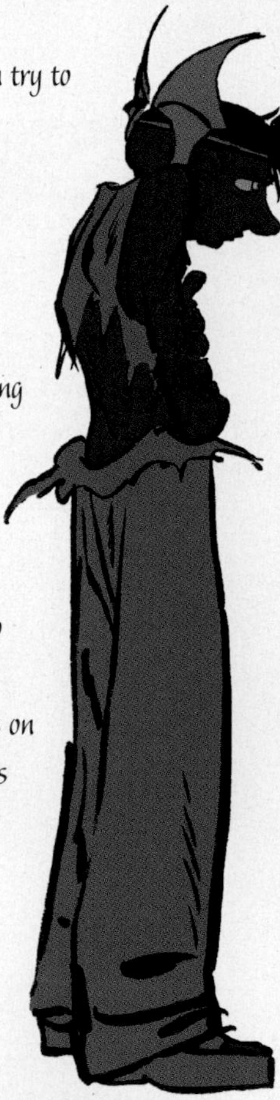

"You can't marry me, sweetheart. But you can try to marry someone just like me."

"Then that's what I'm going to do."

"Sure," says Jonathan, "break your mother's heart."

From the doorway: "David, the donkey's blocking traffic. The guards will impound it.'

"Are you still here, boy?" asks Saul. "You may go."

"Your majesty , excuse me, please. I'm sorry to bother you with this triviality," says David. "I know you have much more important matters on your mind. A simple youth such as myself has but two concerns. One is to please my lord the king."

"Oh, brother," snickers Jonathan.

"What's the second?"asks Michal.

"To make my father proud."

"I wish I had a son like you,"says Saul.

Jonathan rolls his eyes. "Oh, come on!"

"I can't show up at my father's farm after three months away without bringing some money," says David. "He'll think I've been on vacation instead of helping him with the harvest."

"Jonathan, get my box of gold pieces from my bedchamber," says Saul. "This boy's father should be proud."

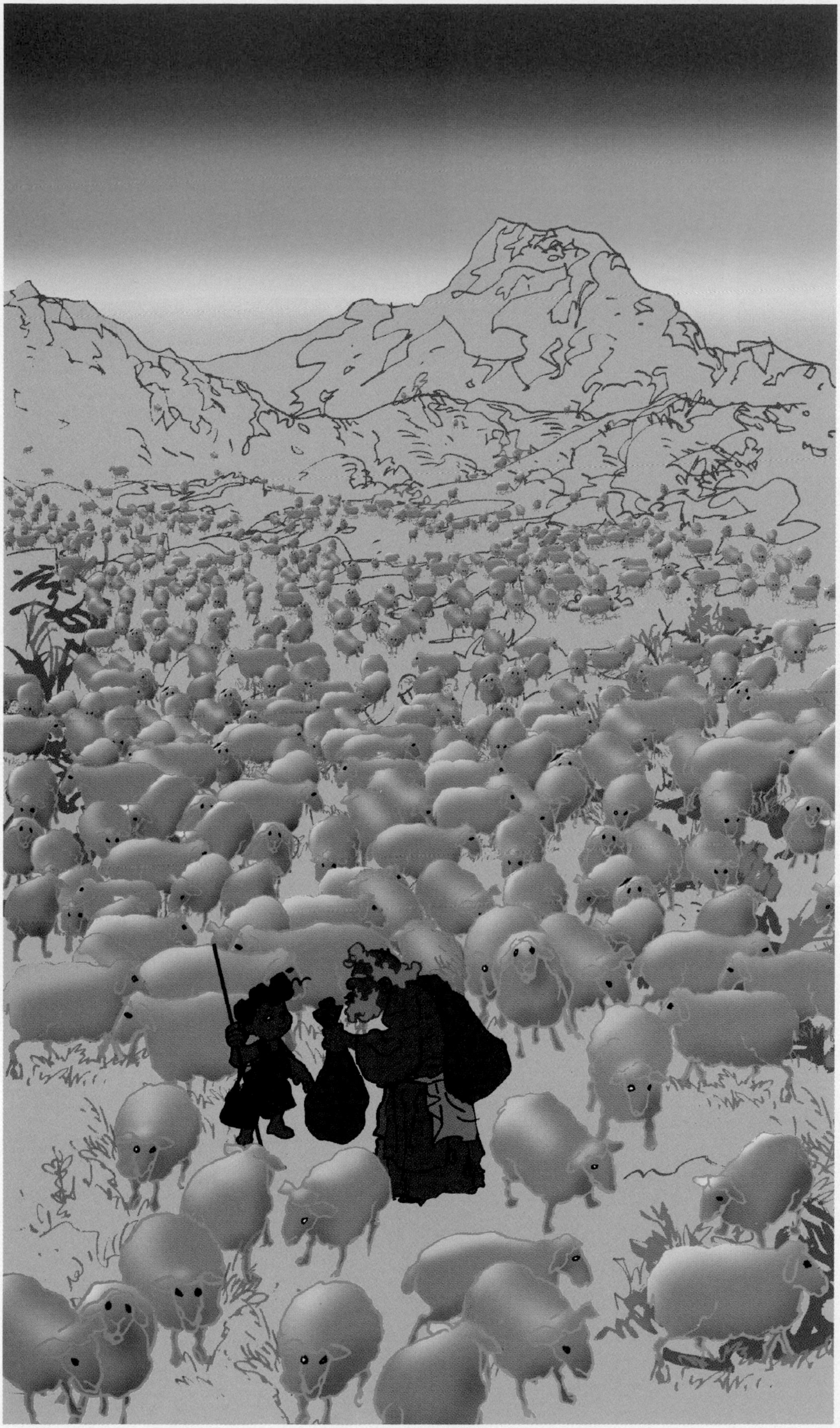

Months pass.

"David, take this food to your brothers' camp. They're with Saul in the Elah valley," says Jesse, David's father.

"You are sending me into the war zone?"

"Hey, your mother wanted me to go! With my knee!"

"I was not protesting, father."

"Your mother says, 'I know those boys are just eating junk while they're away. I don't even want to think what their laundry must look like.'"

"With all due respect, father, I am not carrying their laundry back."

"No, no. So the grain and bread are for your brothers, but these cheeses are for their commander."

"Mother is wise indeed."

"Tell your brothers I know they're busy young men but if it wouldn't be too much trouble to possibly take a few seconds out of their very important schedules to send a little message back to their dear grey mother just so she knows they're okay, so she can stop picturing them lying dead somewhere it would be greatly appreciated. Doesn't have to be much, just a few words. For the woman who only gave birth to them. If they have time, of course."

"Yes, father. Is there anything else?"

"Be careful, and don't stay out too late. And don't tell your brothers you have cheese."

THE PHILISTINE CAMP

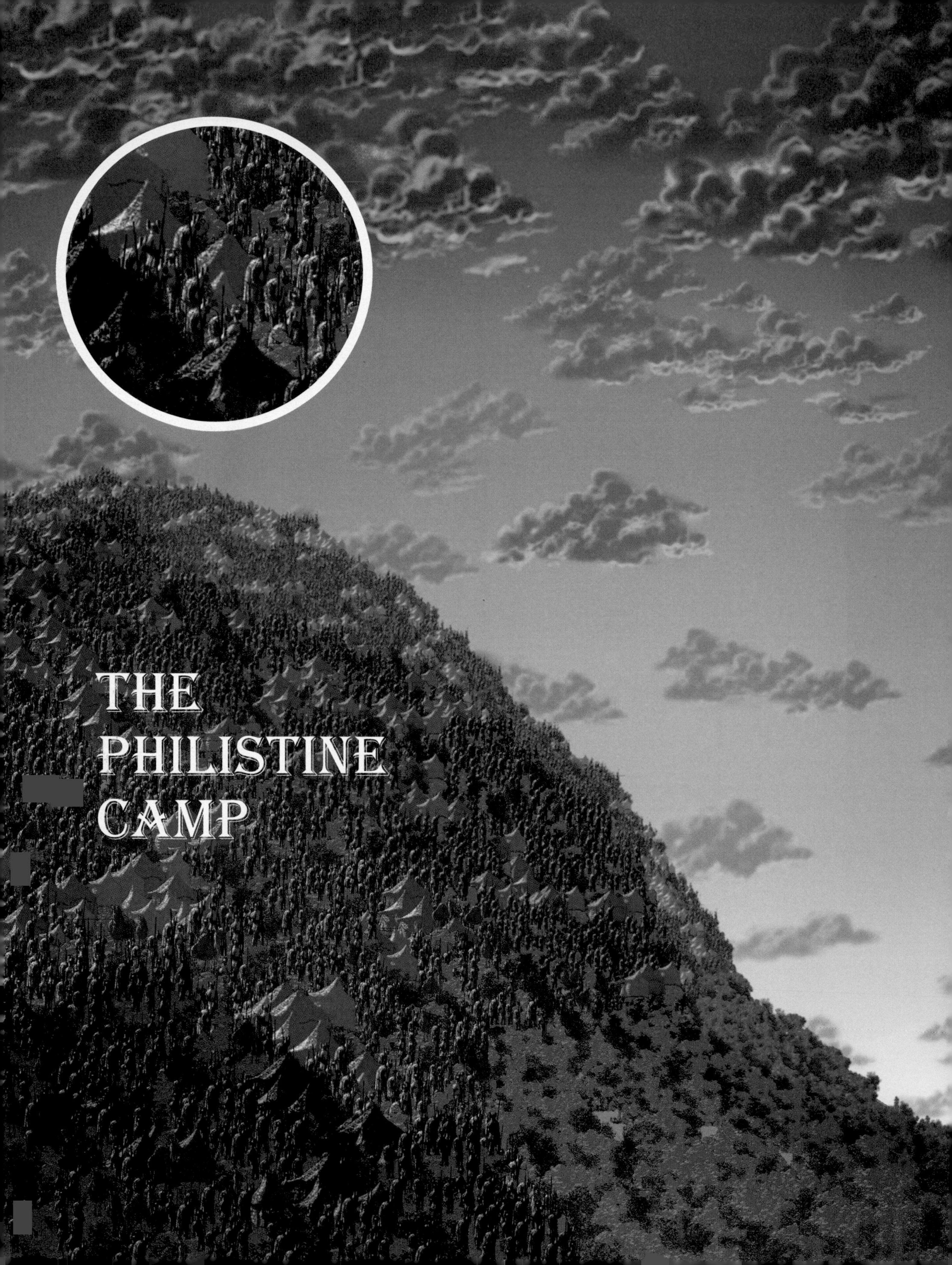

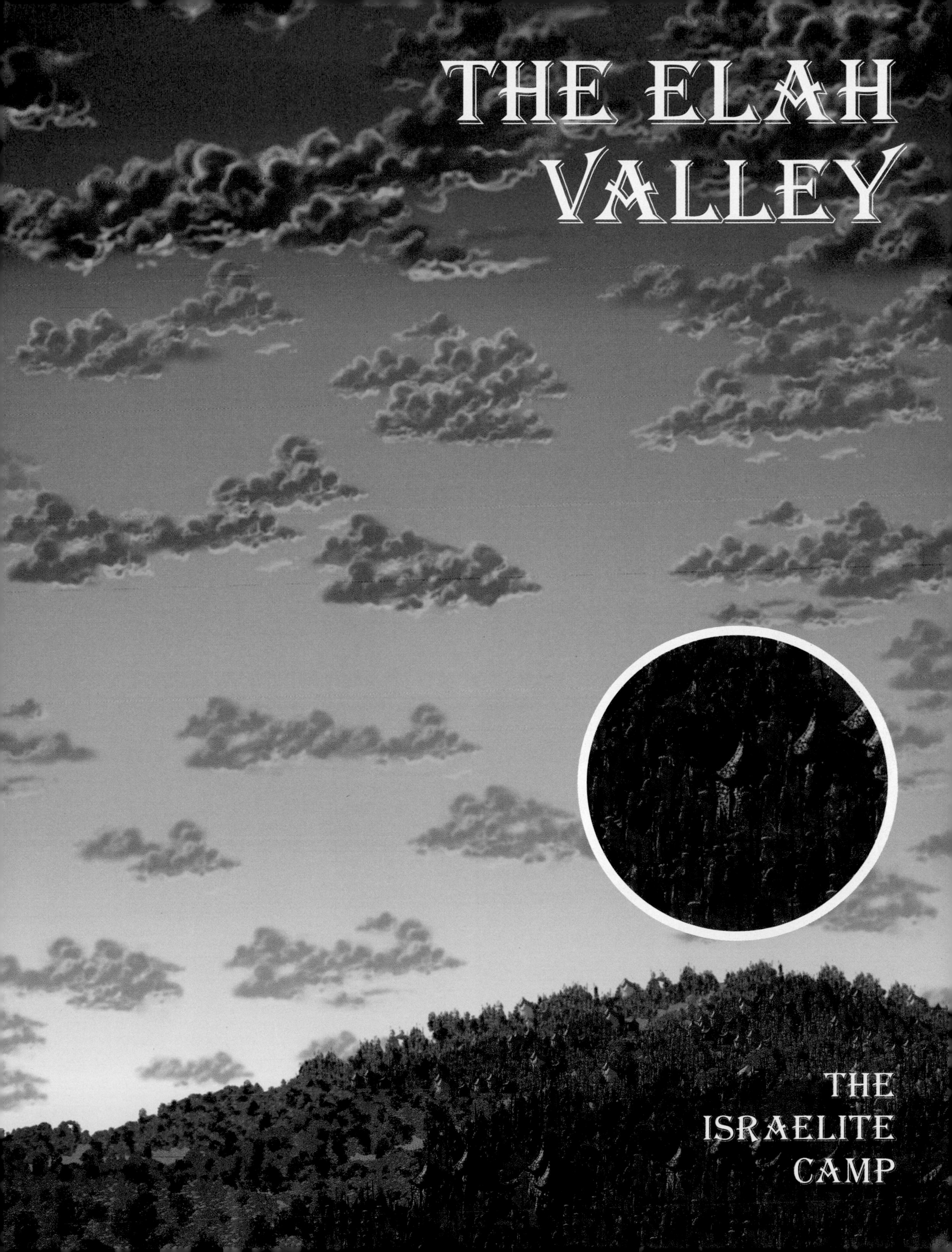
THE ELAH VALLEY
THE ISRAELITE CAMP

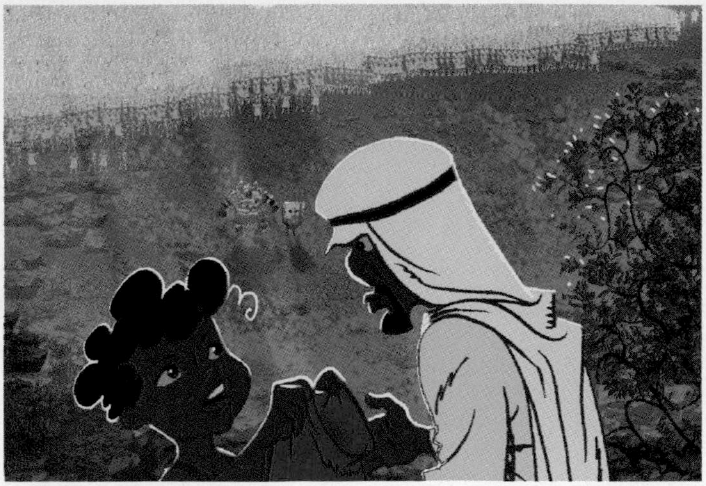

"Eliab. Father sent me with--"

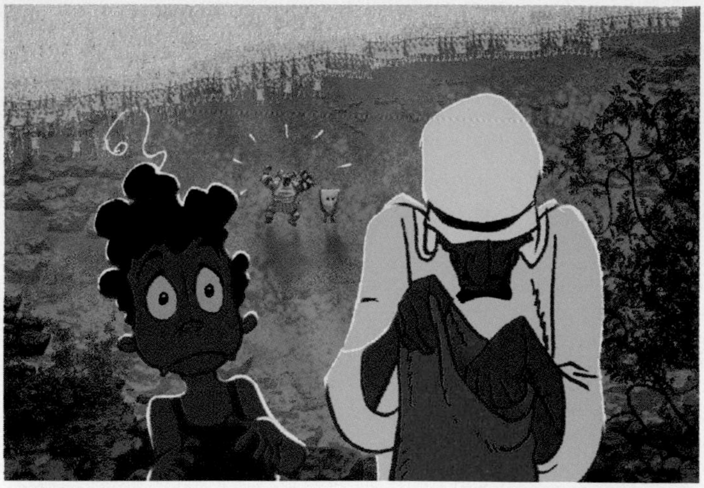

A Philistine shouts from the valley, "FOLLOWERS OF SAUL! COWARDS! WEAKLINGS! TREMBLE IN FEAR BEFORE THE MIGHT OF THE LEGENDARY GOLIATH!"

"Hey! Food!" says Eliab.

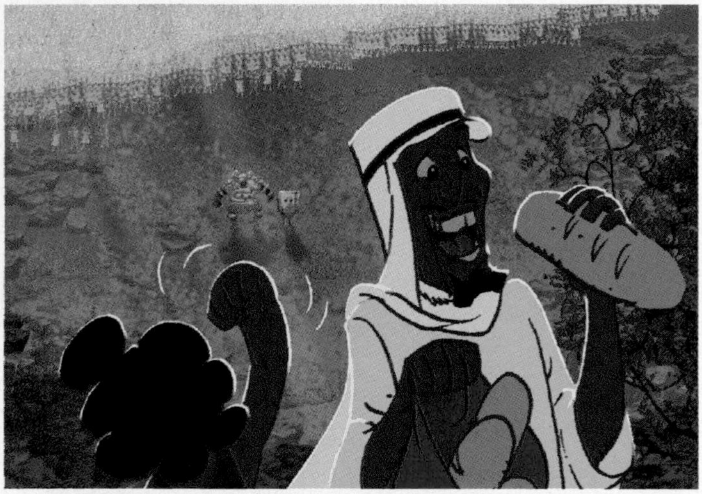

"Philistine trash! You shall die before night!"

"Is this mom's bread? You know I've missed that!"

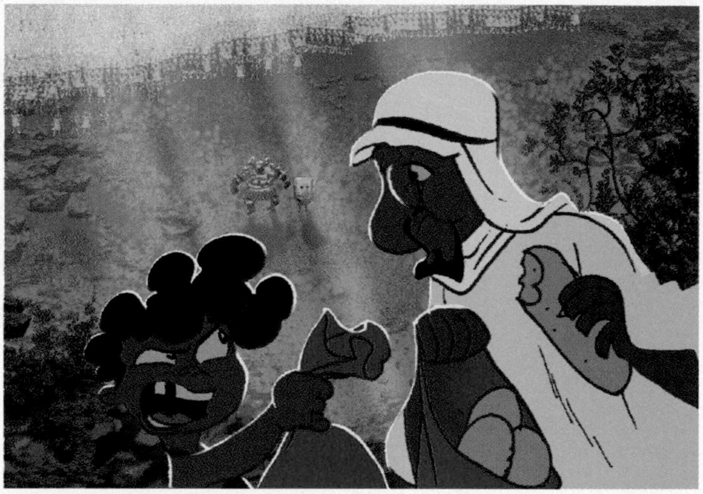

"Yes. And some roasted grain. Father asked if you could--"

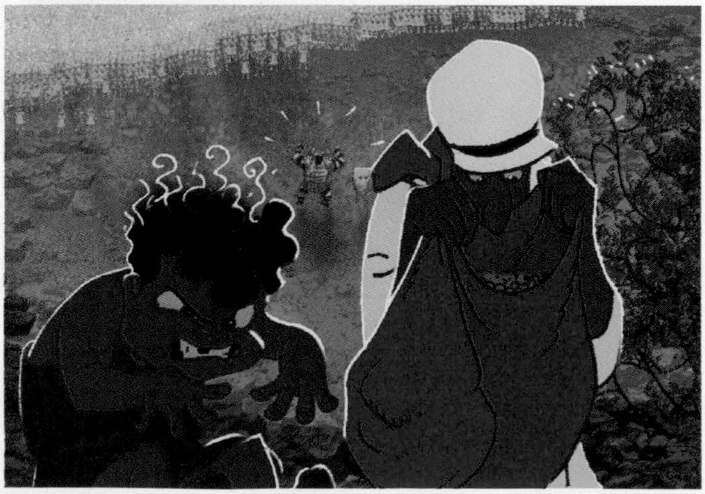

"SAUL'S PUNY FEIFDOM IS DOOMED! YOU WHO FOLLOW HIM ARE DOOMED! WE WILL CRUSH YOU. BEG US NOW FOR MERCY, THAT WE MAY BE GENEROUS AND SLAUGHTER YOU QUICKLY! BEG LIKE THE COWARDS YOU ARE!"

"Roasted grain? Ick. I hope she at least put a little spice in."

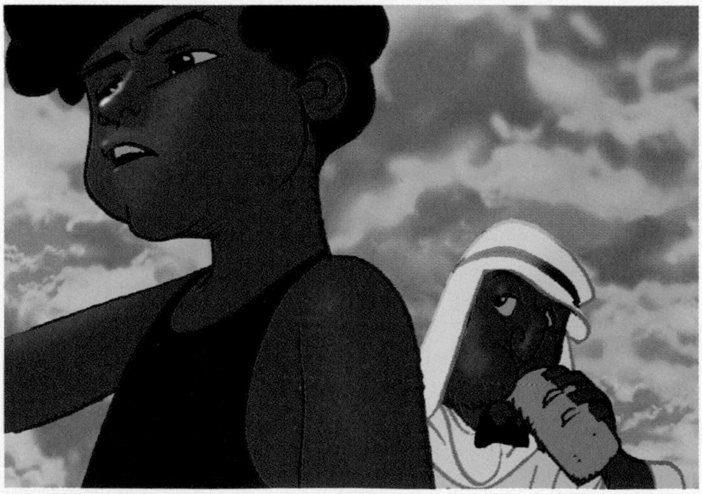

"Who is that Philistine?"

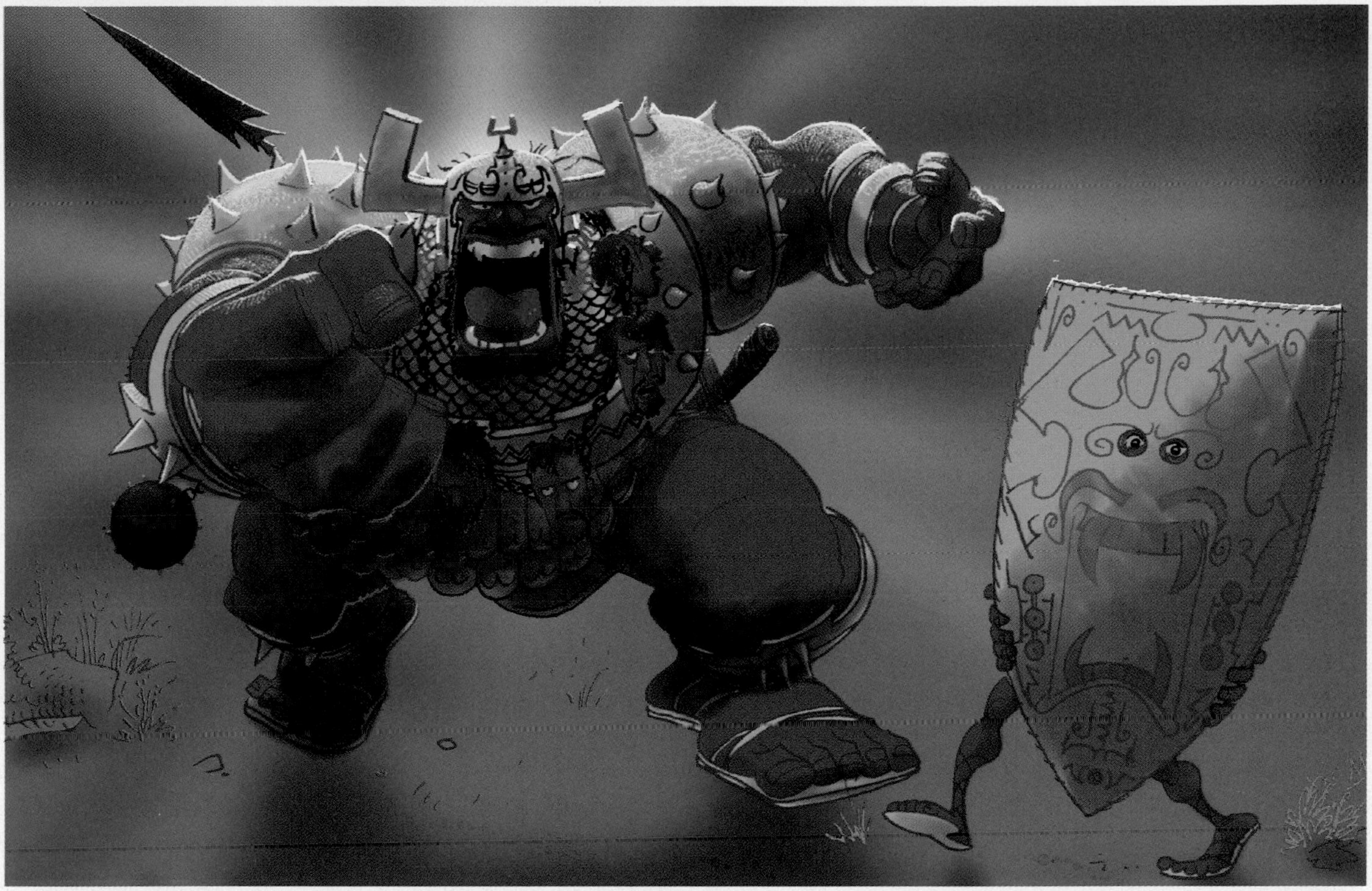

"Oh, him?" says Eliab. "That's just Goliath. The 'Champion of Gath'. He's all talk. Except when he's slaughtering us. Is this it? Bread and grain?"

"His coat of armor weighs a hundred twenty-five pounds!" says a nearby Israelite.

"His spearhead weighs fifteen pounds!" observes another.

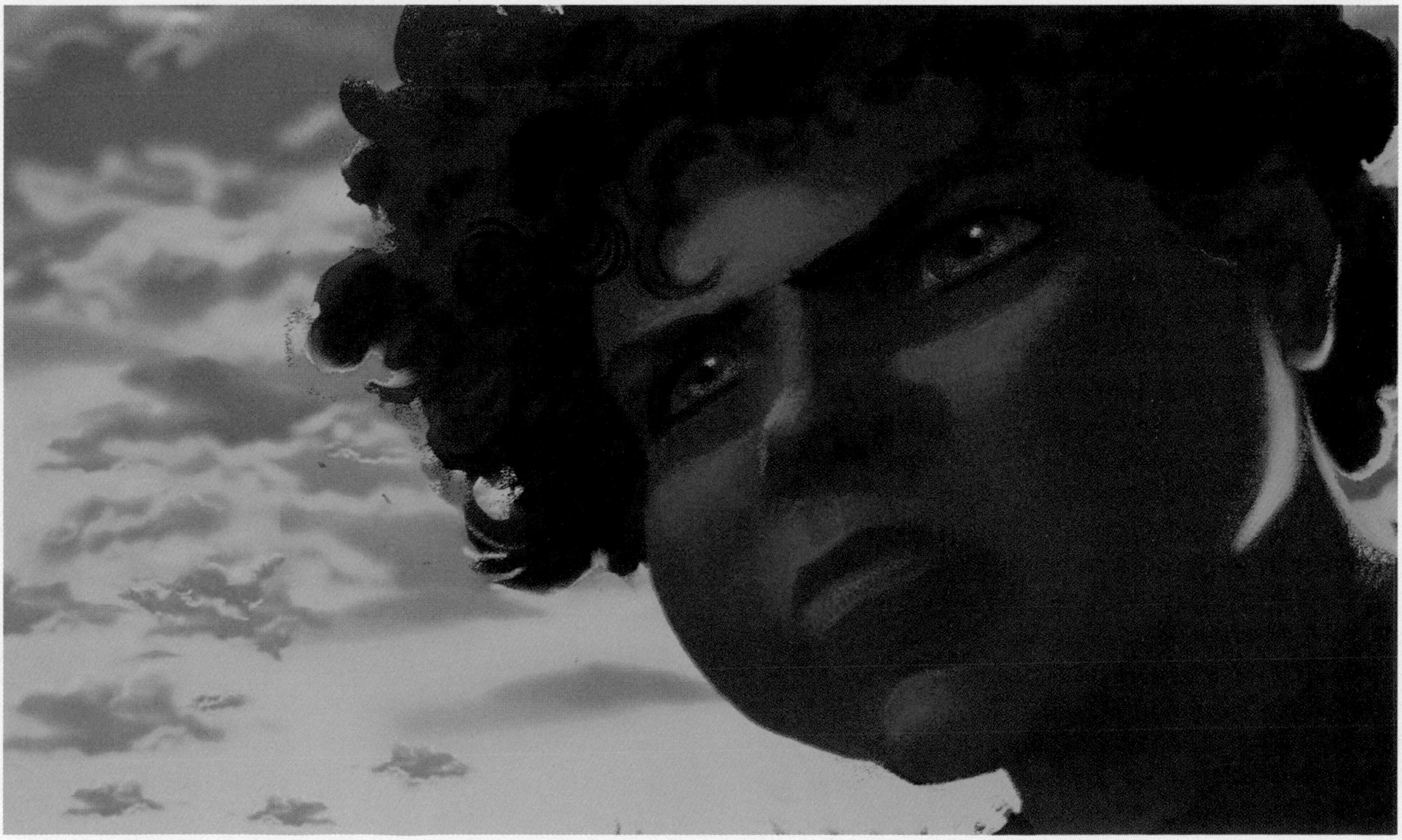

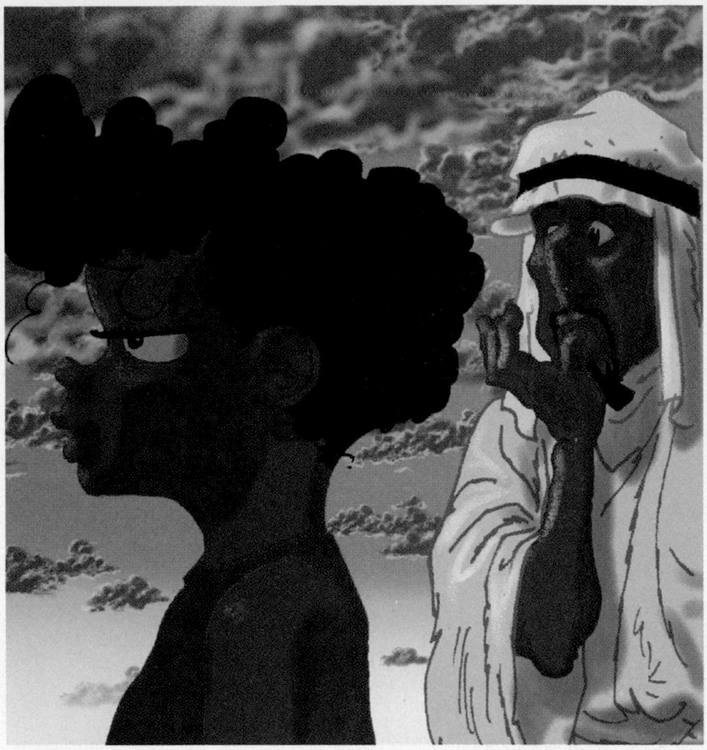

"I suppose he thinks his armor and spear will save him. You good men will show him his error."

"I knew it. No spice. Tell mom to send us some cheese next time."

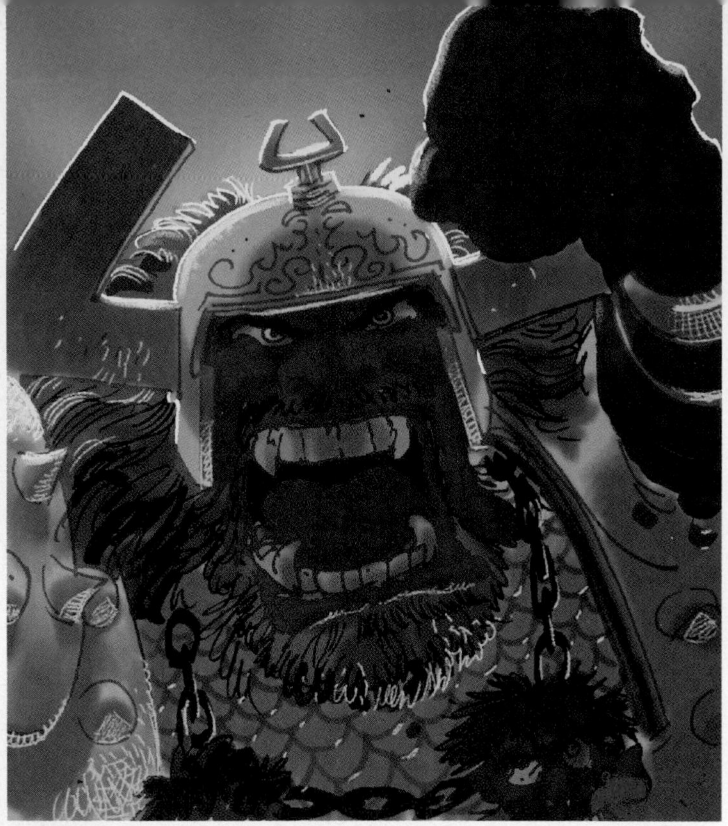

"Why do you come out and line up for battle? Am I not a Philistine, and are you not the servants of Saul? Choose a man and send him down to me. If he can fight and kill me, we will become your subjects; but if I kill him, you will become our servants!"

"He's lying. He doesn't have that kind of authority," says Eliab. "If our guy won, those Philistines would go back on the deal. They're liars."

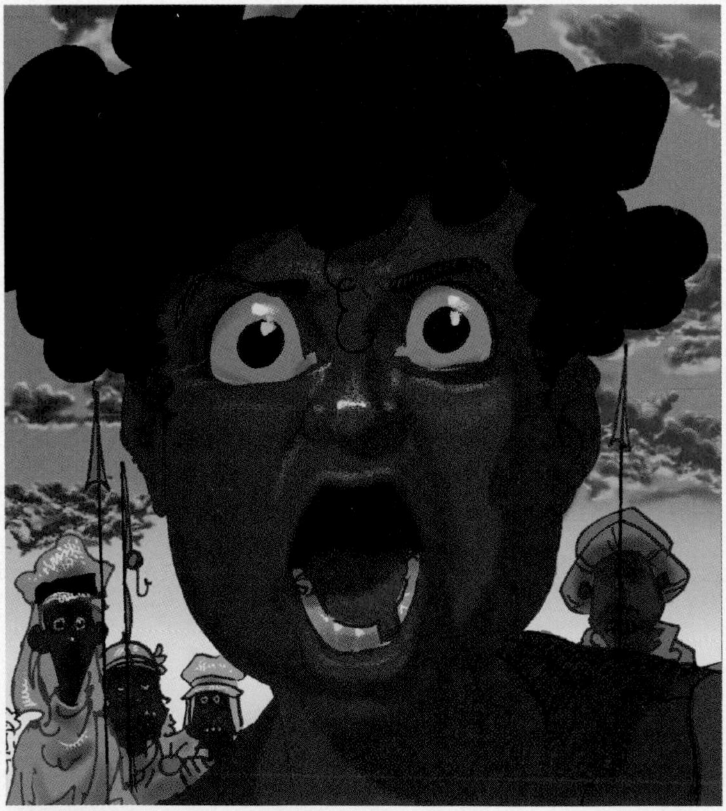

Goliath shouts, "THIS DAY I DEFY THE RANKS OF ISRAEL! GIVE ME A MAN AND LET US FIGHT EACH OTHER!"

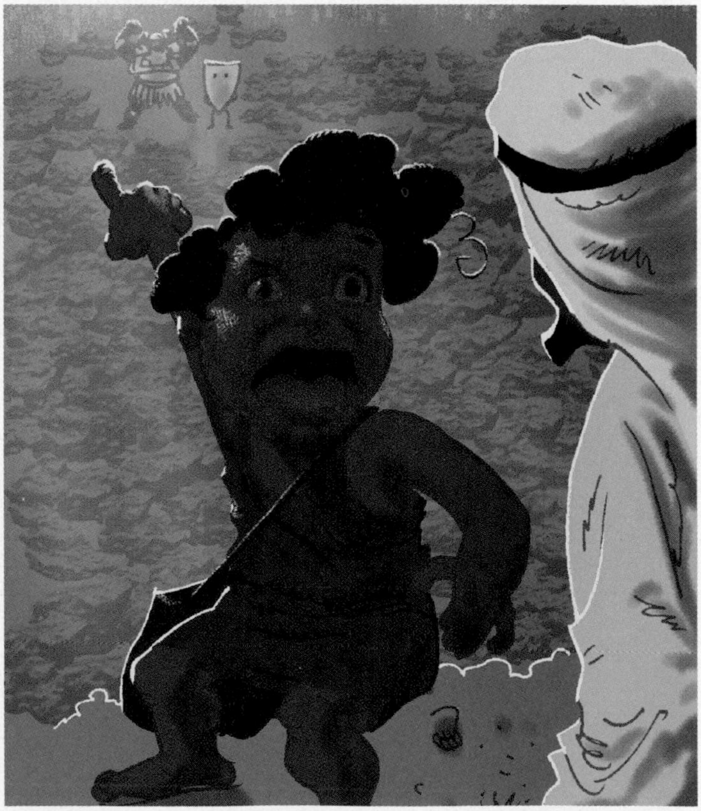

"Do you hear him?" says David, He comes out to defy Israel!"

"He does that every day. It's been over a month now."

"A month!"

"Forty days, actually. Some of us have a pool going on how long till he stops."

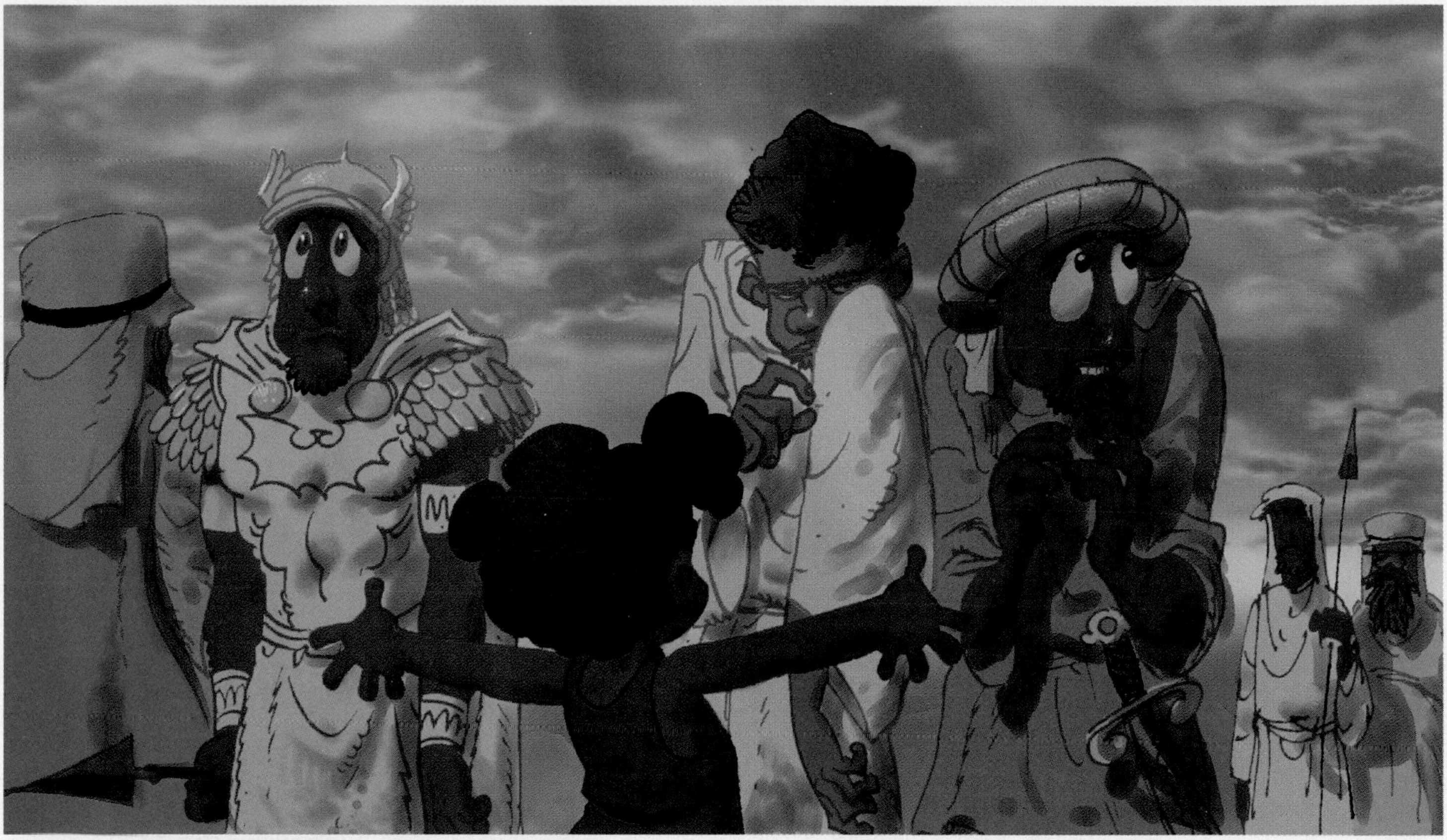

"Who is this uncircumcised Philistine that he should defy the armies of the living God?" asks David. "What will be done for the man who kills this Philistine and removes this disgrace from Israel?"

"To be honest, the king will give great wealth to the man who kills him."

"But you know what they say: You can't take it with you."

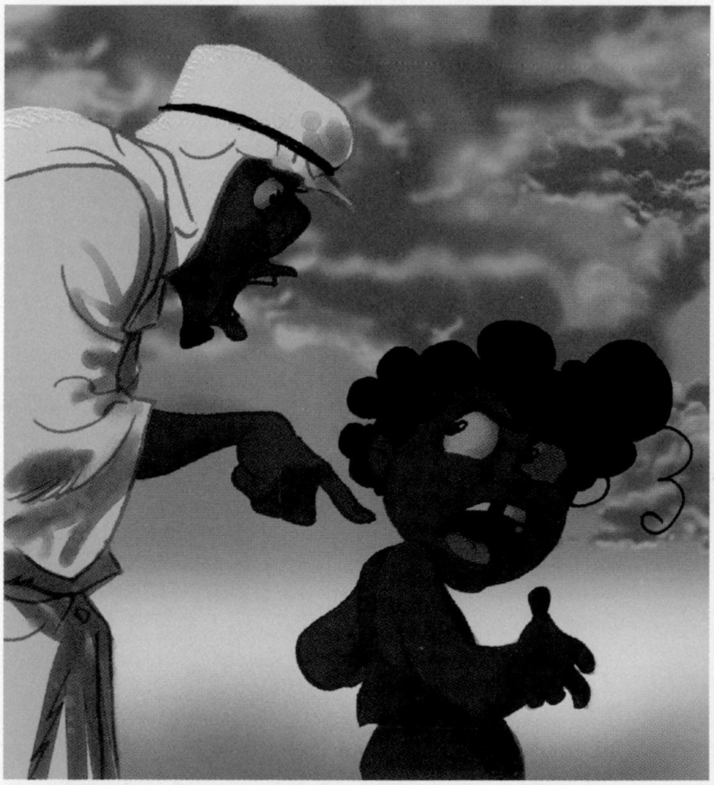

"Why'd you come down here, anyway?" asks Eliab. "Where'd you leave those sheep you're supposed to be watching? I know how you are! You sneaked down here just to watch the battle!"

"Now what did I do? Can't I even talk?"

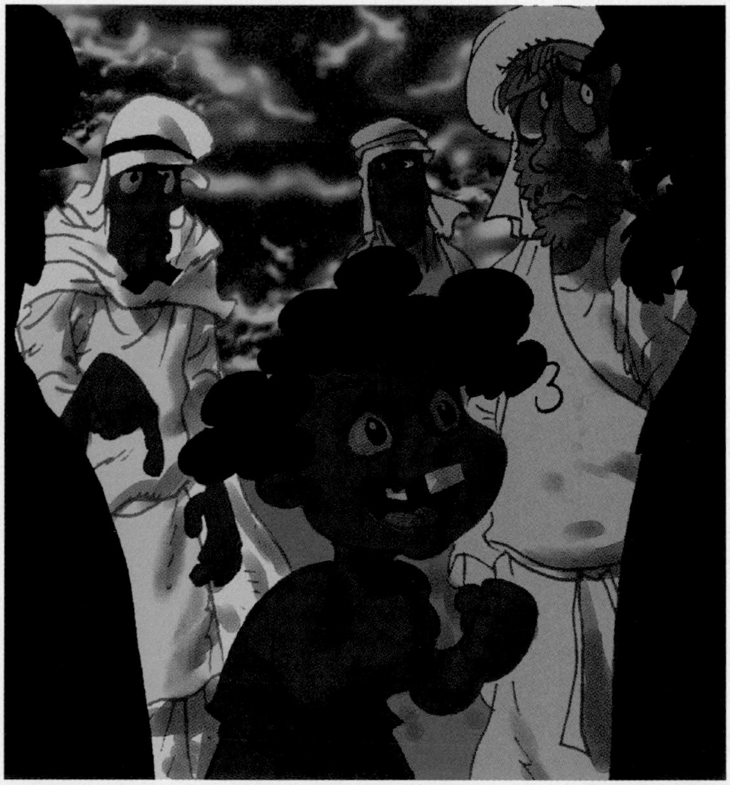

"How much wealth?"

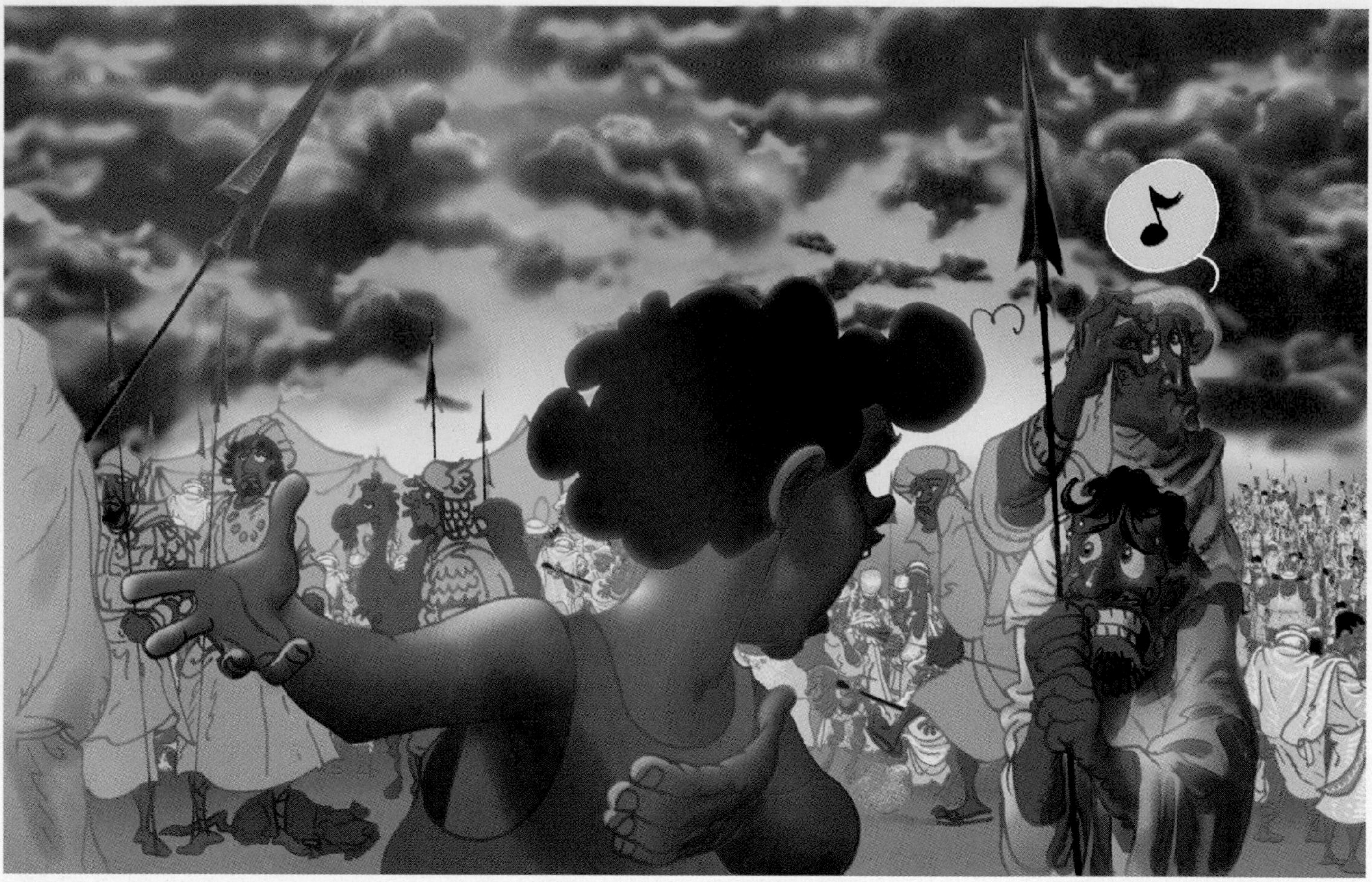

"Plenty," answers one man.

"He will also give him his daughter in marriage," says another.

"He will exempt his father's family from taxes in Israel," adds a third man.

"Who among you shall claim these riches?" asks David.

"Goliath's awfully big."

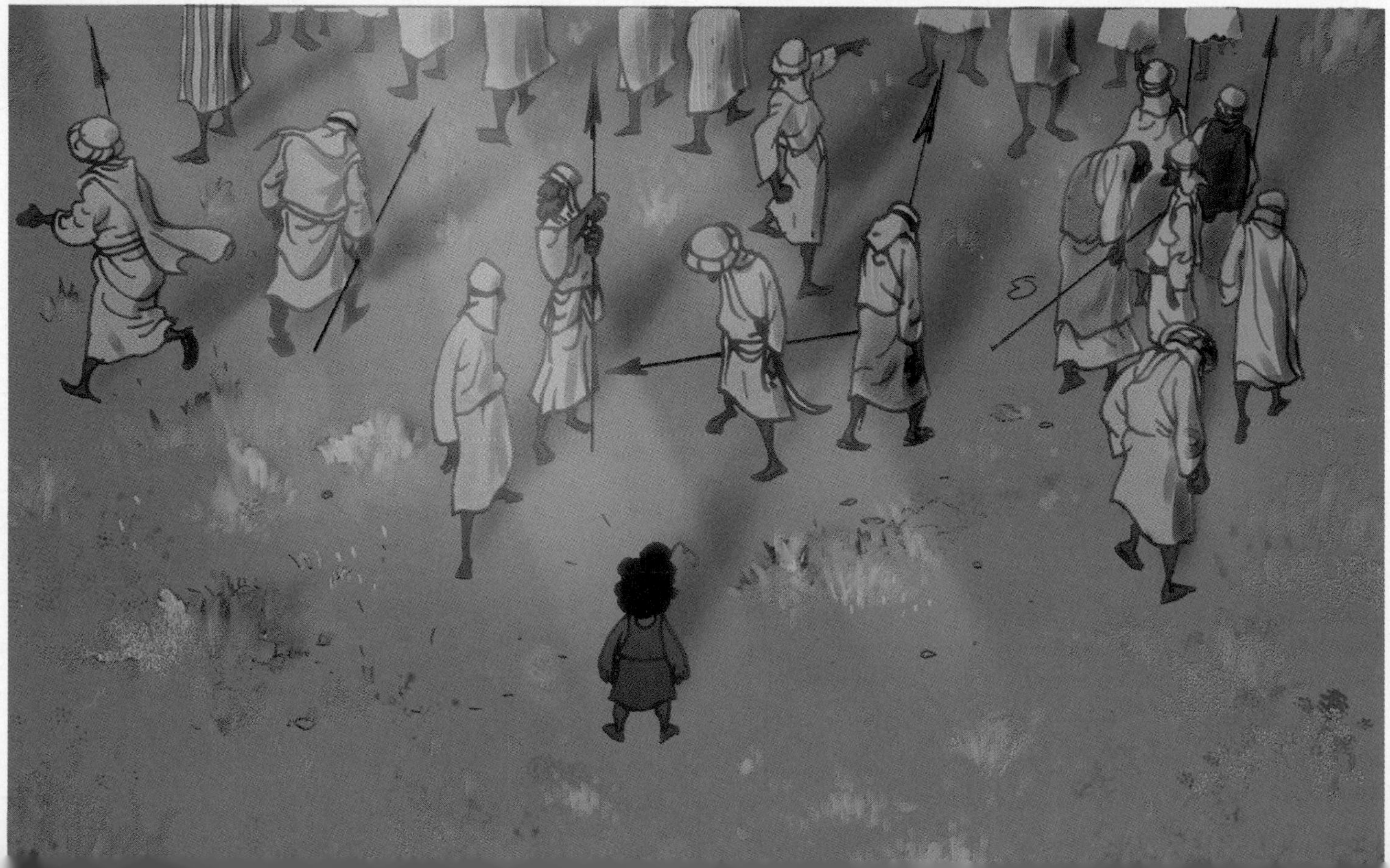

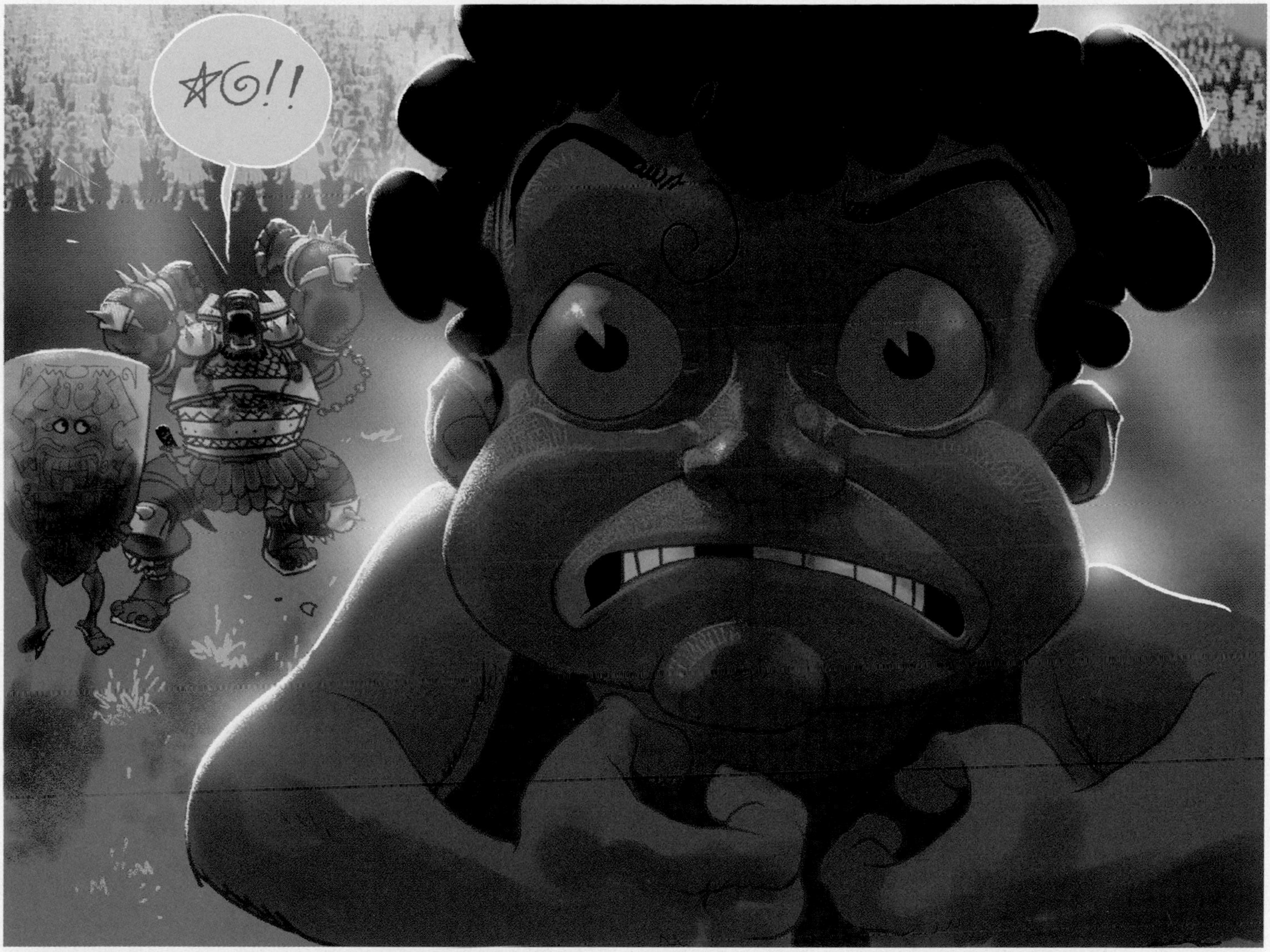
☆@!!

Goliath curses the Israelites by his Gods.

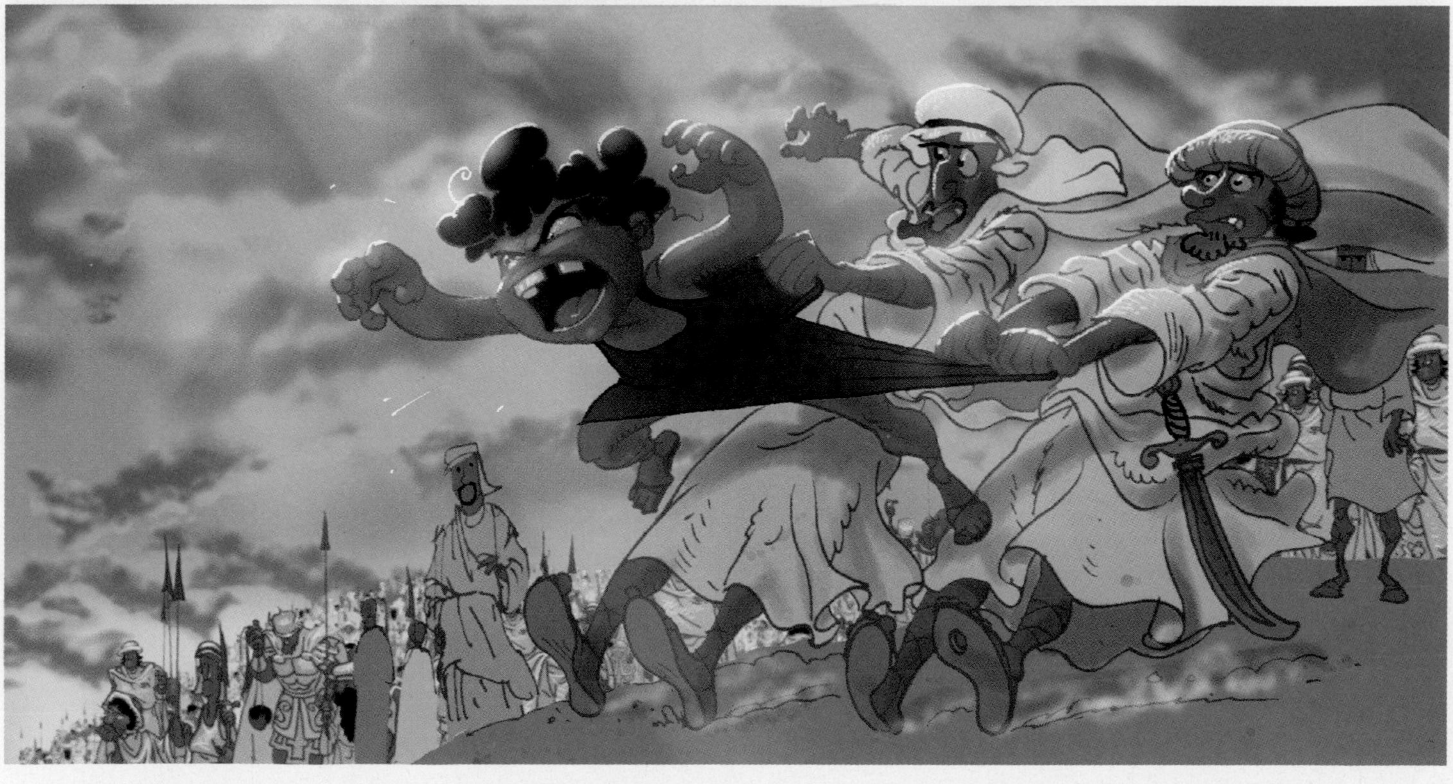

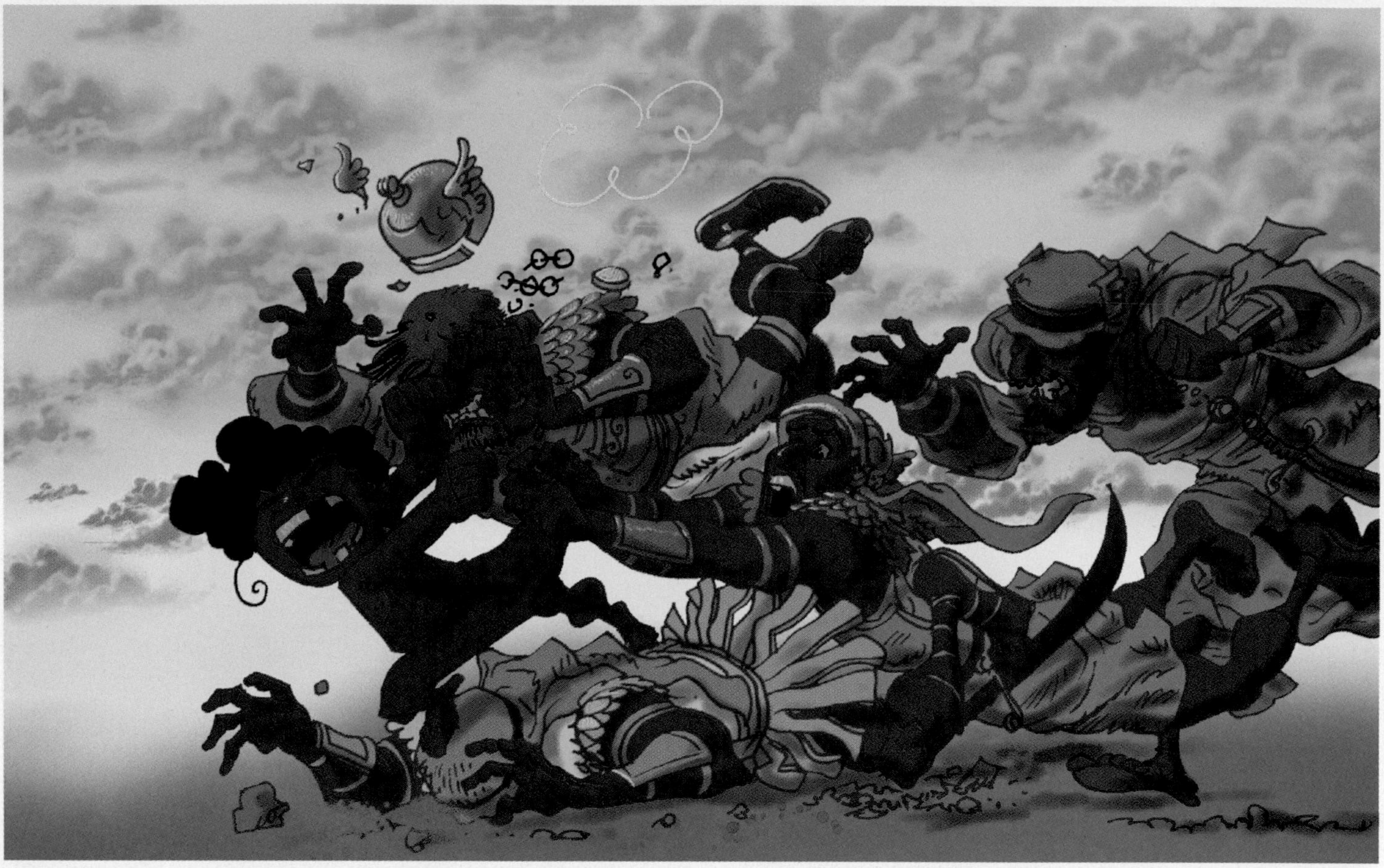

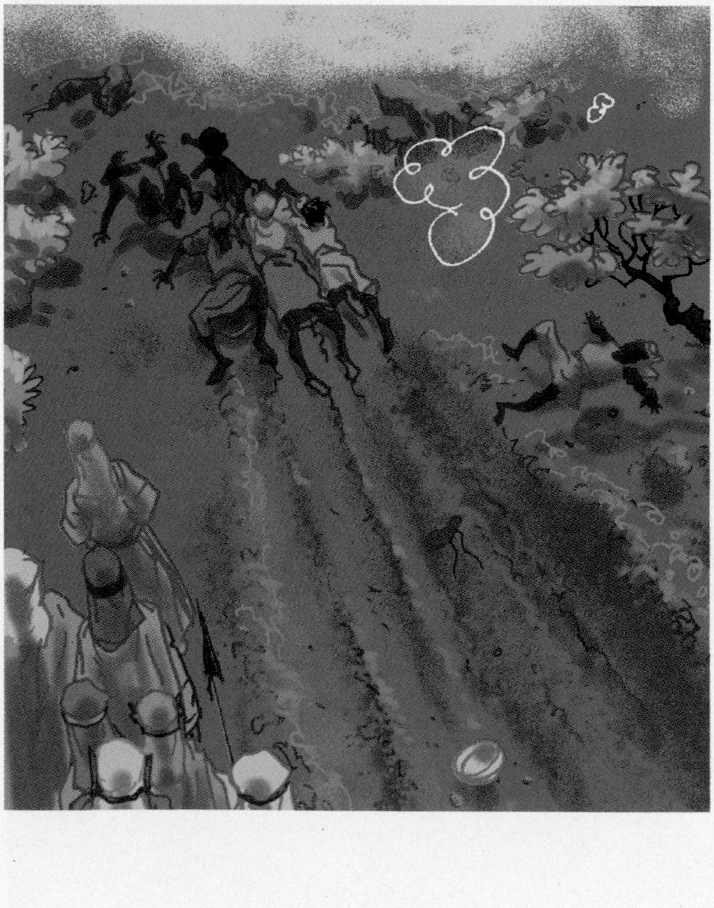

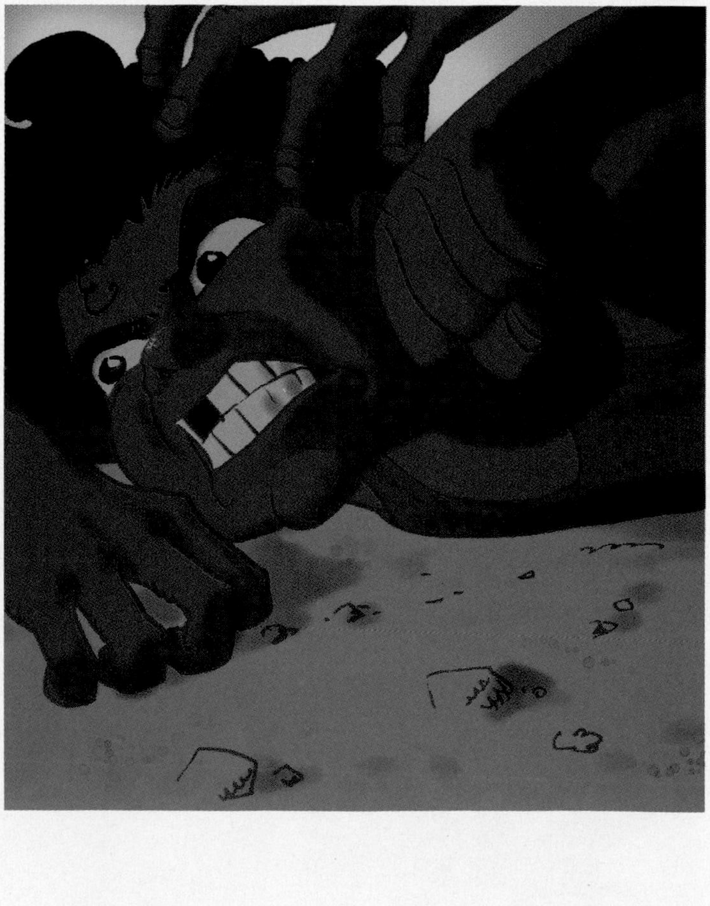

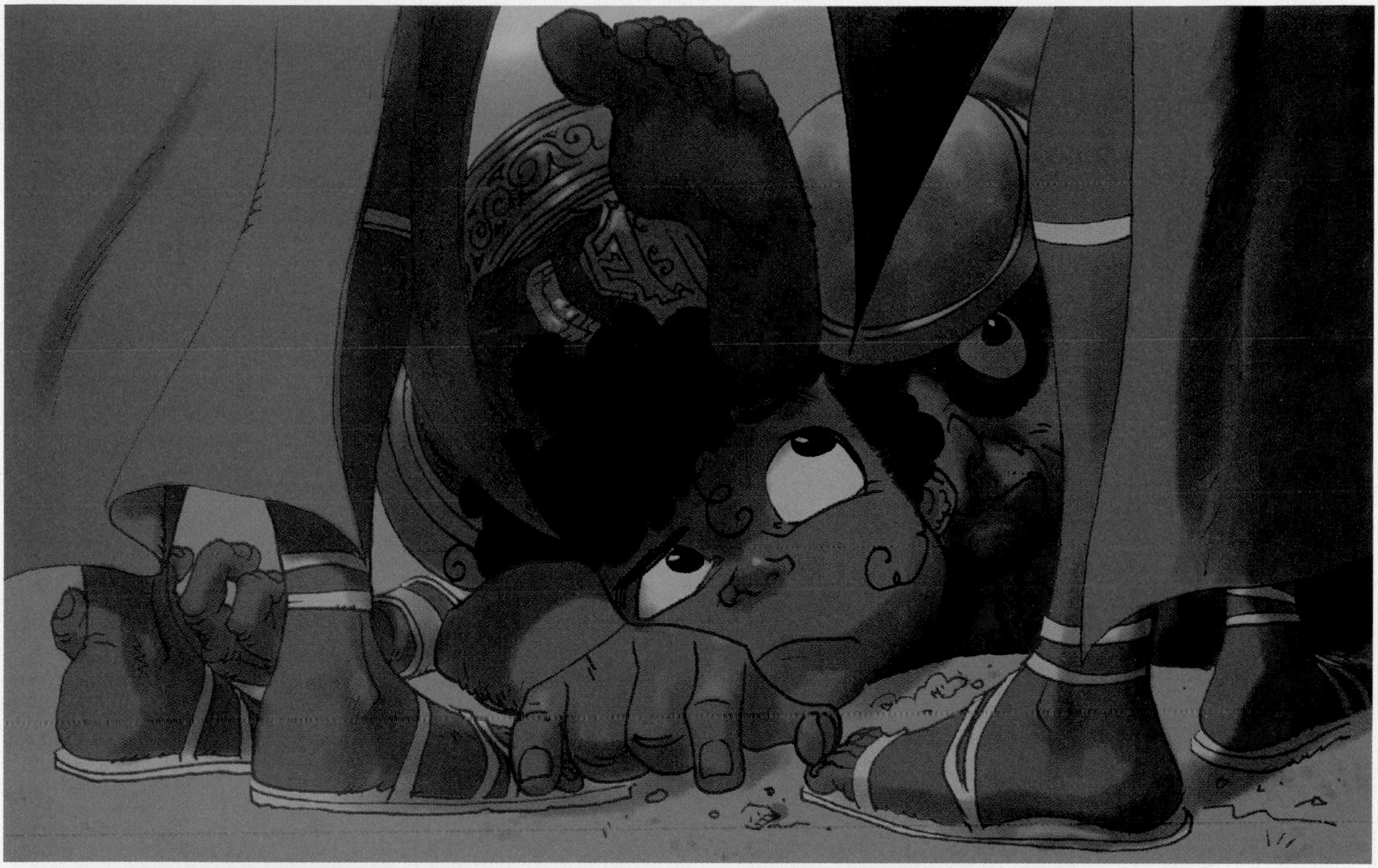

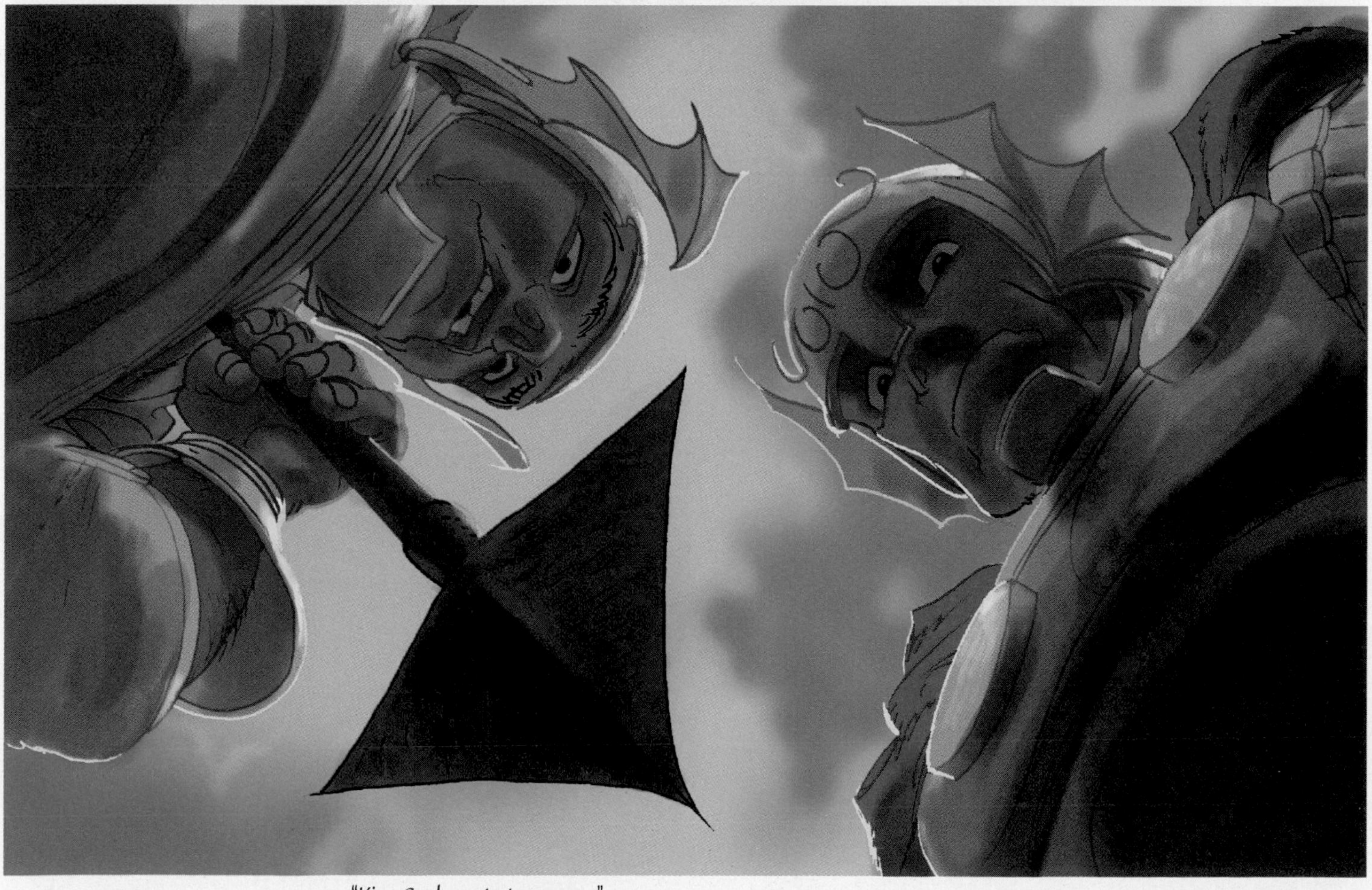

"King Saul wants to see you."

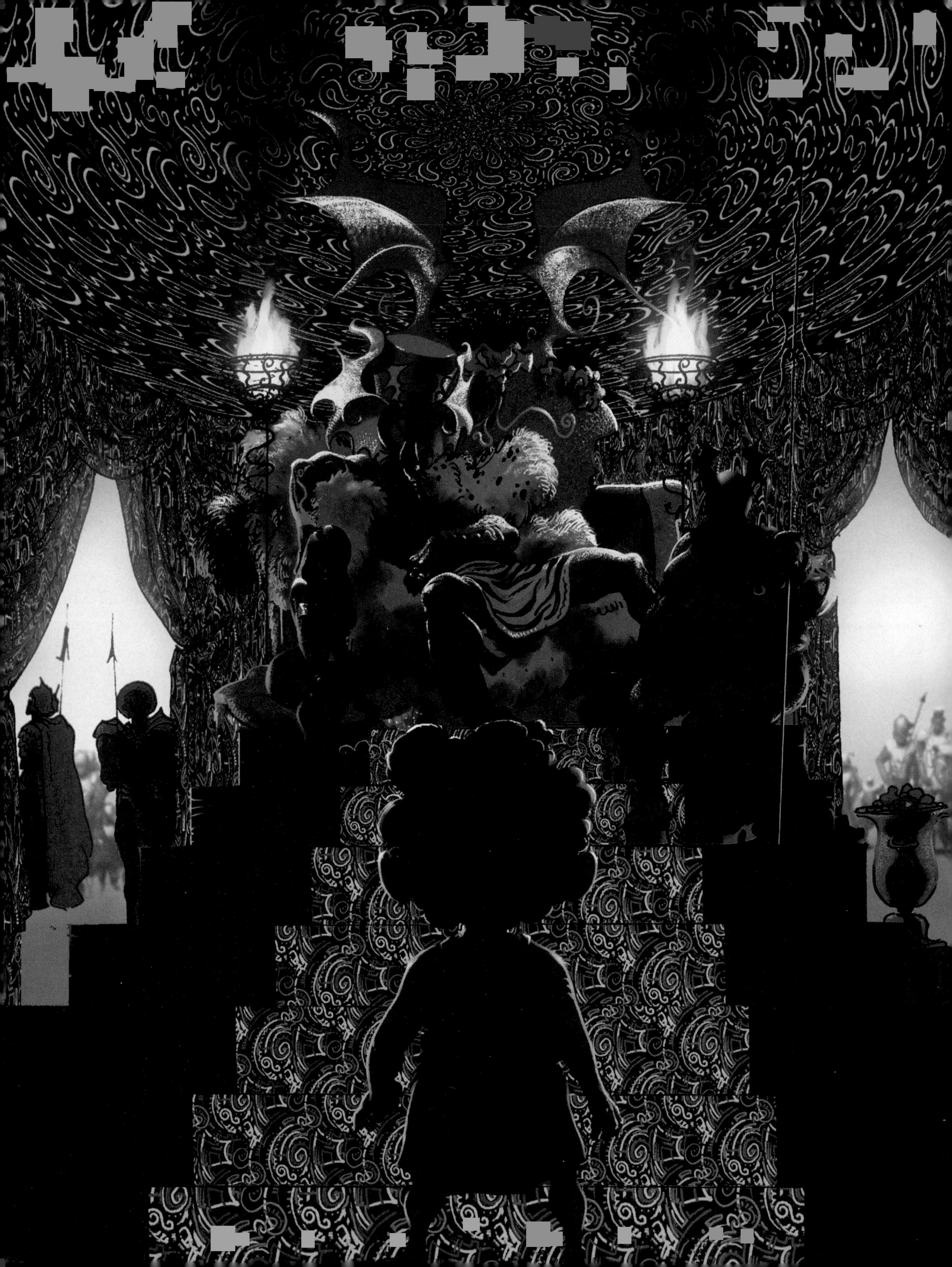

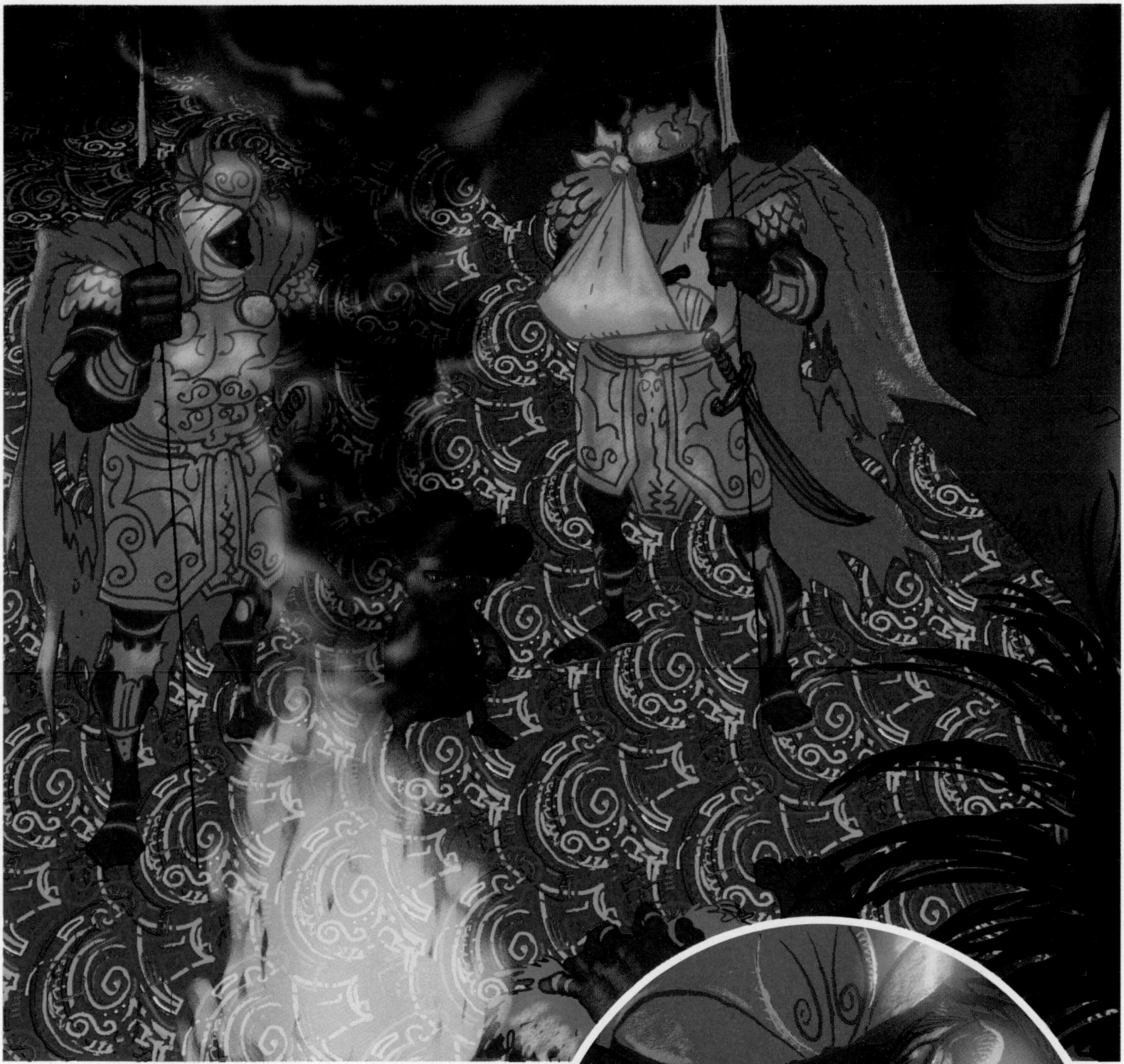

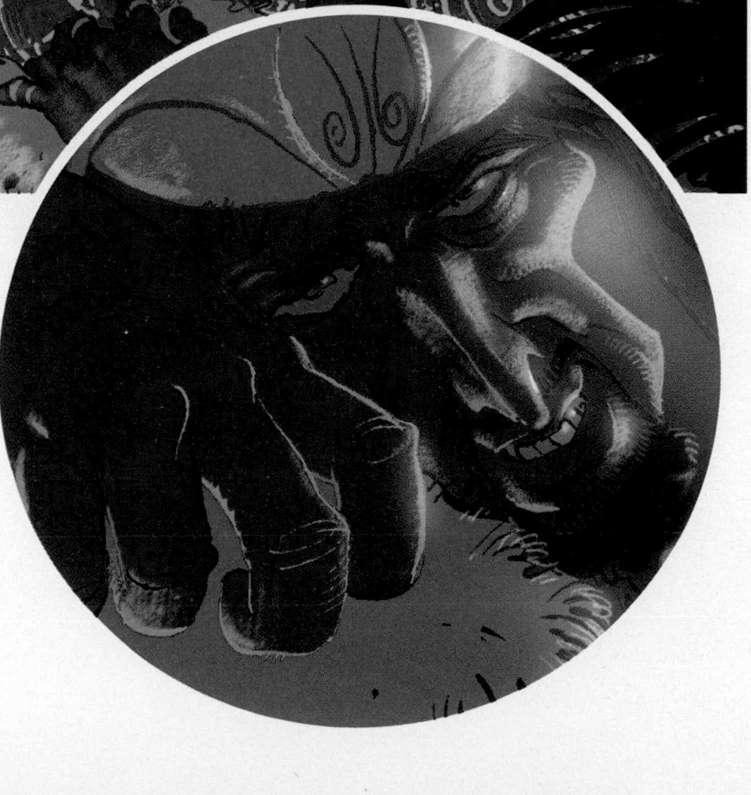

"Young man, you surprise me. Nice little harp boy. My perfect, wholesome, perky little armor bearer. What is this I hear about you now?"

David says, "Let no one lose heart over this Philistine; your servant will go and fight him."

"You can't fight him, you're just a boy. Goliath has been a soldier since his youth."

David replies, "Your servant has been keeping his father's sheep. When a lion or bear carried off a sheep, I went after it, struck it, and rescued the sheep from its mouth. When it turned on me, I seized it by the hair, struck it, and killed it. Your servant has killed both the lion and the bear; this uncircumcised Philistine will be like one of them, because he has defied the armies of the living God. The LORD who delivered me from the paw of the lion and the paw of the bear will deliver me from the hand of this Philistine."

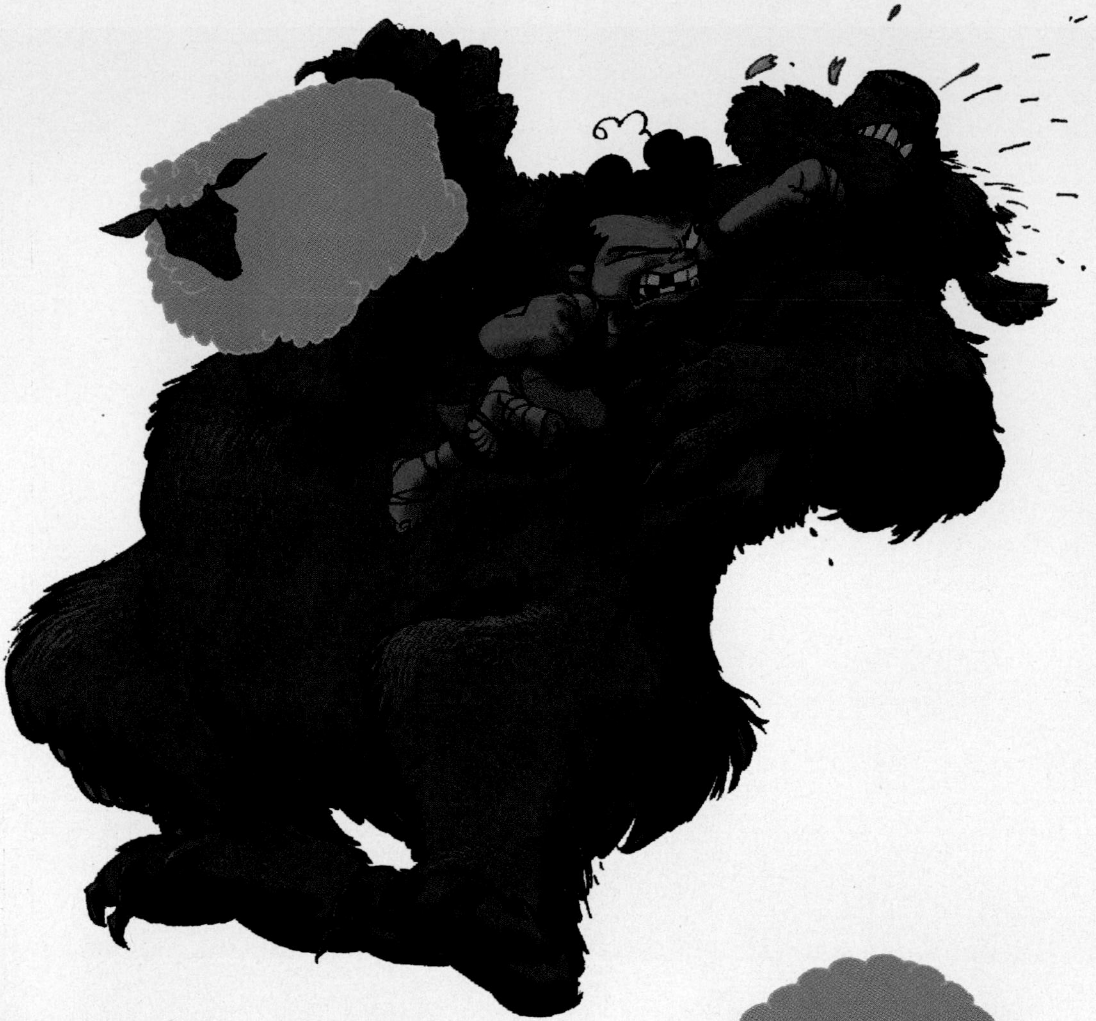

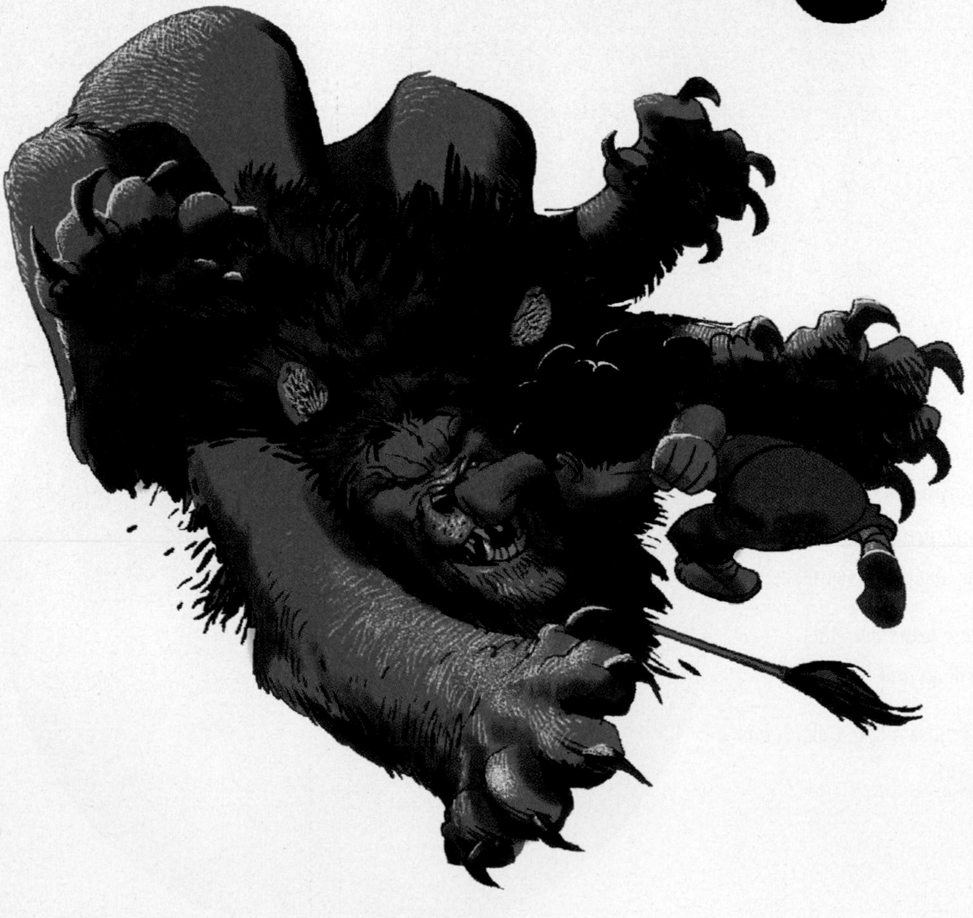

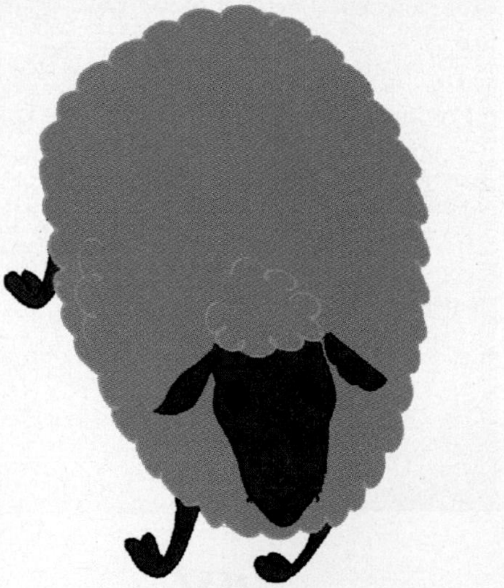

Such a sweet child, thinks Saul. Such faith. Such innocence.

He will have to learn the hard way.

"Go," says Saul, "and the LORD be with you."

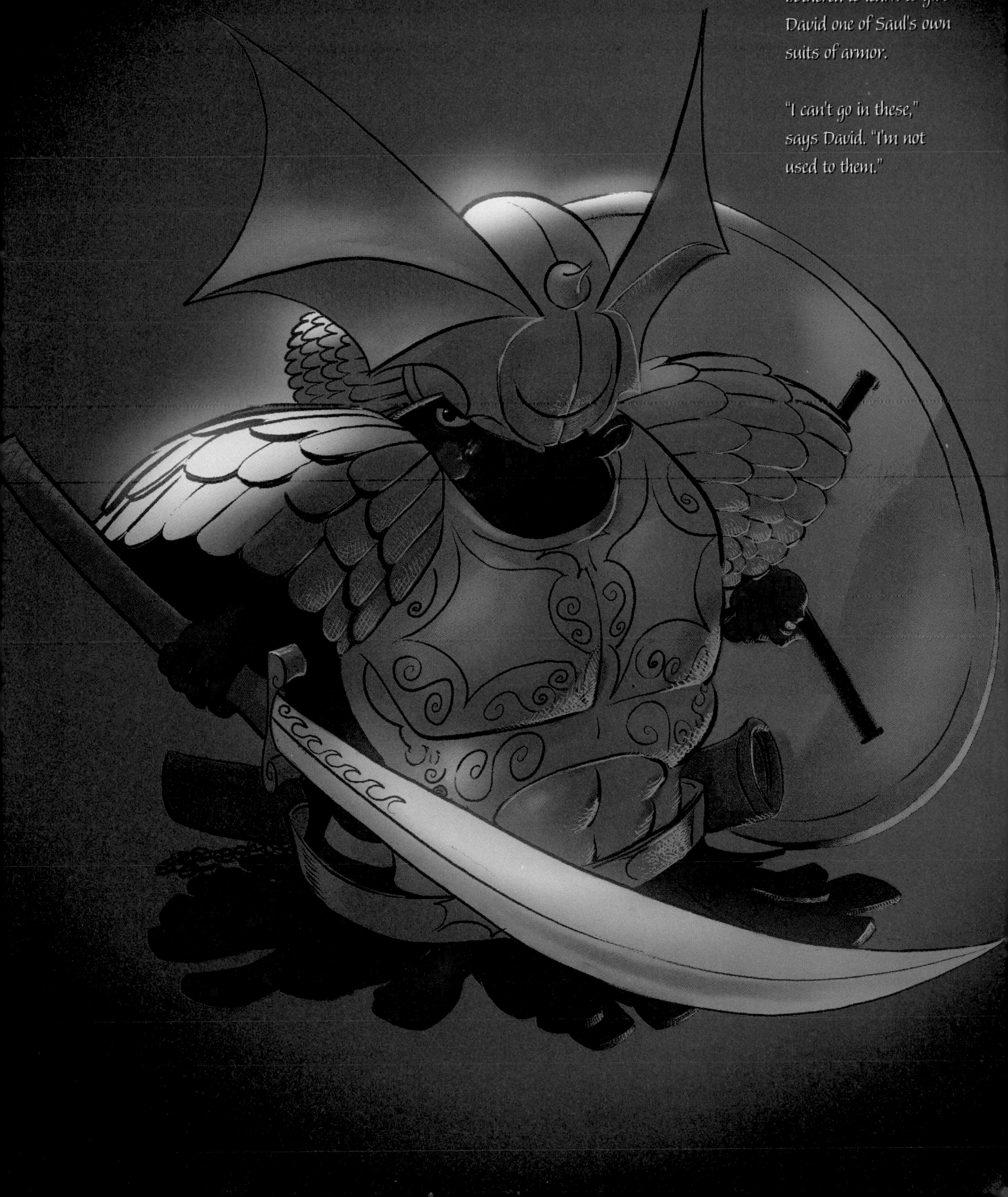

Saul orders some guys whose names he never bothered to learn to give David one of Saul's own suits of armor.

"I can't go in these," says David. "I'm not used to them."

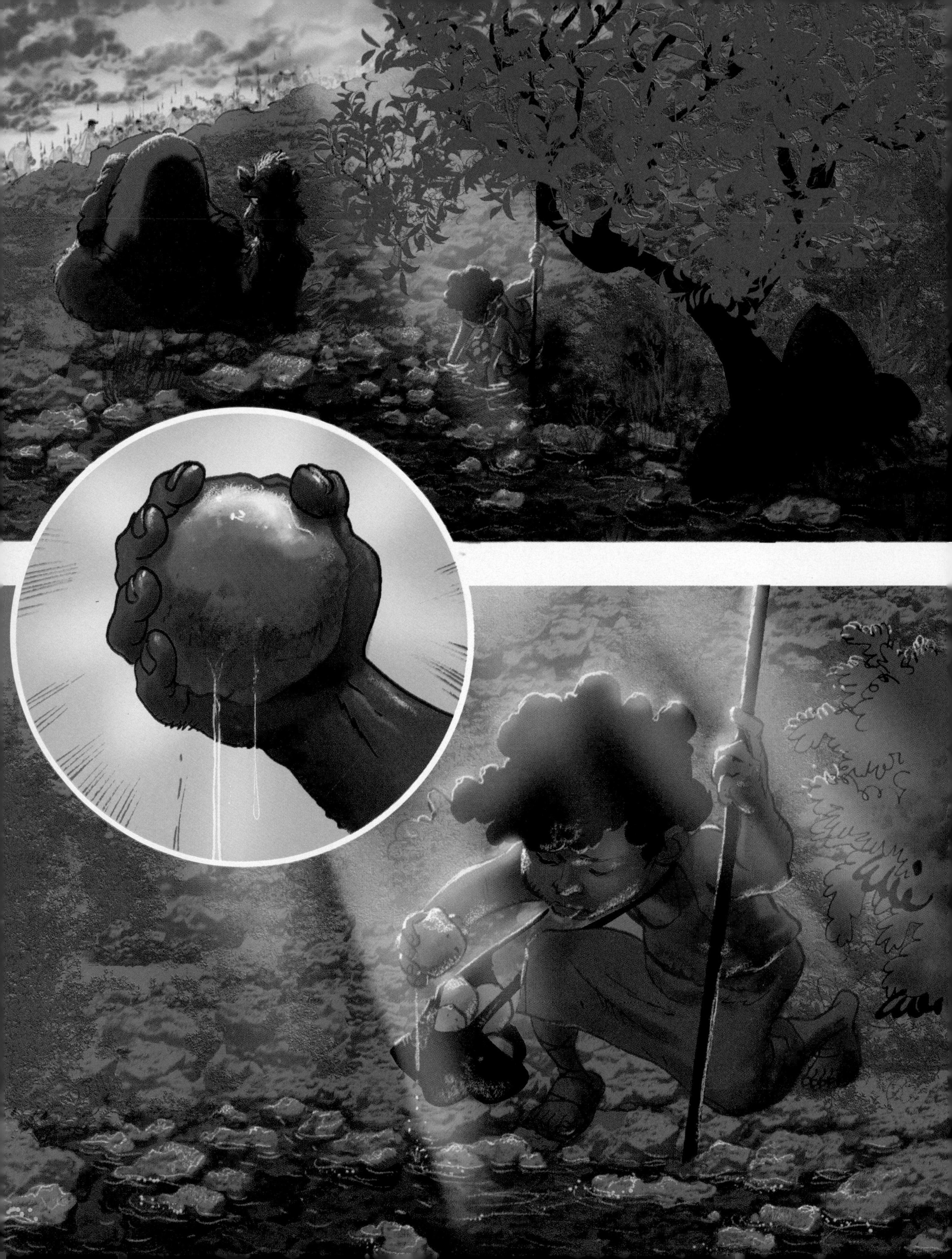

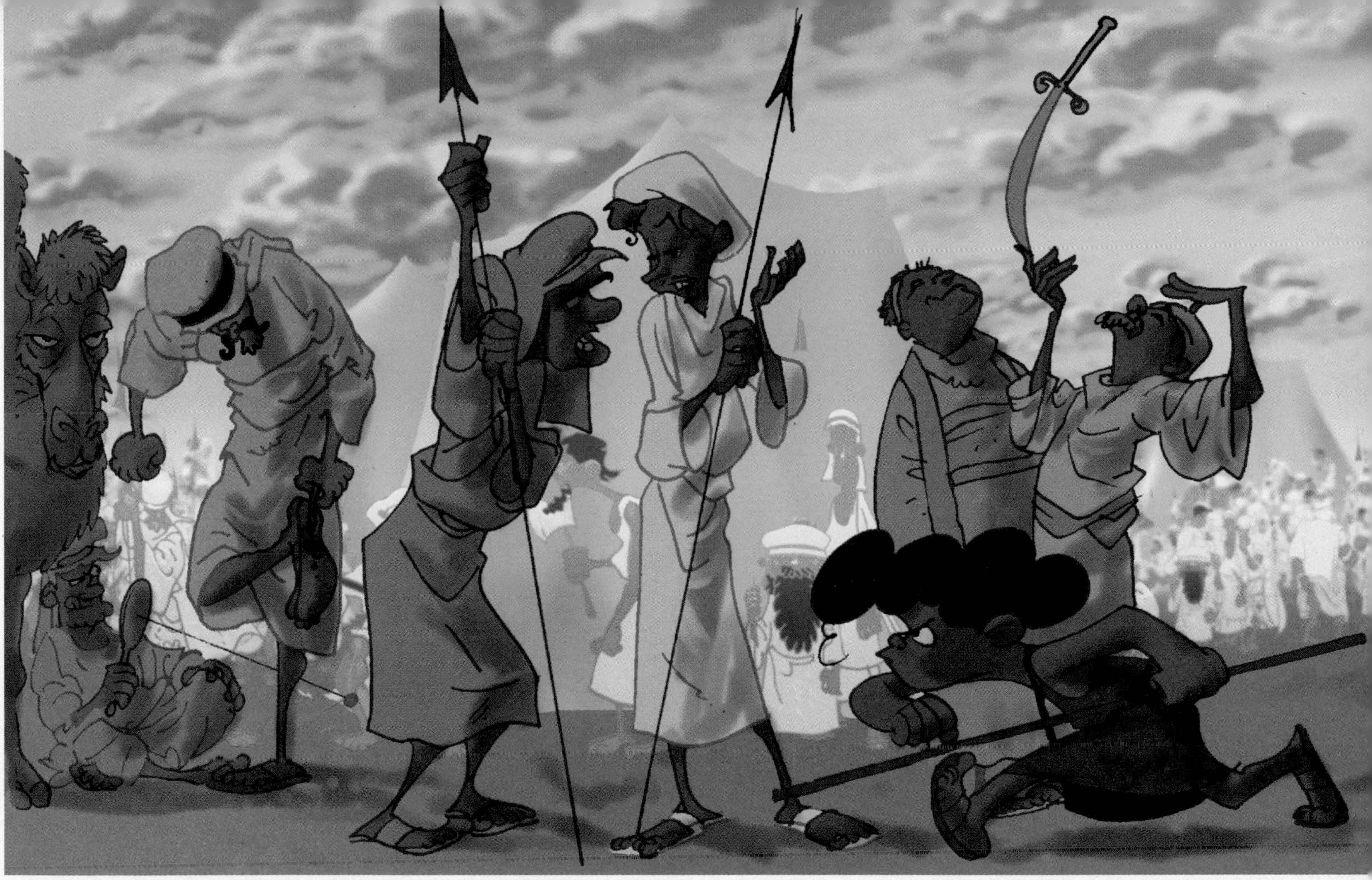

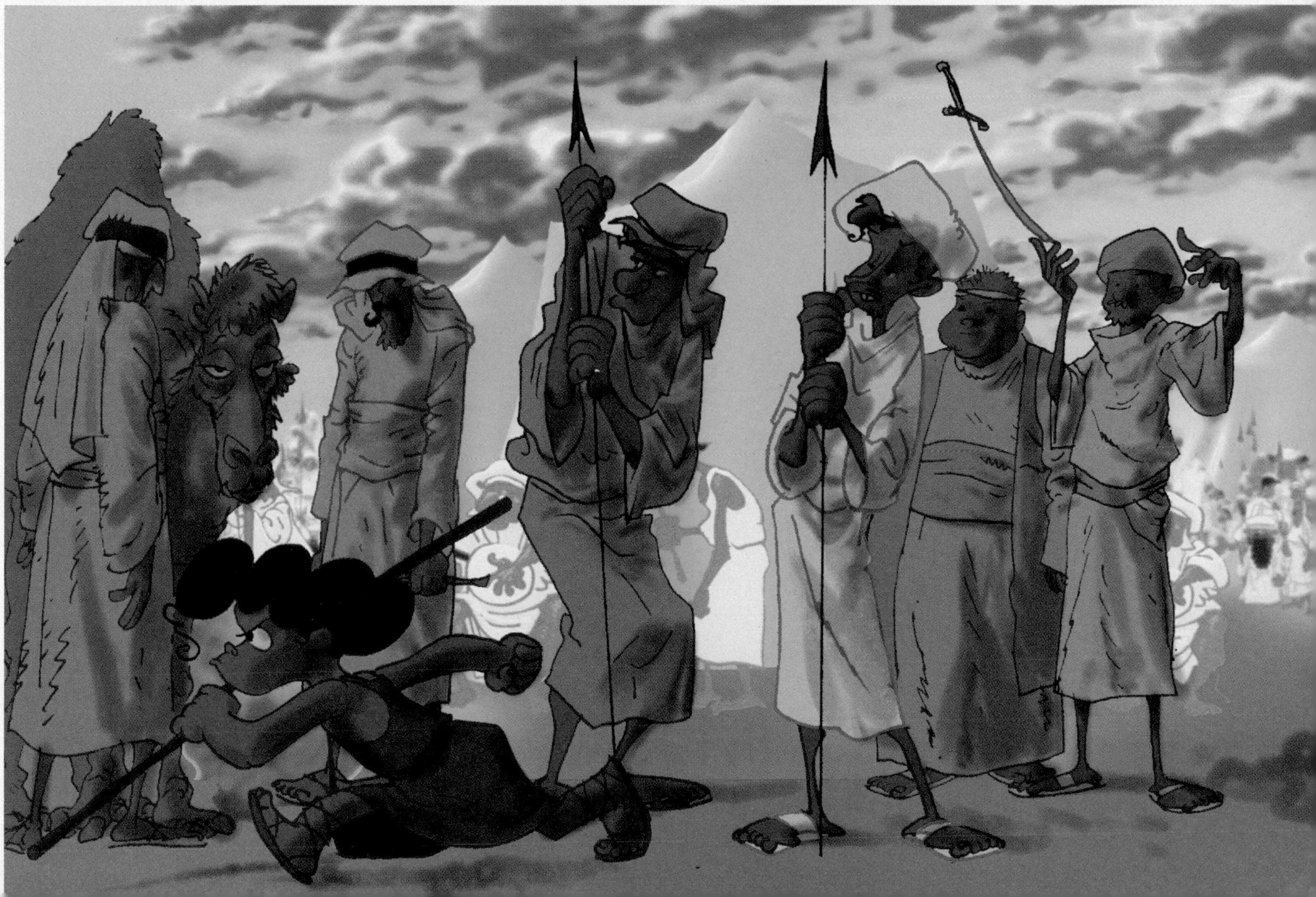

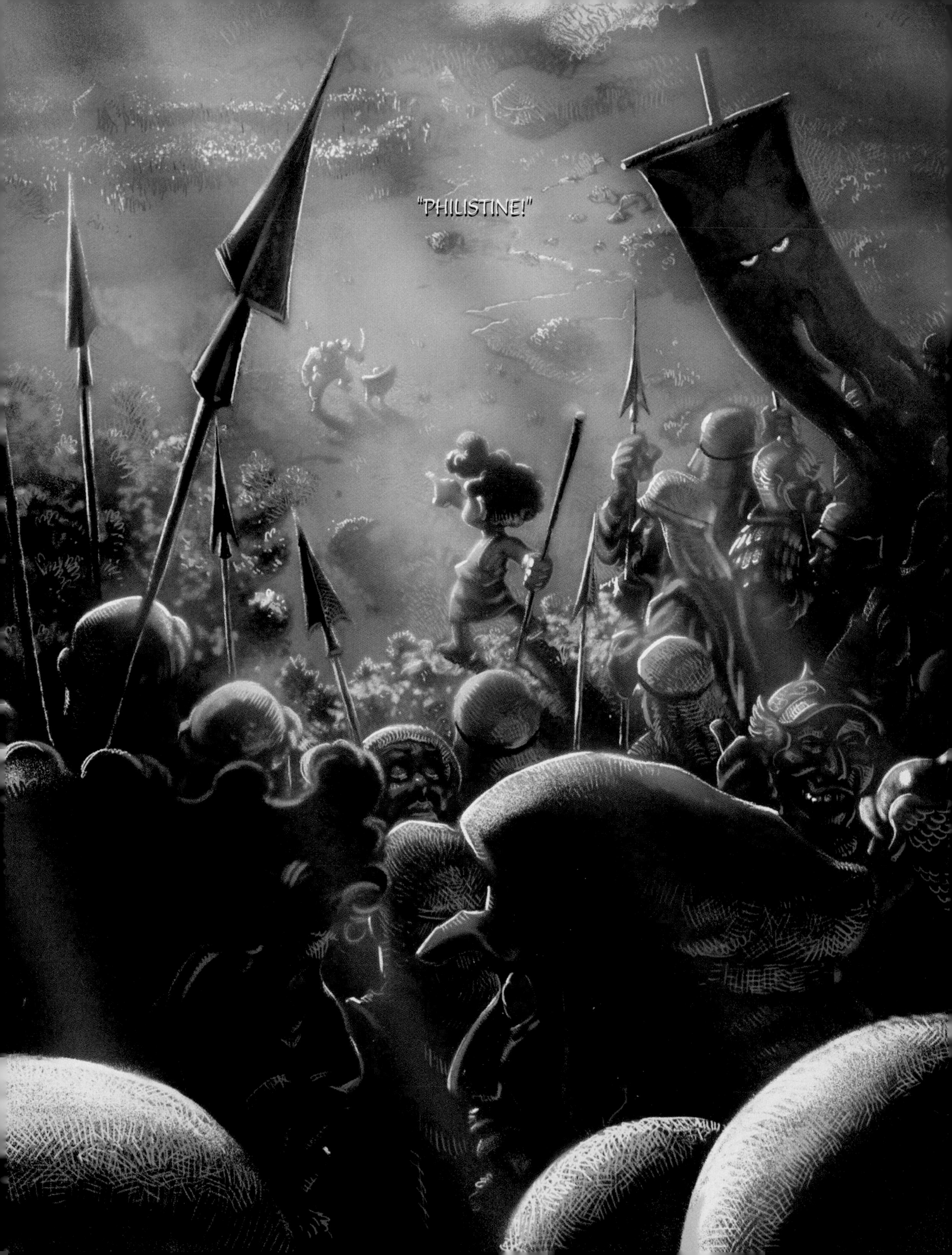
"PHILISTINE!"

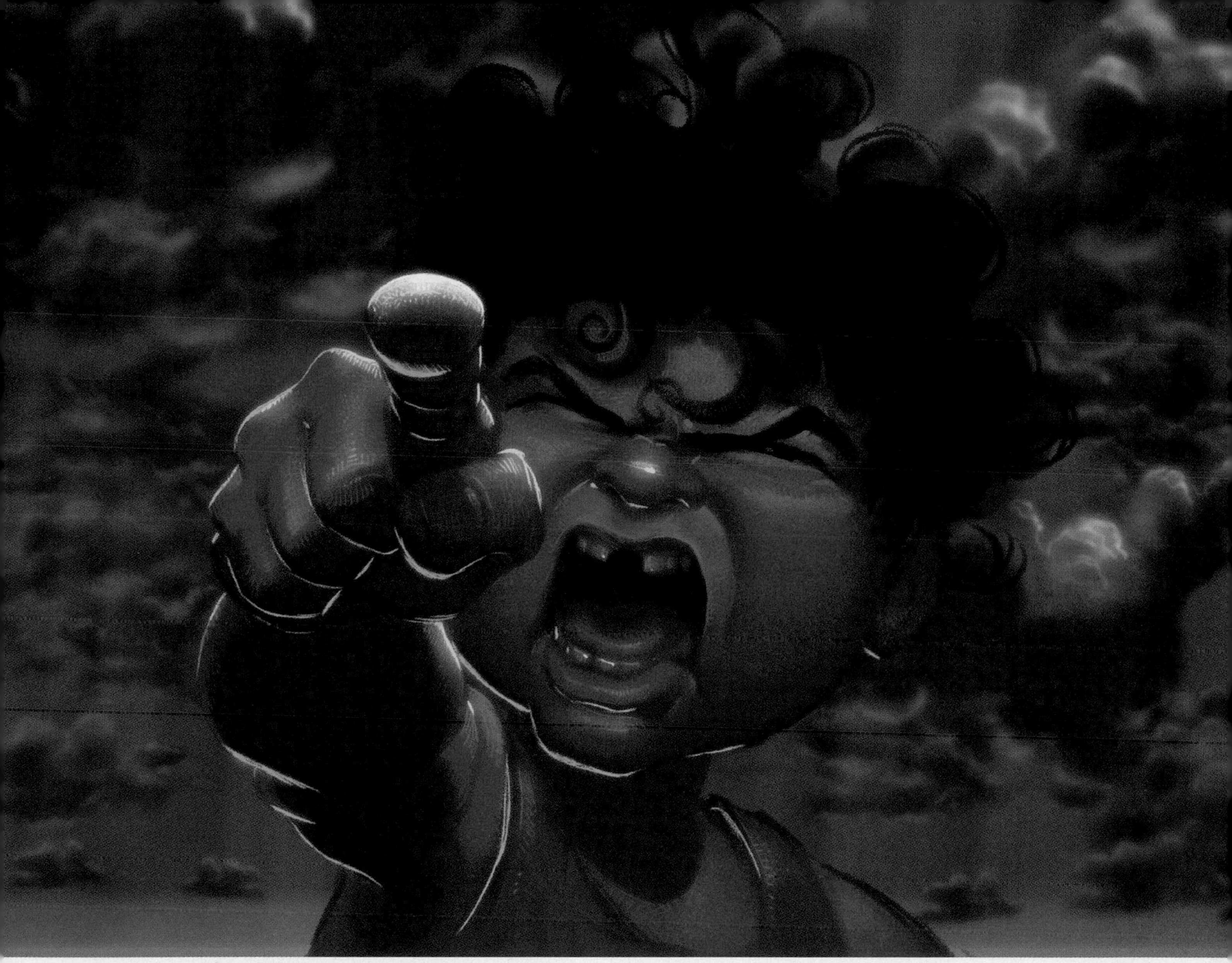

Goliath looks up at David on the hill, and says, "Am I a dog, that you come at me with sticks? Come here, and I'll give your flesh to the birds of the air and the beasts of the field!"

David calls back, "You come against me with sword and spear and javelin, but I come against you in the name of the LORD almighty, the God of the armies of Israel, whom you have defied. This day the LORD will hand you over to me, and I'll strike you down and cut off your head. Today I will give the carcasses of the Philistine army to the birds of the air and the beasts of the earth, and the whole world will know that there is a God in Israel. All those gathered here will know that it is not by sword or spear that the LORD saves; for the battle is the LORD's and he will give all of you into our hands."

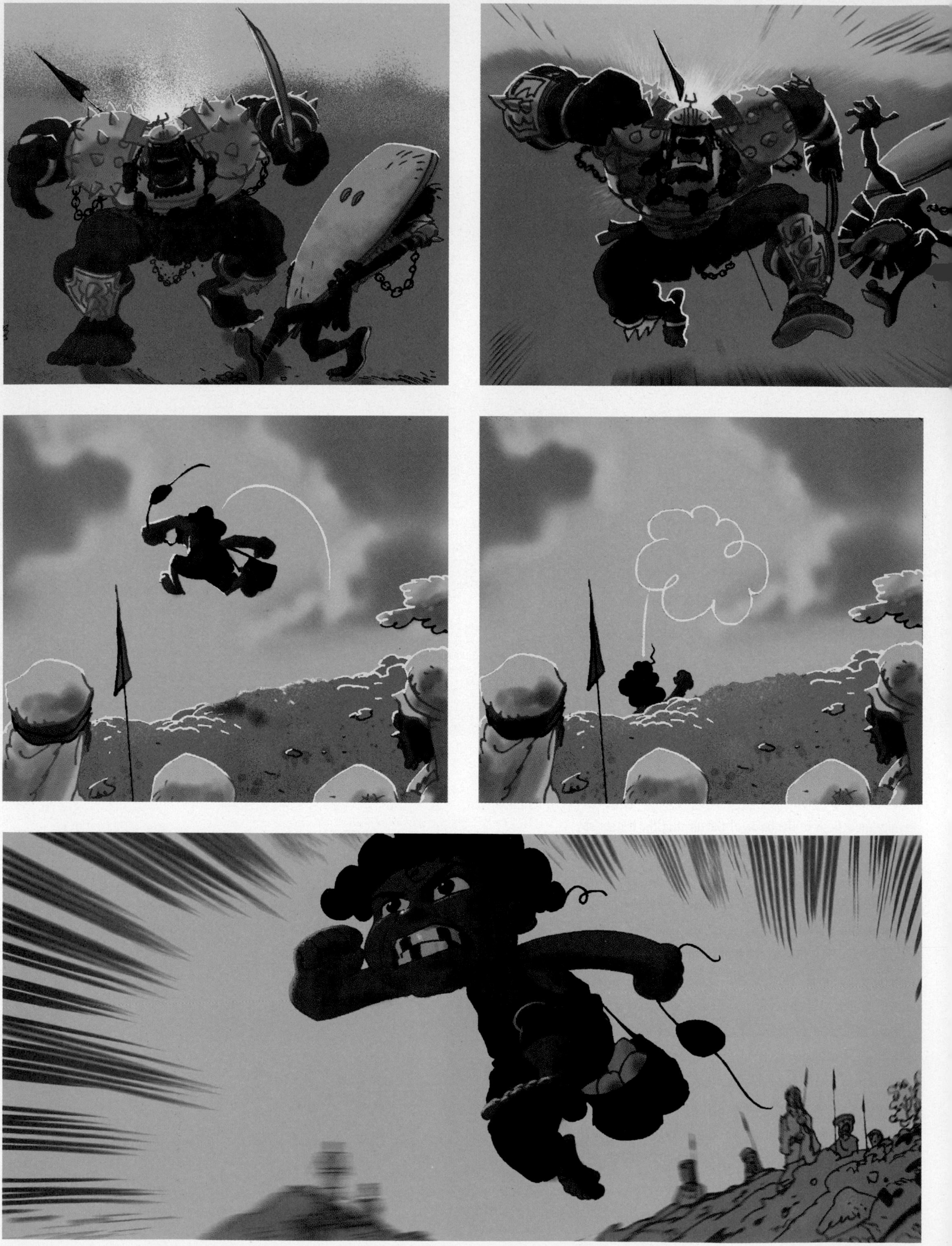

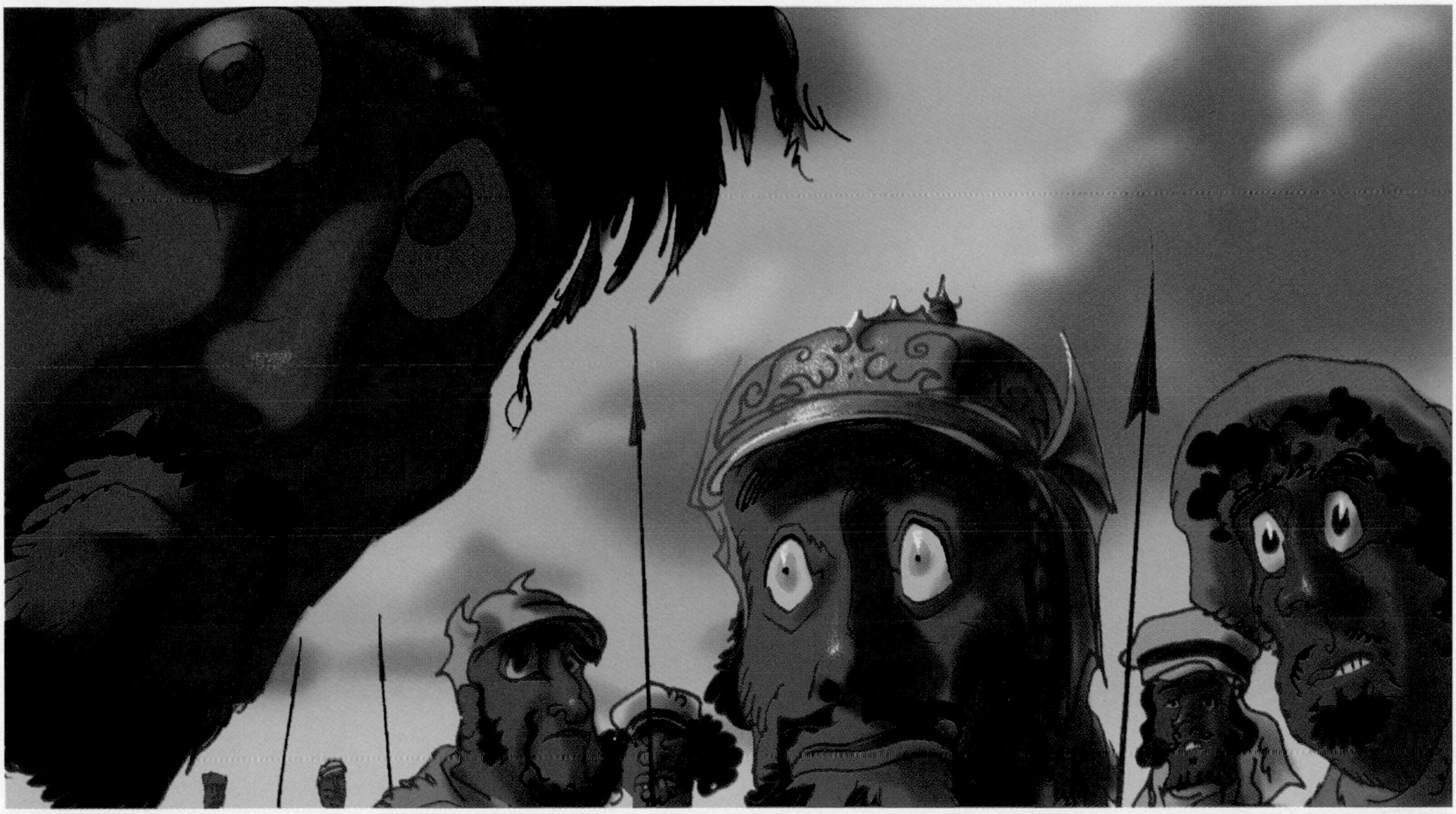

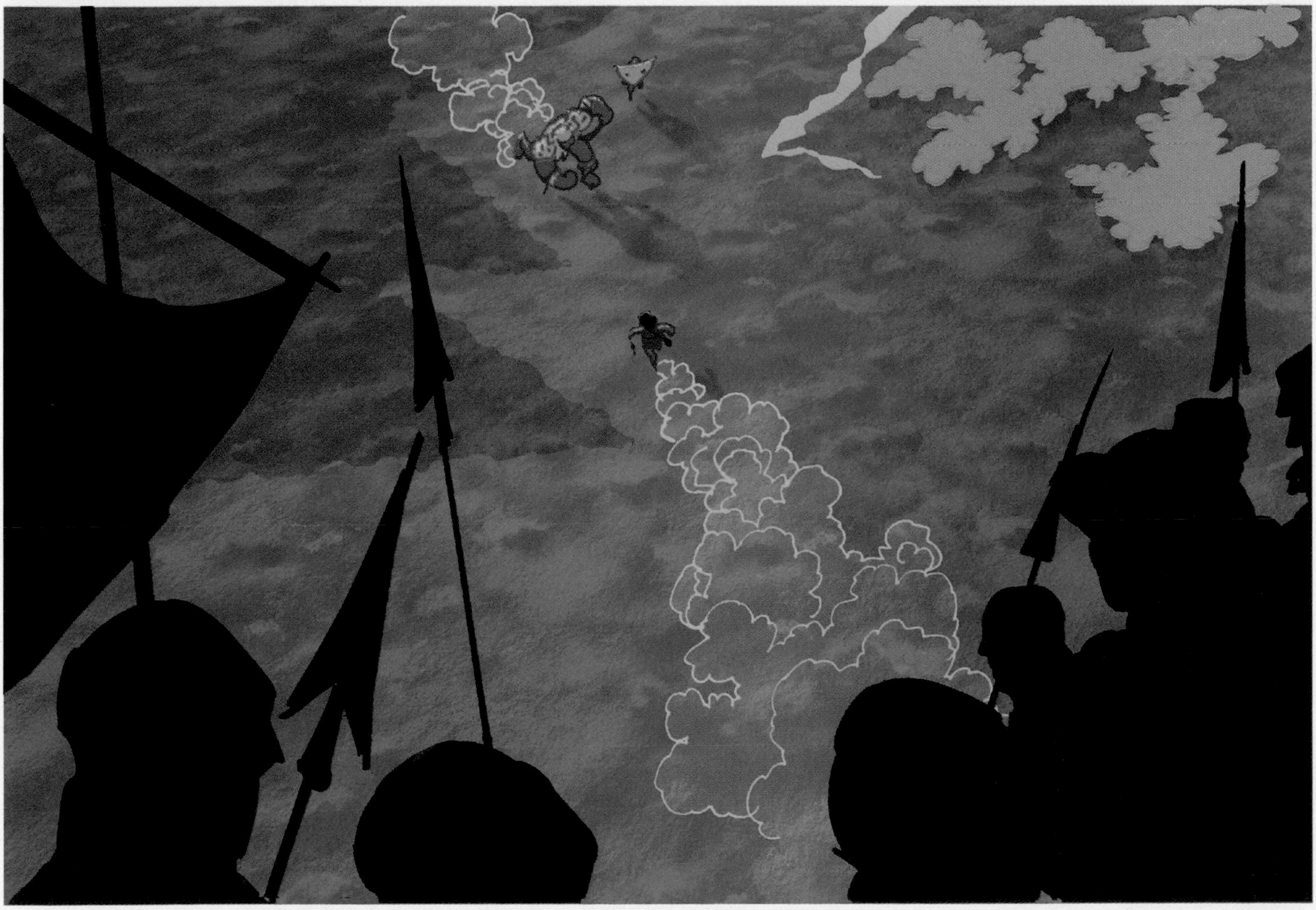

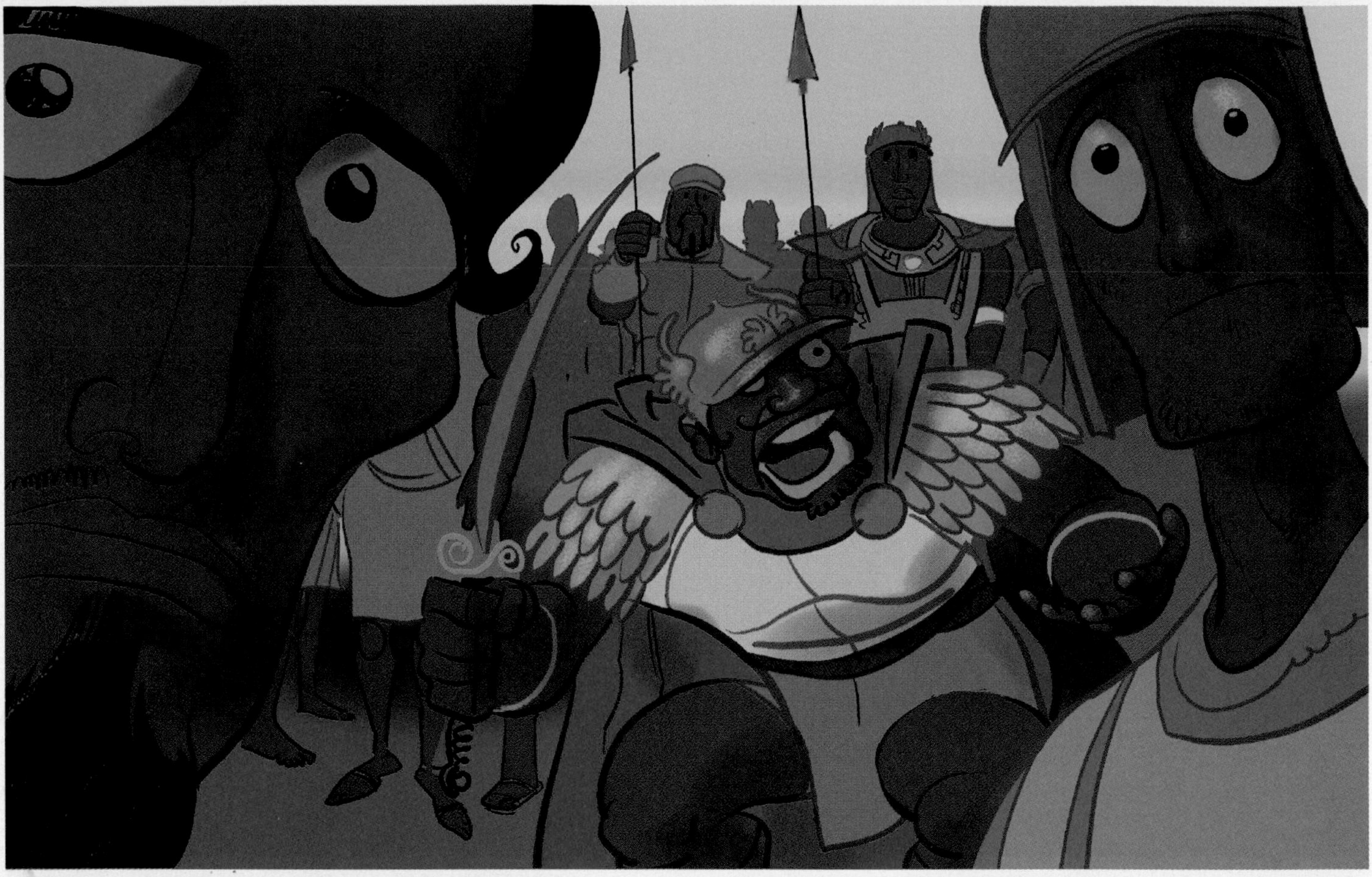

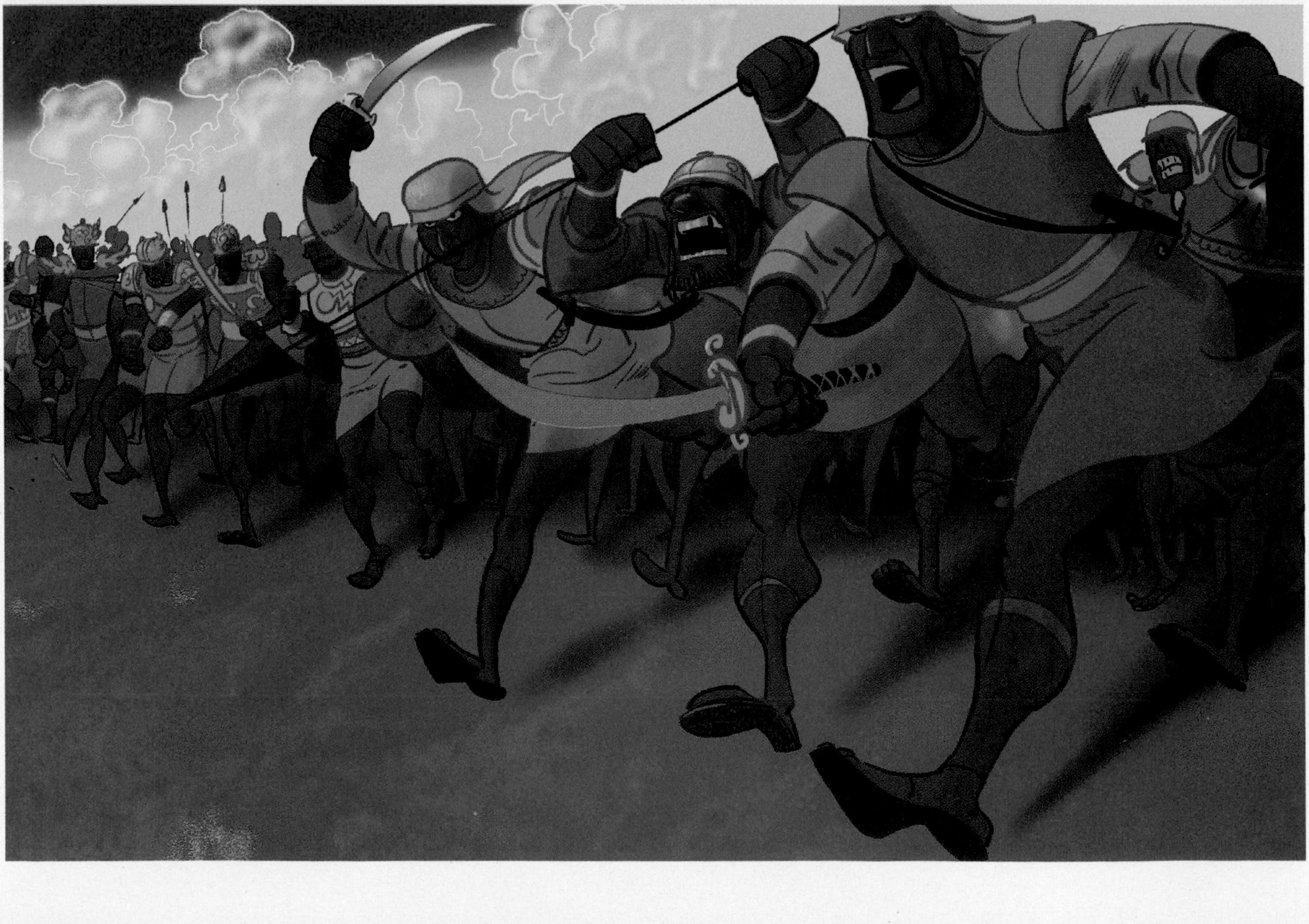

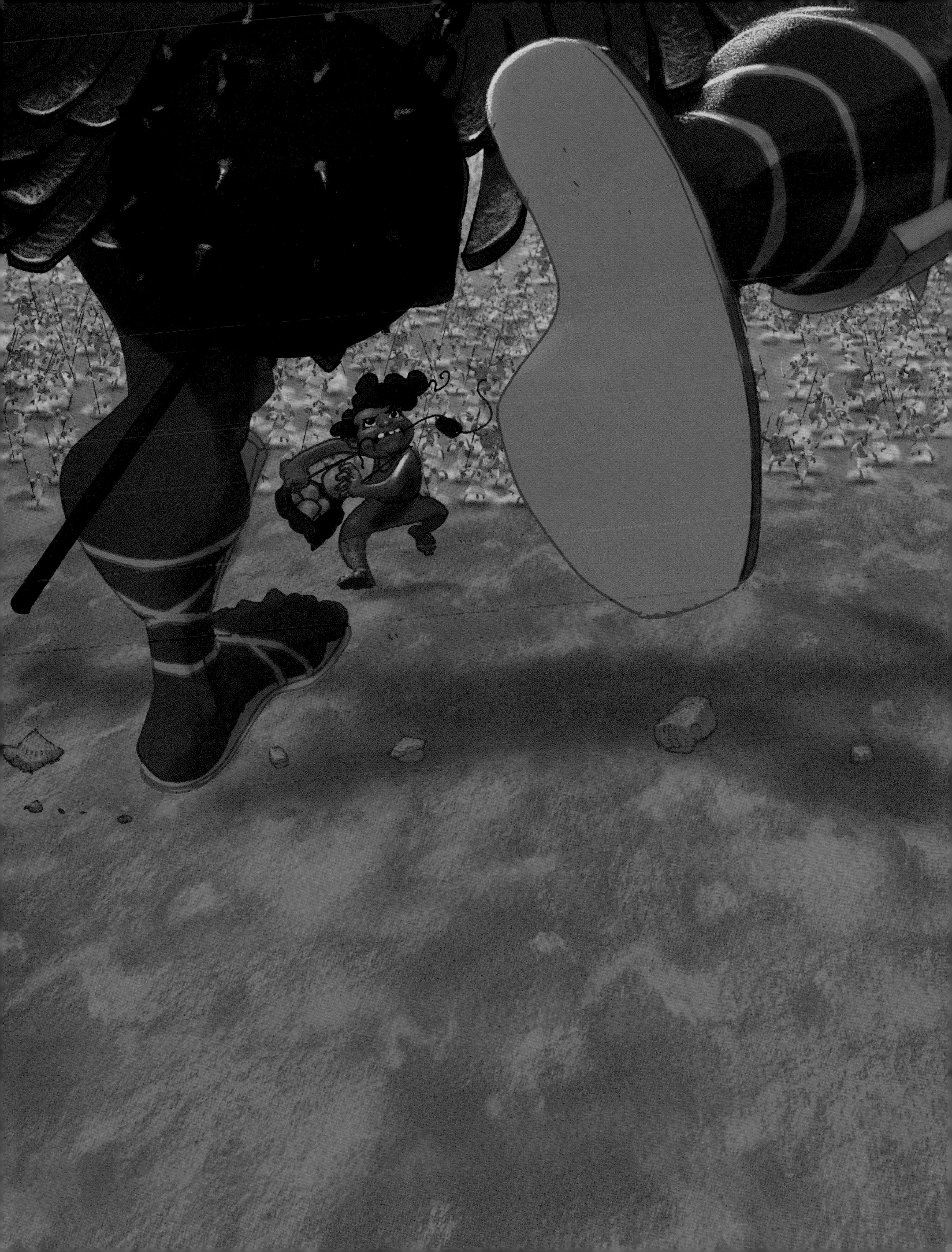

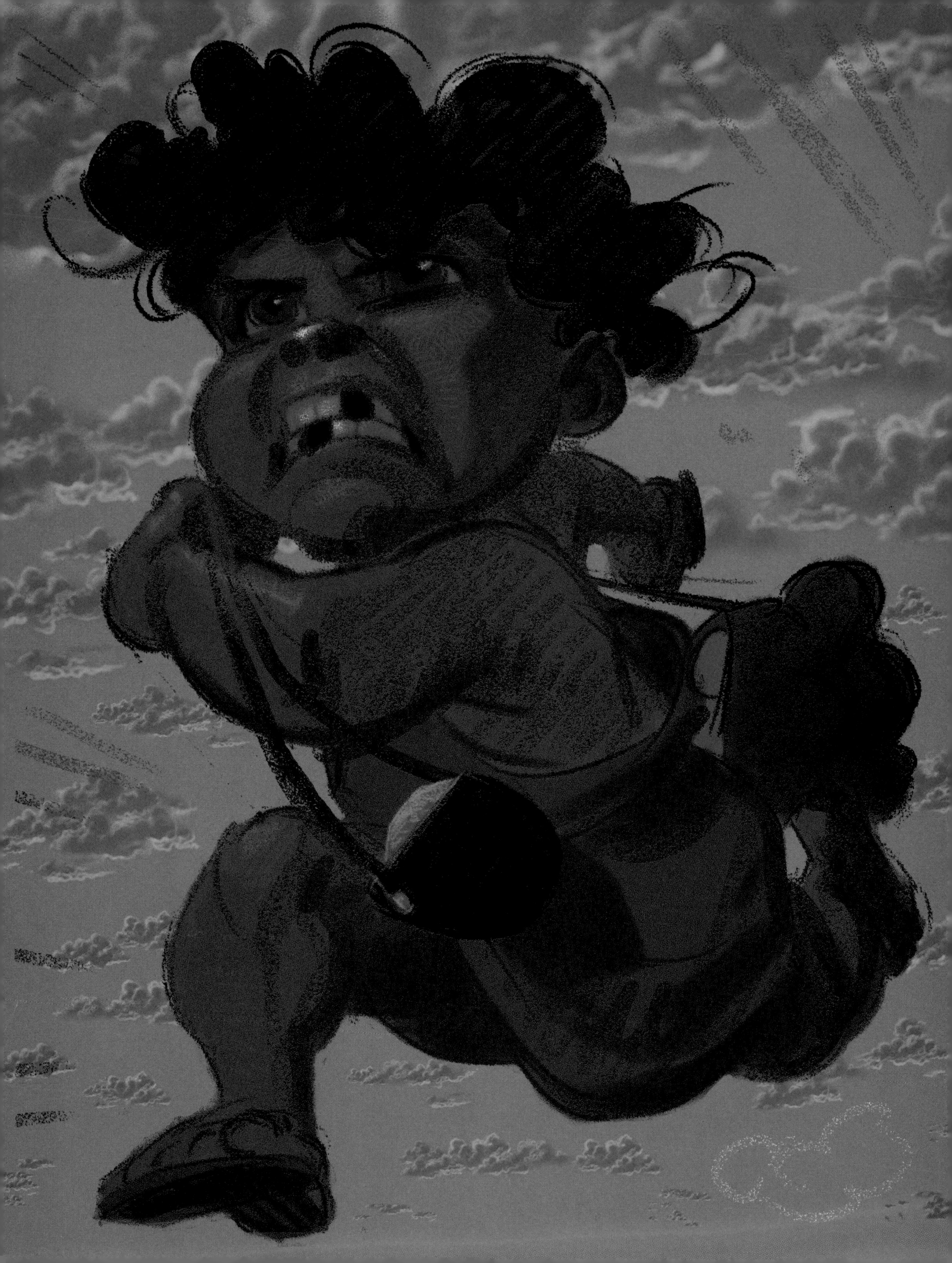

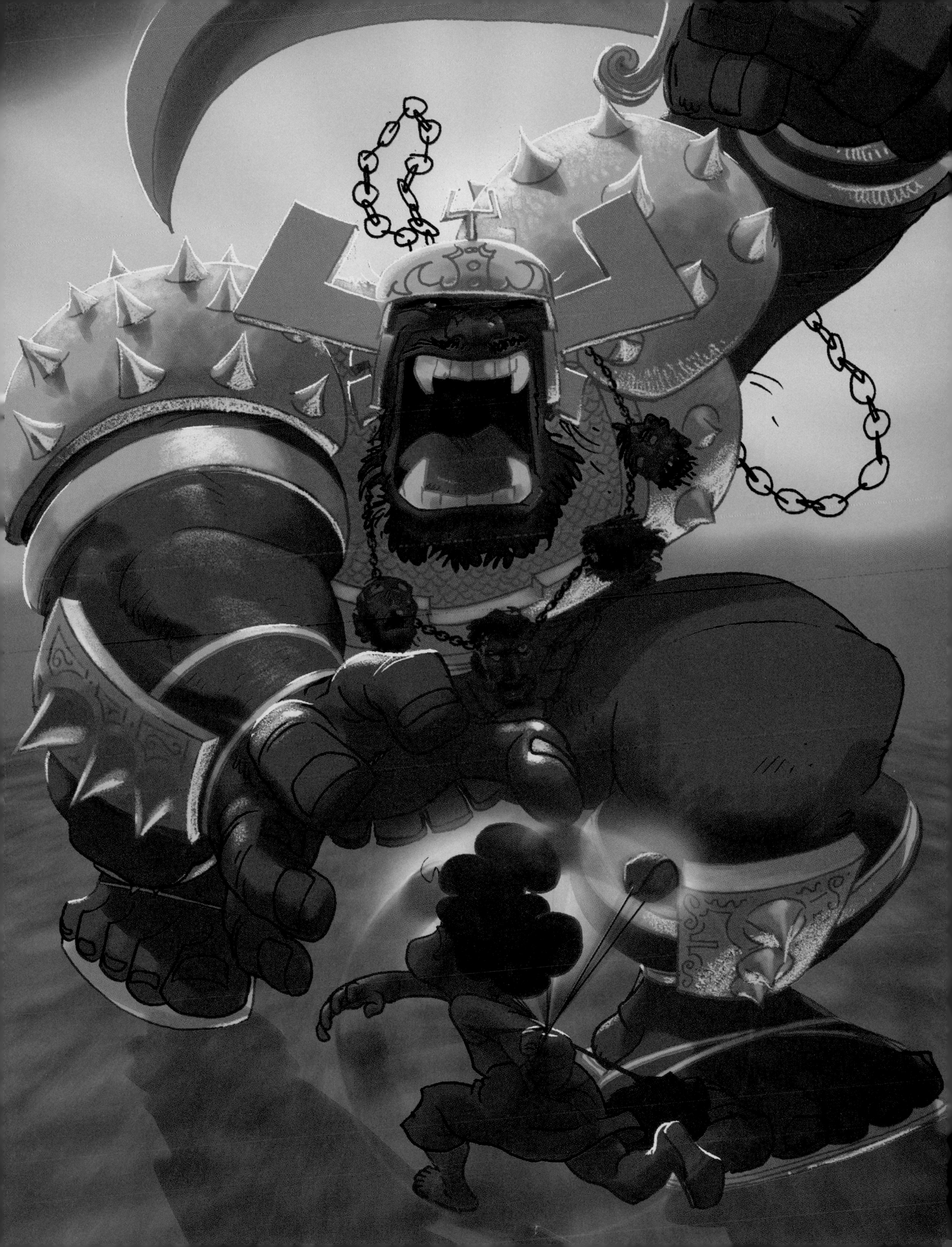

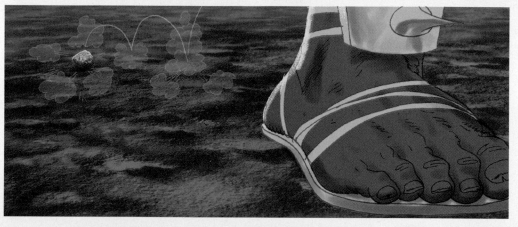

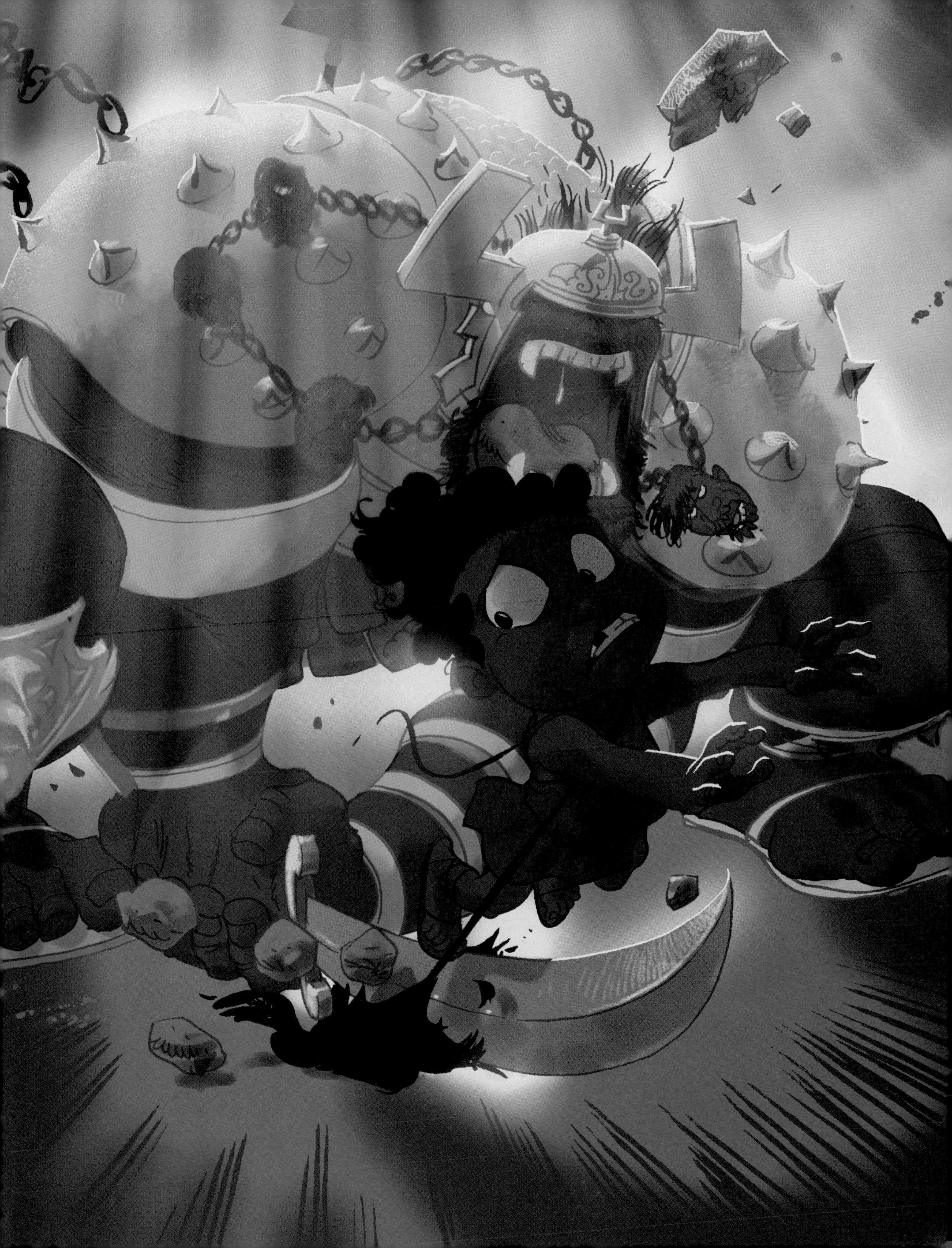

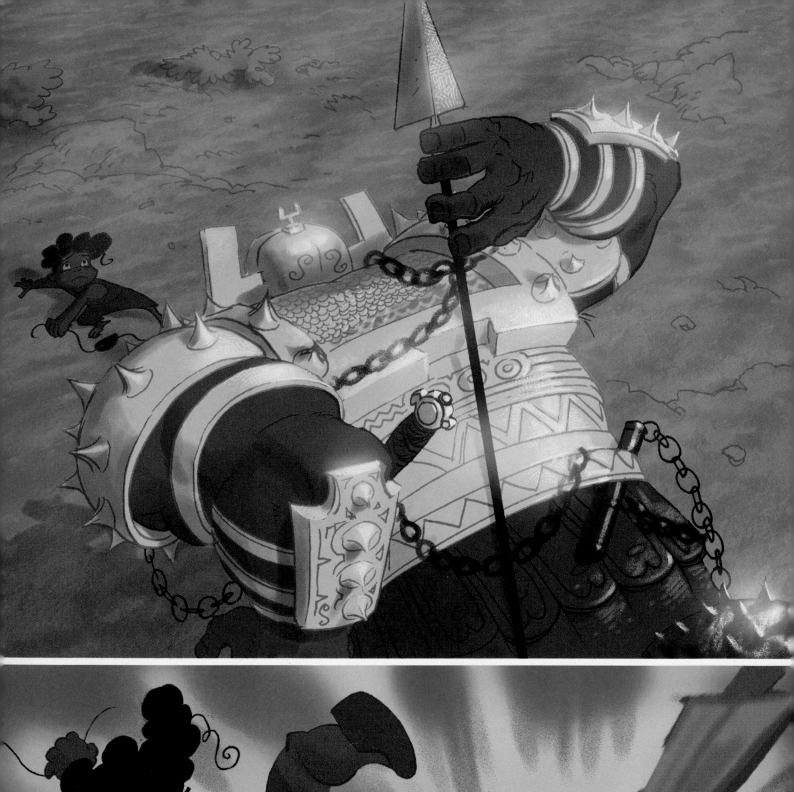

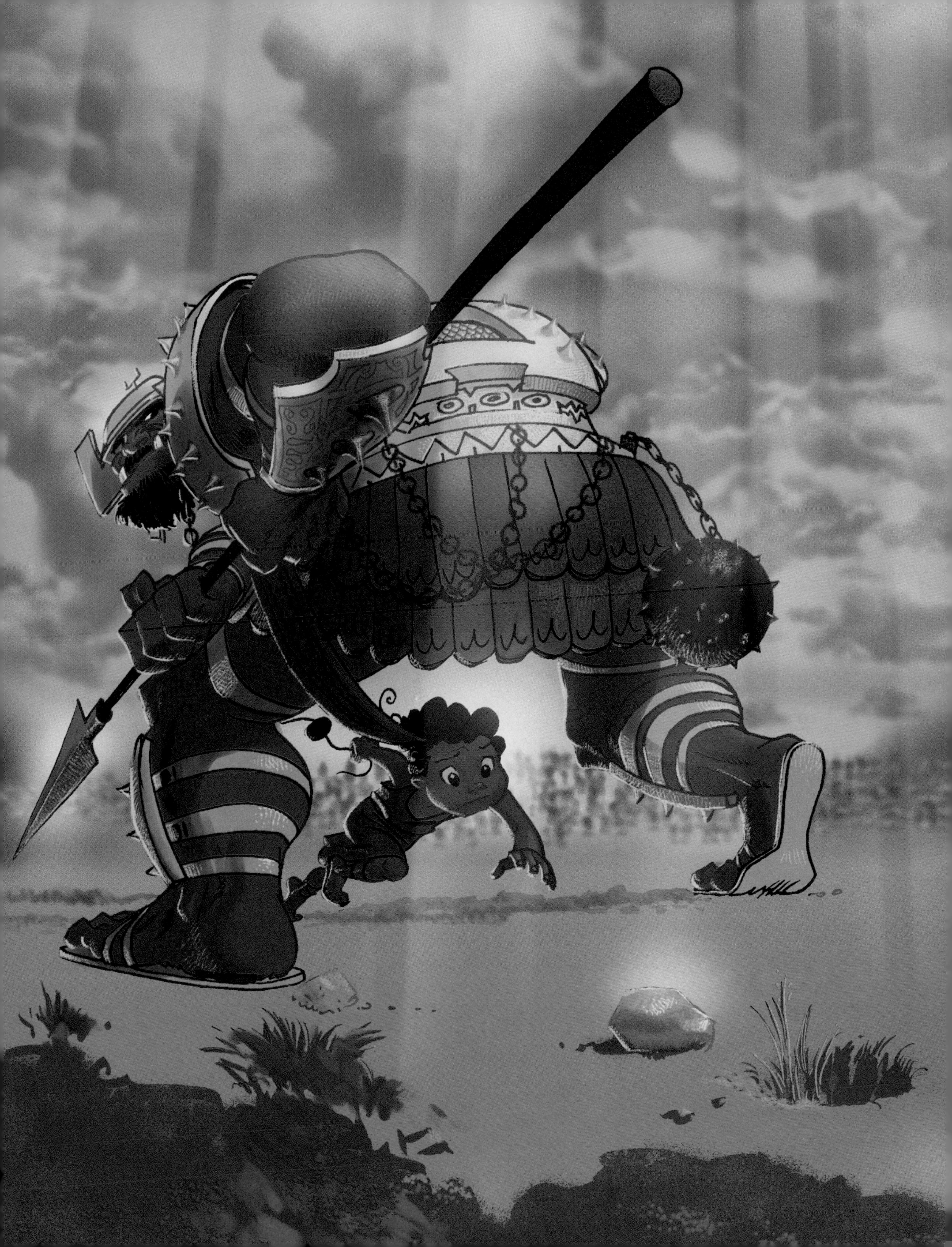

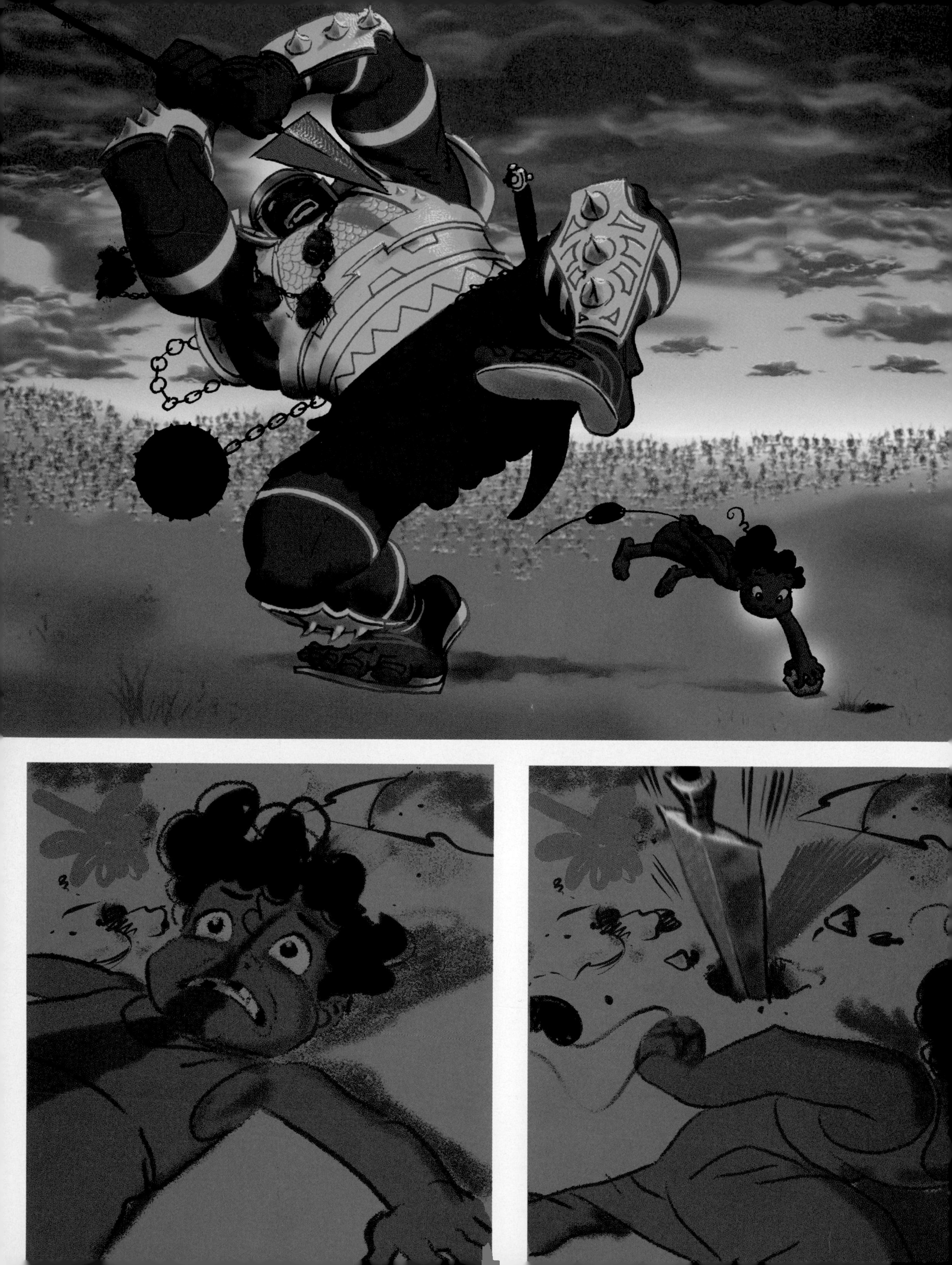

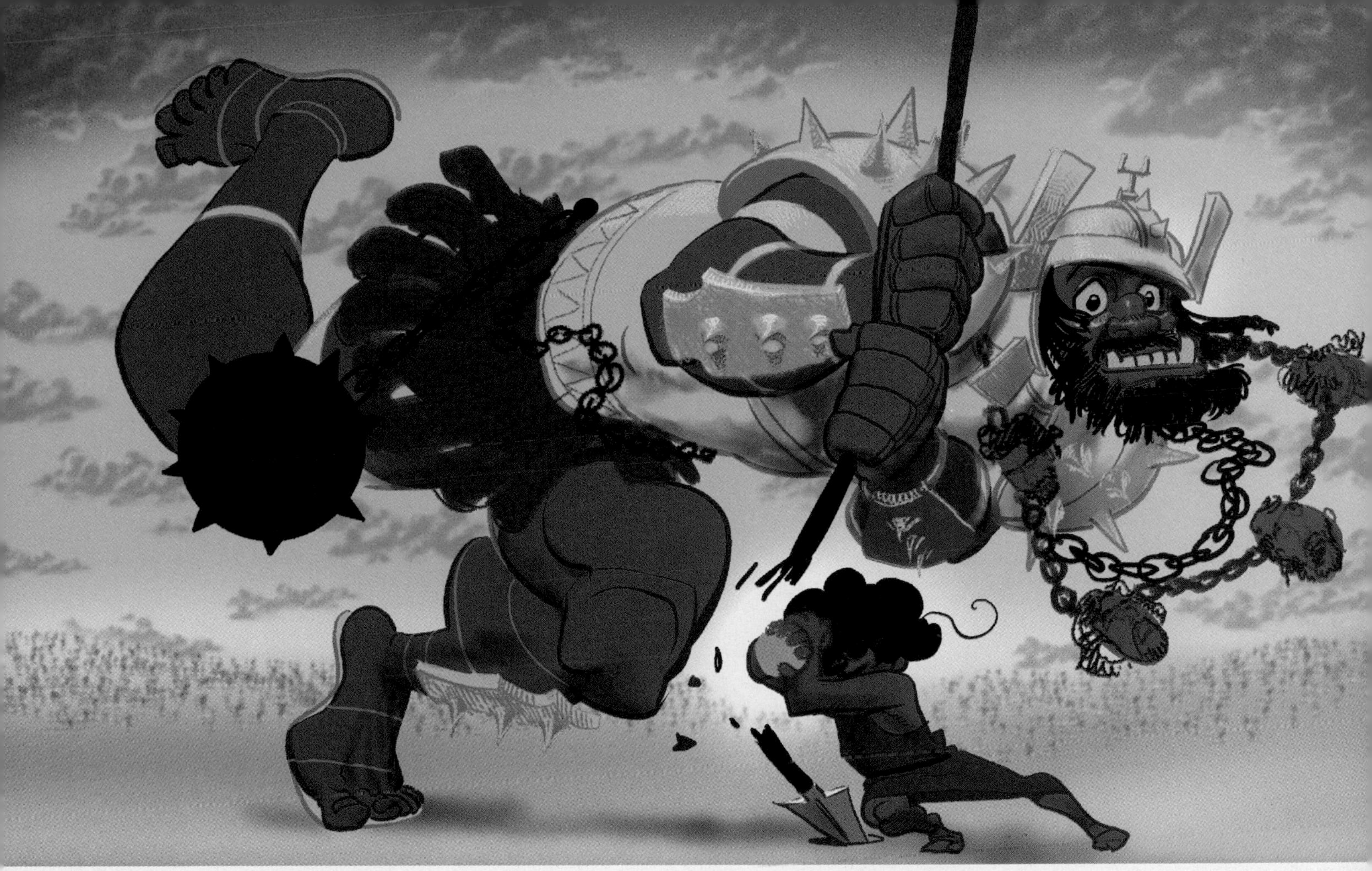

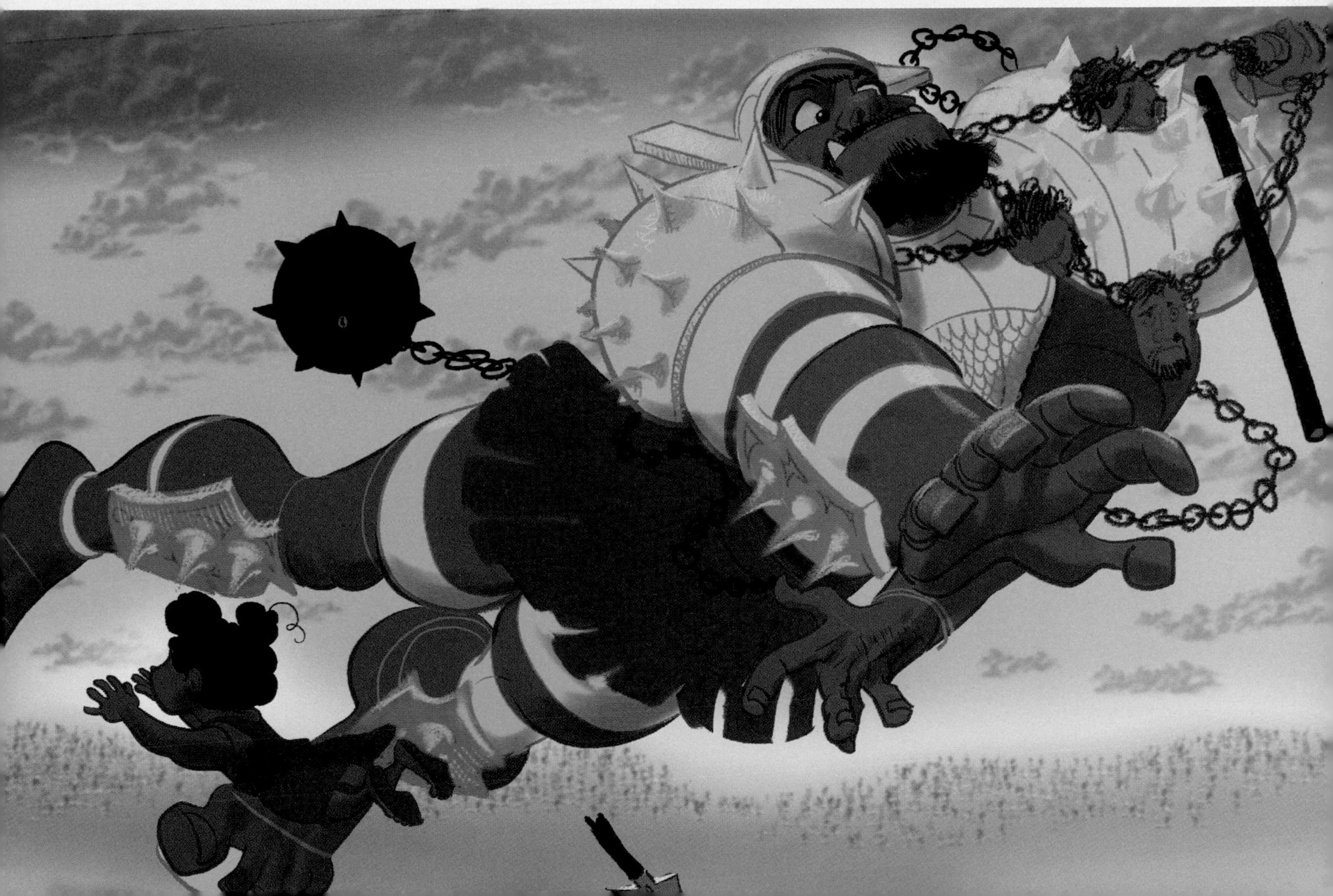

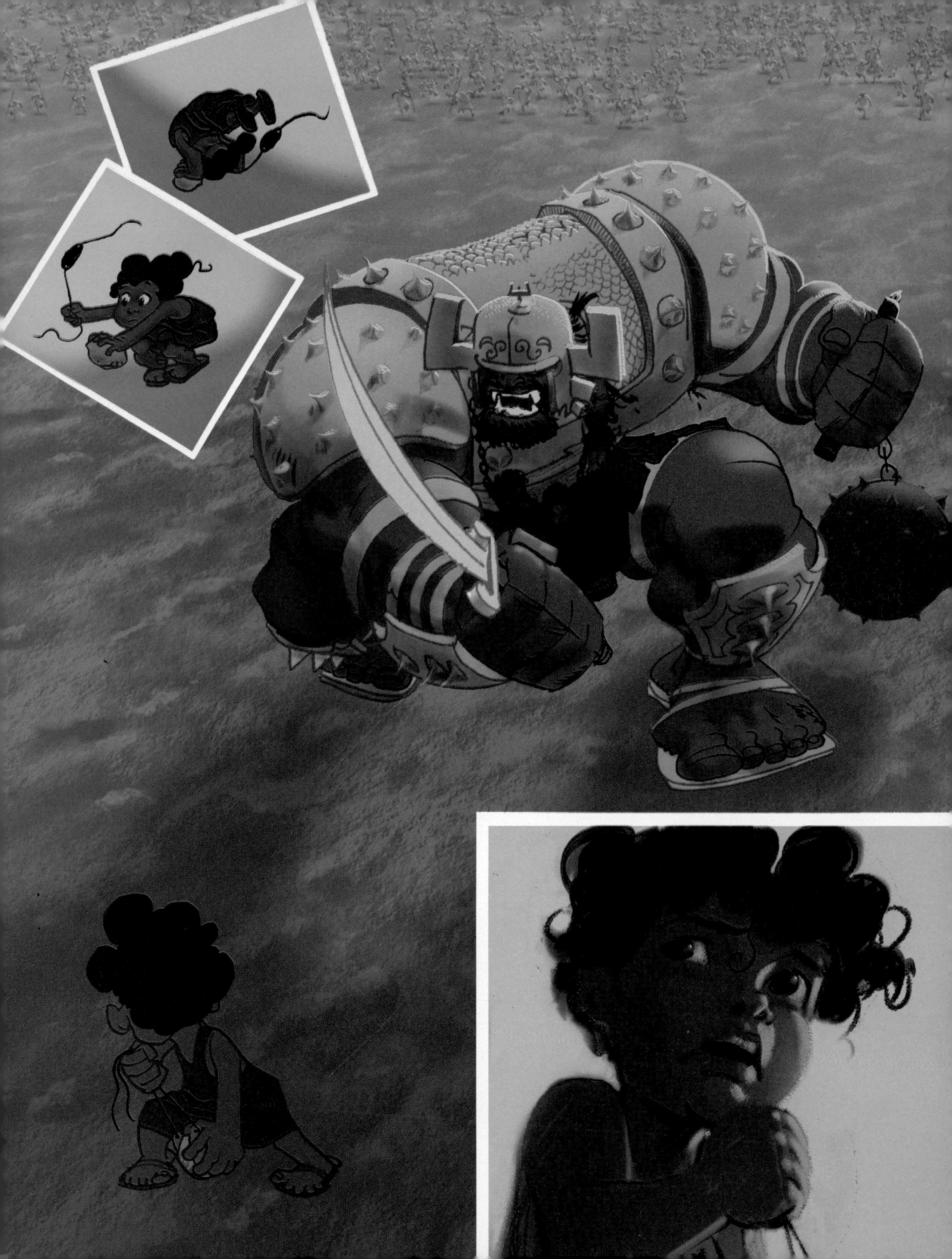

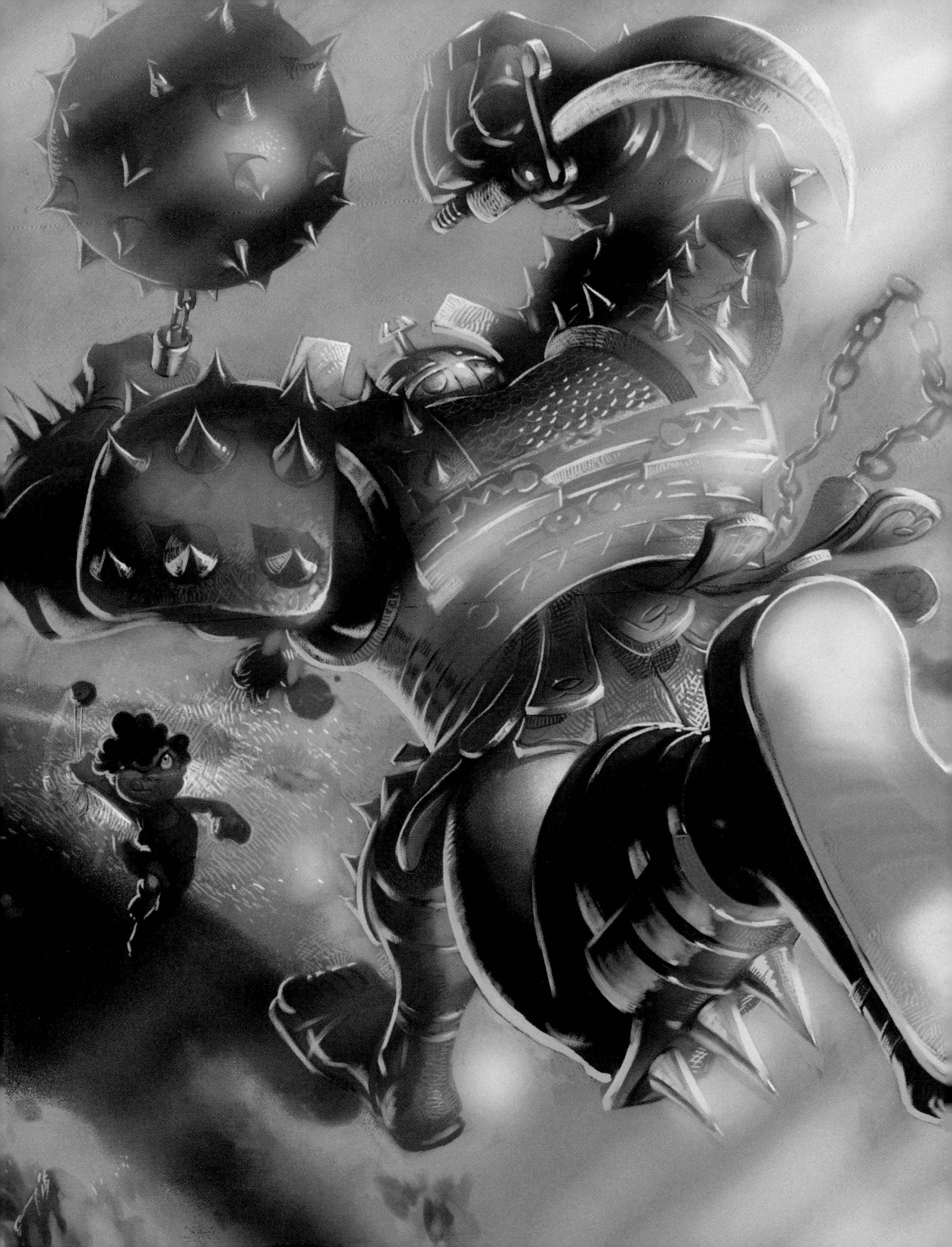

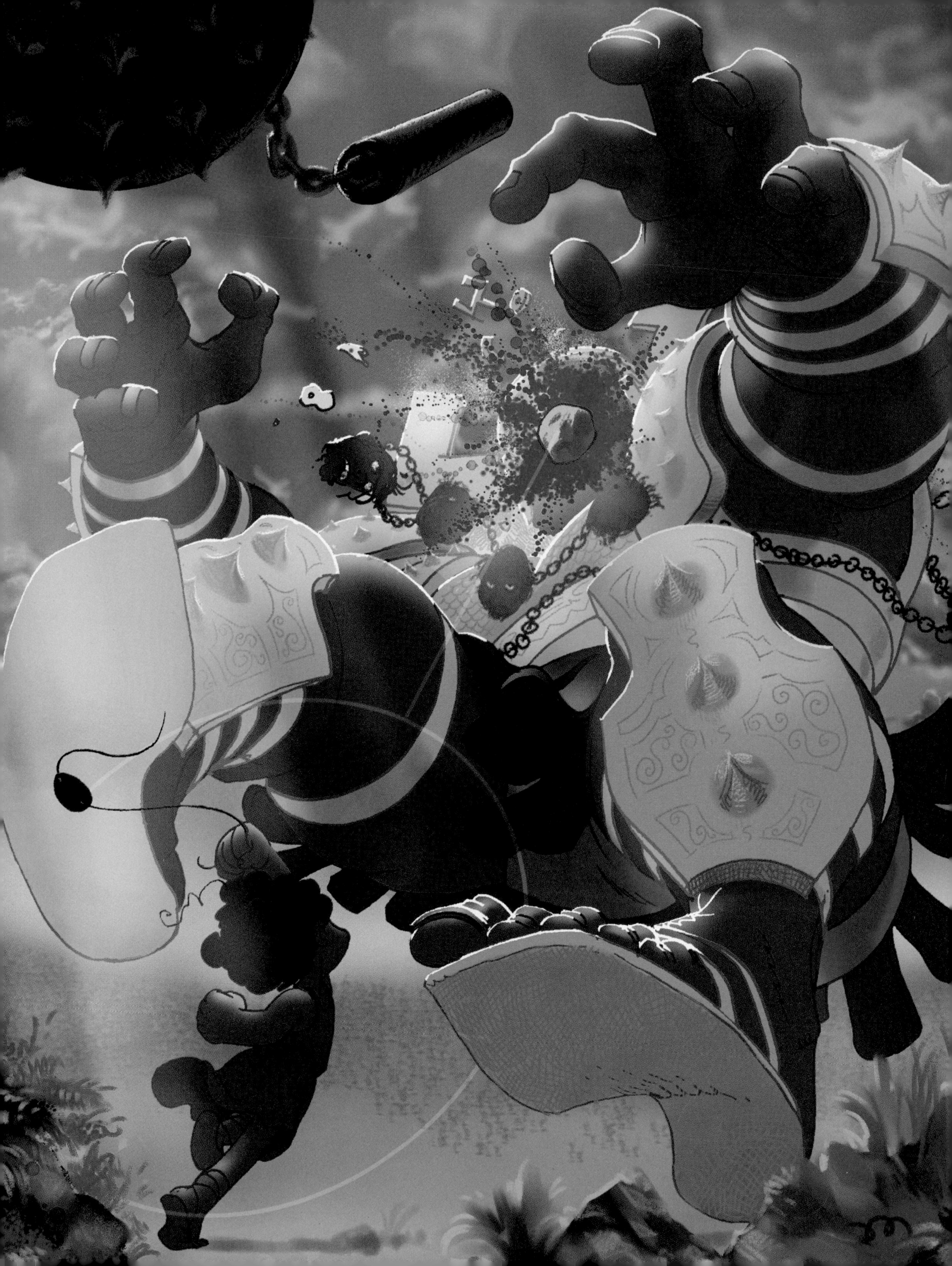

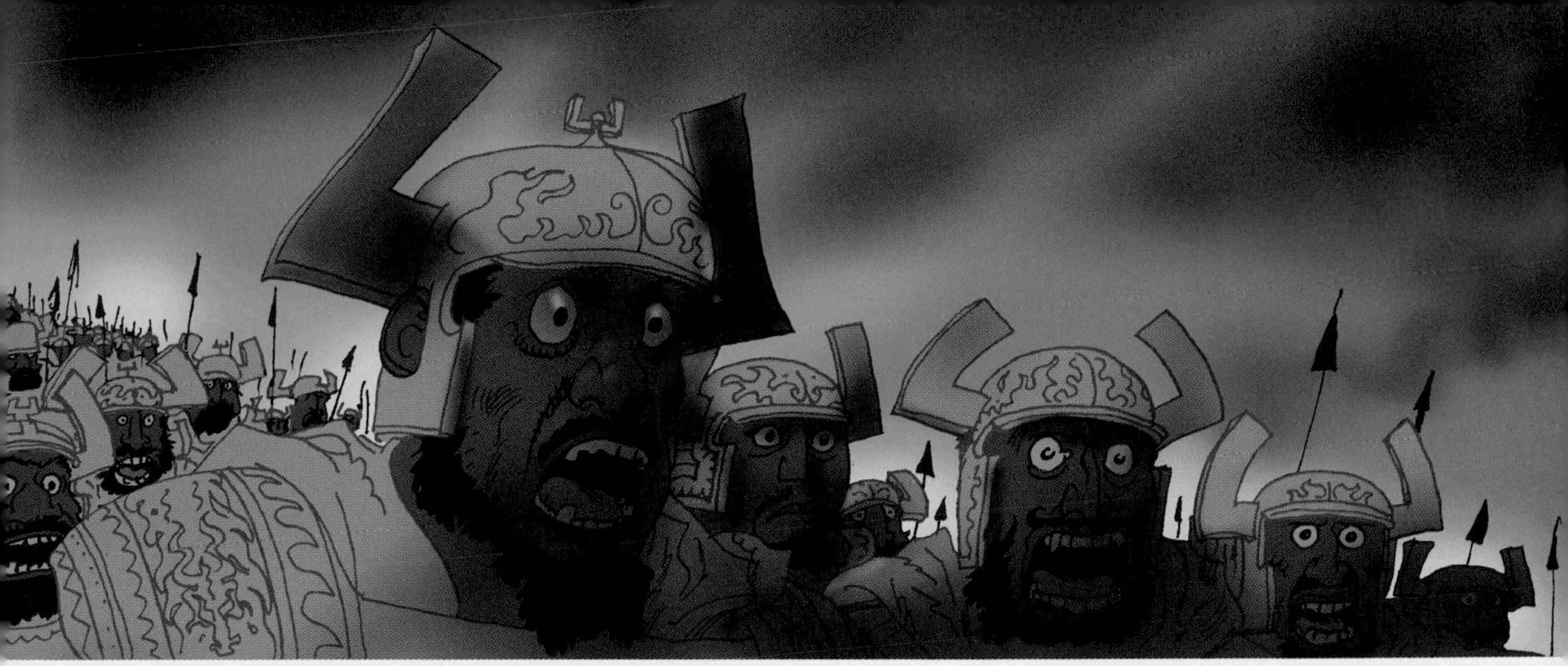

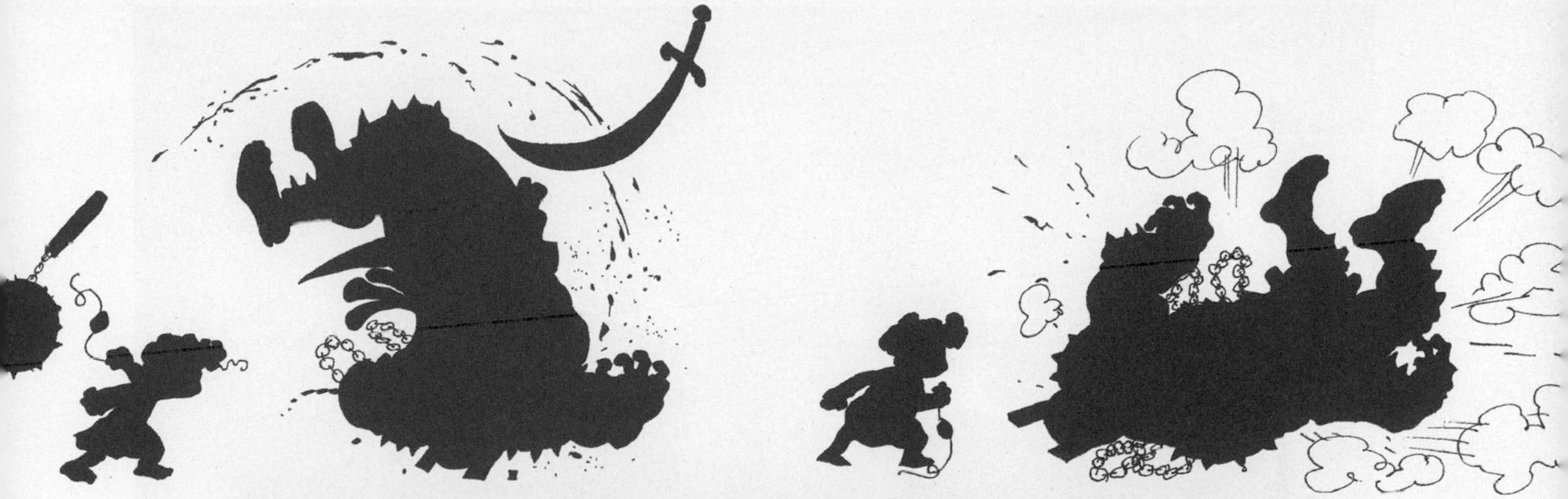

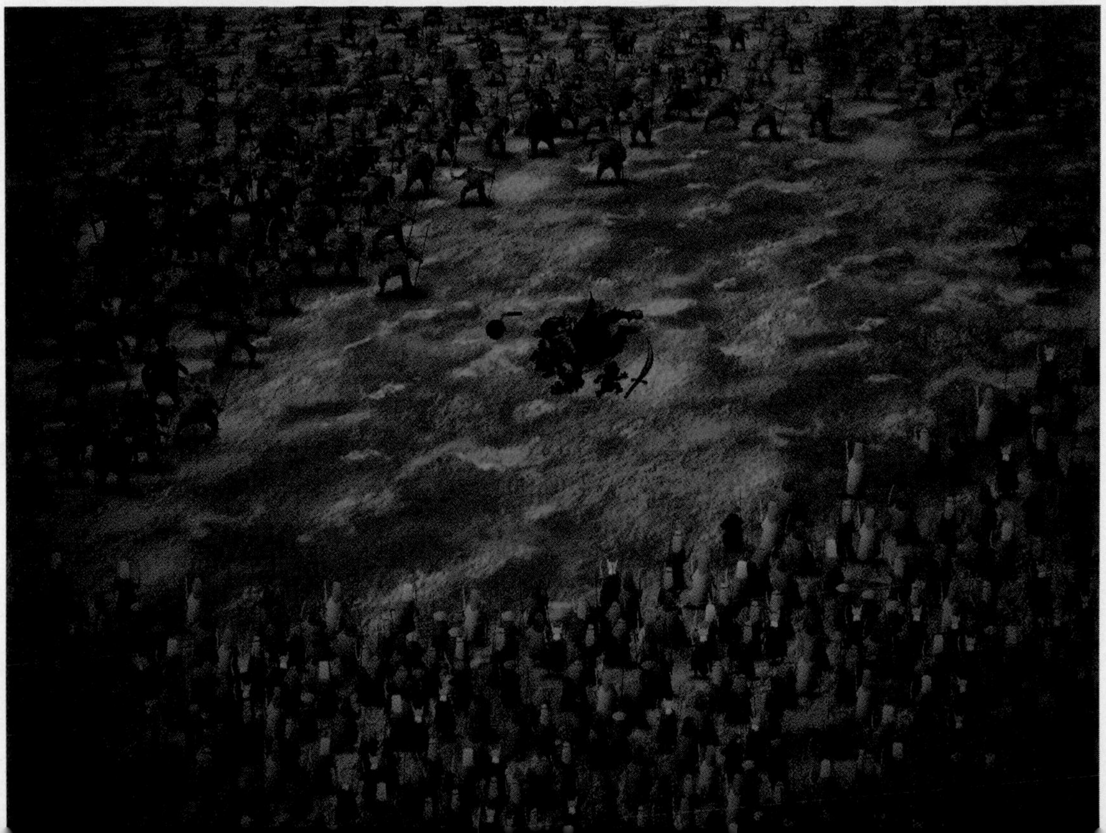

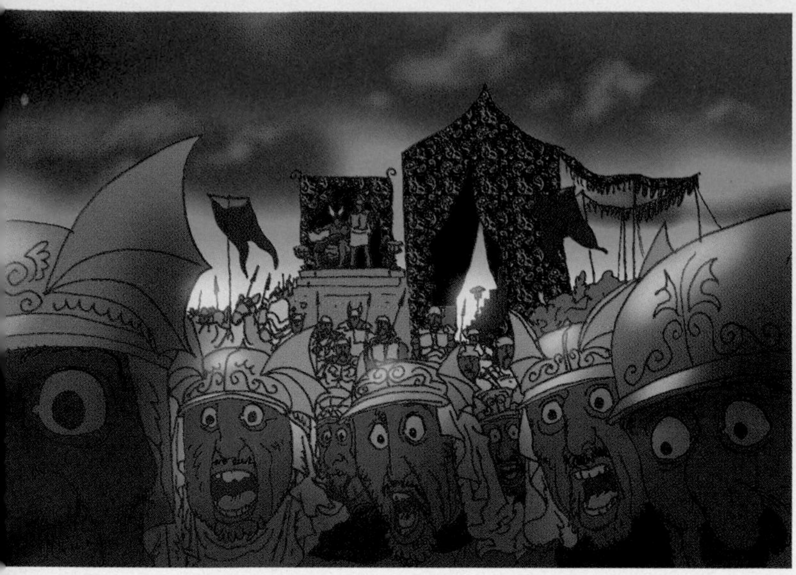

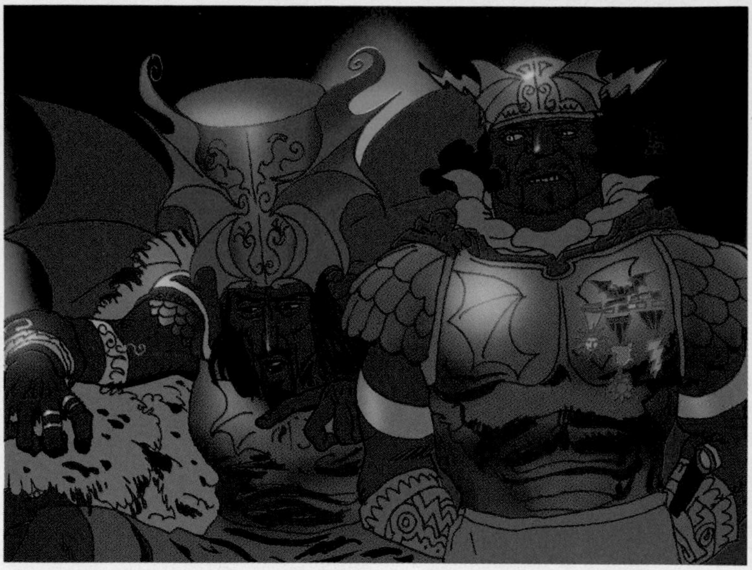

"Abner, whose son is that young man?" "By my soul, O king, I don't know."

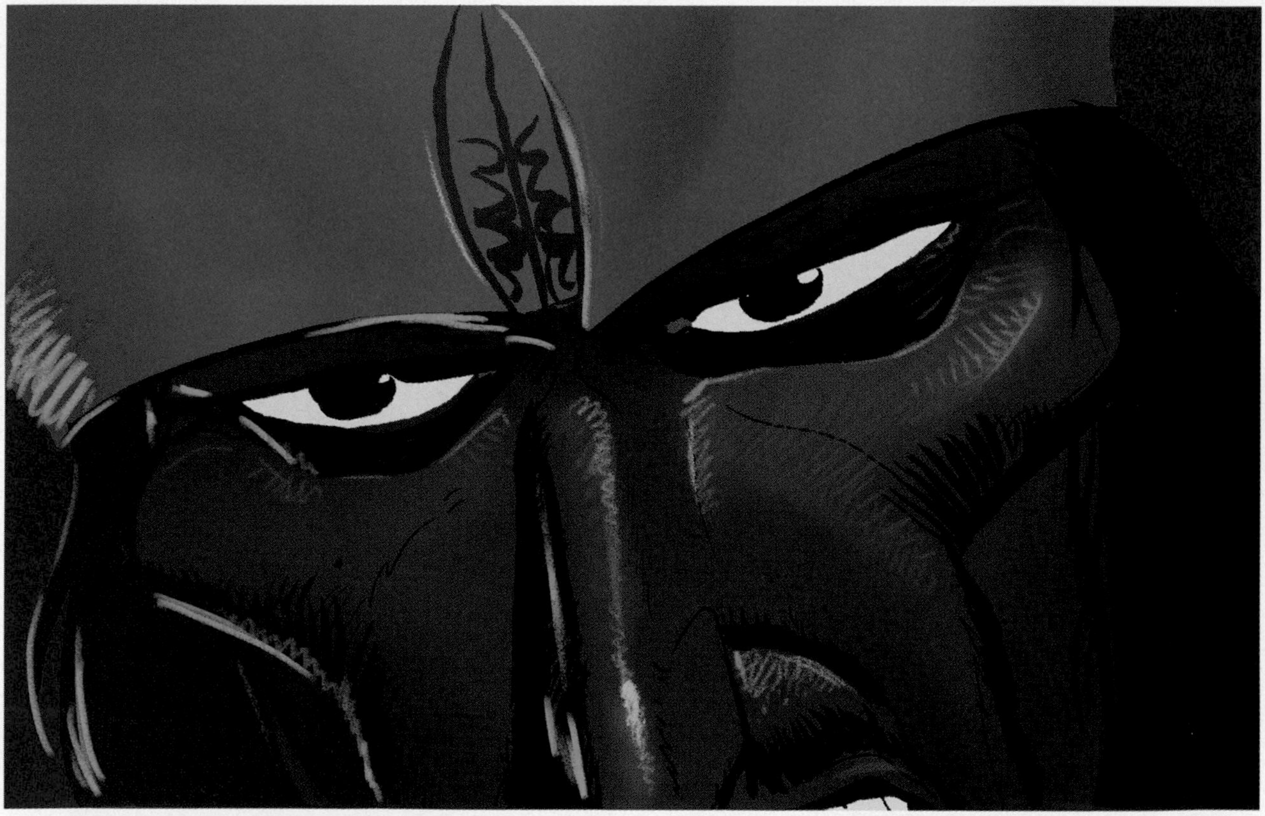

"Find out whose son he is."

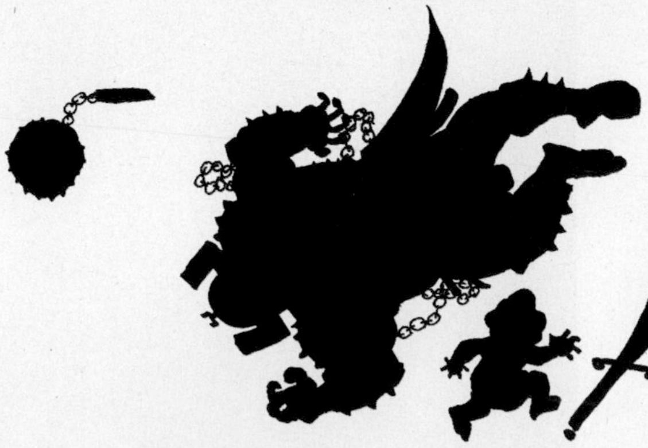

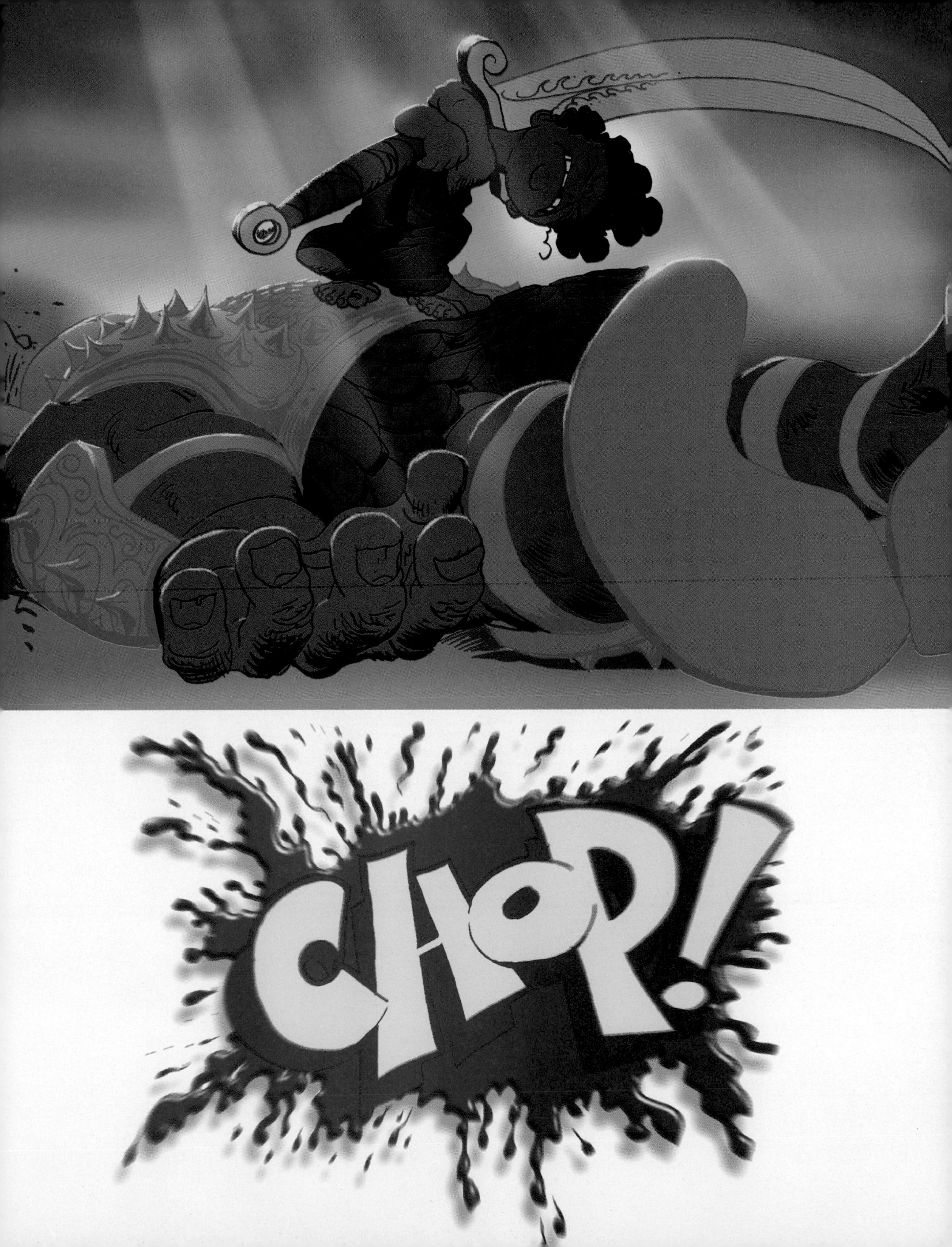
CHOP!

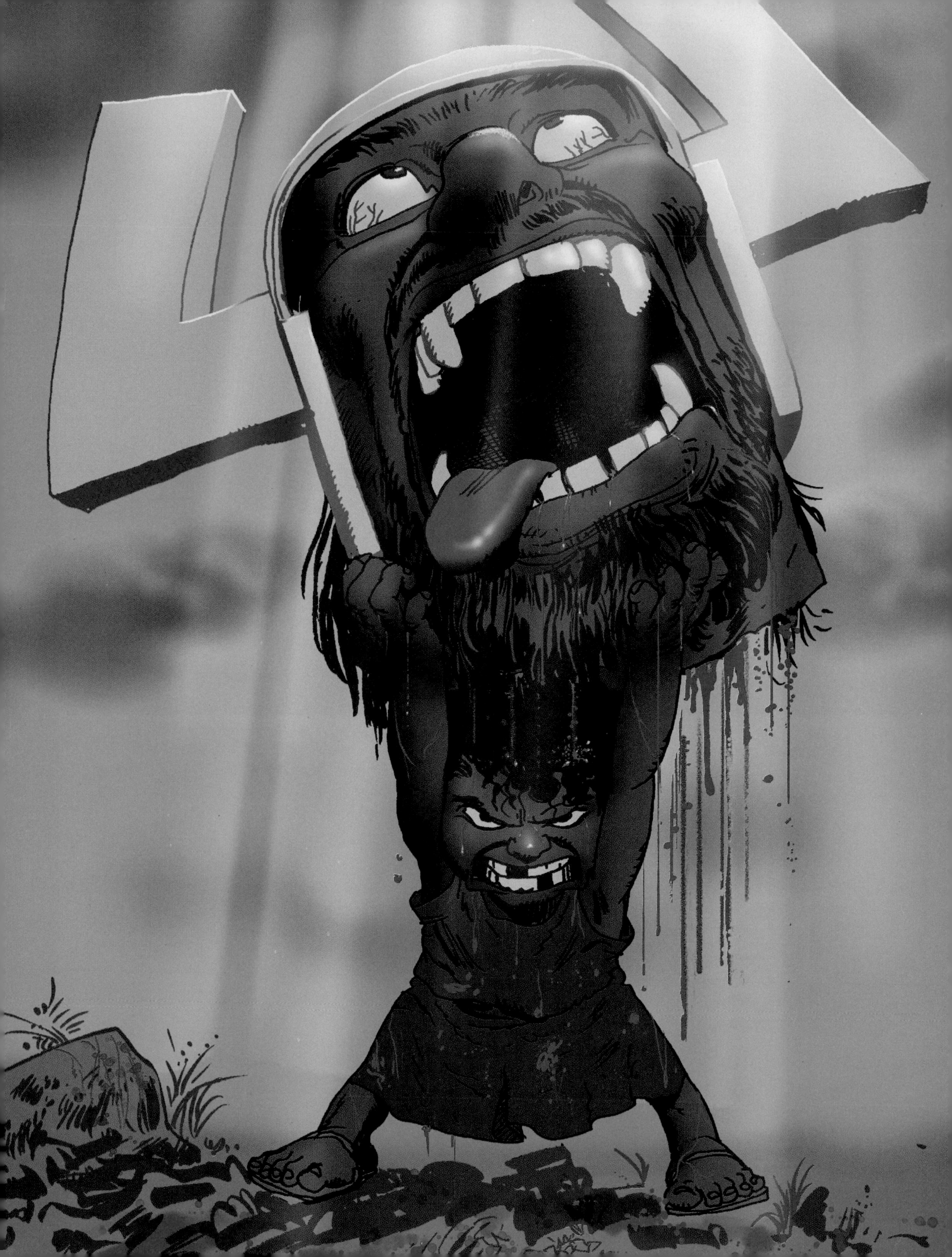

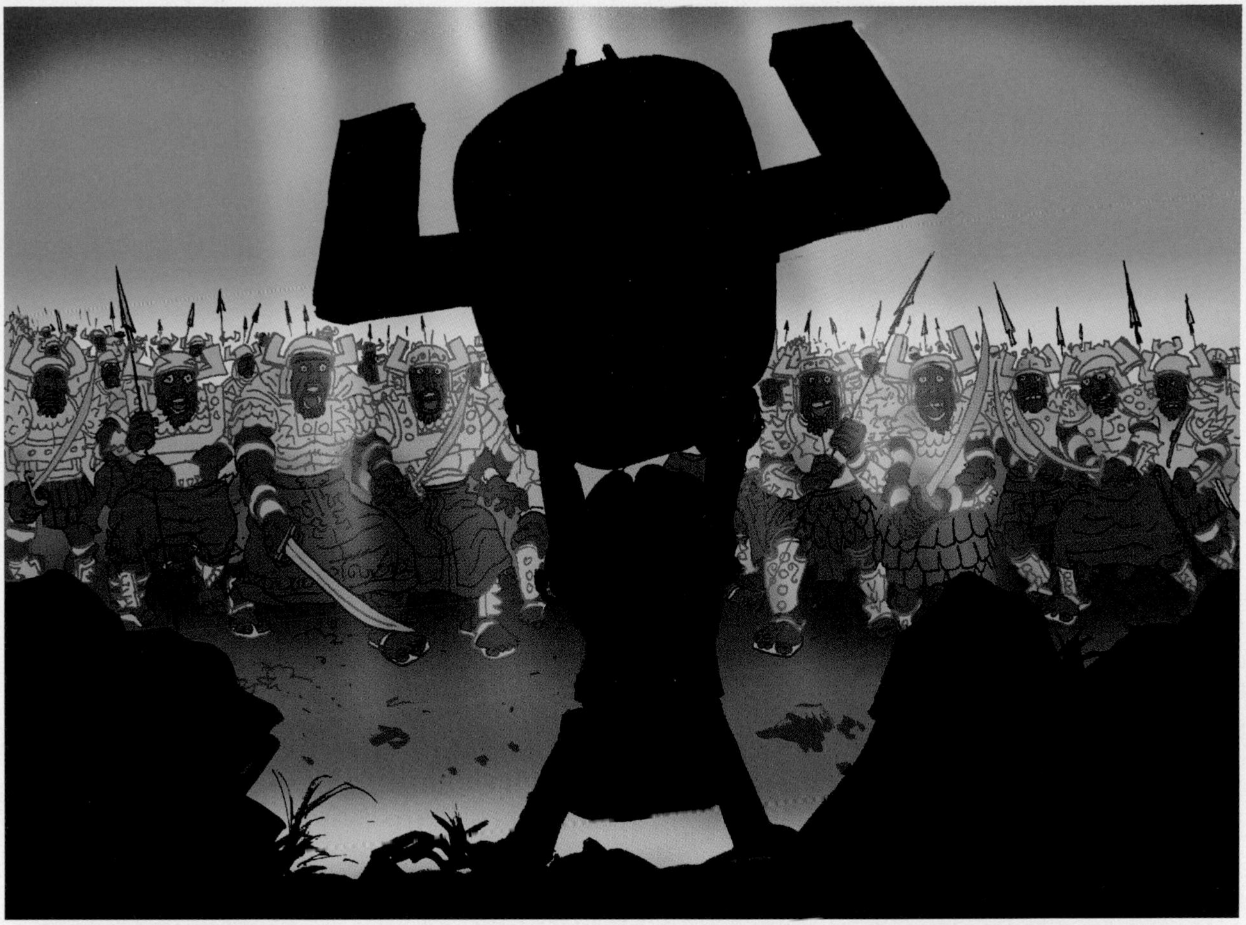

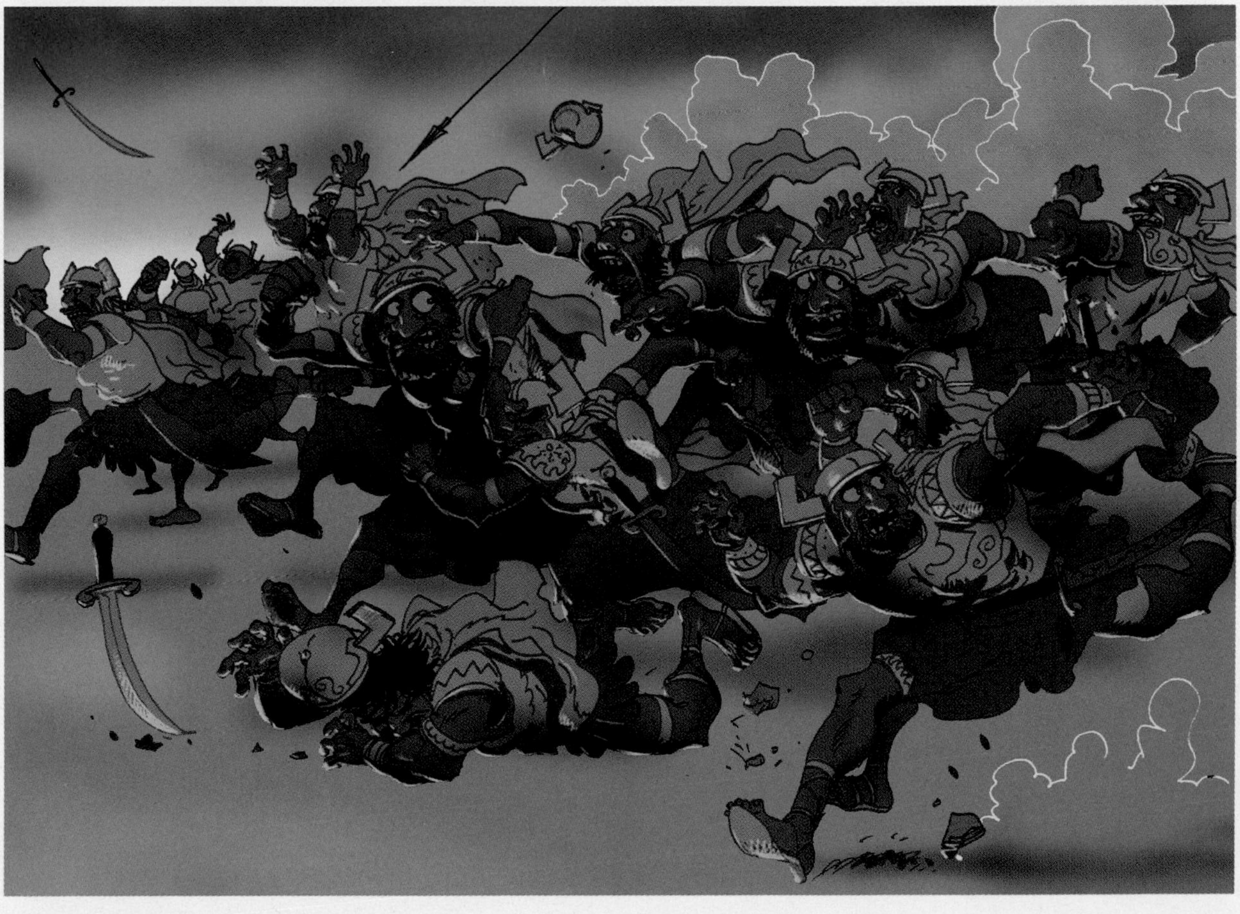

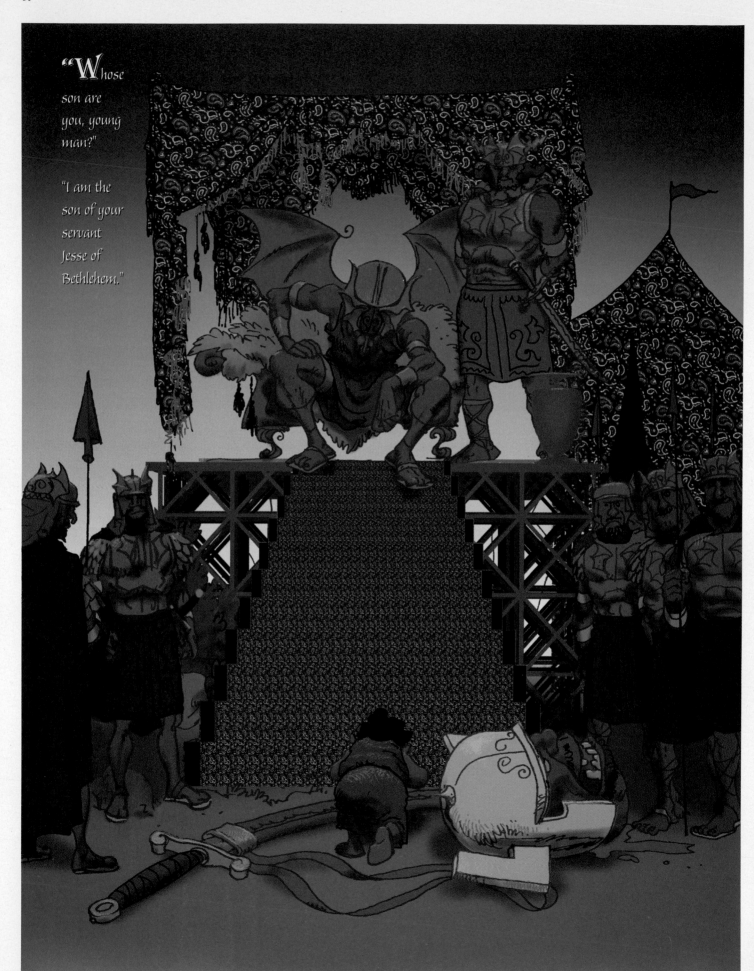

"**W**hose son are you, young man?"

"I am the son of your servant Jesse of Bethlehem."

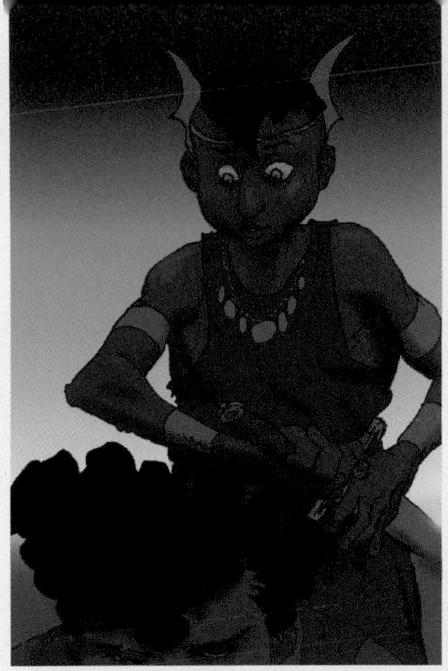
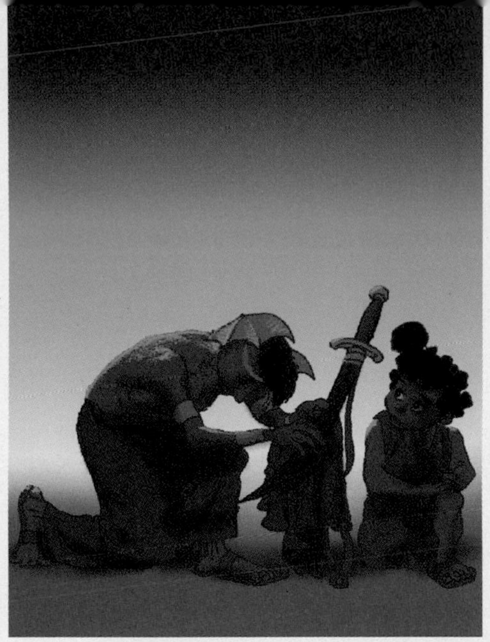
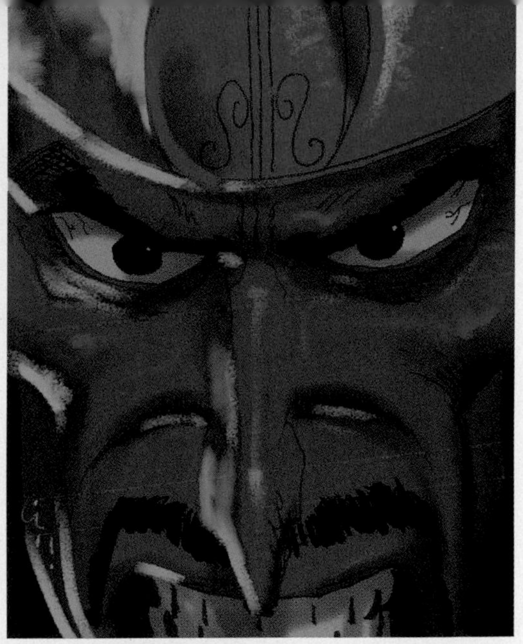

Jonathan steps forward.

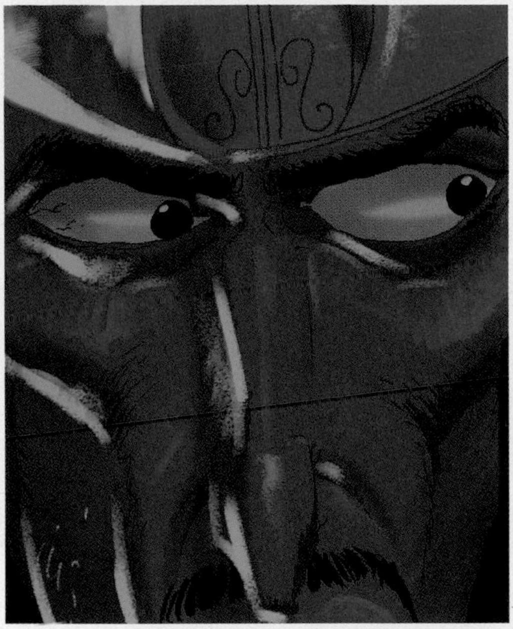
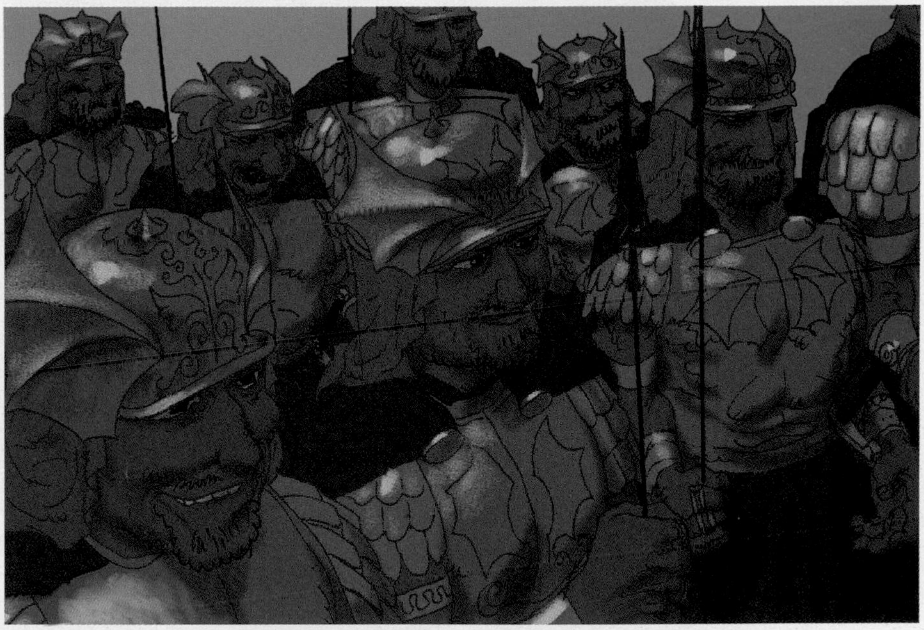
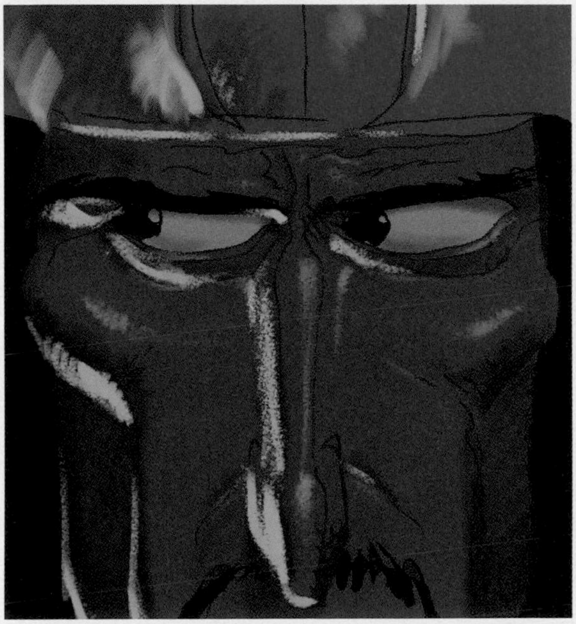
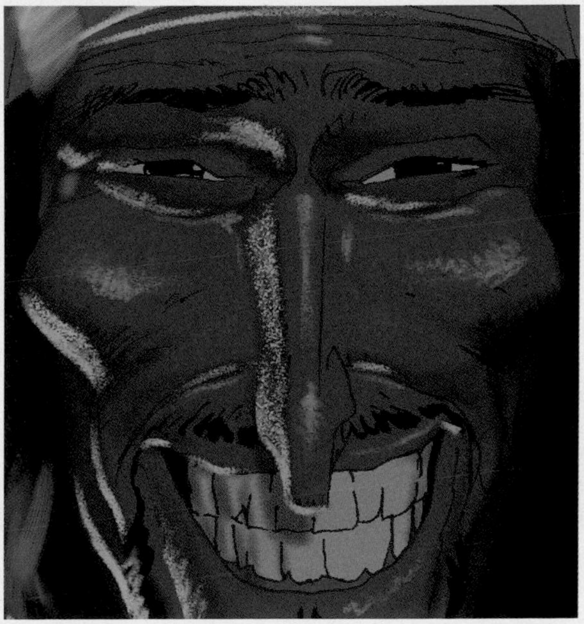

"I love victory parades, Abner," says King Saul. "Moments like this make it all worthwhile. All the pretty girls of the kingdom come out and dance and sing for me. Listen."

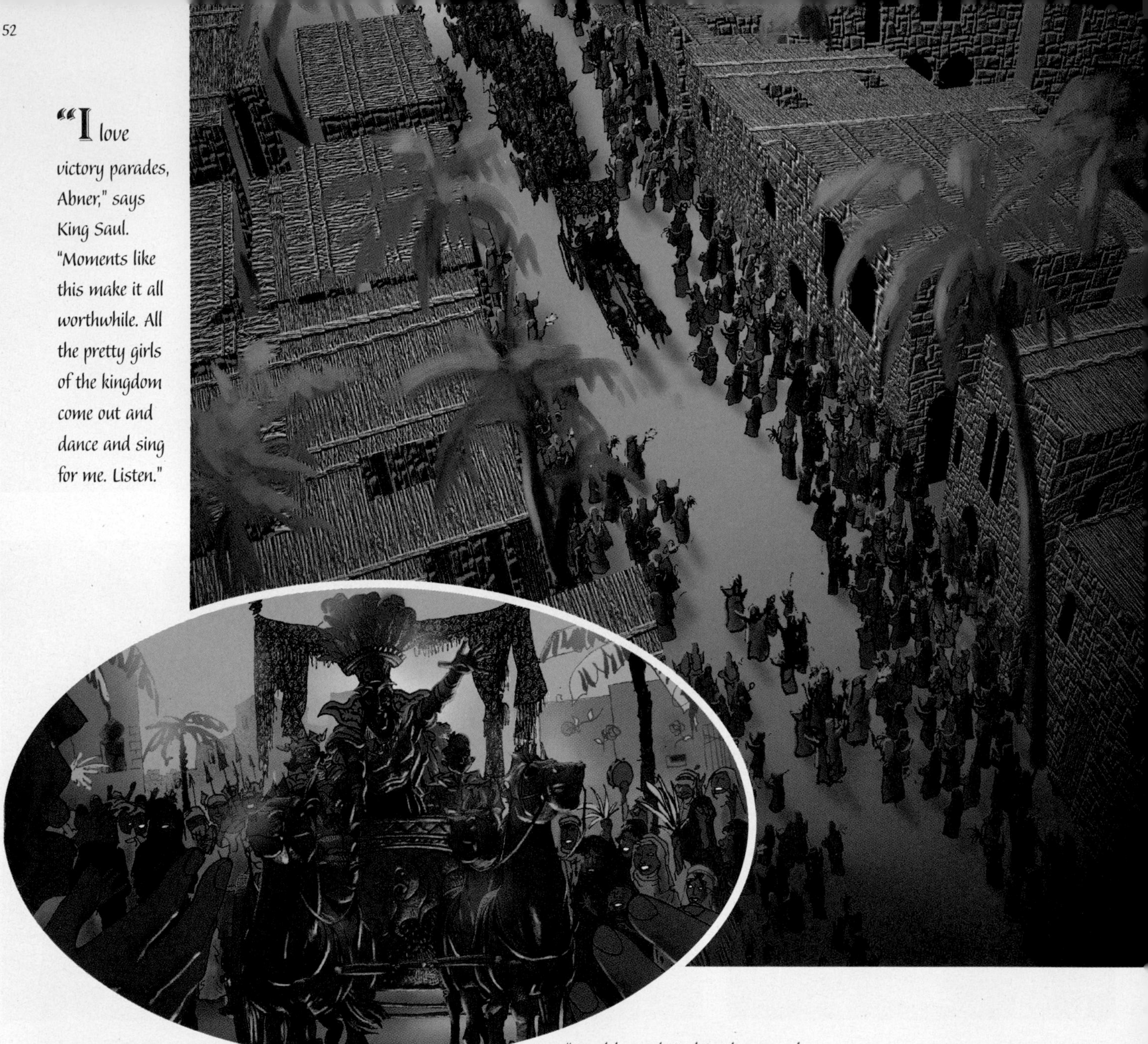

"Saul has slain his thousands,

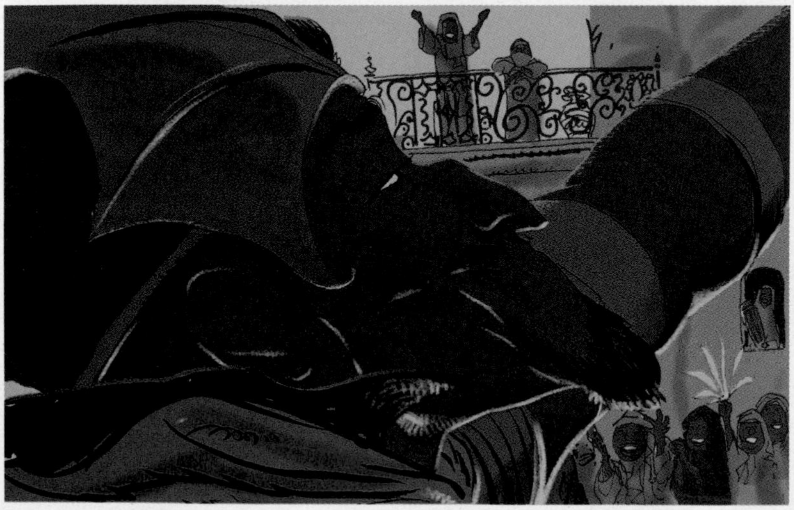

"Saul has slain his thousands,

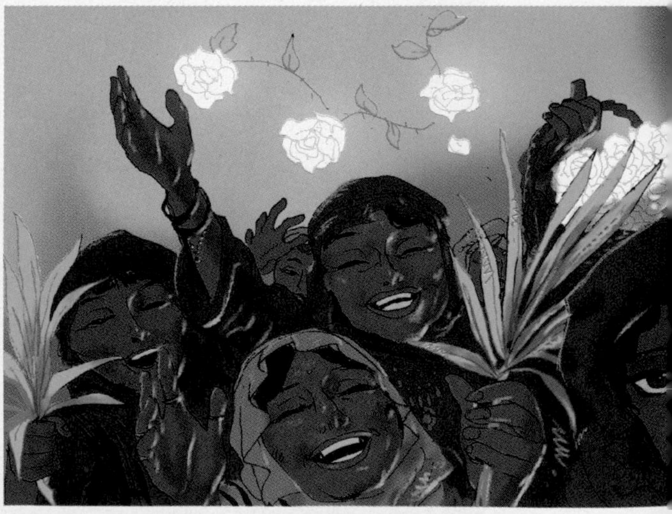

"Saul has slain his thousands,

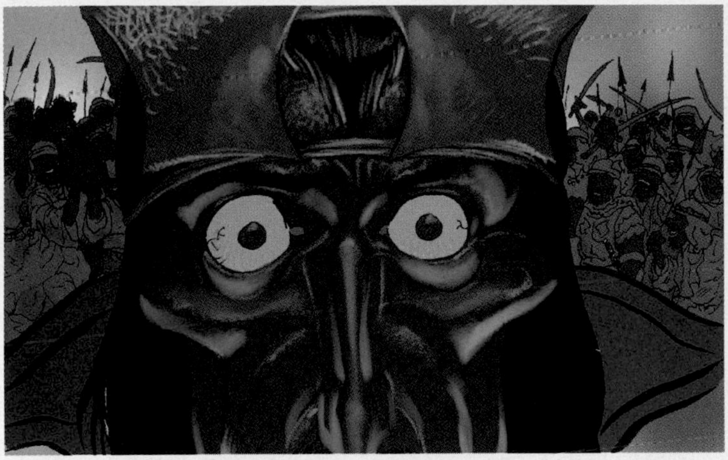

"and David his tens of thousands."

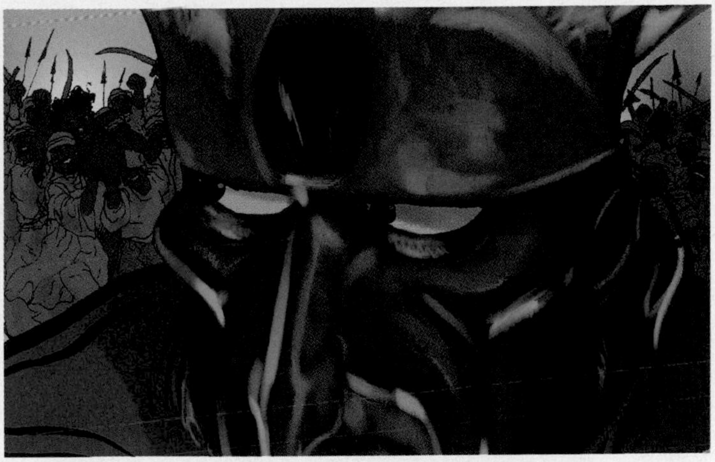

"Saul has slain his thousands,
Saul has slain his thousands,

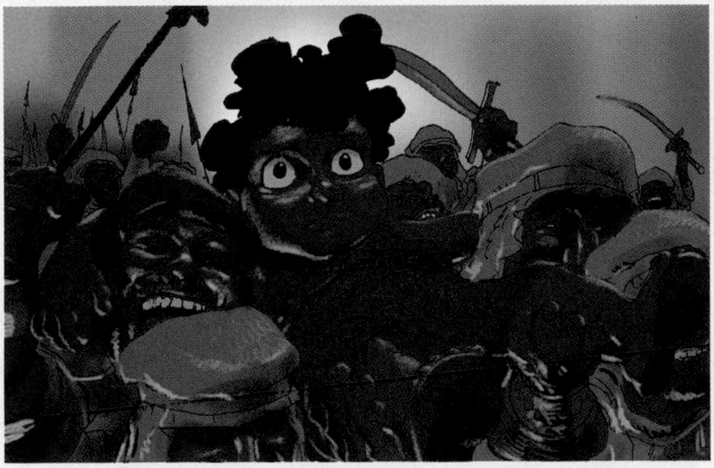

"Saul has slain his thousands,

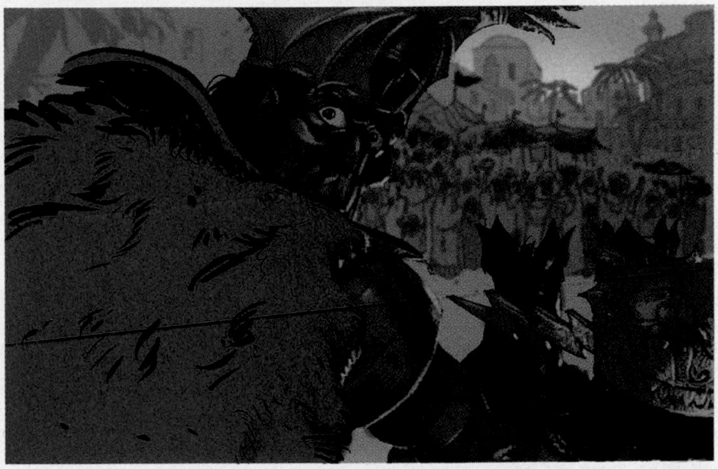

"and David his tens of thousands."

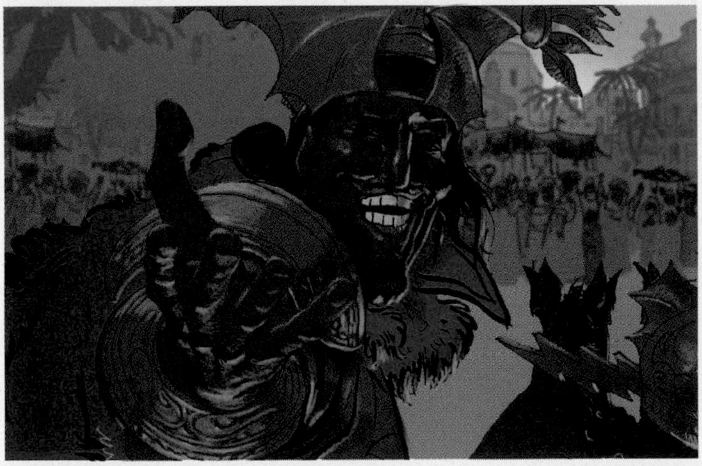

The crowd
cheers.

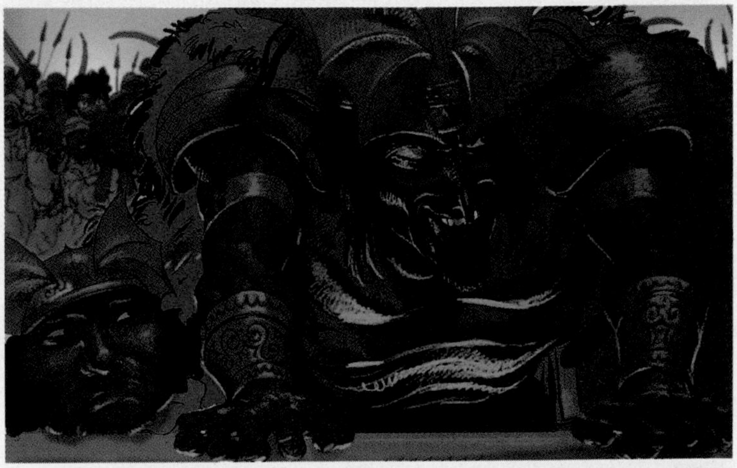

They've credited David with tens of thousands, but me with only thousands, thinks Saul. What more can he get but the kingdom?

Later, at the palace, King Saul is revisited by the tormenting Evil Spirit. David plays the harp to calm Saul's nerves.

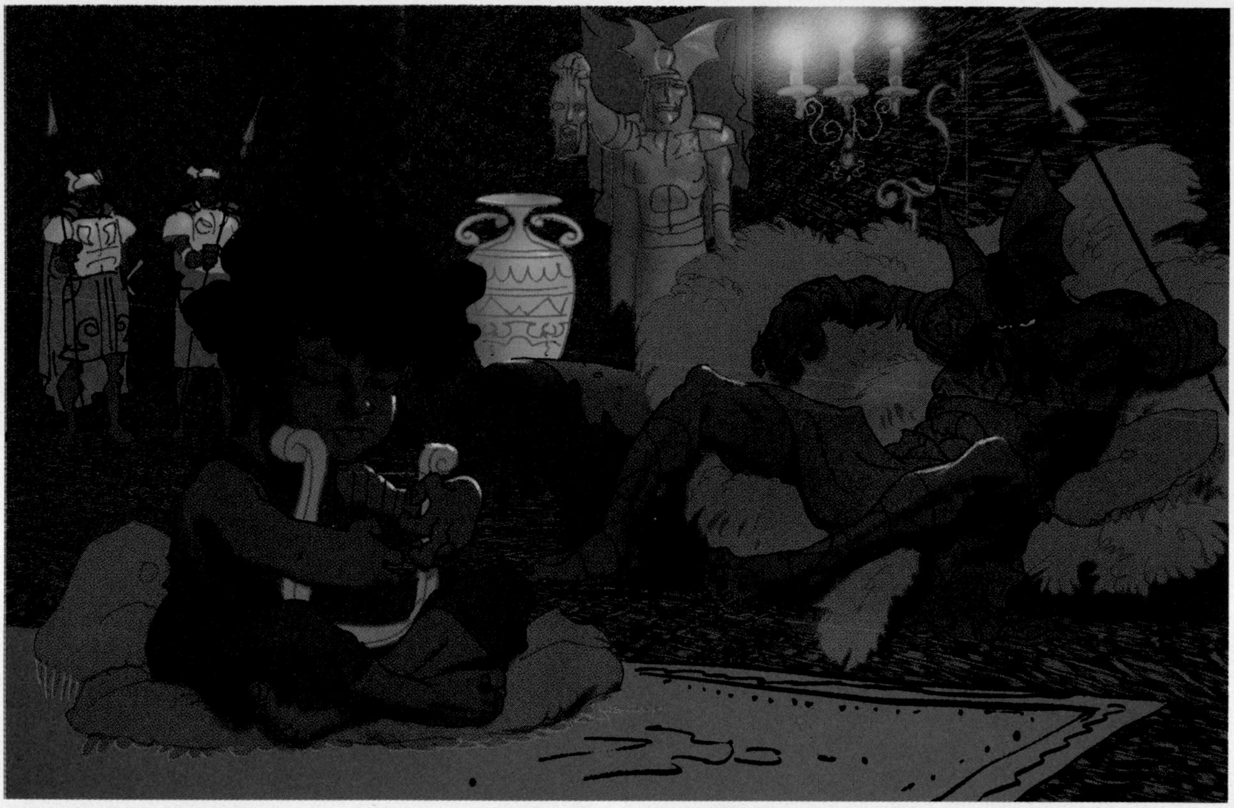

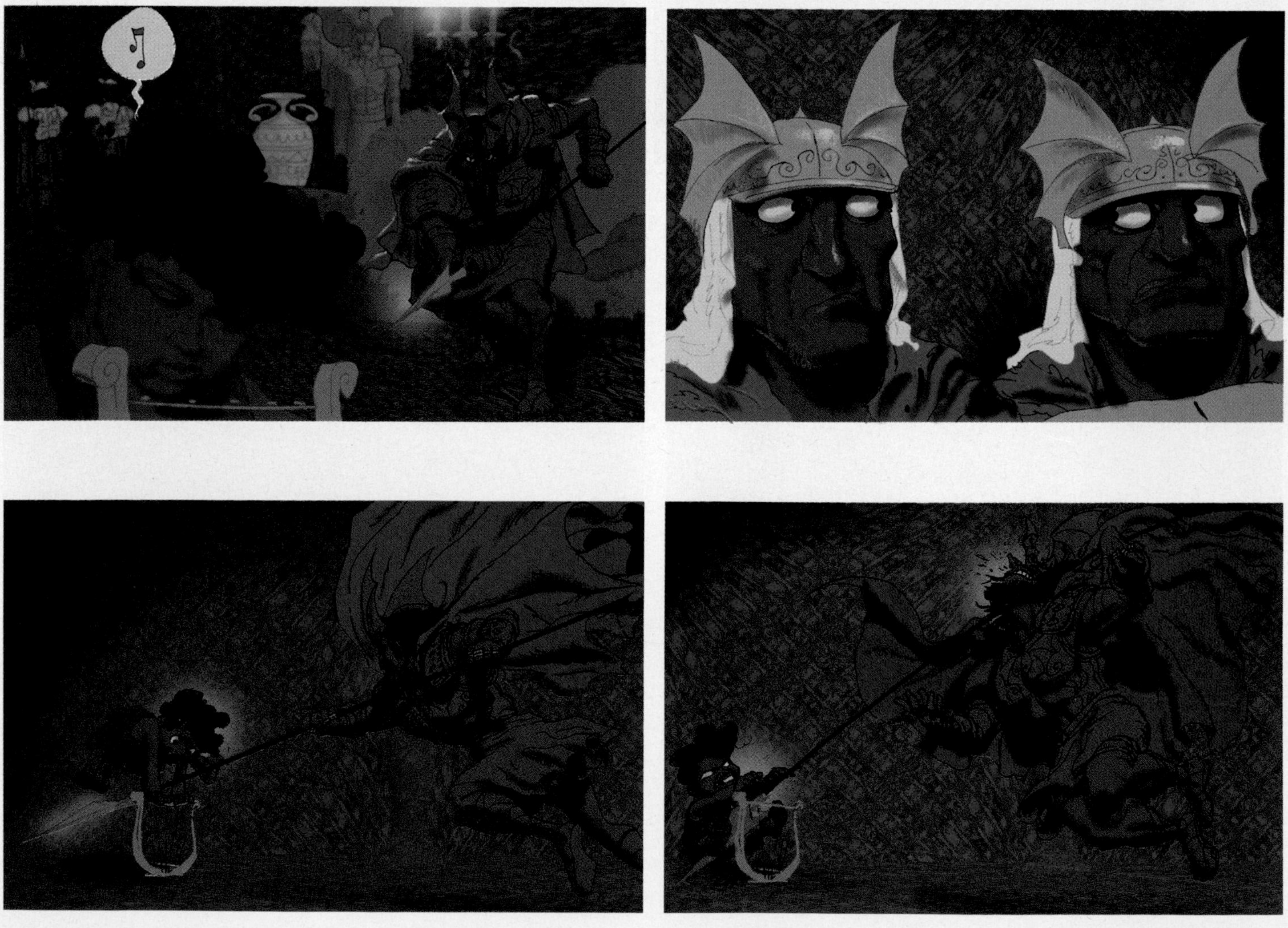

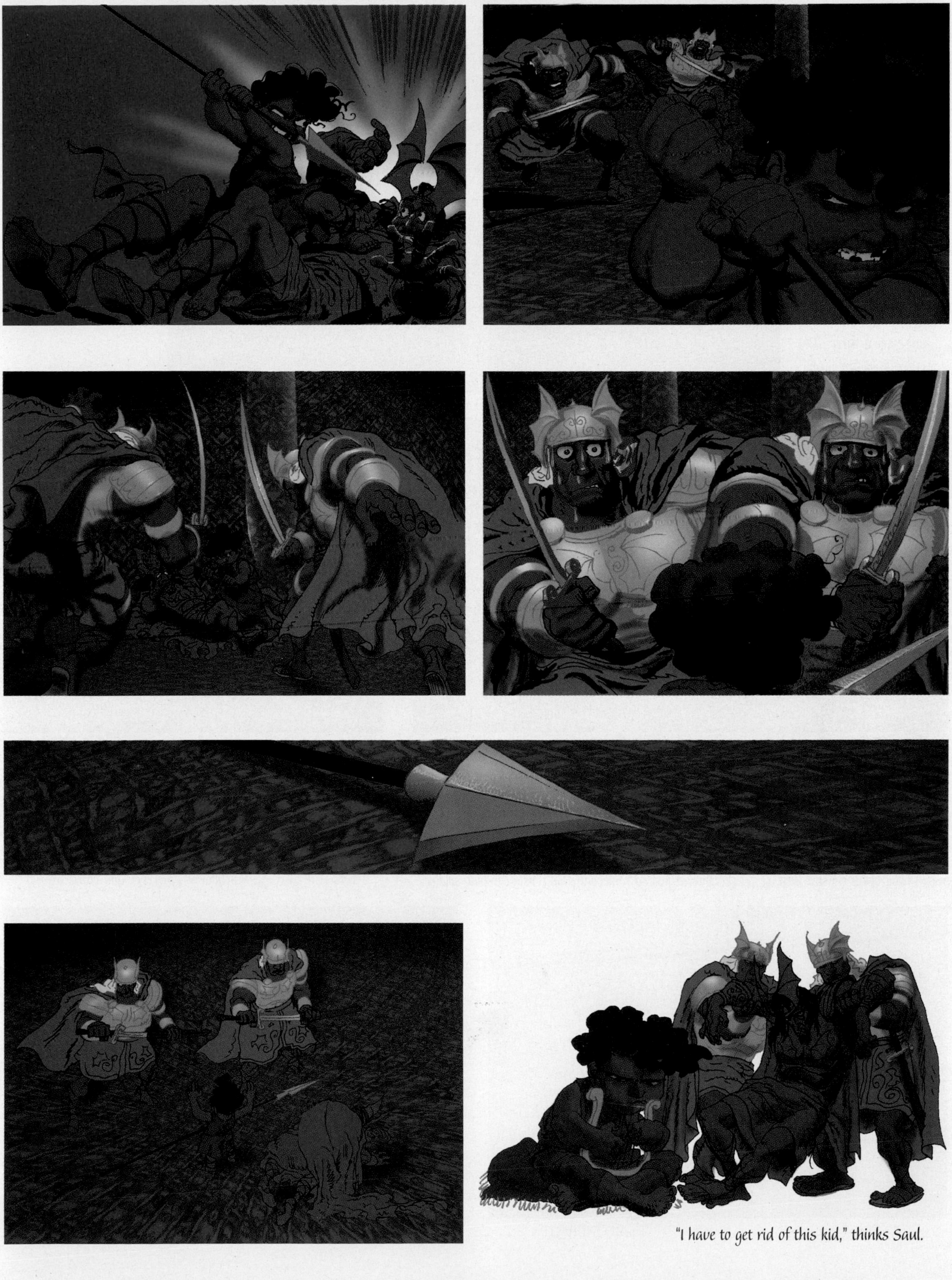

"I have to get rid of this kid," thinks Saul.

"You gotta be joking," says the General.

"In case you cannot read," says David, "you are addressing a superior officer."

"This is a gag, right? I mean, I've seen bureaucratic foul-ups before, I once saw a horse get a three-day pass, but come on!"

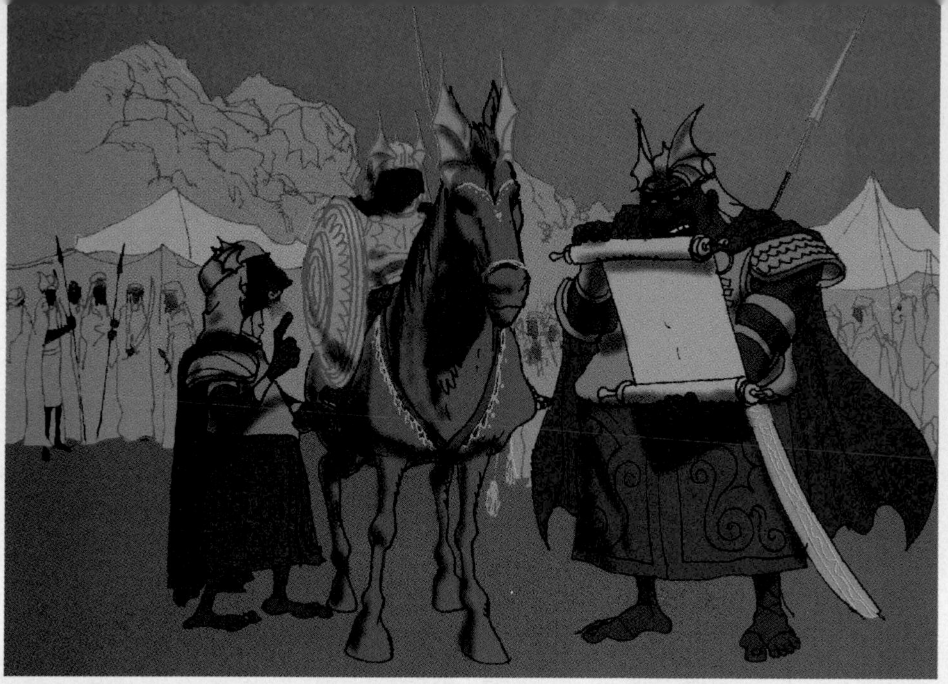

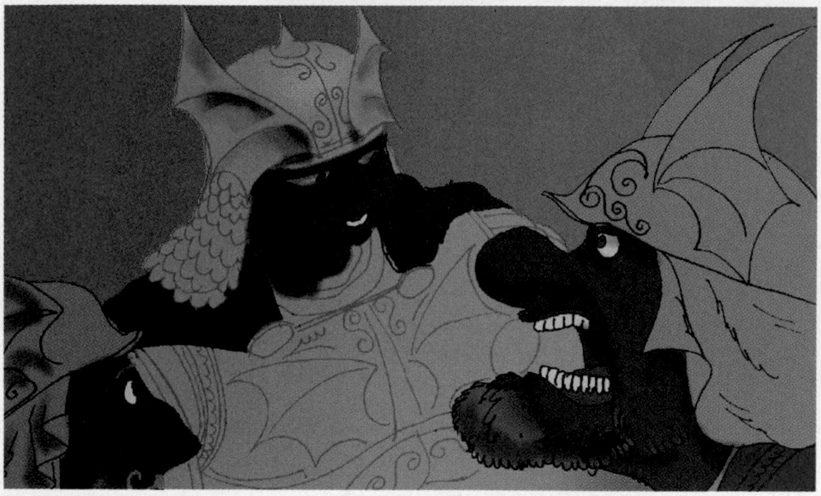

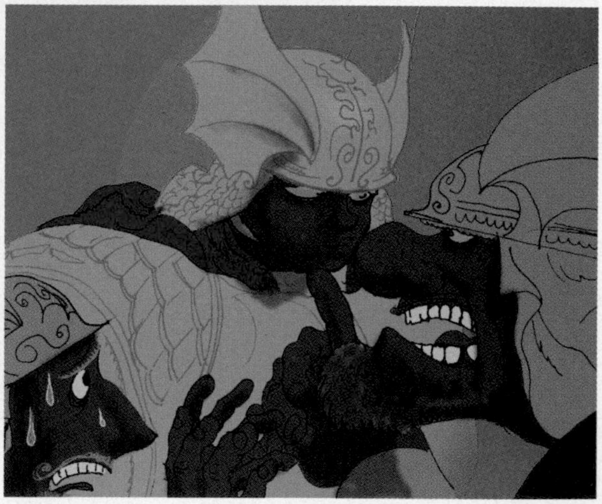

"I have read your record, General,"David says, "It would be a shame if I were forced to lose an officer of your abilities in order to assert my authority. Don't defy me in front of the enlisted men."

"Look, son, no offense, but this isn't a game. We've got orders to attack a walled city, we're hopelessly outnumbered, and we've got no supplies. I don't care whose relative pulled some strings at headquarters to get you promoted, I'm not about to get myself and my men slaughtered just so somebody's kid cousin can play soldier!"

"Uh, sir? Do you know who this--"

"SHUT UP! Look, kid. I'm doing you a favor. This is a war. A kid your age shouldn't have to see the kind of horrors we see. Trust me, you'll be a lot happier back at that fancy private school or wherever you come from."

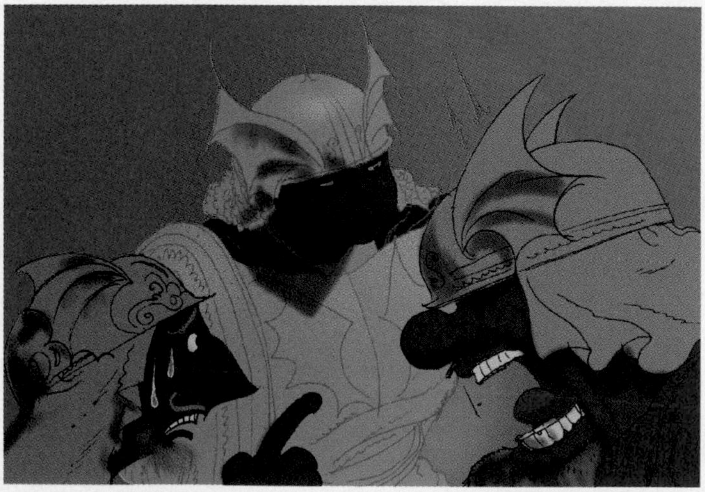

"Sir?"

"I SAID STOW IT!"

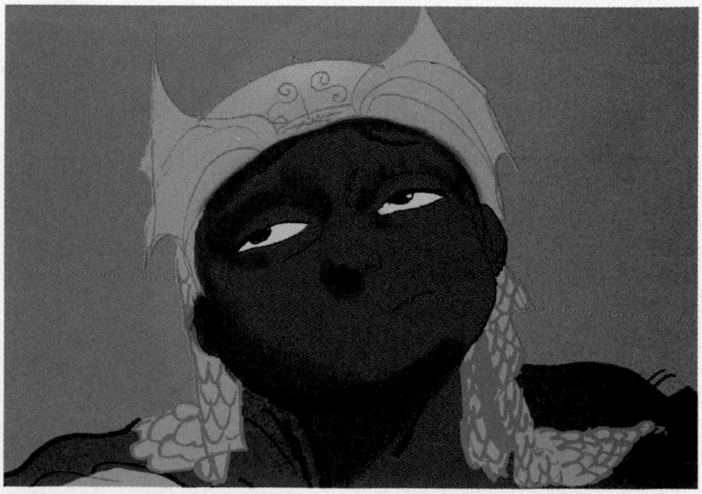

David sighs. "Very well. We'll do it your way."

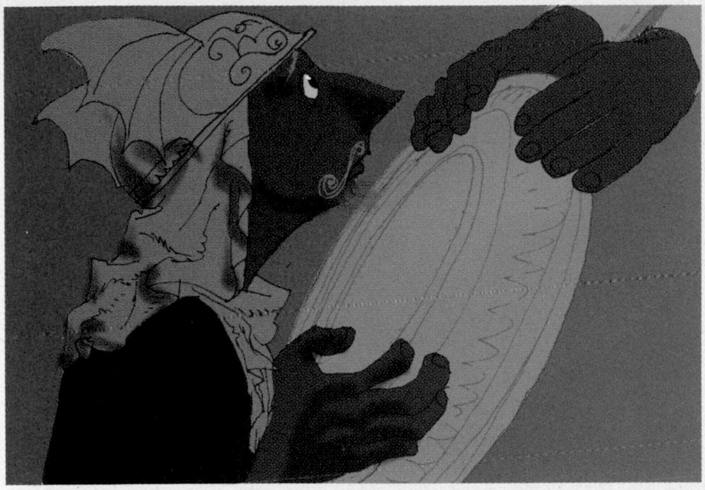

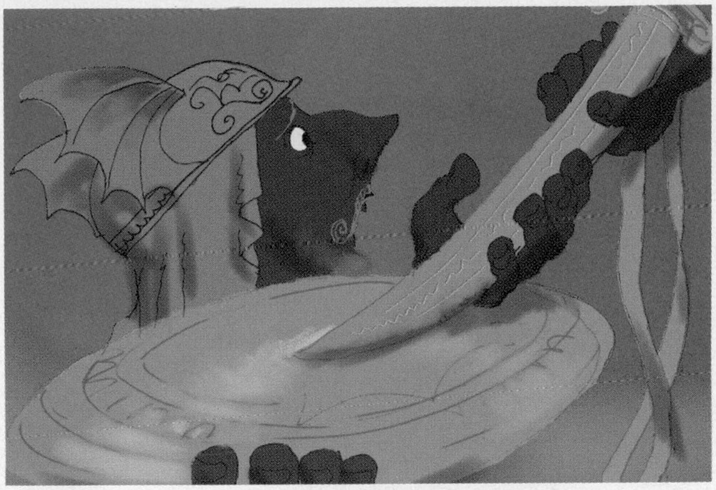

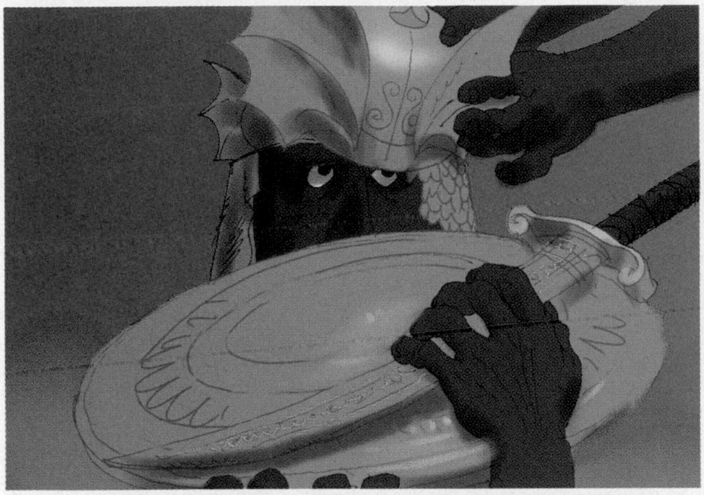

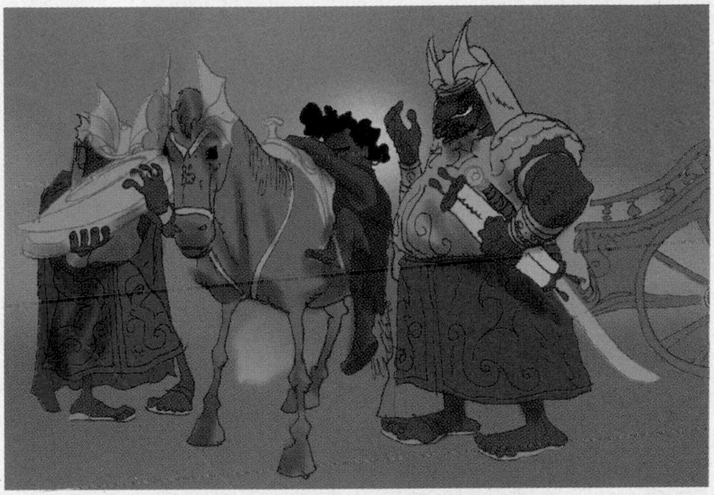

"Now you're being sensible, son. Trust me, it's for the best."

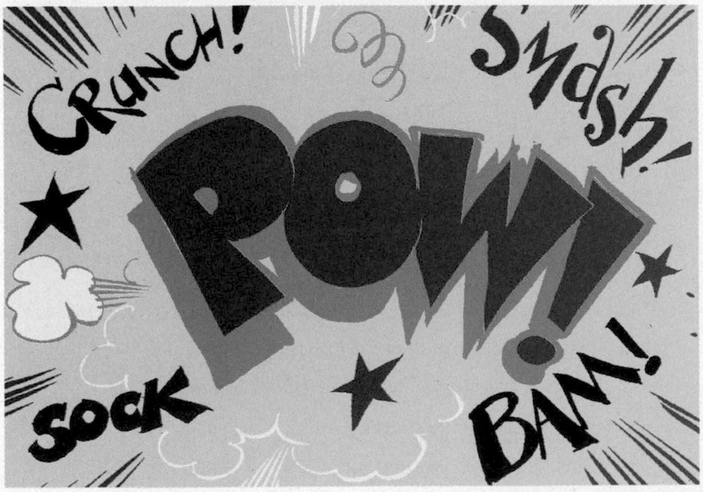
CRUNCH!
Smash!
POW!
SOCK
BAM!

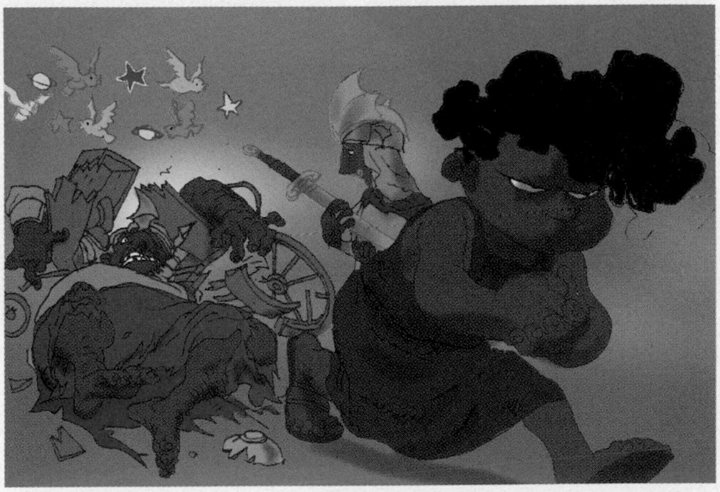

"Oh. You're THAT David."

"Next time, I will kill you. We attack the city at dawn. Pull yourself together by then."

Time passes.

Commander Abner briefs the king: "David and his men have been continually successful in their campaigns. Israel is triumphant, your majesty."

"Curses!" says King Saul. "I mean, let's not be overconfident. The enemy still holds the southern hills. Intelligence reports it is heavily fortified, with troops outnumbering David's men a thousand to one."

"Not anymore, your majesty. David decimated the Philistine ranks at dawn today."

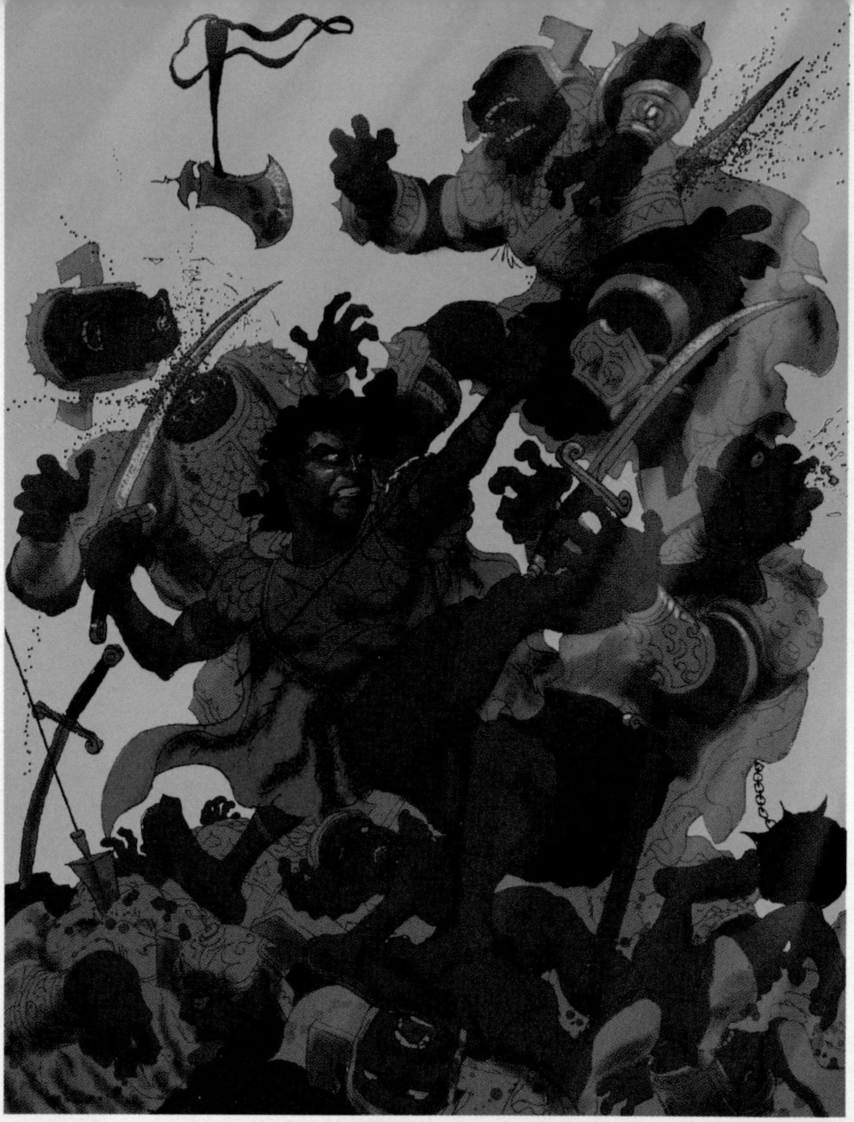

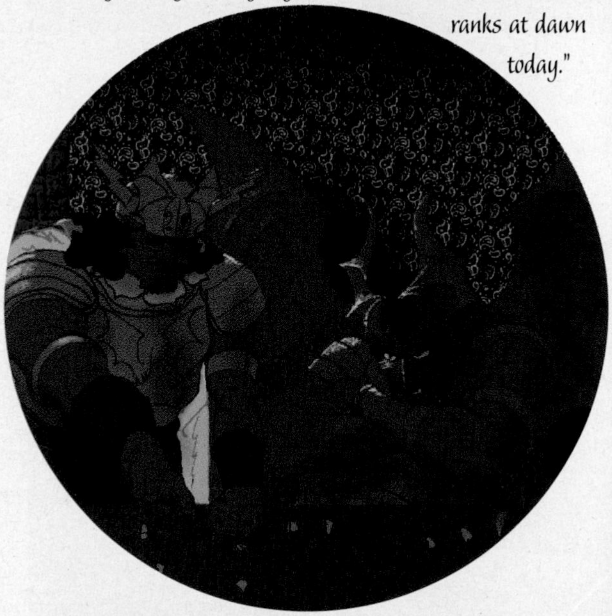

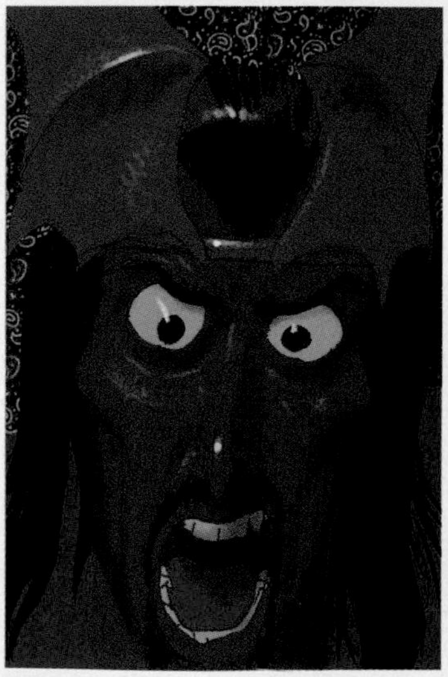

"What? I thought that was a suicide mission! Didn't you tell him it was a suicide mission? Can we have David killed for disobeying orders?"

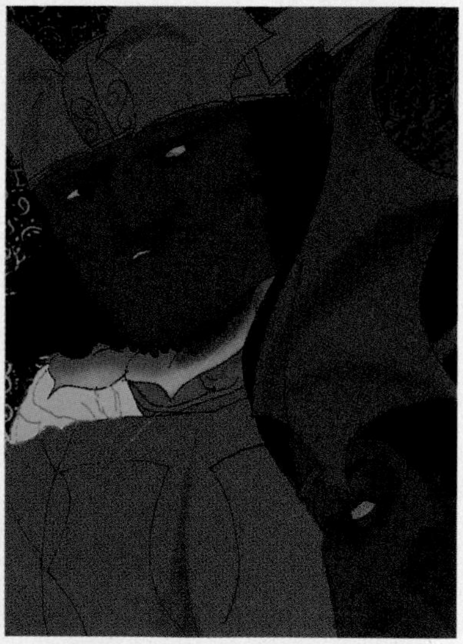

"I didn't actually tell him it was a suicide mission. That would have been tacky.... Permission to speak freely, your highness?"

"Sure, Abner, we're alone."

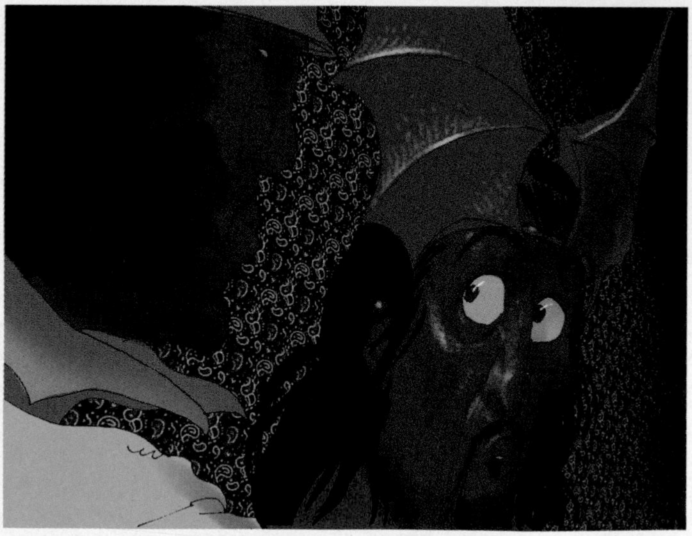

"I know you are a noble man of the highest moral character, but in my line of work it pays to be suspicious. You may not realize it, but if this David kid gets any more popular, he might try and steal your job."

"Really? I hadn't considered that."

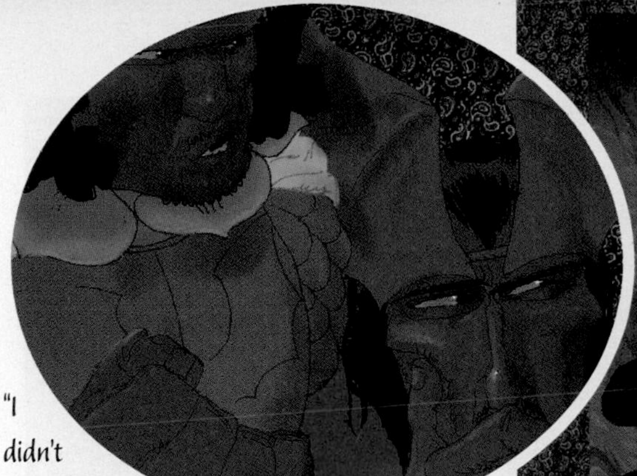

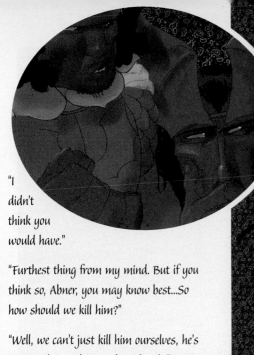

"I didn't think you would have."

"Furthest thing from my mind. But if you think so, Abner, you may know best...So how should we kill him?"

"Well, we can't just kill him ourselves, he's too popular. He has to die in battle."

"That hasn't worked. I mean--he's too skilled in battle."

"If he could be lured into doing something reckless...Perhaps he has a weakness."

"No, he's perfect. There is no bait that would tempt him."

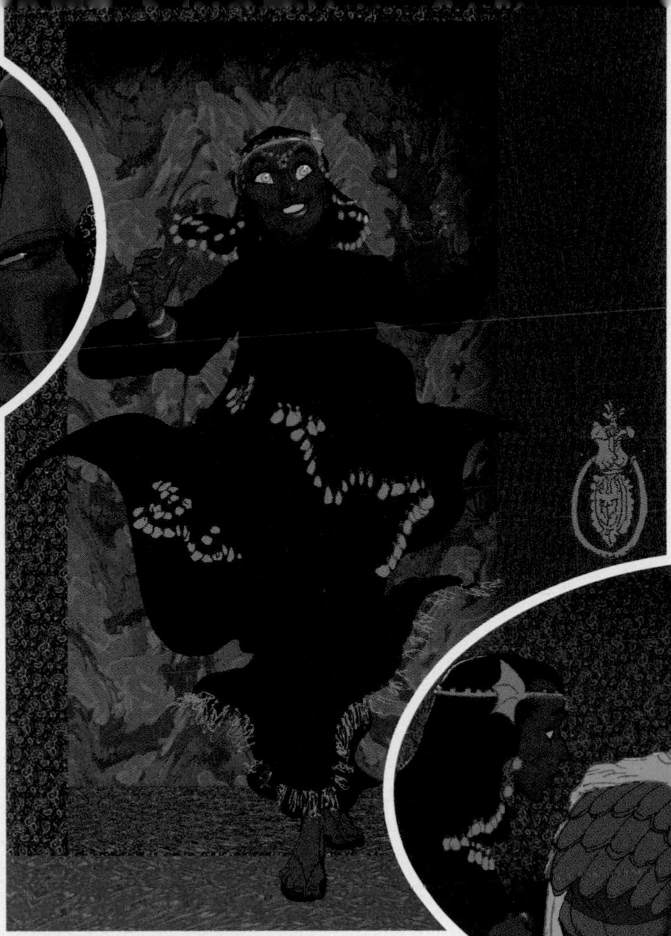

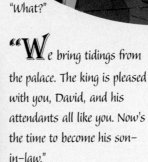

Michal rushes in. "Daddy! I just heard that David won the south for us! Isn't he wonderful?"

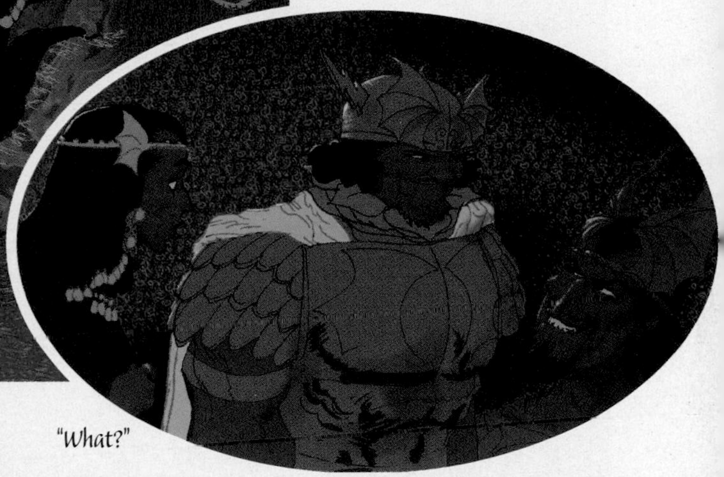

"What?"

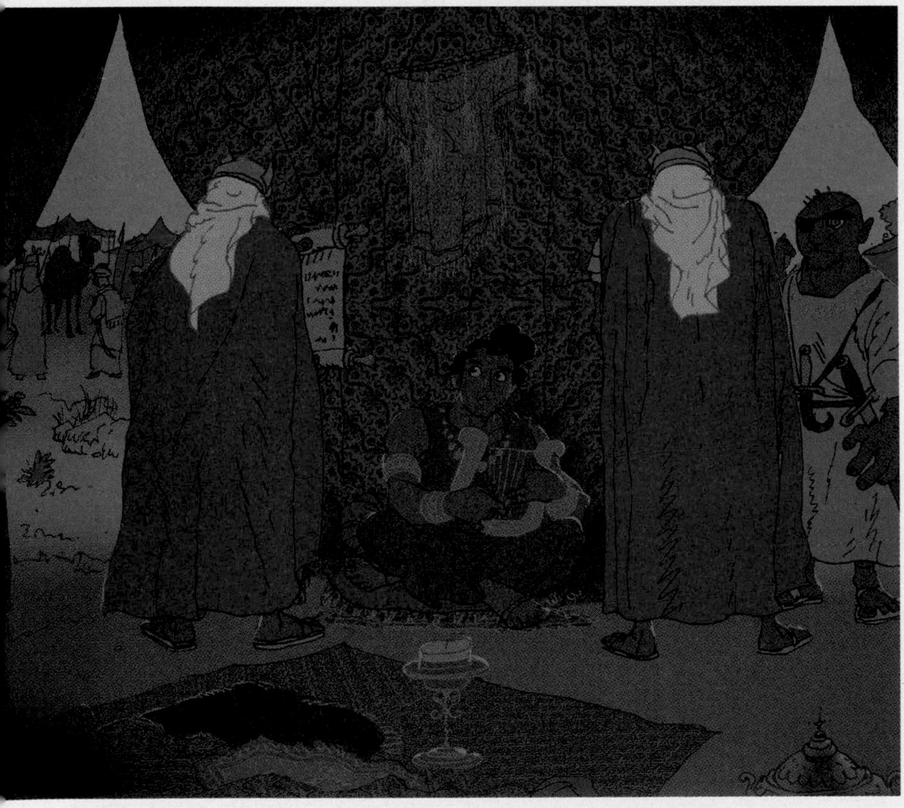

"We bring tidings from the palace. The king is pleased with you, David, and his attendants all like you. Now's the time to become his son-in-law."

"Don't mock me," says David, "Do you think it is a small matter to become the king's son-in-law? I am only a poor man, a nobody! I have nothing to offer her family."

"The king wants no other price for the bride than a hundred Philistine foreskins, to take revenge upon his enemies."

"Excuse me?"

"Purely a symbolic gesture."

"That's it? A hundred Philistine foreskins? When does he want them? Is tomorrow okay?"

"The thing is, since technically this is peacetime, and the treaty is being negotiated, the procurement can not be a full military action, you understand."

"We mean, how would it look, the king orders troops to chop a bunch of foreskins off?

"You'll have to do the job alone."

Pause.

"Which daughter are we talking about?"

"The pretty one. Michal."

"I wish we had taken prisoners."

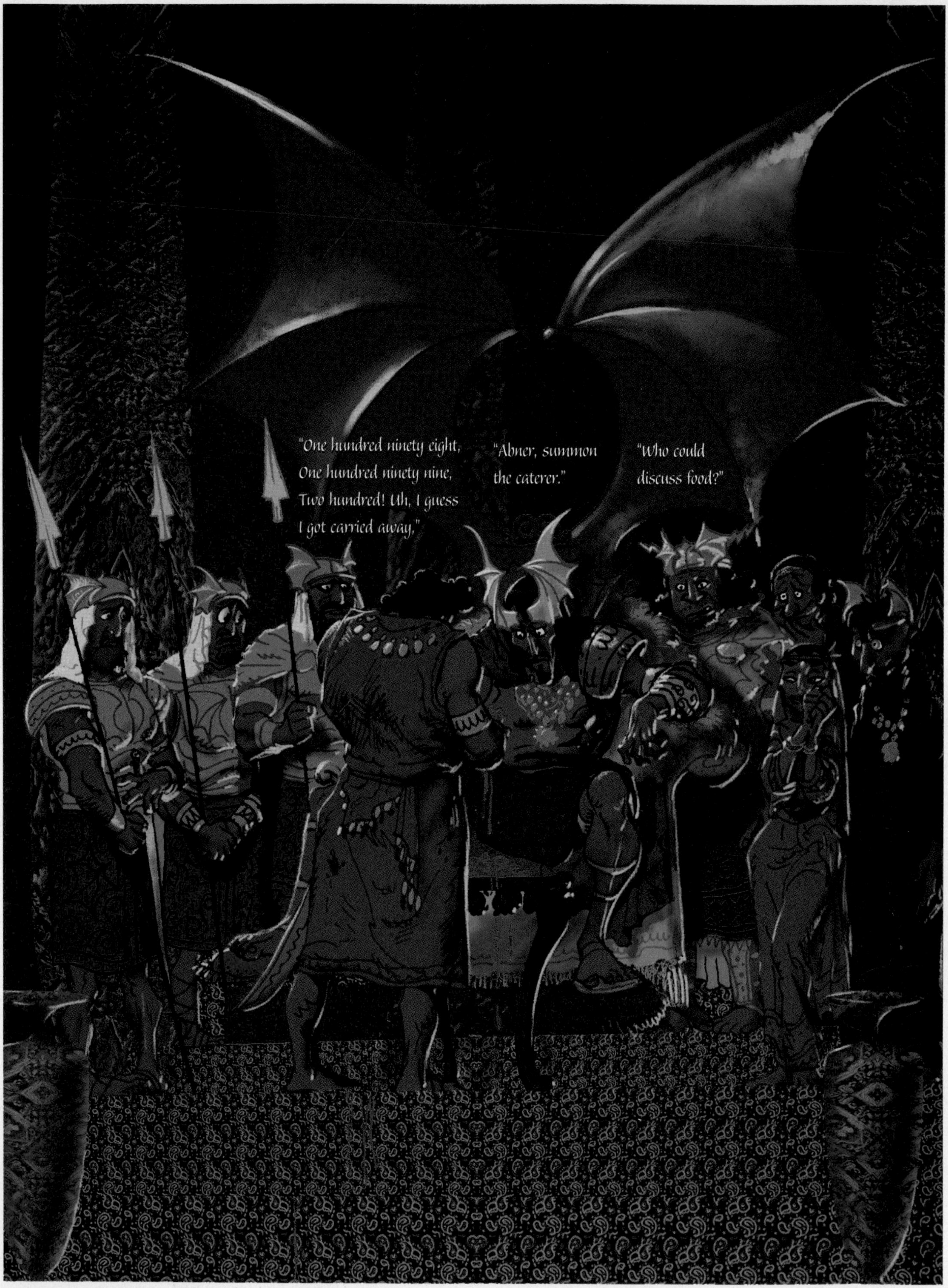
"One hundred ninety eight, One hundred ninety nine, Two hundred! Uh, I guess I got carried away,"
"Abner, summon the caterer."
"Who could discuss food?"

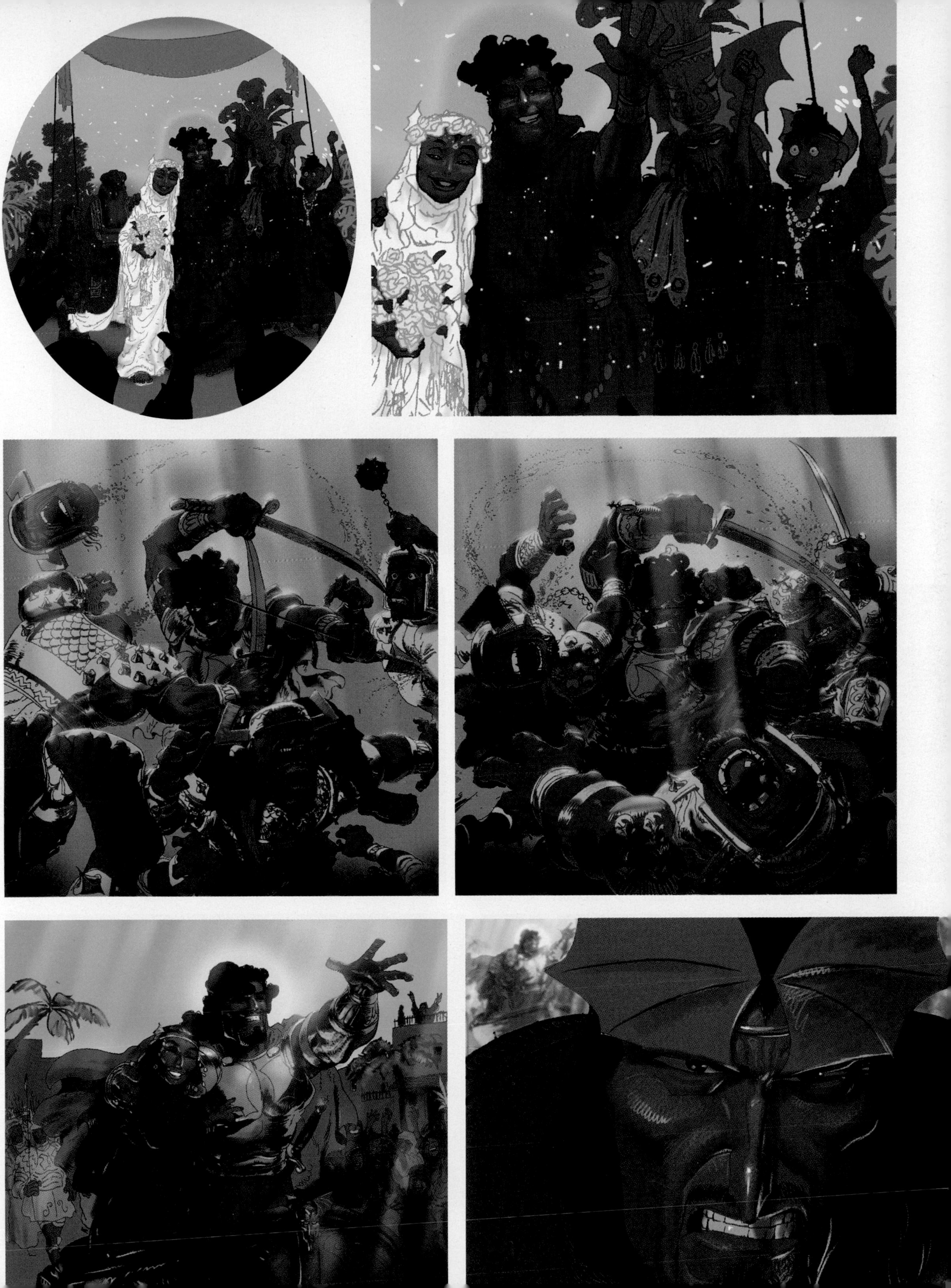

"I'm sick of trying to trick him and trap him and set him up. That little punk has weaseled his way into my home, he's wormed his way into my family, he's gnawing his way into my people's hearts. He's a disease! It ends tonight. Go to David's house and kill him."

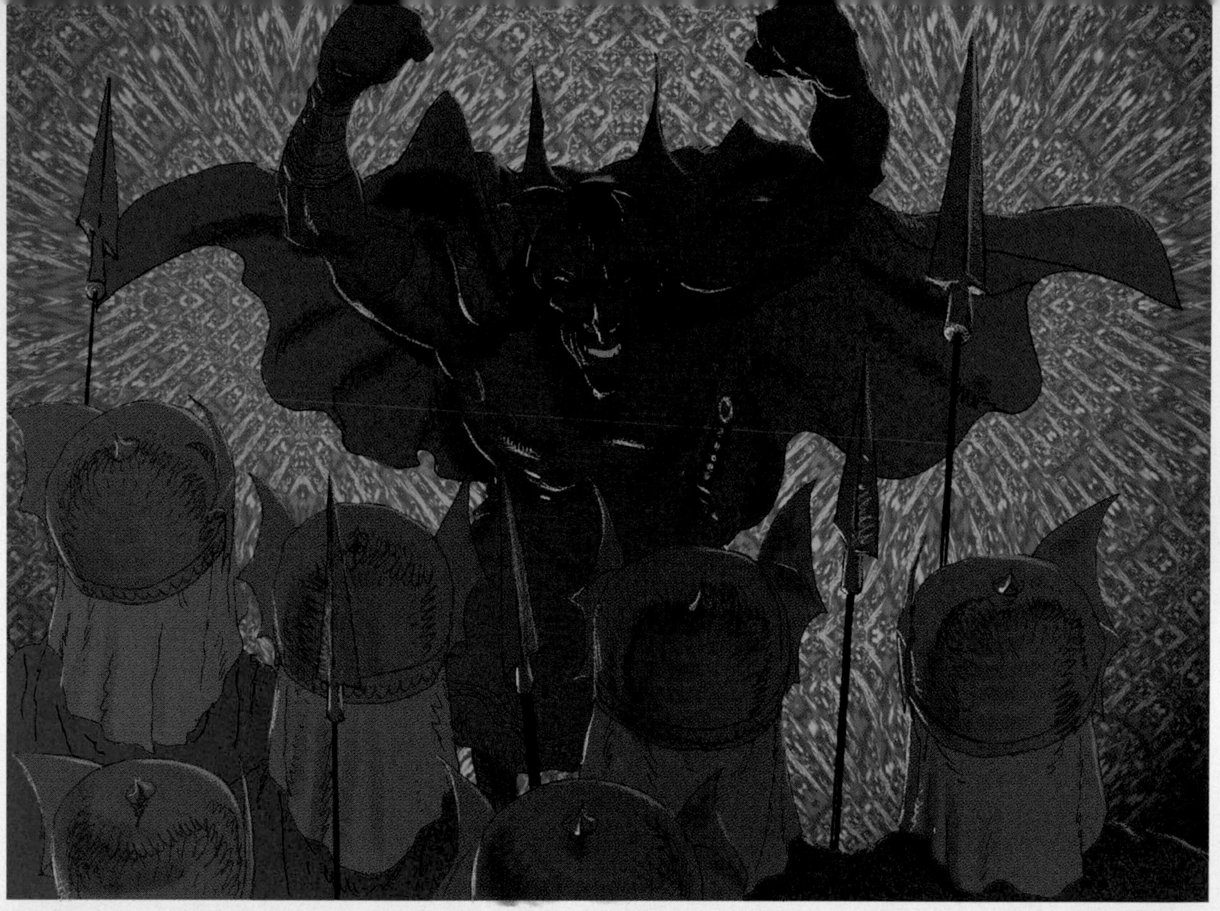

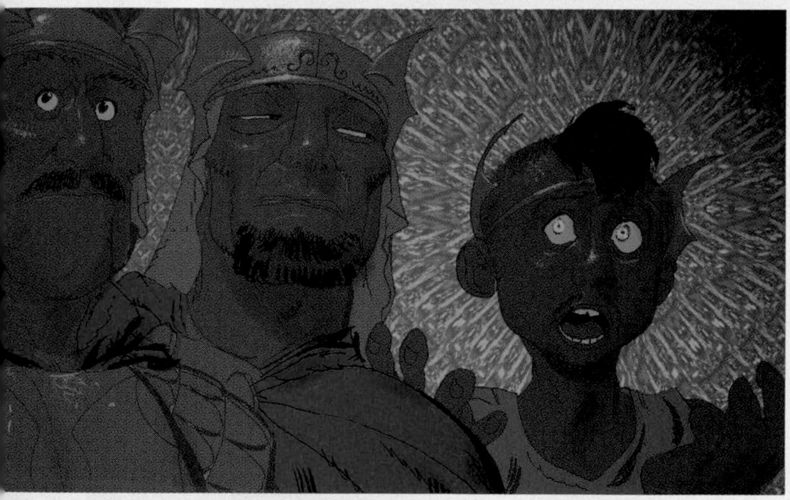

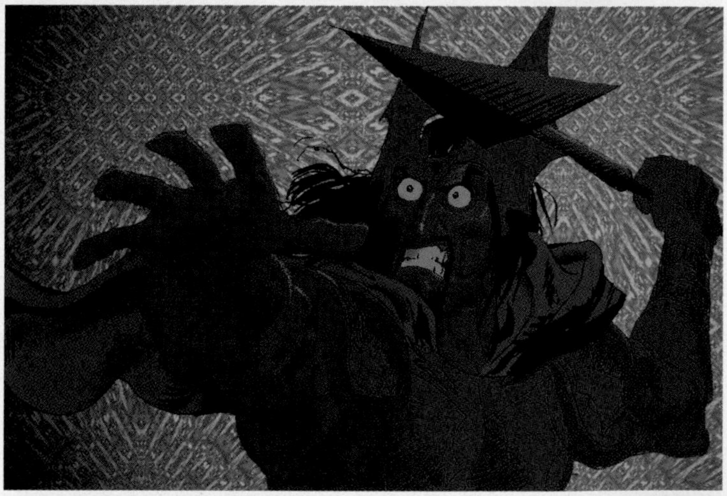

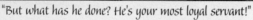

"But what has he done? He's your most loyal servant!"

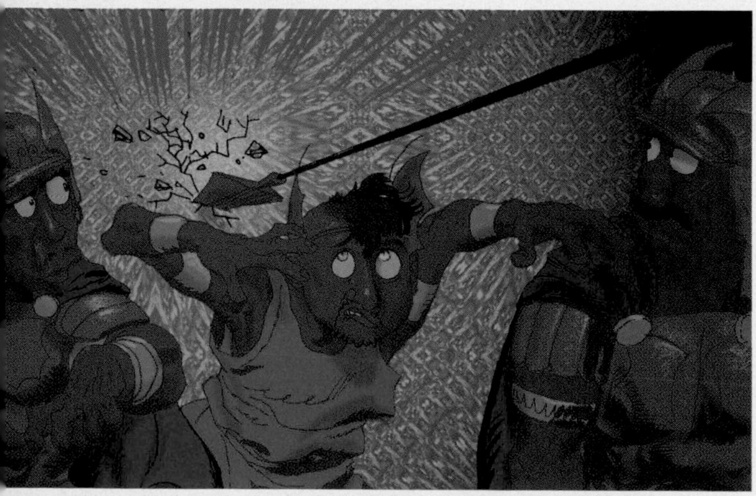

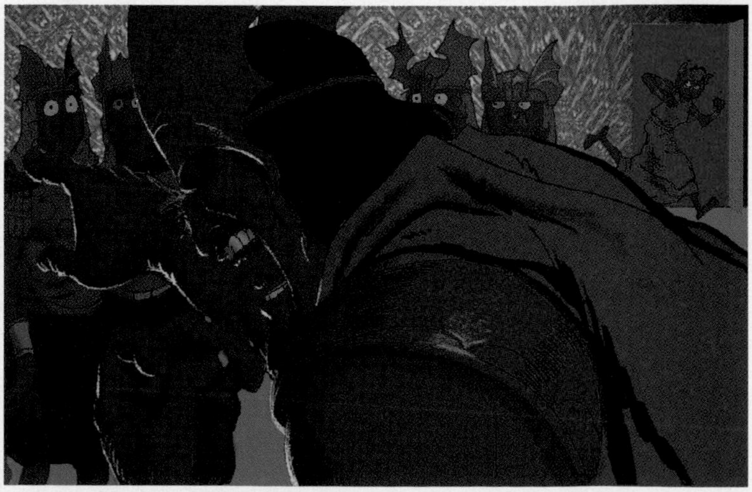

"Kill David NOW!"

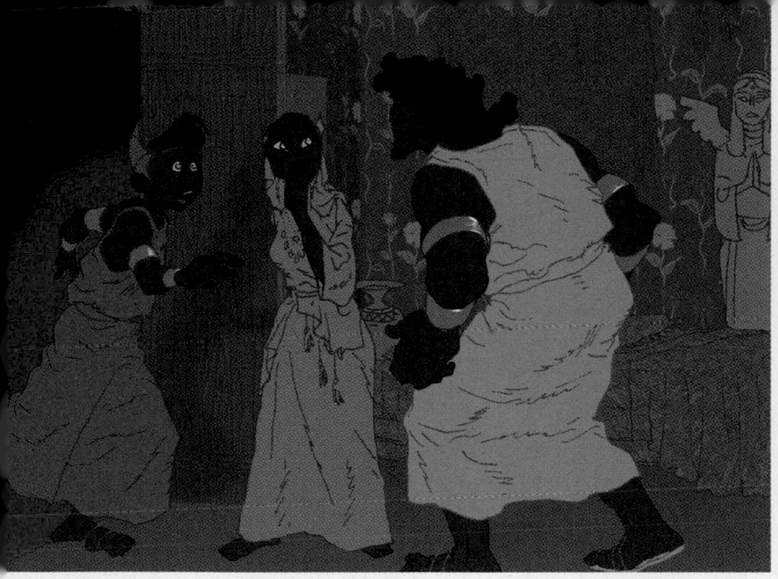

"David--"

"Did you hear? Daddy tried to spear David again today!"

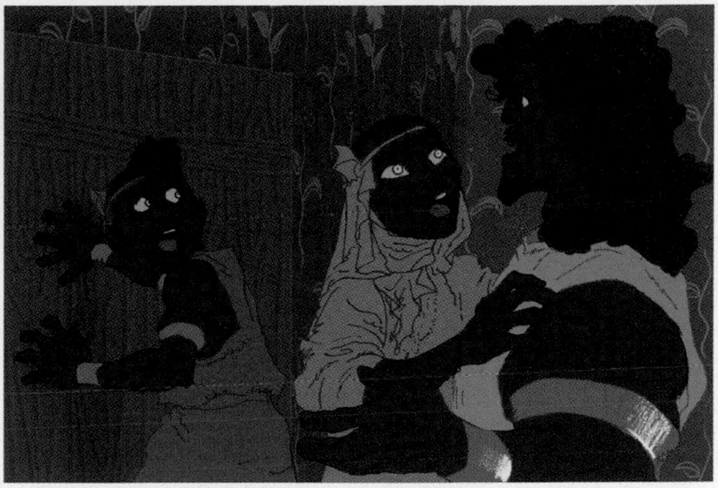

"And there's a hundred guys on their way here to finish the job!"

"What have I done?"

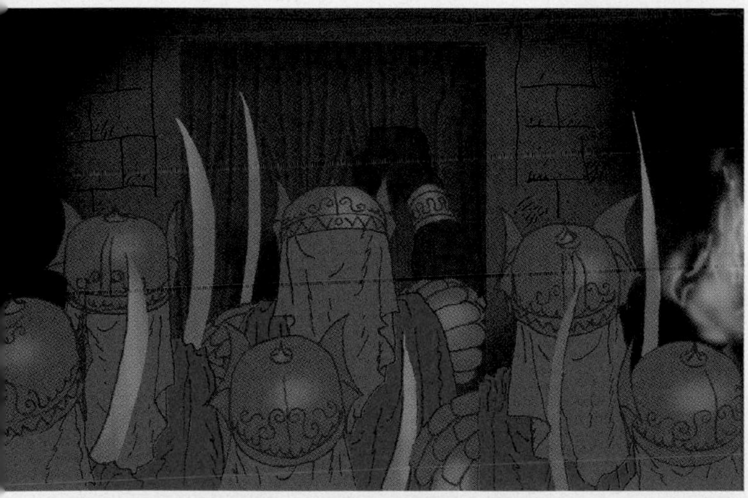

A knock on the front door.

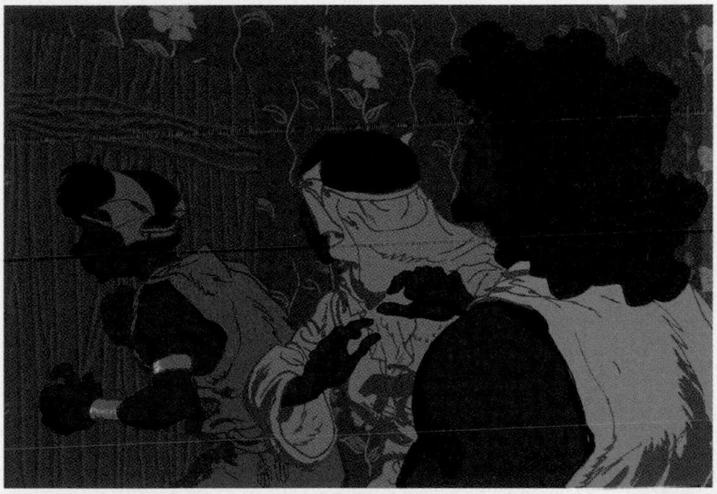

They whisper.

"It's them!"

"I thought you said you talked to Dad."

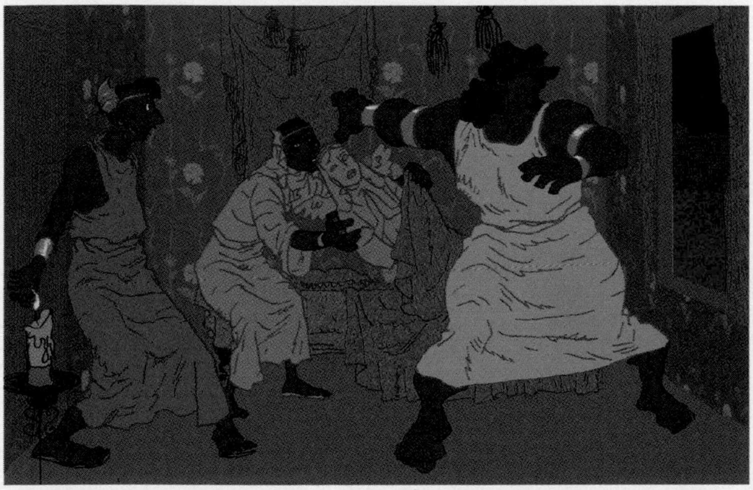

"I did! The last time he was talking about killing David, I asked him why, and reminded him about Goliath, and he says, "Okay, you're right. I swear I won't kill David." But you know Dad, he says one thing then turns around and does the opposite! Totally passive-aggressive."

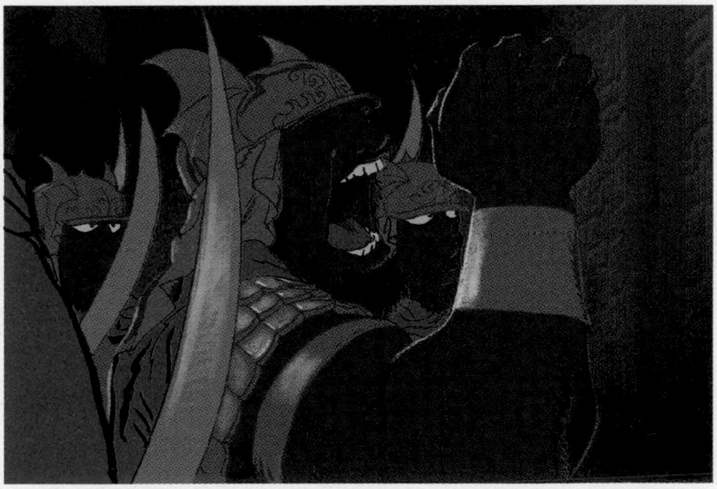

Another knock.

"Open this door!"

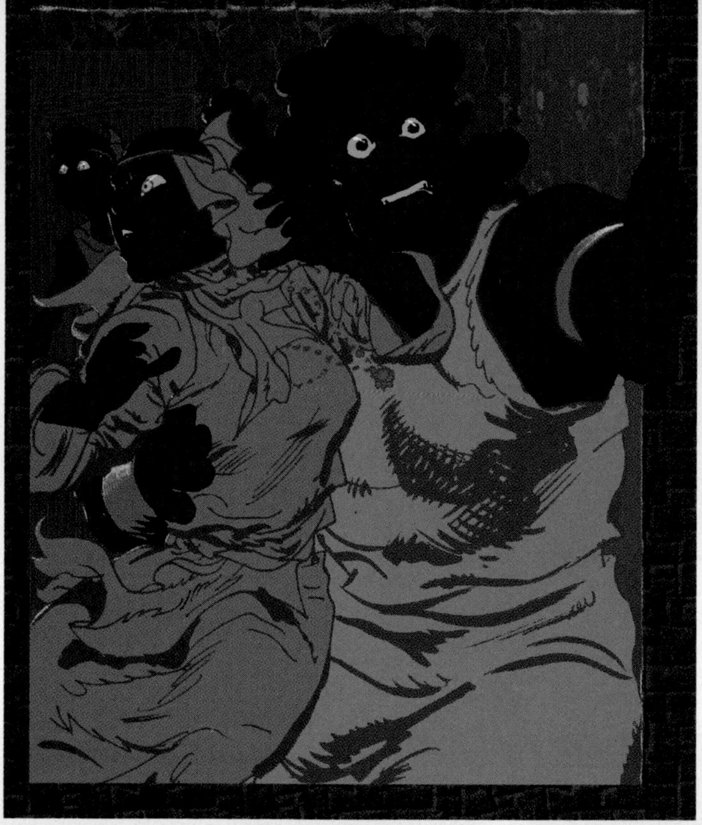

"Hurry!"

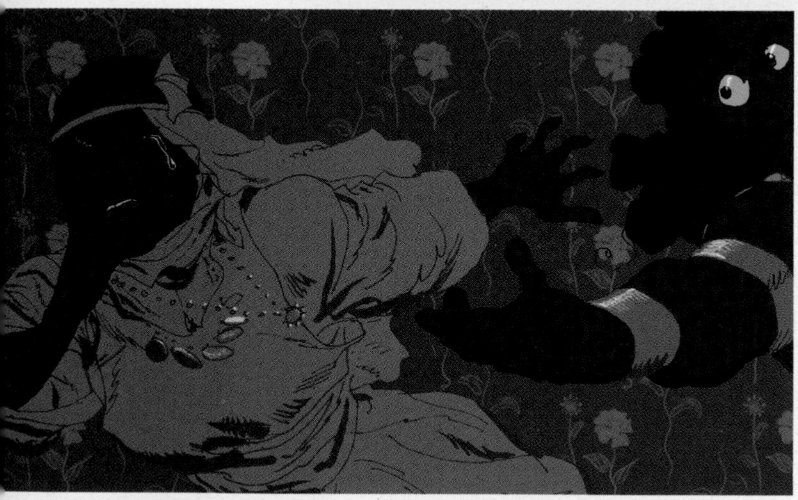

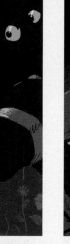

"I can't leave my father!"

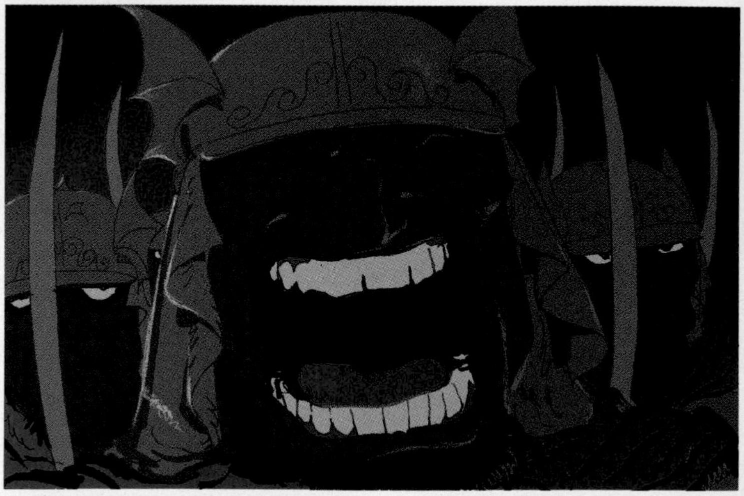

"Open this door in the name of King Saul!"

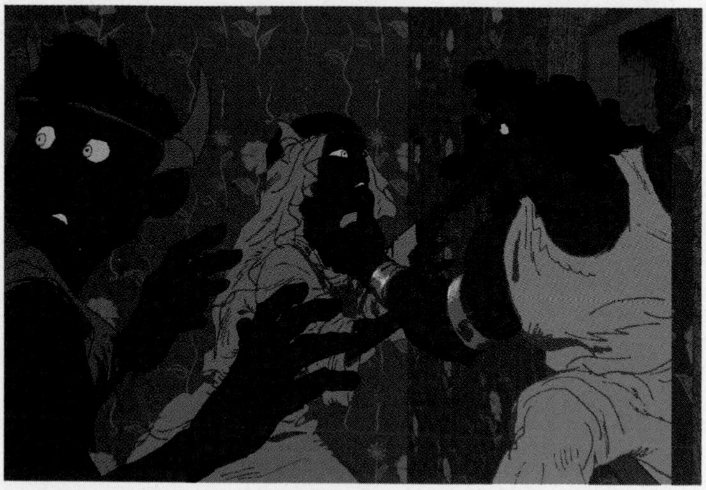

"Honest, David. We'd love to flee with you, but it's out of our hands. We have to honor our parents. Ten Commandments and all that. Sorry."

"David."

"Michal."

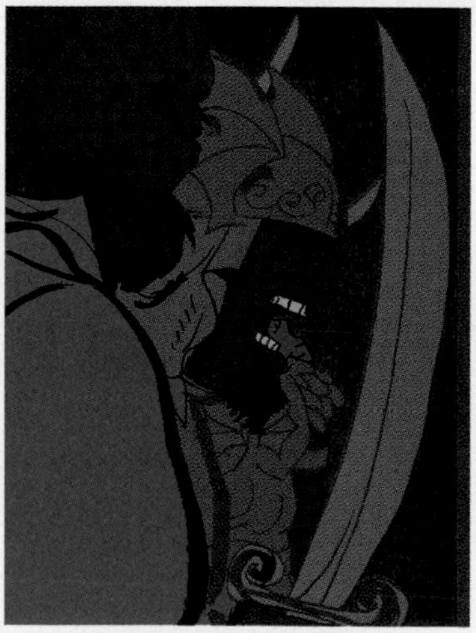

"Don't make me knock this door down. You'll only get me angry."

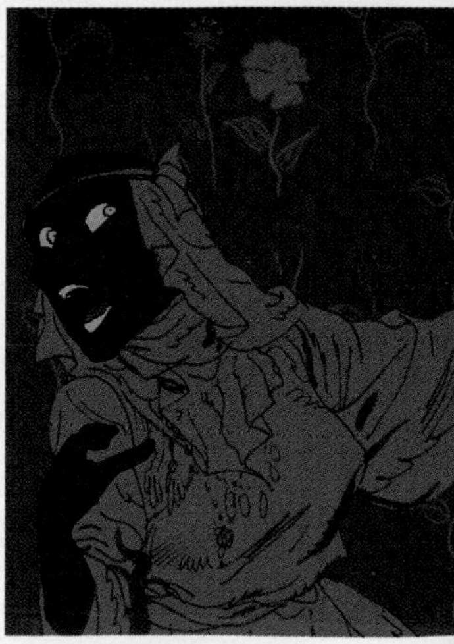

"You can't come in. My husband is very sick."

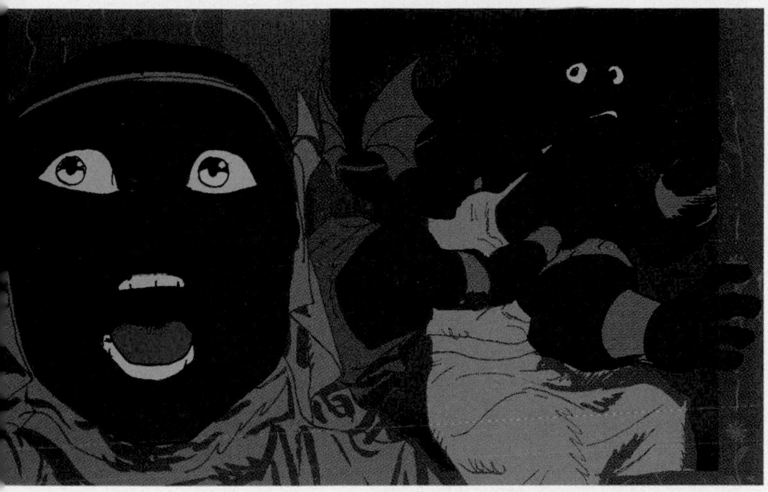

"We have orders to kill David."

"Did you hear me? He's sick! You want to catch leprosy?"

"Go!"

"I'll come back for you, Michal!"

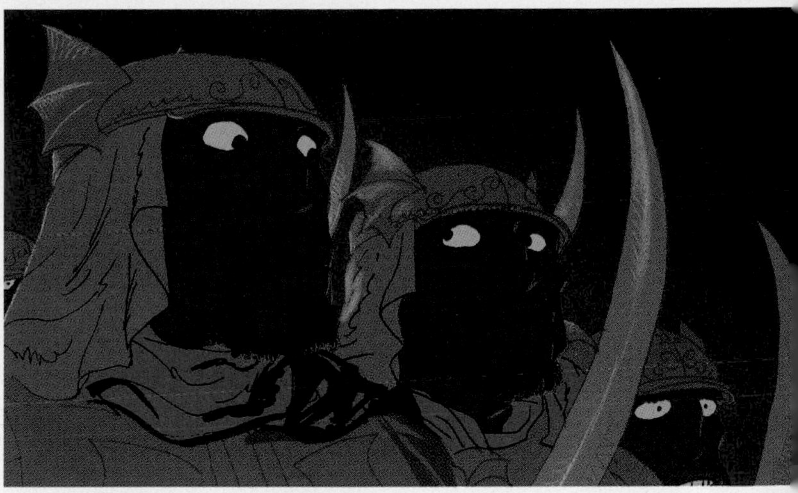

"Are you sure it's leprosy?"

"Not really," answers Michal. "Tell you what, why don't you come in and if your flesh starts rotting in a few days, we'll be positive."

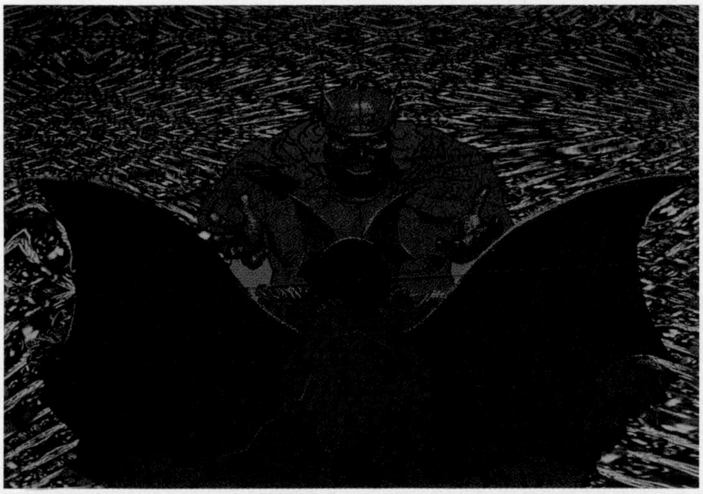

"He's sick."

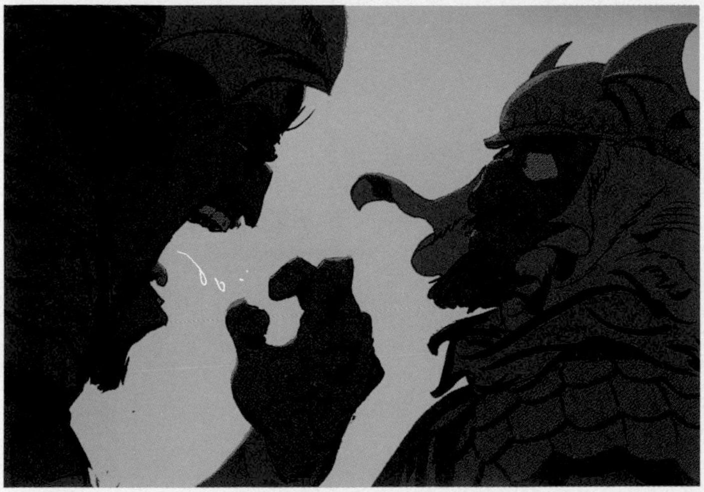

"Bring him to me in his bed and I'll kill him myself!"

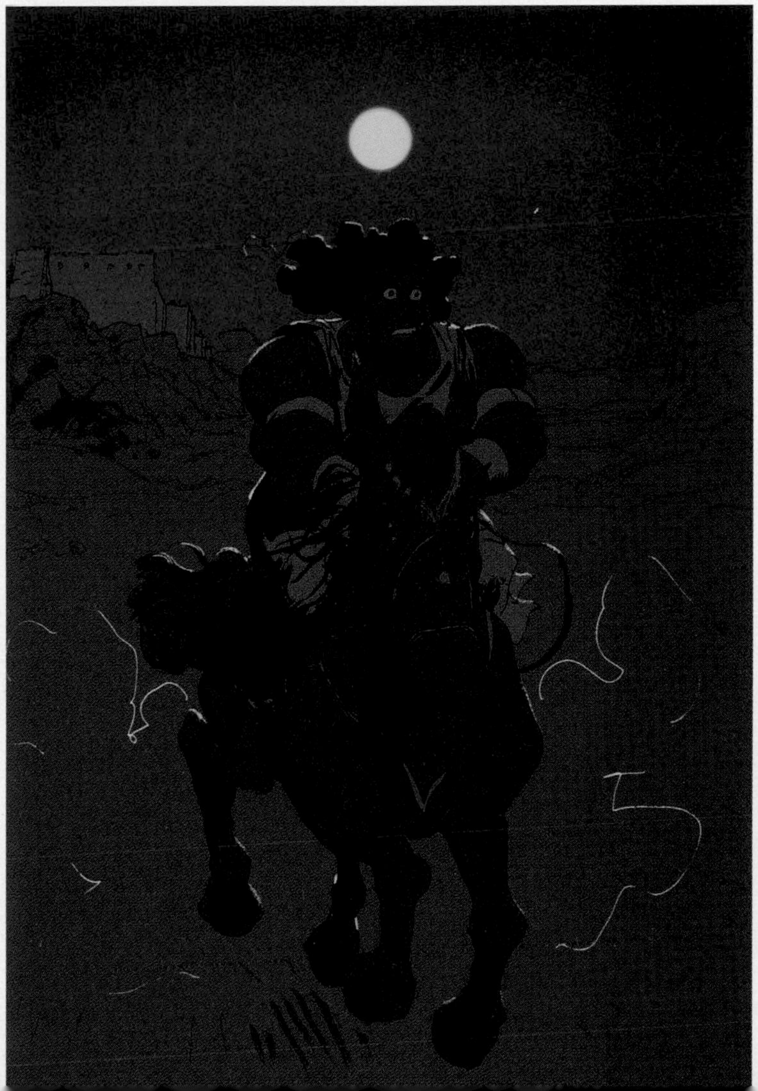

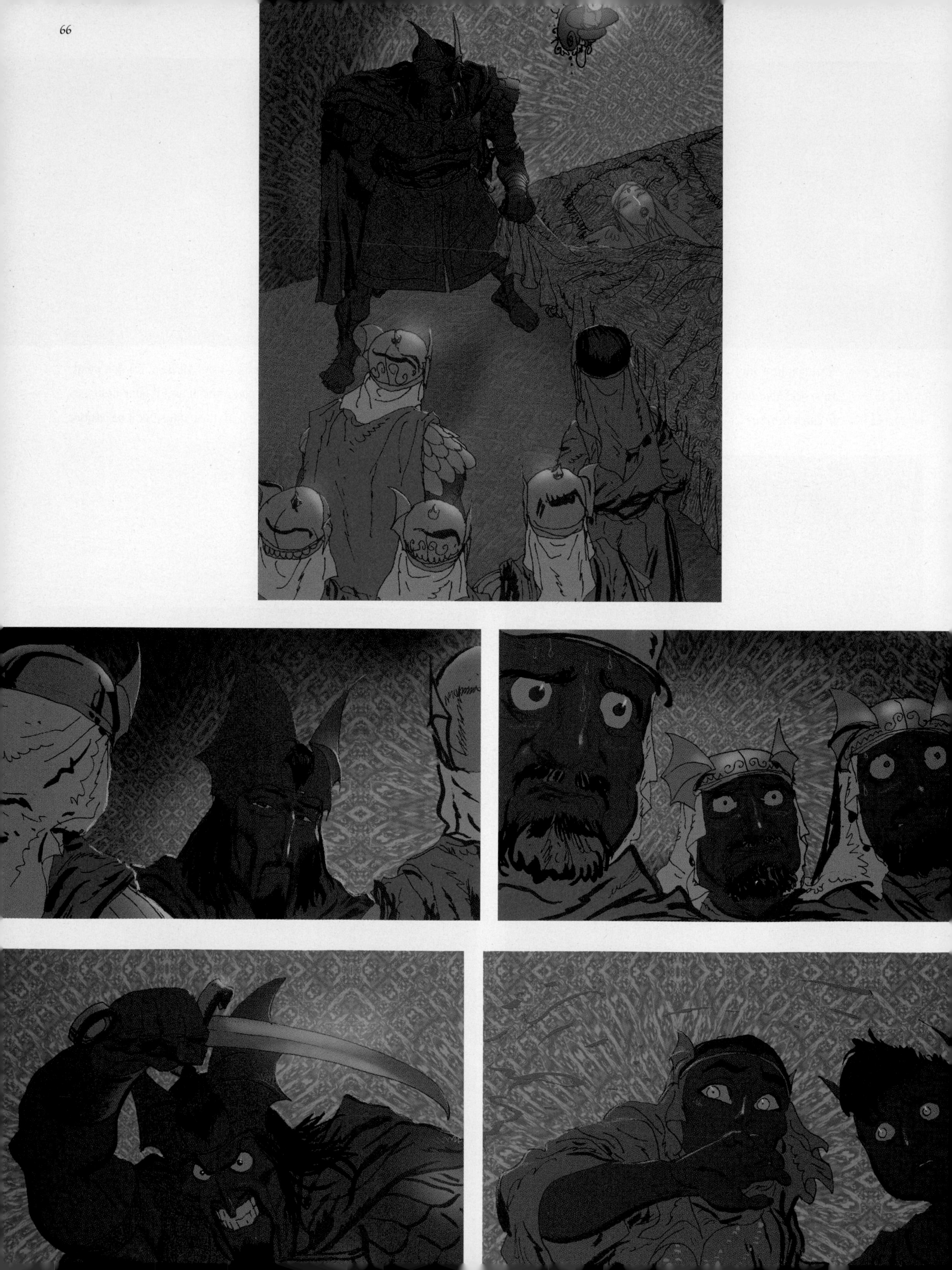

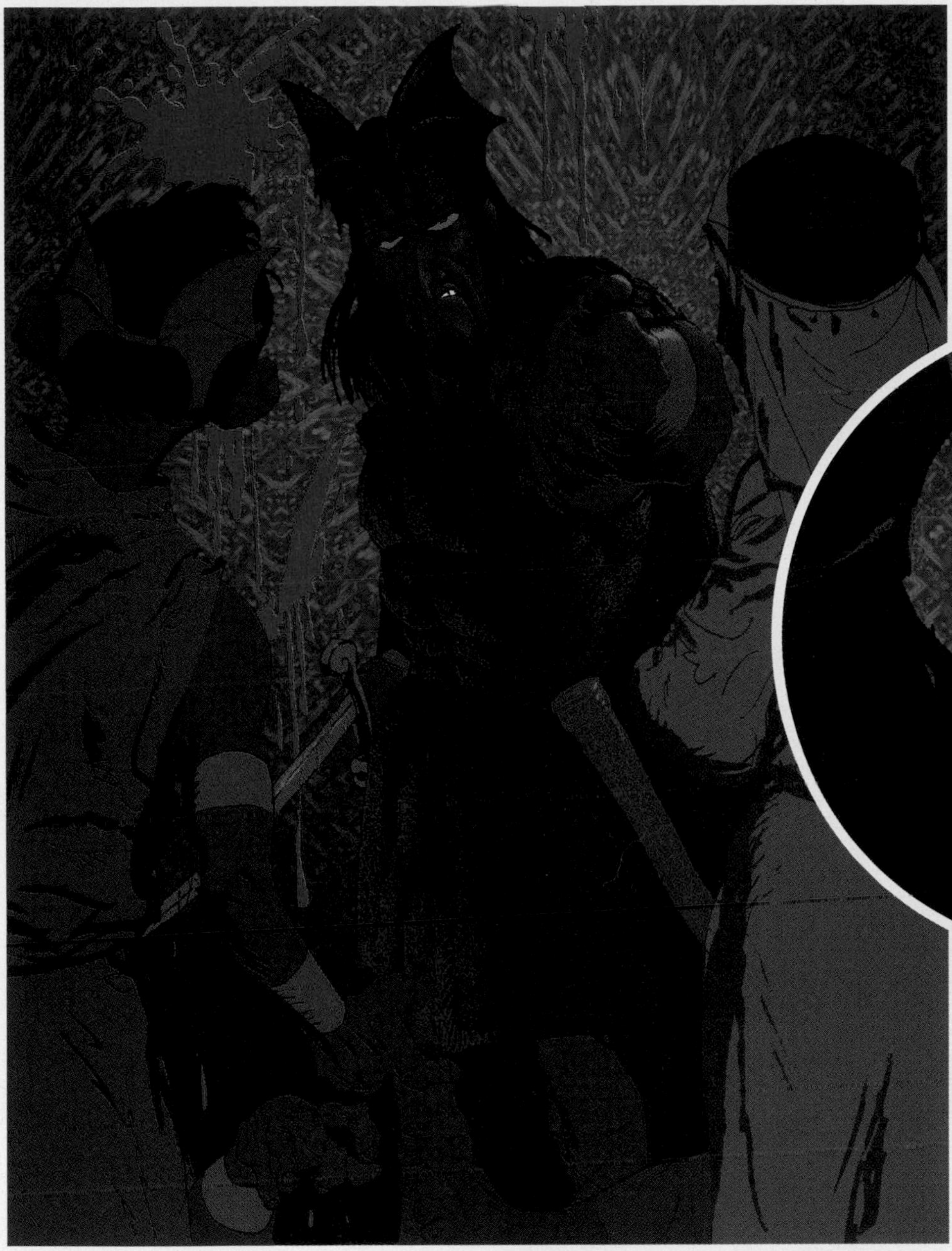

" Why have you,
my own children,
deceived me this
way," asks Saul,
"that you have sent
away my enemy,
and he has
escaped?"

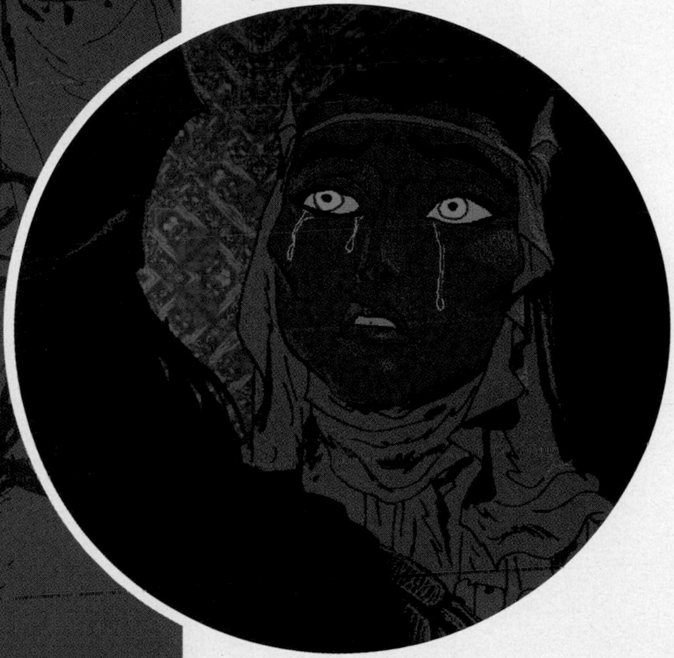

"He said to me,
'Send me away;
why should I
kill you?'"

David approaches the town of Nob.

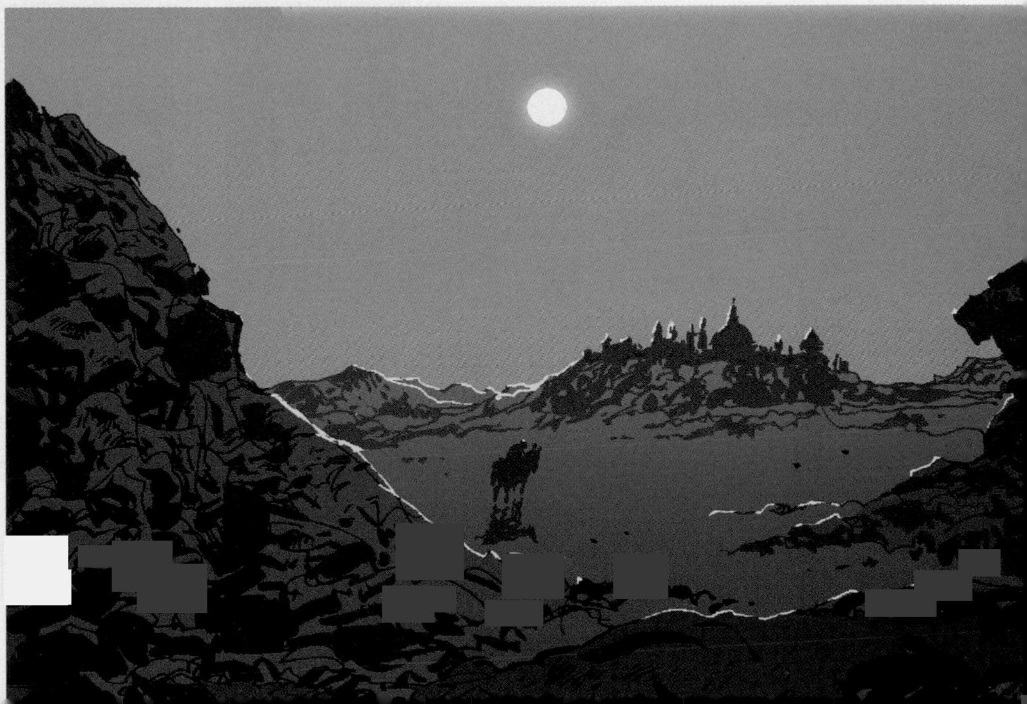

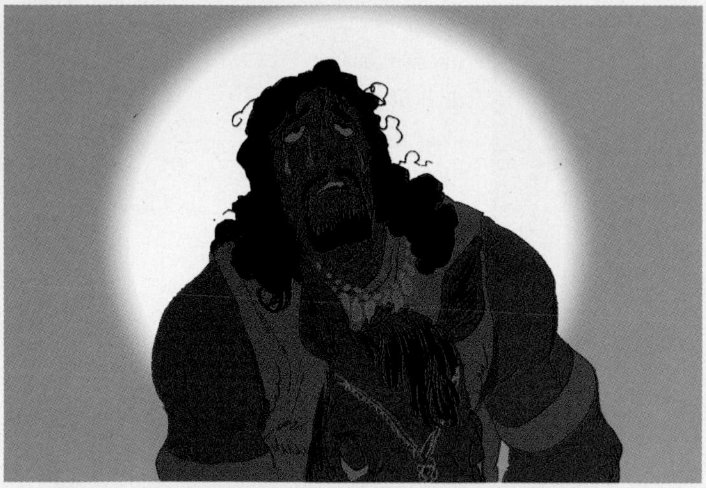

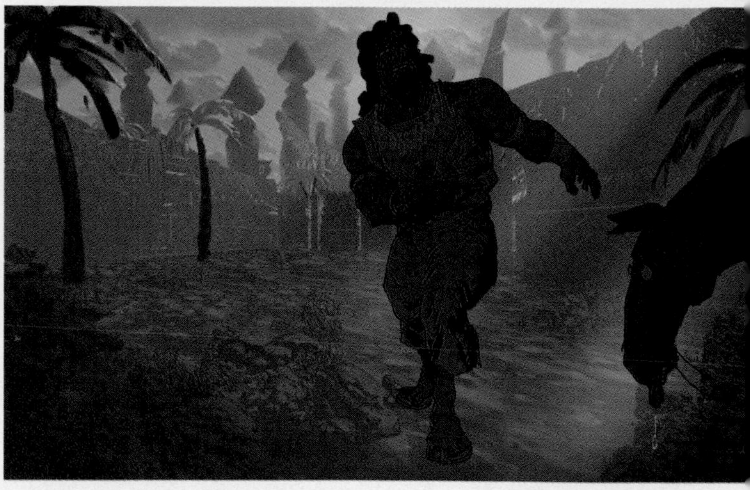

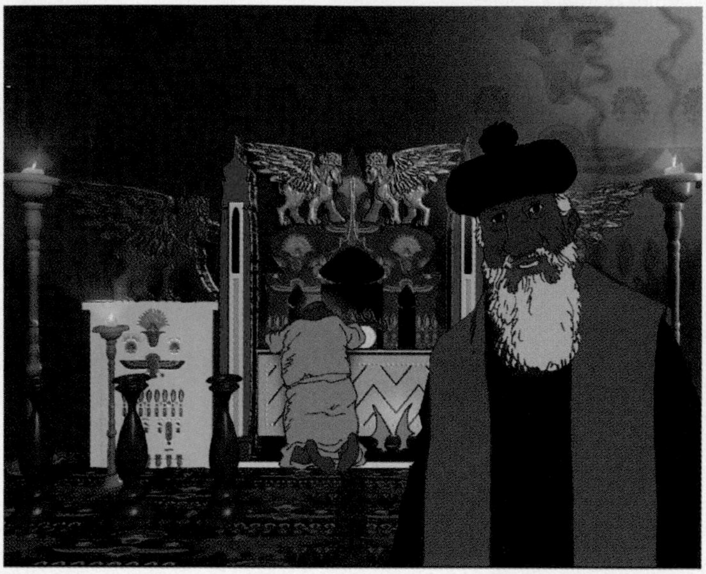

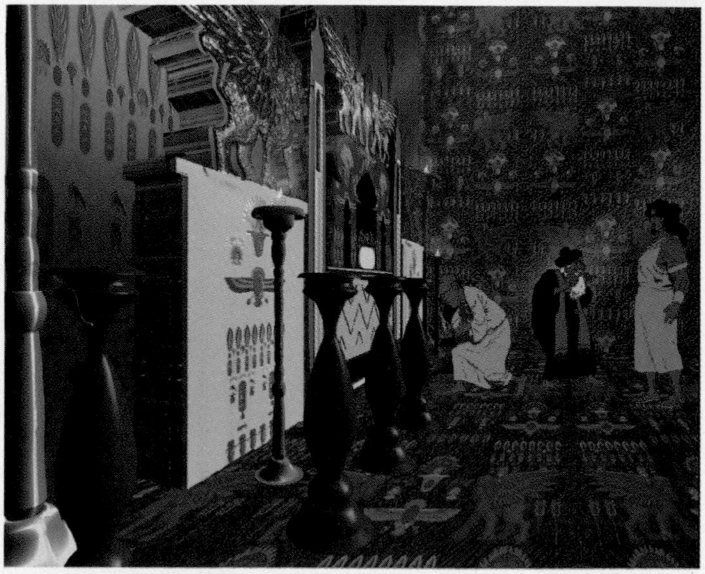

"David. Why are you by yourself, and no man with you? Am I in trouble?" says Ahimelech the priest.

"I'm on a top secret mission for King Saul," says David, "so top secret I can't even hint at its nature. I've sent the rest of my men ahead to...I can't tell you where. Now, then, what do you have on hand? I could use five loaves of bread, or whatever you have."

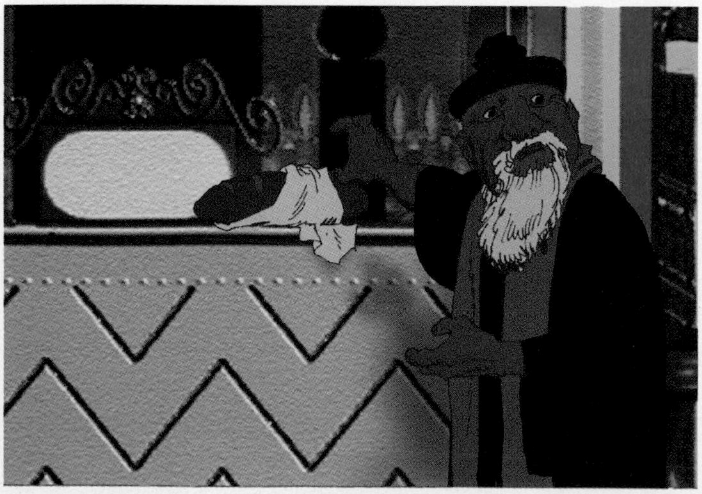

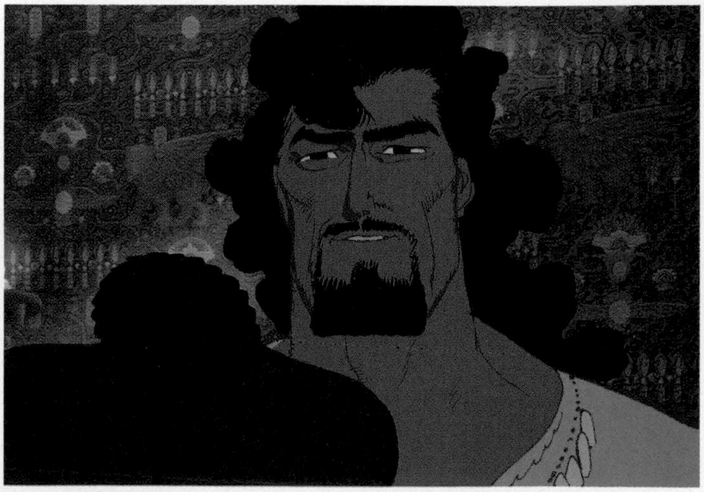

"I have no common bread, only the holy bread. I can give it to you only if your men have been kept from women lately. "

"My men and I always keep ourselves ritually pure when on top secret missions for the king. We haven't been with women for days."

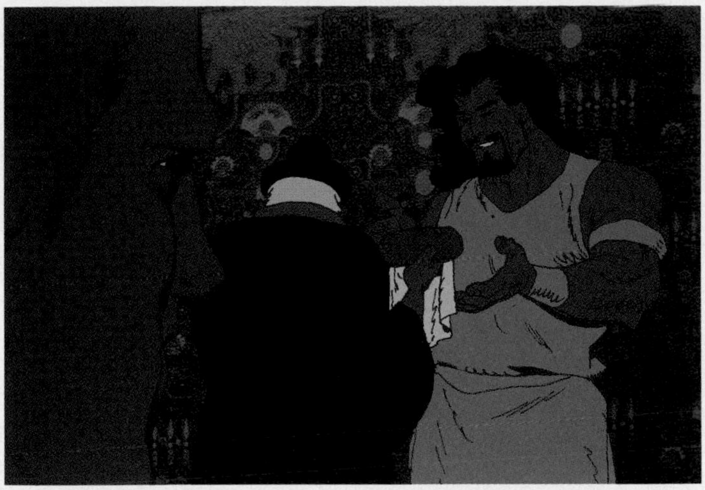

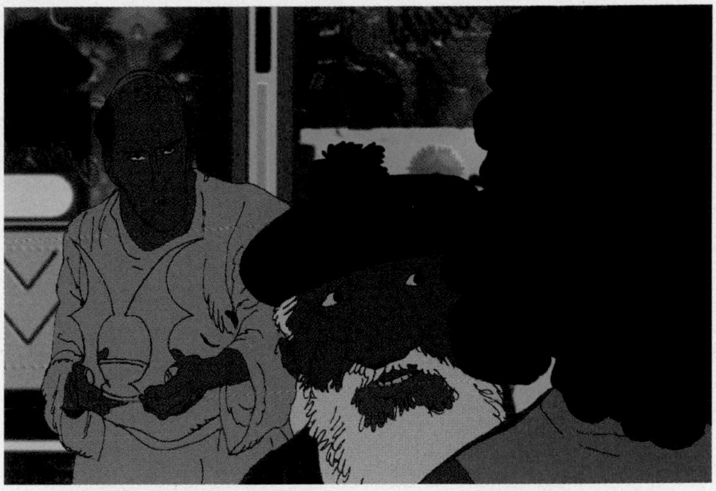

"Thank you. You know, Ahimelech, this top secret mission my men and I are on was so important that we had to leave in a hurry, and I rushed out so fast I forgot to bring a weapon! Would you happen to have any weapons lying around, perhaps? Anything will do."

"How strange it is to leave on the king's business with no weapons and then ask a holy man for one!"

"It happens. Hello Doeg."

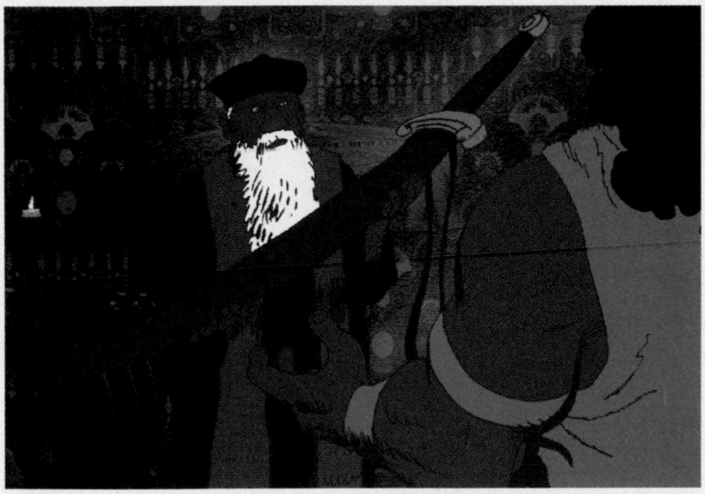

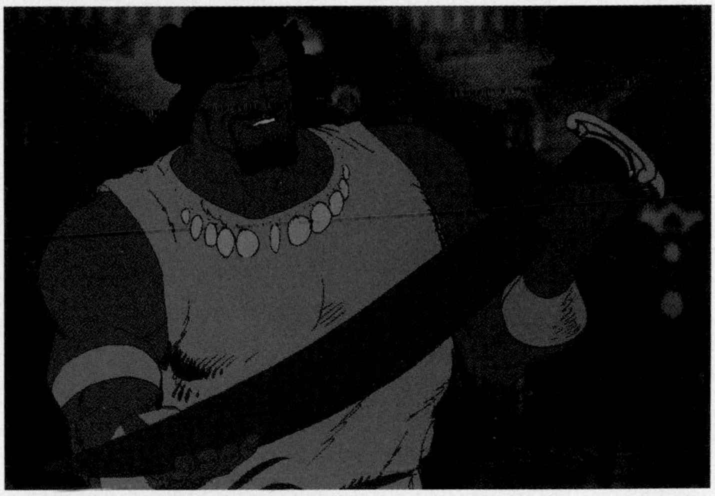

"I have no weapons, except the sword of Goliath the Philistine, whom you struck in the valley of Elah. If you desire, take it."

"There is none like it. Give it to me."

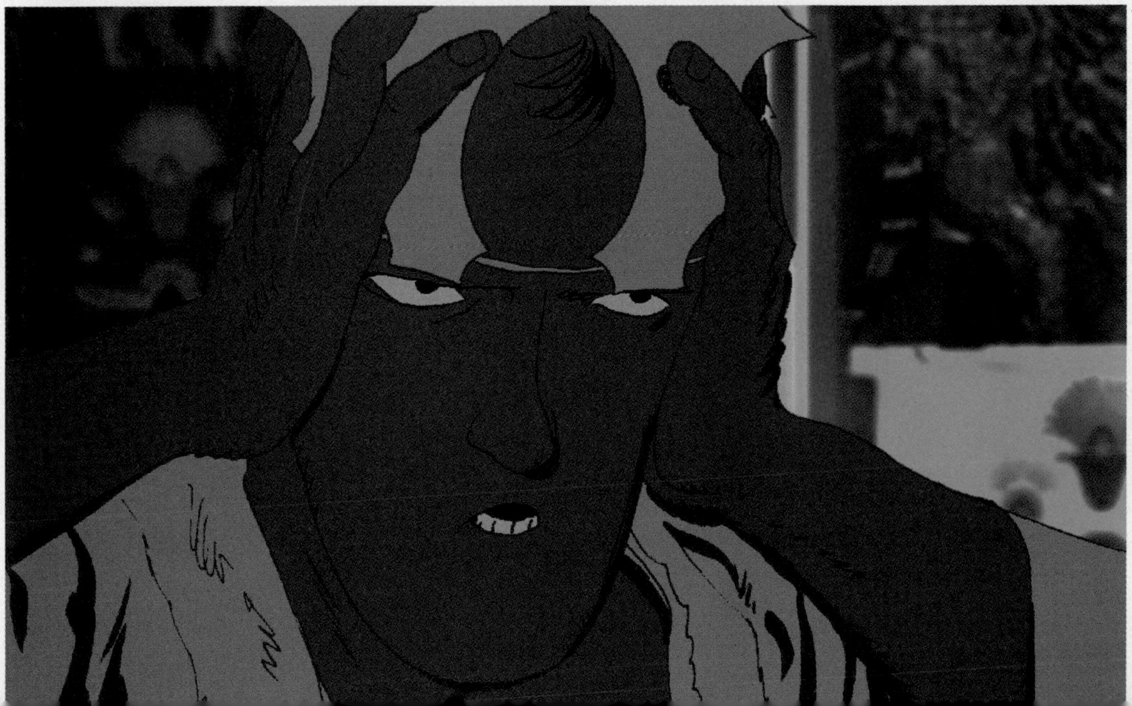

Doeg wonders silently if King Saul might like to know about David's "secret mission for the king."

From Nob, David flees to King Achish of Gath.

"Isn't that David?" say Achish's advisors. "The one who everyone sings about? 'Saul has killed his thousands, and David his tens of thousands'?"

David suddenly questions the wisdom of fleeing to the hometown of Goliath while wearing Goliath's sword.

David becomes afraid. He quickly decides that the best solution is to fake insanity.

David babbles, drools spittle down his beard, and scribbles on the gates.

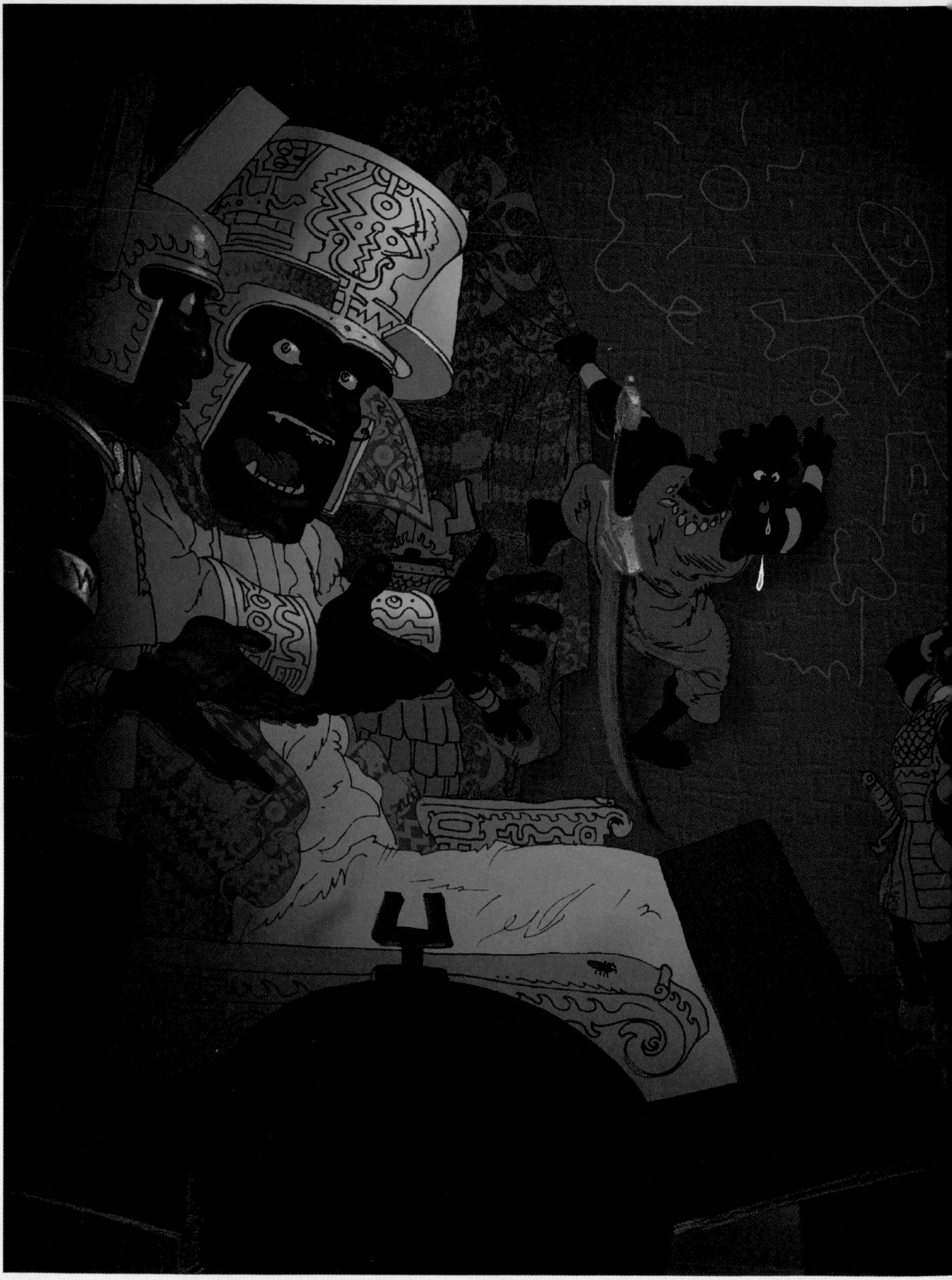

King Achish yells at his servants. "This man is obviously insane! Do I lack crazy people, that you have to bring one into my house? Get him out of here!"

"Why have you conspired against me with the son of Jesse?" asks Saul. "Why did you give David food and a sword and even inquire of God for him?"

Ahimelech gasps, "Who of all your servants is as loyal as David? Was that day the first day I inquired of God for him? Of course not! Let not the king accuse your servant or his father's family of any wrong-doing, for your servant knows nothing at all about this whole affair."

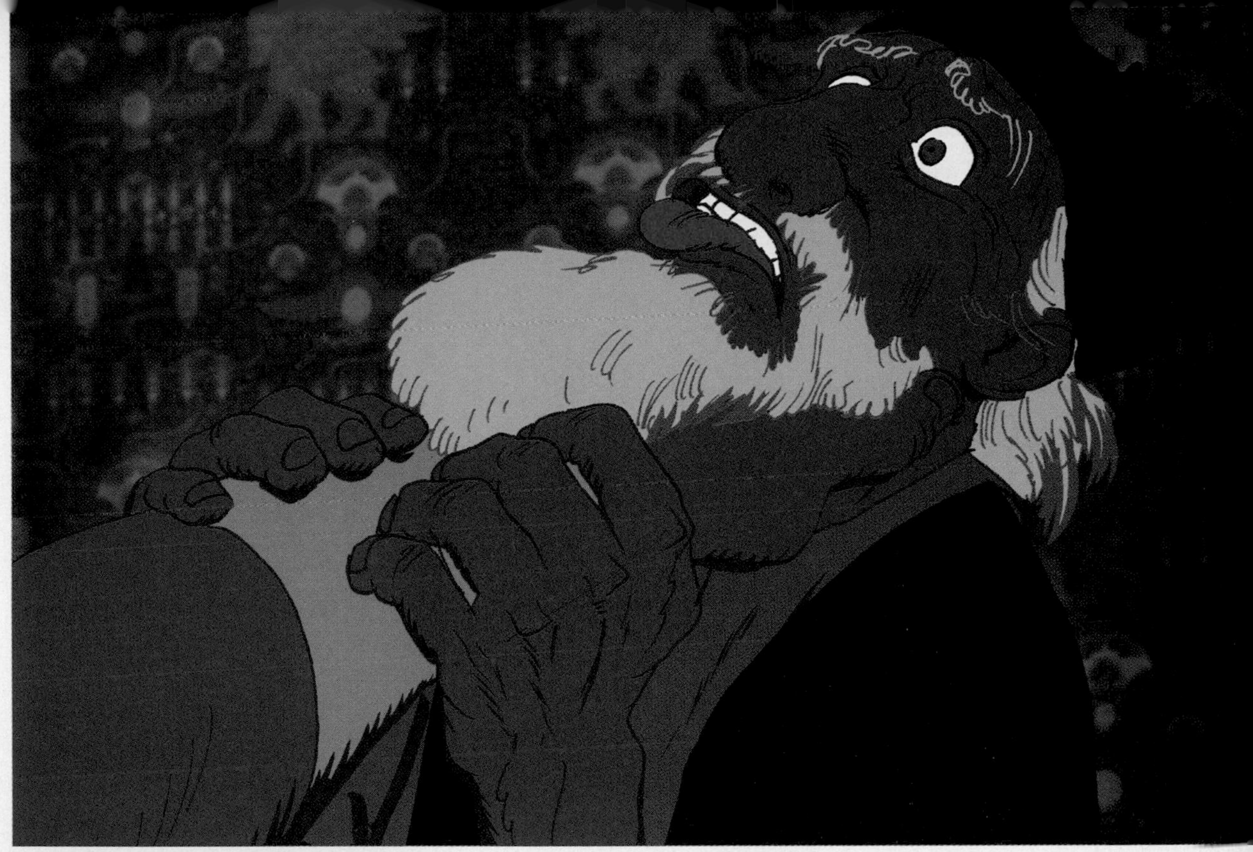

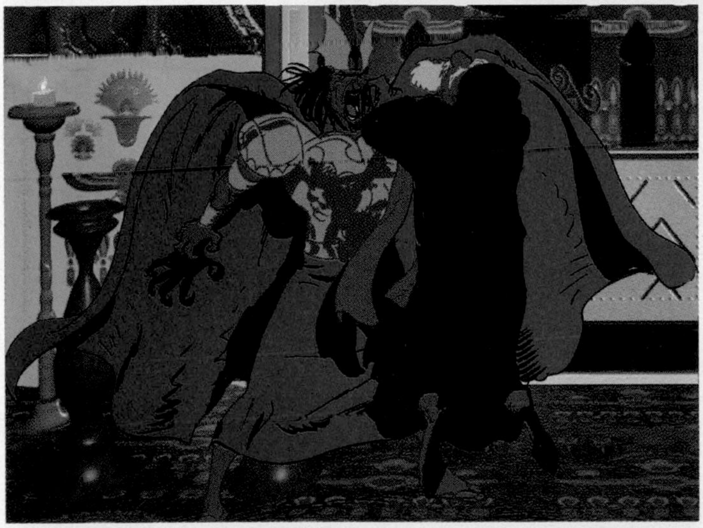

Saul says, "You will surely die, Ahimelech. You and your father's entire family shall die."

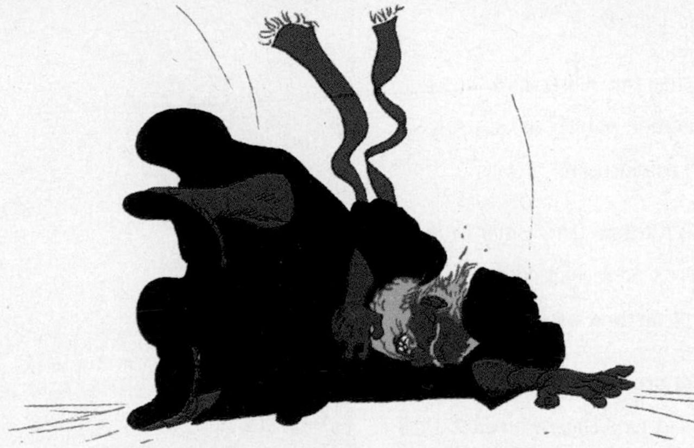

Saul throws Ahimelech to the floor.

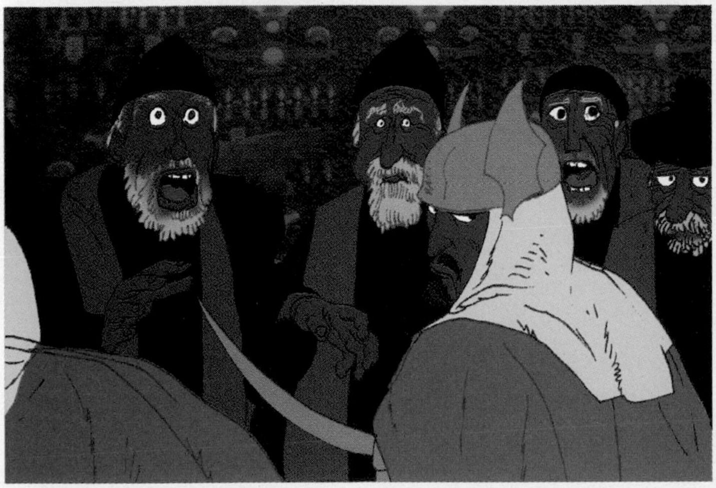

"Soldiers! Kill all the priests," commands Saul.

The soldiers hesitate.

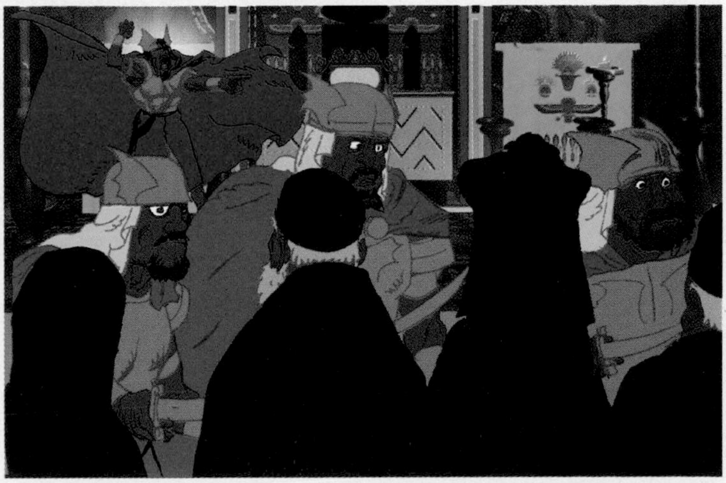

"Have you all lost your hearing? Kill the priests!"

"I'd never be able to face my mother again." says one soldier.

MEANWHILE, David has hidden in the cave of Adullam.

David's brother Abinadab shouts, "David! We heard you were hiding in here!"

"You and everyone else," says David, referring to the crowd of 400 families also packed into the cave.

"Who are all these people?" asks Abinadab.

"I have no idea. Apparently, everyone who is in debt, or in distress, or discontented."

"In my day we called them bums," says Jesse, David's father.

"Dad! Mom! You got my message," says David.

"Excuse me, when does the revolution start?" asks a soft-spoken old man.

"I keep telling you," says David, "there's no revolution. Where are people getting these ideas?"

Eliab preaches to a rapt crowd, "David was chosen by God, I tell you! I was there when the prophet Samuel anointed him king!"

"For this you give up a nice job with King Saul." Jesse says to David.

"I didn't give it up!"

"You got fired? By your own father-in-law?"

A follower interrupts Jesse to say, "Good news, David. We just heard back from the king of Moab. He says your parents can stay with him until this whole thing's settled."

"Don't be ridiculous," grumbles Jesse. "We've got a harvest in two

weeks. David, go talk to Saul. What was so terrible that you couldn't apologize?"

"He's trying to kill me!" says David.

"Who likes their boss?" Jesse shrugs. "The man asks you to do a little hard work, you say he's trying to kill you. King Saul is a very good person to know."

David's mother interjects. "I told all my girlfriends, 'My son has a very

good career playing harp at the palace. For his father-in-law, the king!' What am I supposed to say now?"

"What do I care what you tell your girlfriends, Ma?"

"Oh, pardon me. You know everything. That's why you live in a cave full of bums."

"Maybe I could talk to King Saul," says Jesse.

"He wants to kill you too," says David.

"He wants me dead too? What did you do to the man?"

"Nothing!"

"I know your nothing. Your nothing is always something."

"You hear how he talks to his mother," says his mother, "you think he's going to show a king respect?"

"You call yourselves soldiers," bellows Saul. "Can't even bring yourselves to kill unarmed priests! Losers! Thank goodness there's one man here with some guts!"

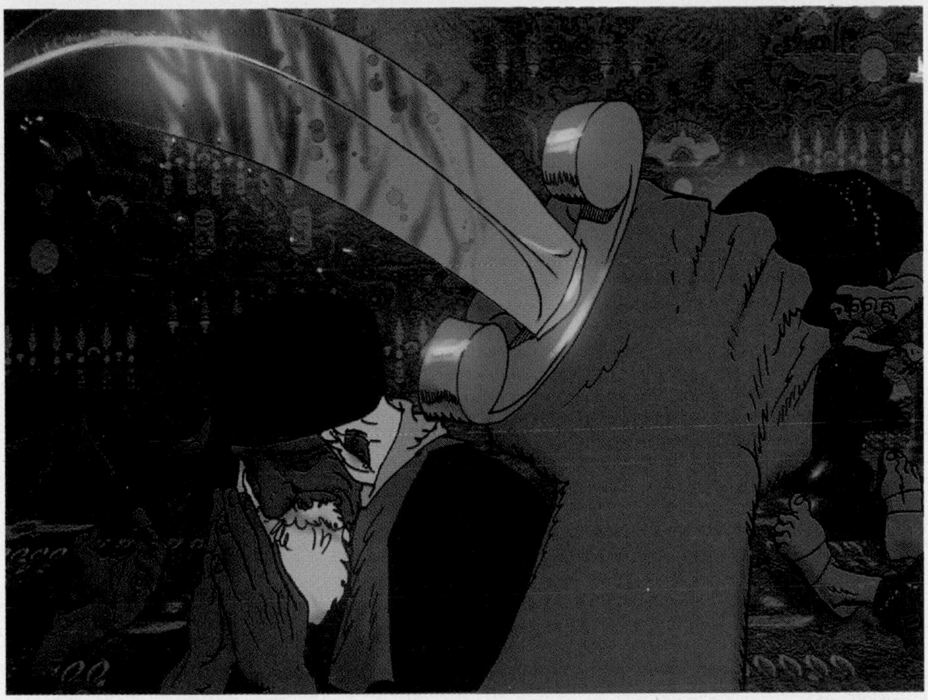

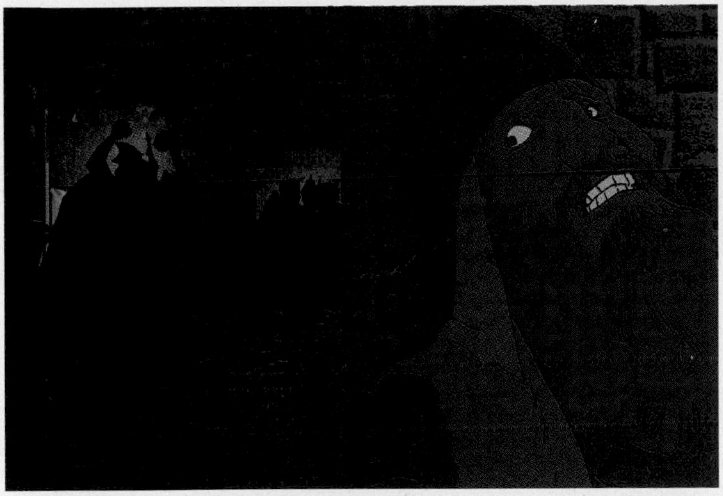

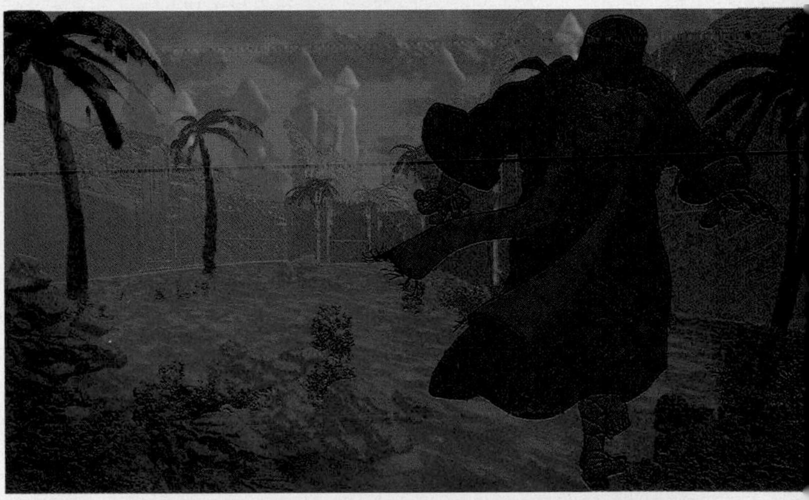

Abiathar, son of Ahimelech, escapes while the other priests die.

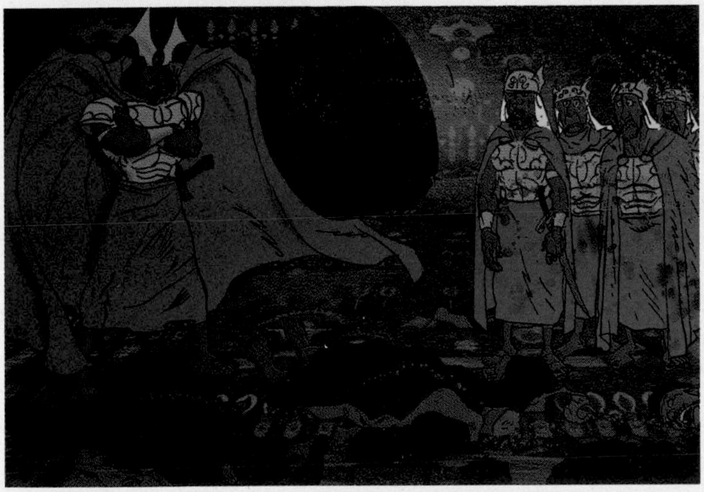

"Thank you, Doeg, for doing my soldiers' job for them." says Saul. "Now go destroy Nob, town of the priests. Leave no one alive. No man, woman, child, baby, cattle, donkeys, sheep. Destroy them all."

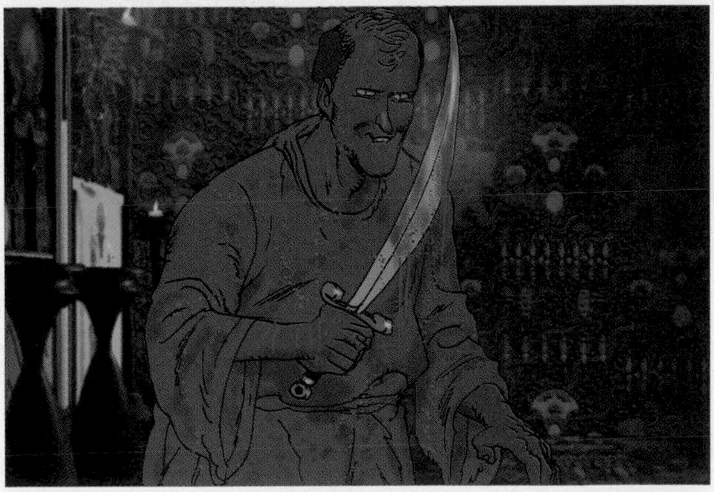

"It will be done, my king."

"Next, we find and kill the son of Jesse," Saul tells his soldiers.

Abiathar runs to join David, and tells him what happened in Nob.

"That day, when Doeg the Edomite was there in Nob," says David, "I knew he would be sure to tell Saul. I am responsible for the death of your father's whole family. Stay with me; don't be afraid; the man who is seeking your life is seeking mine also. You will be safe with me."

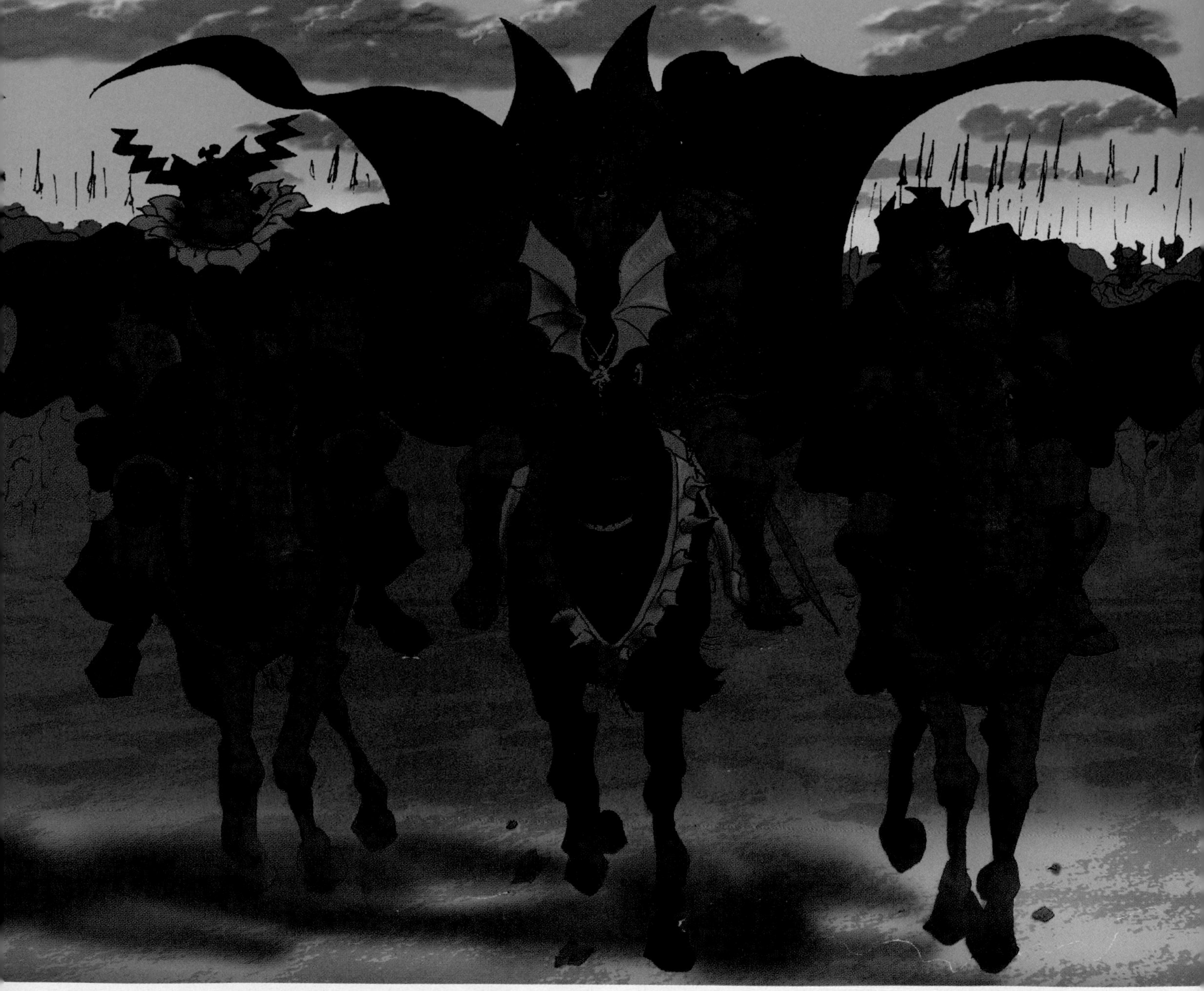

Saul pursues David in the desert of En Gedi.

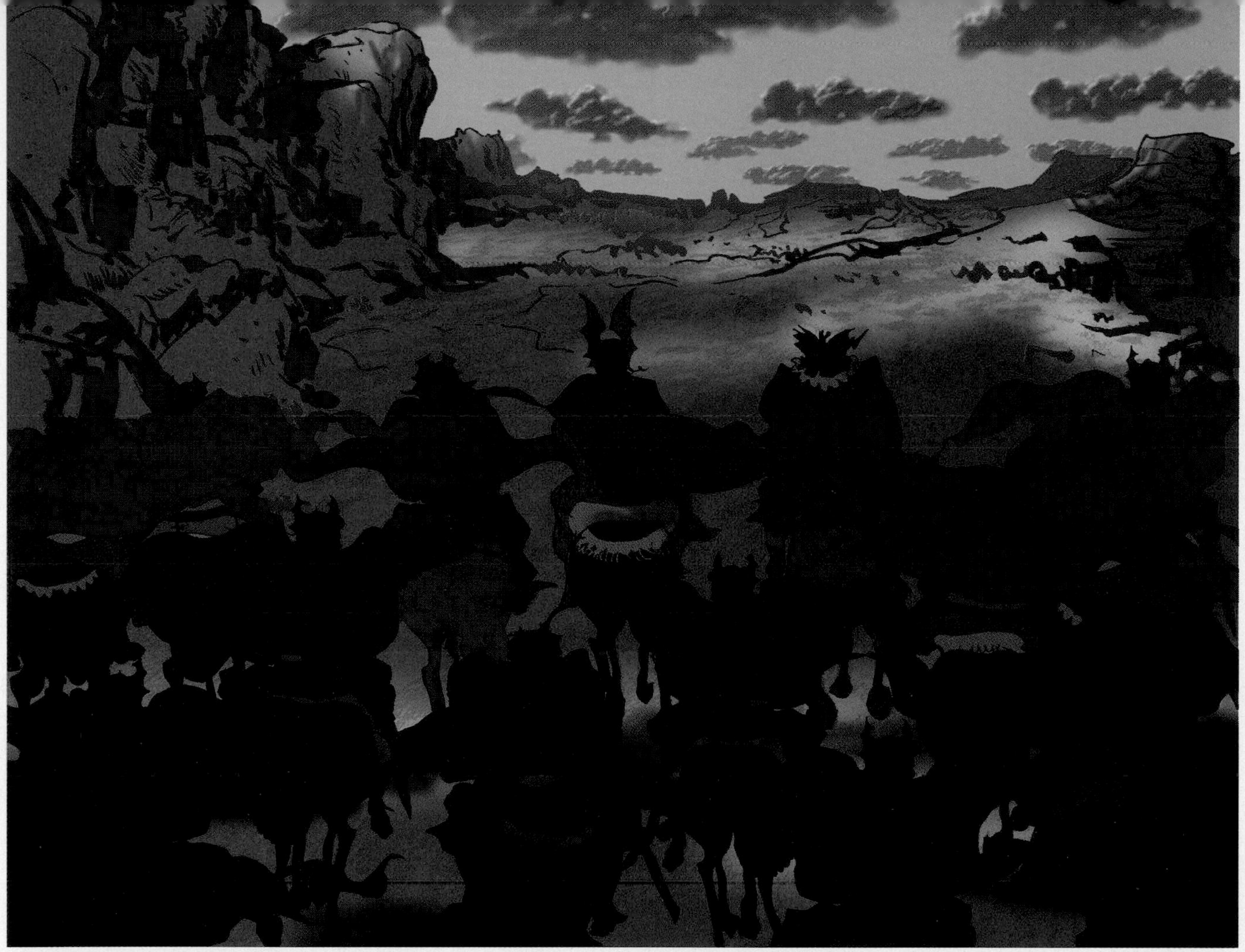

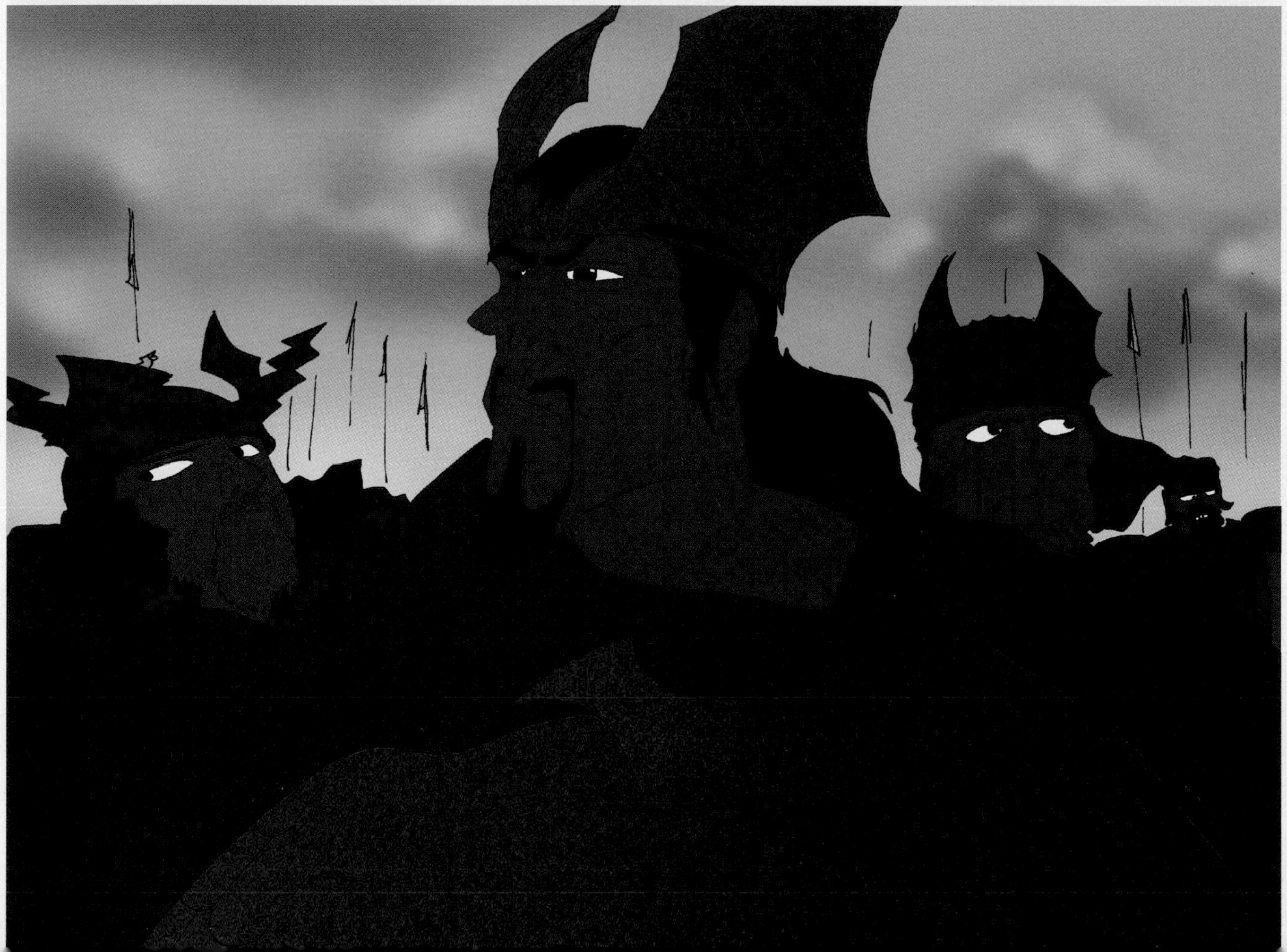

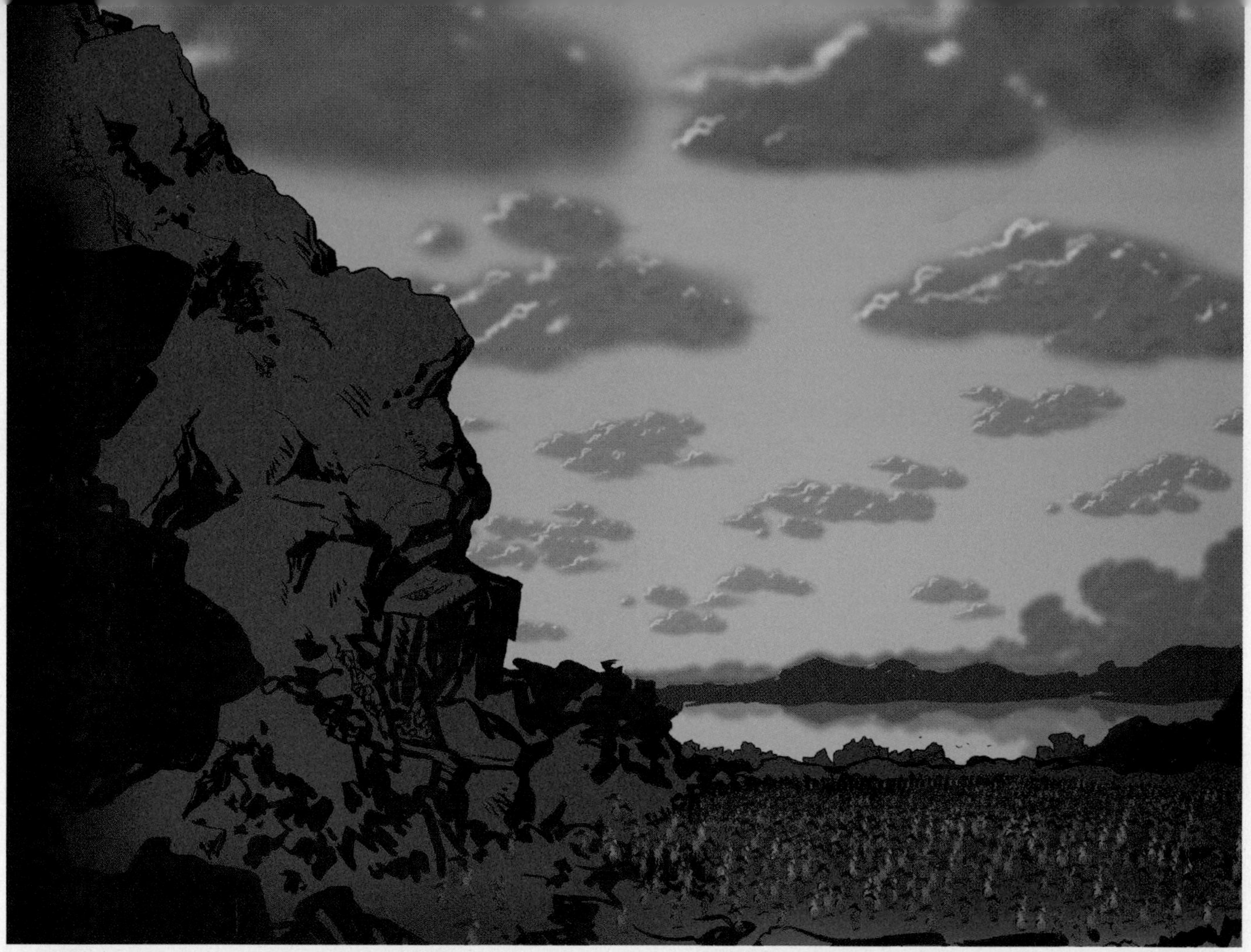

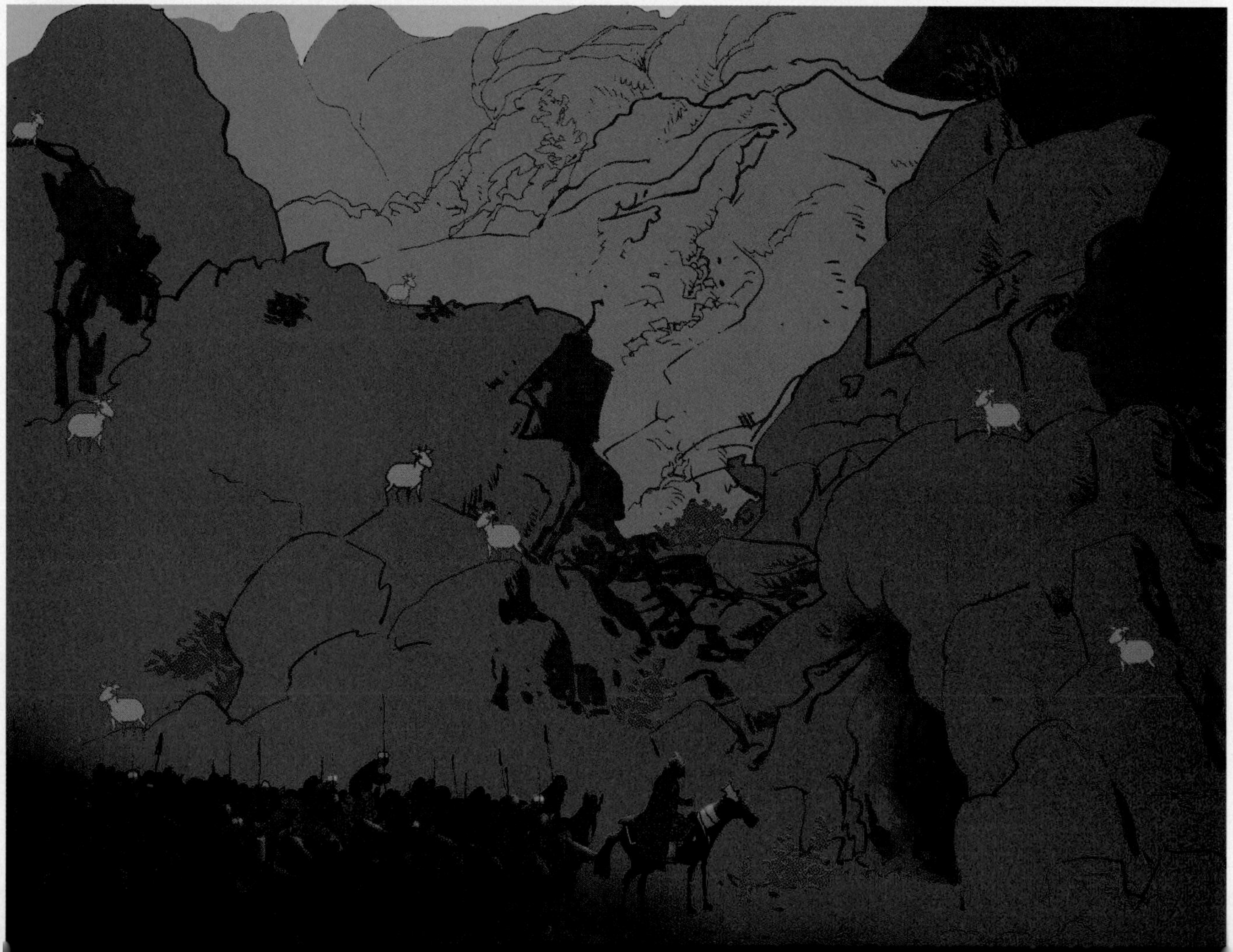

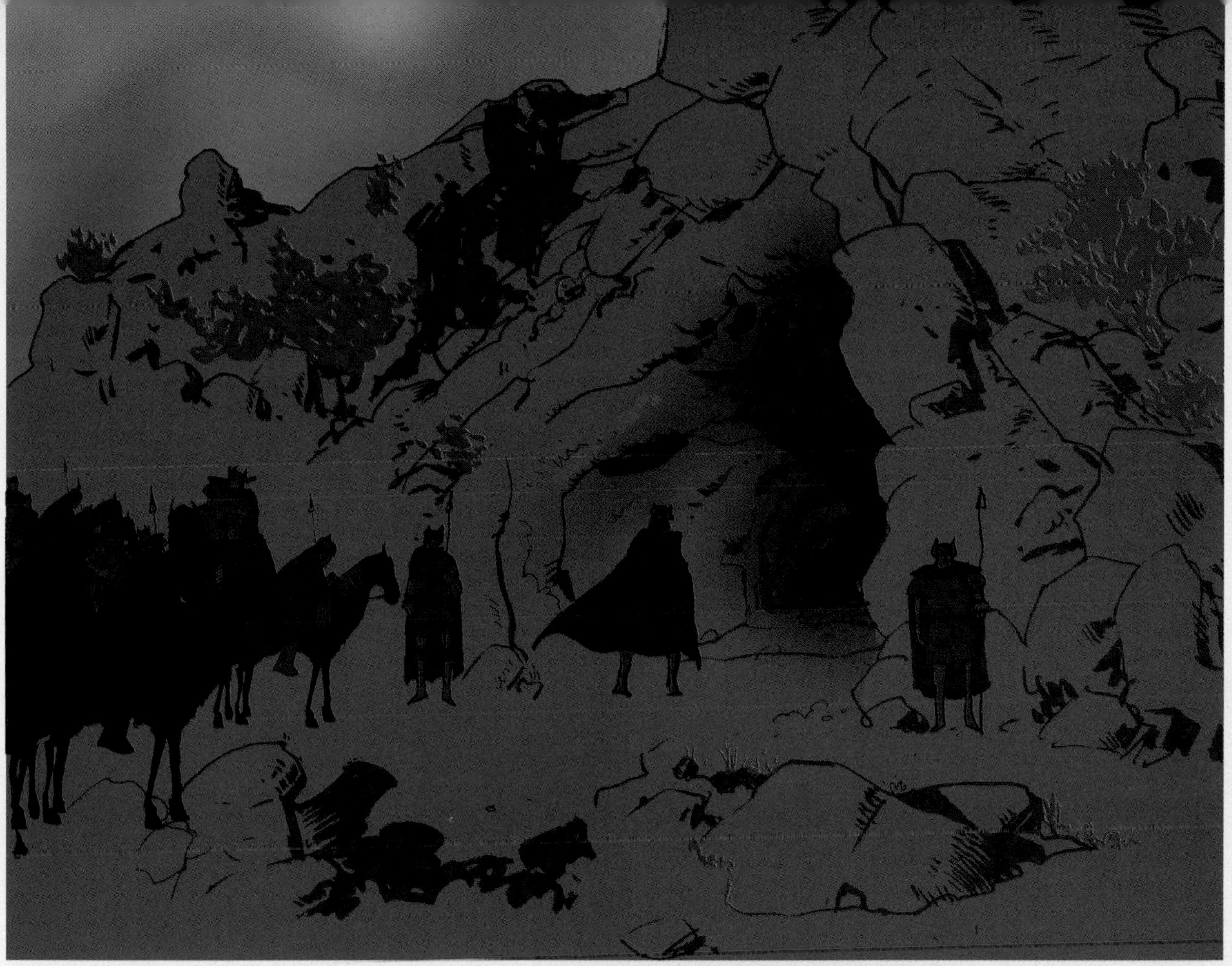

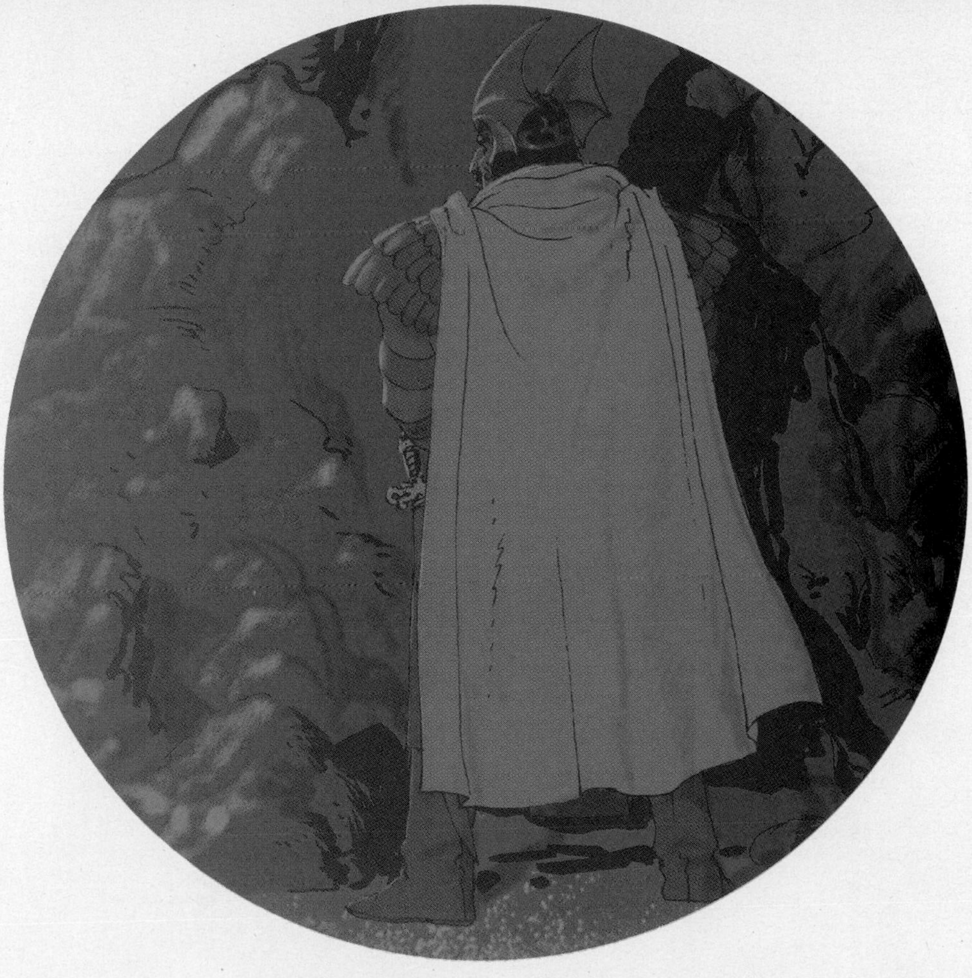

Saul pauses to relieve himself.

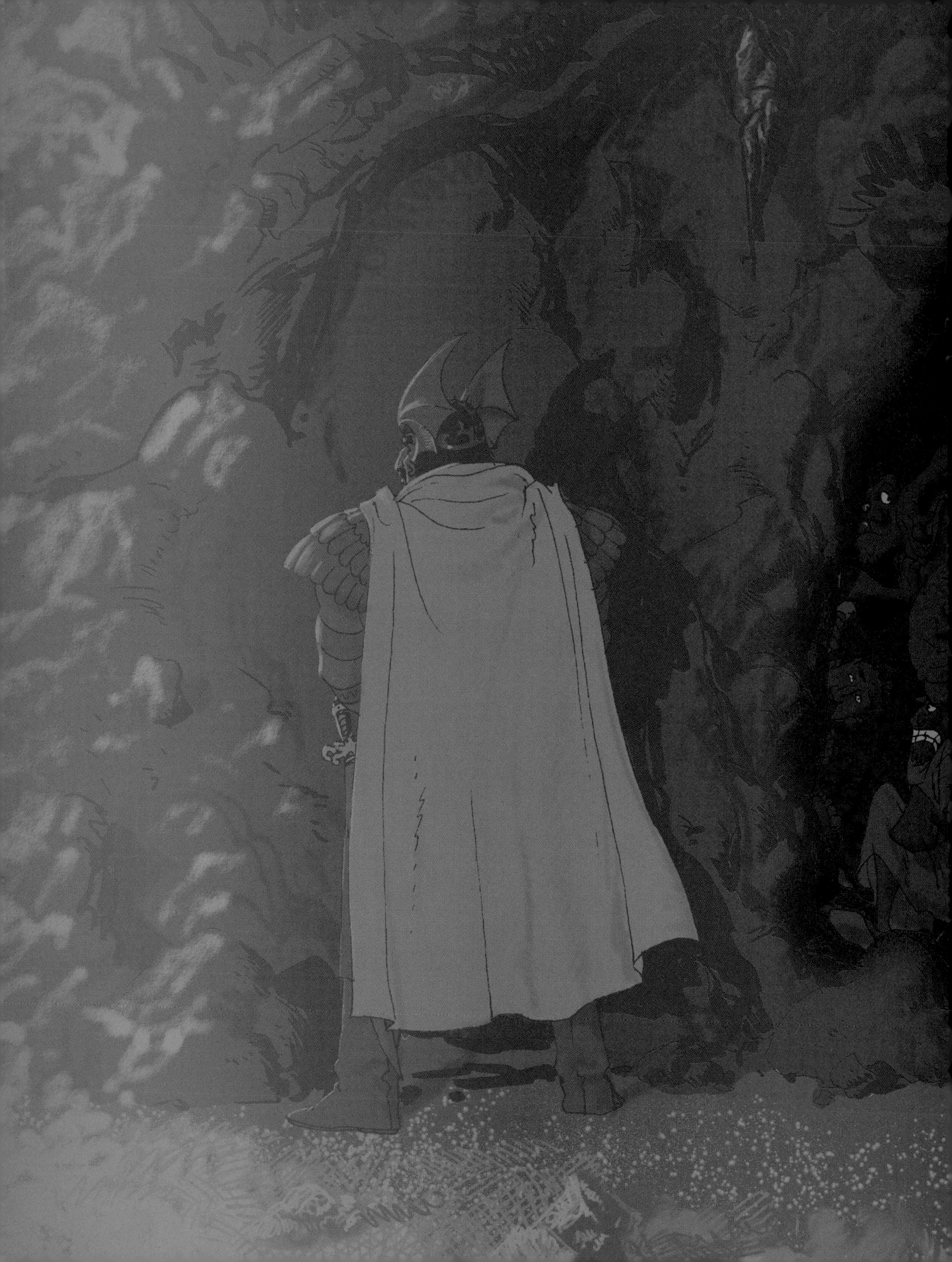

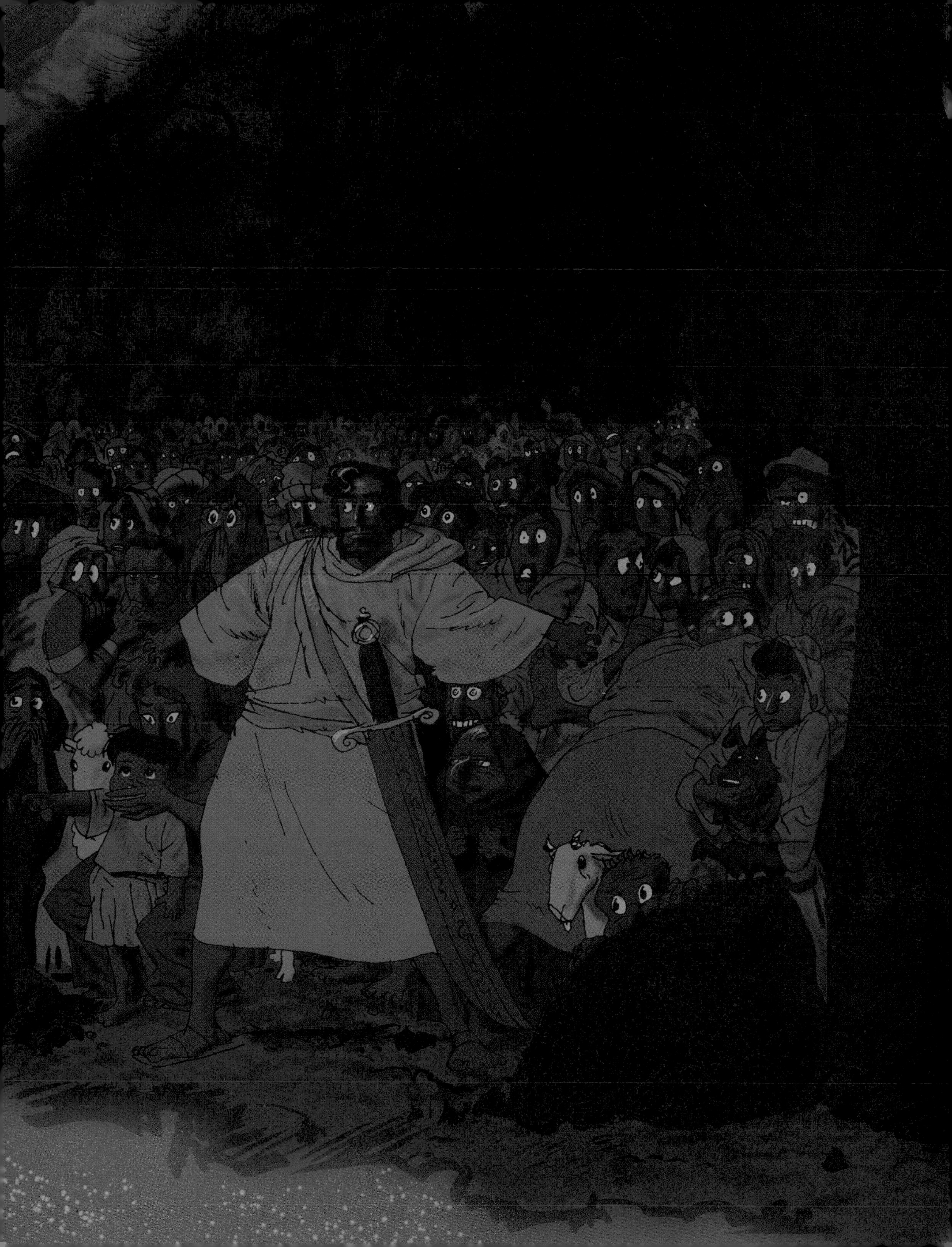

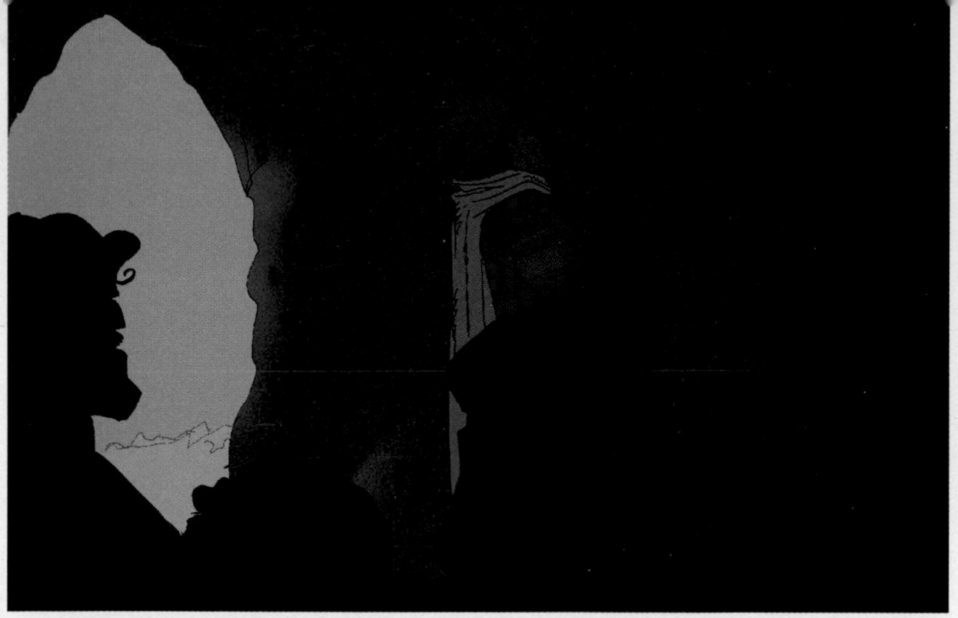

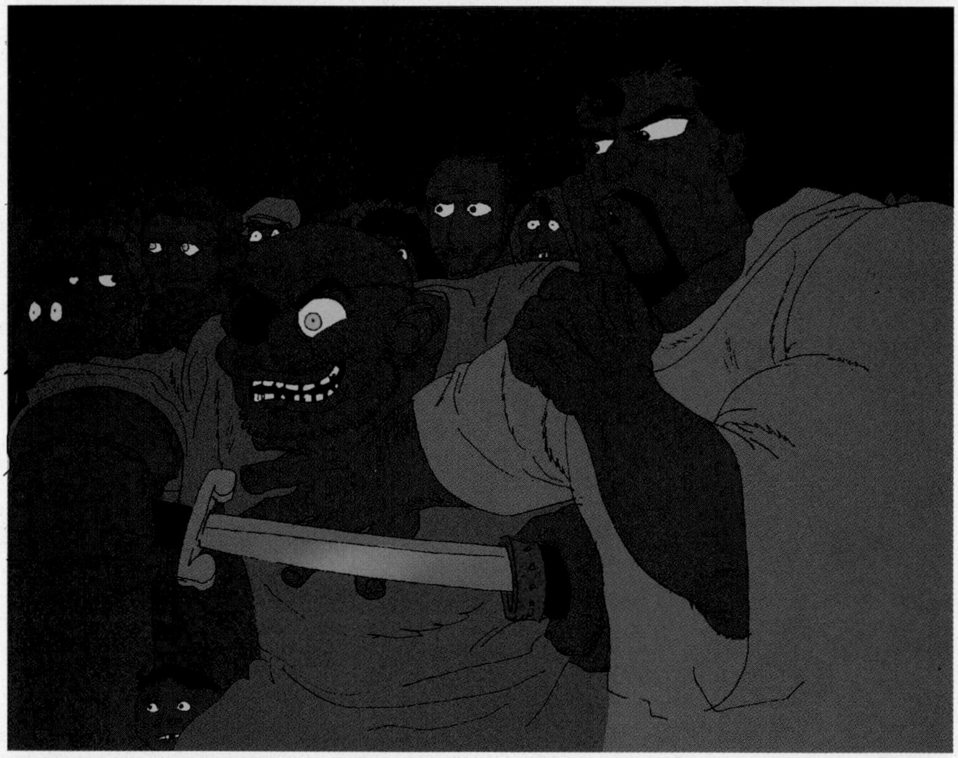

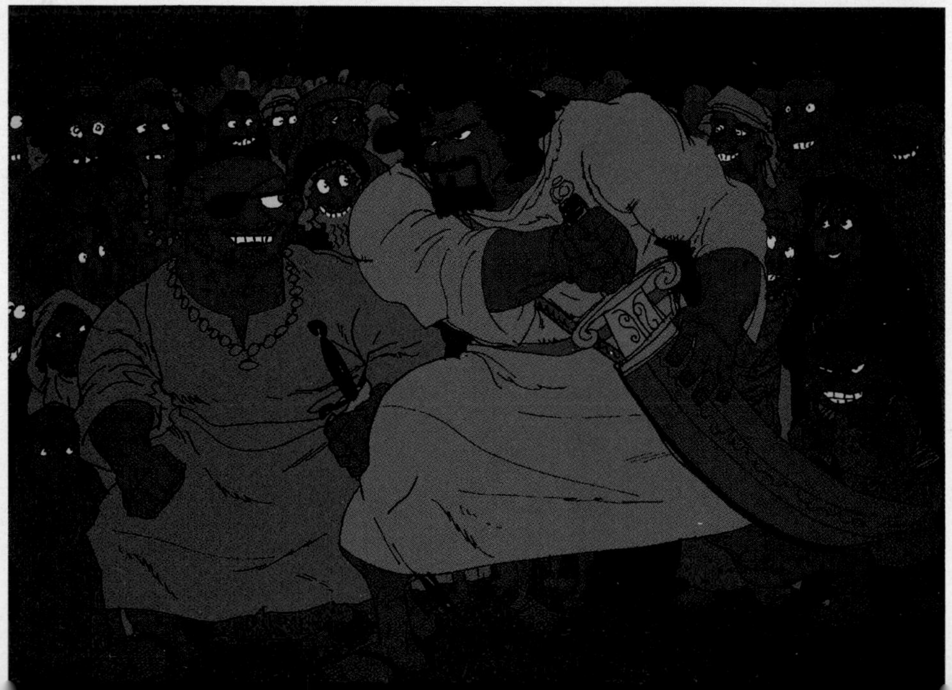

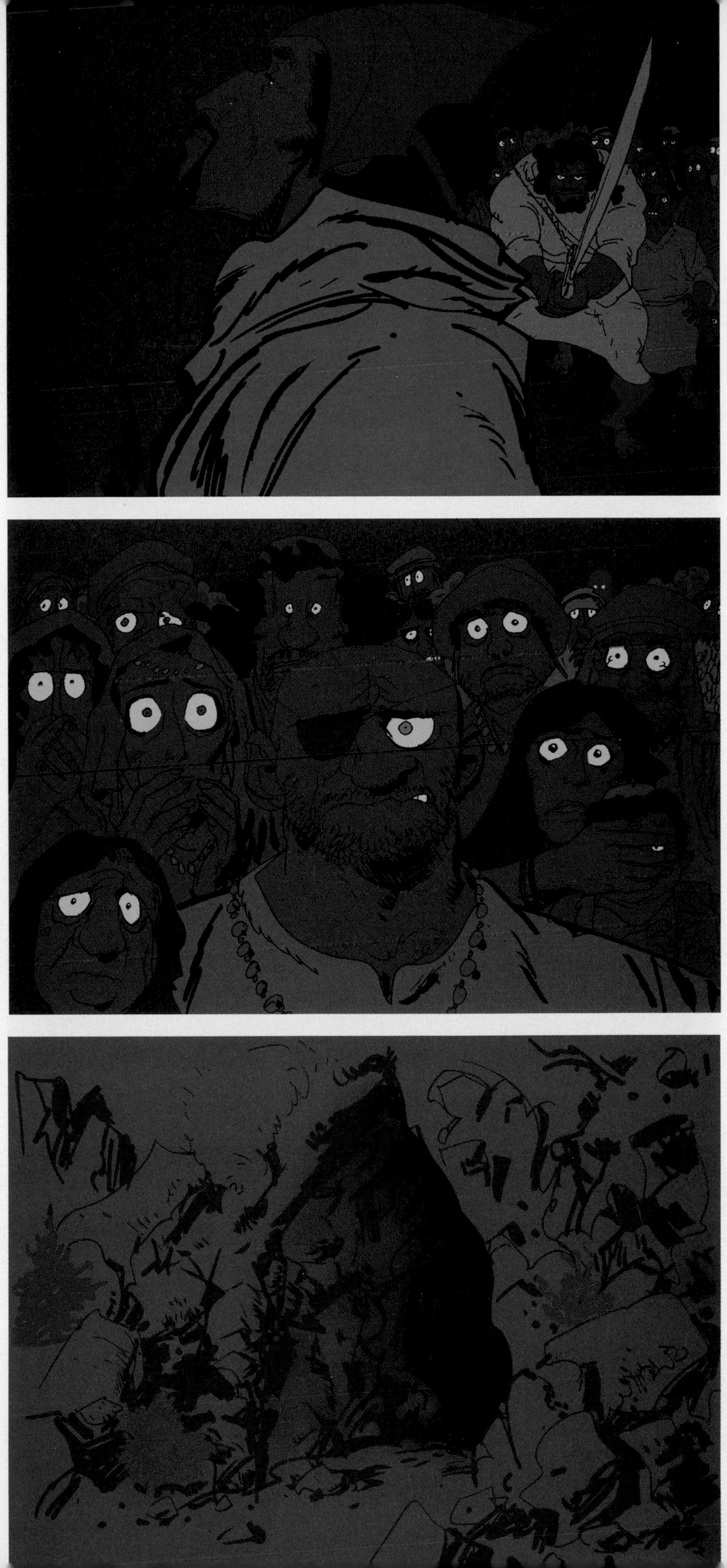

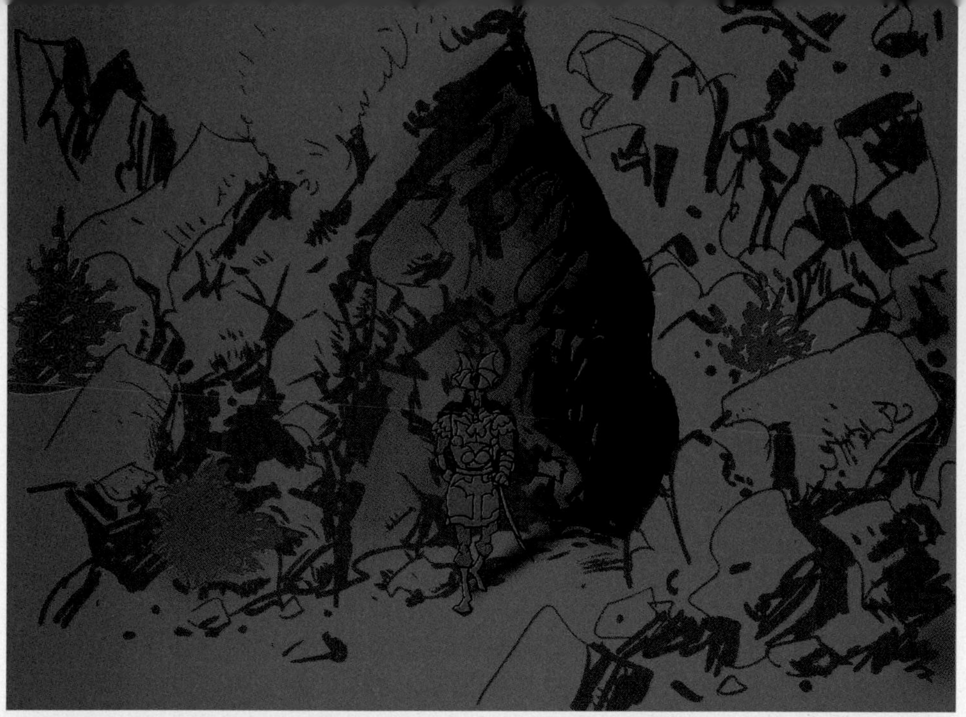
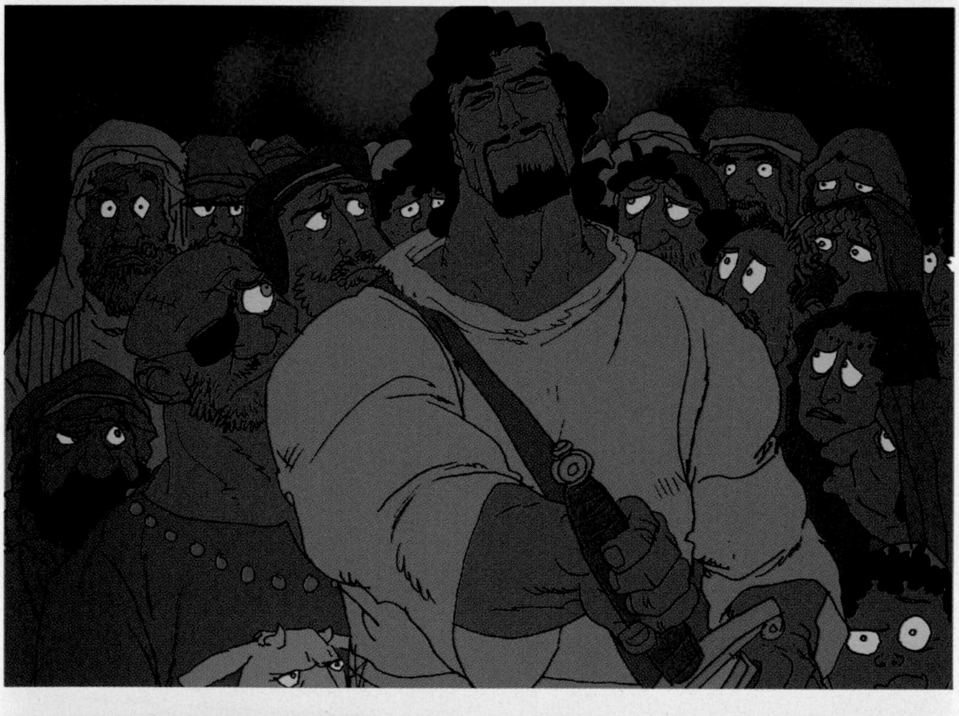
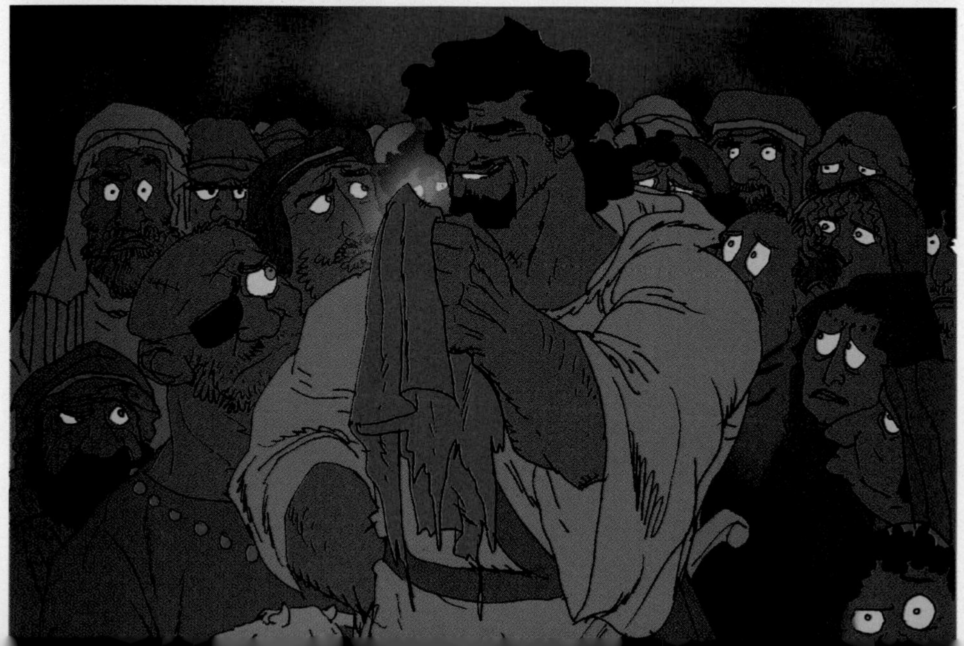

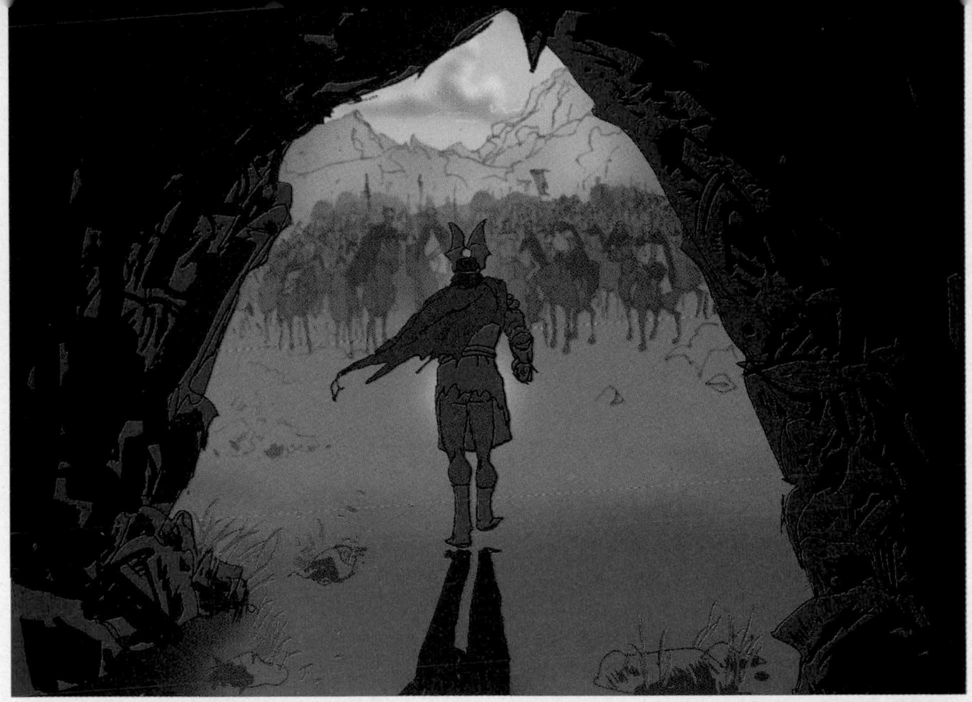

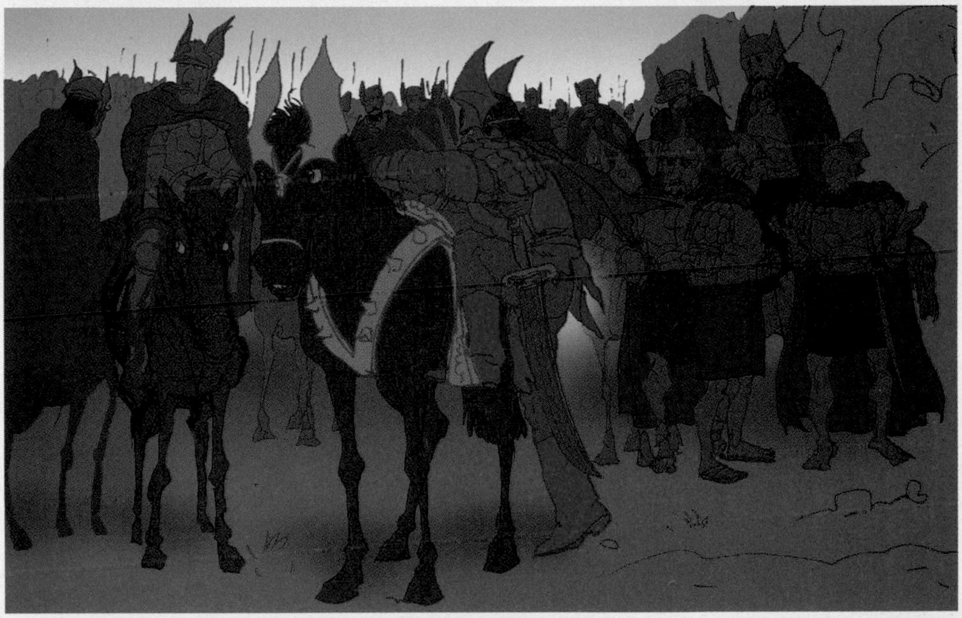

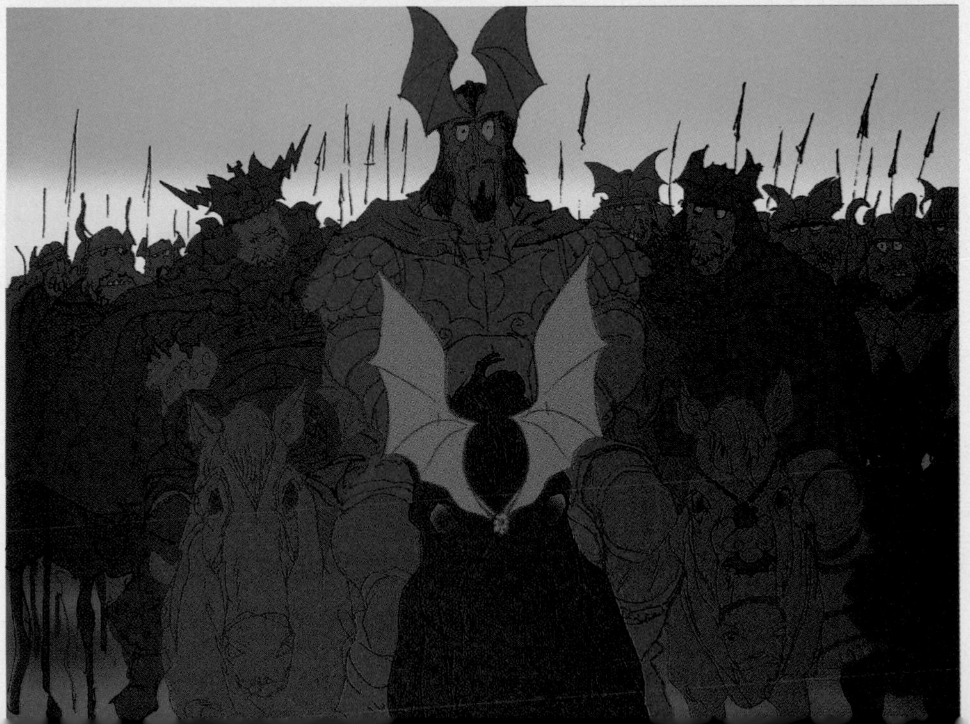

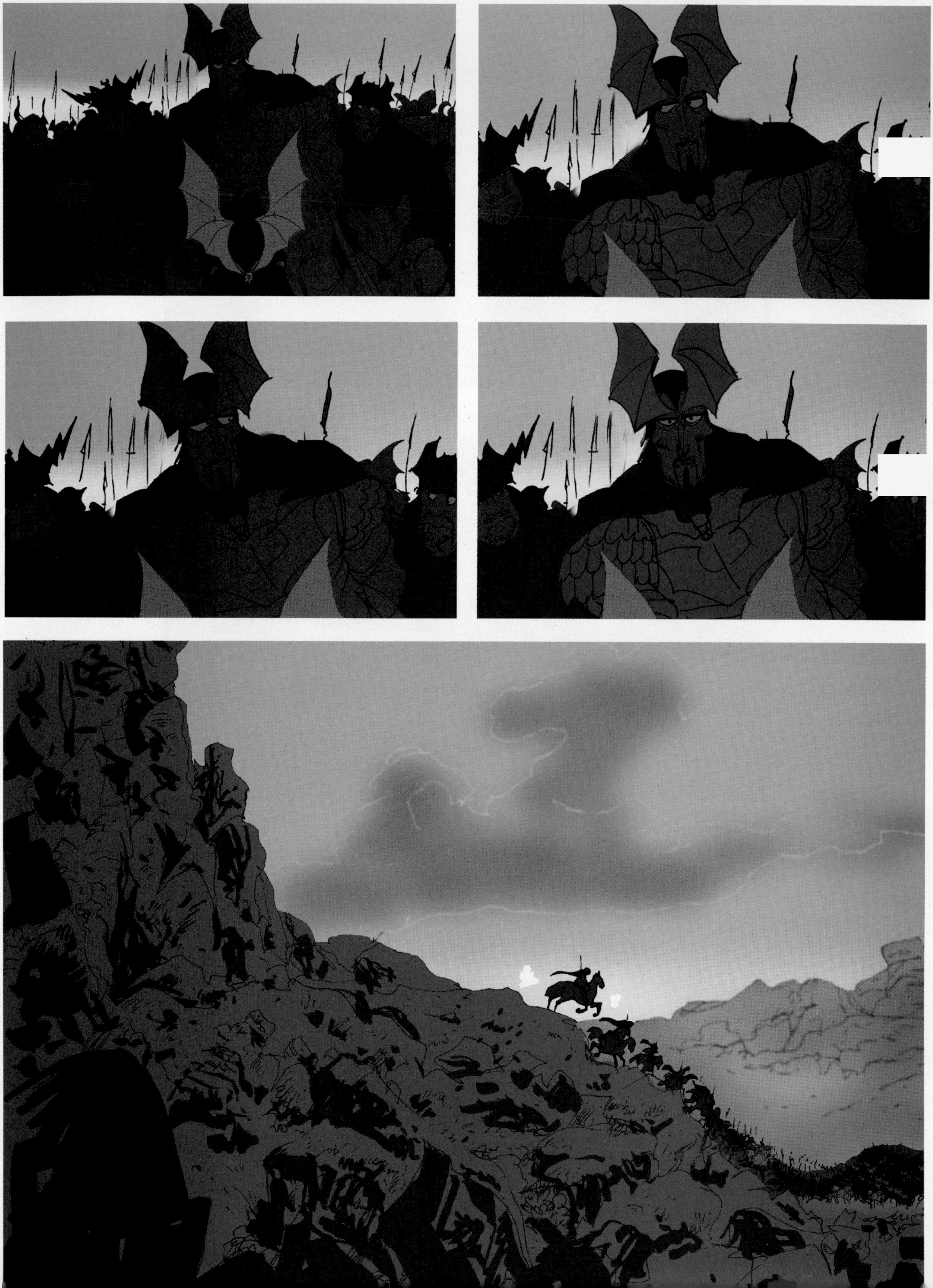

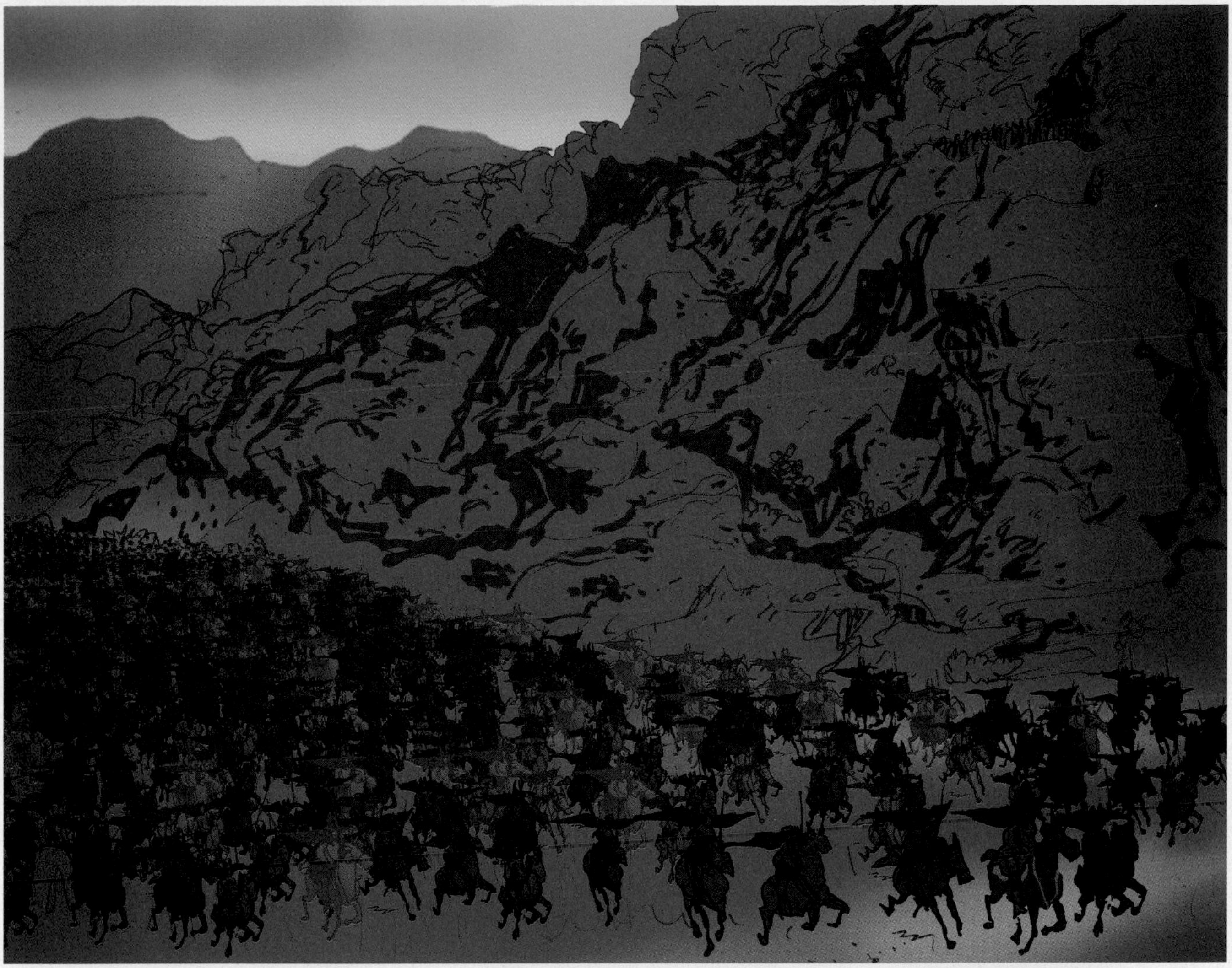

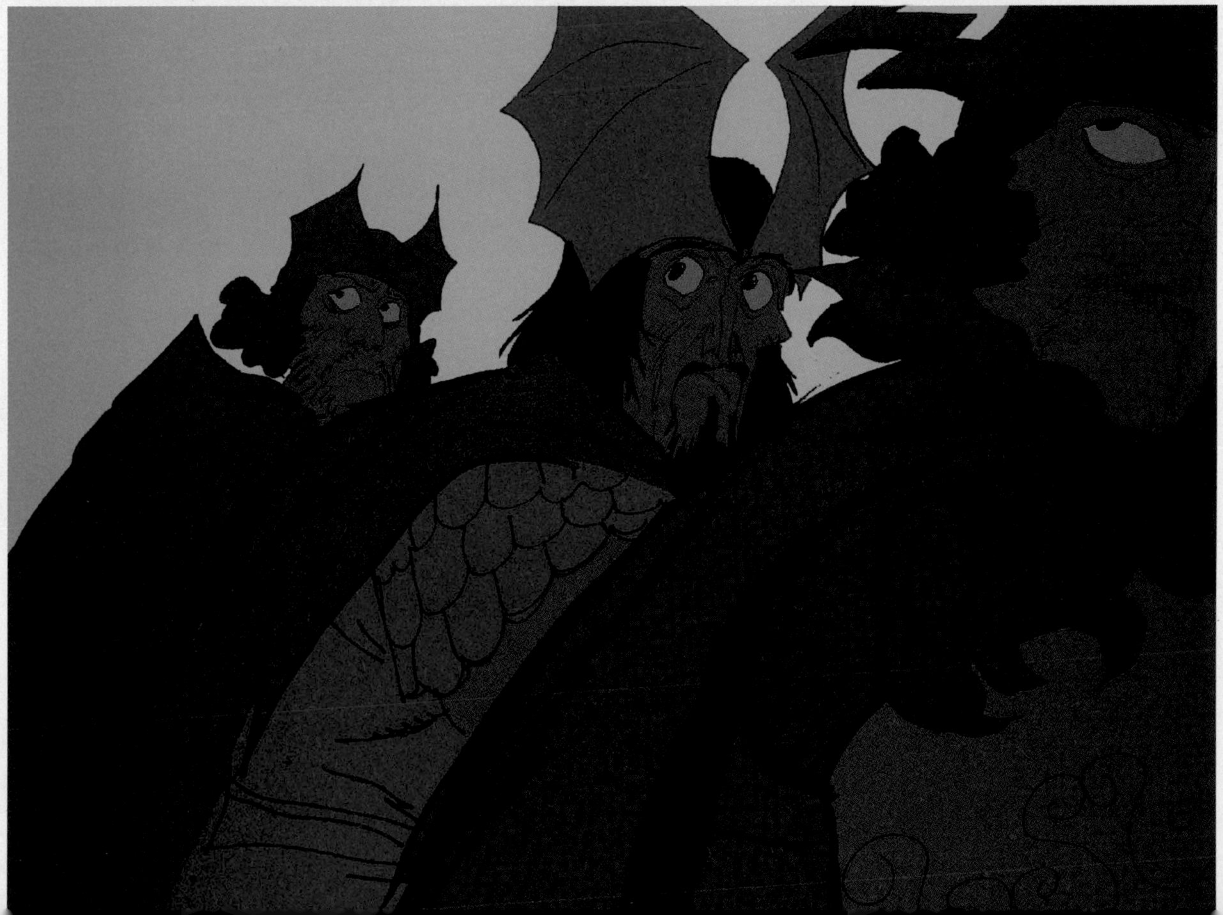

"My lord the king!" calls David.

"Why do you listen when men say 'David is bent on harming you'? This day you have seen with your own eyes how the LORD has delivered you into my hands in the cave. Some urged me to kill you, but I spared you; I said, 'I will not lift my hand against my master, for he is the LORD's anointed!'"

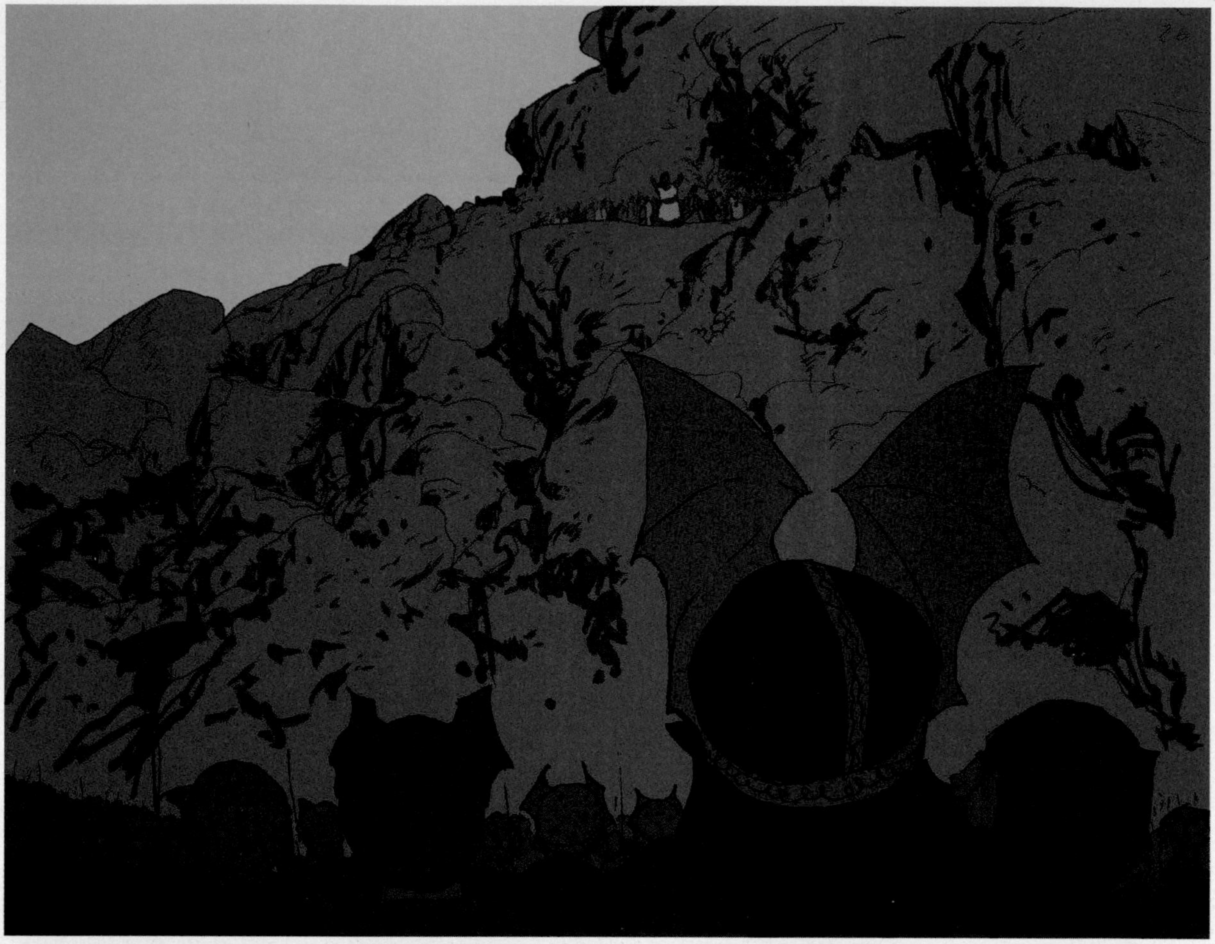

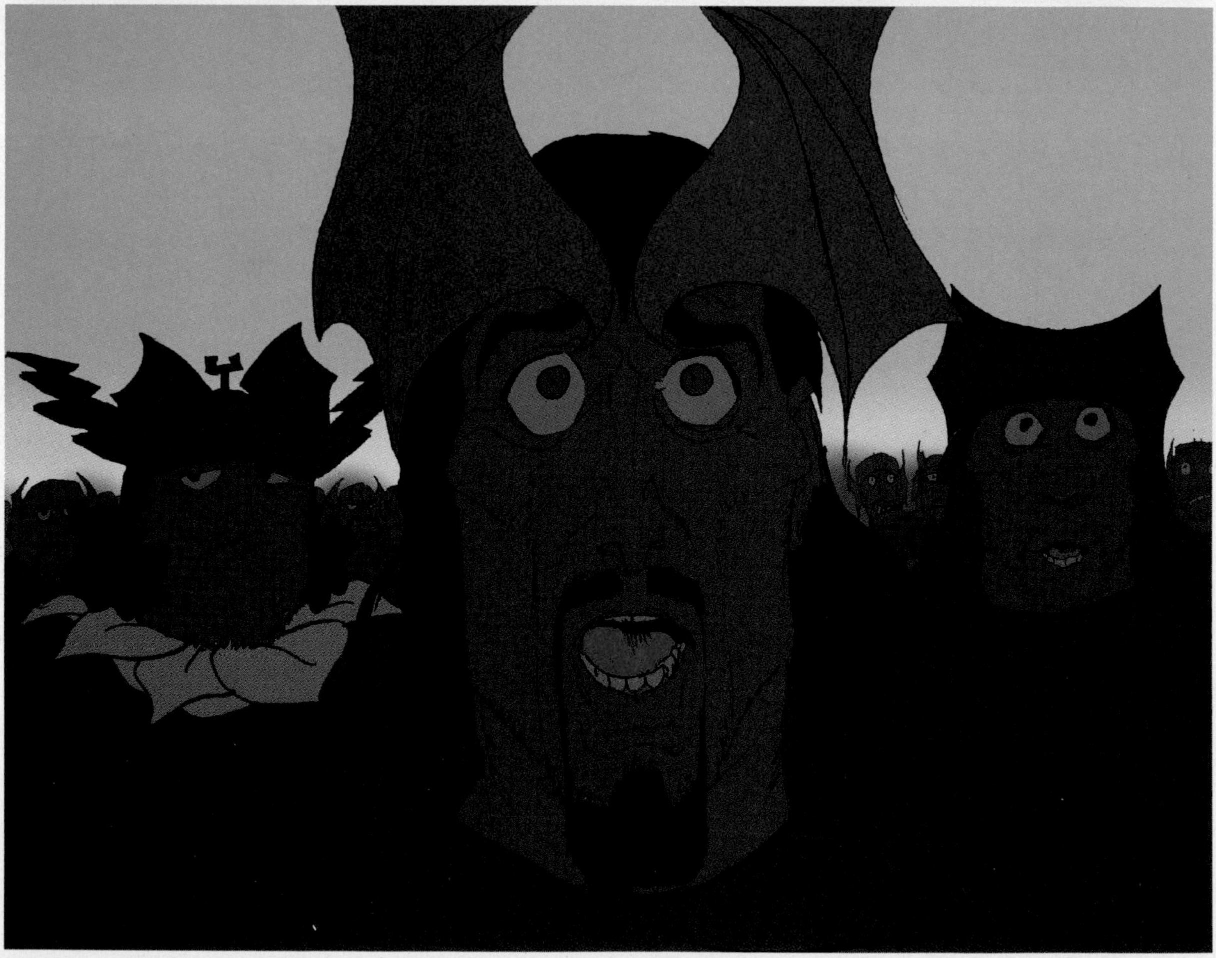

"See, my father, look at this piece of your robe I cut off with my hand! I cut off the corner of your robe but did not kill you!"

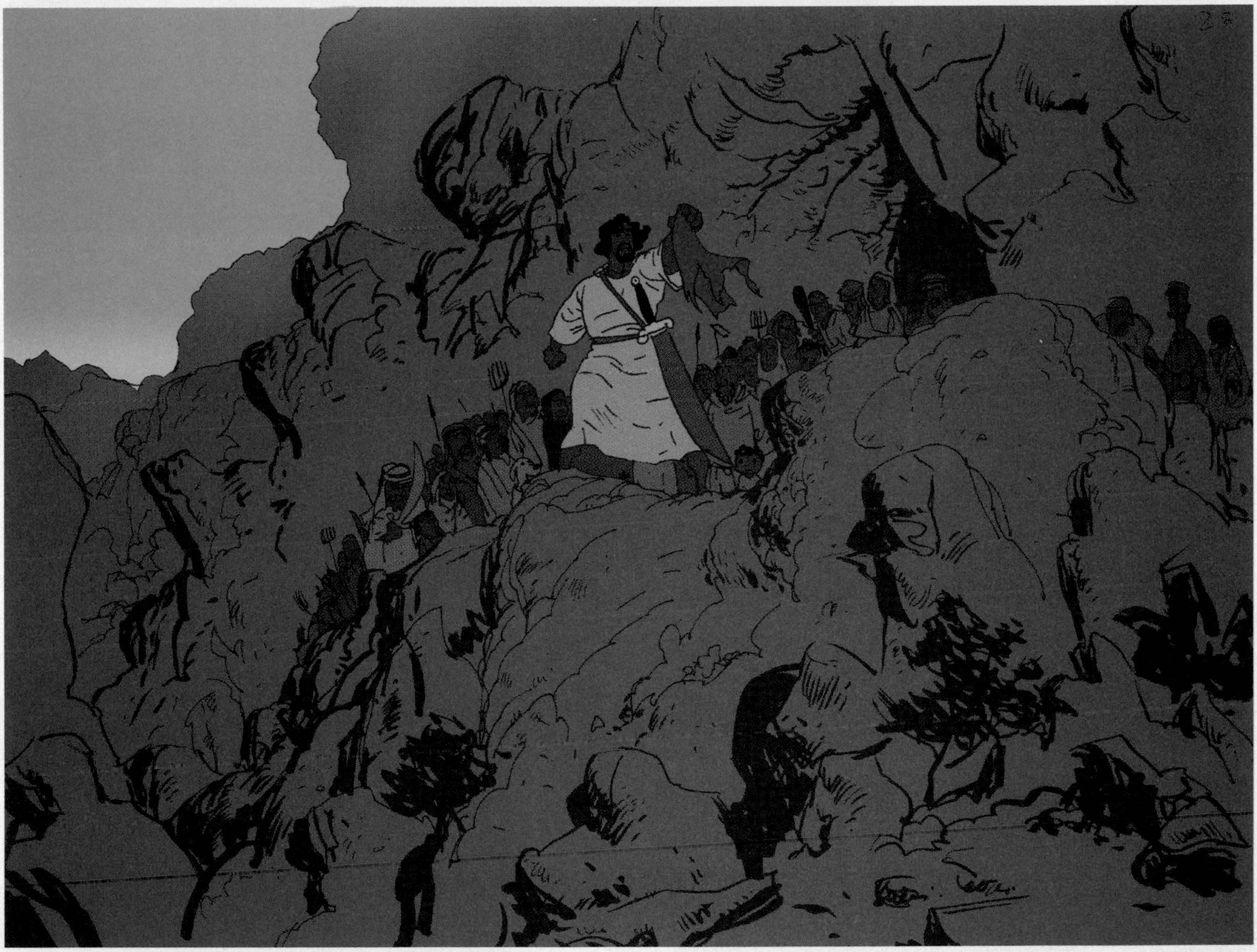

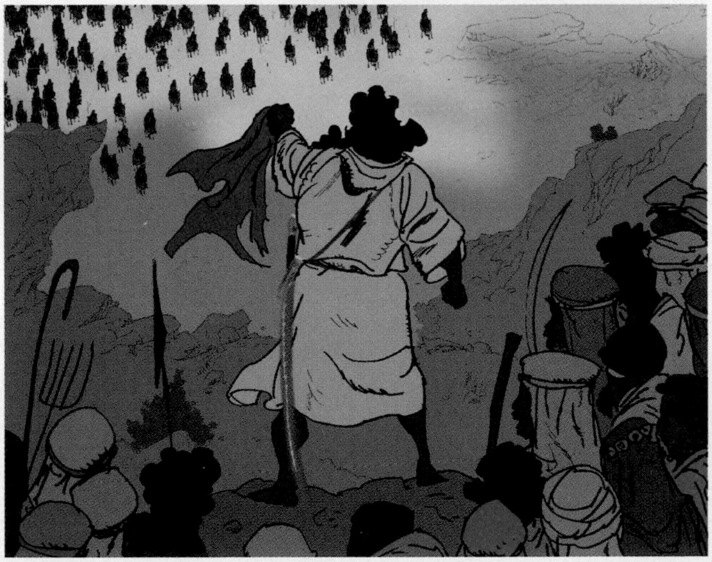

"Now understand and recognize that I am not guilty of wrongdoing or rebellion! I have not wronged you, but you are hunting me down to take my life! May the LORD judge between you and me, and may the LORD avenge the wrongs you have done to me, but my hand will not touch you! After whom has the king of Israel come out? Whom are you pursuing? A dead dog? A flea? The LORD shall be judge, and shall judge between you and me. Yea, He shall see and contend for my cause, and shall deliver me out of your hand."

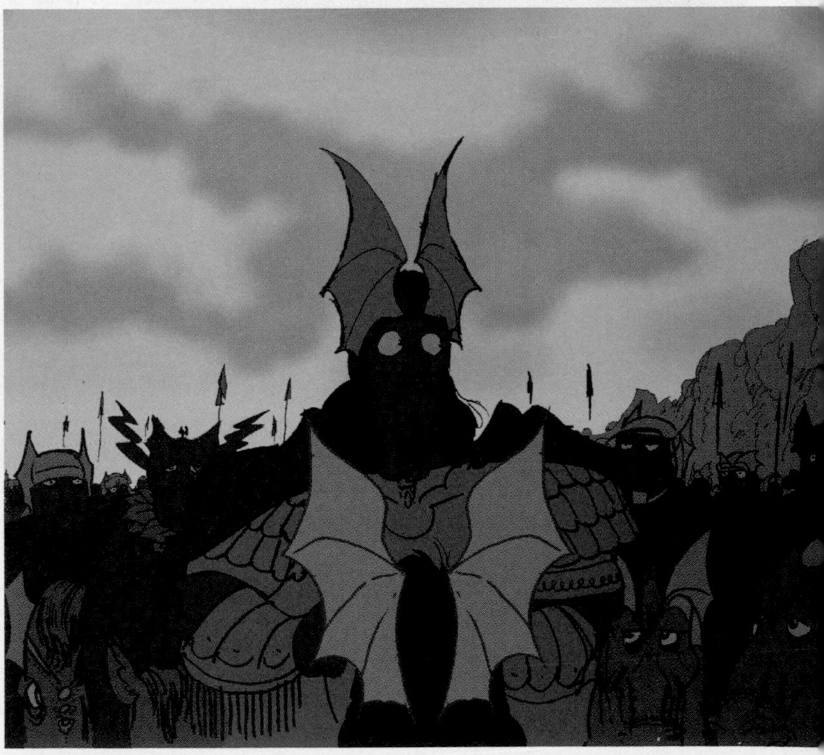

"Is that your voice, my son David? You are more righteous than I. For you have done good to me, and I have rewarded you with evil. And you have today shown that you have dealt well with me, in that the LORD shut me up into your hand, and you did not kill me. For if a man finds his enemy, does he let him get away unharmed? The LORD will repay you good for that which you have done to me today.

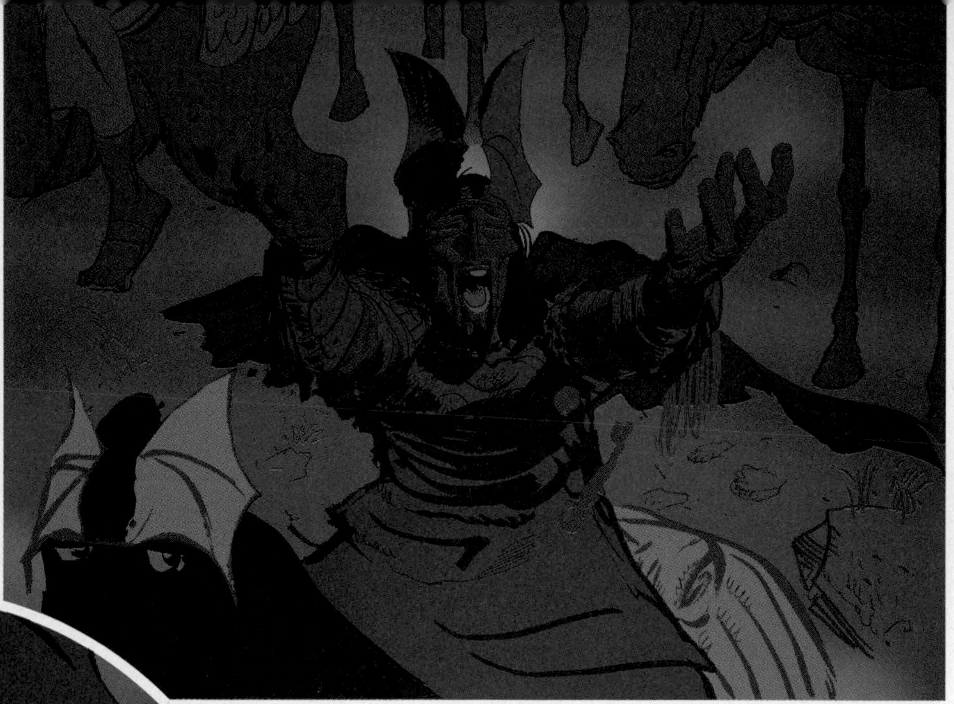

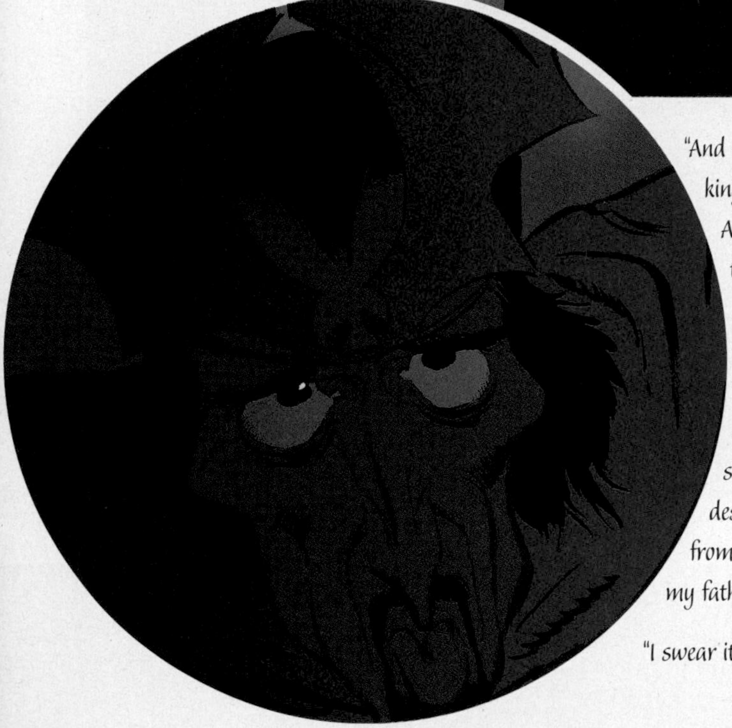

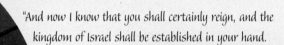

"And now I know that you shall certainly reign, and the kingdom of Israel shall be established in your hand. And now, swear to me by the LORD that you shall not cut off my seed after me, nor shall you destroy my name from the house of my father."

"I swear it," says David.

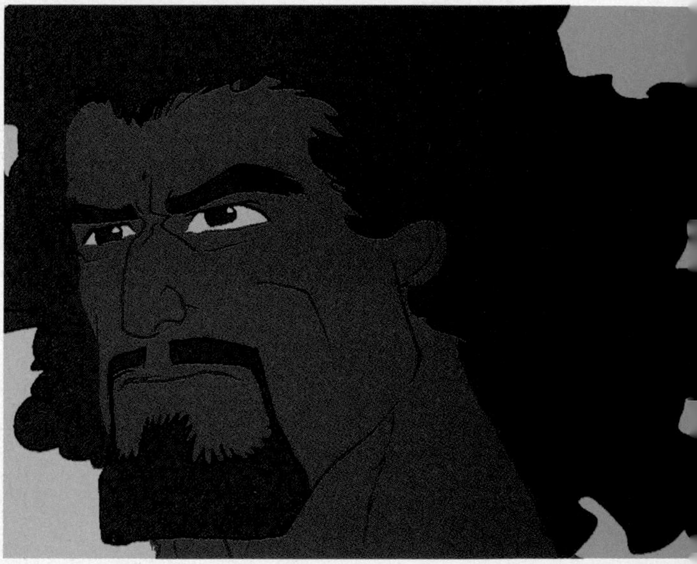

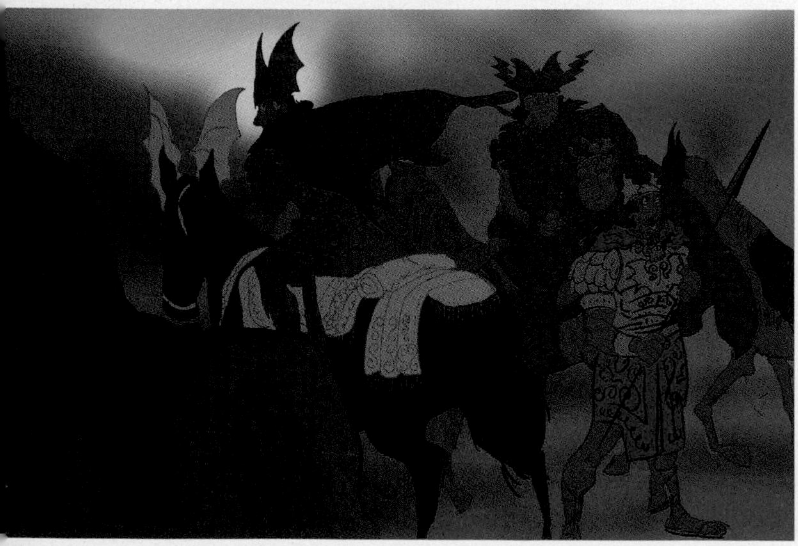

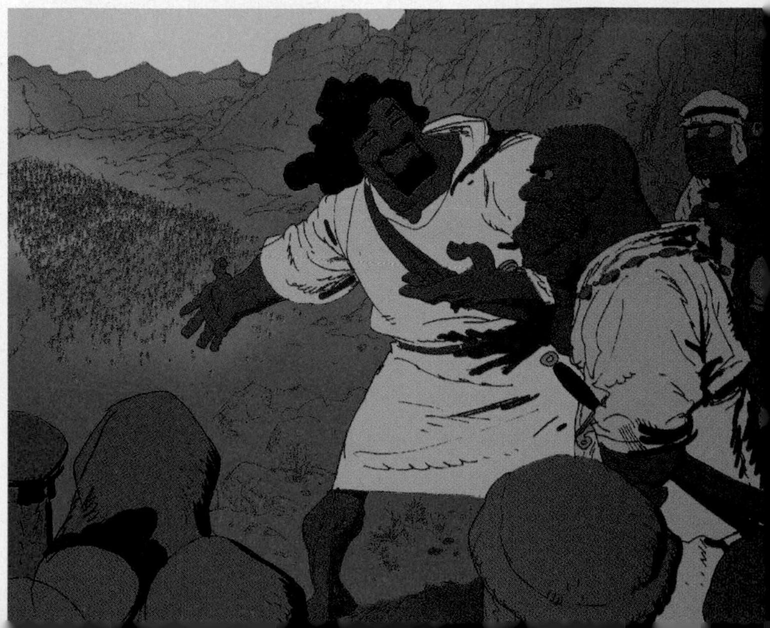

The wilderness of Paran.

"How long are we supposed to hang out in this wilderness, anyway?" asks Joab. "It's been months."

"We should have killed Saul," says the guy with the axe.

"I'm starving," says Abiathar.

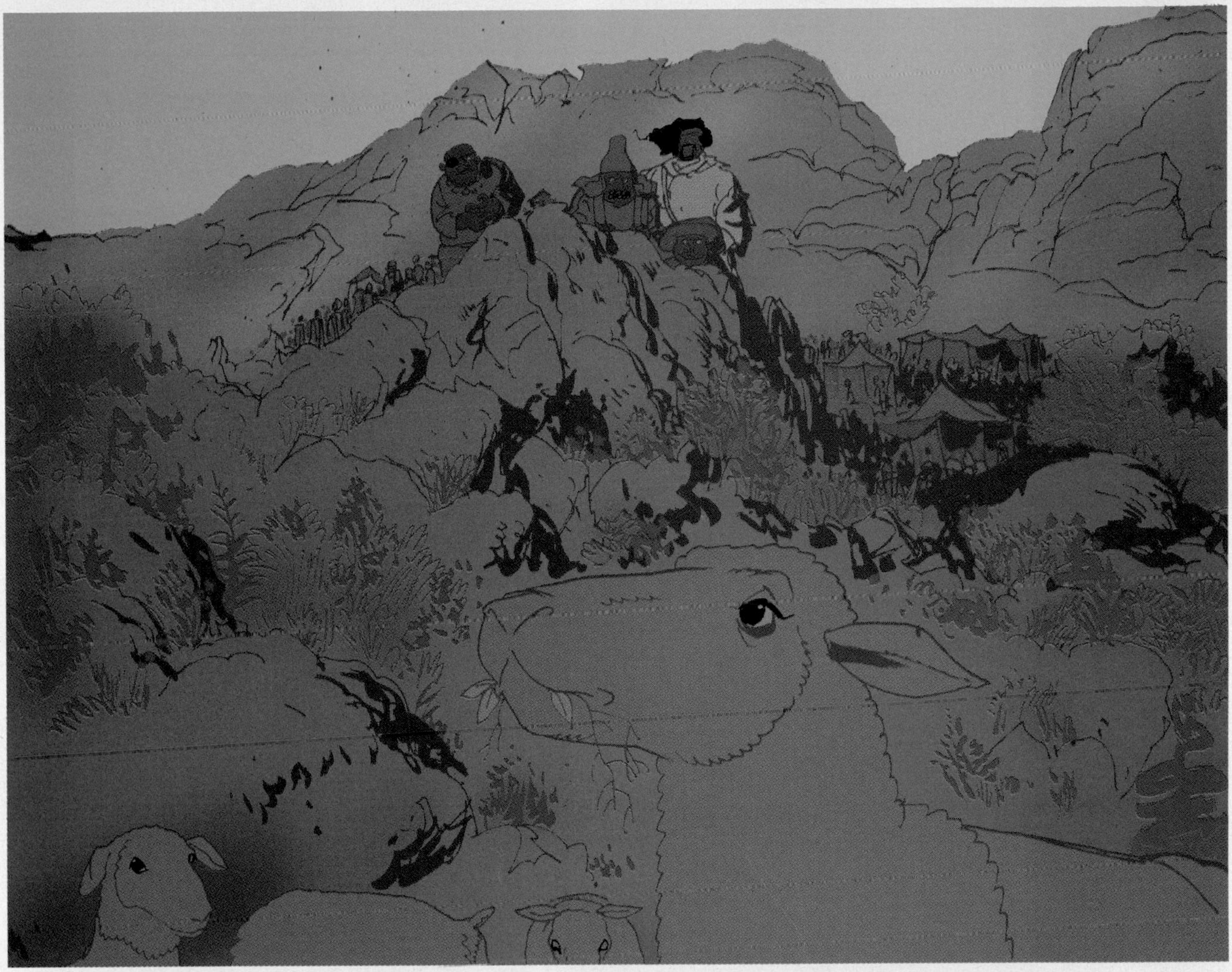

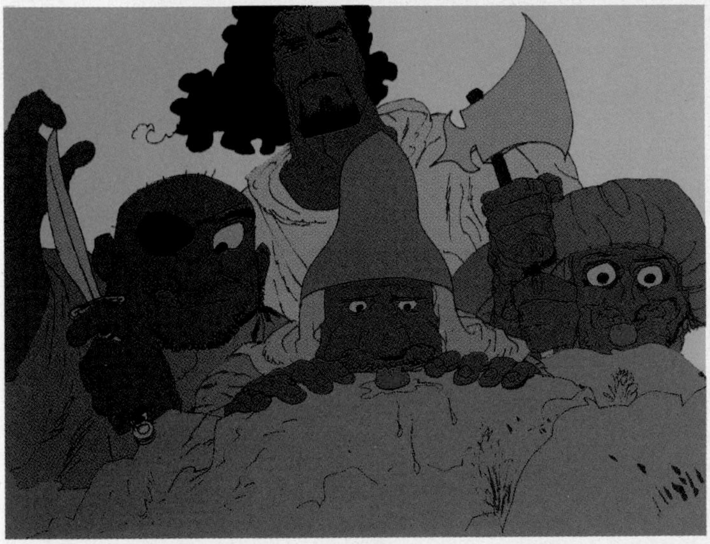

"We're all starving," says Joab. "Look at those fat, juicy sheep. There must be three thousand. One sheep wouldn't be missed."

"With a little wild onion."

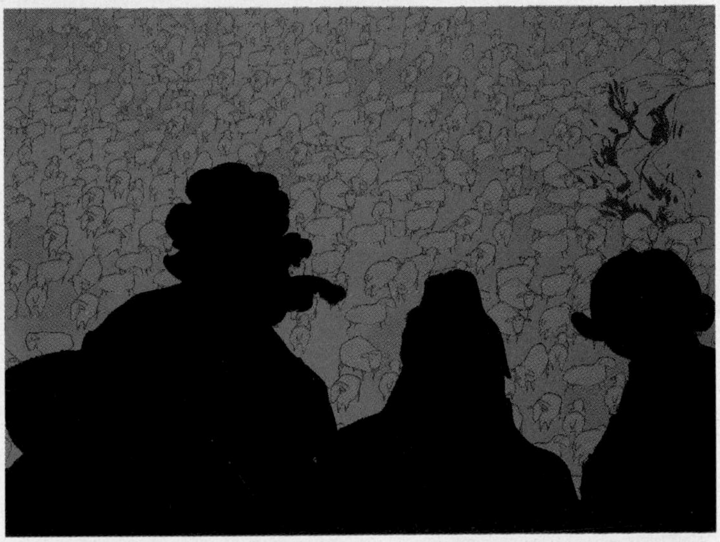

"No," says David. "It wouldn't be fair to the shepherds. If a shepherd loses a sheep, he has to pay for it himself. Those guys have it hard enough."

"So we make a deal with the shepherd," says Joab. "We leave him a leg and an ear. He could say a lion took the rest."

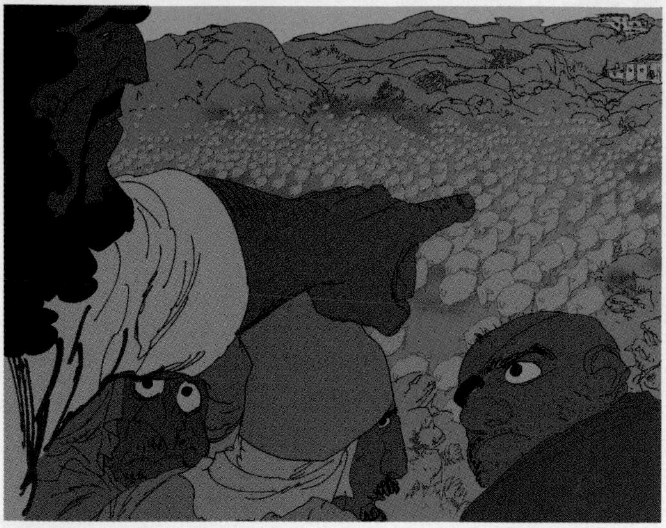

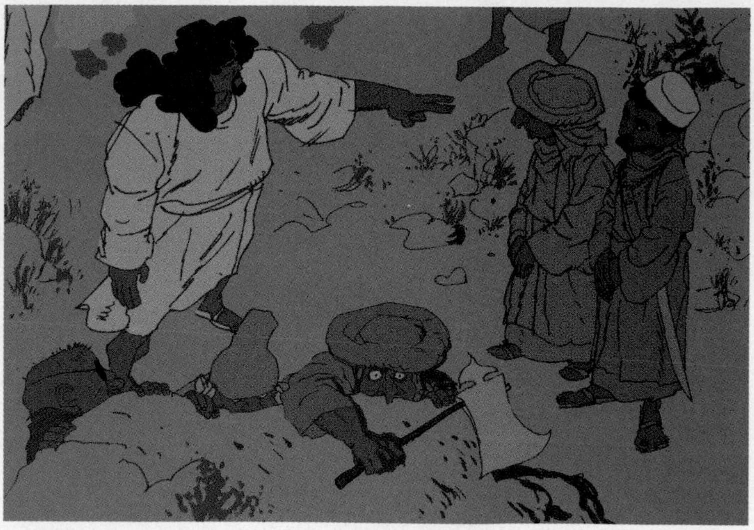

David shakes his head. "His reputation would suffer. He might lose his job. Look, I've been talking to the shepherds--"

"What is it with you and shepherds anyway? "

"These sheep are the property of a man, Nabal. We are in luck, because he happens to be in Carmel for sheep-shearing. Now, you city folks might not know this, but sheep-shearing is always a big event, full of festivals and feasts to celebrate the fact that a year of hard work is over, and payday has arrived. This Nabal fellow is probably very happy right now, and feeling generous."

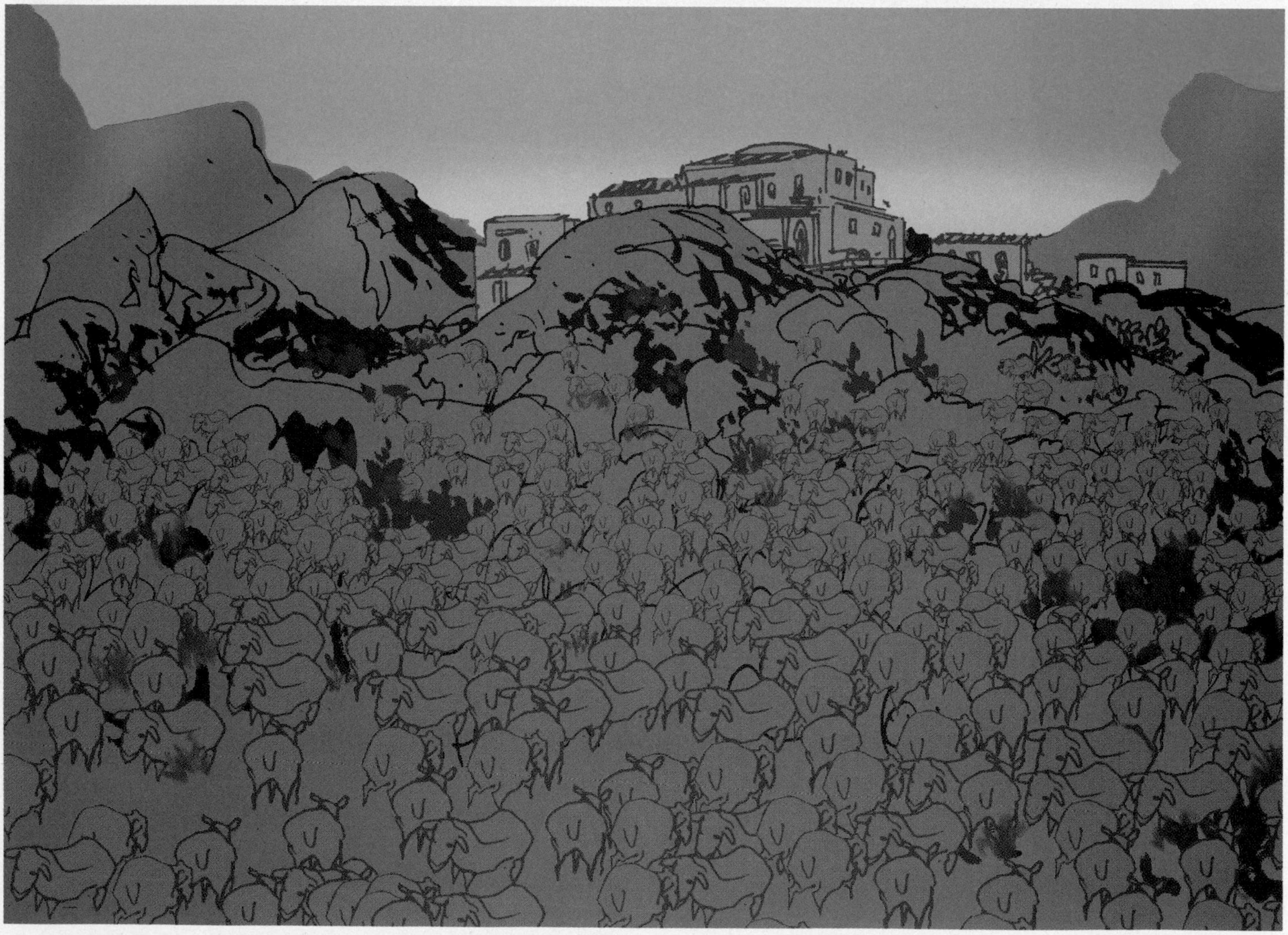

"So here's what we'll do: I want you two men to go with eight more to see Nabal in Carmel, and say..."

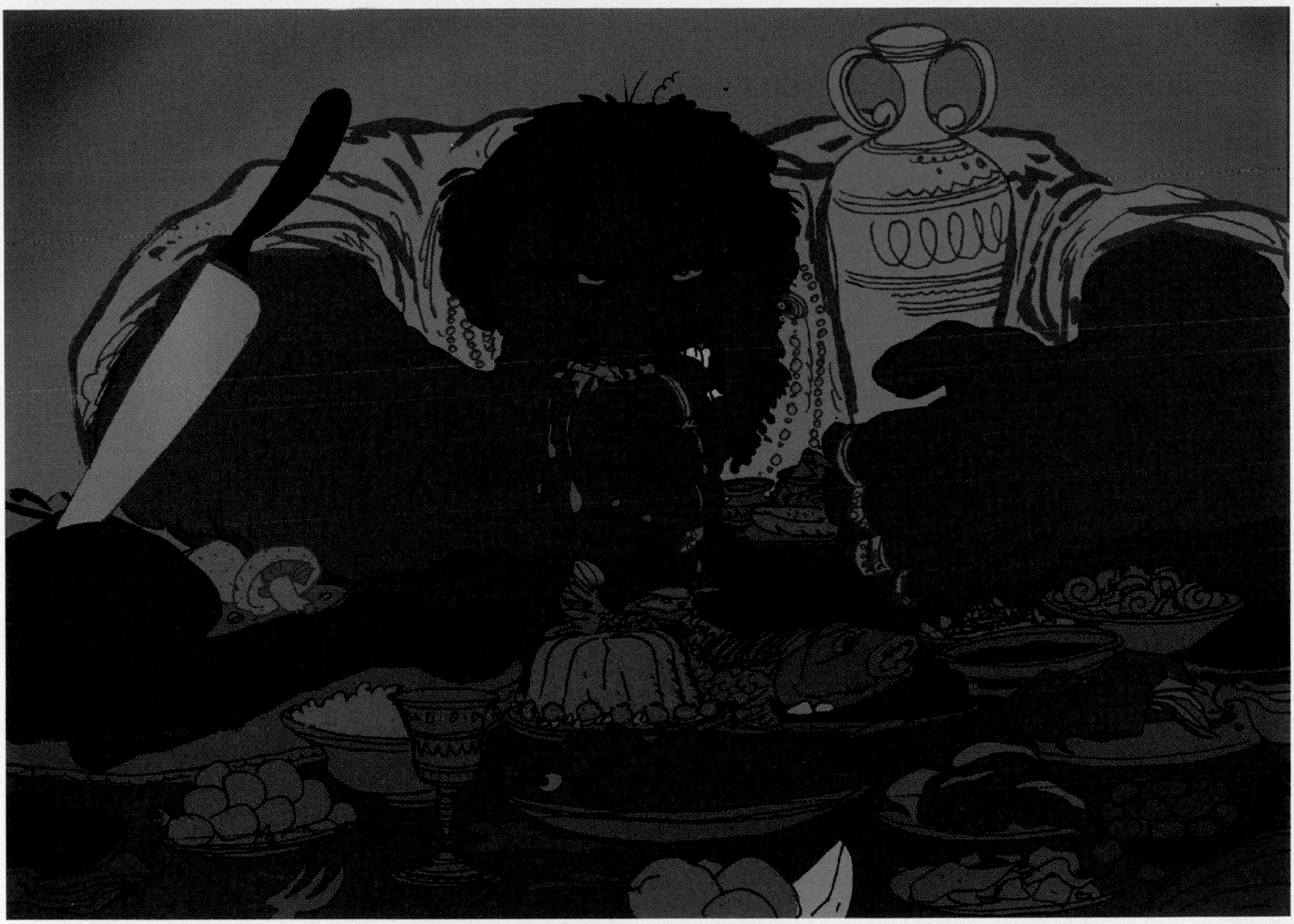

"...We come in the name of David, son of Jesse. Long life and peace to you! And peace to your house, and peace to all that you have.. And now, David has heard that you have shearers. And your shepherds have been with us; we have not harmed them, nor was anything of theirs missing all the days they were in Carmel."

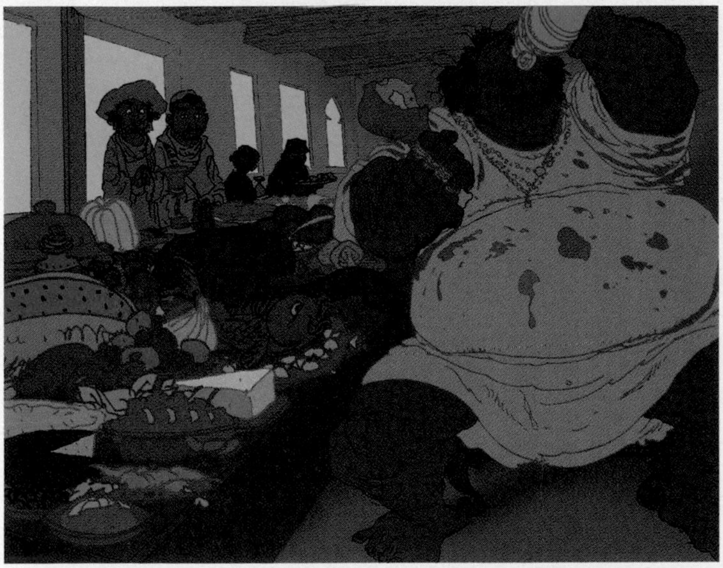

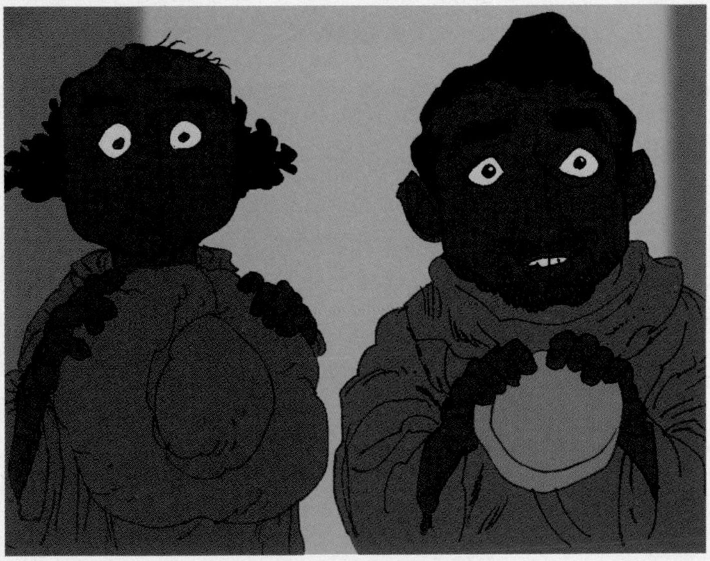

"Ask your young men, and they will tell you. And may we find favor in your eyes, for we have come at a good day. Please give that which your hand finds to us, your servants, and to your son, to David."

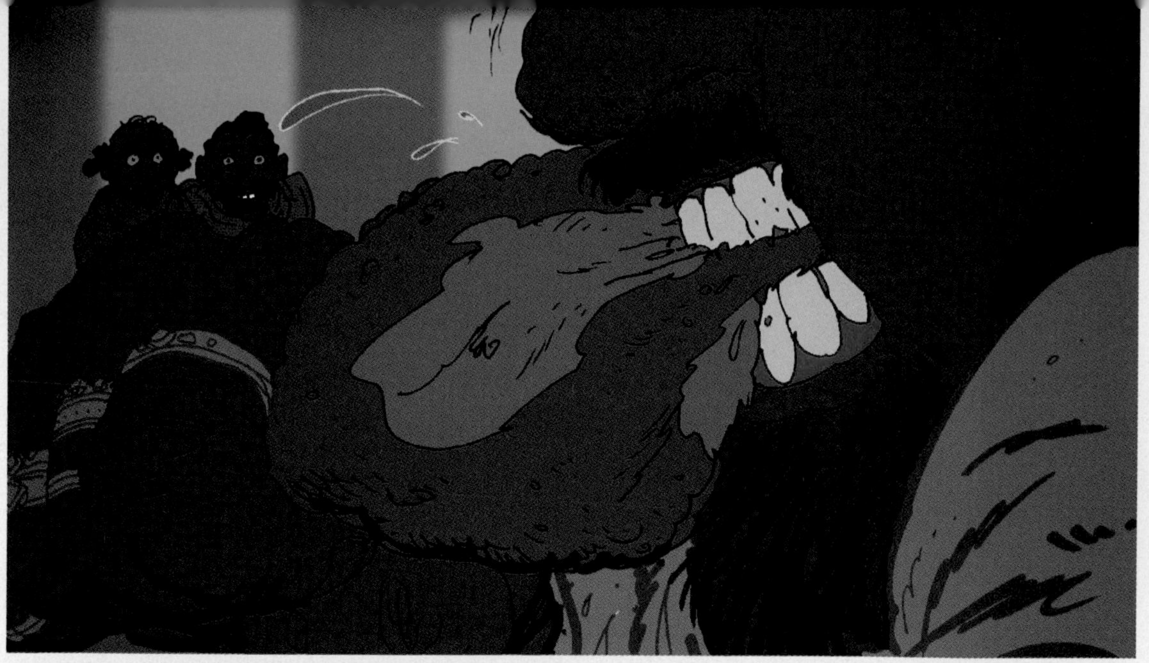

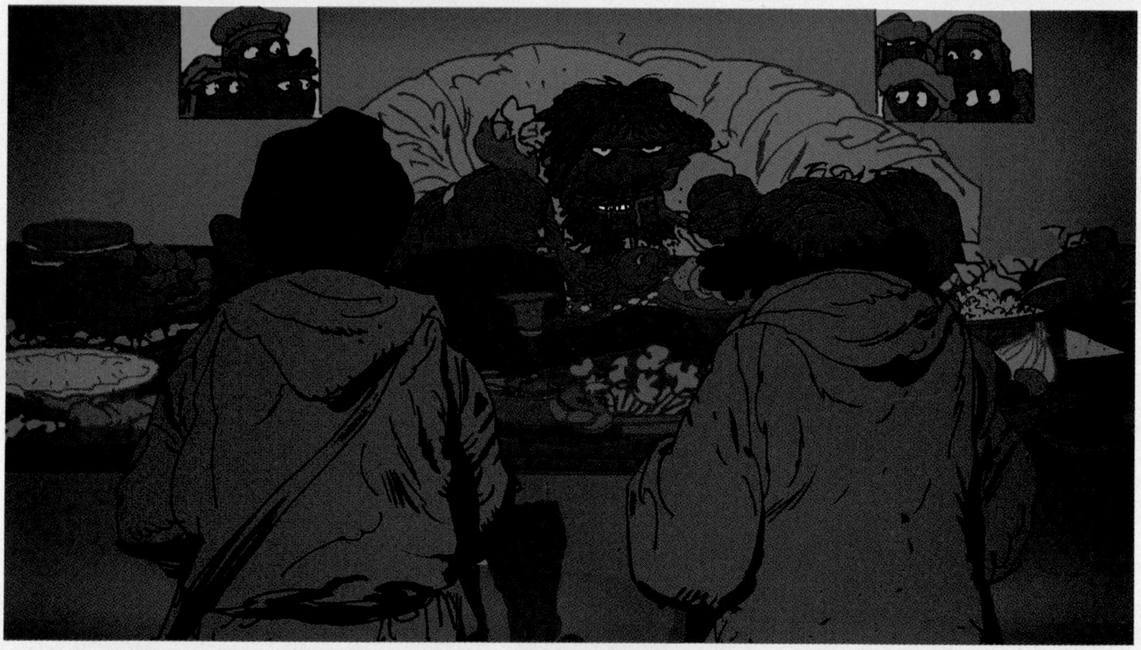

"Who is this David, and who is the son of Jesse? The desert's full of servants who have run away from their master. I'm supposed to take my bread, and my water, and my meat which I have killed for my shearers, and give them to some runaway slave I never met from who knows where? Get out of here!"

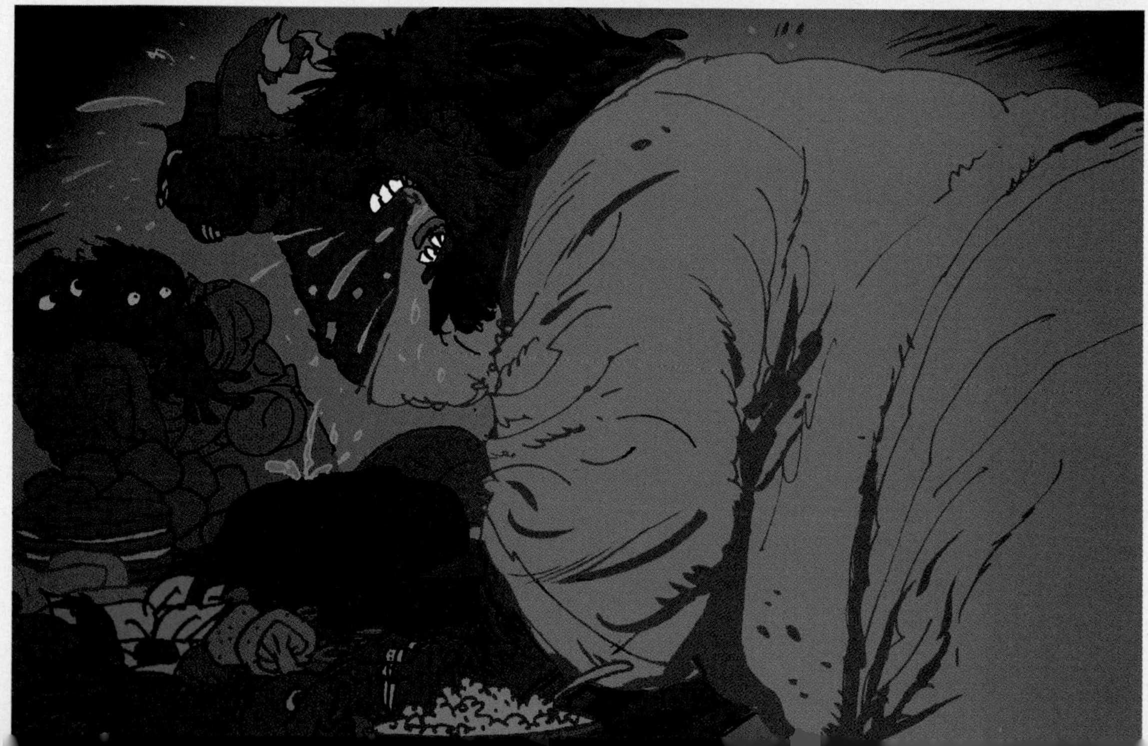

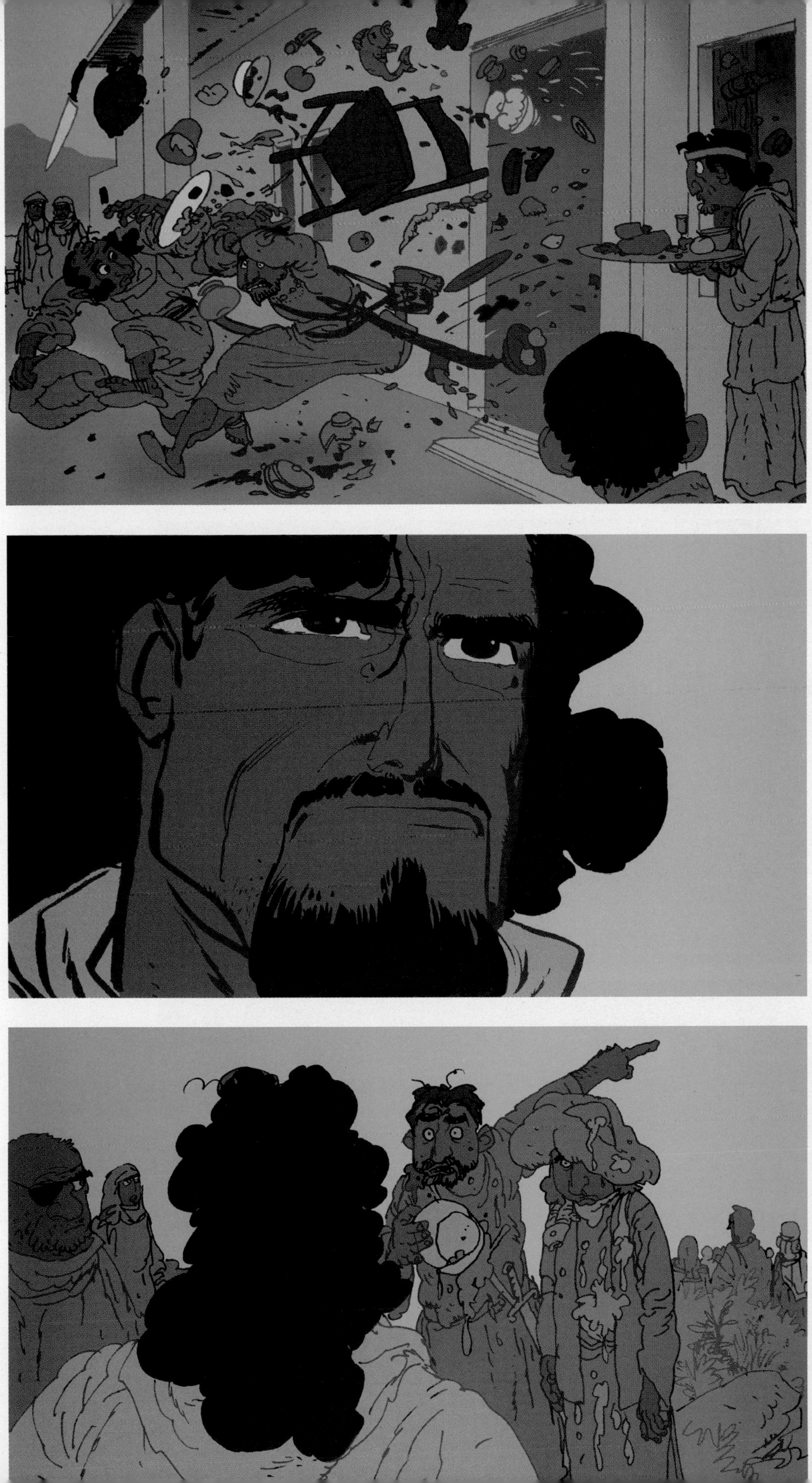

"...And then he said, 'Get out of here!'"

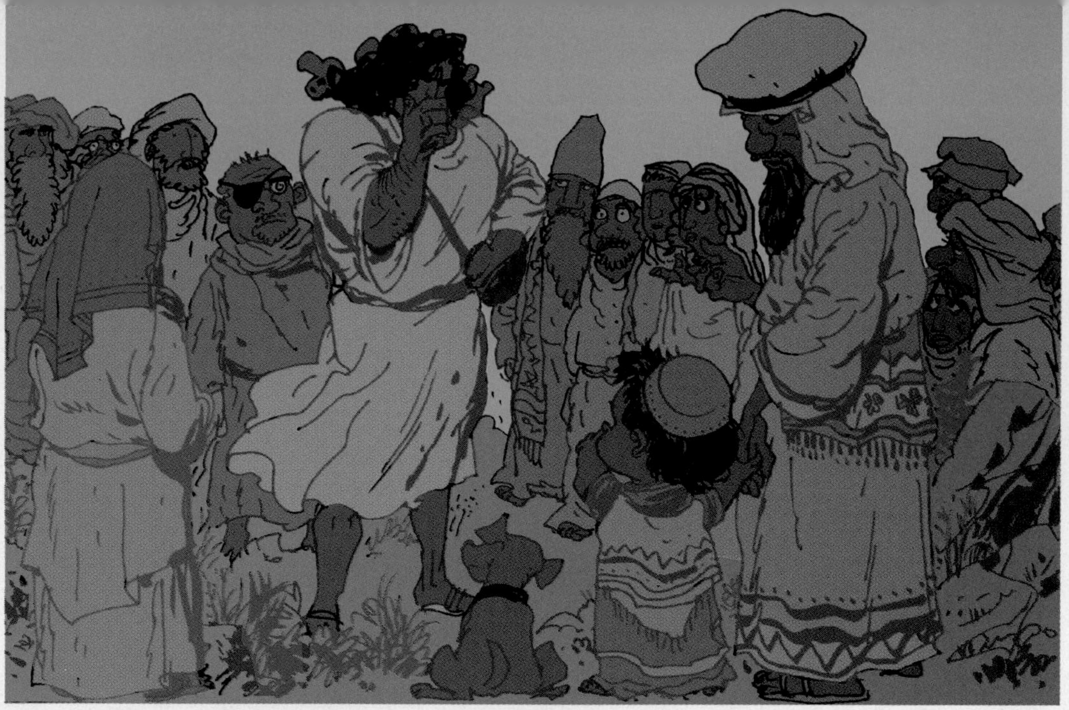

"Such concentration. You are watching the great David at work, son. Remember this moment."

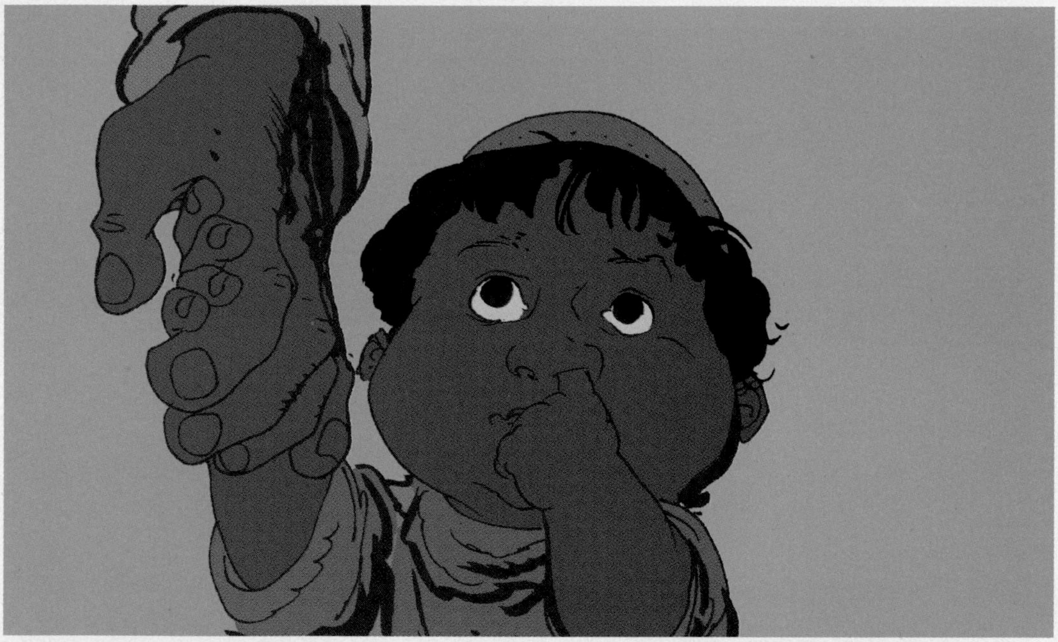

"Watch. He'll figure out exactly the right thing to say. Some clever diplomatic solution which would elude a common ruffian."

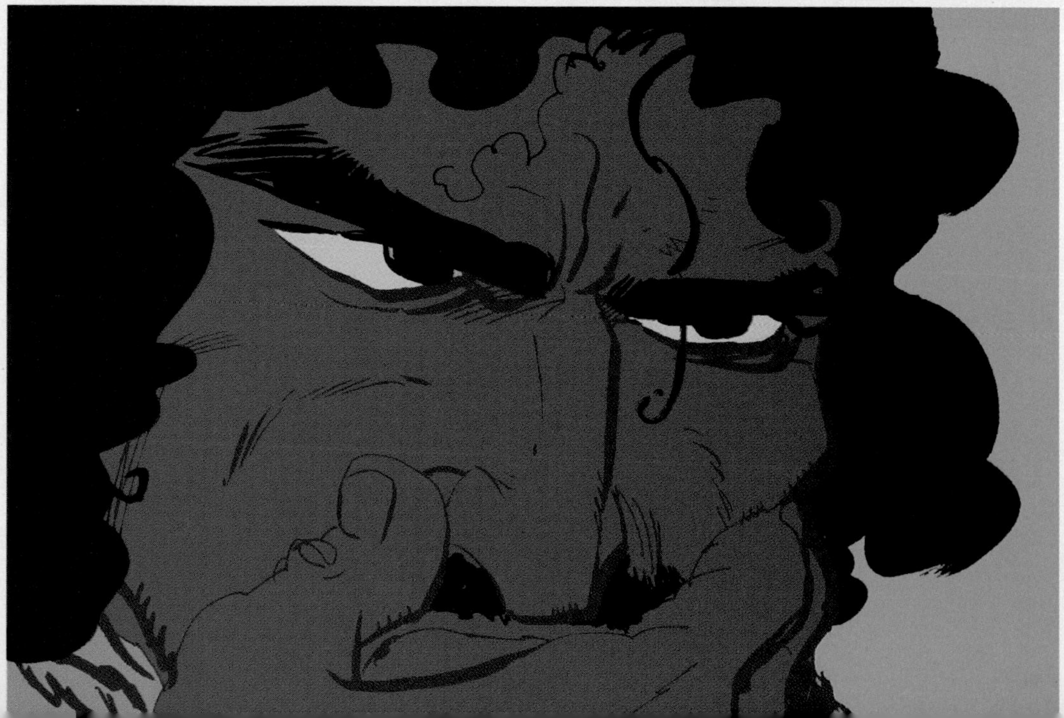

"Men, put on your swords."

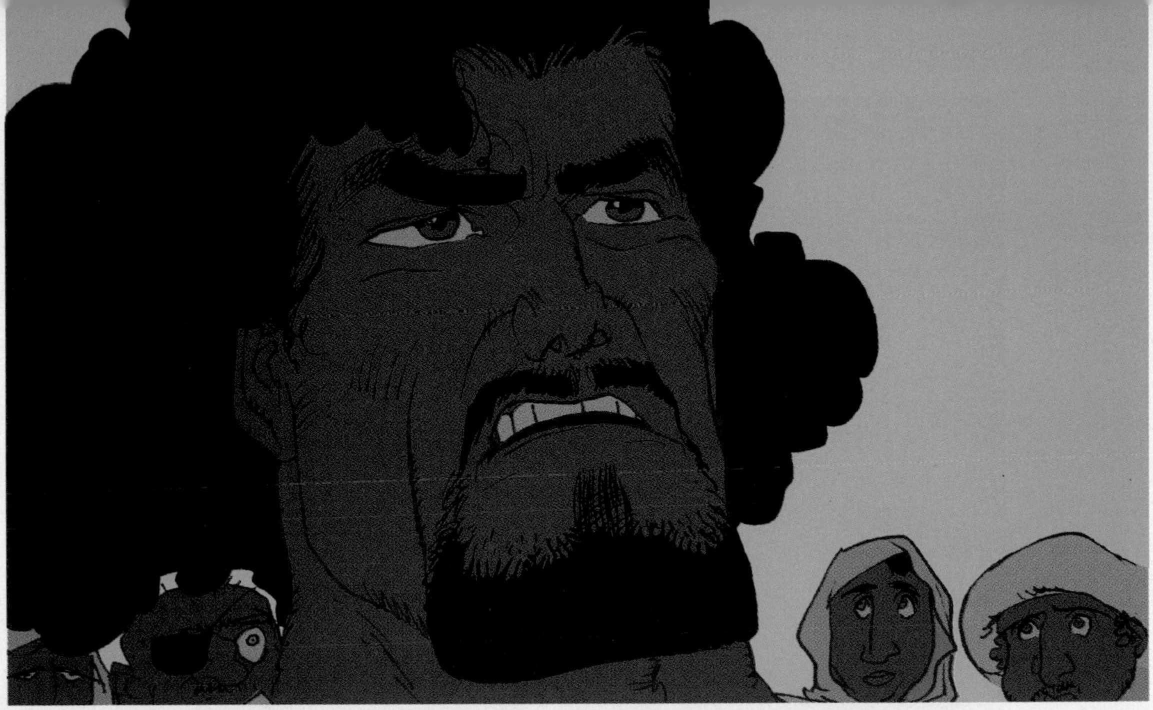

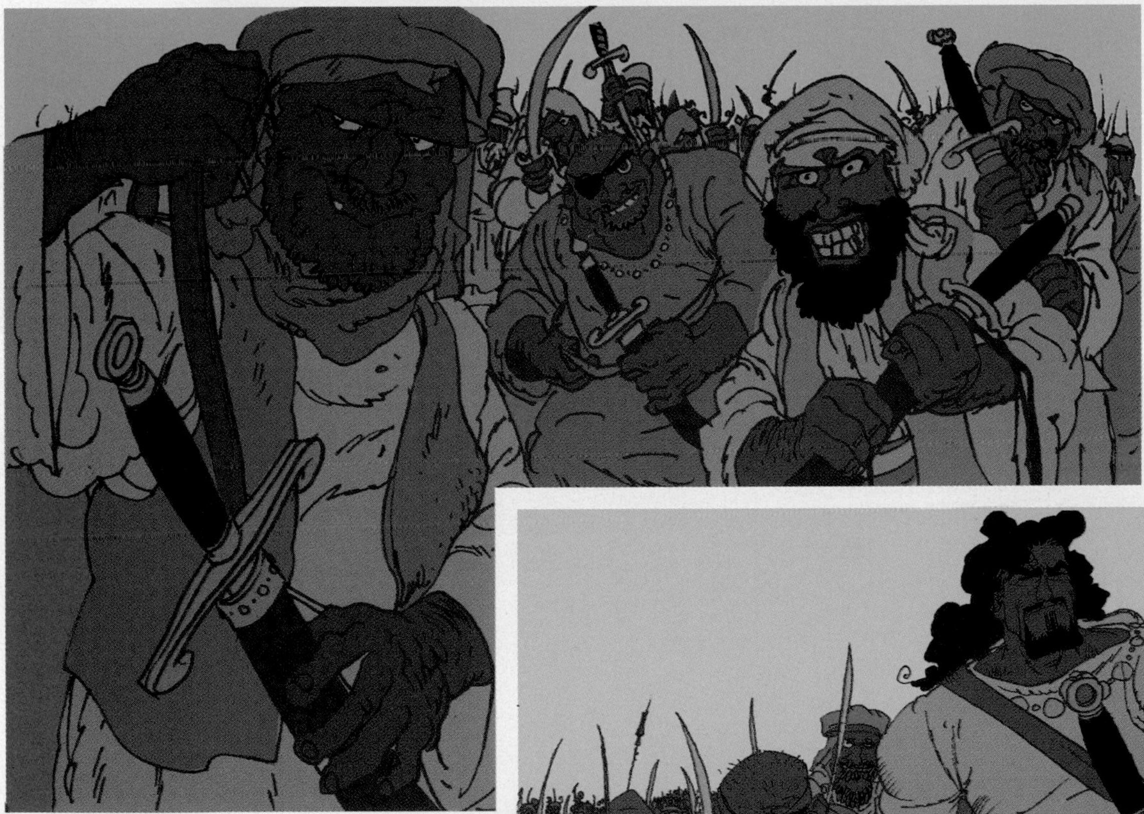

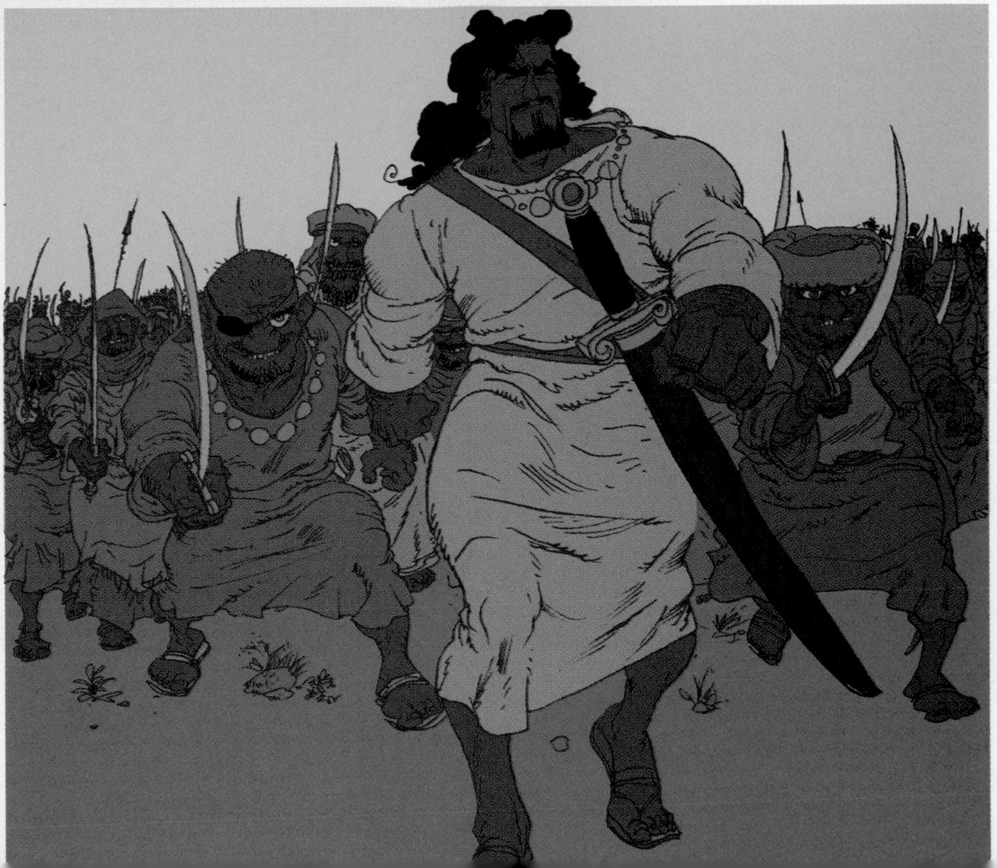

Abigail enters. "You screamed for me, dear?"

"Take this meat back. Tell the cook if she keeps serving me blood I'll chop her hands off. I hate blood."

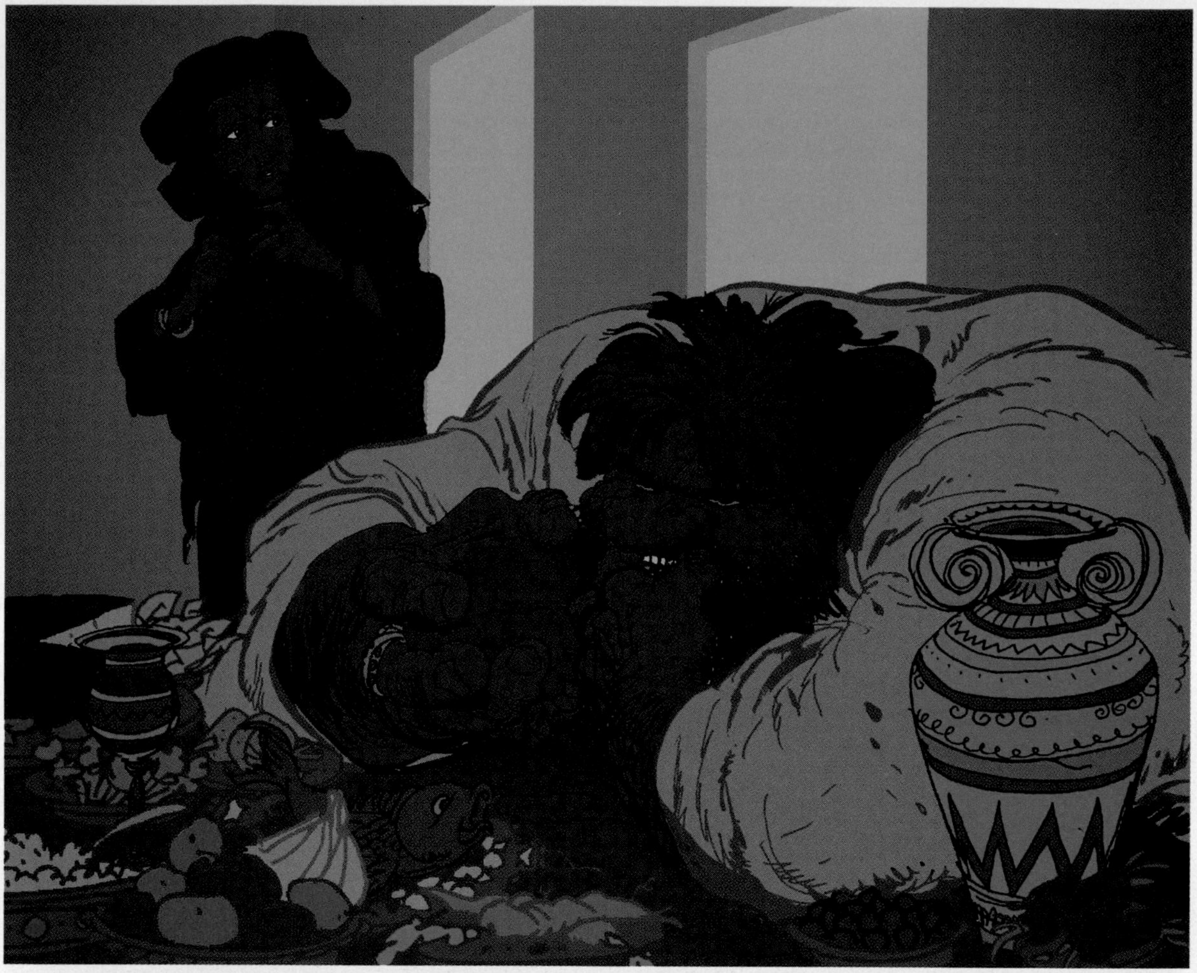

"You know, Nabal, just once it might be nice to have someone besides the two of us at these feasts."

"Tell her not to burn it, though. Burnt's as bad as bloody.."

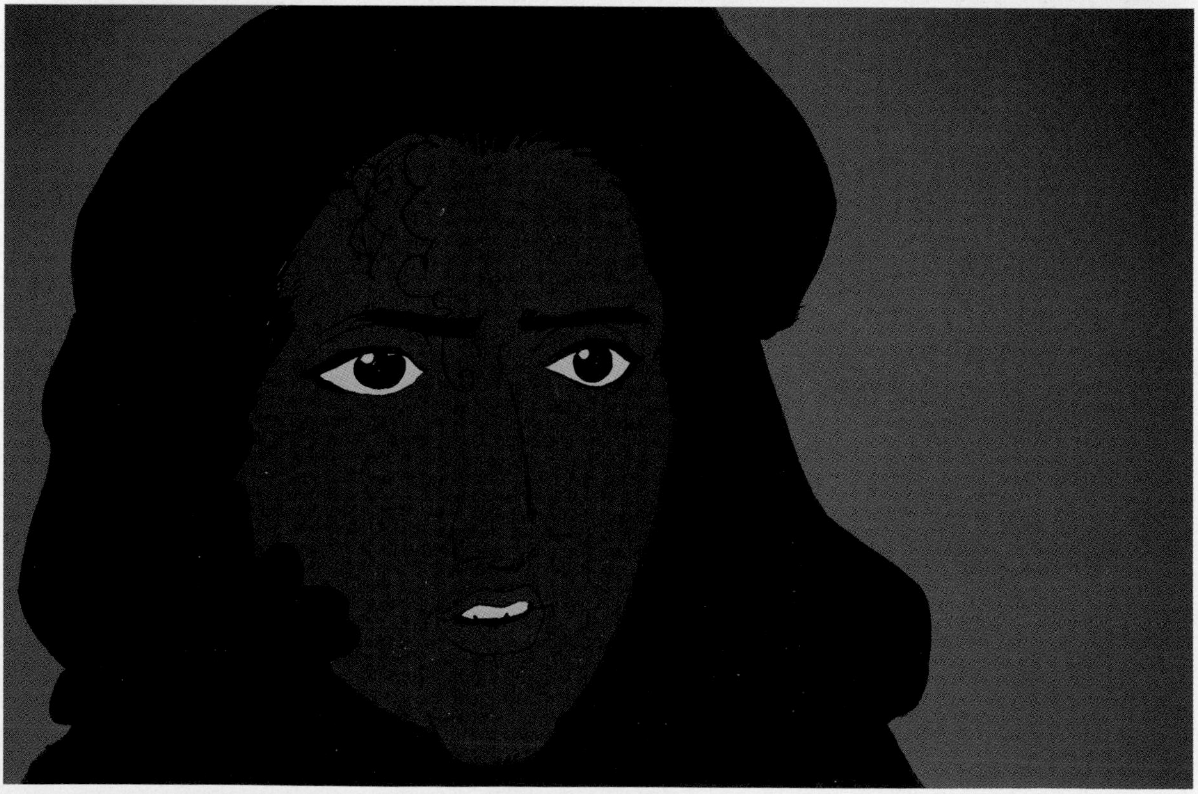

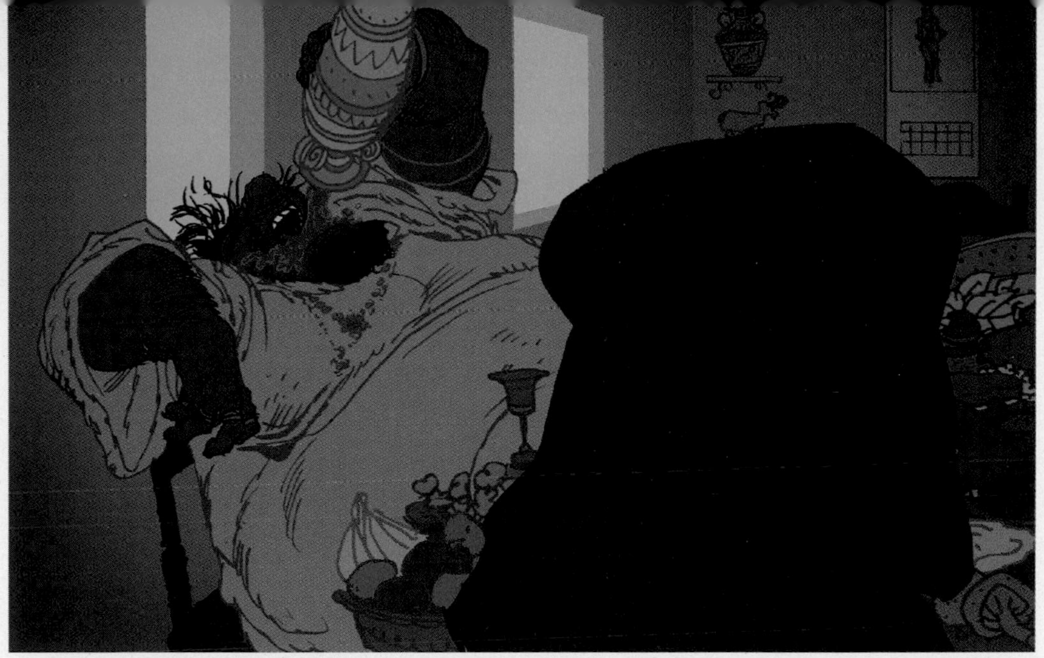

"You have two other roasts in front of you. We'll be eating leftovers for weeks, and still end up throwing most of them in the trash."

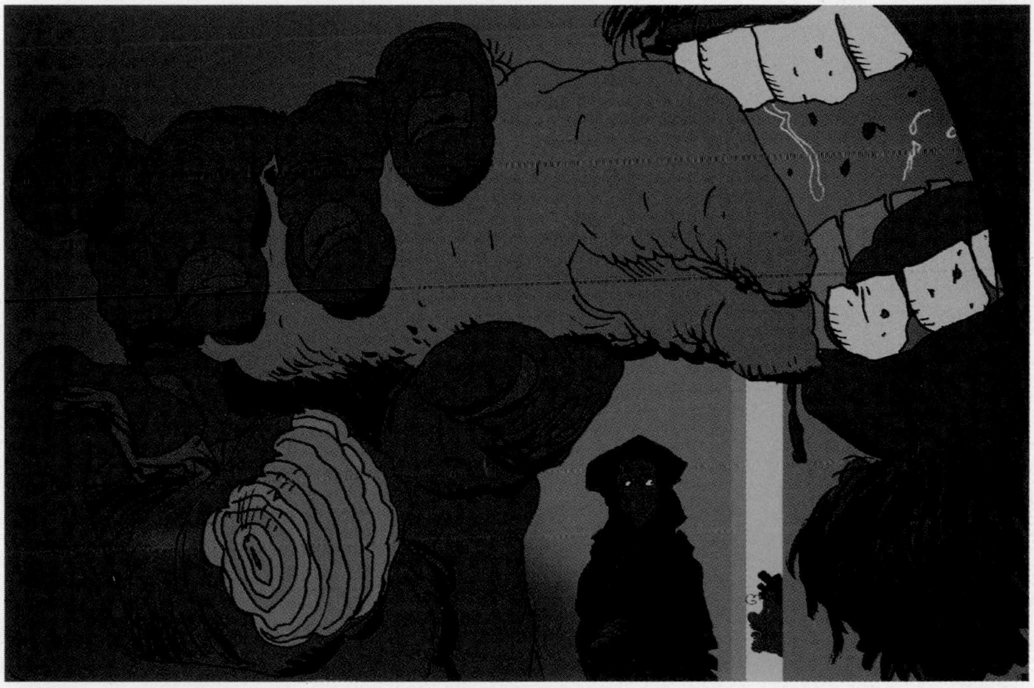

"This one tastes okay, but it looks pinkish. Have the cook flogged just in case. And have yourself flogged while you're at it. And bring me more wine."

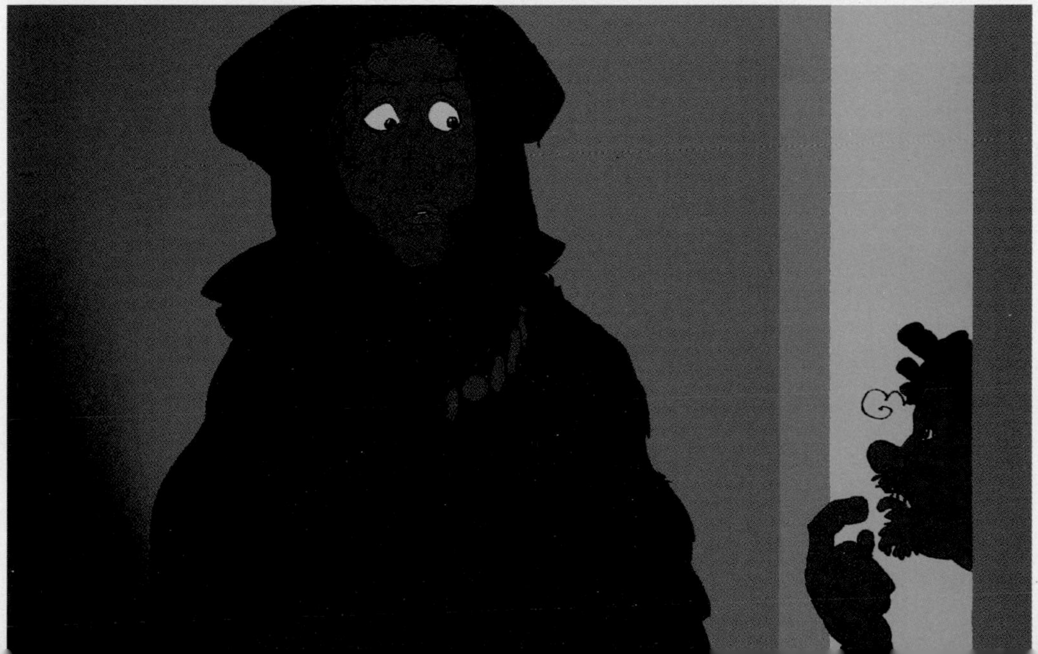

"Psst!"

"I'm sorry you and the other shearers have to eat outside, after all your hard work," Abigail says, "But you know how my husband is."

He whispers. "We know, mistress. And a job is a job...but--Um... You've heard of David? Son of Jesse, David and Goliath? That David?"

"Like in the song? David has slain his tens of thousands? That David?"

"Yeah!"

"Only an ignoramus hasn't heard of him!"

"You said that, I didn't. While you were working in the kitchen, David had sent messengers out of the wilderness to bless our lord, your husband Nabal."

"Well, this is an honor! Where are they? Washing up for dinner? I hope Nabal won't embarrass us as usual."

"Your husband screamed at them and sent them away."

"He screamed at the guy in the song? The tens of thousands guy?"

"Well, at the messengers. The messengers have gone and screamed at David, I suppose."

"Only if they're as stupid as Nabal. And that is virtually impossible!"

"And David's men had been good to us, they had not harmed us, and nothing was stolen from us all the days we had gone up and down with them when we were in the field. They have been a wall to us both by day and by night, all the days we have been with them, feeding the flock."

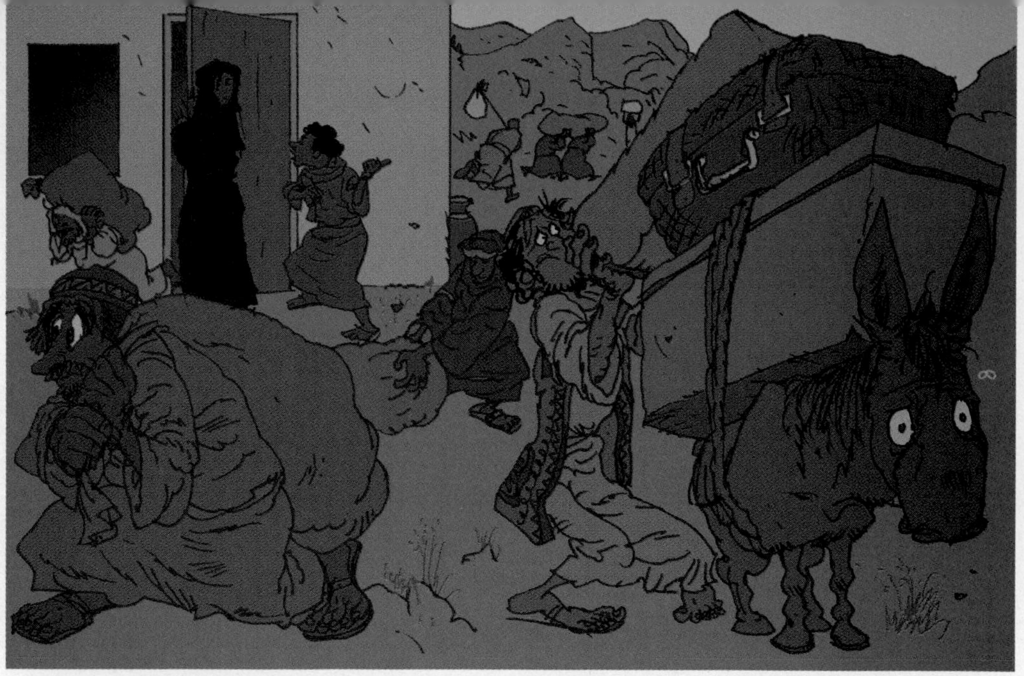

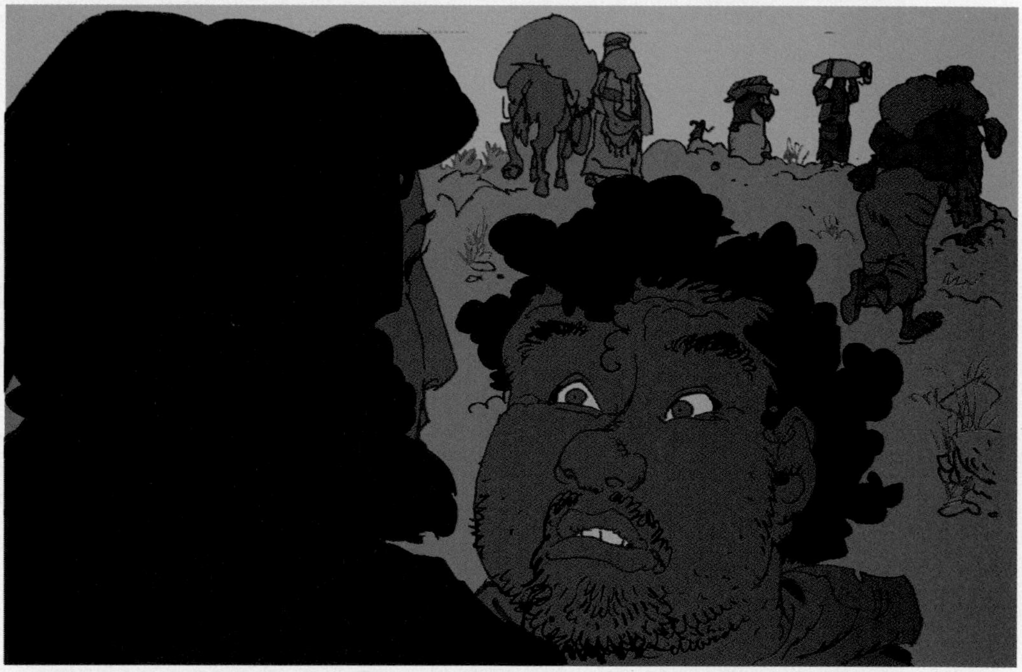

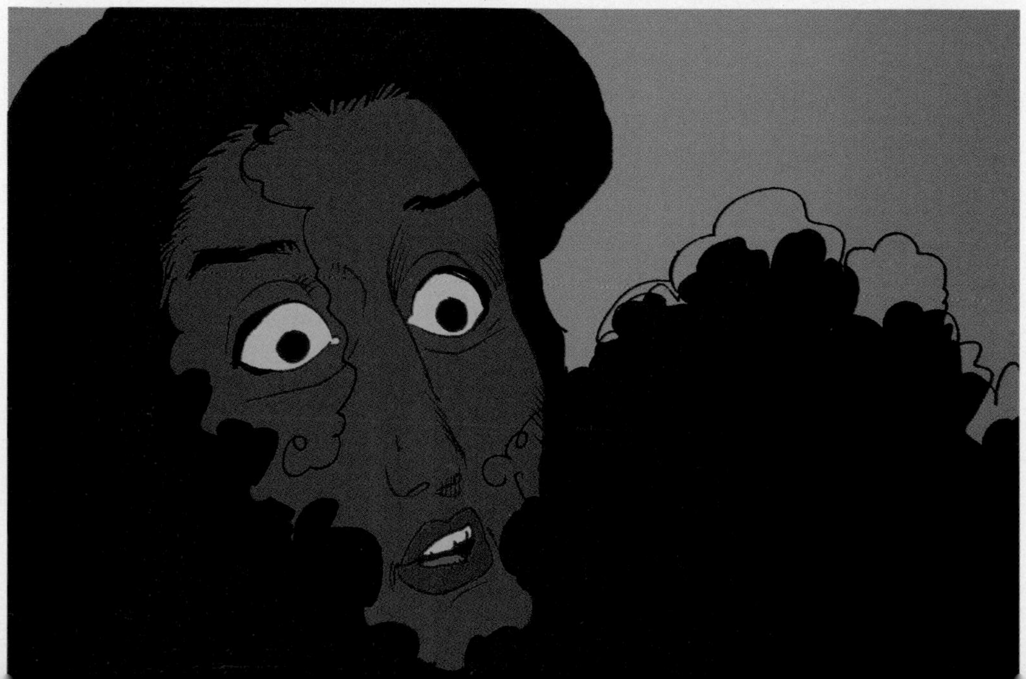

"We're doomed!" says Abigail.

"We're all fleeing, but we thought you should know before we left, since you've always done right by us. Now, consider what you should do; for evil has been determined against our lord Nabal, and on all his house. And he is a son of worthlessness, no one can speak to him."

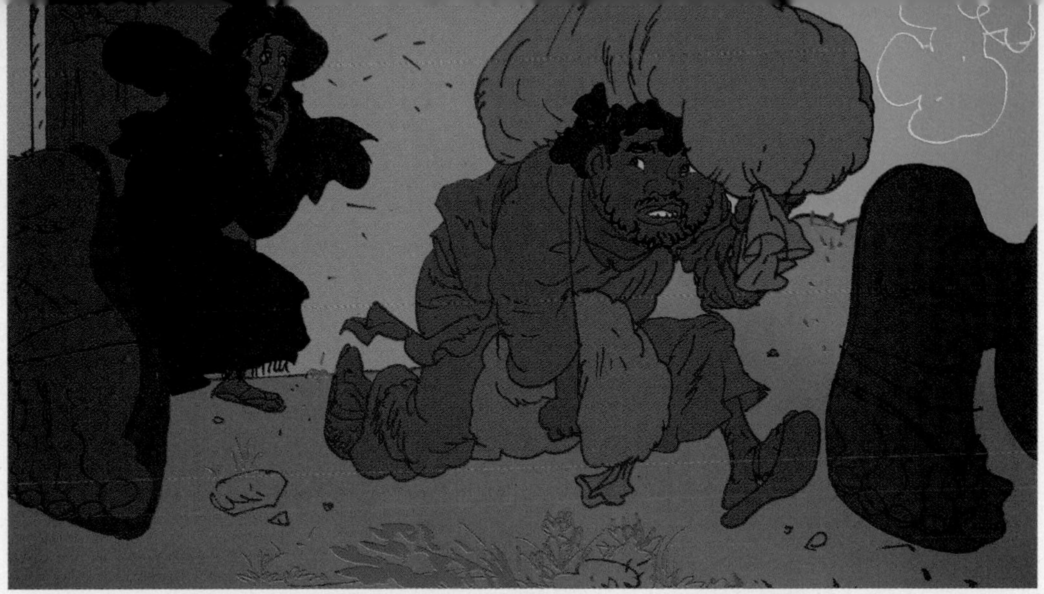

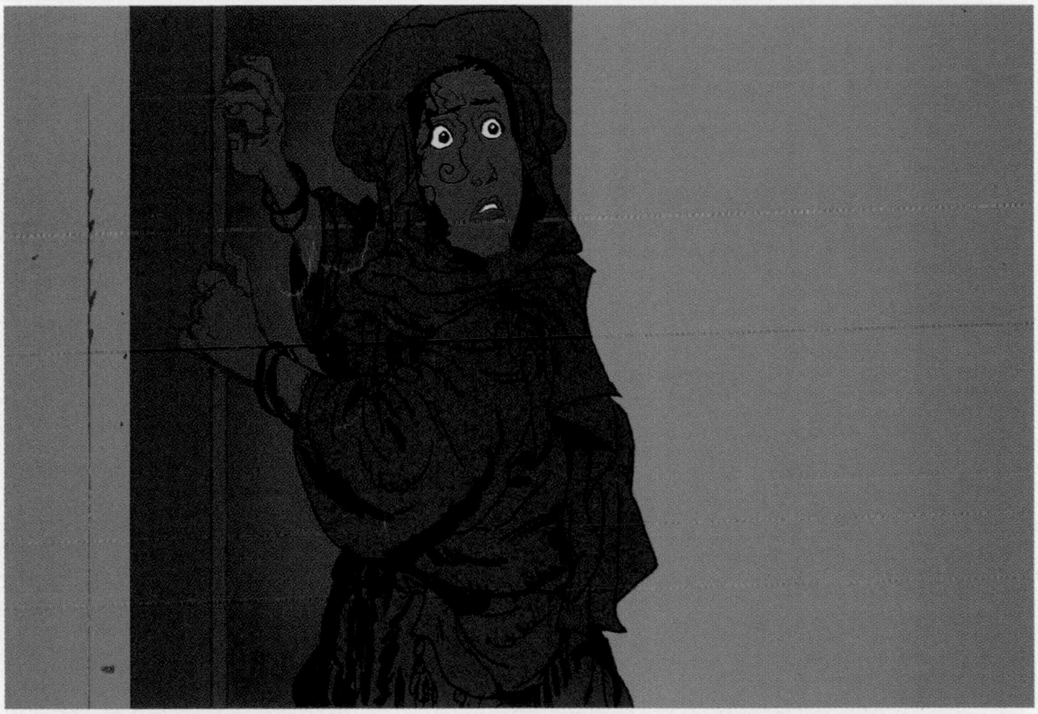

Nabal shouts from inside, "Abigail! Get your fat lazy butt in here! I need more wine, you shiftless cow!"

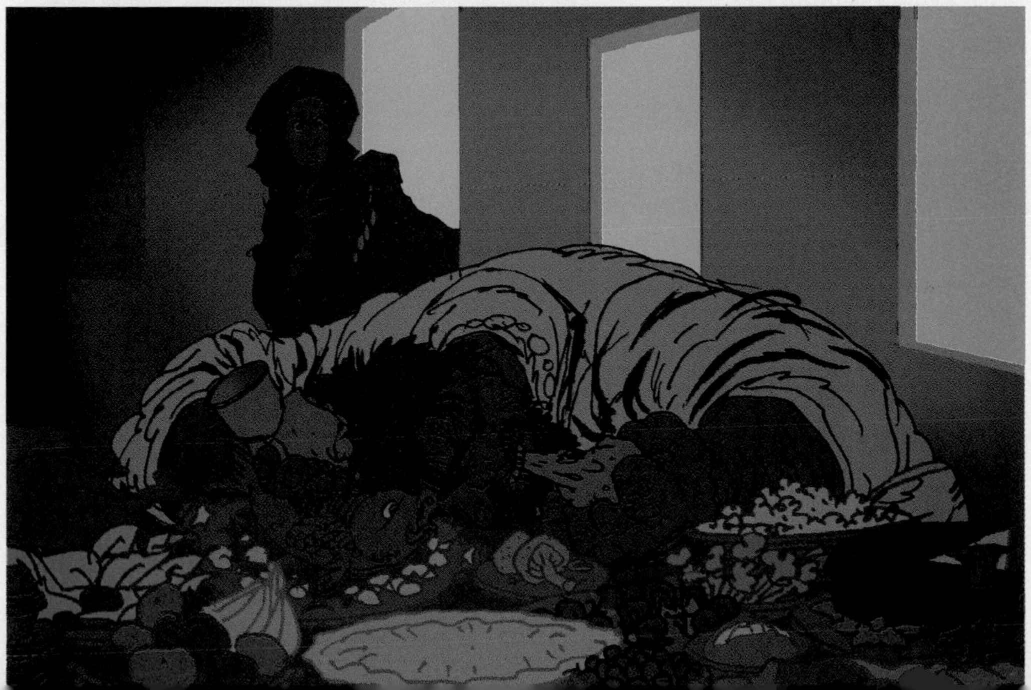

"I'll be right back, darling. I have to go to the shed for it."

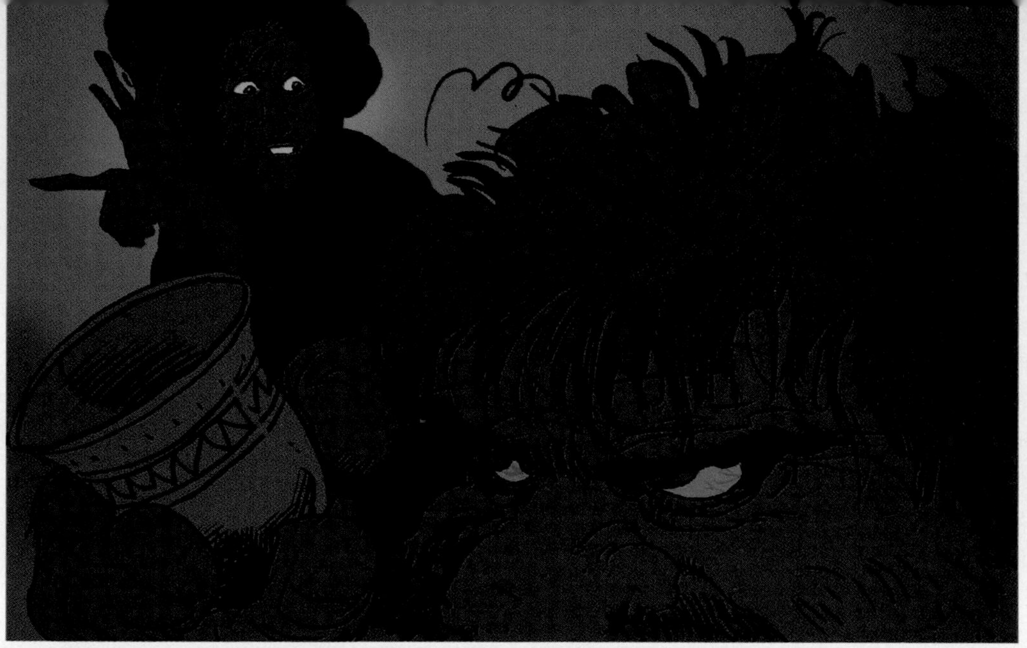

"Wait! I've got an idea!"

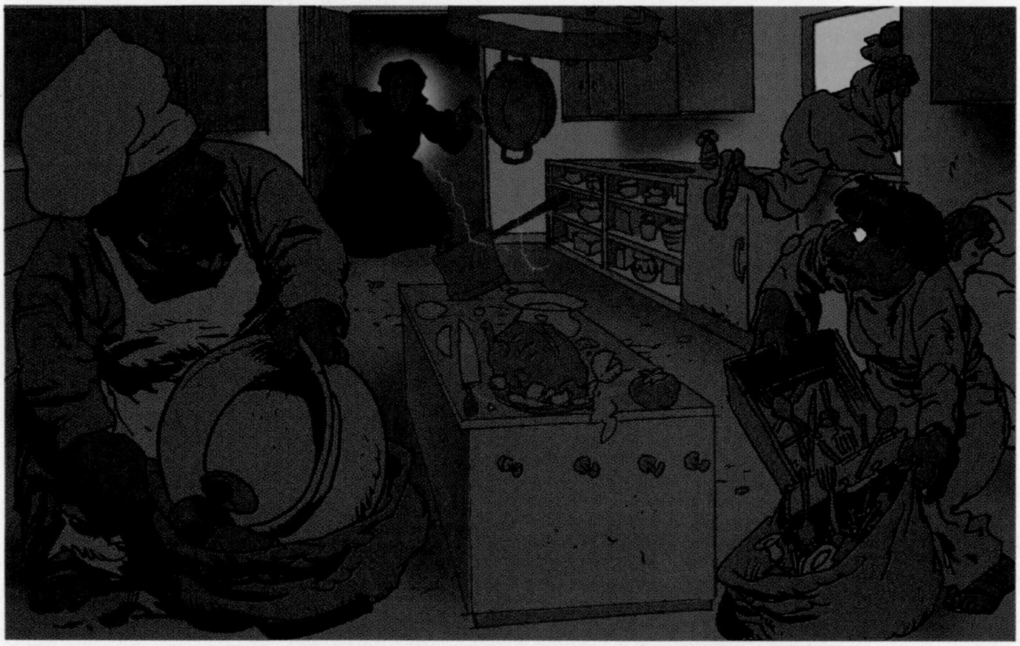

"Surely, in vain I have guarded all that belongs to this fellow in the wilderness, so that nothing was taken of all that was his. And he has returned to me evil for good. May God strike me dead if I leave any of all that is to Nabal to the light of the morning, of one who urinates against a wall."

"What?" asks Joab.

"Men. We're killing every man in his house."

"And then we eat, right?"

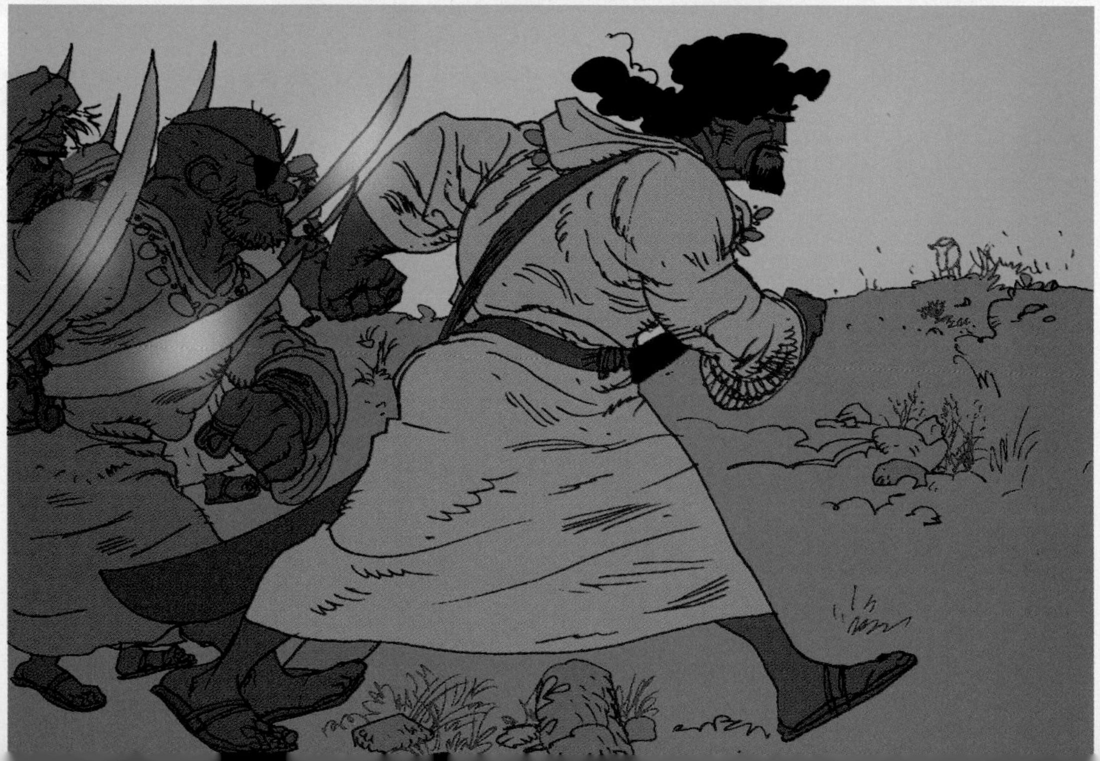

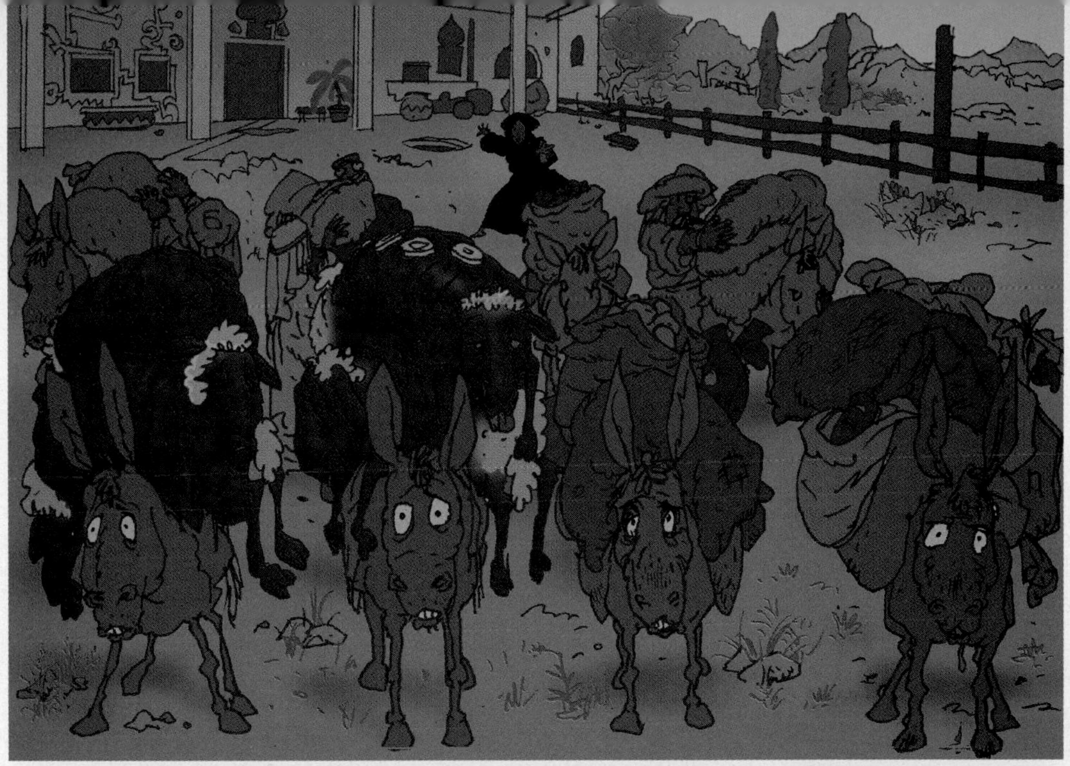

"Hurry! Hurry!" Abigail says, "Okay, let's see, that's two hundred loaves, two skins of wine, five prepared sheep, and five measures of roasted grain, a hundred bunches of raisins, and two hundred cakes of figs. I pray that's enough."

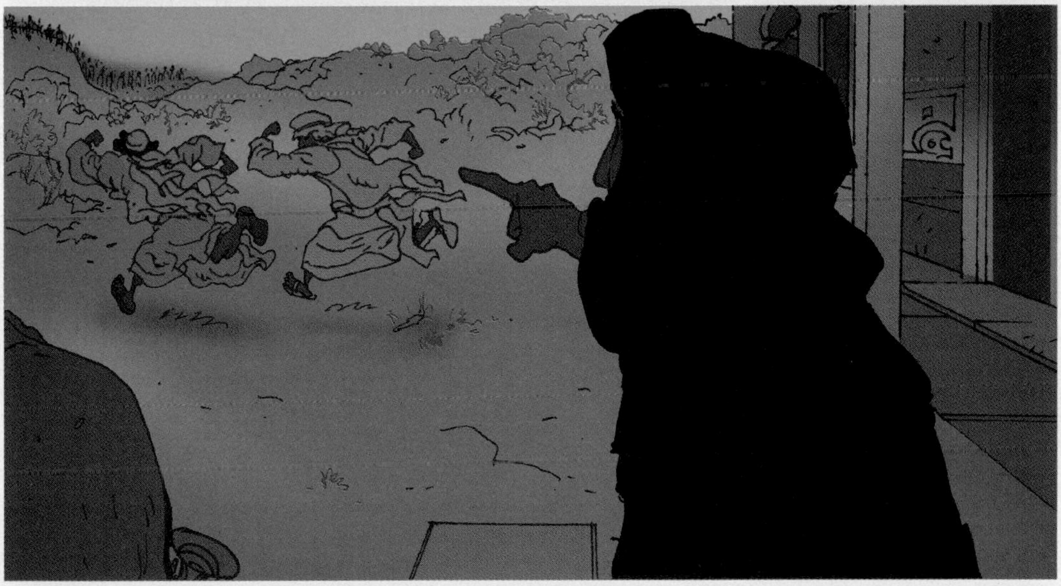

"You young men, pass on before me. I am coming after you!"

To the other servants, she says, "Nobody tell Nabal."

"Who can talk to Nabal?" one answers.

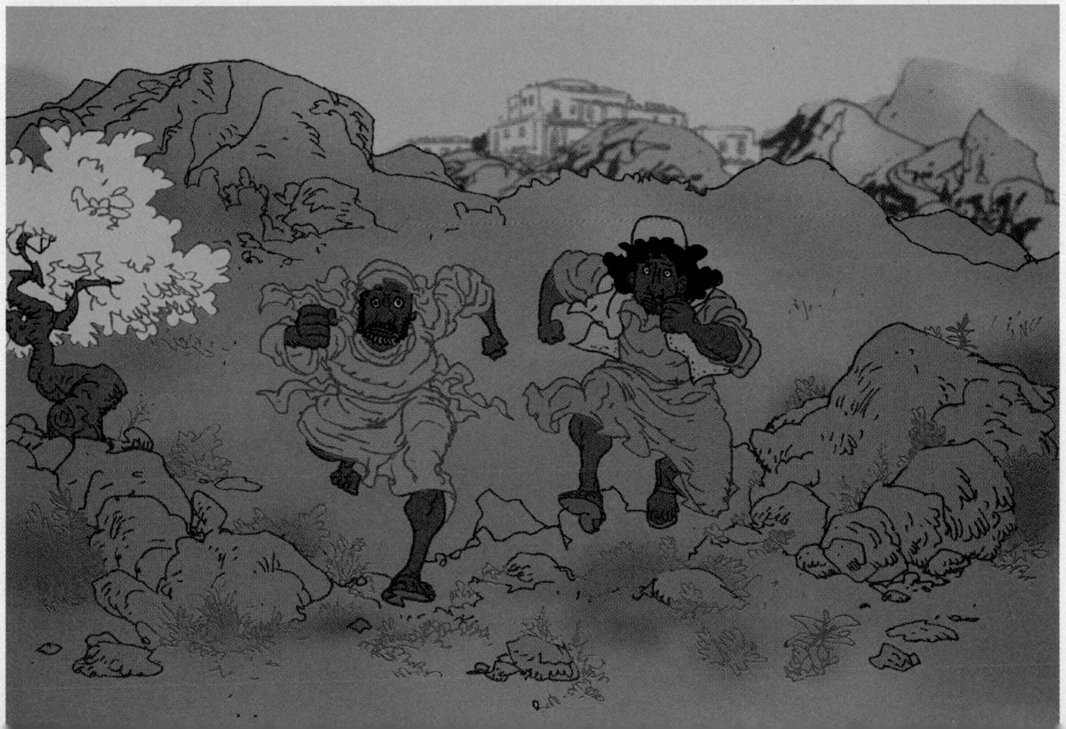

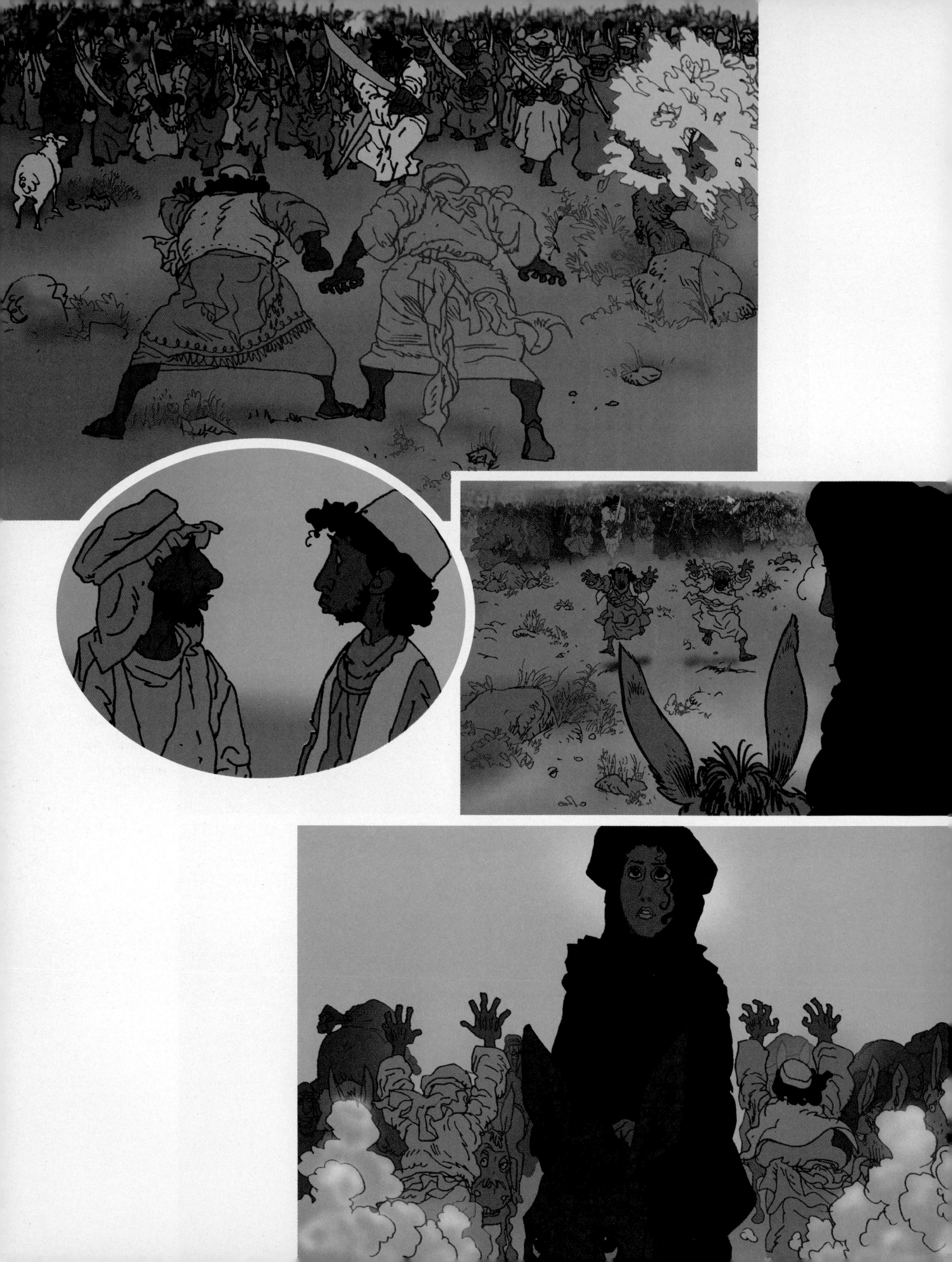

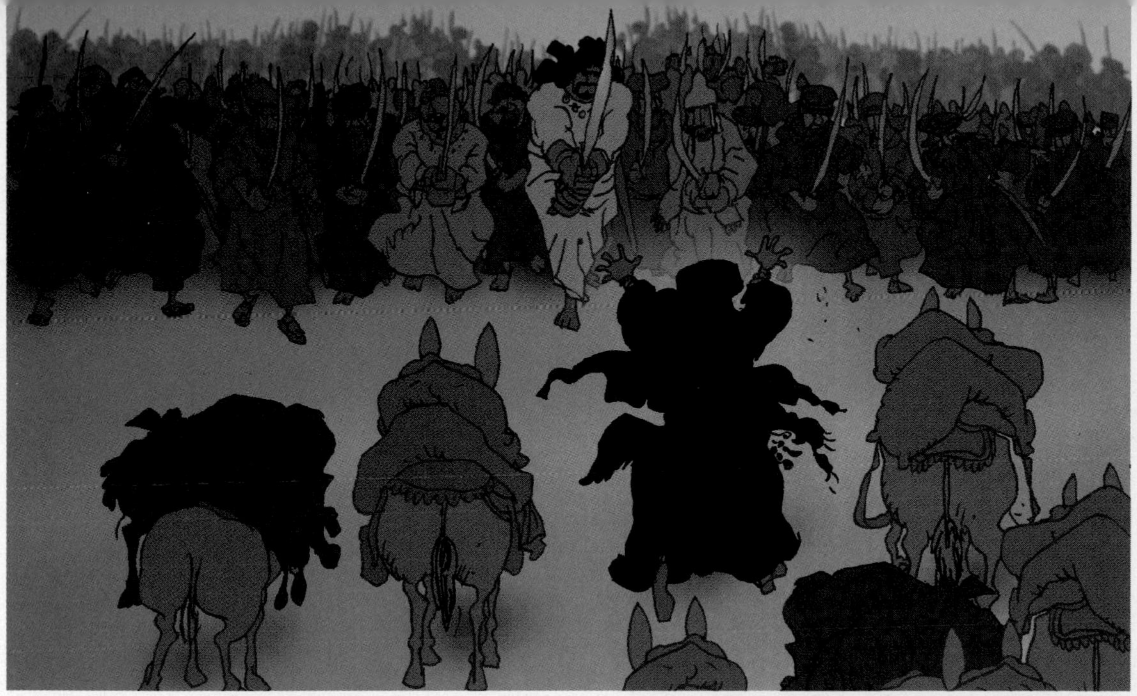

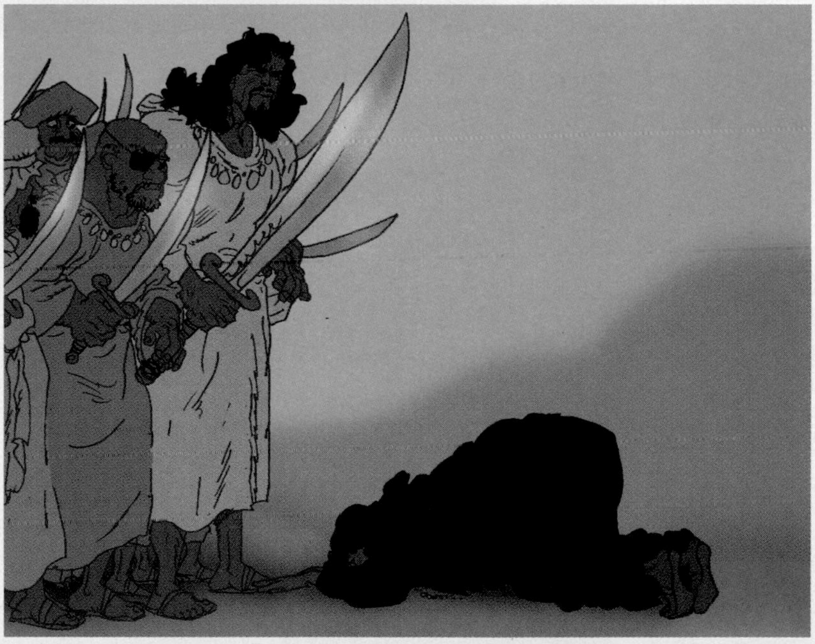

Abigail says, "On me, even me, my lord, be the iniquity. And please, let your handmaid speak in your ears; and hear the words of your handmaid. Please, do not let my lord set his heart toward this man of worthlessness, on Nabal. For as his name is, so is he. Nabal means fool, and foolishness is with him. And I, your handmaid, did not see the young men of my lord whom you sent. And now, since the LORD has withheld you from coming in with blood, and avenging yourself with your own hand; as surely as the LORD lives and as you live, even now let your enemies be as Nabal, even those seeking evil to my lord. And now these gifts which your handmaid has brought to my lord, let them be given to the young men who go after my lord. Please, forgive the transgression of your handmaid, for the LORD shall certainly make a lasting dynasty for my lord. For you have fought the battles of the LORD, and evil has not been found in you all your days. And if a man rises up to pursue you and to seek your soul, the soul of my lord will be bound up in the bundle of life with the LORD your God; and the souls of your enemies, He shall sling them from the hollow of the sling. And it shall be, when the LORD does to my lord according to all the good which He has spoken concerning you, and has commanded you to be ruler over Israel, that this shall not be for a cause of staggering, or of stumbling of heart to my lord, either to shed blood for nothing, or that my lord saved himself. And may the LORD do good to my lord, and you remember your handmaid."

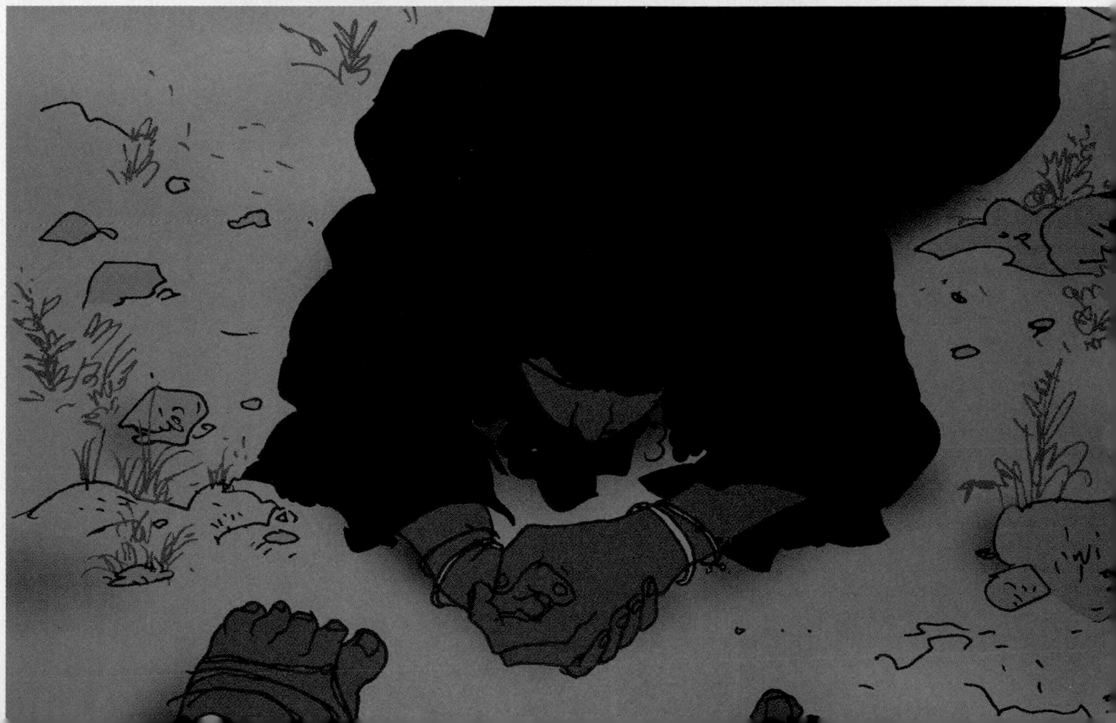

"Blessed is the God of Israel," says David, "who has sent you to meet me today.

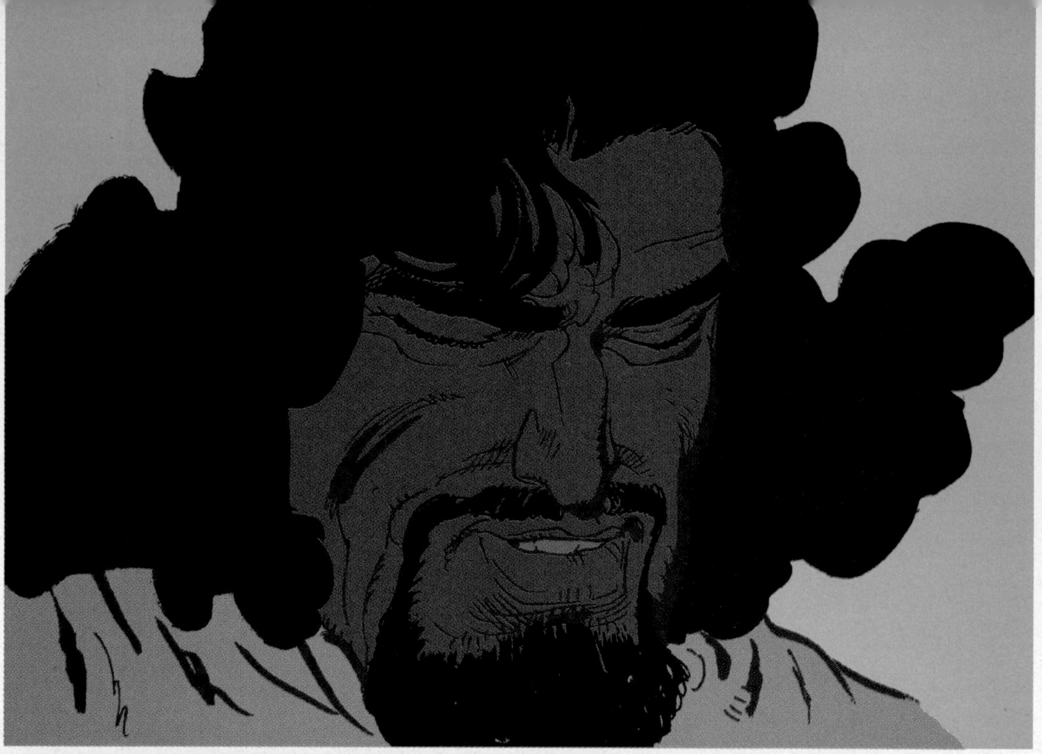

"And blessed is your discernment. And blessed are you in that you have kept me from coming in with blood this day, and from delivering myself with my own hand. And, indeed, as the God of Israel lives, who has kept me back from doing evil to you, unless you had hurried and had come to meet me, surely there would not have been left to Nabal one who urinates against the wall till the light of morning."

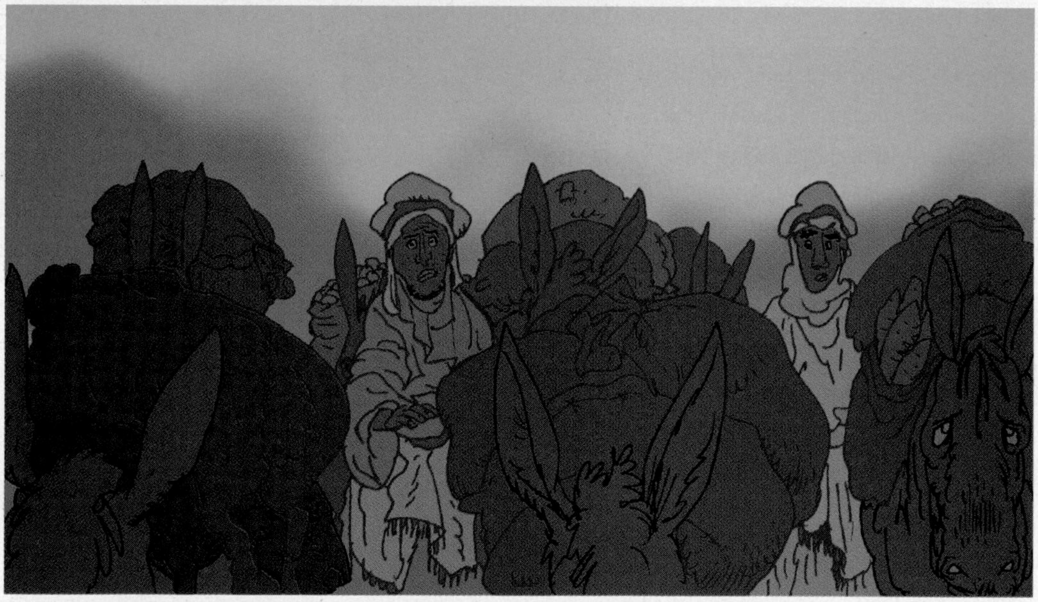

"He means men," adds Joab.

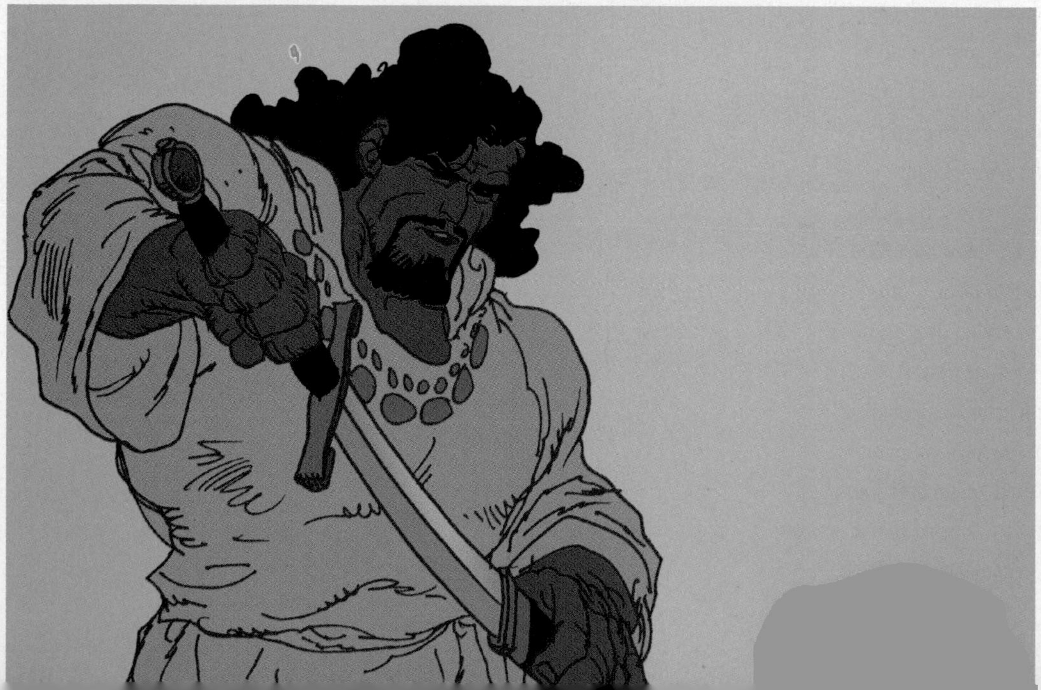

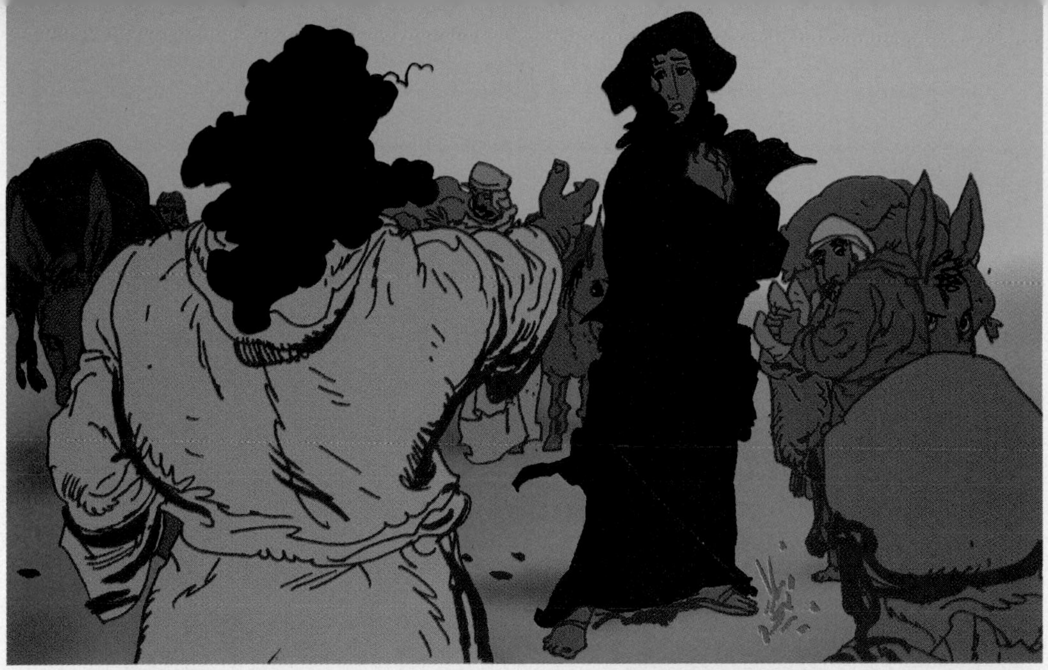

"Go in peace to your house," says David. "See, I have heard your voice, and have accepted your face."

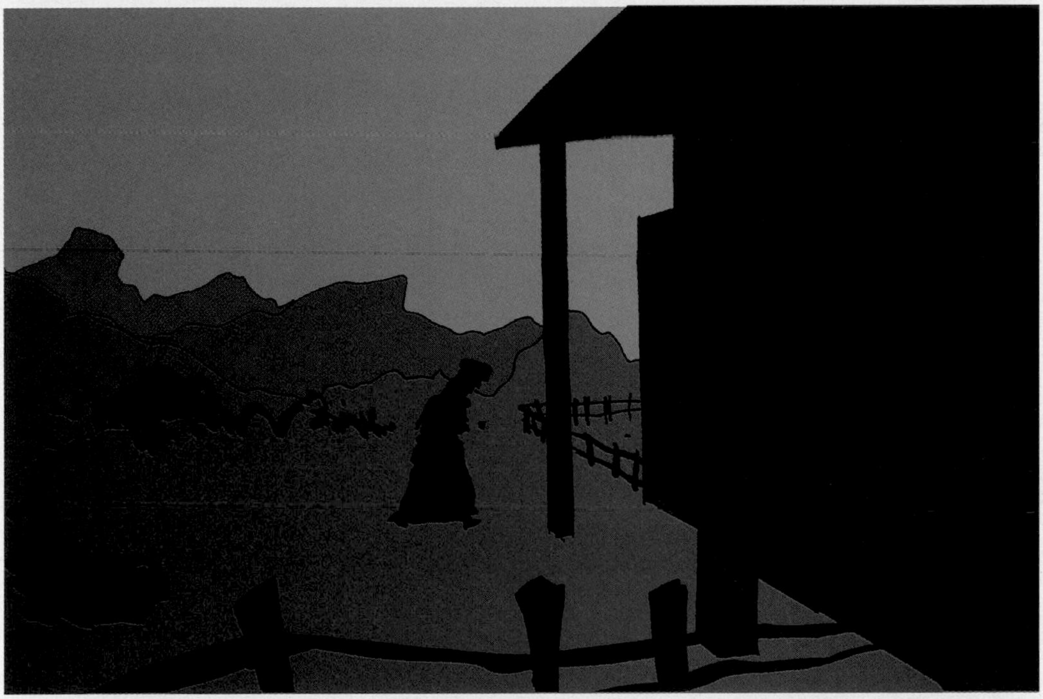

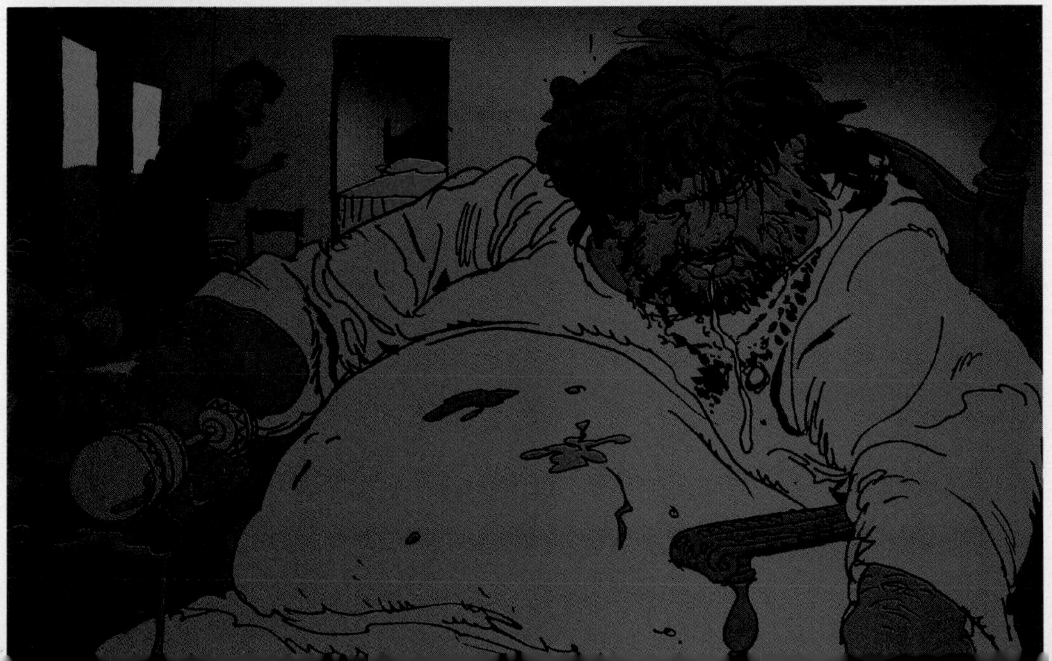

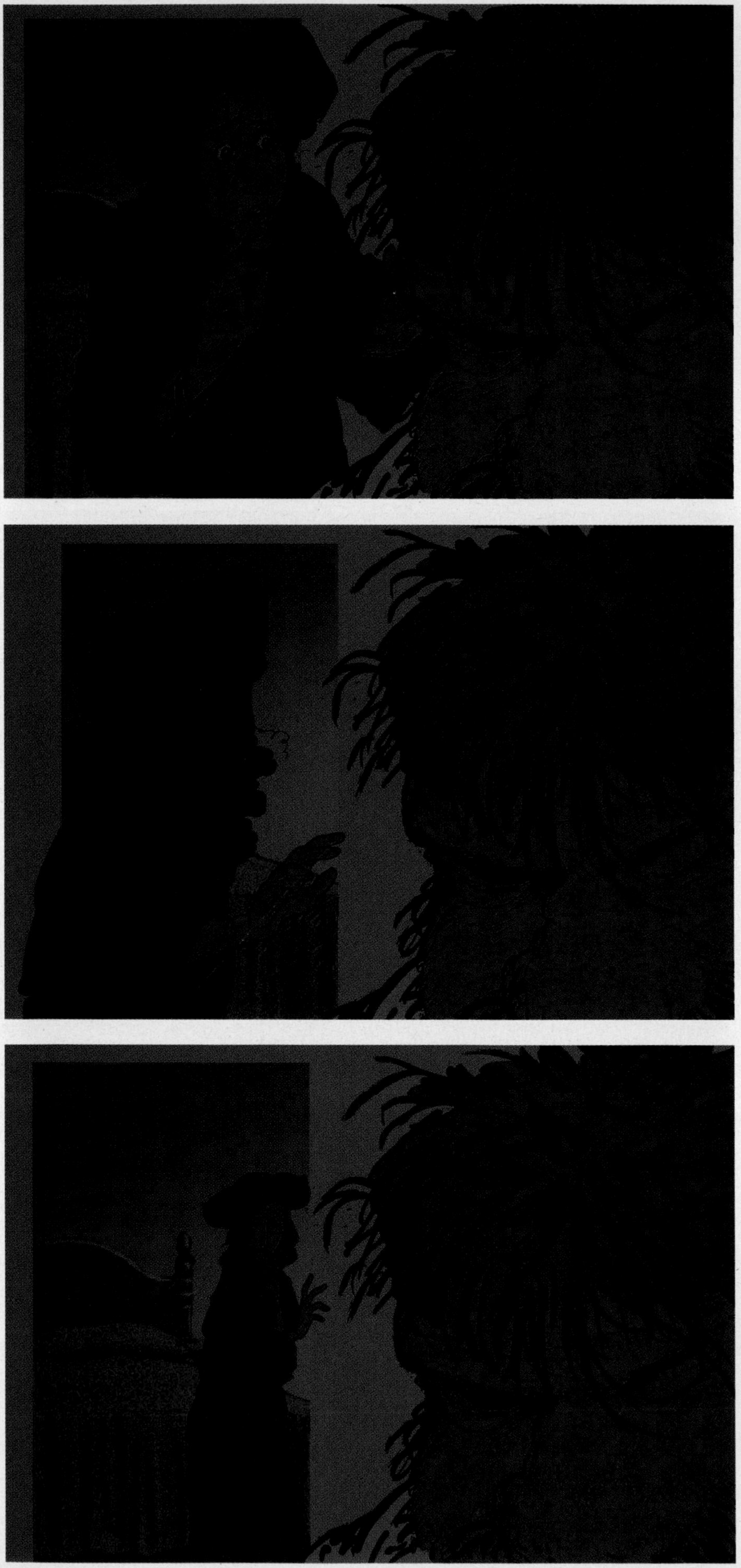

"Oh, my head."

"You're awake. You want breakfast?"

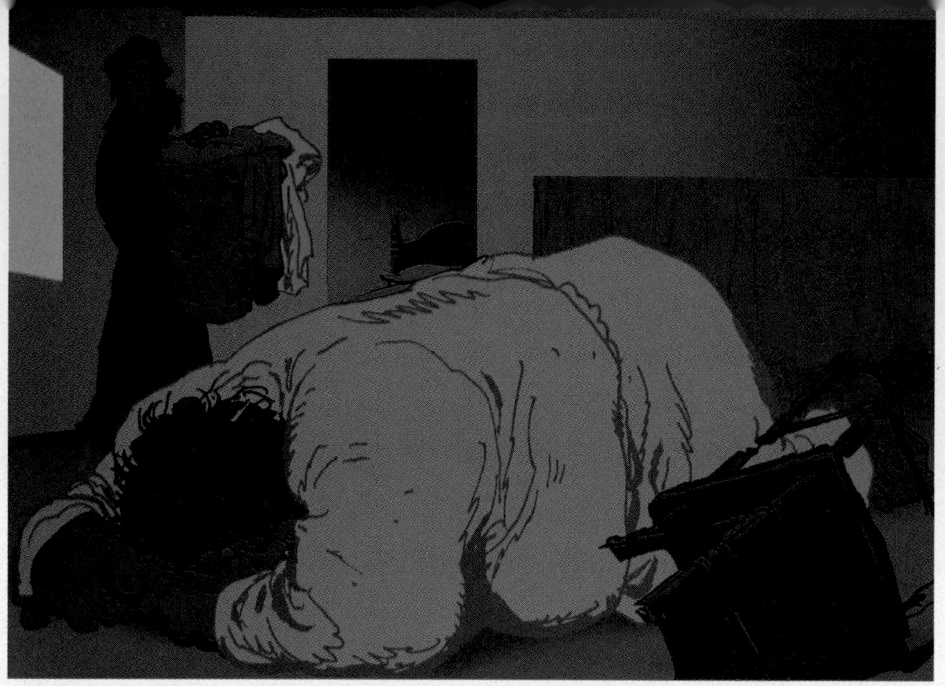

"Urg. Gonna be sick."

"I'll get your bucket. Look, Nabal, you probably don't remember, so I should tell you..."

"All this food. Can't stand the smell."

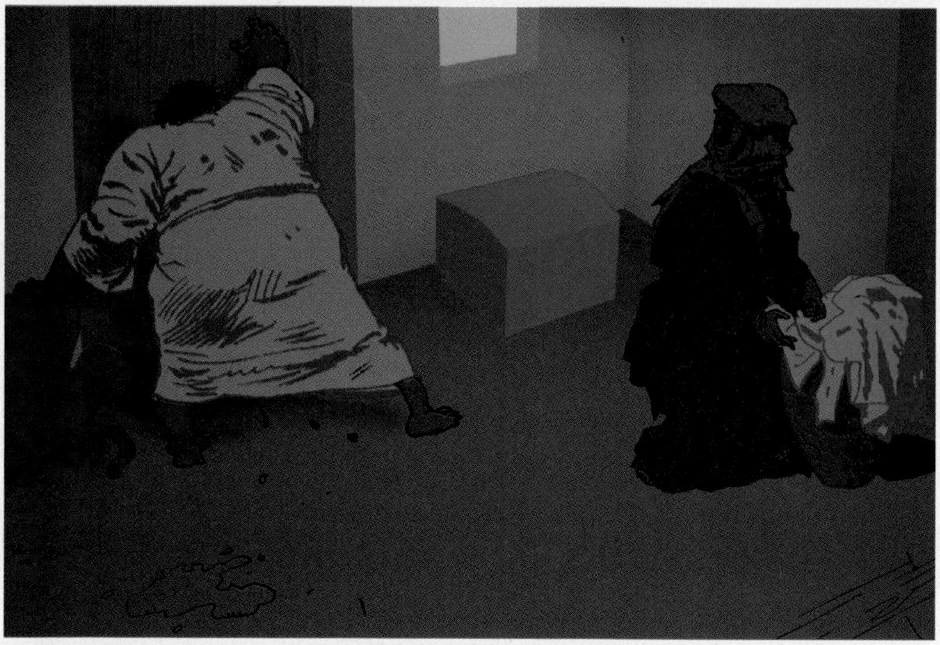

"Yesterday, some messengers came and you screamed at them, and, uh, here's the thing. You ever hear that song, Saul has killed his thousands, and David--"

"Need air."

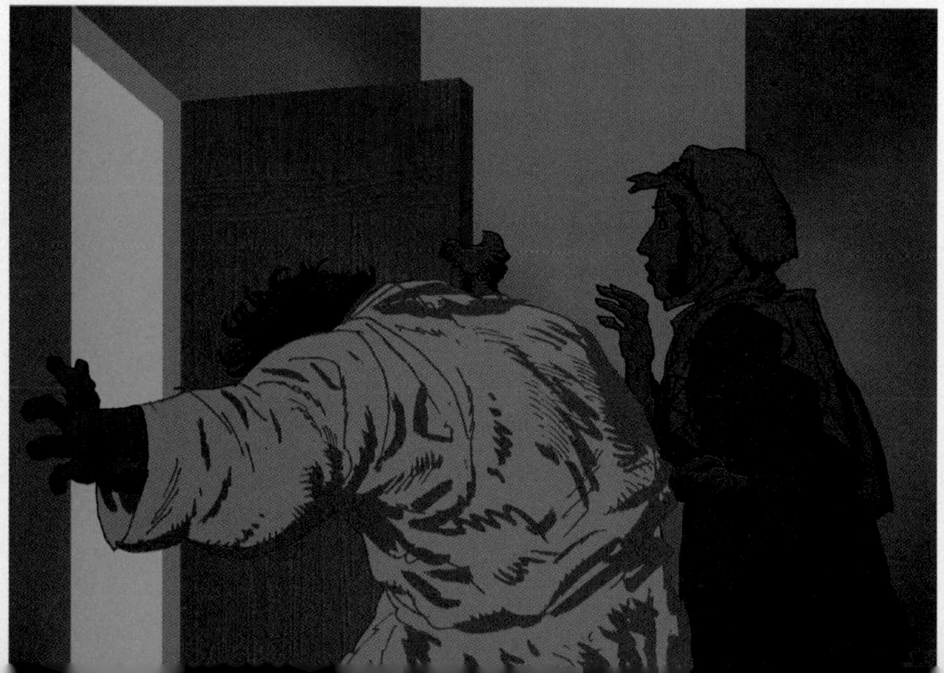

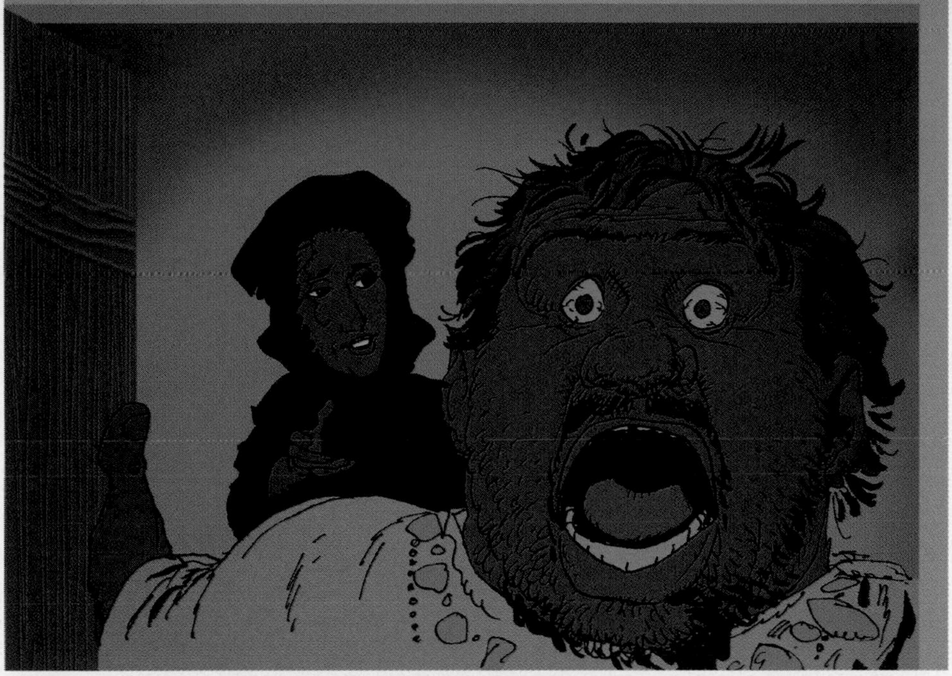

"Nabal, that's the David you insulted. From the song."

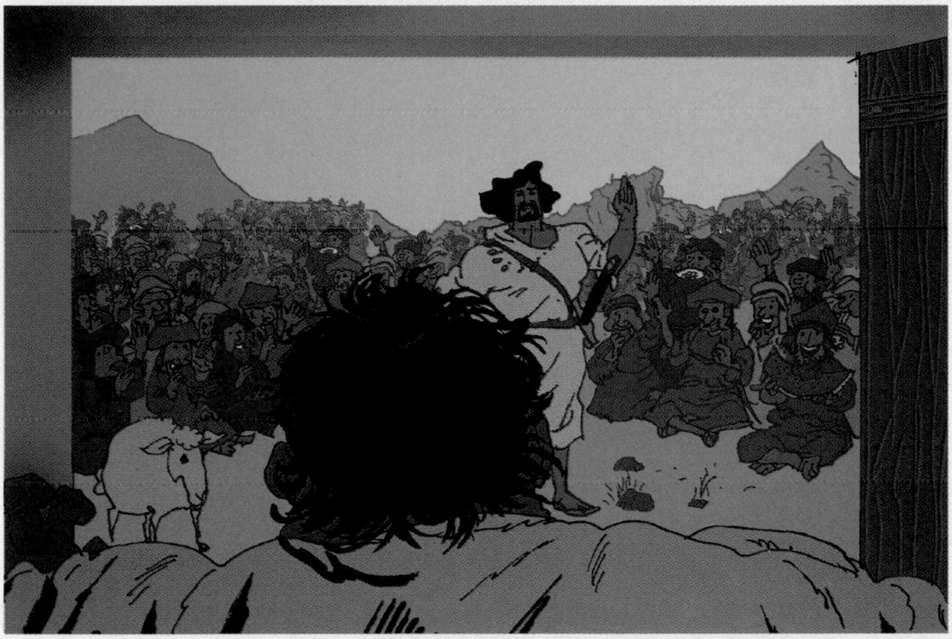

"Good morning, Nabal!"

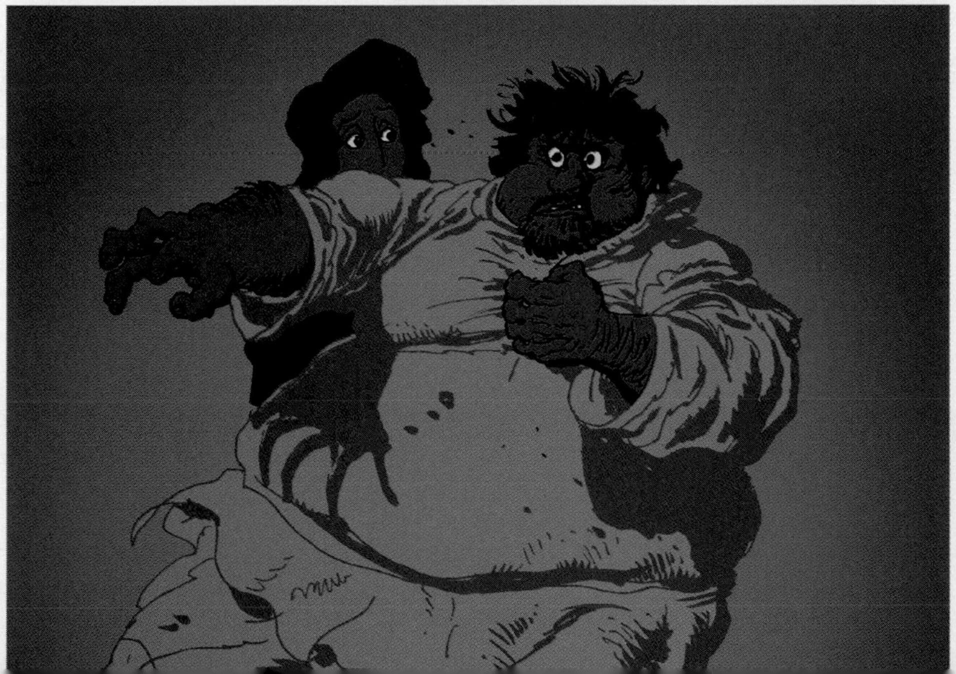

"**B**lessed be the LORD who has avenged the insult I received from the hand of Nabal; and His servant has been kept back from evil; the LORD has caused the evil doing of Nabal to return on his head." says David.

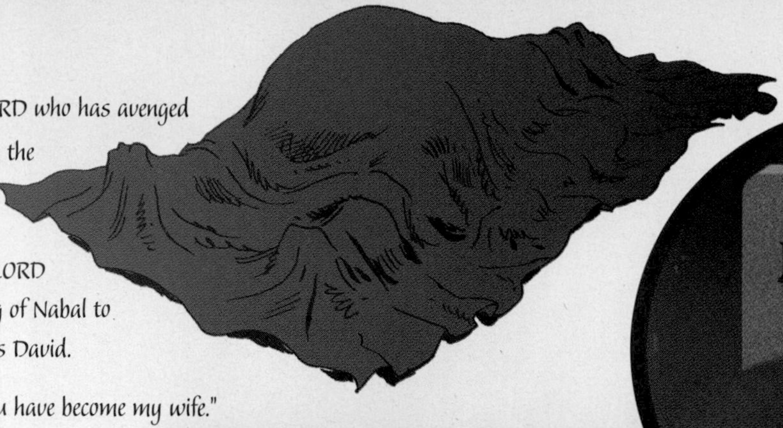

"It is only fitting that you have become my wife."

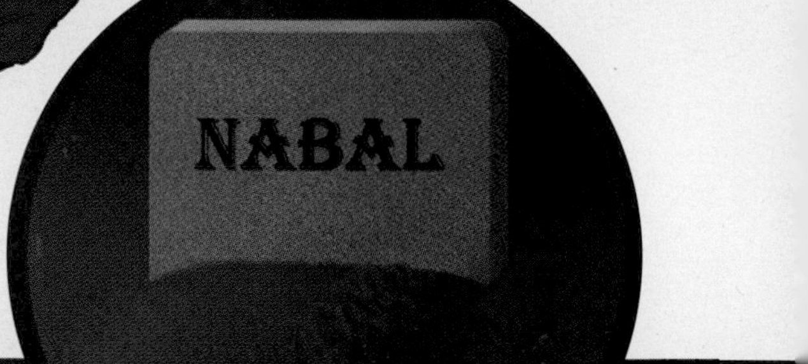
NABAL

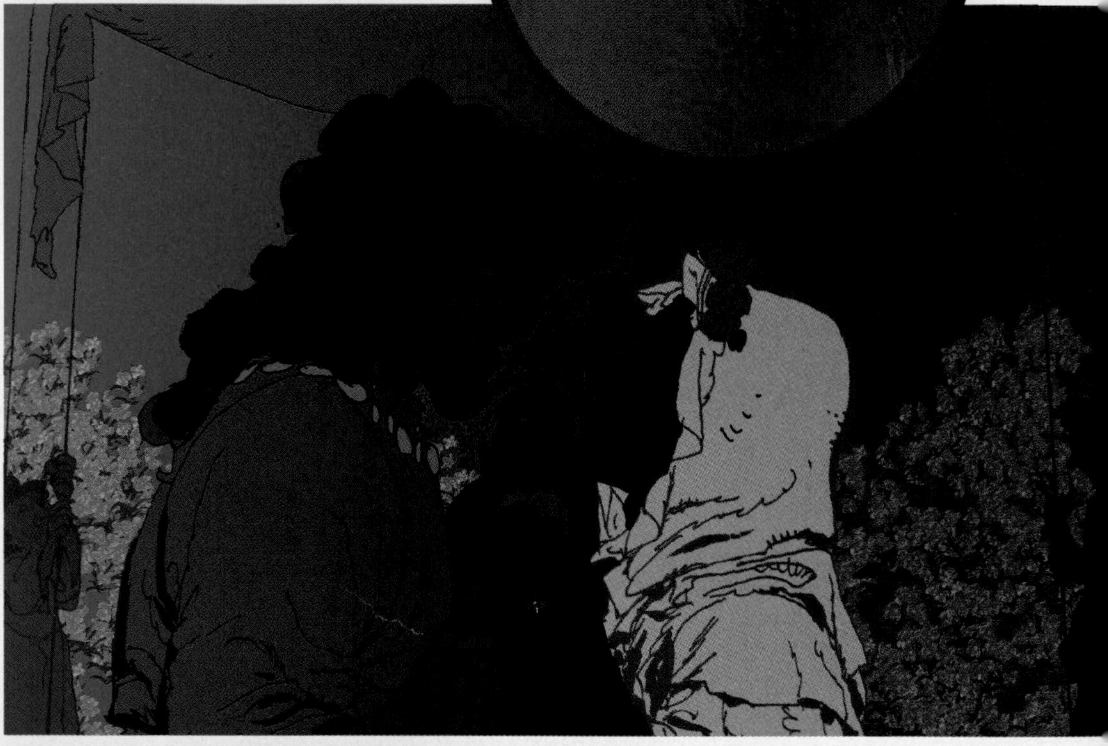

Two elders of the six hundred families following David in the wilderness discuss their hero's good fortune:

"Can you believe that guy? Two wives."

"Three. Don't forget Michal, daughter of Saul."

"I was counting her. Who's the third?"

"Ahinoam from Jezreel."

"Her I forgot. Three wives. Can you imagine?"

"I would destroy my own eardrums with a hot poker."

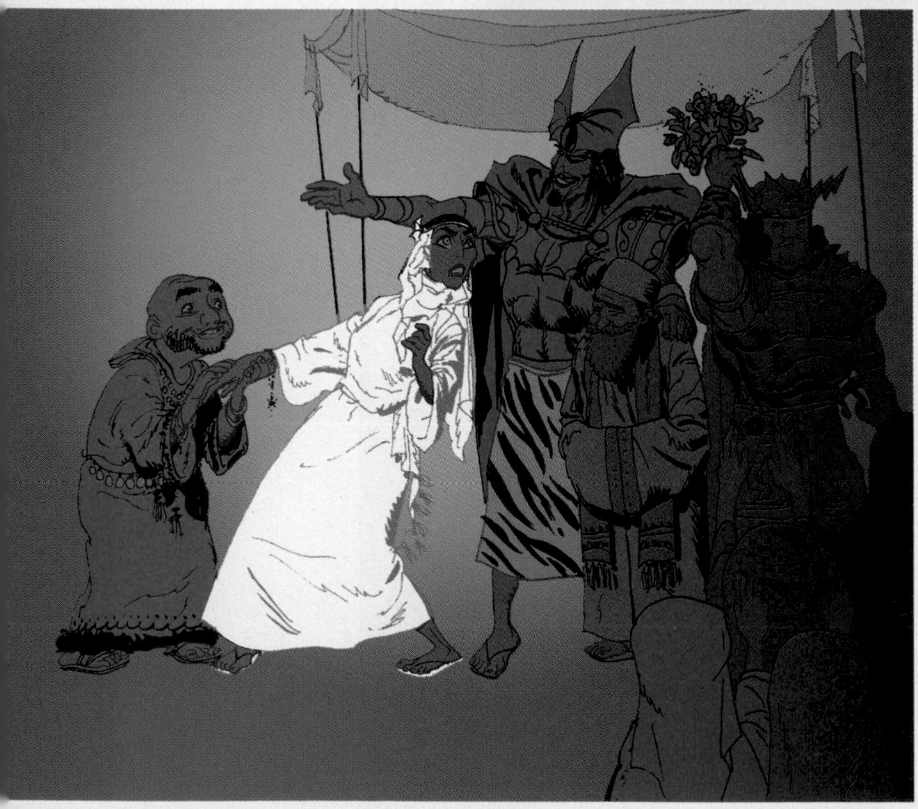

Saul says, "Mazel Tov. You had a lovely wedding. I'll pay the rabbi."

"You call that a wedding?" says Michal. "I wasn't even here!"

"Is it my fault you showed up late? I told you about this last night! Go, Phalti, son of Laish, take your new wife back to Gallim. I'll tell the relatives where to send the gifts."

"But Daddy! I've already got a husband. David!"

"Some husband. He's never home, hasn't got a job...your mother wants grandchildren! Phalti, take her."

"Thank you, sire. You're, uh, sure I don't have to cut off anyone's--"

"Nah, your money's fine. Take her and be gone!"

"Daddy!"

"If I may be so bold, princess Michal, let me assure you that I will do everything in my power to ensure that your life with me will be long and happy." Phalti says.

"Thanks. What'd you say your name was?"

"ABNER! Do you not answer, Abner?"

"What's all the noise?" Joab asks Abishai.

Abishai points at the army below. "Three thousand of Saul's finest. Showed up last night."

Abner shouts from below, "Who are you, the one calling?"

"Again?" asks Joab. "I thought that was taken care of! What's going on?"

David shouts, "Are you not a man? And who is like you in Israel? But why have you not watched over your lord the king? For one of the people came in to destroy your lord the king."

Abishai tells Joab, "Me and David sneaked into Saul's camp last night. Everyone was asleep. Even the guards."

David yells at the valley, "This thing which you have done is not good. As the LORD lives, you also are sons of death, in that you have not watched over your lord, over the anointed of the LORD."

"So I'm looking at Saul sleeping. He's as close to me as you are right now. His spear stuck in the ground near his head."

"Again the lord delivered Saul into our hands!"

"That's what I said! I said, 'David, let me stab him! I won't have to do it twice!'"

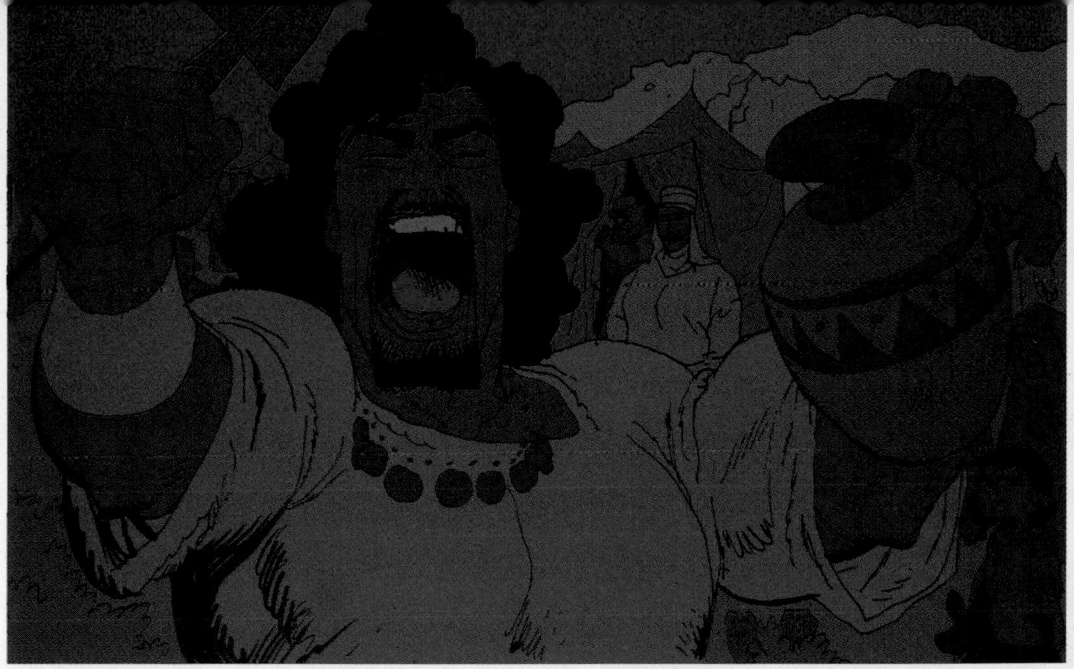

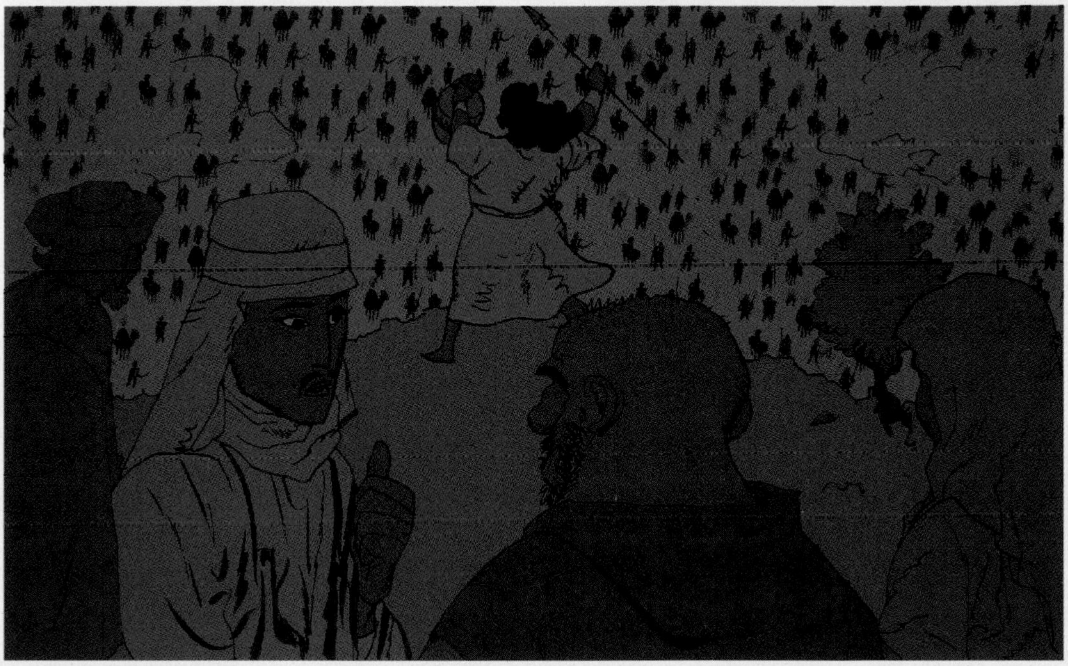

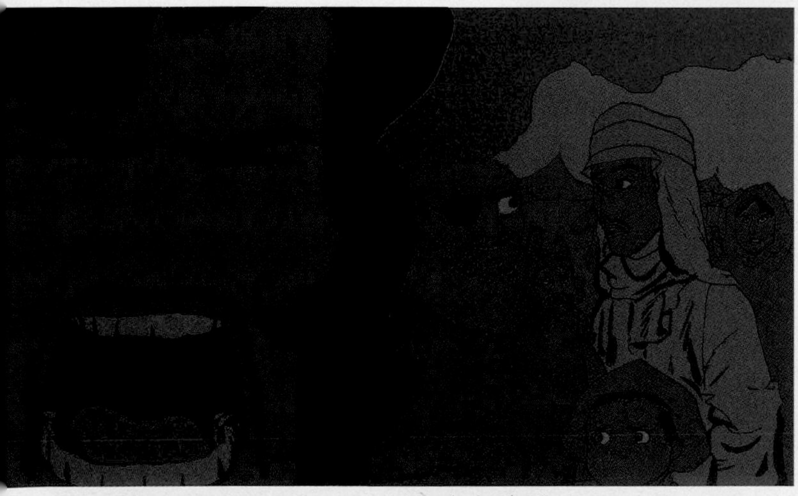

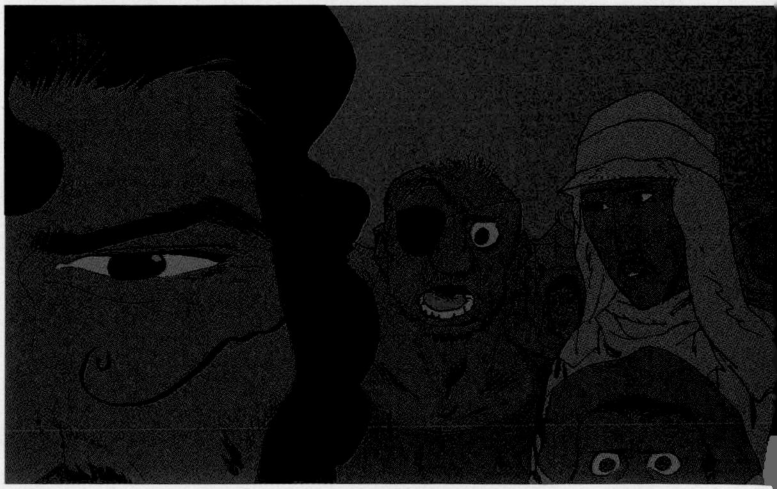

David yells at Abner below, "And now, see where the king's spear is, and the jar of water which was at his head-place?"

"You lucky dog!" says Joab. "You're a hero!"

Saul calls from the valley below. "Is this your voice, my son David?"

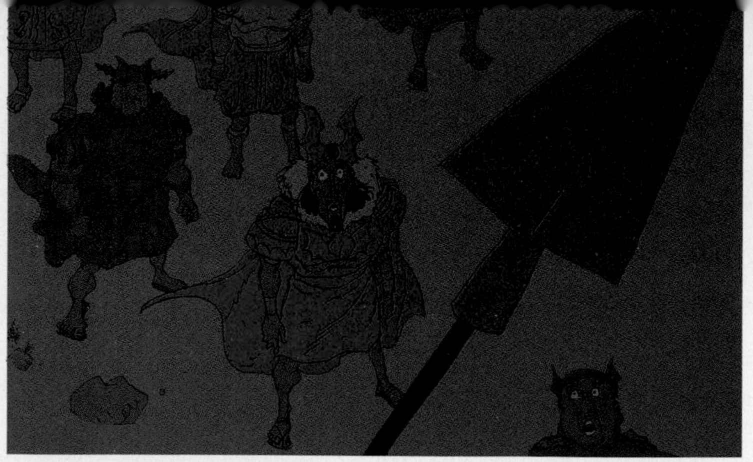

Abishai says, "David wouldn't let me kill Saul! Gave me his usual, 'Who can destroy the LORD's anointed and remain guiltless,' bit."

"Again? What is it with him?"

"It's sick."

David shouts, "My voice, my lord, O king! Why is this, that my lord is pursuing his servant? For what have I done, and what in my hand is evil?"

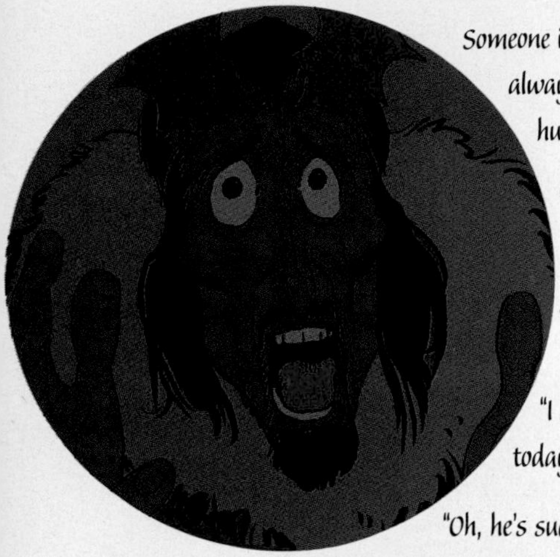

Someone in David's camp mutters, "It's always about him. There are six hundred families here following him! Why? To starve in the wilderness until Saul's army finally slaughters us?"

"And now, please let my lord the king hear the words of his servant. If the LORD has moved you against me, let Him accept an offering. But if men have done it, let them be cursed before the LORD; for they have driven me out today from joining myself with the inheritance of the LORD, saying, Go, serve other gods. And now, let not my blood fall to the earth before the face of the LORD, for the king of Israel has come out to seek a flea, as one hunts the partridge in the mountains."

"I have sinned. Return, my son David, for I shall not do evil to you anymore, because my life has been precious in your eyes today."

"Oh, he's such a liar!" says a little old lady in David's camp.

"Blessed be you, my son David. Both you shall surely do, also you shall surely be able."

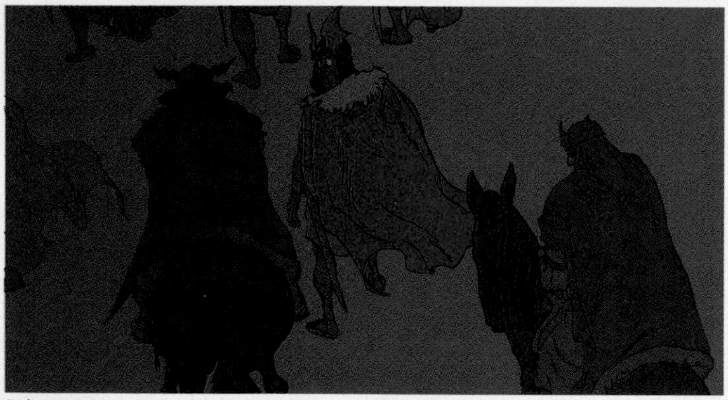

"They're leaving," says Abishai. "Should've let me kill him."

"Now what?" asks one of David's followers. "Keep starving in the desert?"

"Maybe we should go back to Israel," a woman suggests. "We were starving in Israel, but at least soldiers weren't trying to kill us."

"Well, not all of us, they weren't," says a young man.

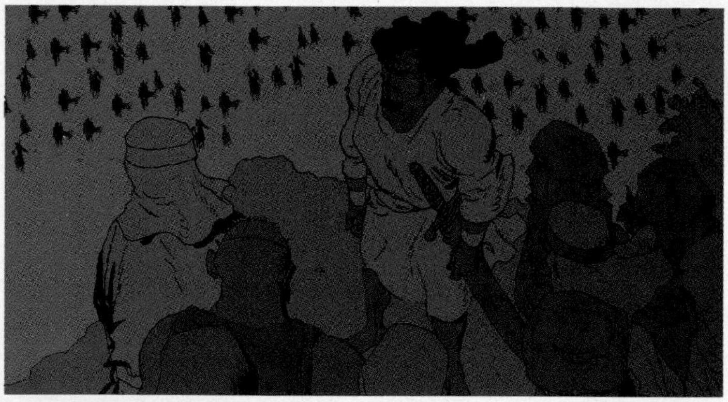

"I thought David was going to be king of Israel someday!" says one man..

"You want to stay here and hope Saul dies of old age before we starve?" asks his wife.

"Shh. Don't mention starving in front of the children," the man answers.

Joab tells David, "Saul will be back, you know. He'll keep chasing us. We're not safe here."

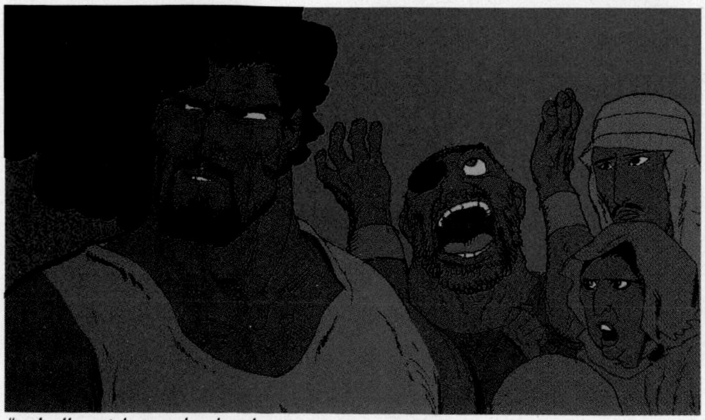

"I shall perish one day by the hand of Saul, I see that now."

"Finally! What was your first clue?"

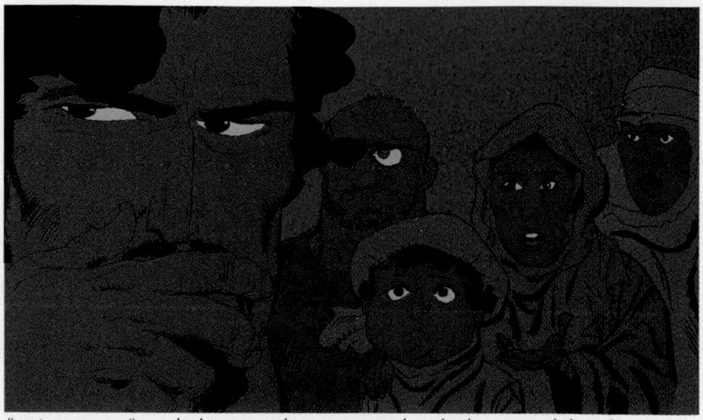

"Quiet. Let me think."

"Watch this, son. The great David is thinking. Watch how he employs wisdom to solve what appears to be an impossible problem."

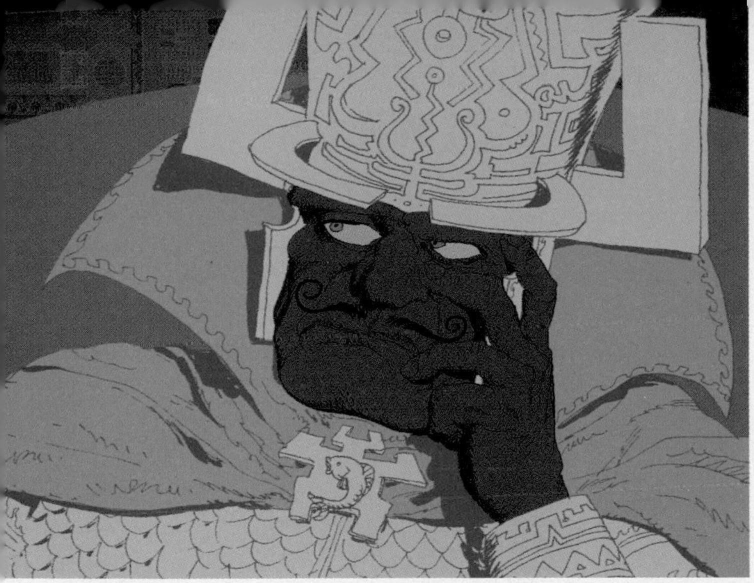

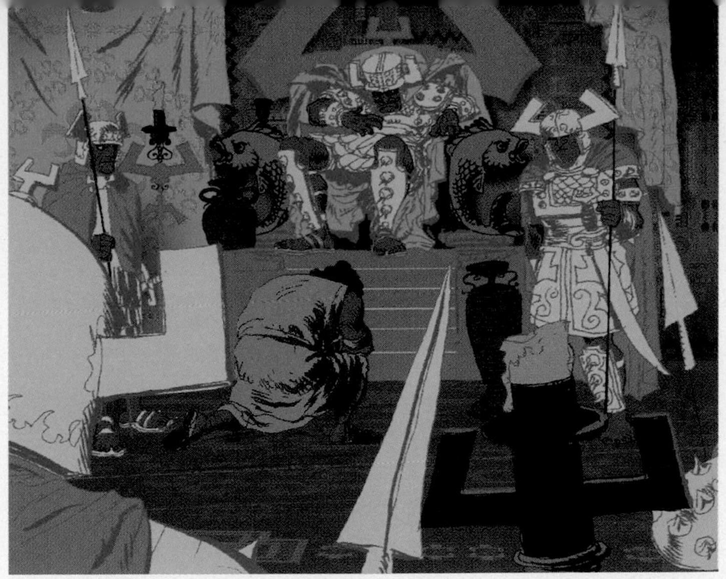

"I was right. You are insane," says King Achish.

"Hear me out, your majesty," David says, "I pretended to be mad last time we met. I was afraid for my life. But since then six hundred men and their families have somehow fallen into my care. I'm sure you have heard as all the region has, that Saul seeks my death. You may also have heard that my small band has bested Saul's vast army twice. You have also probably heard of how we saved the town of Keilah--"

"--From the Philistines! From us!" shouts Achish.

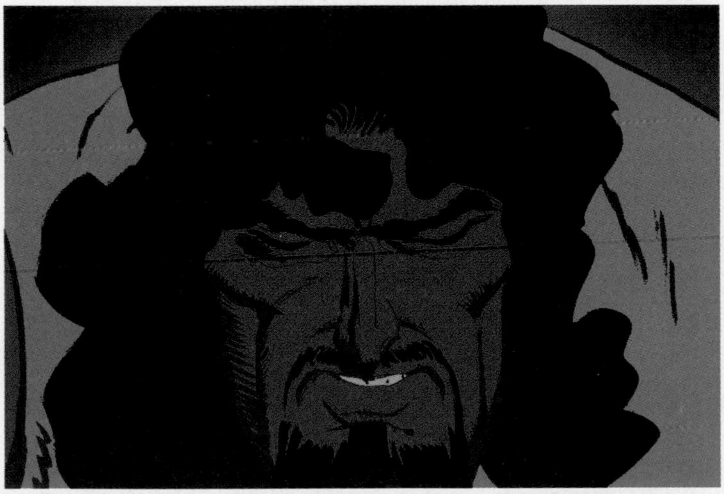

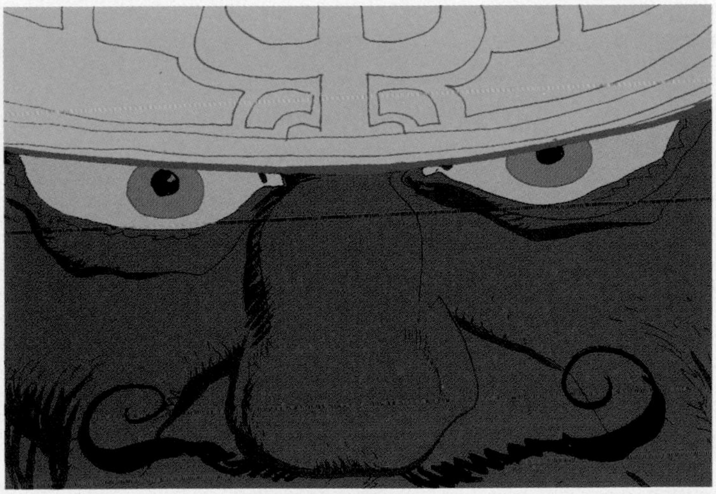

"Yes, and those ungrateful Keilites wanted to turn us over to Saul! My point is, I have a considerable force of fighting men and acknowledged skill as a military commander. Surely these assets are of as much value to you as they are despised by your enemy Saul."

"Suppose I decide, as Saul has, that you and your forces are too dangerous to live?"

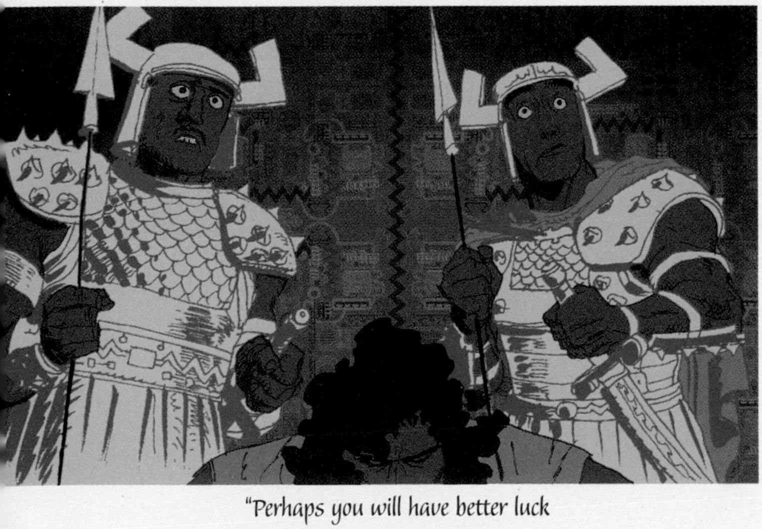

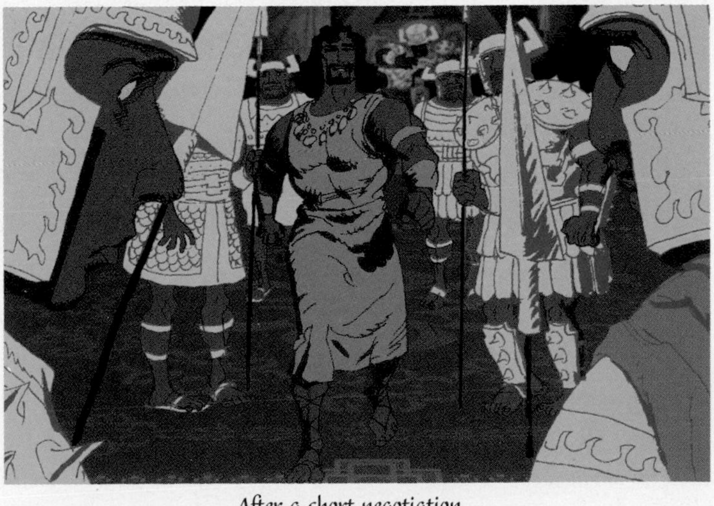

"Perhaps you will have better luck than Saul at killing us."

After a short negotiation, David exits smiling.

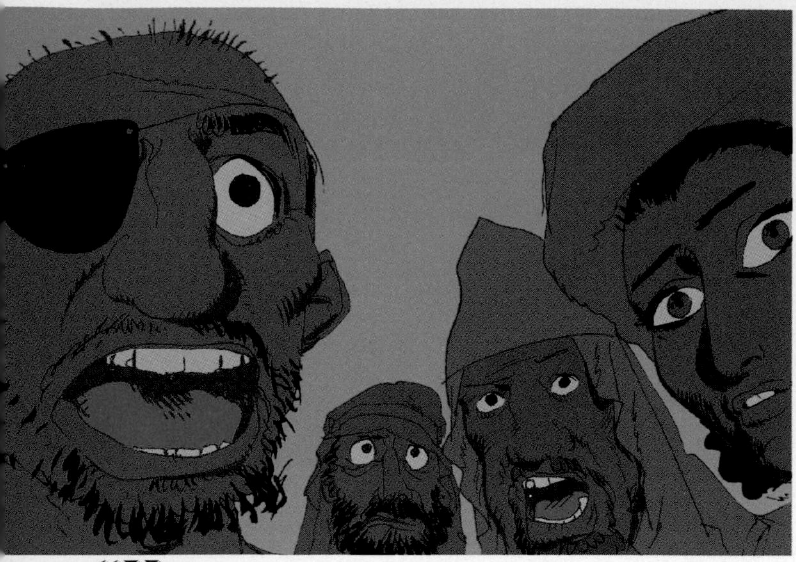

"He gave us a town?" asks Joab, "A whole town? How did you pull off that little transaction?"

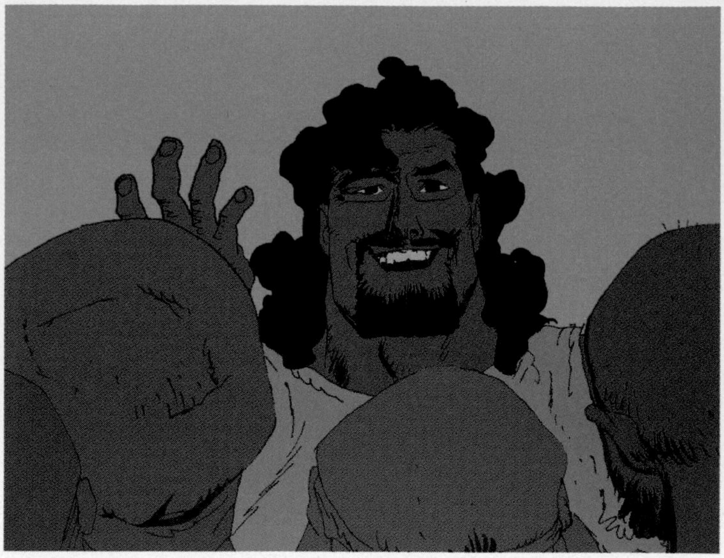

"I said, 'Why should your servant live in the royal city with you?' King Achish figures we might do him some good, but he's not stupid. He doesn't want me any closer than I want him. So he gave us the town of Ziklag."

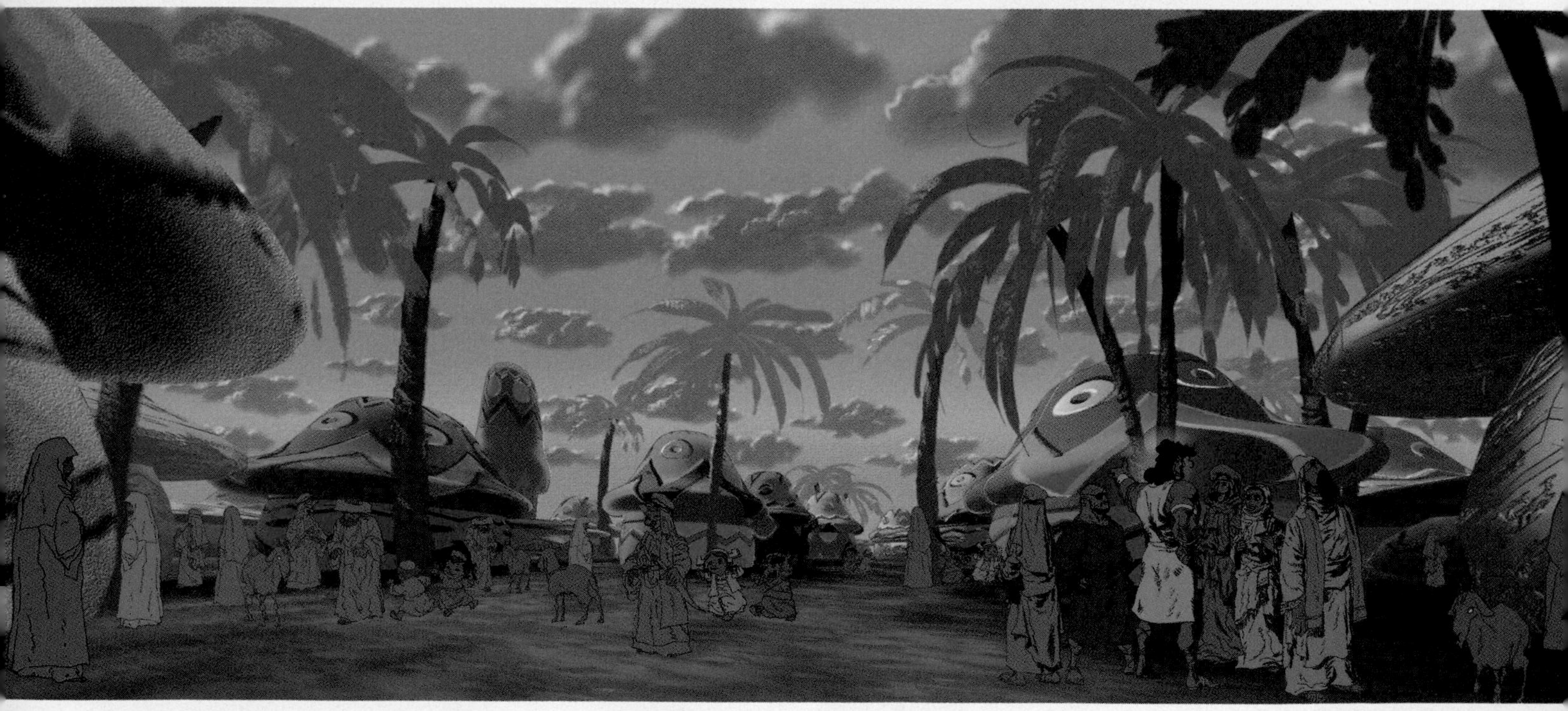

"David, I saw the perfect house for us," says Ahimoam.

"Don't listen to her," says Abigail, "The kitchen's a joke. I found the house for us over there."

"Ziklag. Was this town empty yesterday?" asks Joab.

"Evacuated after the last war," says David. "It's a terrible location. Too close to Israel for the Philistines, too close to Philistia for the Israelites. Good for us, though."

"Your house has no light, Abigail," Ahinoam says, "David, you have to see the windows on the house I picked. Gorgeous views.

"After a year in the wilderness, who needs views?" says Abigail, "Give me a kitchen."

Joab says, "So that's it, then. I hear Saul's given up chasing us. And we now have our new home. All's well that ends well."

"Not exactly," says David. "Nothing is free in this world. Achish is understandably suspicious of us, and he expects to be paid for this town and his protection."

"But we don't have anything!" says Joab.

David says, "We have swords. Achish expects loot."

"All I know is we'd better have a good kitchen and bathroom," says Abigail.

"All I know is we'd better have a picture window and closets!" says Ahinoam.

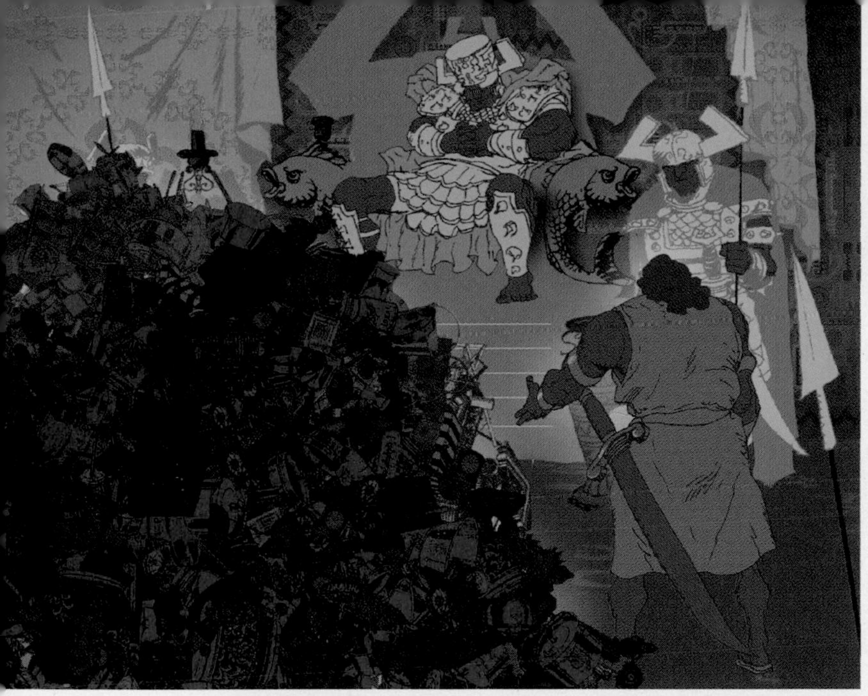

"Quite a fortune!" says Achish. "Where did you make raids this week?"

"Against the south of Judah, and against the south of the Jerahmeelites, and to the south of the Kenites, my lord."

"Wonderful. Keep up the good work."

After David and his men leave, Achish tells an advisor, "David has made himself so hated among his people in Israel, surely he has become my servant forever."

Outside the palace, Abishai says, "We'll never get away with this."

"We'd better," says David.

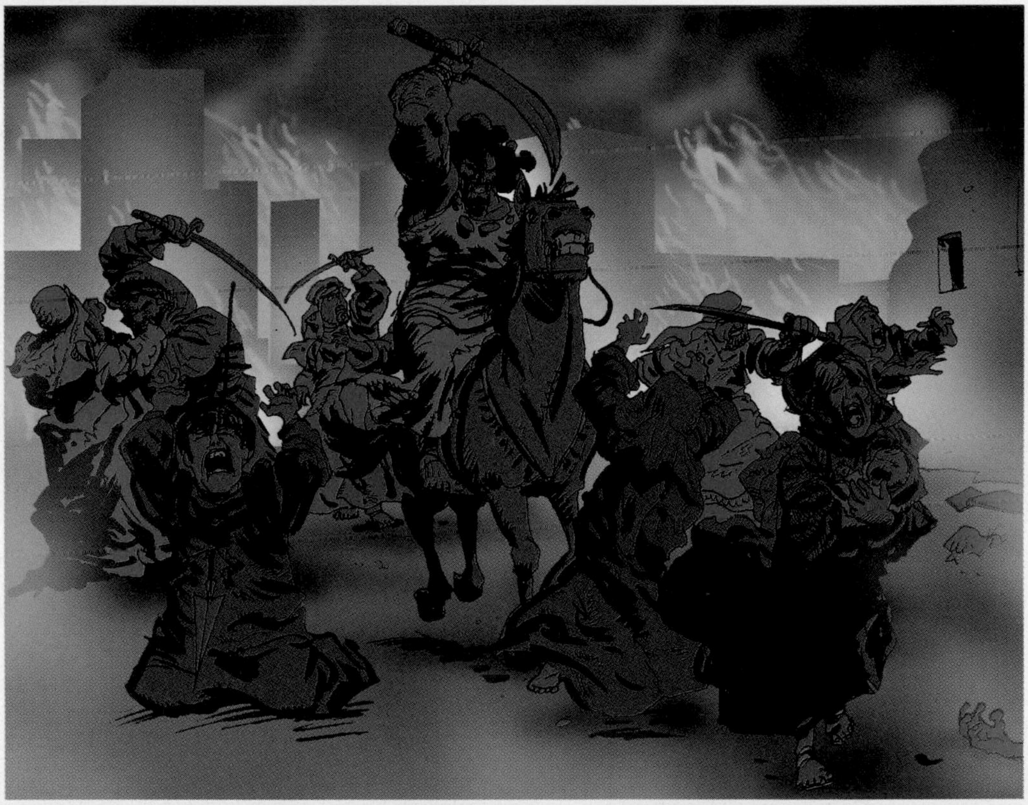

Shur, land of the Amalekites.

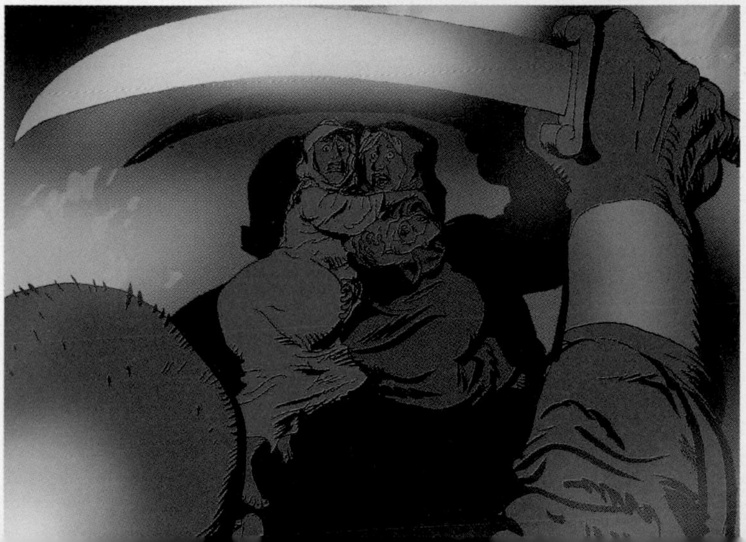

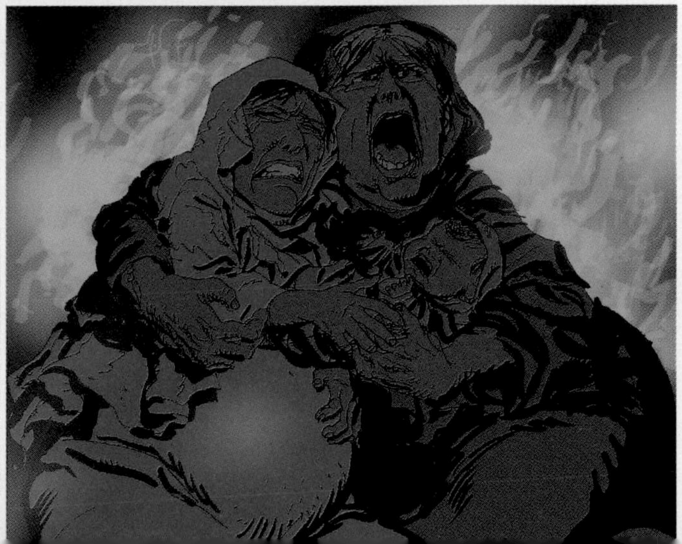

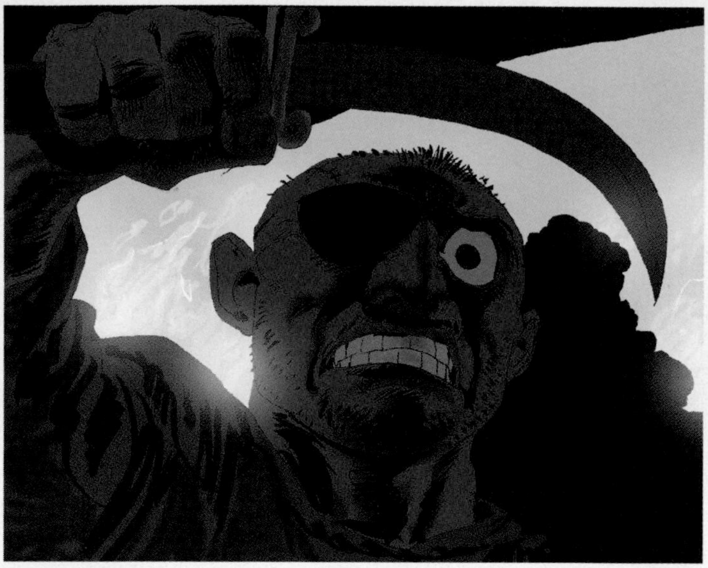

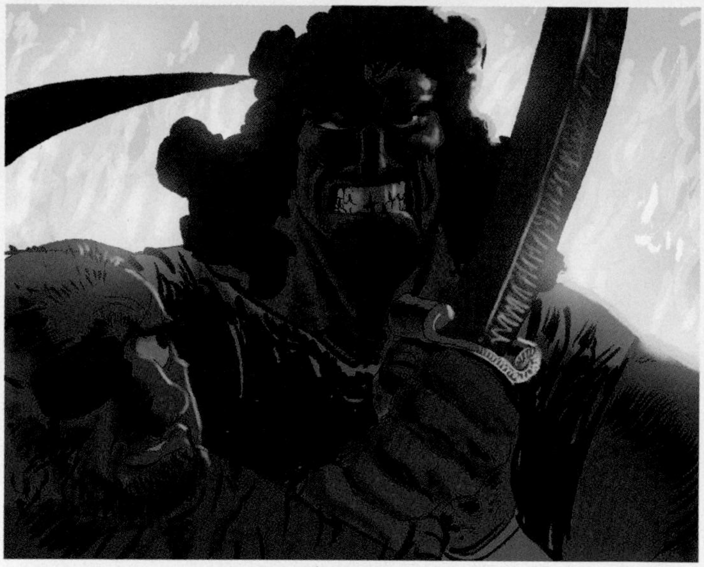

"I said no prisoners."

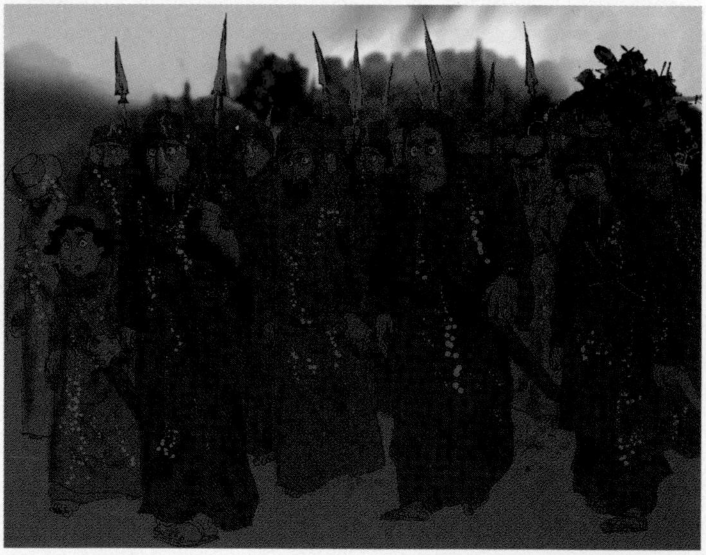

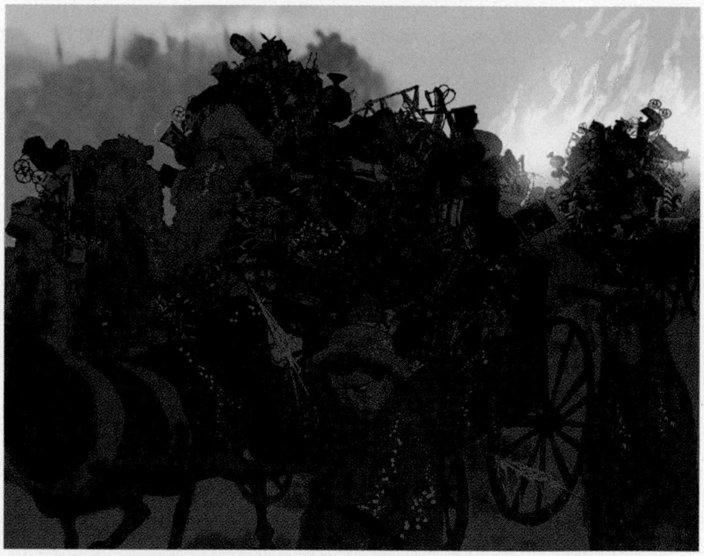

"What's wrong with you?" says David. "Use your head! If Achish ever finds out we've been raiding Philistines and not Israelites, we'll all be dead! Do you want to go raiding against your own people? You want to kill Jews?"

"We've been living like this for over a year," says Joab. "Is this how the rest of our lives will be?"

"It's them or us. We can't risk leaving anyone alive who could report back to Achish. It's them or us."

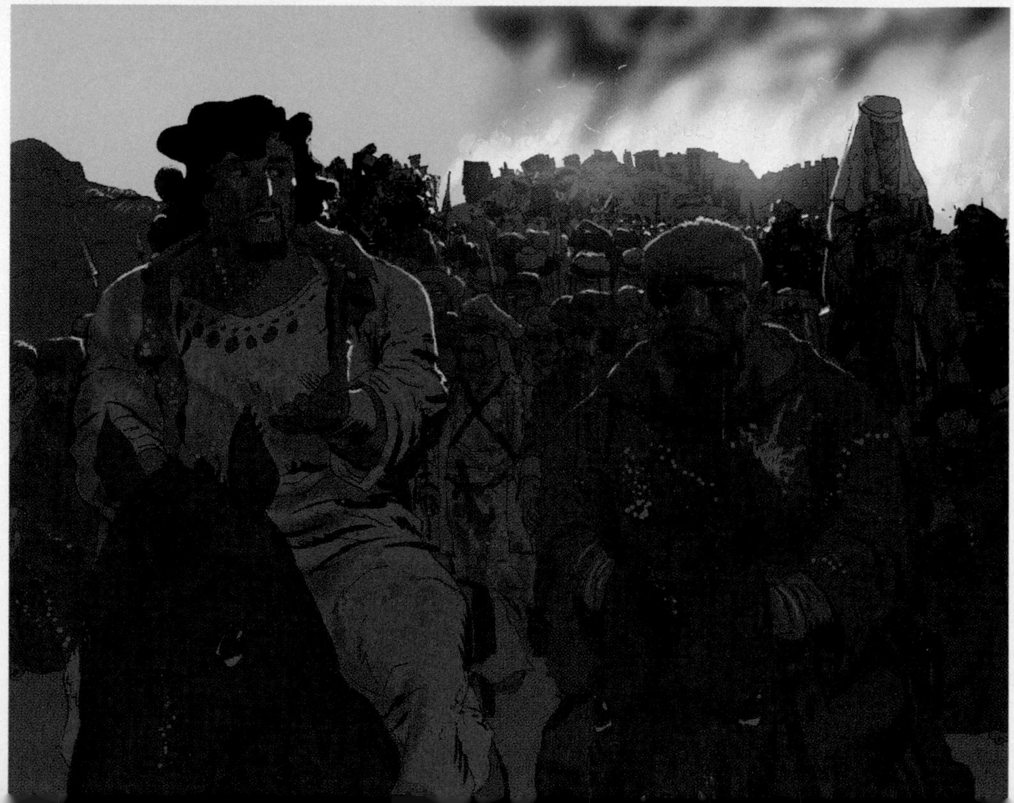

After delivering more loot to Achish in Gath, David and his men return to Ziklag, reuniting with wives and children.

A chariot approaches. "David, son of Jesse. King Achish requests the presence of you and your soldiers at Gath immediately."

"We have just returned from Gath! Is anything wrong?"

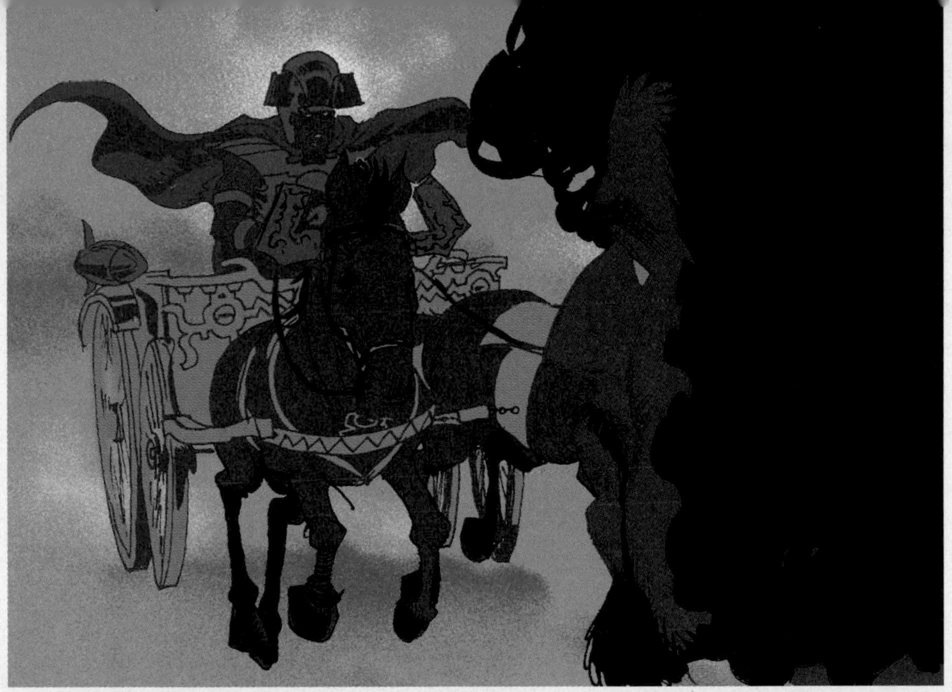

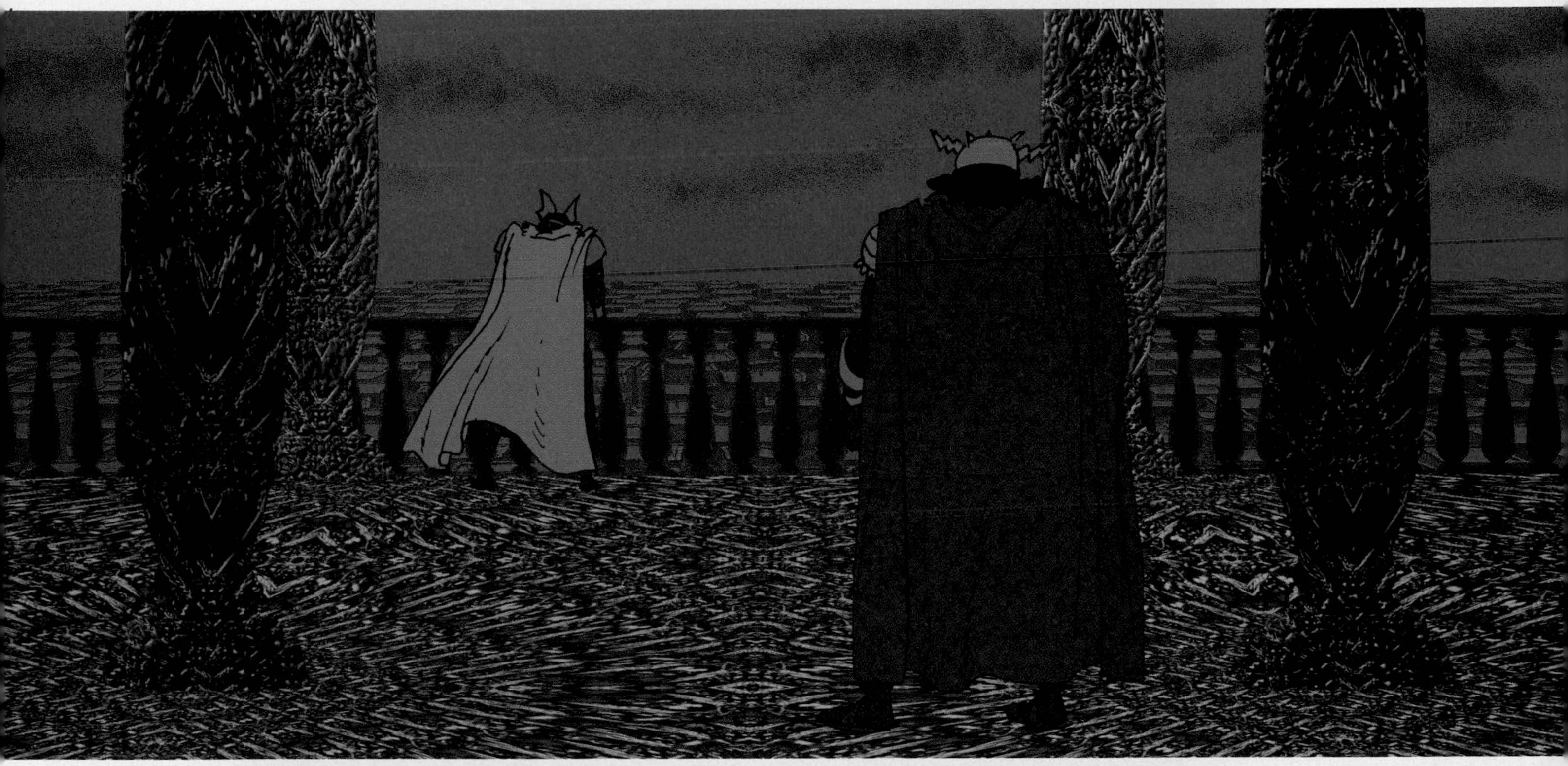

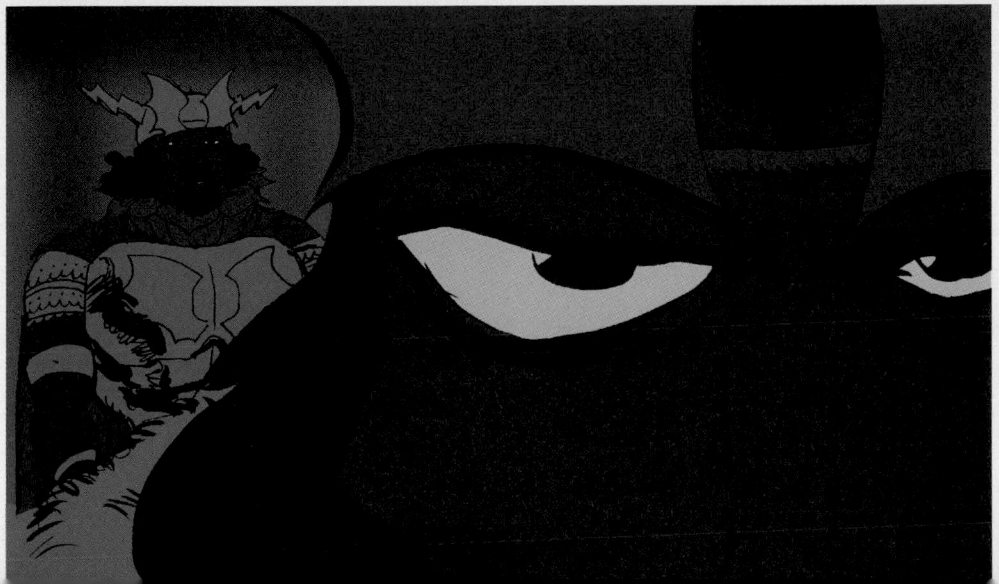

Saul's palace.

Abner enters. "Your Majesty, the Philistines are gathering their armies once again, preparing to war against us."

"And David is with them," says Saul.

"Most likely."

"David is with them."

"I can't believe this," says one of David's followers. "My parents still live in Israel! My brothers are in the Israeli army! I can't fight them!"

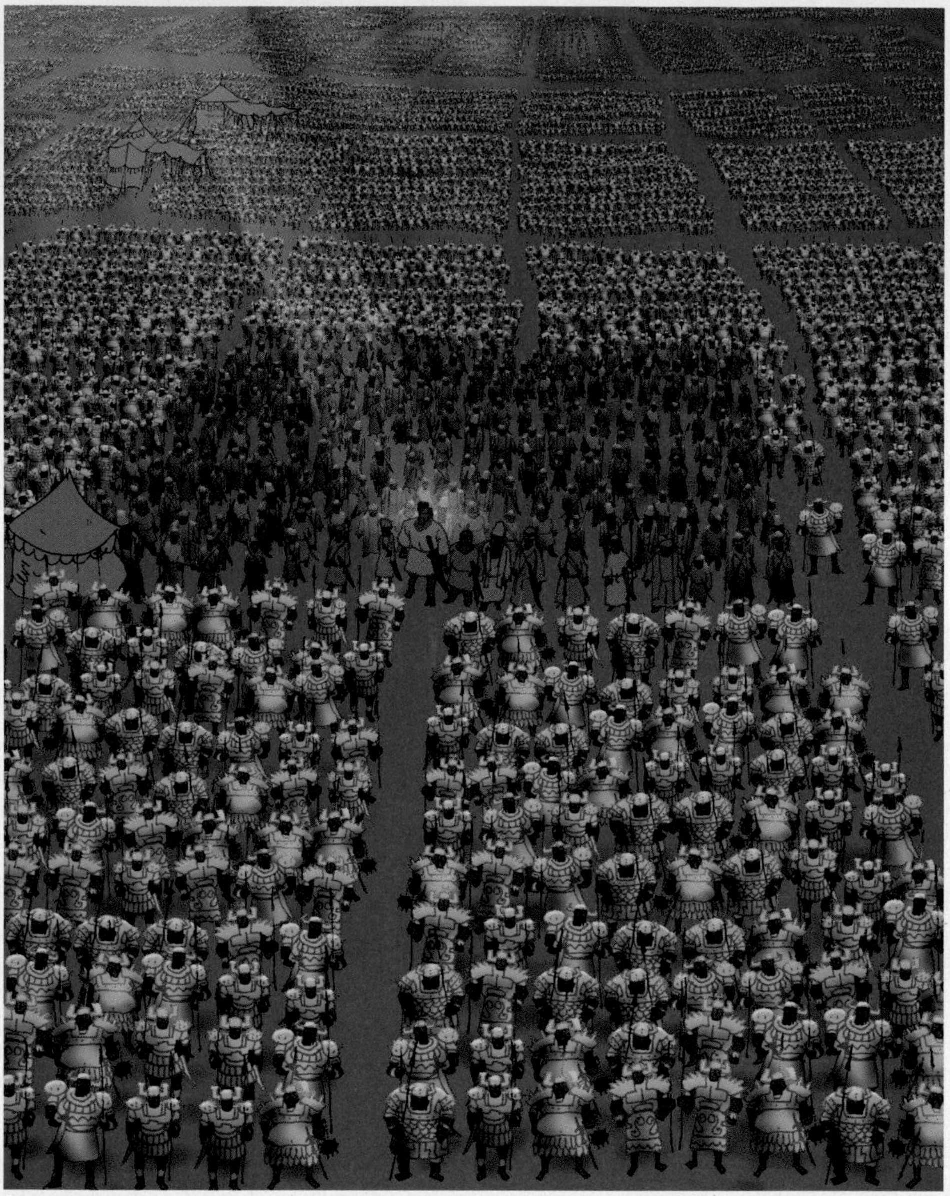

"It's the same with all of us," says Abishai. "My wife didn't want me to go."

"You told your wife?" says another man. "My wife thinks I'm on a fishing trip."

Joab says, "What are we gonna do? We're surrounded by the entire Philistine army! They'll kill us if we don't fight!"

"This is all David's fault," says Abishai.

A young man says, "Don't give up on David. Maybe he's got a plan."

"How can you say that?" asks Abiathar.

"He got us this far, didn't he?"

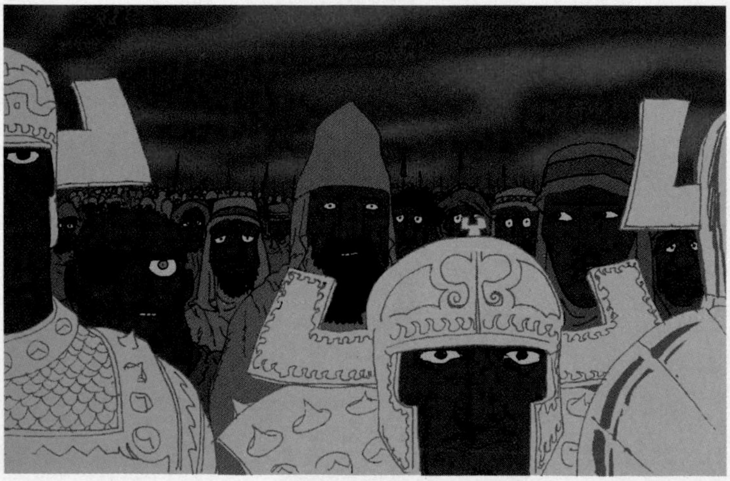

"You're an idiot," says Abiathar.

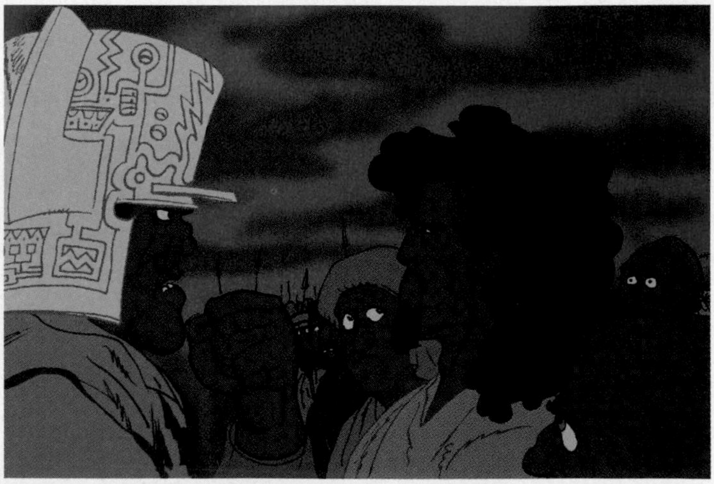

Achish says, "David, you shall go out with me in the army, you and our men. Together you and I shall destroy the Israelites and have our revenge."

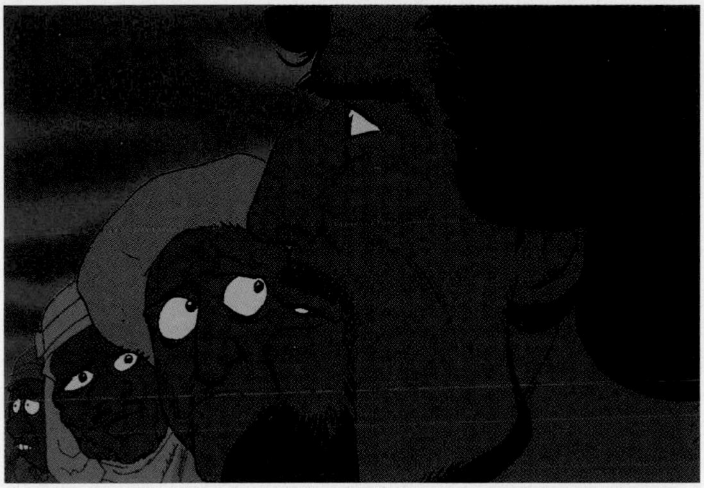

"You shall see for yourself what your servant can do."

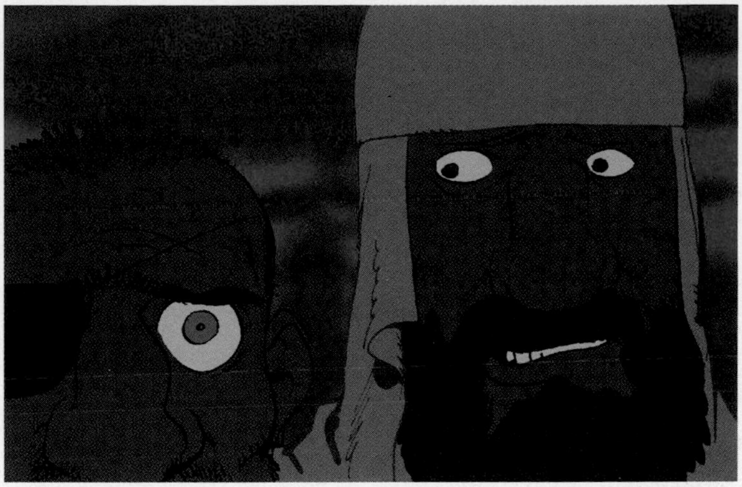

"What is that supposed to mean?"

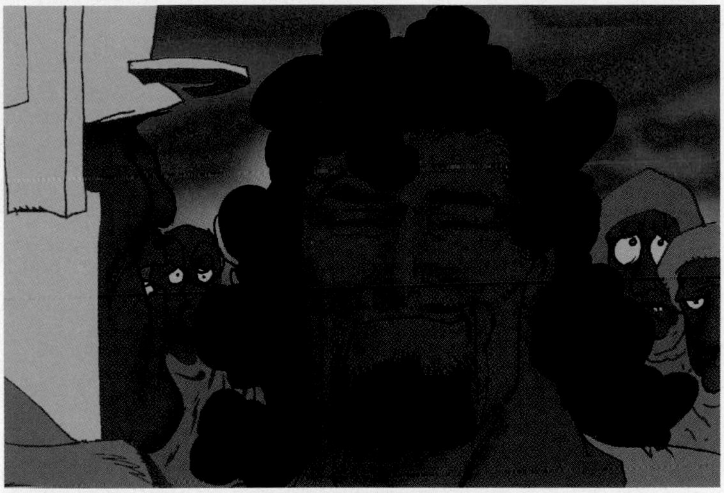

Achish smiles. "Then, David, I appoint you my official bodyguard for life."

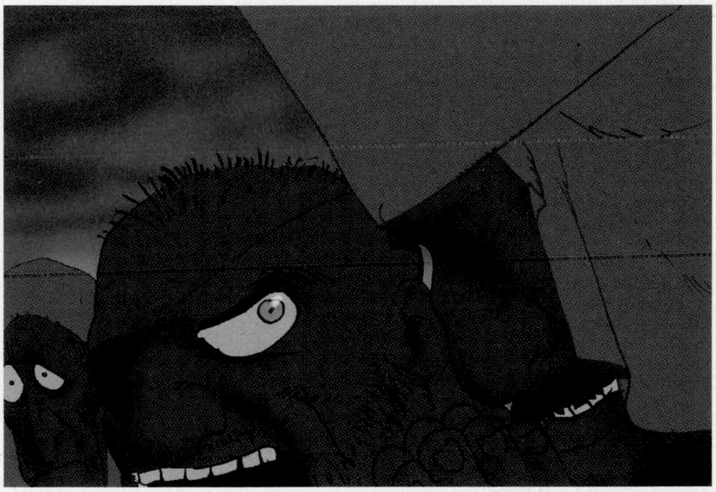

"What are you doing?"

"What can I do? I'm praying we lose."

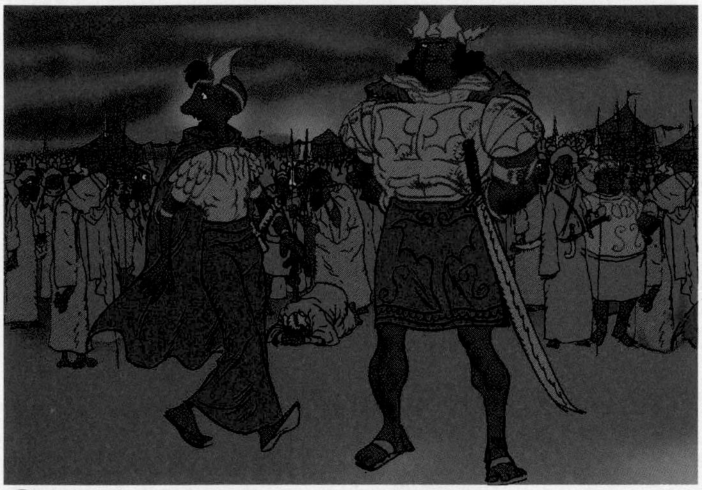

Saul's camp.

"The men look worried," says Jonathan.

"They only look worried. Inside they're terrified."

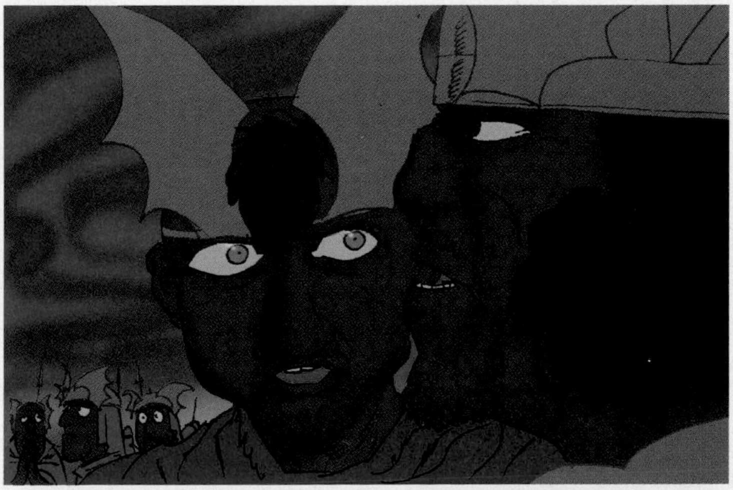

"Attitude is ninety percent of any battle. Perhaps my father should make a speech to inspire the troops."

"He already made the speech. You're witnessing the result...By the way, I think you should know-- Your father went to a medium last night."

"A what?"

"You know, a medium? Talks to dead people for money?"

"I thought he had all the mediums and spirit-knowers outlawed."

"He did. He had to go all the way to Endor to find one. The king was wearing a disguise, since he didn't want to be spotted breaking his own law, and then the old witch didn't want to help him because she thought he was a cop. Imagine the old woman's face when she found out it was the king."

"I don't understand. Why did he do that?"

"He wanted to talk to the prophet Samuel."

"Samuel?"

"See, God hasn't spoken to your father personally in years, except for sending the occasional evil spirit to torment him. And with all the priests dead, there's no way to communicate with God."

"So the old woman couldn't help Dad, which put him in a deeper funk, eh?"

"No, Samuel's ghost told the king we were going to lose, that Saul was going to die today, and that his crown would be given to David. Hence the funk, as you so quaintly put it."

"And Dad paid the old lady for this?"

"Actually, she fed him. Baked some cakes, killed a calf...She felt sorry for him. She begged him to eat. To be fair, this was all after Saul fainted."

"Is it possible for us to reschedule this war? Just push it back a day?"

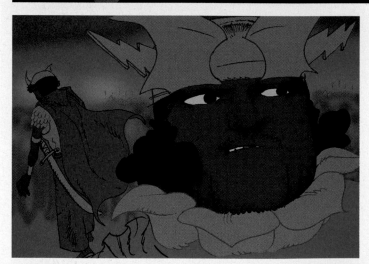

"Sure. I'll send a note to the Philistines. I'm sure they wouldn't want to fight us when we aren't at our best."

"I'll talk to Dad."

"You do that. I'll give the troops another pep talk. Mine is titled, 'Deserters Will Be Executed'."

"David's out there somewhere. Waiting to finally kill me. He can't fool me. He only let me off the hook those other two times because I had a bigger army."

"Are you all right, Dad?"

"I can tell you the exact moment God turned against me. I remember it vividly."

"Come on, Dad. Think positive. You always told me––"

"It was when we destroyed the Amalekites. Remember? When we went and killed every man, woman and child of the Amalekites. That's when God abandoned me."

"Okay, look, Dad. I'll admit, maybe it was wrong to kill the women and children, but––"

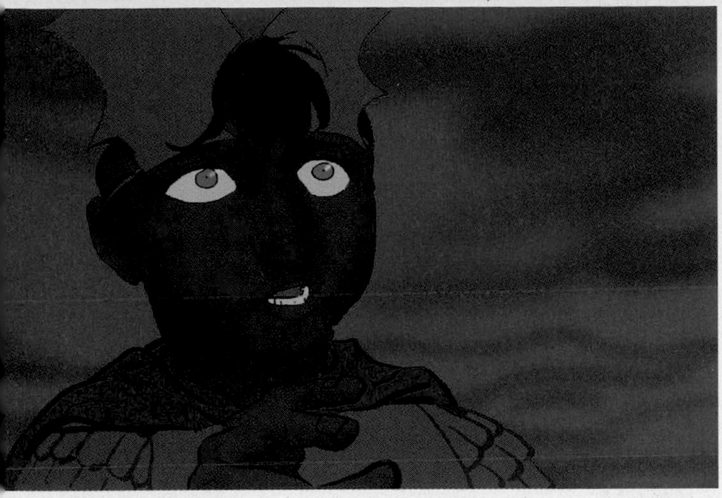

"I should have killed the livestock also."

"I don't think I'll ever understand you, Dad."

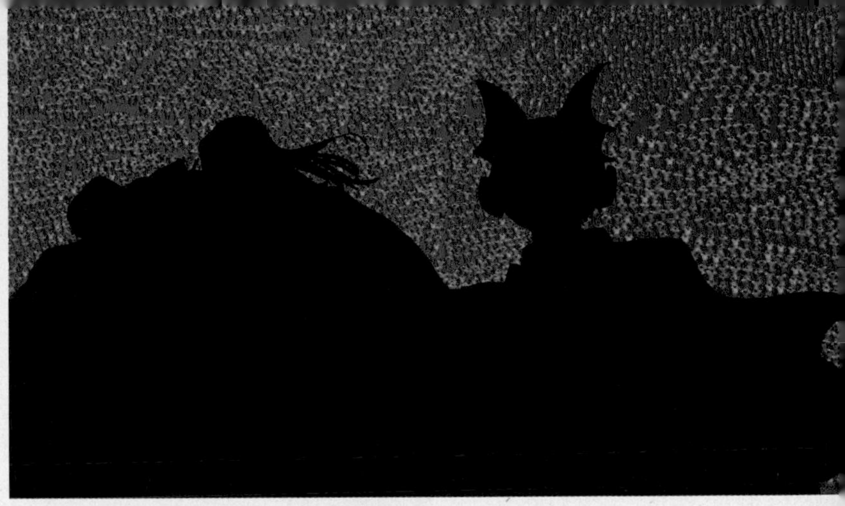

Saul says, "God had told me through Samuel, 'You shall put to death all from man to woman, from little one to suckling, from ox to sheep, from camel to ass.' But my troops refused to waste perfectly good livestock. I mean, were they supposed to fight for free? The winner always gets the loot! That's the whole point!"

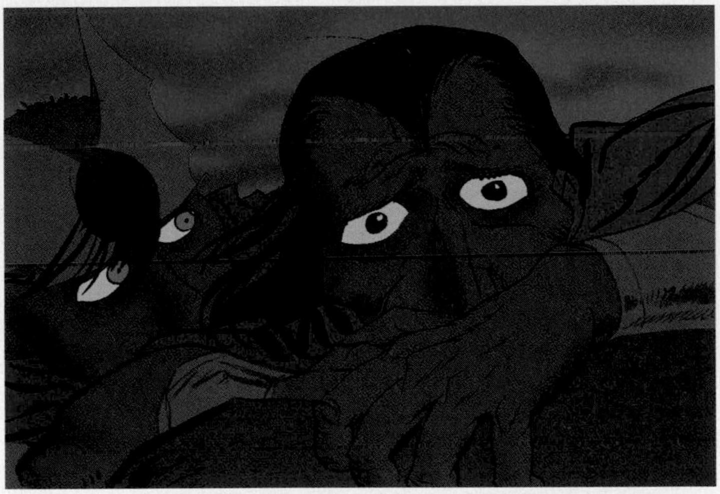

"Dad, about today's battle--"

"You try telling ten thousand blood-soaked foot soldiers that they can't have their cattle, or a free ox! I'll admit it, those guys scared me. I let them keep the animals. That's when God turned against me. That's when Samuel, right before he quit, said the kingdom had been taken from me by God and given to another."

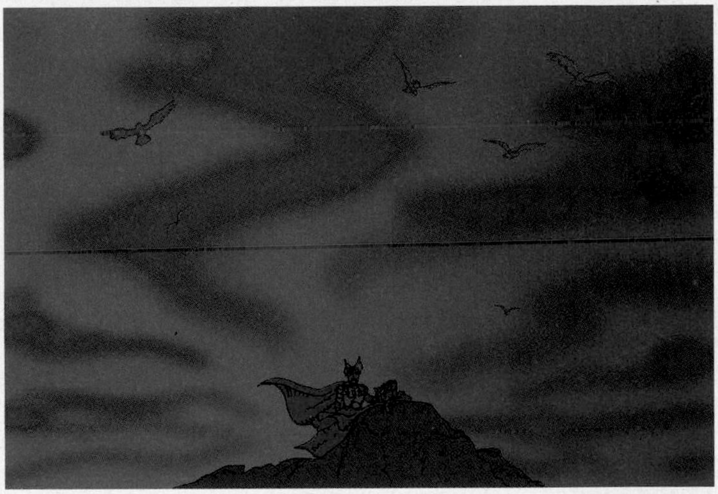

"Dad. That was years ago."

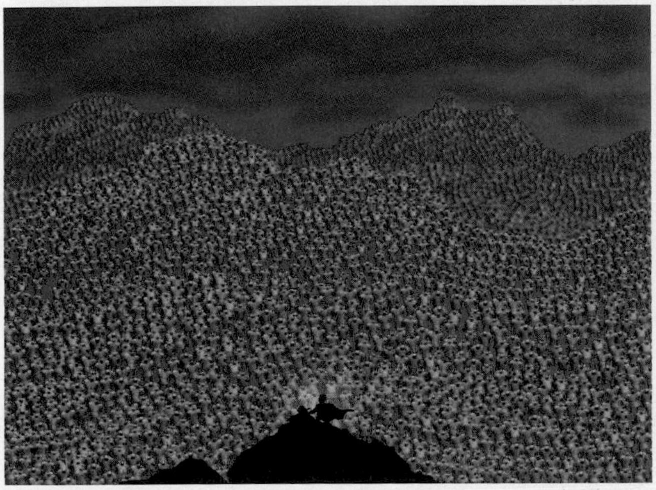

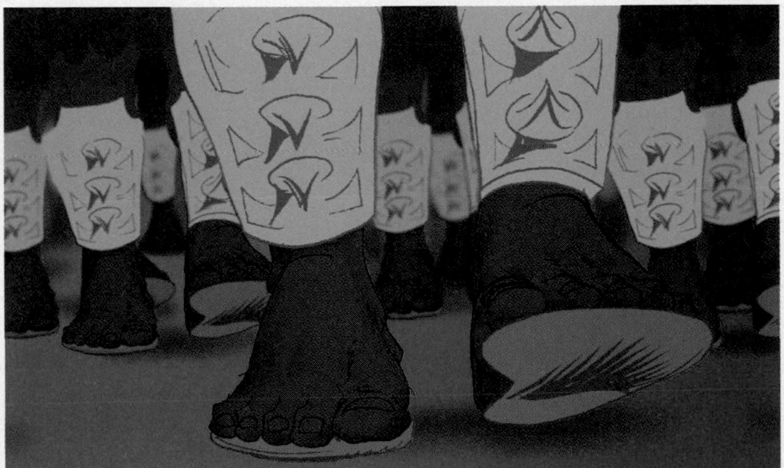

"Who does God have to hurry for? At any rate, it ends today."

"Here we go," mumbles Joab, "Off to destroy our own kind."

"What do we do? What do we do?" worries another of David's men.

"We should have killed Saul when we had the chance," says Abishai.

"Well, here comes another chance!" says Abiathar.

"But this time if Saul loses, Israel loses!" says Abishai.

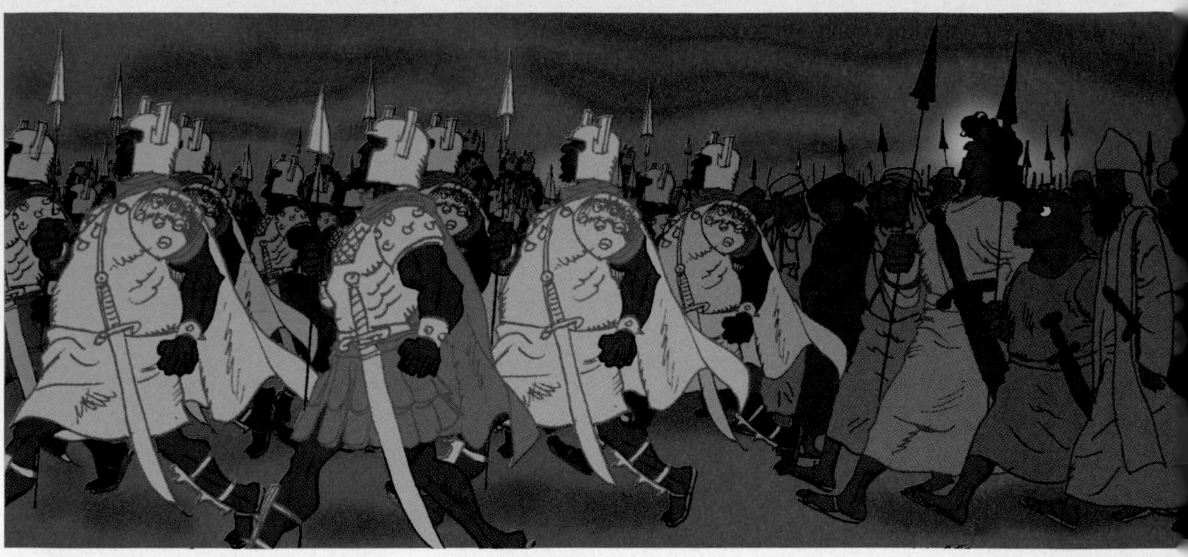

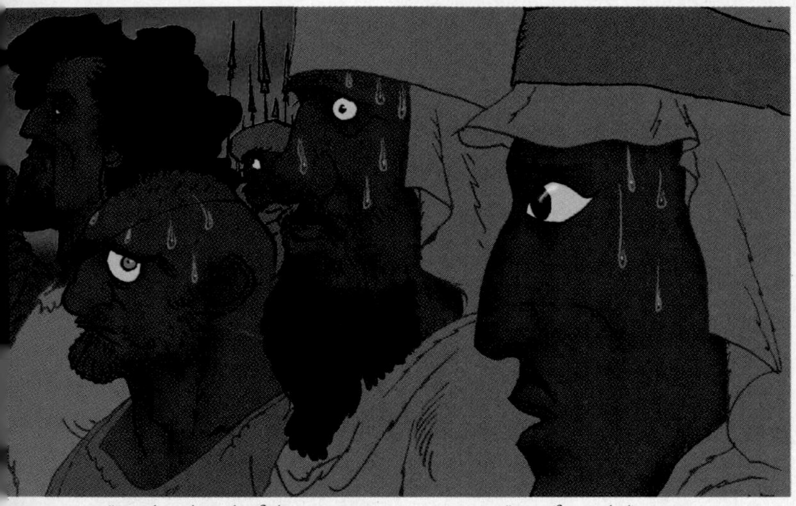

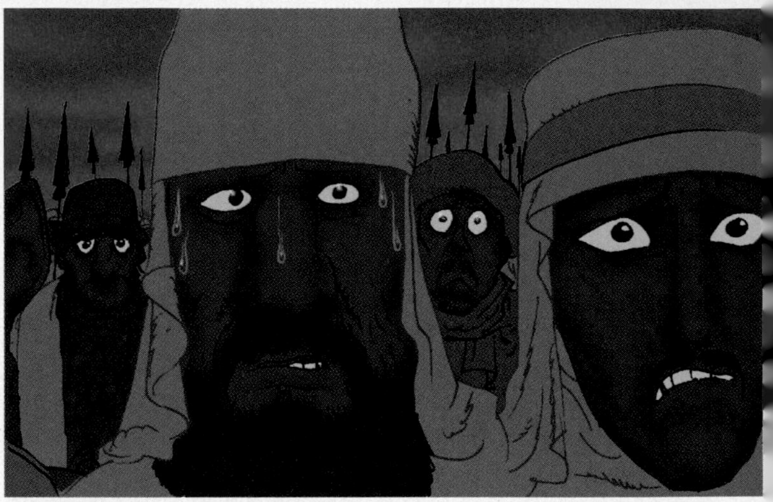

"Maybe when the fighting starts, we could start killing Philistines," says Joab. "We'd get killed, but at least we could take a bunch of them with us."

"But if we rebel against Philistia," aks Abishai, "what will happen to our wives and children in Ziklag?"

"You're right," says Joab. "We have to destroy Israel. It's them or us."

"We're damned if we do, and damned if we don't."

"And this is our priest saying this!"

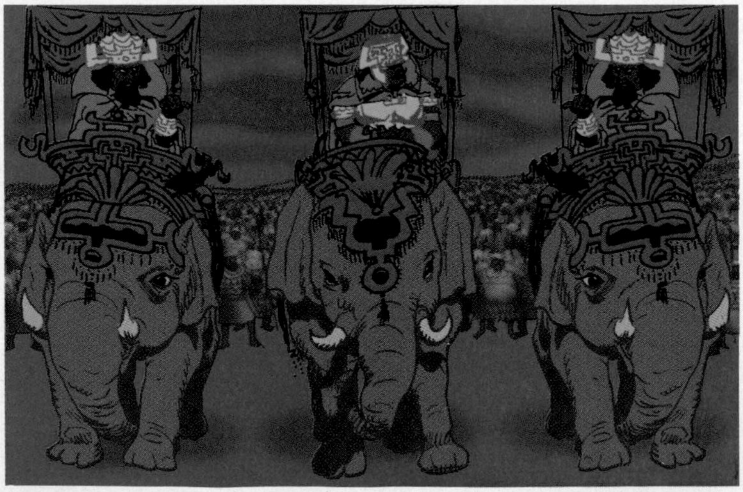

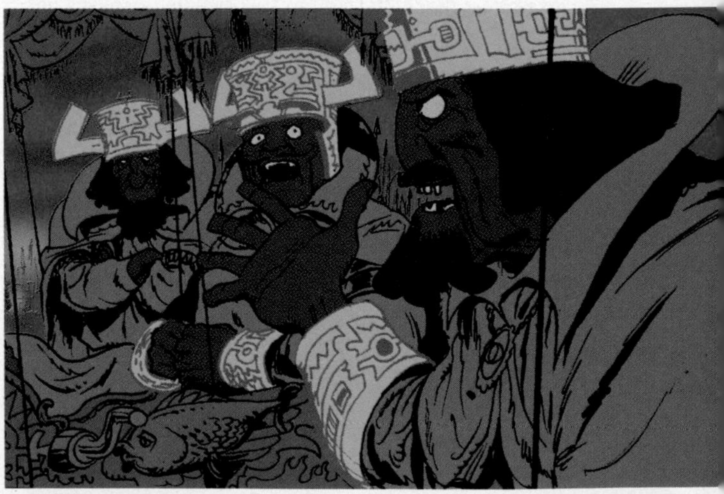

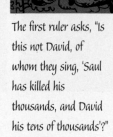

"What are these Hebrews doing here, Achish?" asks a Philistine ruler.

Achish responds, "Is this not David the servant of Saul the king of Israel who has been with me for over a year? And I have not found anything evil in him from the day he fell away until today."

"What are you, stupid?" says a second ruler. "He can't go down with us into battle! He'll start fighting against us! What better way to regain the favor of his master Saul, if not with the heads of our men?"

The first ruler asks, "Is this not David, of whom they sing, 'Saul has killed his thousands, and David his tens of thousands'?"

The second ruler says, "I hate that song. Everywhere I go I hear it."

The first ruler says, "Send David and his men back to that town you gave them."

"When I was young, they knew how to write songs. This new stuff's just a bunch of noise," says the second ruler.

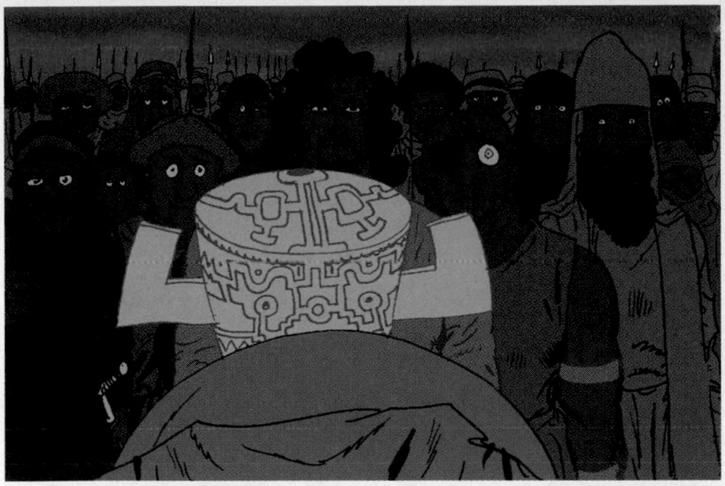

"As God lives," says Achish, "surely you have been loyal and I would be pleased to have you come with me out to the battlefield. For I have not found evil in since you joined me."

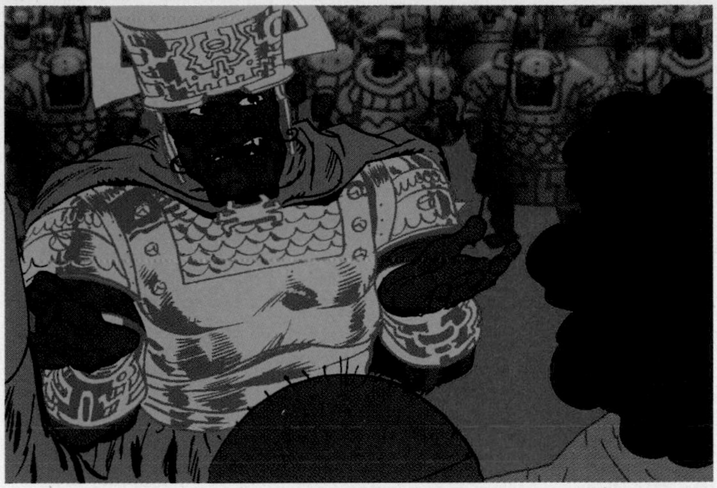

"But the other rulers don't like you. And now return, and go in peace, that you not do evil in the eyes of the rulers of the Philistines."

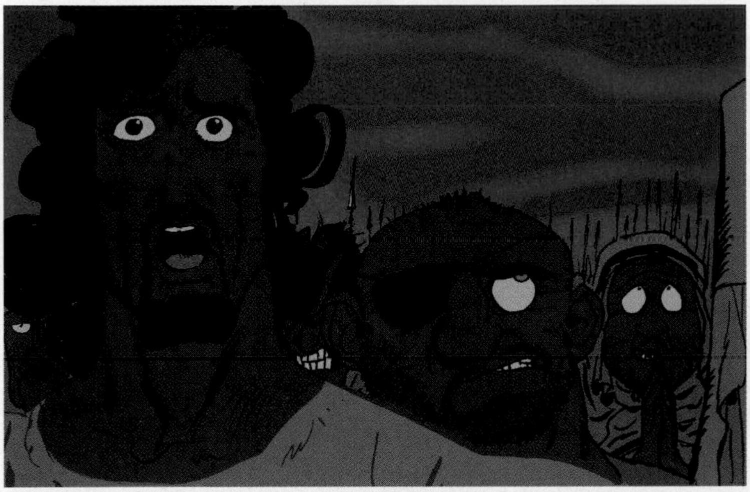

"But what have I done? And what have you found in your servant from the day that I have been in your presence until today, that I may not go in and fight against the enemies of my lord the king?"

"I know, I know," says Achish, "you've been wonderful, like an angel of God. It's not me, it's the other rulers. So you have to go."

Joab whispers, "Keep your mouth shut, David. Please!"

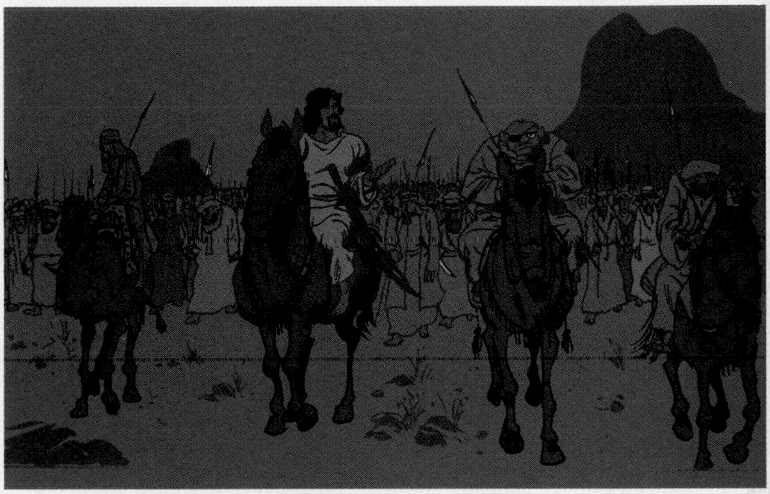

On the journey home, David tries to relieve the palpable tension of his men. "Well, all's well that ends well, eh?"

"That was way too close for comfort,' Joab says, "If we hadn't gotten lucky..."

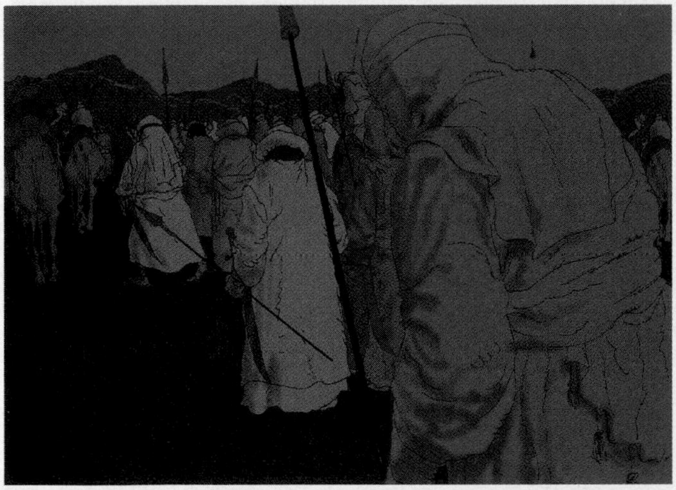

"But we did get lucky!" says David, "God has once again interceded on our behalf."

Abishai asks, "What if Saul wins the war?"

"Or worse, what if Israel loses?" asks Abiathar.

David smiles. "Everything will work out fine. For now we can return safely to our wives and children in Ziklag. Remember, God is always on our side."

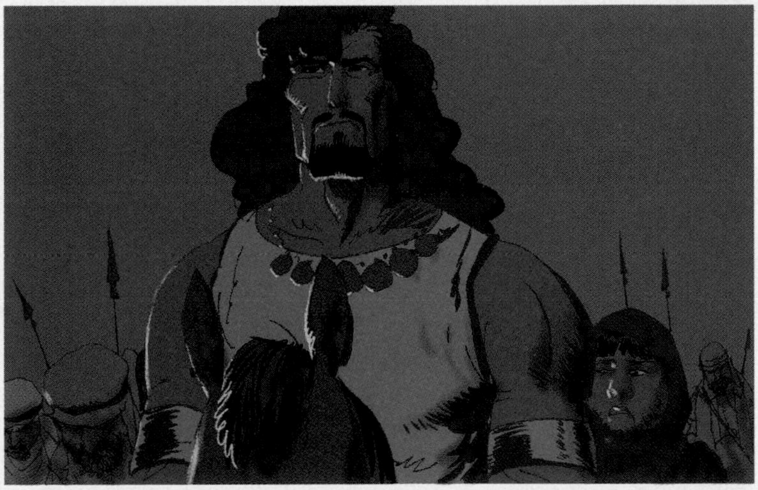

"What's that smoke on the horizon?" someone asks.

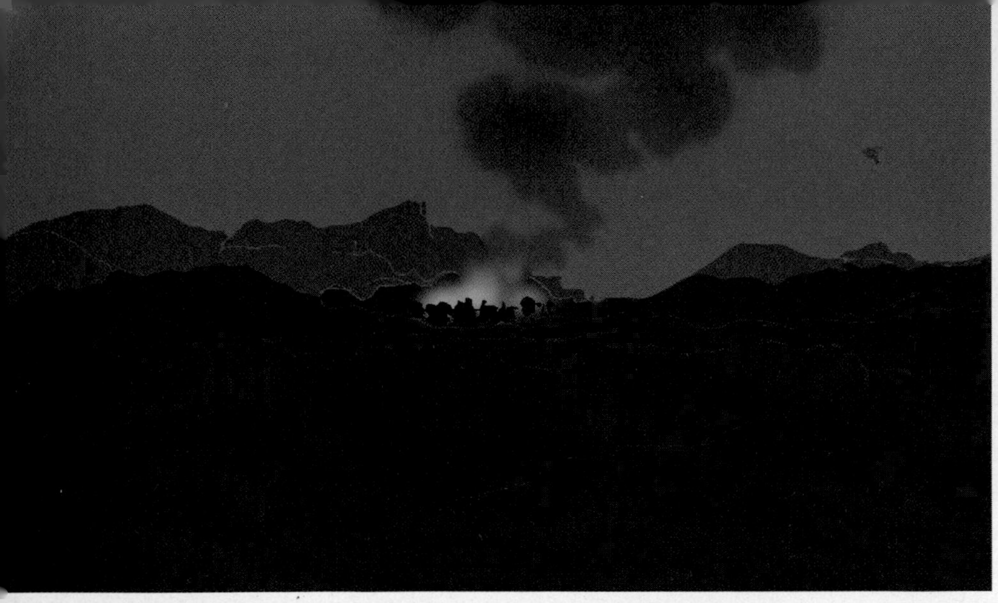

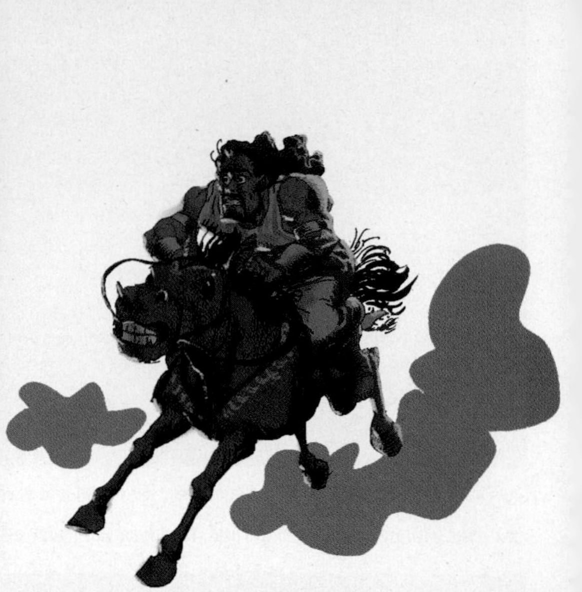

Joab says, "I think it's Ziklag!"

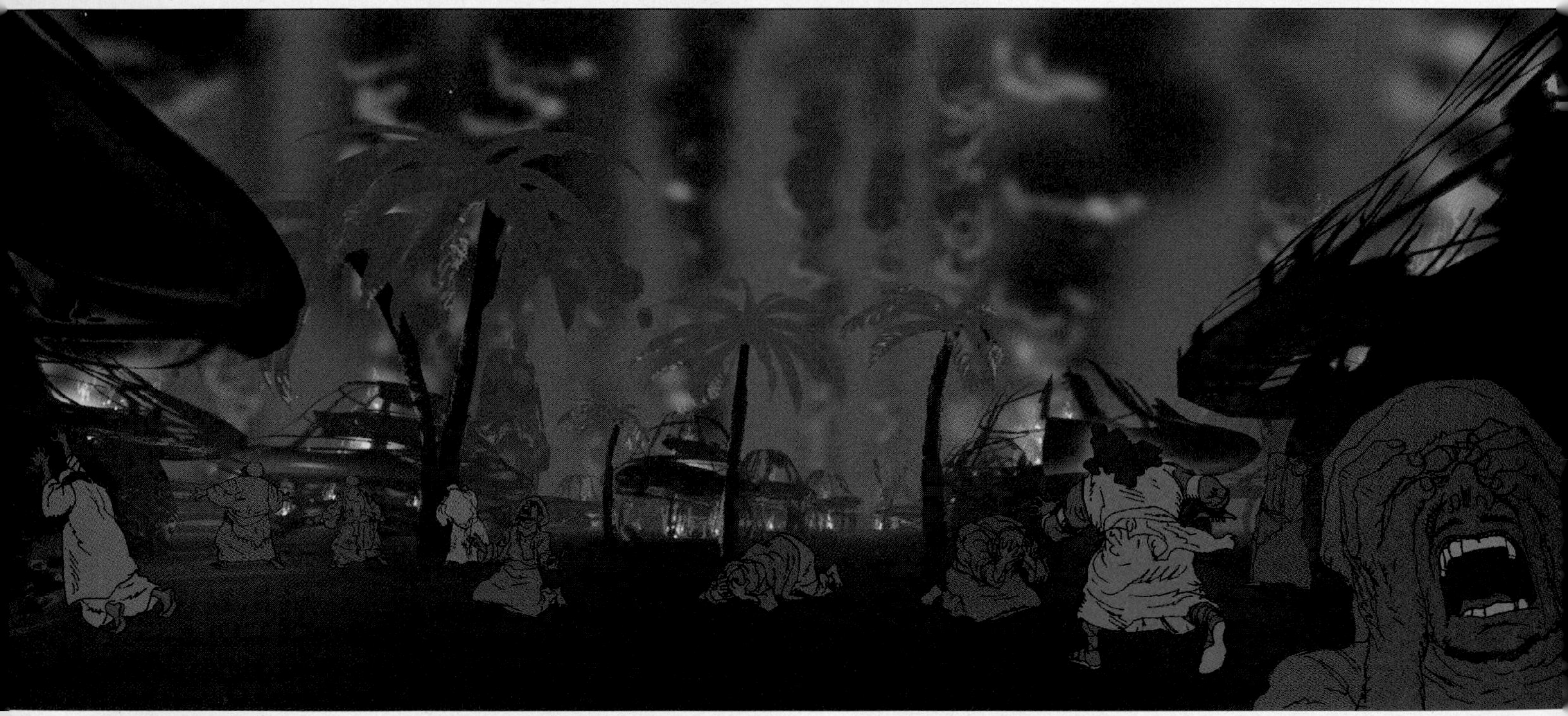

"There are no bodies," says a scout. "My wife, my children..." chokes Abishai.

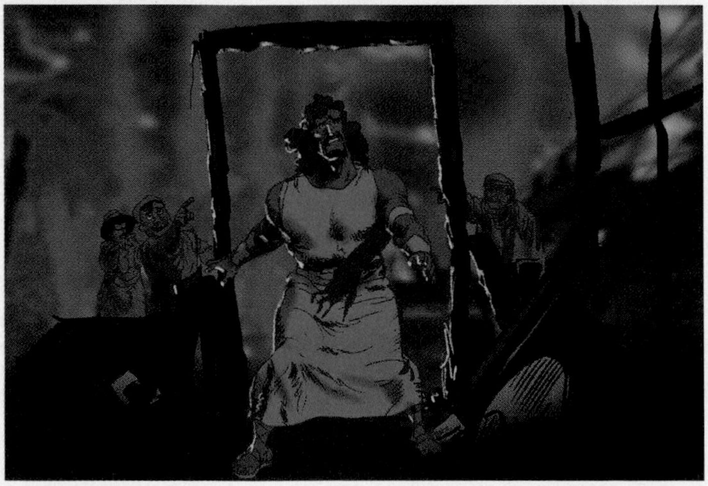

One of David's most ardent followers speaks up. "This is all David's fault!"

"If he had killed Saul those two times he had the chance, we wouldn't be in Ziklag today!" one man growls.

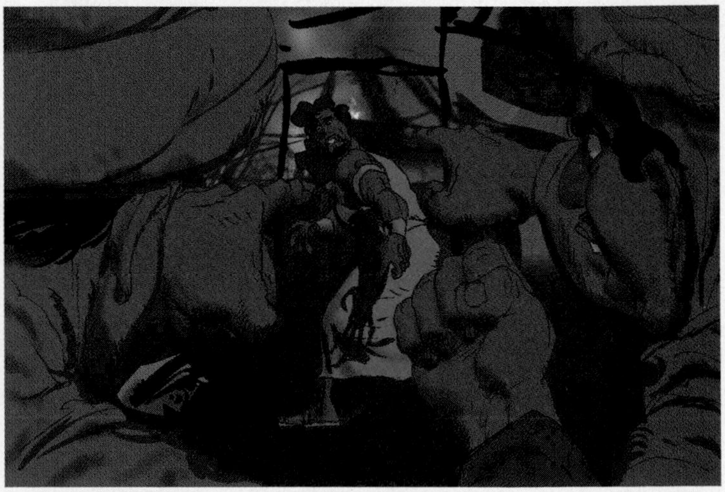

"And we'd still have our children!" says another man.

"My wives have been taken as well," David says.

"Let's kill David! Stone him!"

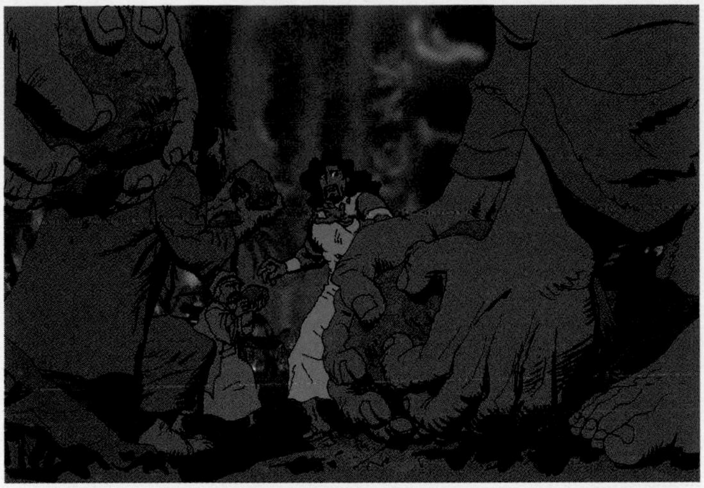

"Wait, men. Listen," pleads David.

"No more lies!"

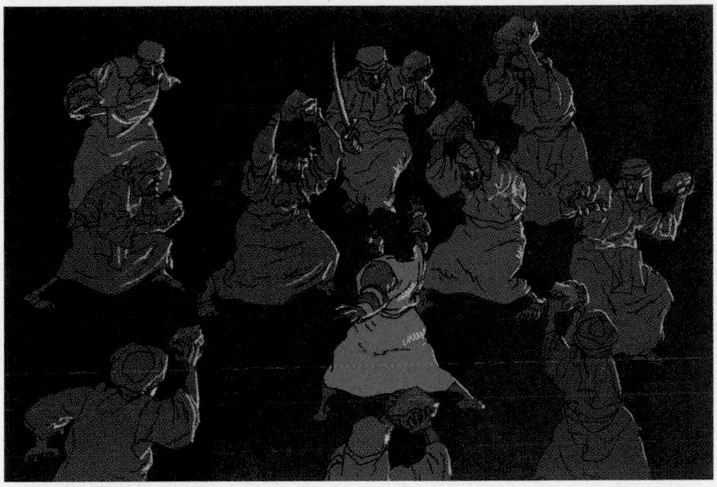

"Another phony politician!"

"Kill him!"

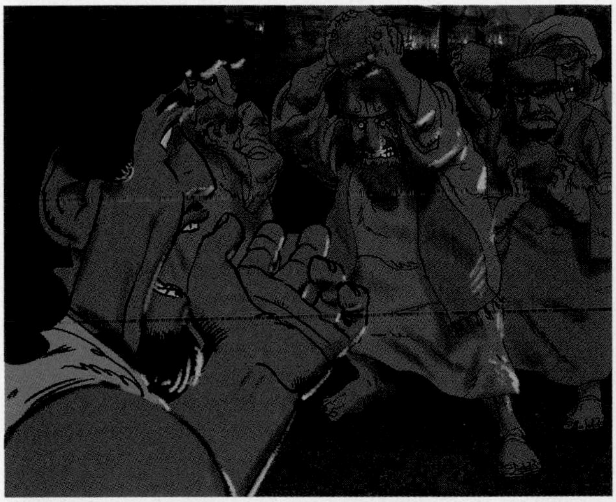

"Abiathar! Fetch the ephod!"

Abiathar says, "Bad enough you got my father killed with your lies along with the other priests! Now look what's become of us!"

"Abiathar!" says David. "This isn't the time."

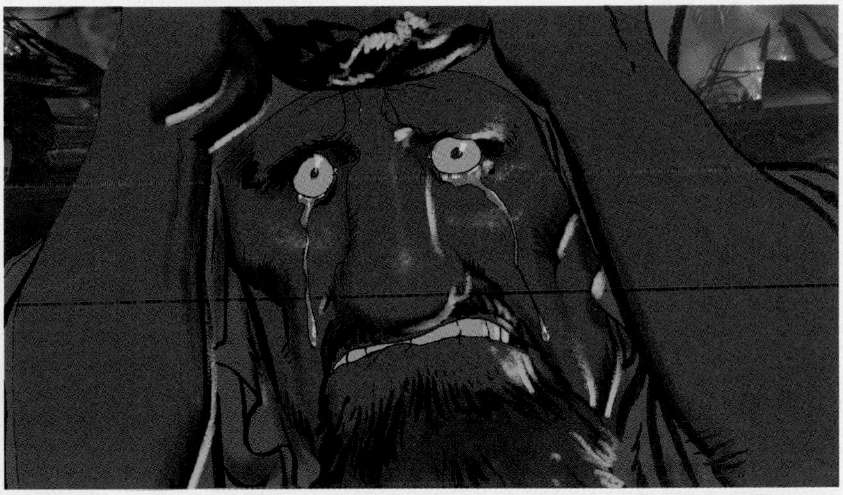

"Chased and hunted everywhere we go," someone says.

"Driven to kill women and children," shouts a big man.

"And for what?" cries another. "Now our own women and children are gone!"

"Abiathar," says David. "Please! Ask the LORD what we should do."

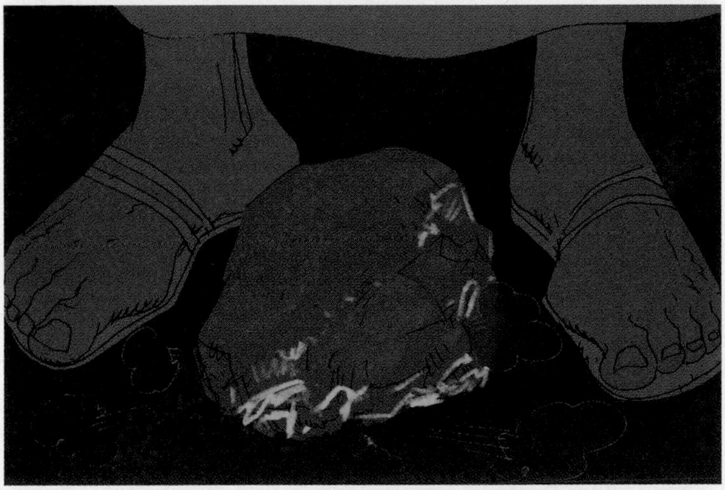

Abiathar realizes David is right.

""We must inquire of the LORD as to what we should do. It's what we should have done in the first place. We have suffered all we have suffered this past year because we placed our faith in David. Could God do any worse job leading us?"

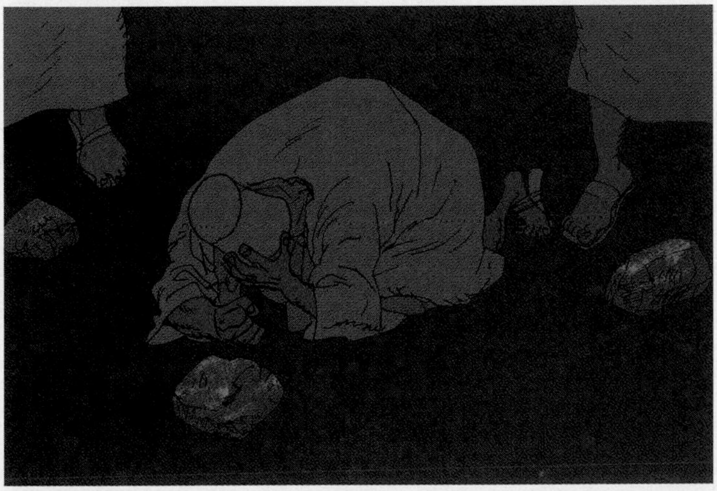

"Thank you, Abiathar," says David, vaguely insulted.

Abiathar inquires of God.

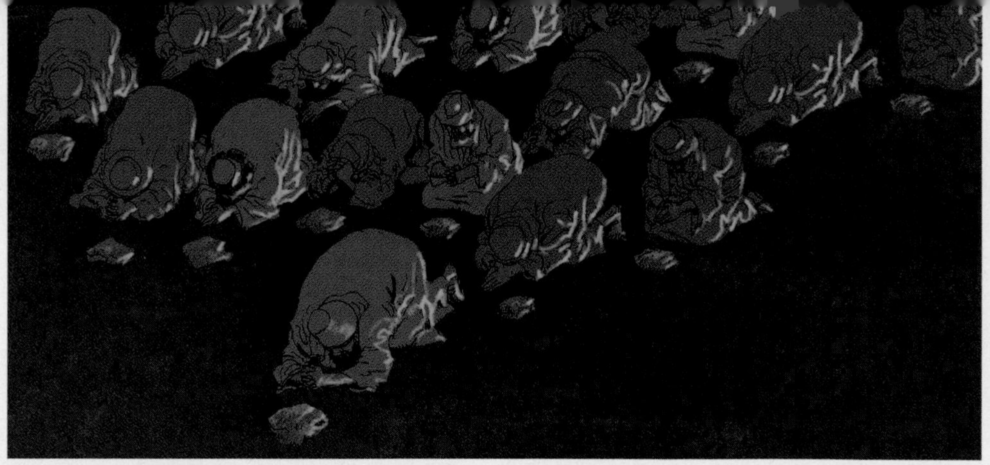

Later, a lone young man is dehydrating to death in the desert heat. Lying on the desolate sand, tongue hanging out, he rasps, "Oh, God. Oh, God. Please save me. I'll do anything you ask. Please God save me."

A foot lands next to him. Weak, he looks up...

David and his army are looking down at him.

A few moments later, the stricken man is drinking water and eating fig cakes and raisins in the shade of David's tent.

"Whose are you?" asks David. "And from where do you come?

"Come on, David," says Joab. "You heard Abiathar. God says our families are still alive! We've got to hurry and rescue them!"

The young man speaks. "I am an Egyptian youth, slave to an Amalekite man."

"Why are we wasting our time saving some slave?" Joab protests. "We have to go find our children!"

"My master abandoned me," says the Egyptian, "for I had been sick three days."

Joab says to David, "Look, let's just leave a sandwich with him and go!"

The Egyptian continues, "We raided the south of the Cherethites, and we burned Ziklag with fire."

Joab asks, "Do you need a ride home, son?"

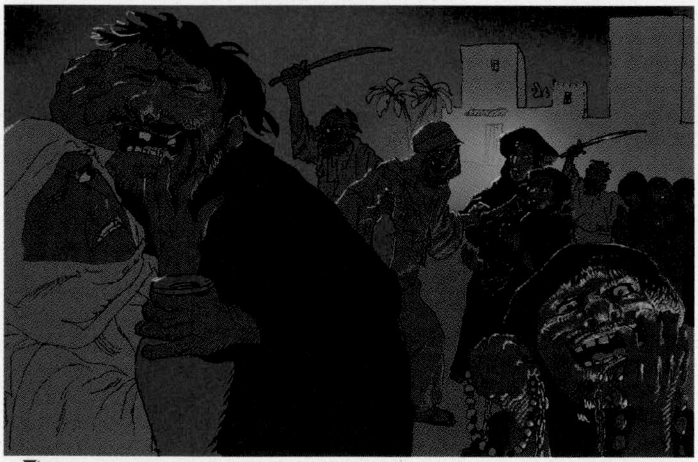

An Amalekite camp. Loot is piled up everywhere. The captive wives and children of Ziklag, shackled, despair as their Amalekite captors party.

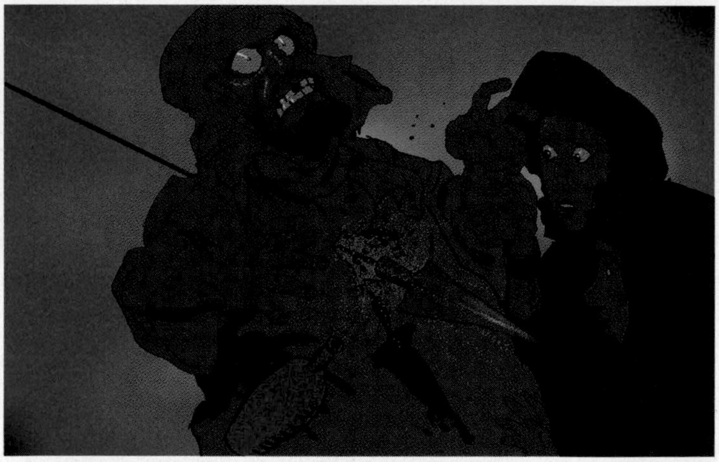

A very drunk Amalekite says, "What do I care if your husband's got a song about--GAK!"

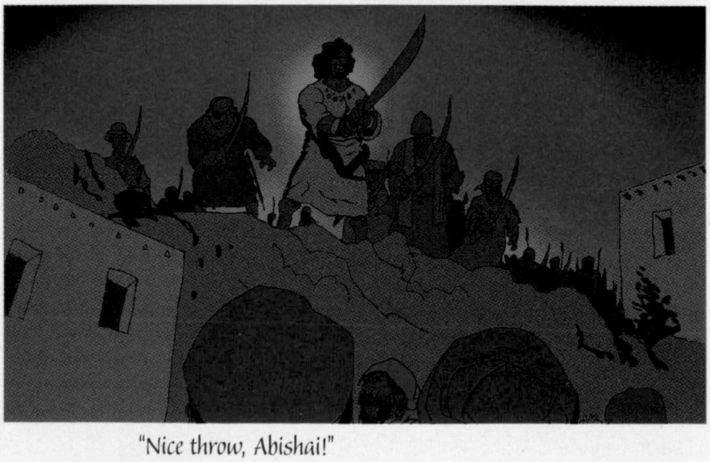

"Nice throw, Abishai!" says Joab.

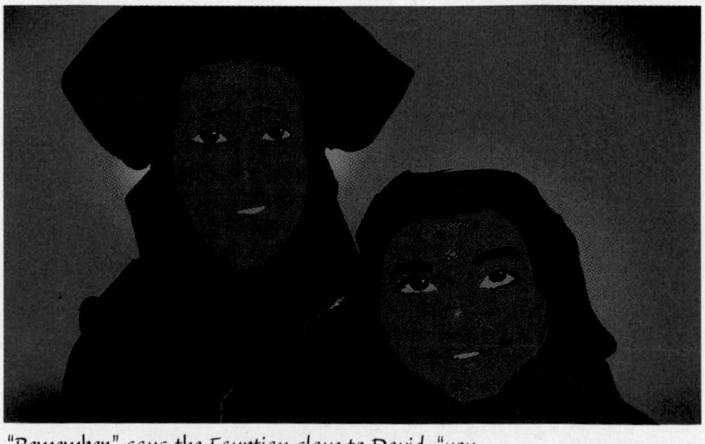

"Remember," says the Egyptian slave to David, "you promised not to kill me if I brought you here, right?"

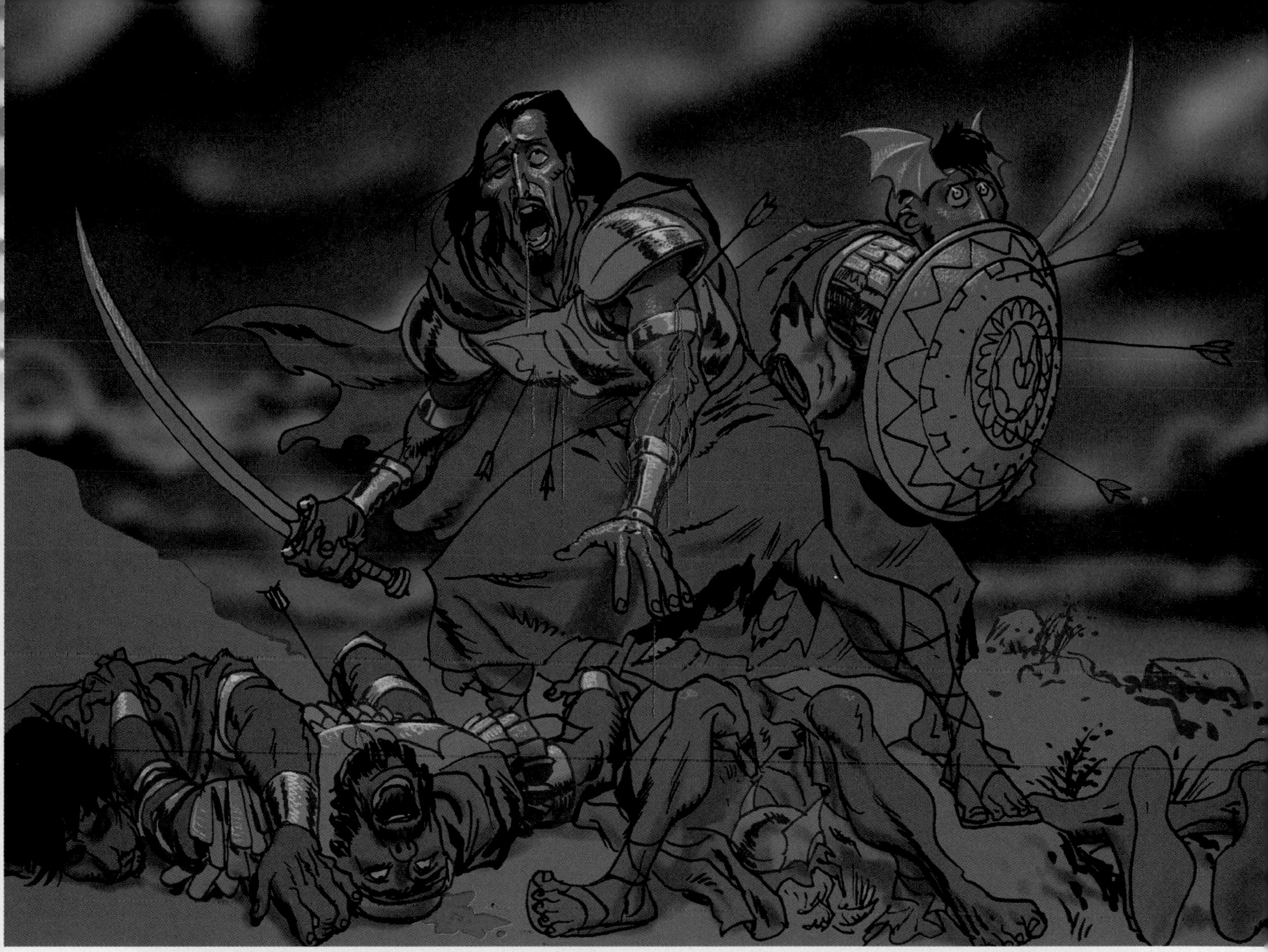
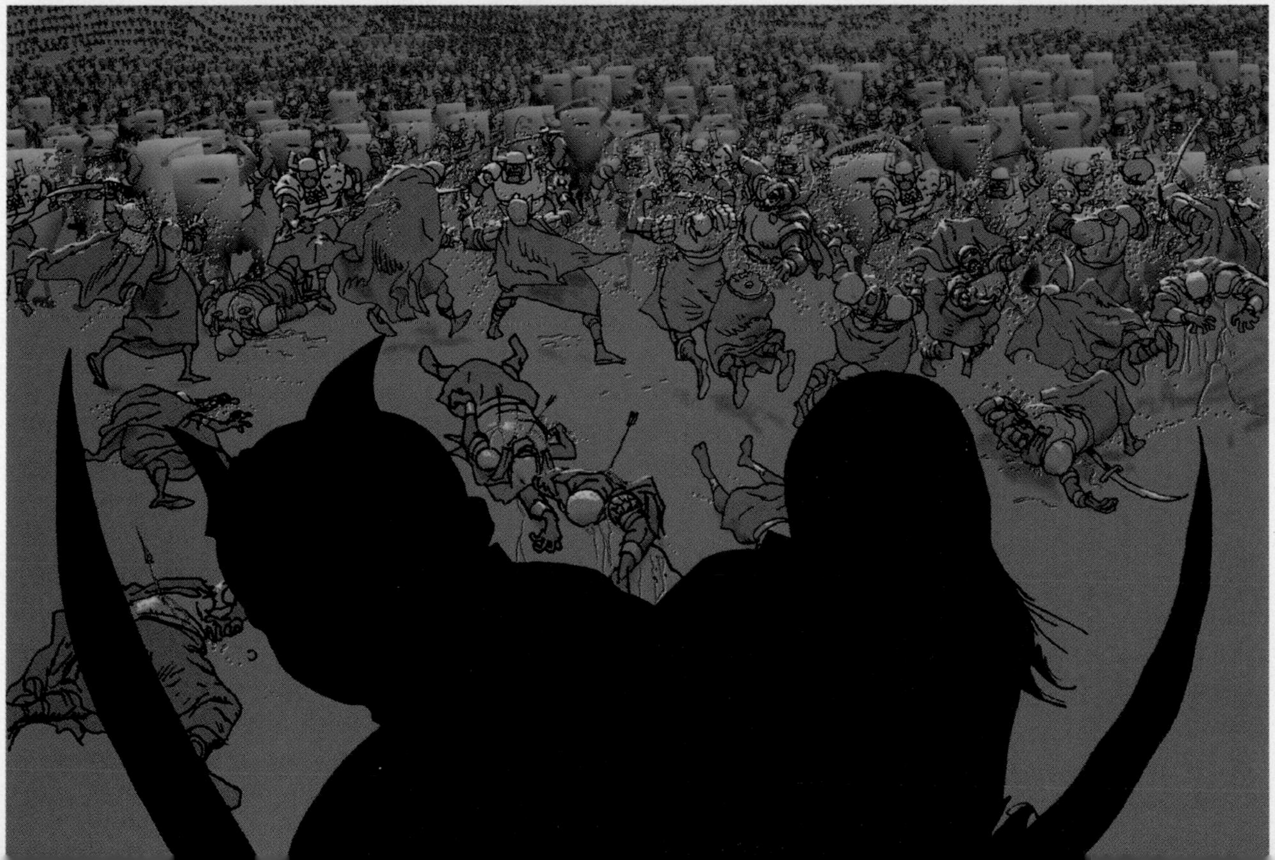

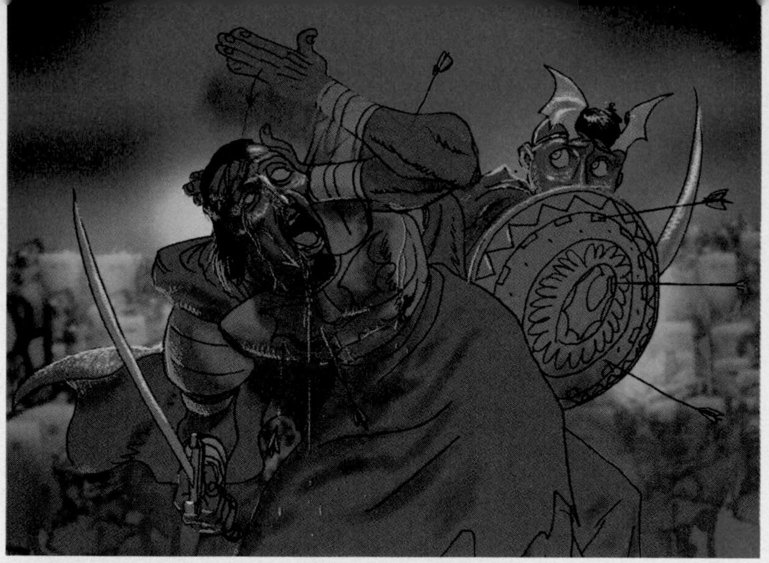

"Slay me with your sword, lest these uncircumcised fellows abuse me."

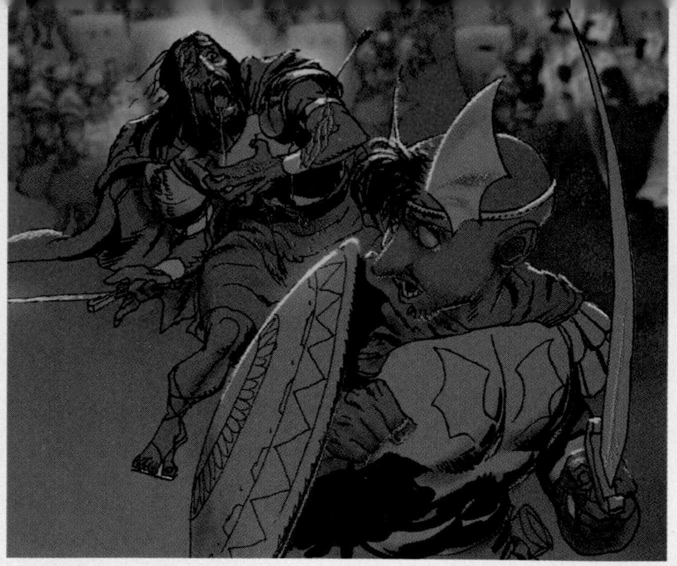

"Please! They won't kill me! They didn't kill Samson!"

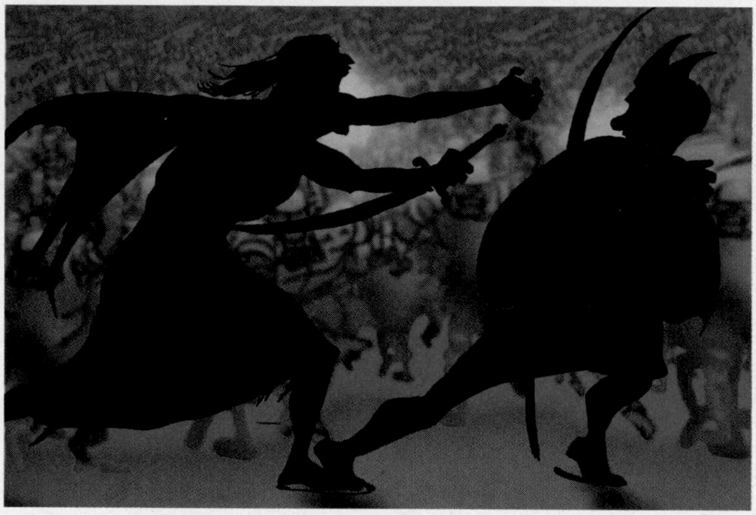

"Kill me! Hurry!"

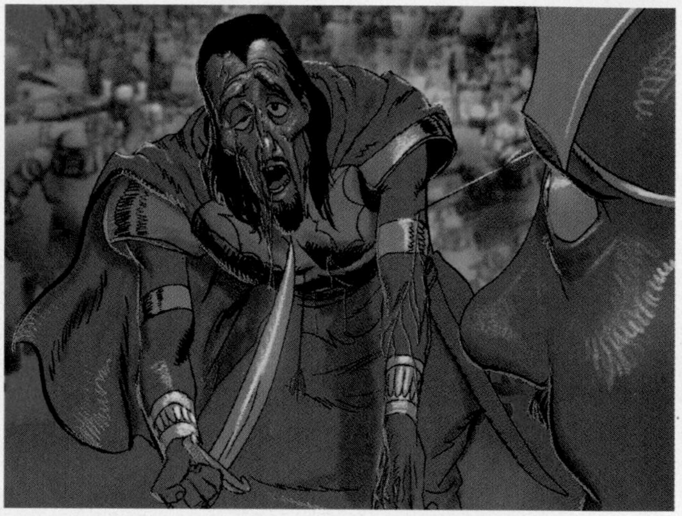

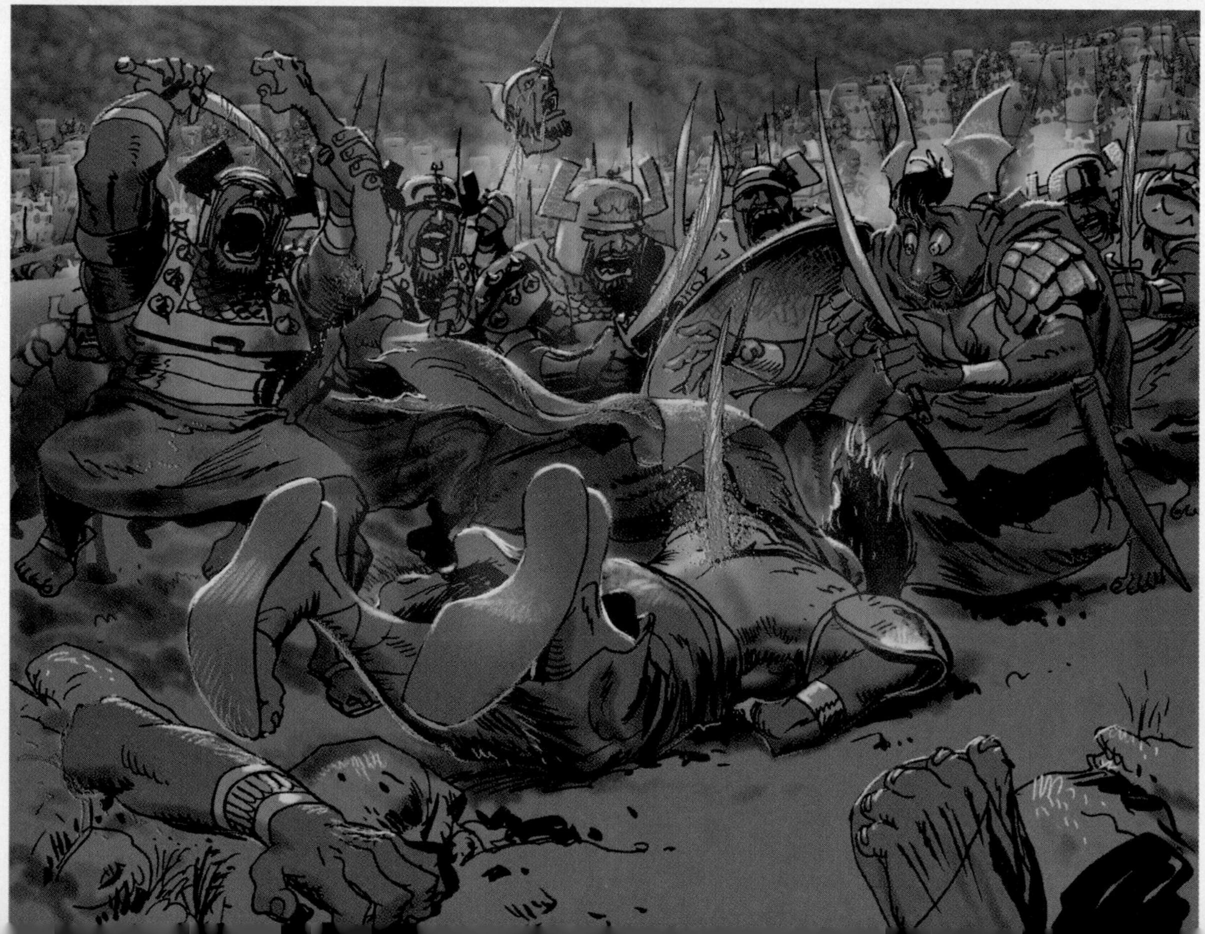

Time passes.

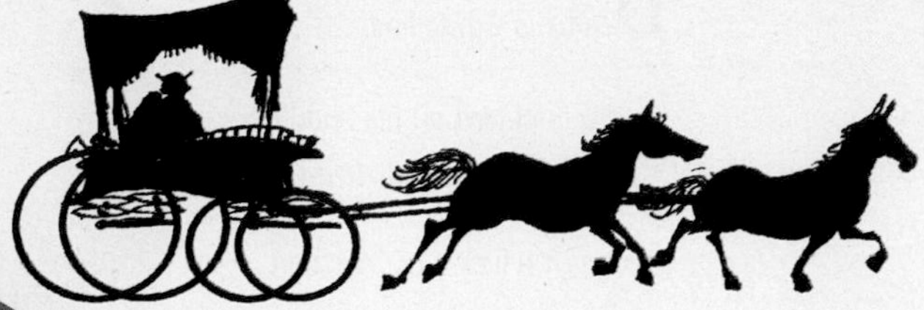

"He's still following us."

"It's been miles. Look at him, crying like a woman."

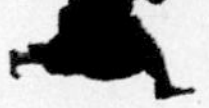

"My husband is crying because he loves me."

"Phalti's not your husband anymore. And David loves you."

"It was kind of David to remember me. I hear that he has acquired six wives since the day I saved his life. The day I betrayed my father, may he rest in peace."

"You want to hear how much David loves you? I sent him a message, offering my influence with the elders to get him crowned king of Israel. He sent back the message, 'Don't even show your face here unless you first bring Michal.'"

"I saw the message. It said, 'Give up my wife Michal the daughter of Saul, whom I betrothed to myself with a hundred foreskins of the Philistines.' How romantic."

"My point is, he loves you more than the crown I am offering."

"Look at Phalti crying. What's he going to do without me?"

"Oh, for..."

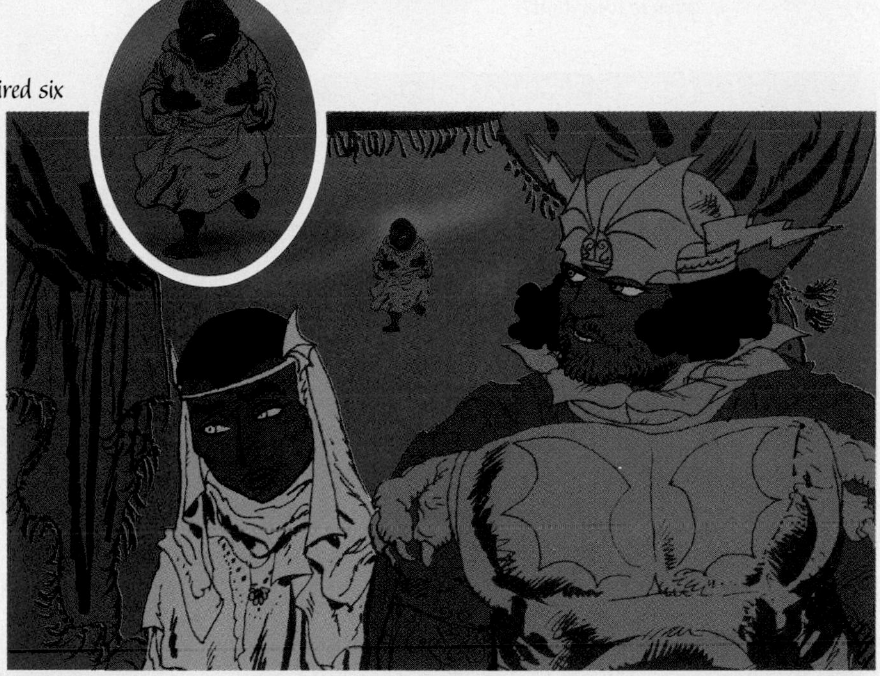

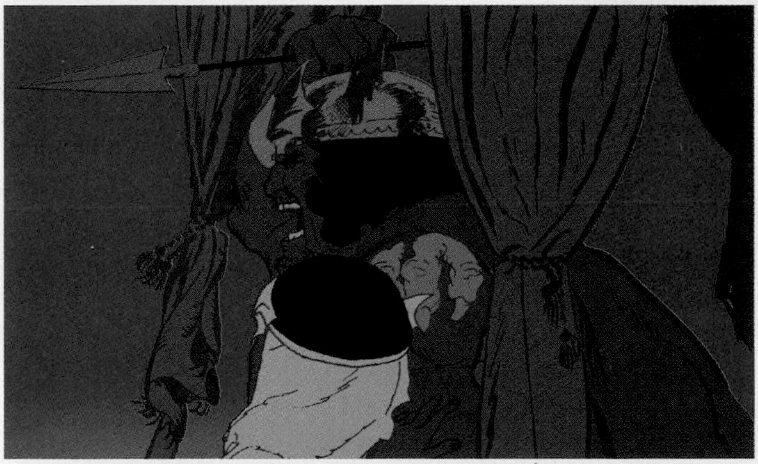

"Go home!"

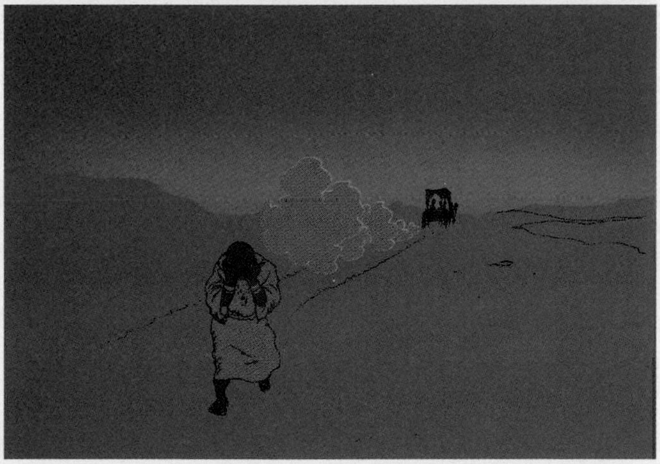

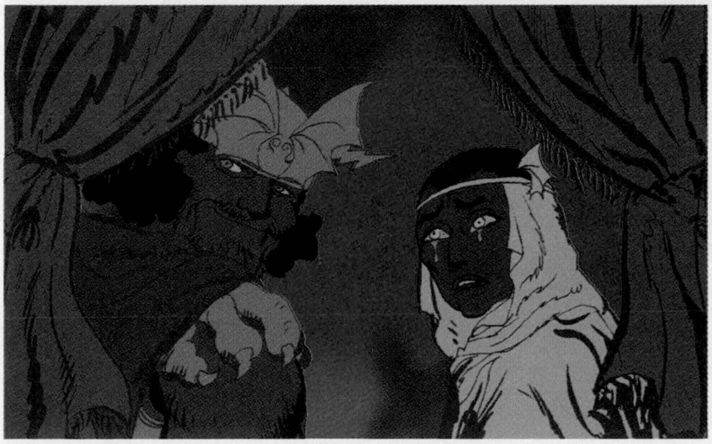

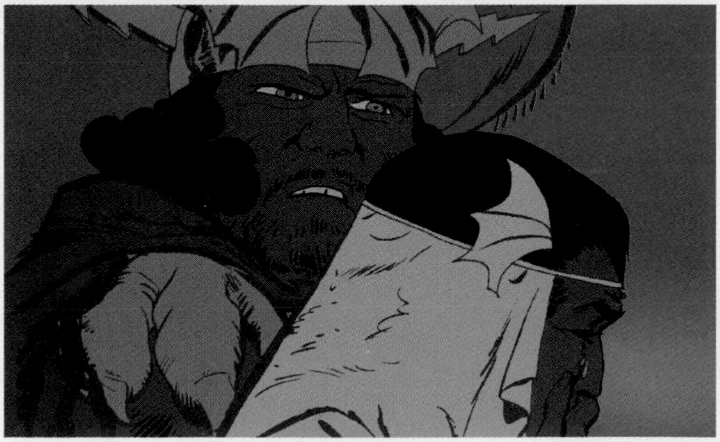

"Oh, don't you start now!"

David is made king.

A cape is placed on his shoulders.
A crown placed on his head.

His seven wives say, "Are you going to wear that?"

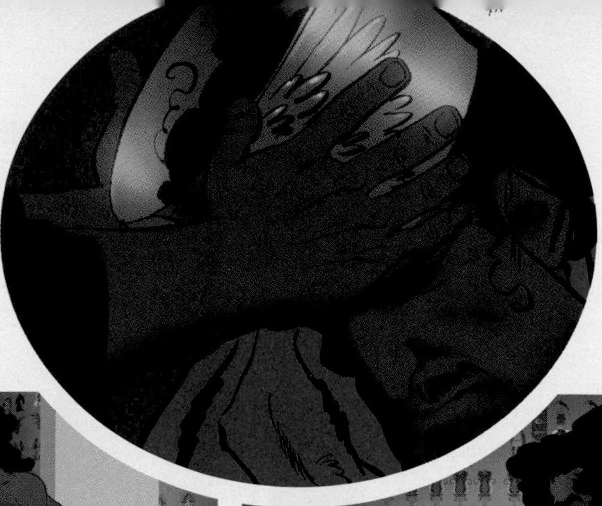

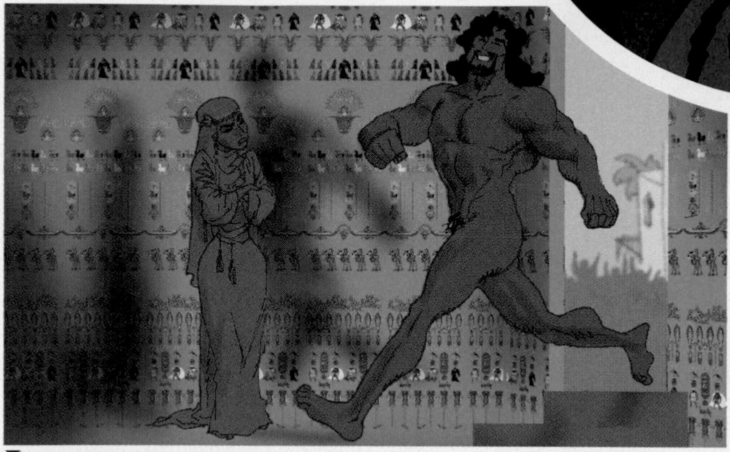

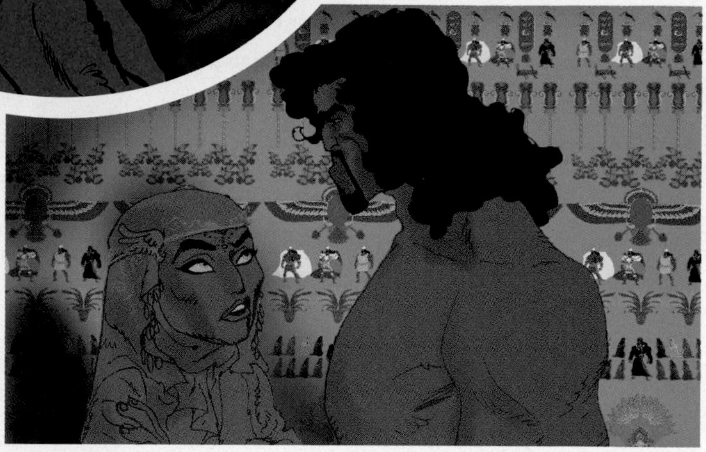

Later, the ark of Jehovah is brought to the city of David. Michal the daughter of Saul looks through the window and sees King David leaping and dancing before Jehovah. She despises him in her heart.

"How glorious was the king of Israel today, who was uncovered today before the eyes of the slave girls of his servants, as one of the vain ones shamelessly uncovers himself."

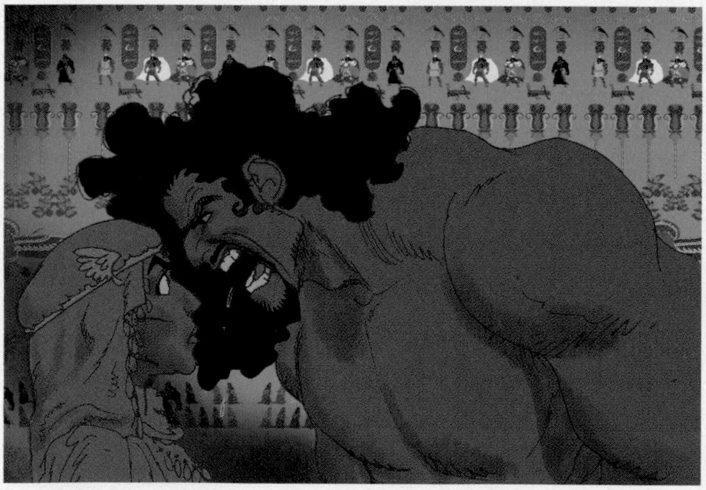

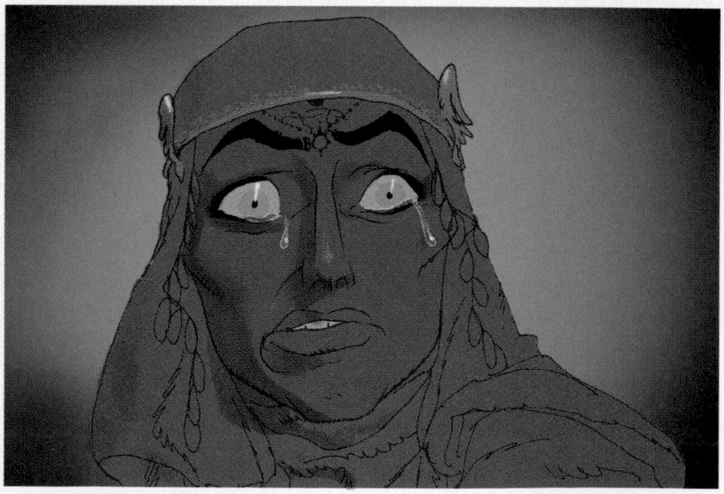

"Before Jehovah, who chose me over your father and over all your father's house, to command me to be leader over the people of Jehovah, and over Israel, so I danced before Jehovah. And I will be yet lighter than this, and shall be lowly in my own eyes. But with the slave girls of whom you spoke, with them I will be honored."

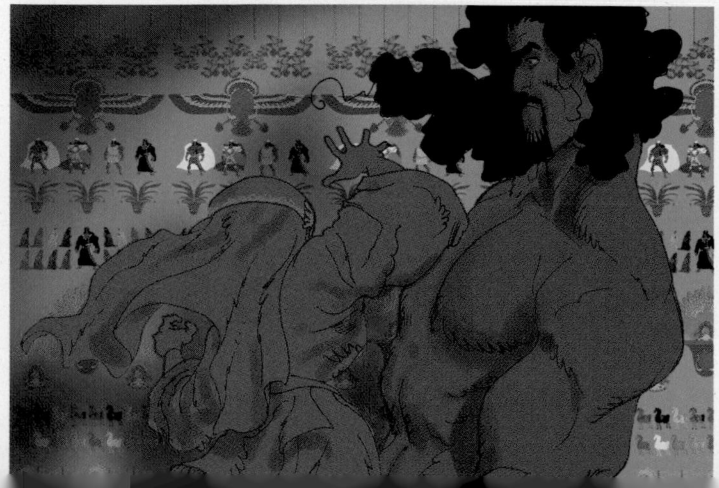

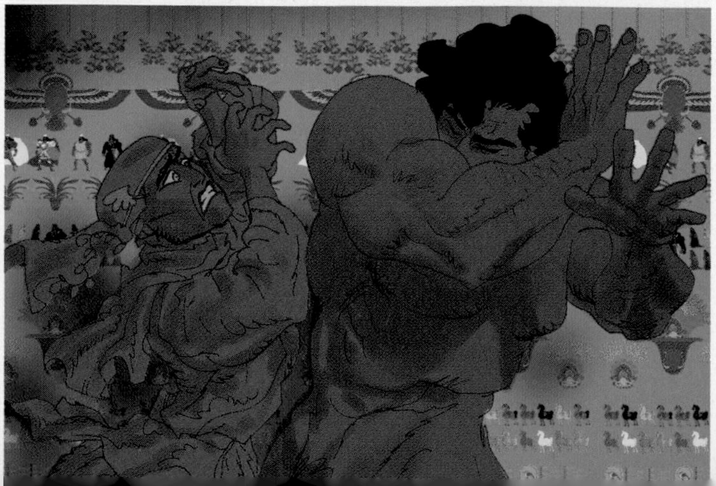

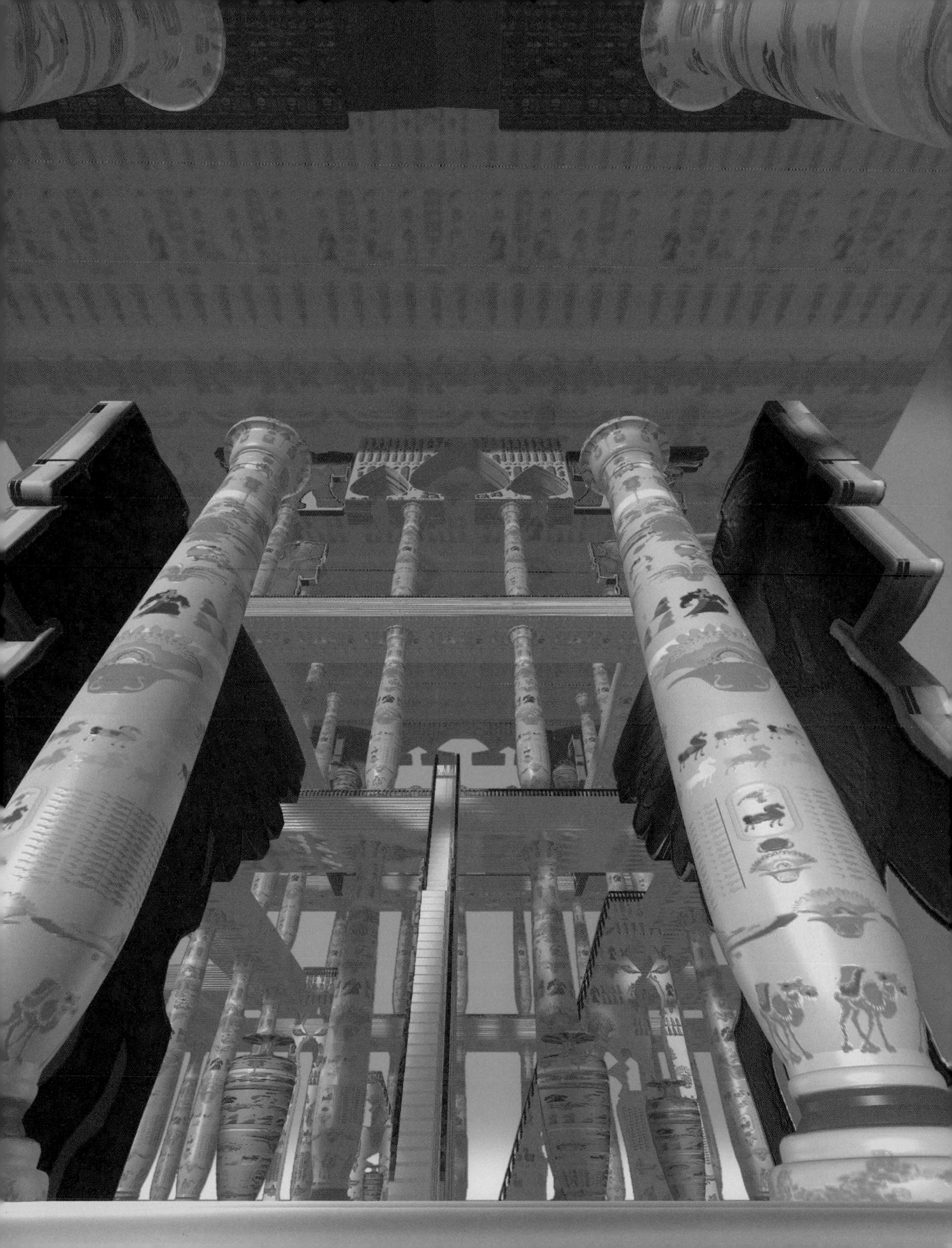

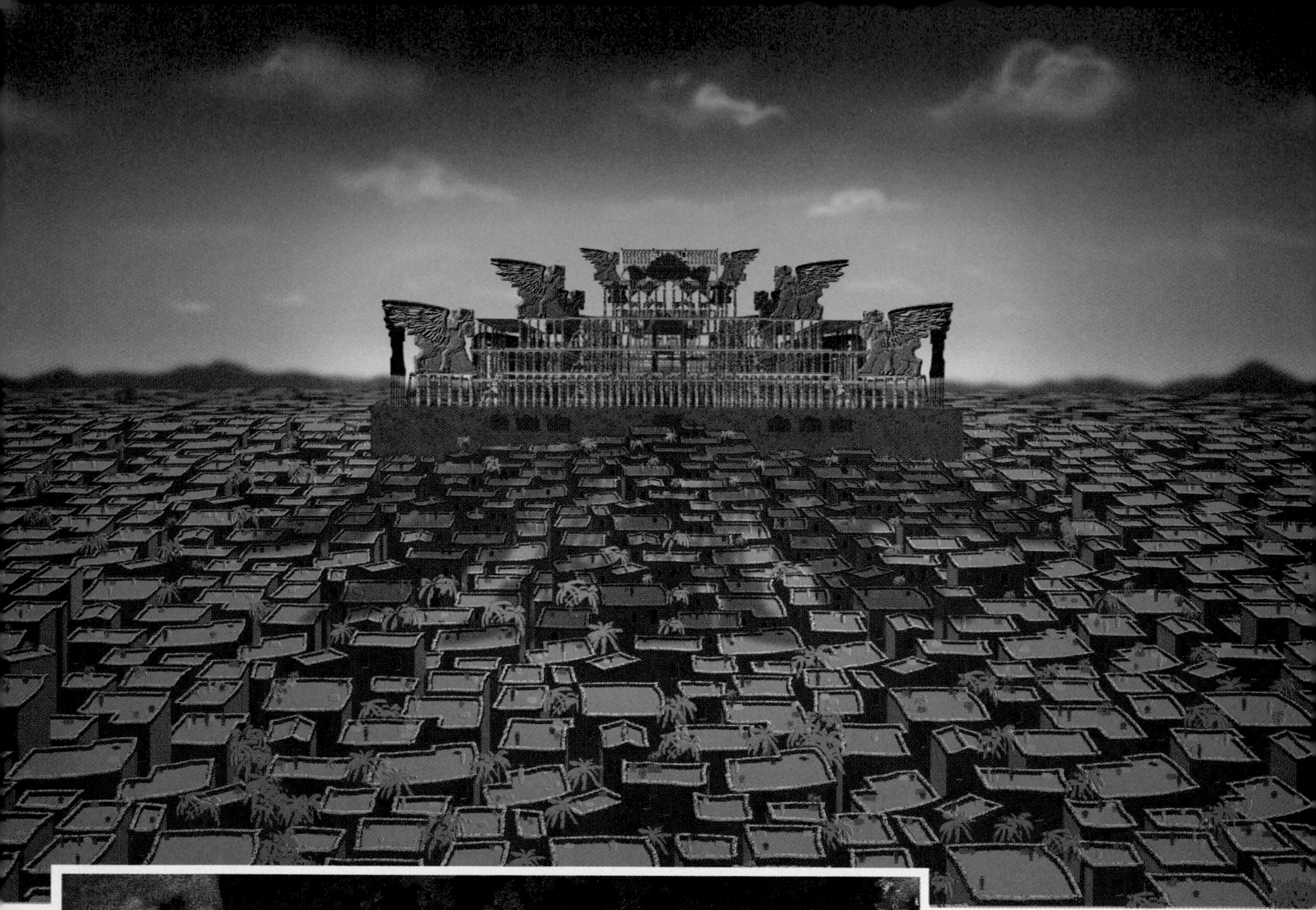

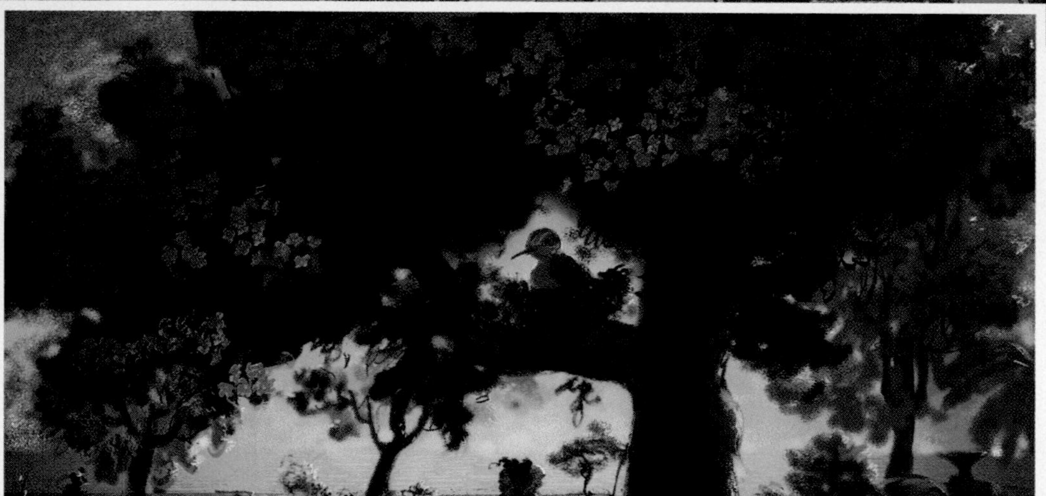

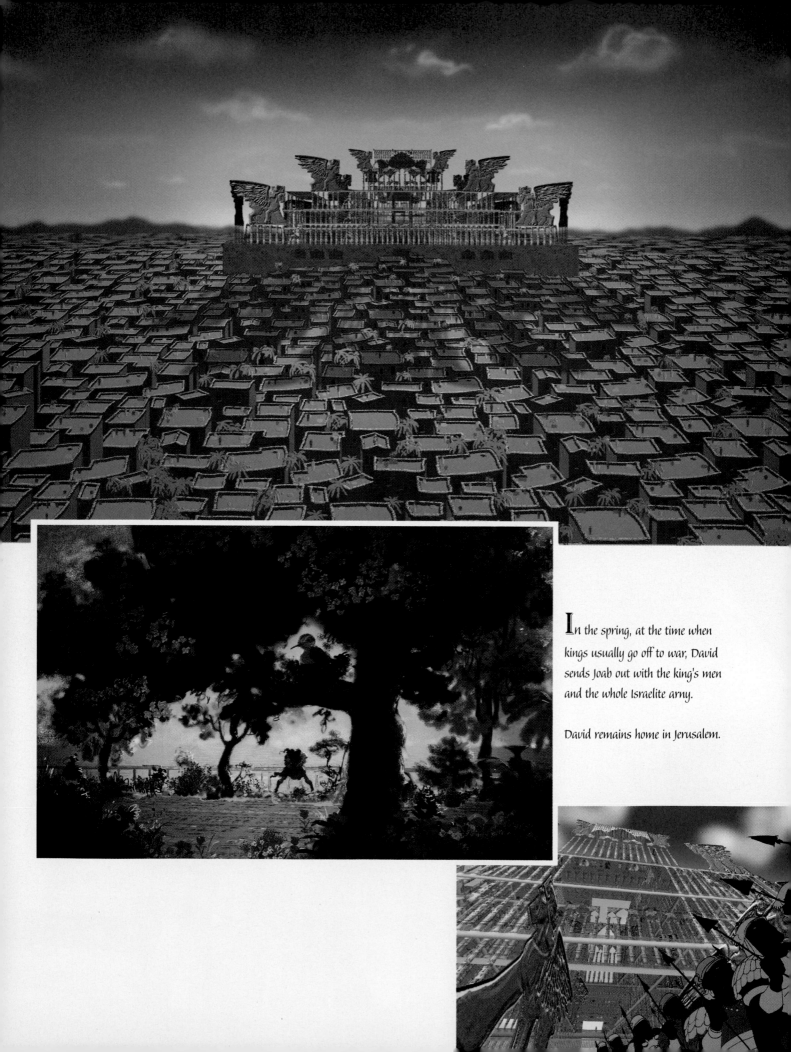

In the spring, at the time when kings usually go off to war, David sends Joab out with the king's men and the whole Israelite arny.

David remains home in Jerusalem.

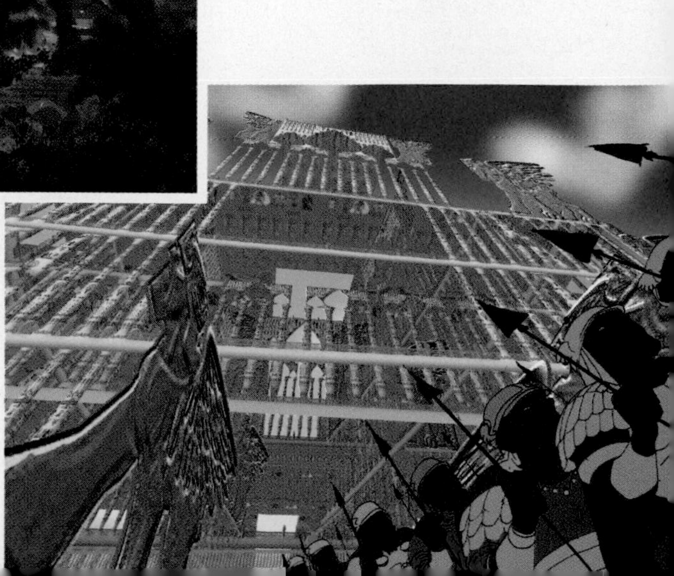

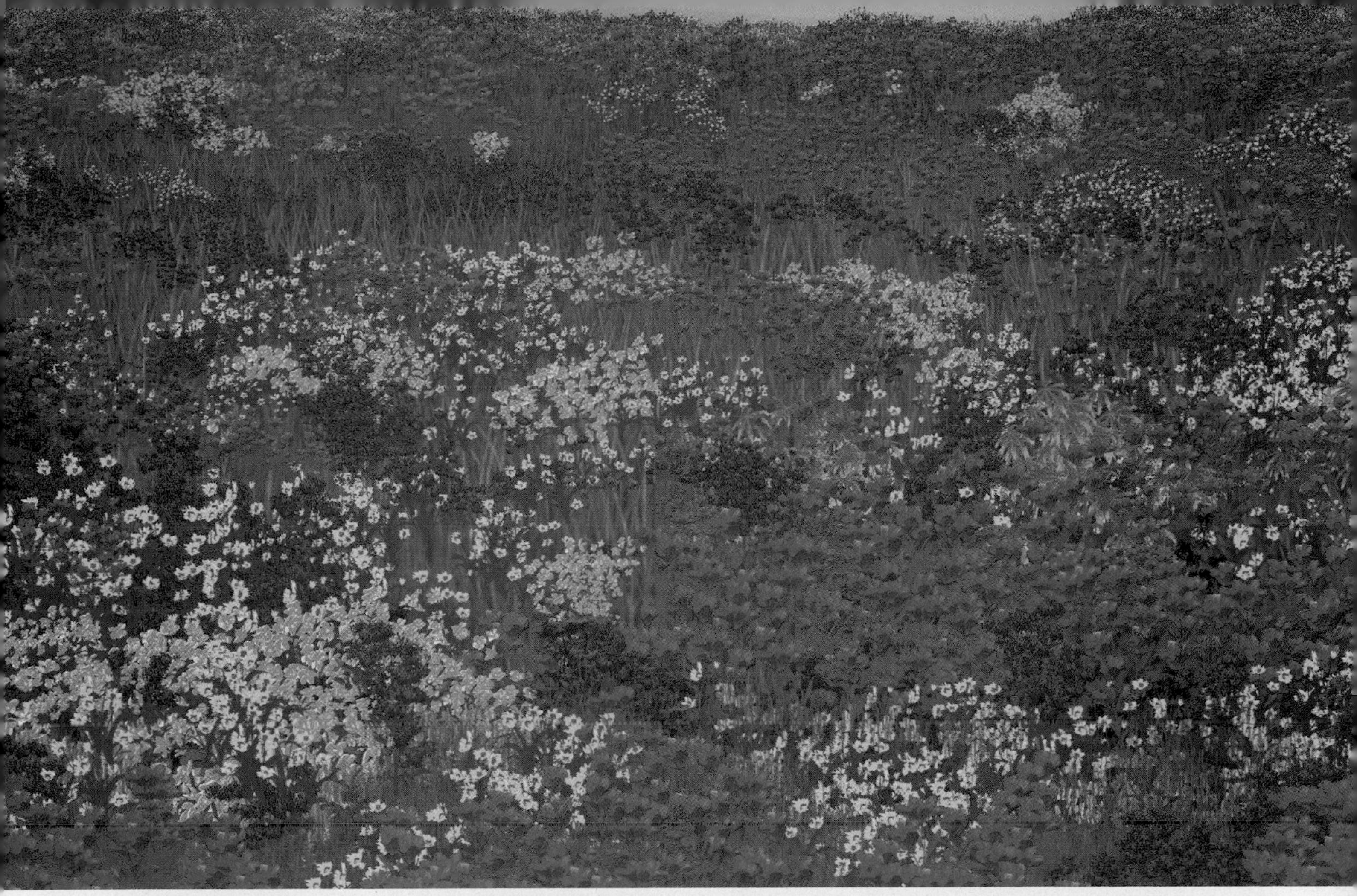

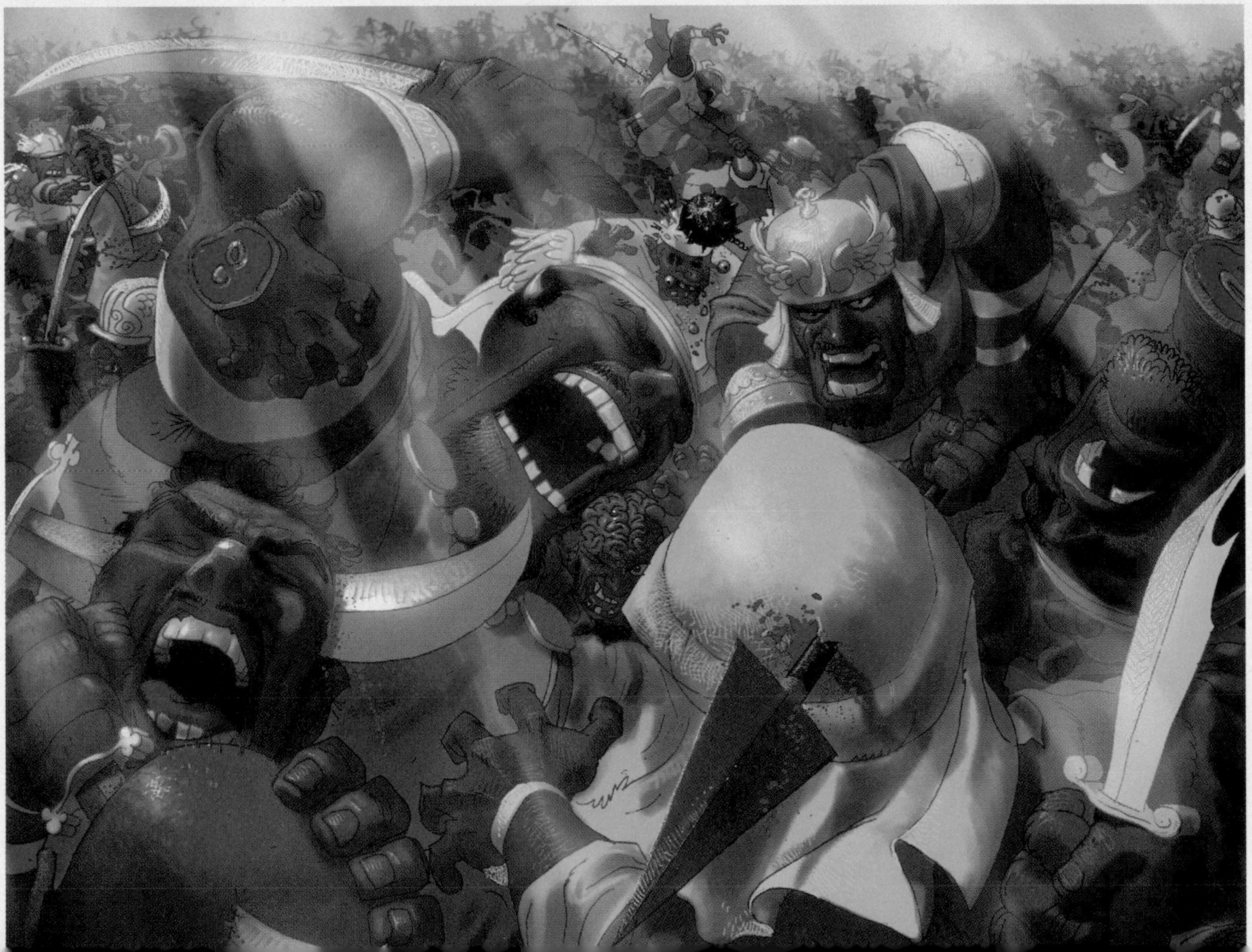

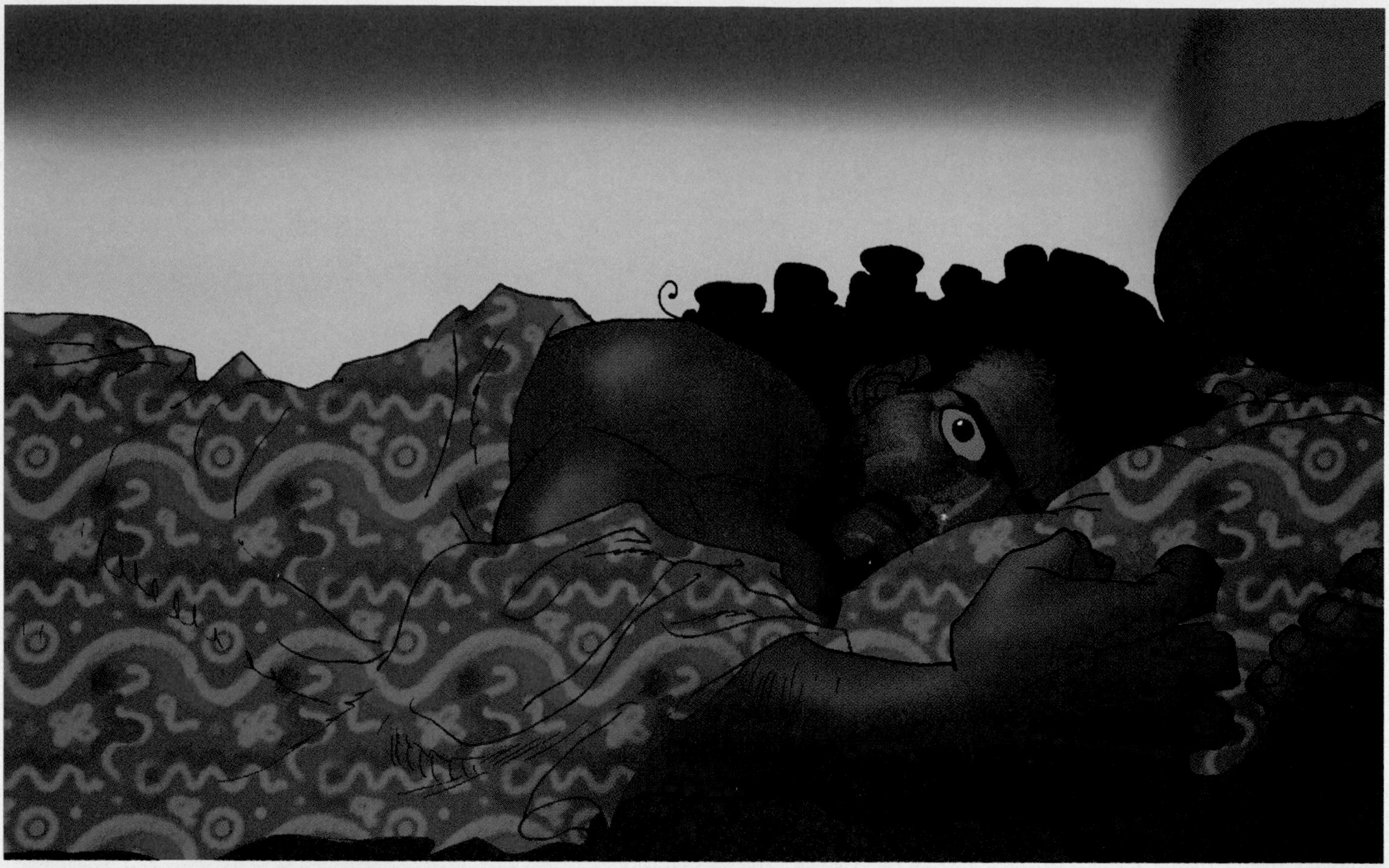

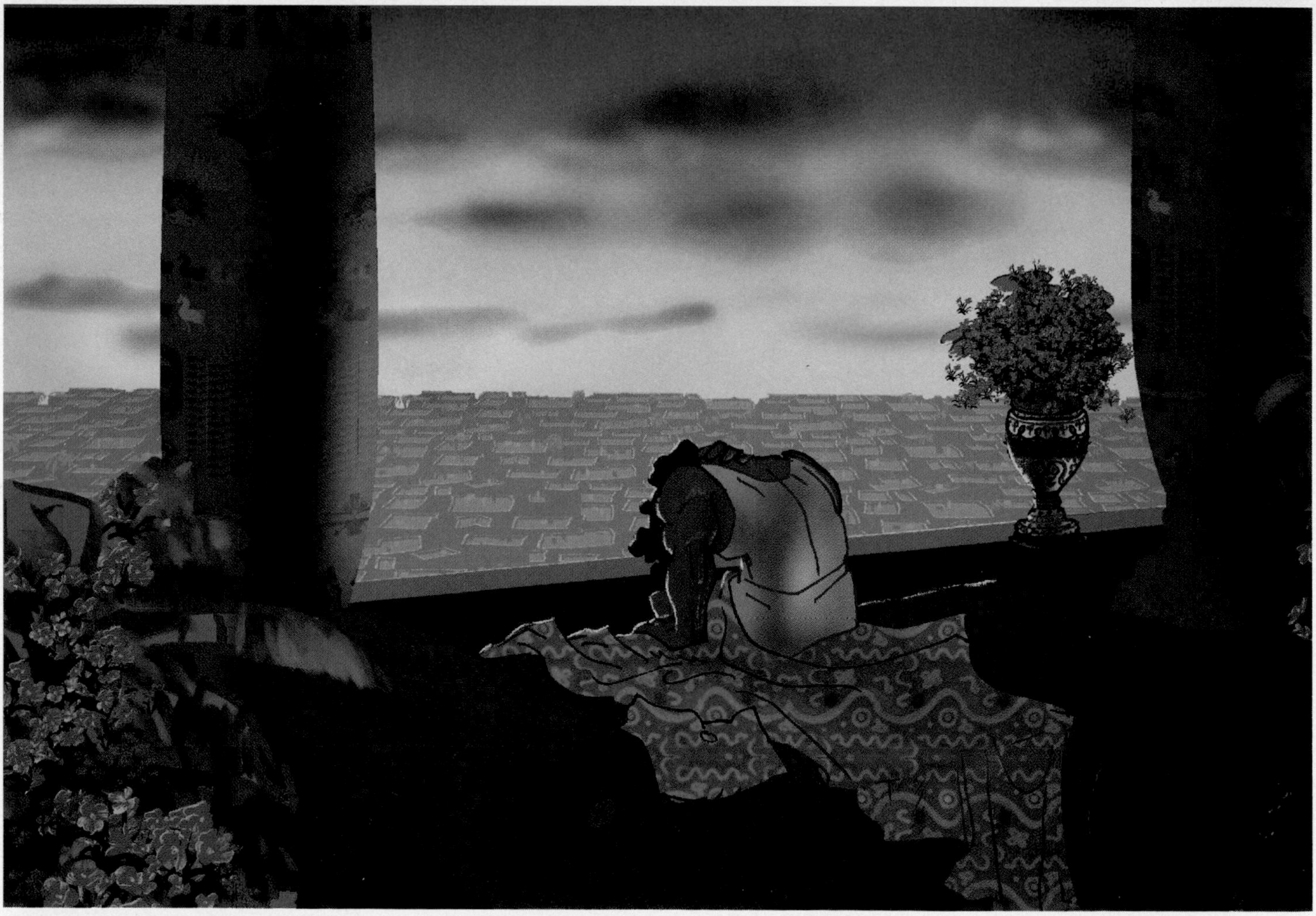

"Yes, your majesty?"

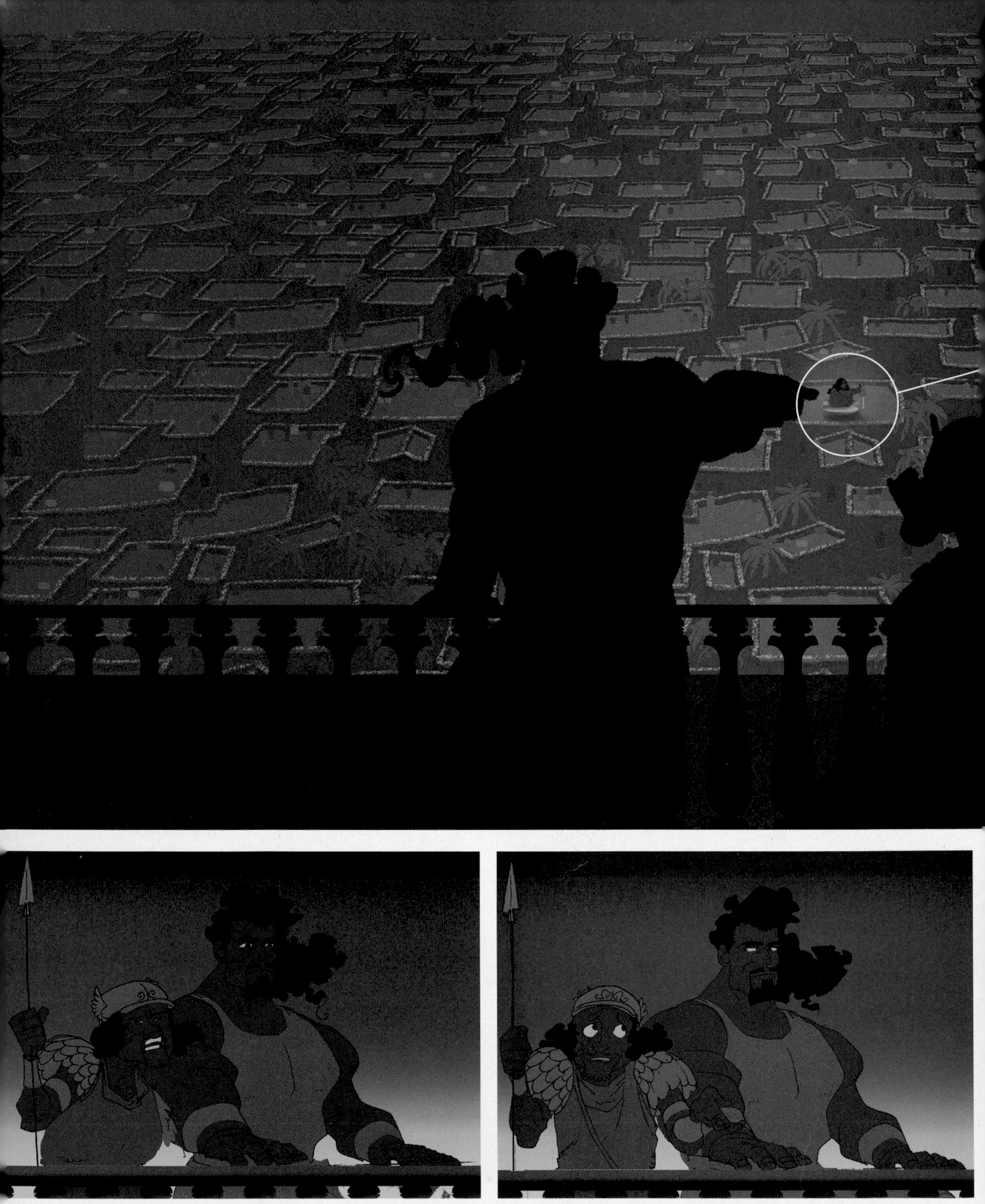

"Is that not Bathsheba, the daughter of Eliam, the wife of Uriah the Hittite?"

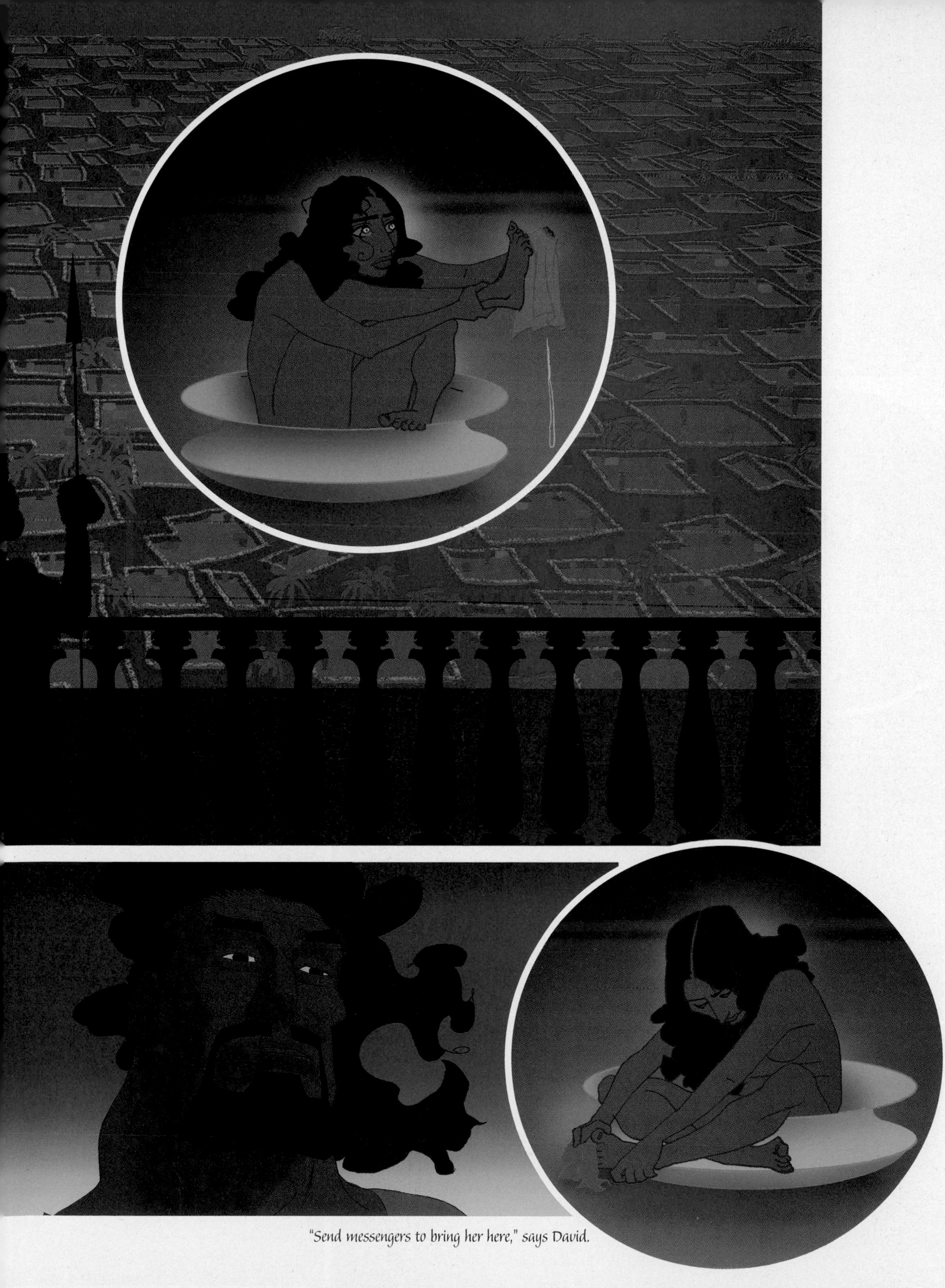

"Send messengers to bring her here," says David.

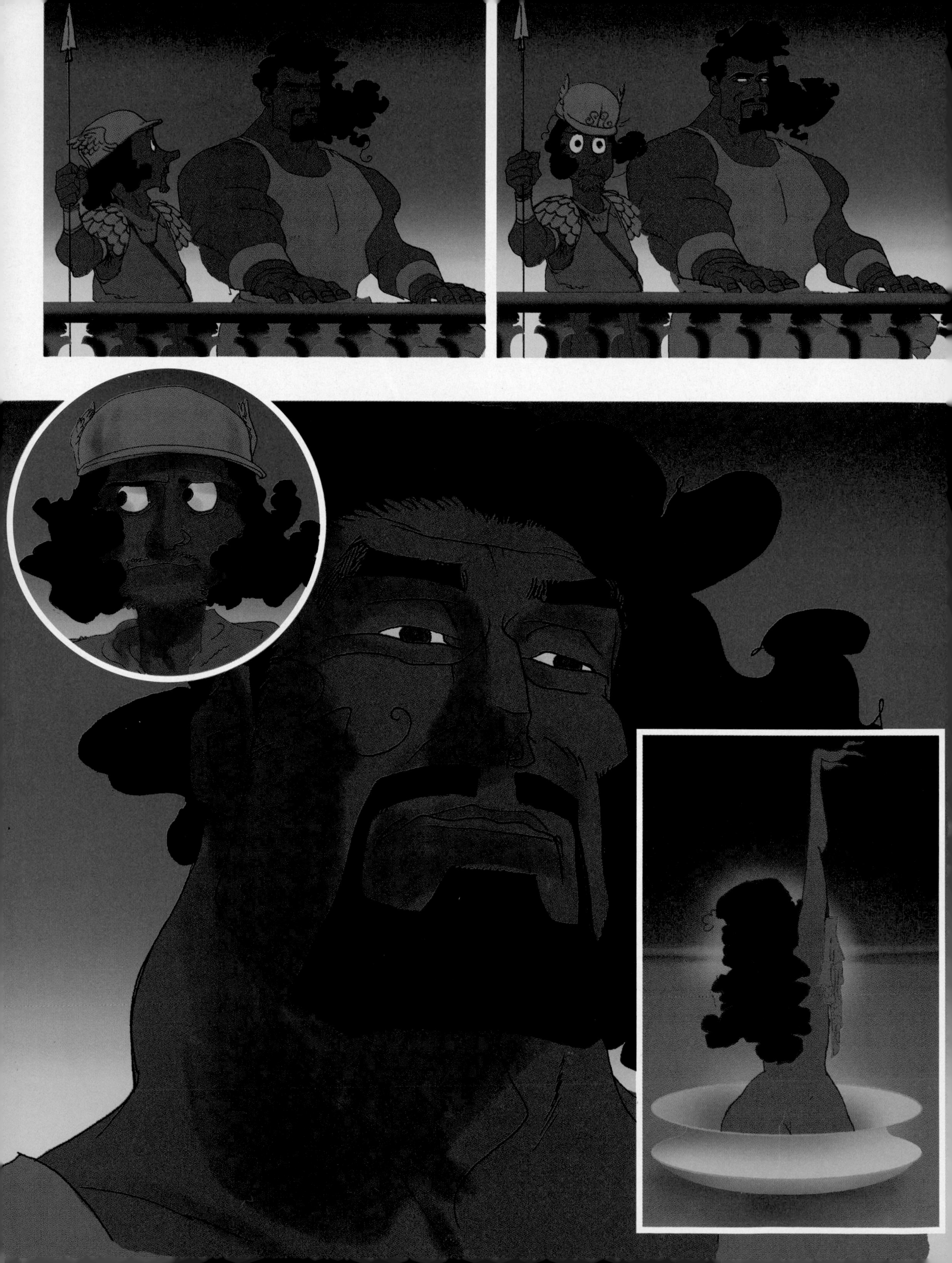

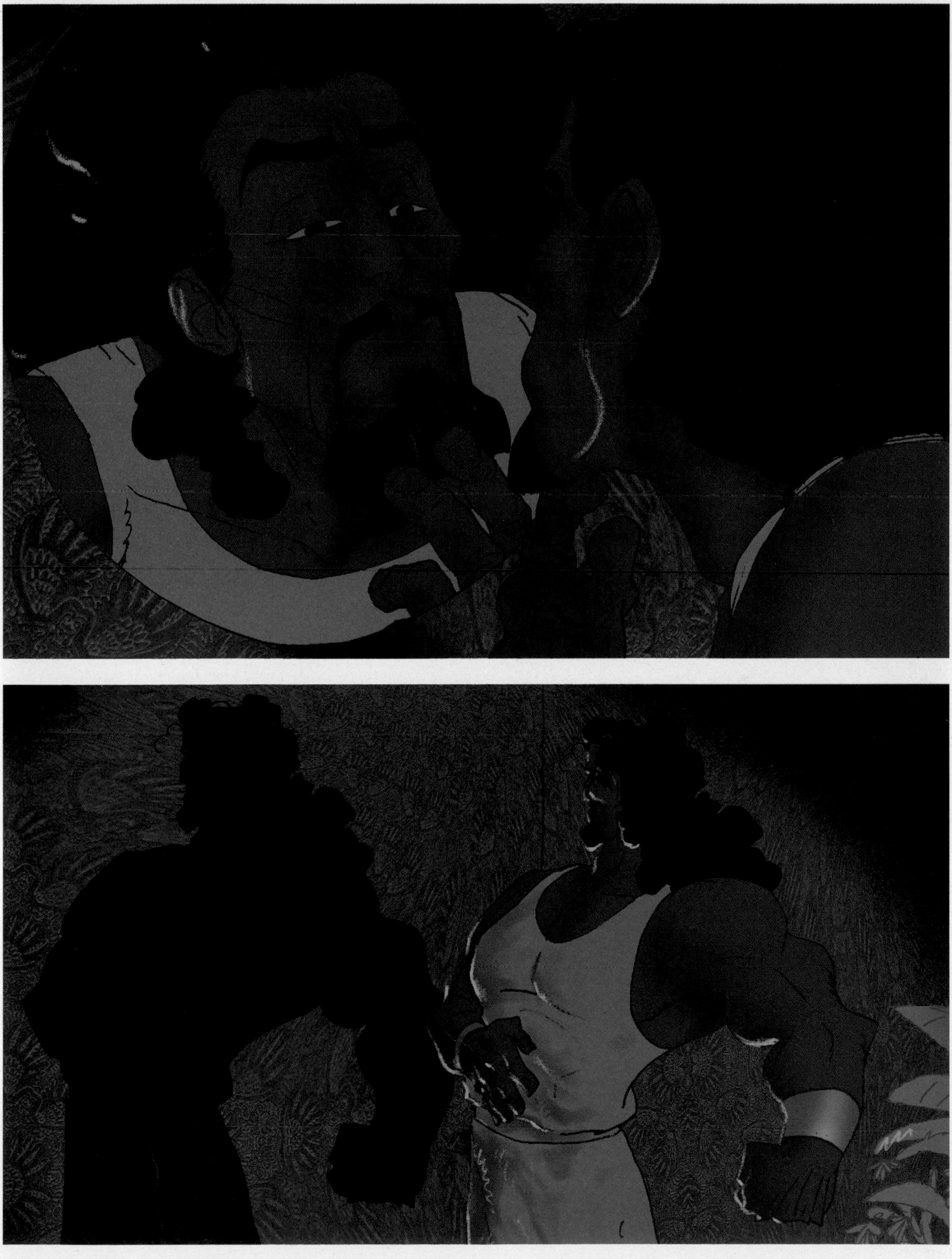

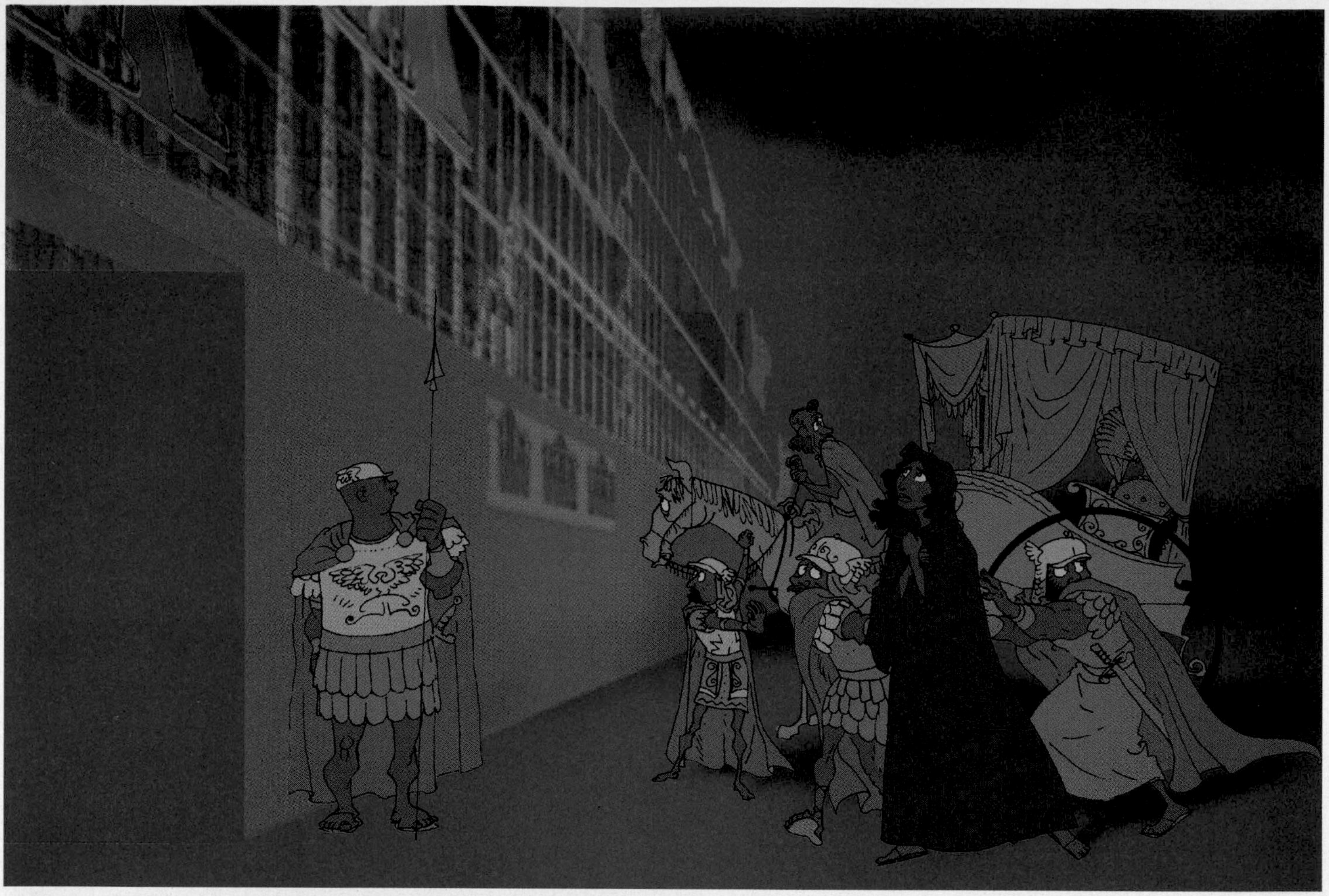

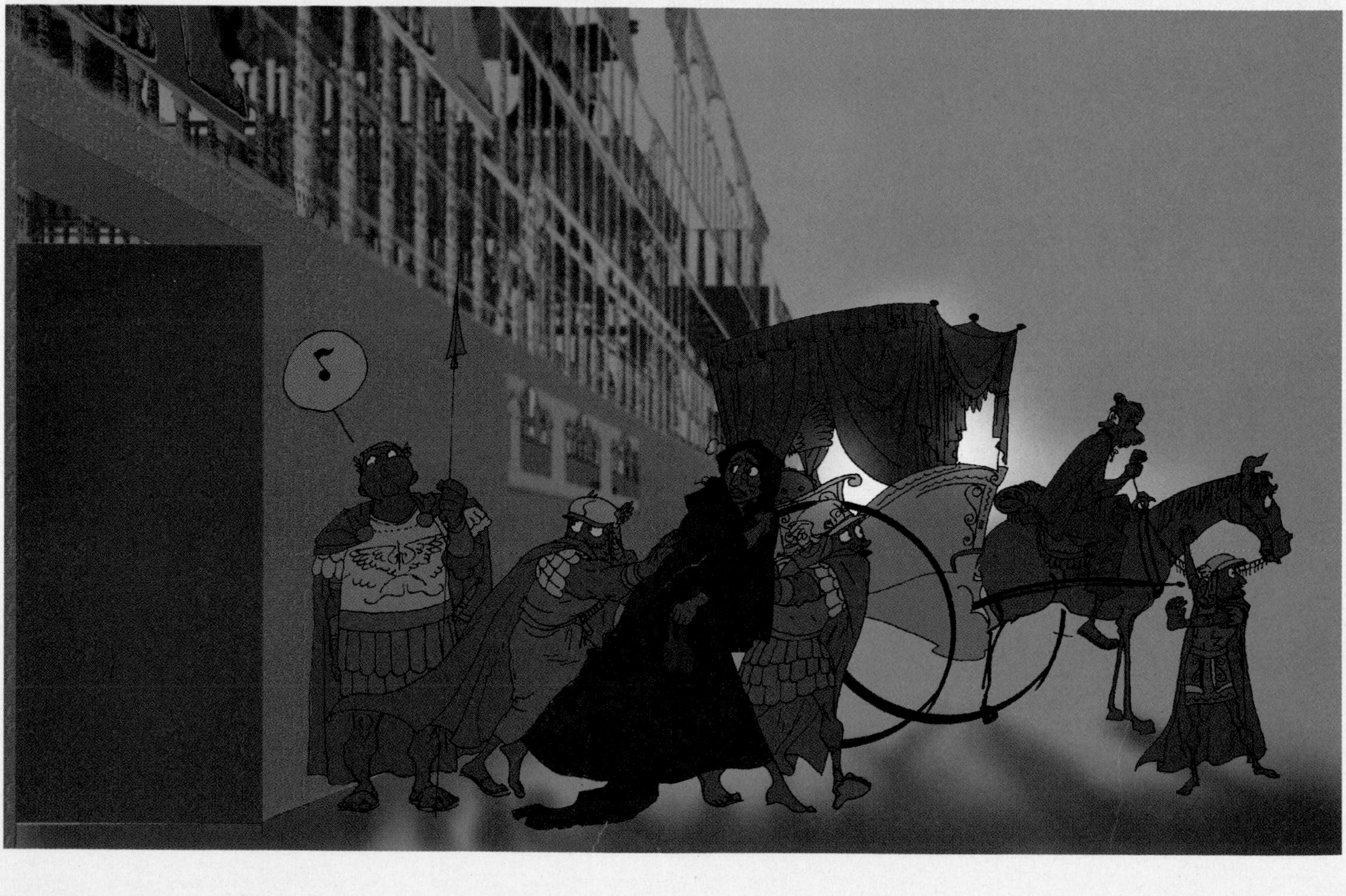
?

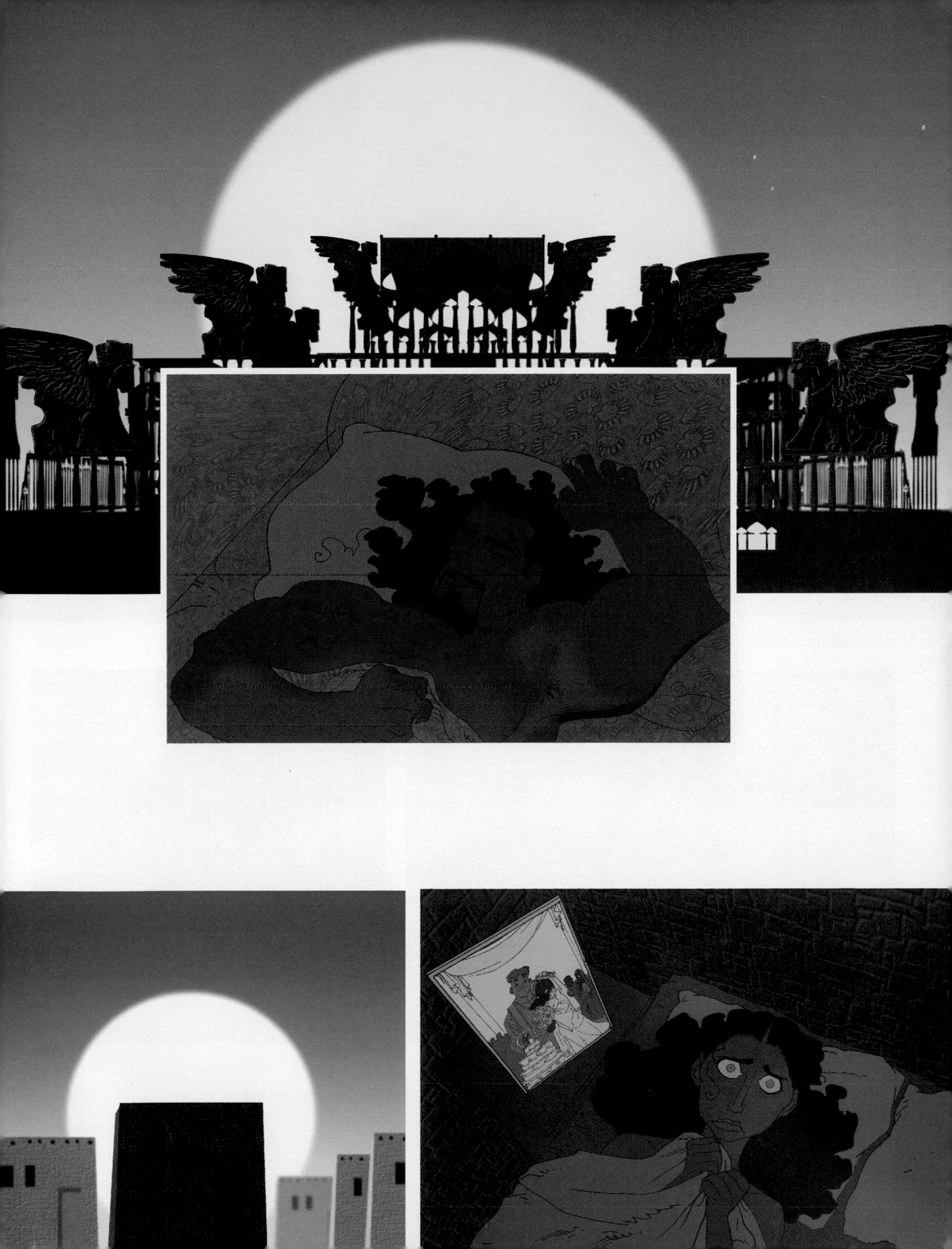

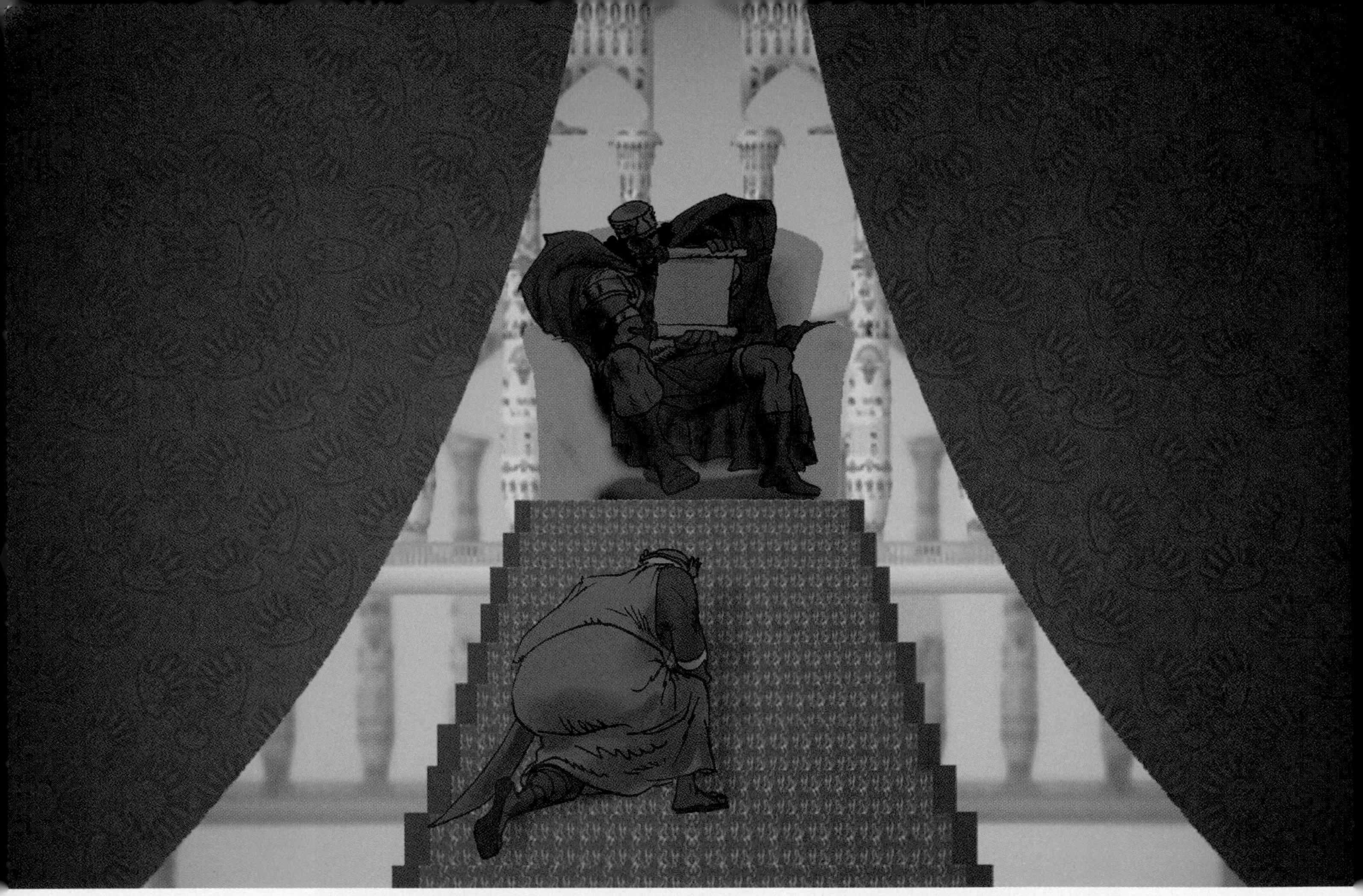

A few weeks later, Bathsheba sends David a message: She is pregnant.

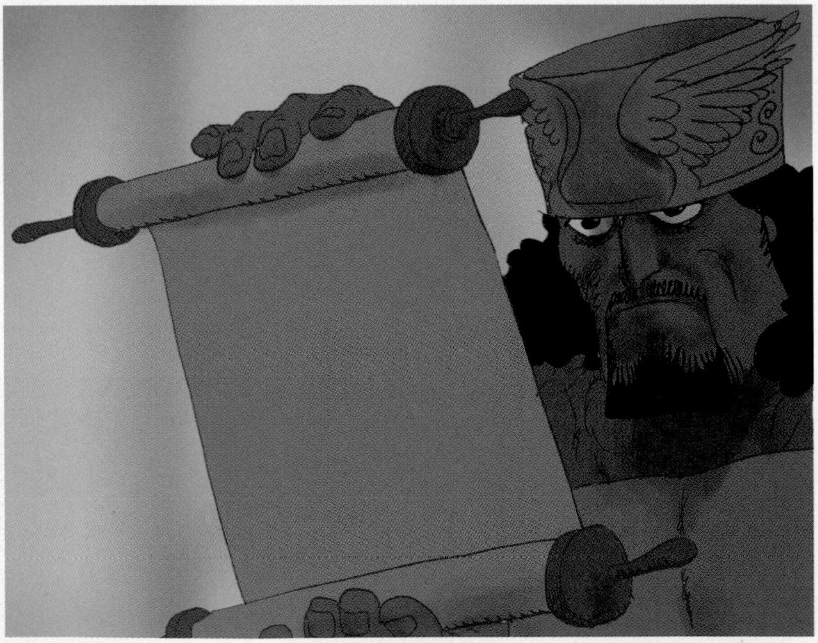

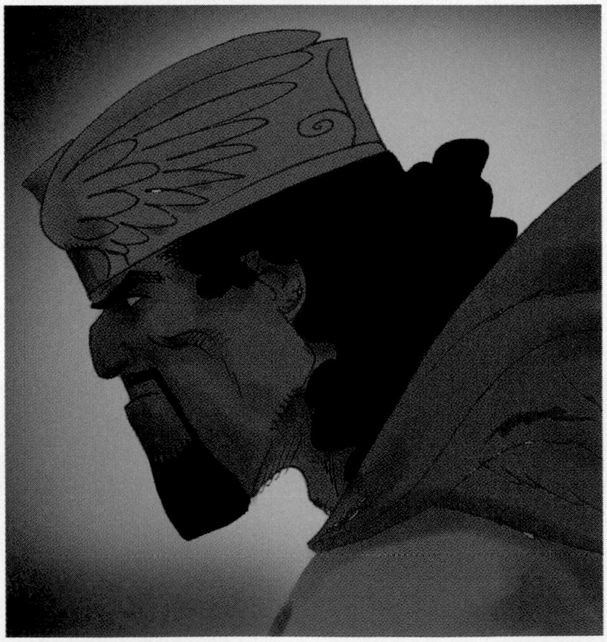

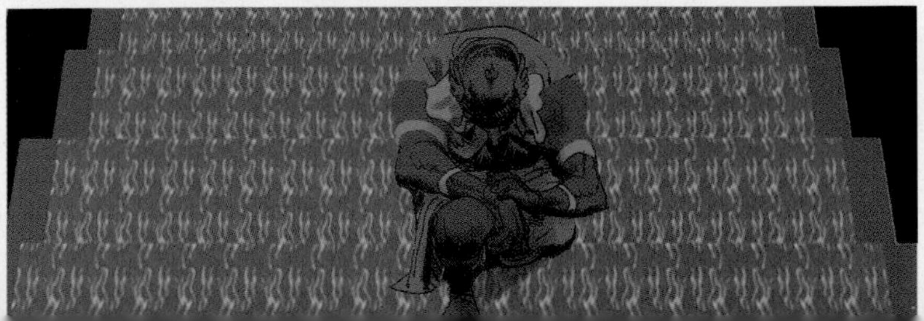

"Take a message to Commander Joab," David says, "Tell him; 'Send me Uriah the Hittite.'"

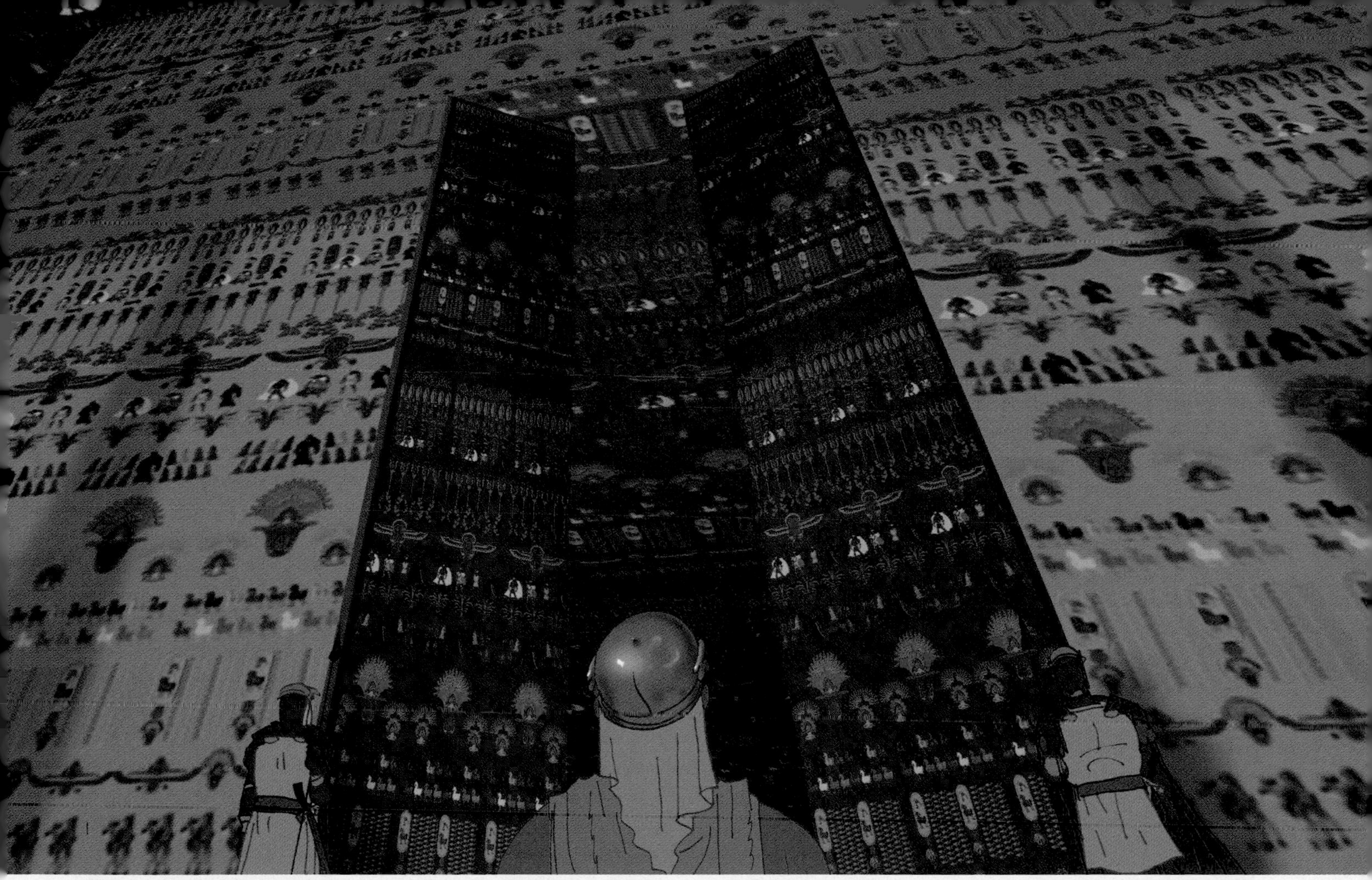
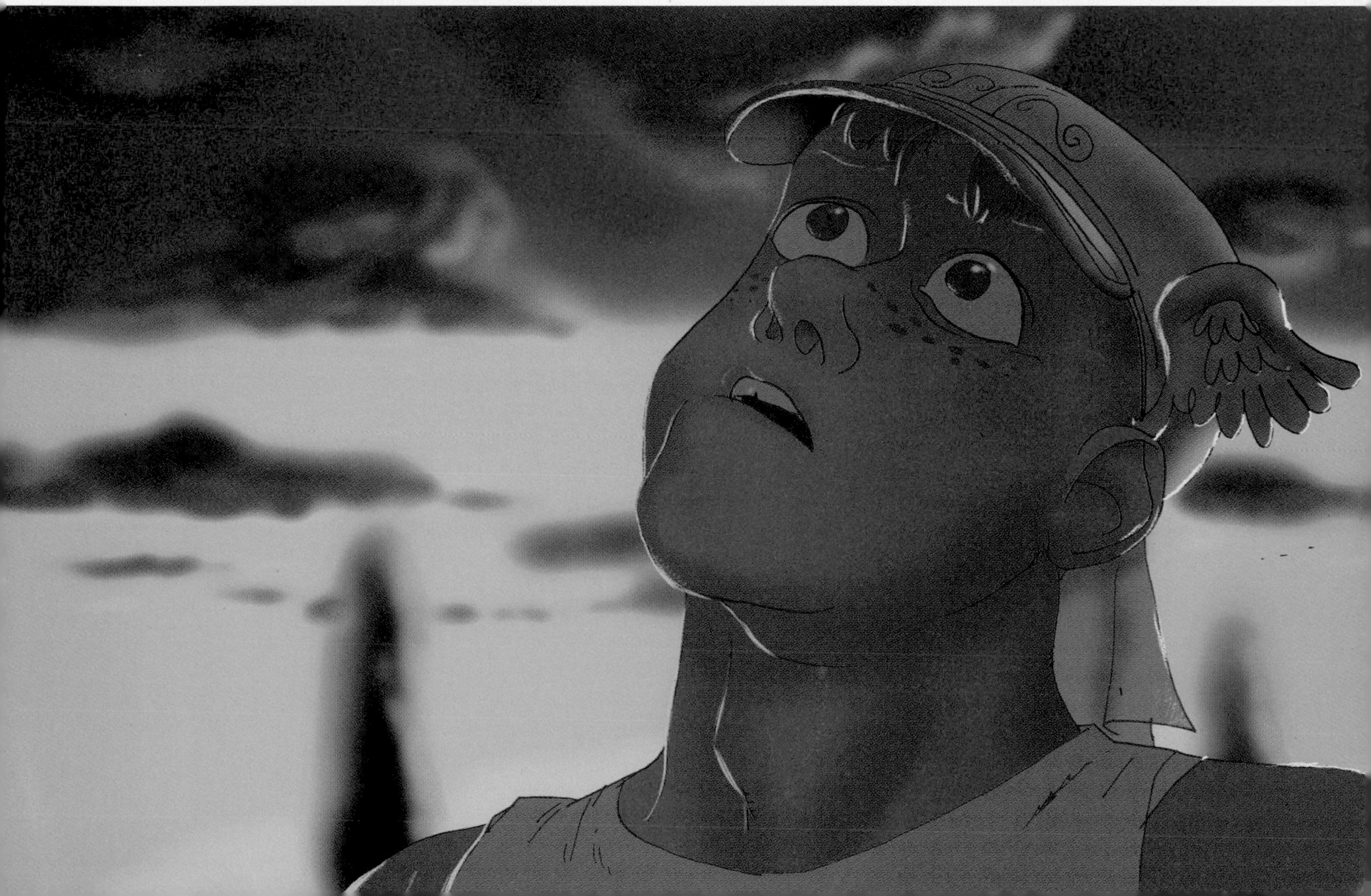

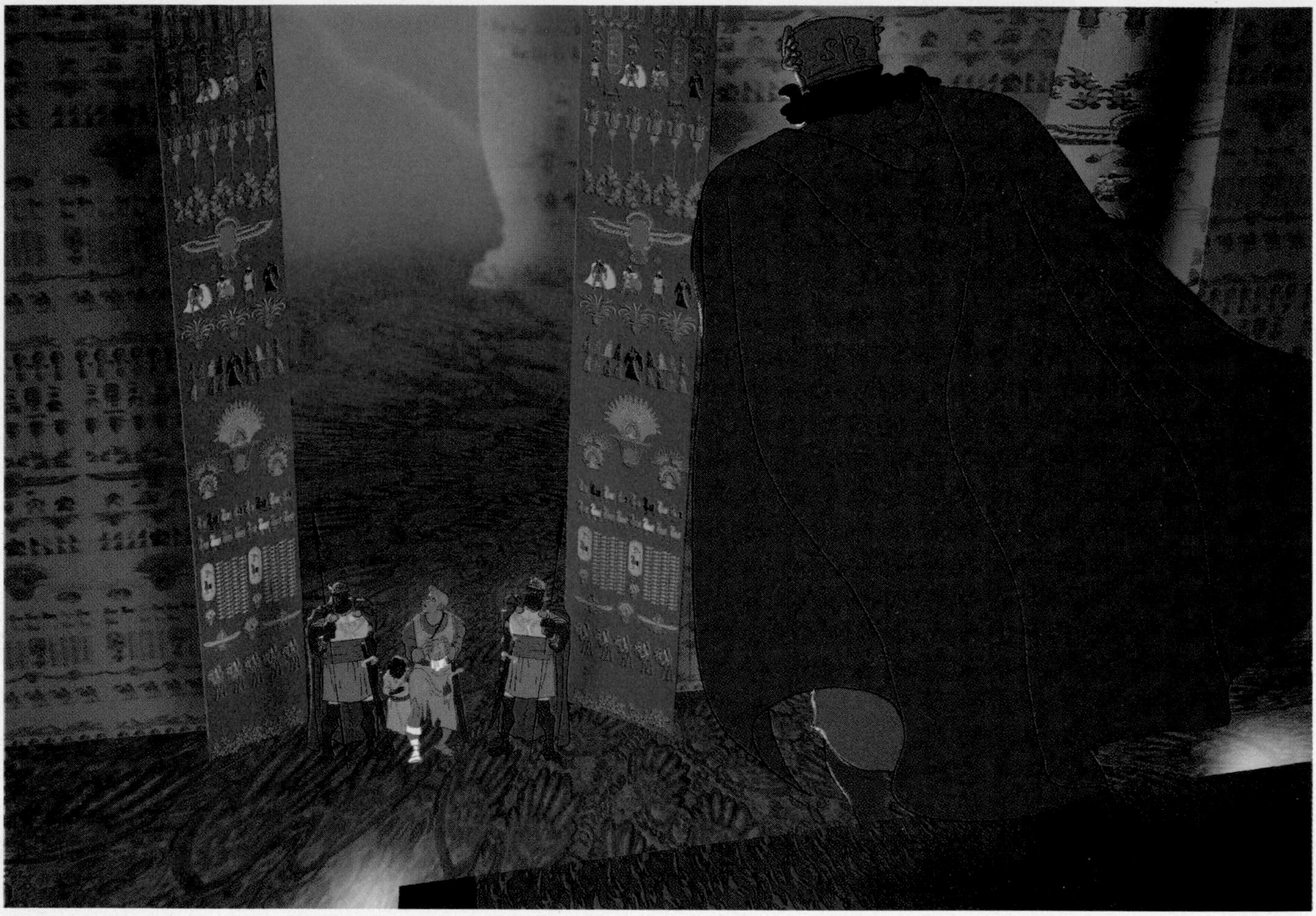

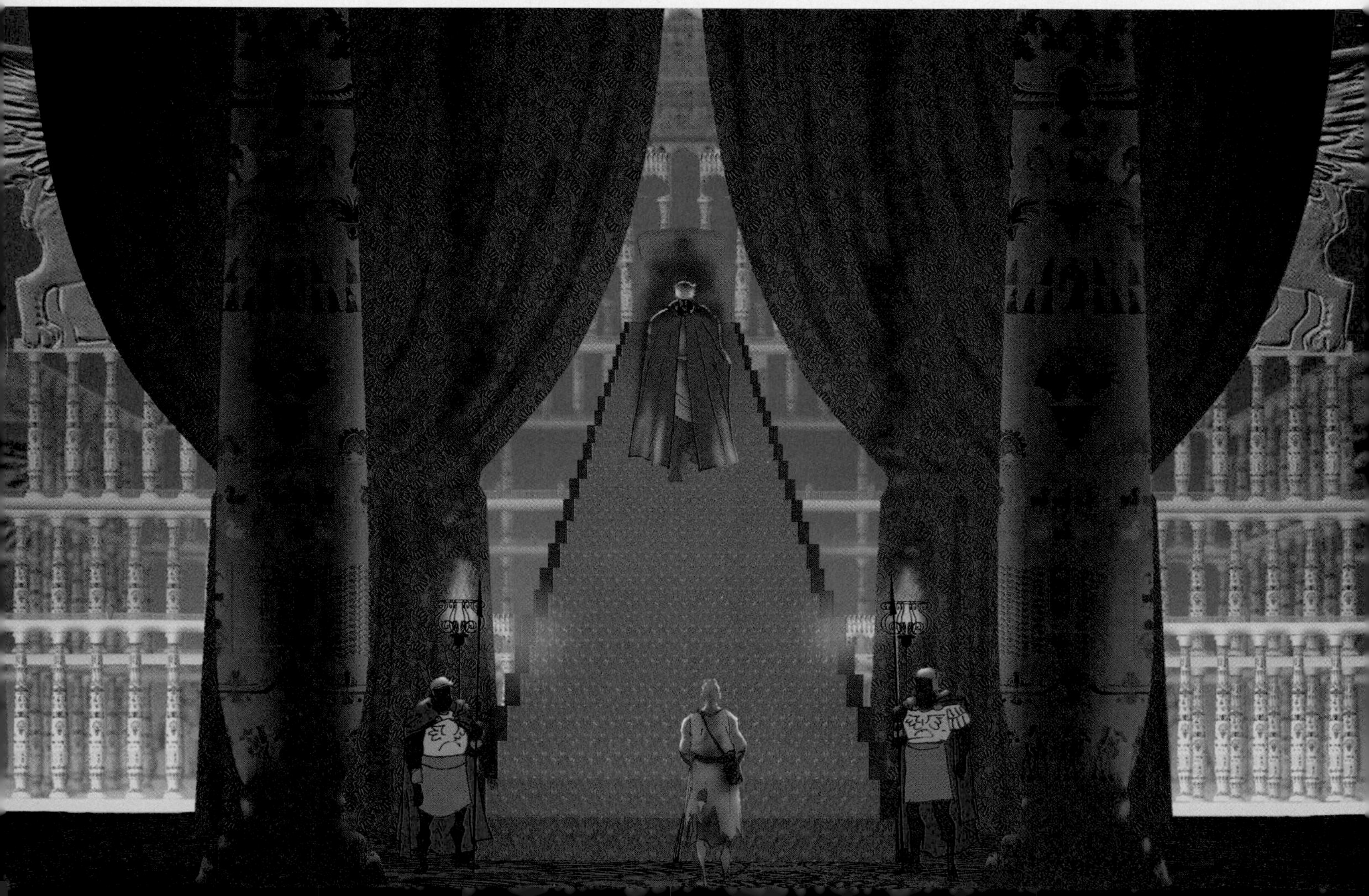

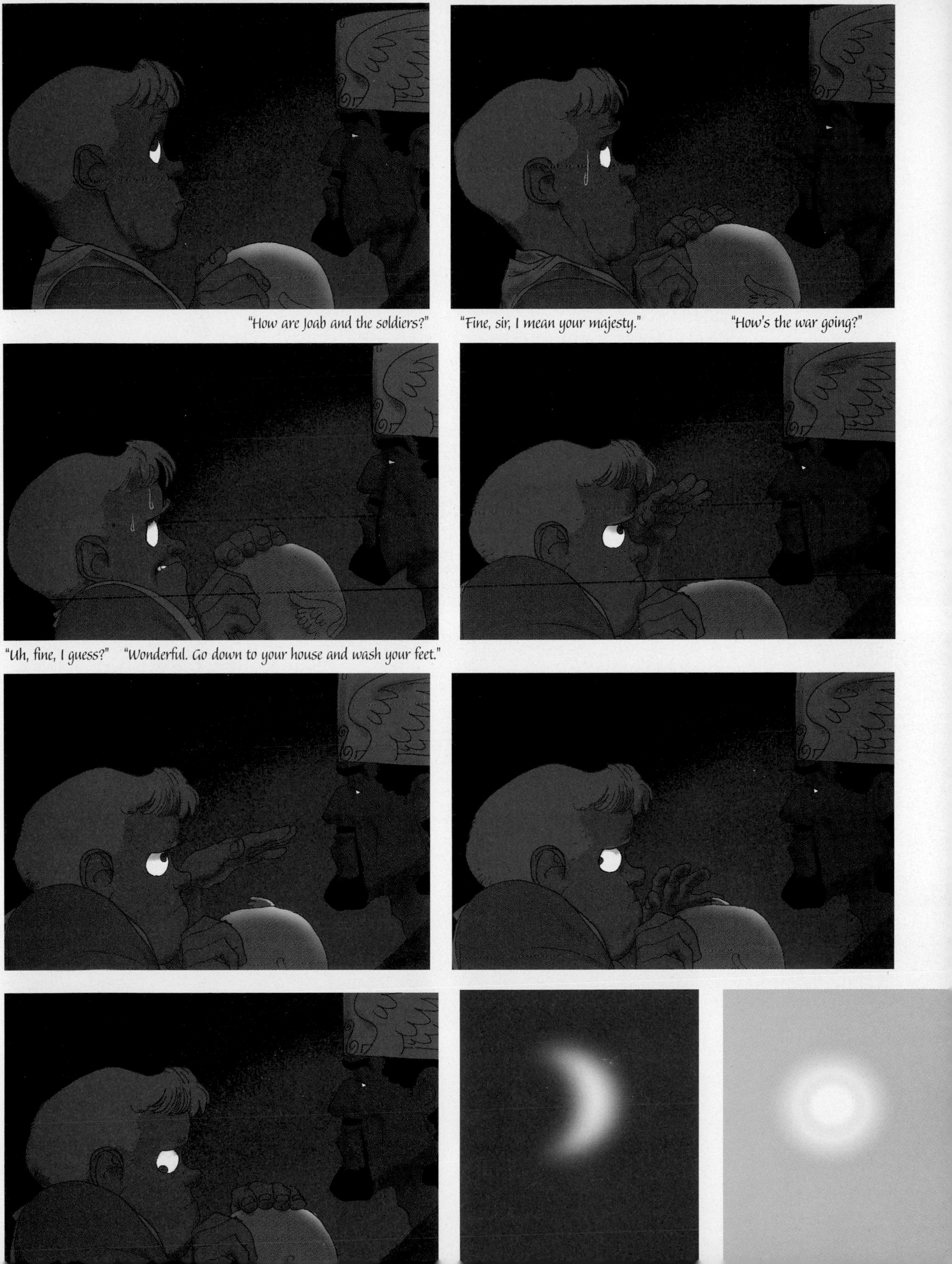
"How are Joab and the soldiers?"
"Fine, sir, I mean your majesty."
"How's the war going?"
"Uh, fine, I guess?"
"Wonderful. Go down to your house and wash your feet."

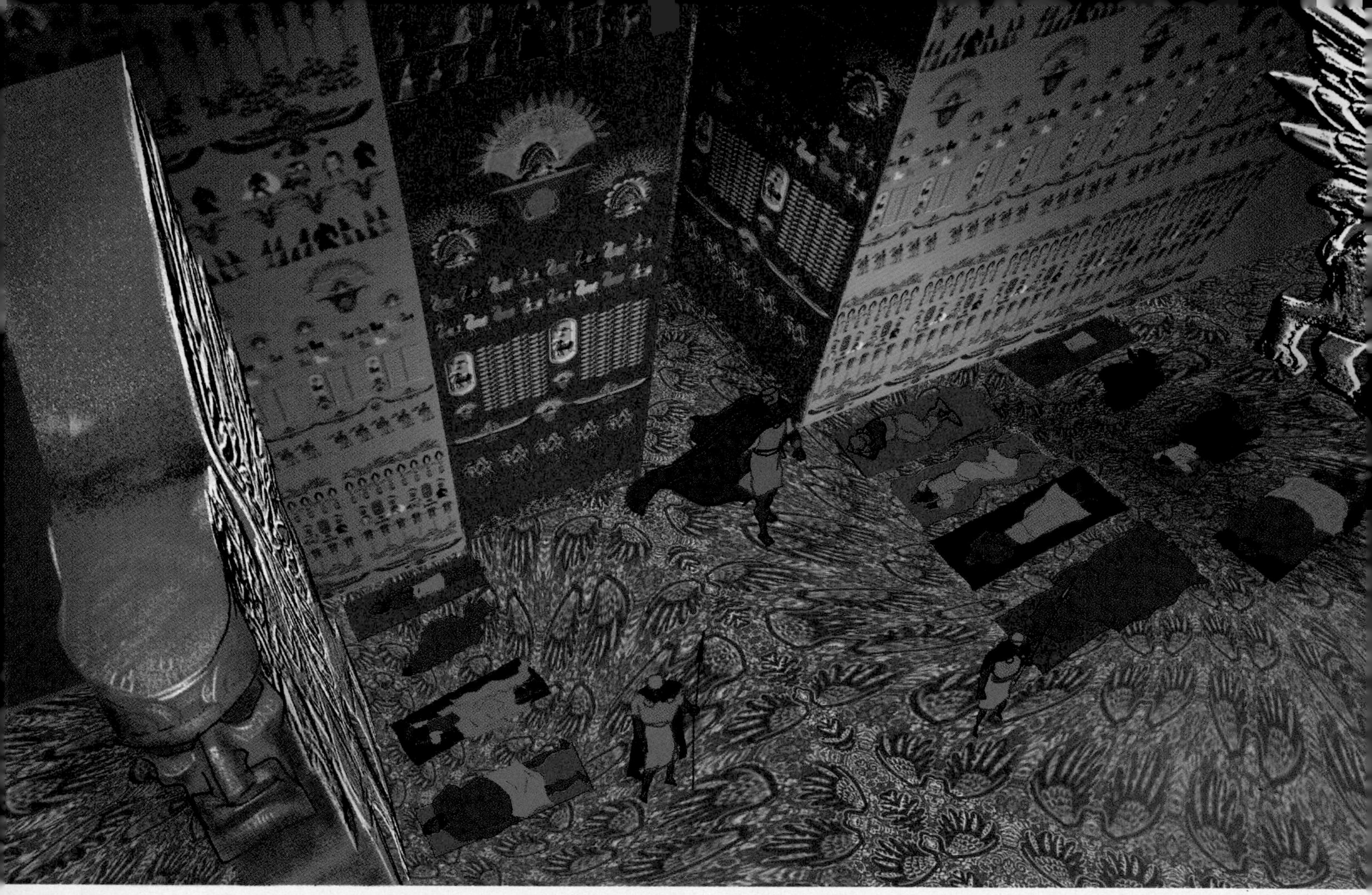

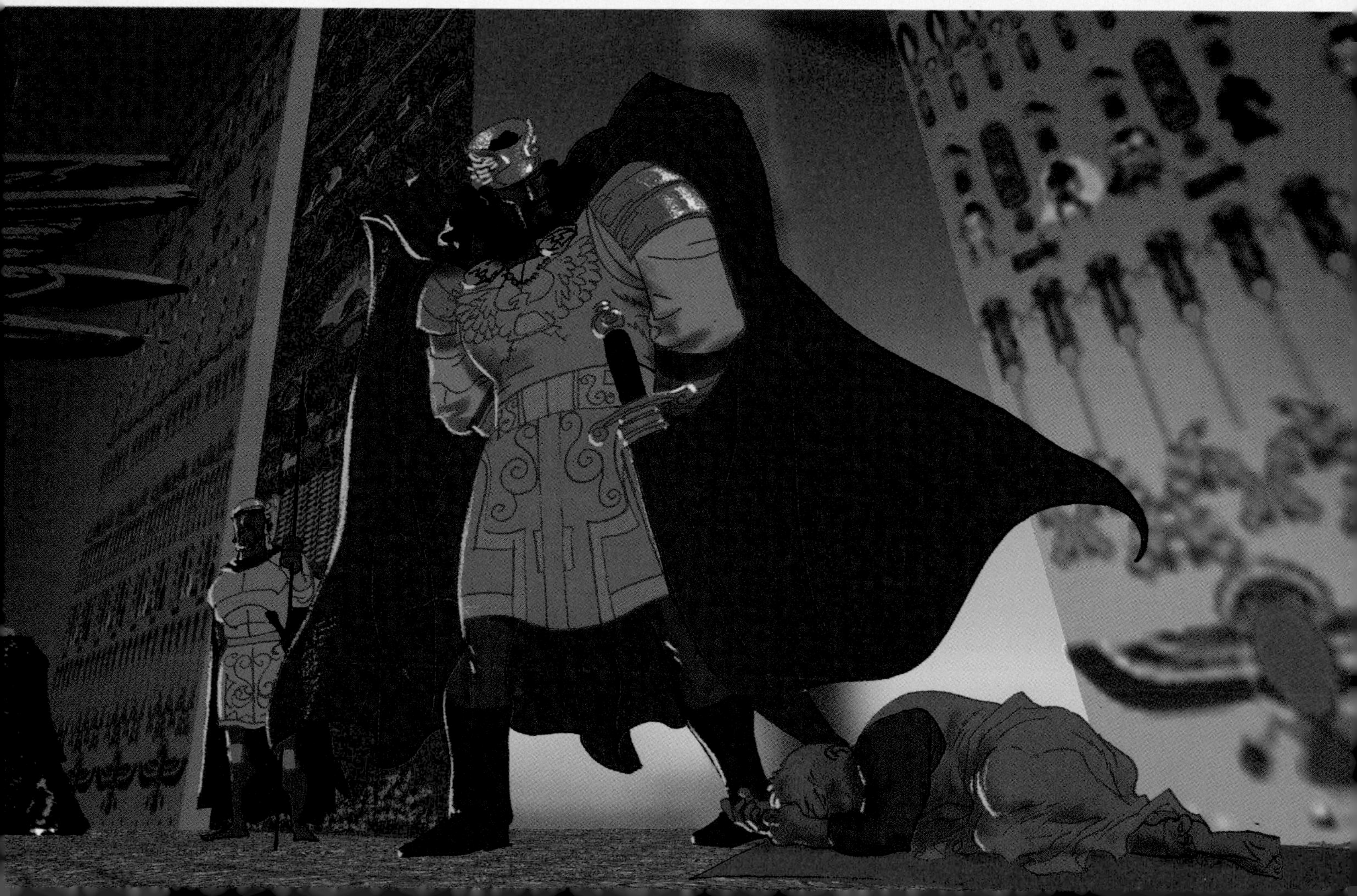

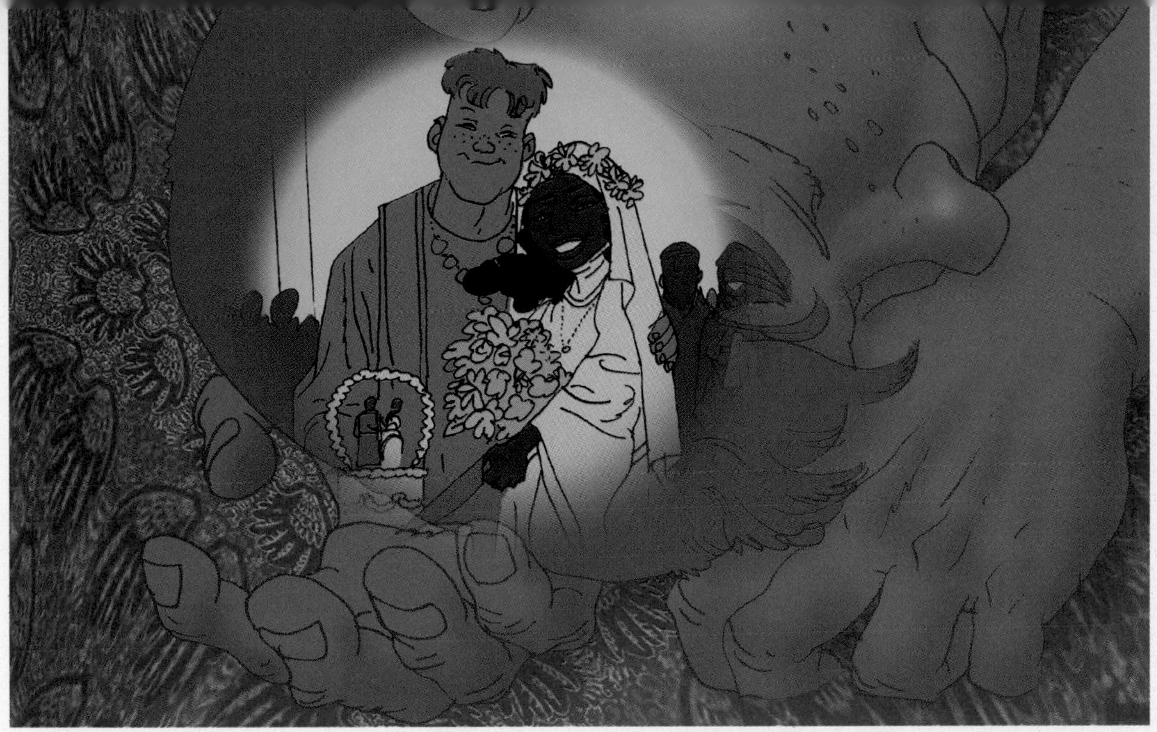

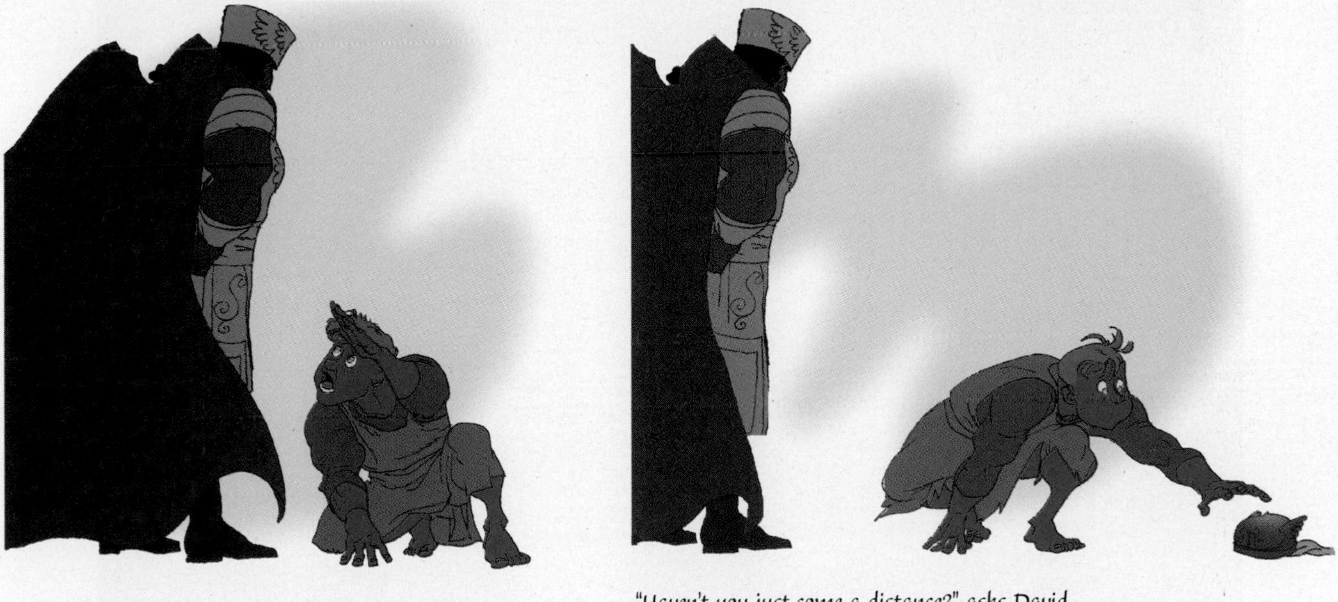

"Haven't you just come a distance?" asks David.
"Why didn't you go home last night?"

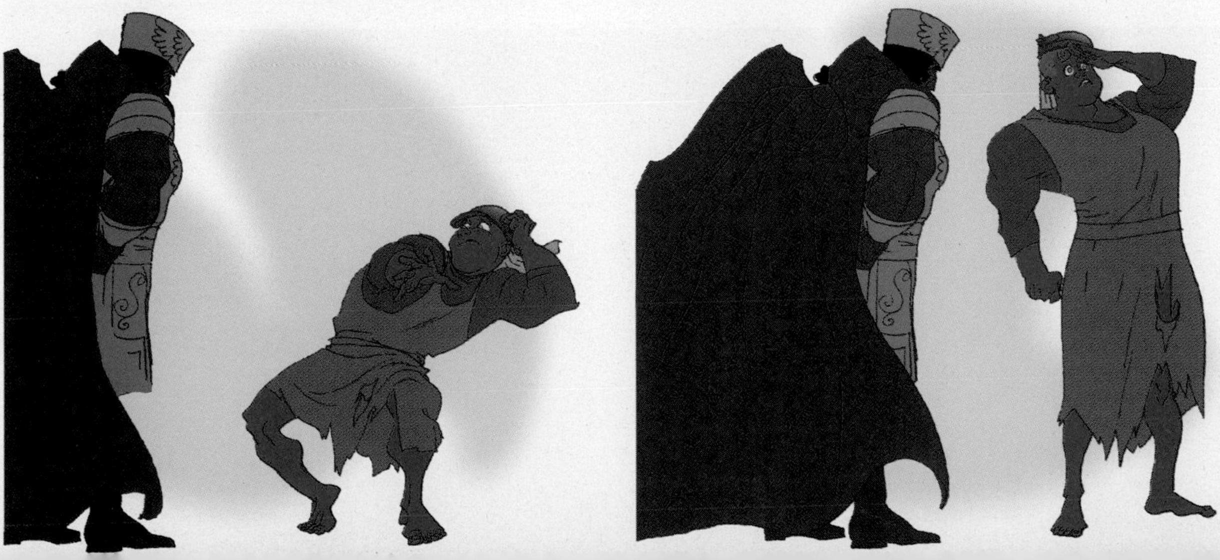

"The ark and Israel and Judah are staying in tents," Uriah says. "And my master Joab and my lord's men are camped in the open fields. How could I go to my house to eat and drink and lie with my wife? As surely as you live, I would not do such a thing!"

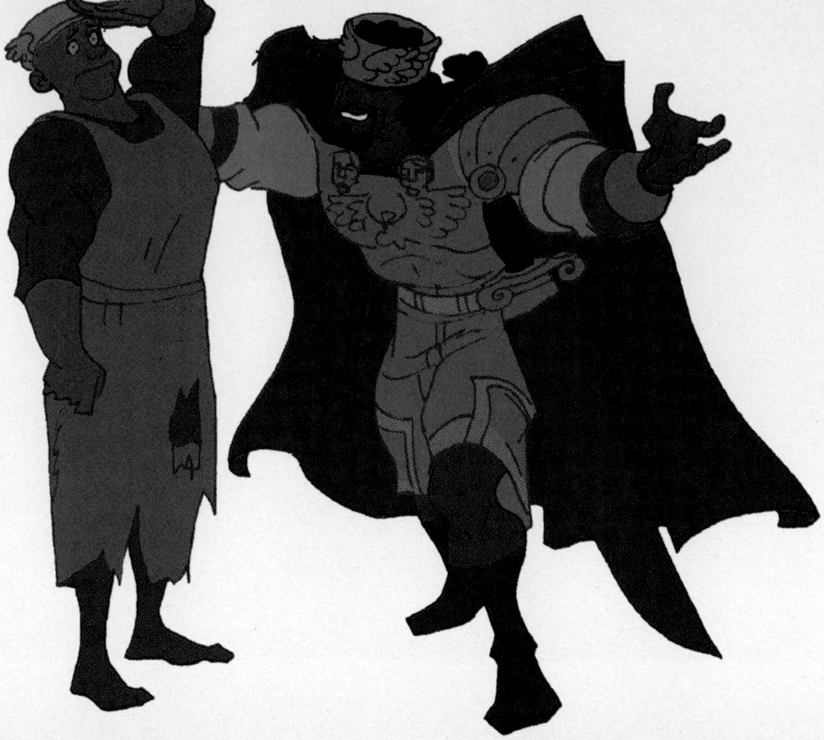

"Stay here one more day, and I will send you back."

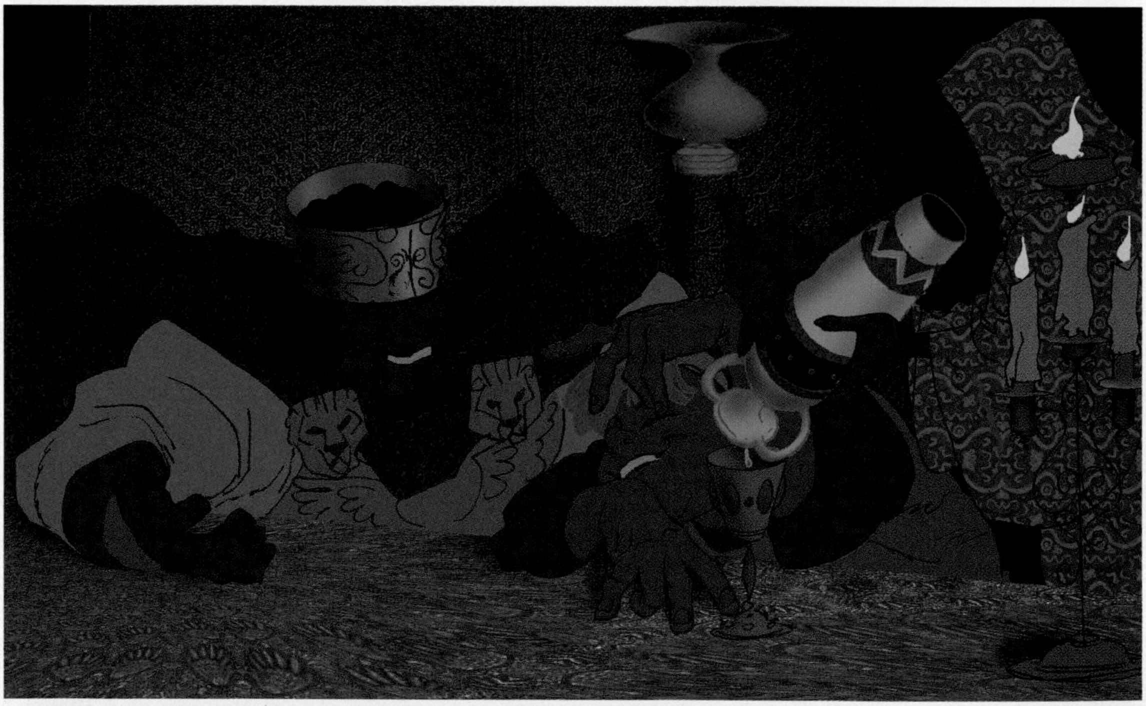

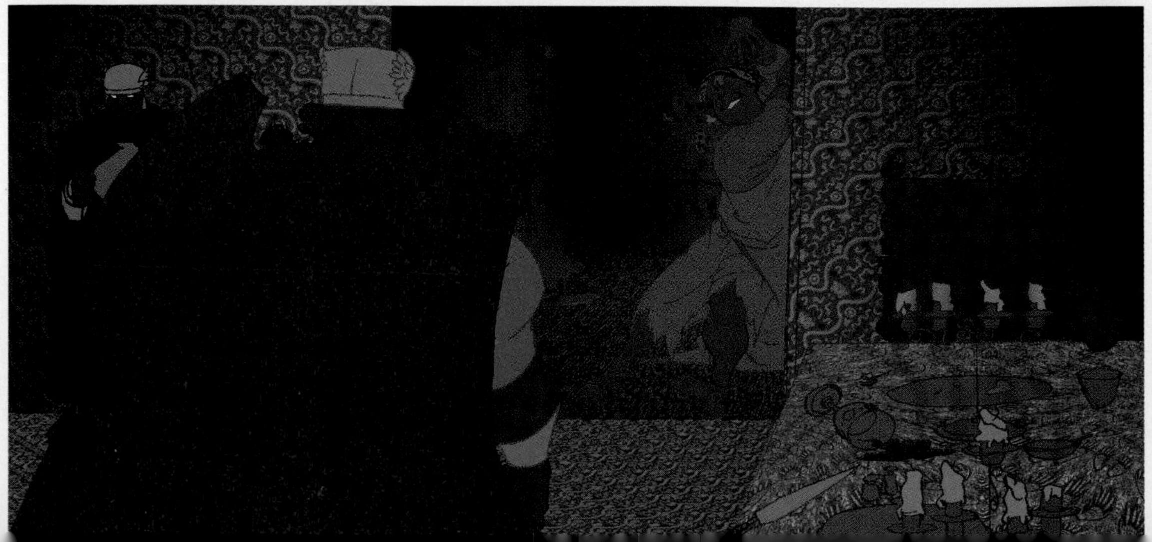

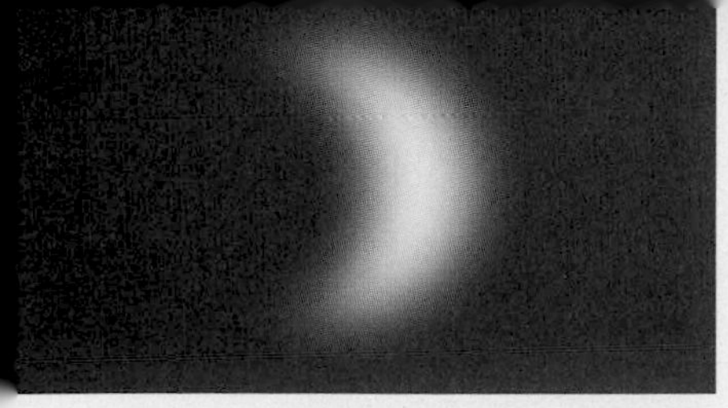
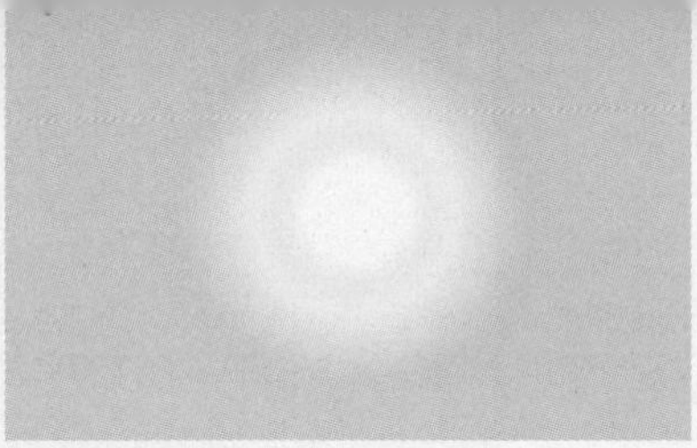
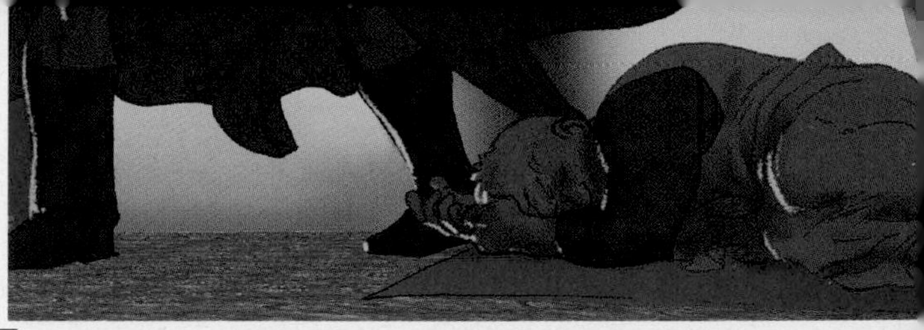

The next morning, David finds that Uriah still has not gone home.

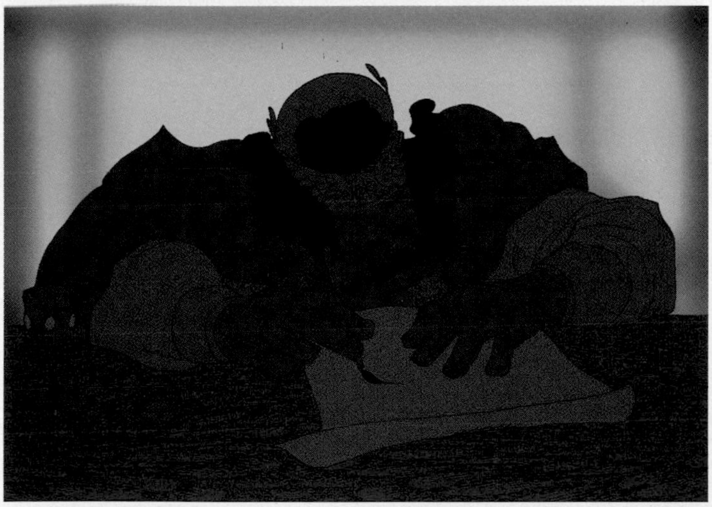
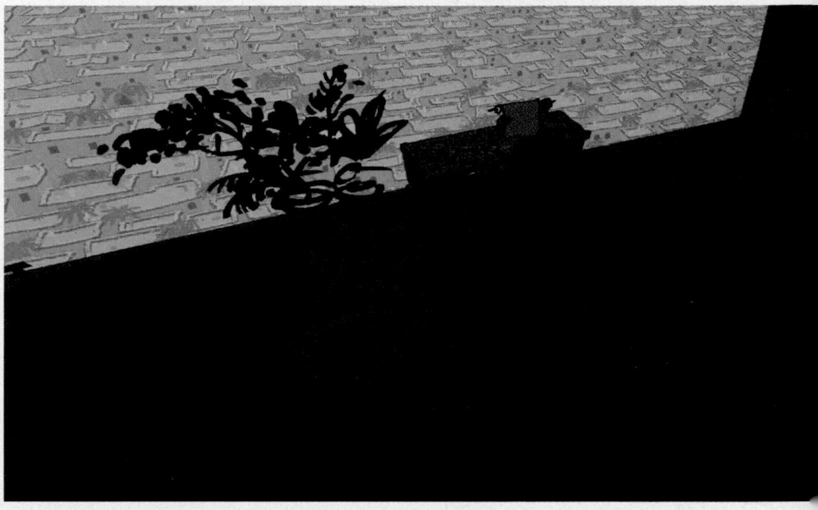

David writes a message to Joab. It says,"Put Uriah in the front line where the fighting is fiercest, then withdraw from him so he will be struck down and die."

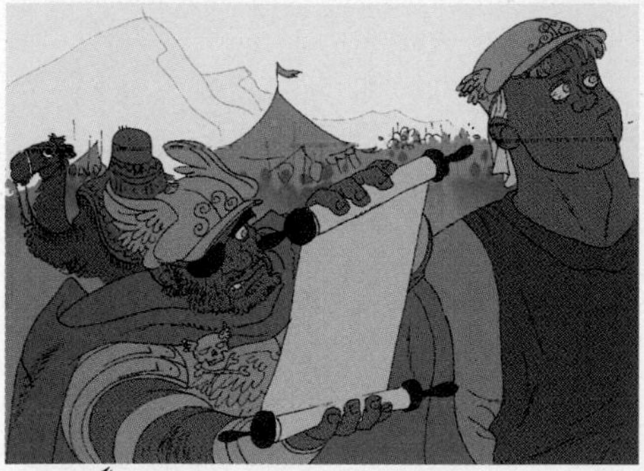

"What did you say your name was?"

"Uriah."

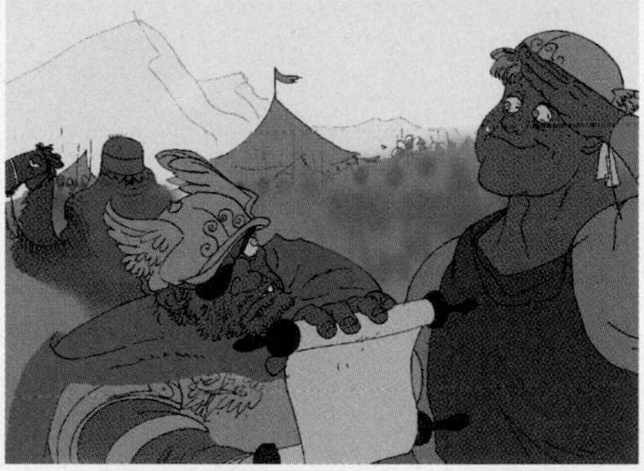

"And David gave you this message to deliver personally?"

"Yes."

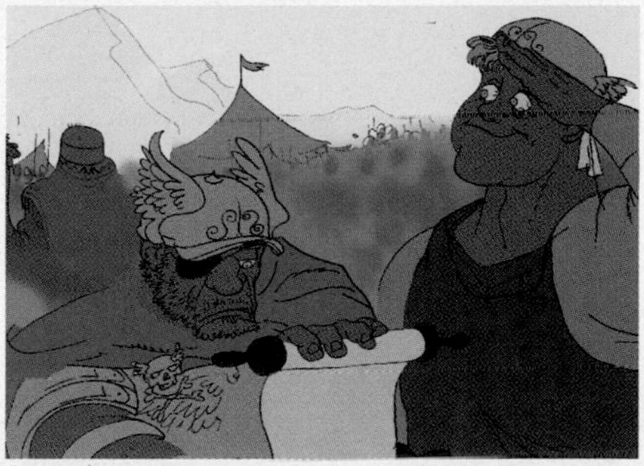

"Now that's chutzpah. Thank you very much, Uriah. Don't go too far. I'll need you later."

"Yes sir!"

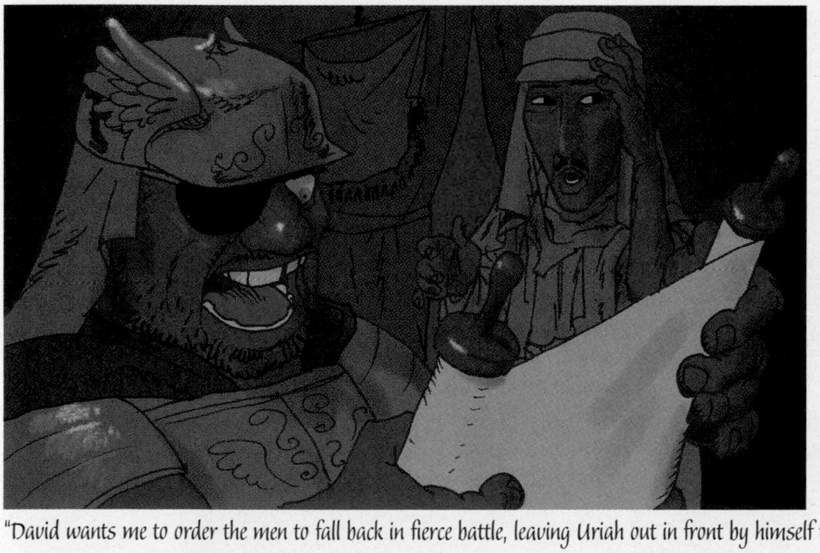

"David wants me to order the men to fall back in fierce battle, leaving Uriah out in front by himself to be killed. Isn't it going to seem a little suspicious when I give that order? Even if I could pull it off without one of the men tipping Uriah off, the rumors would be confirmed: While these men are fighting and dying on the battlefield, the king is back home doing their wives! Not exactly a morale-builder for the troops, is it? Remember Ziklag?"

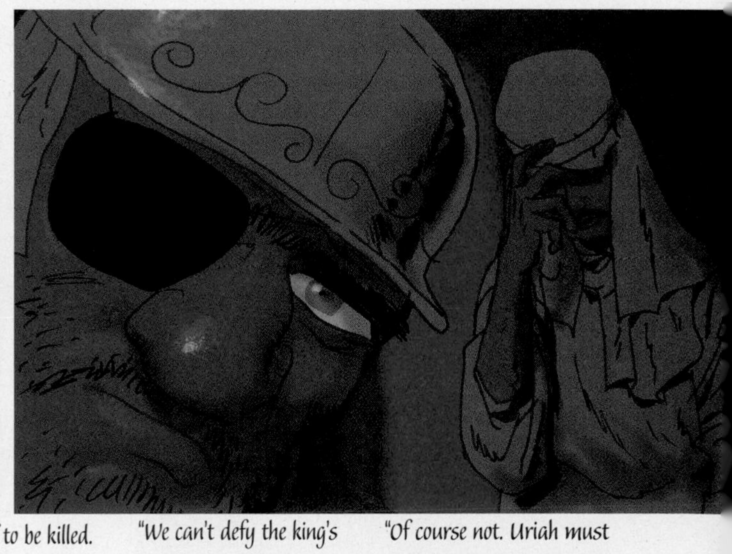

"We can't defy the king's order," says Abiathar. "I'm not dying in Uriah's place."

"Of course not. Uriah must die in battle. I'm just saying we can't give the order for the men to withdraw from him."

The messenger from Joab says, "Surely the men have been mighty against us, and came out to us into the field. And we were on them to the entrance of the gate. And those shooting shot at your servants from off the wall, and many of the servants of the king are dead."

David is angry. "Why did you draw near to the city to fight? Did you not know that they would shoot from off the wall? Who killed Abimelech the son of Jerub-besheth? Did not a woman throw a piece of a riding millstone on him from the wall, and he died in Thebez? Why did you draw near to the wall?"

"Also your servant Uriah the Hittite is dead."

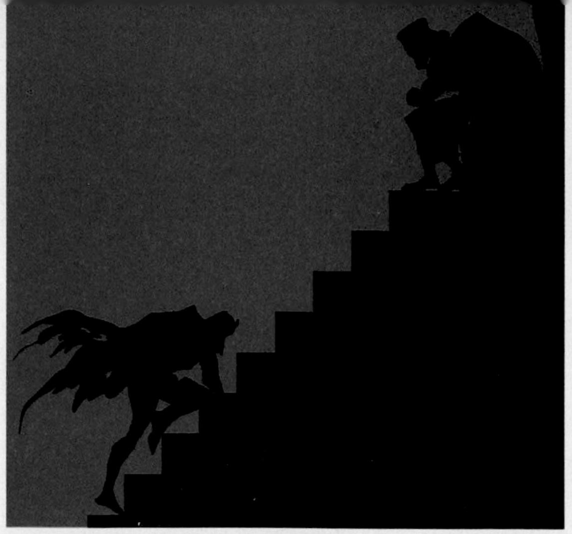

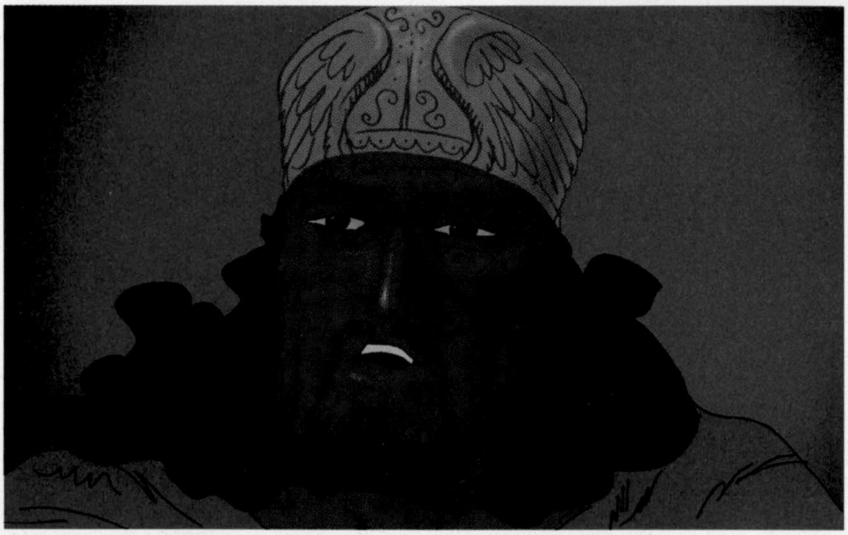

"You shall say to Joab, 'Do not let this thing be evil in your eyes. For the sword devours one as well as another. Make your battle stronger against the city, and overthrow it. And make him strong.'"

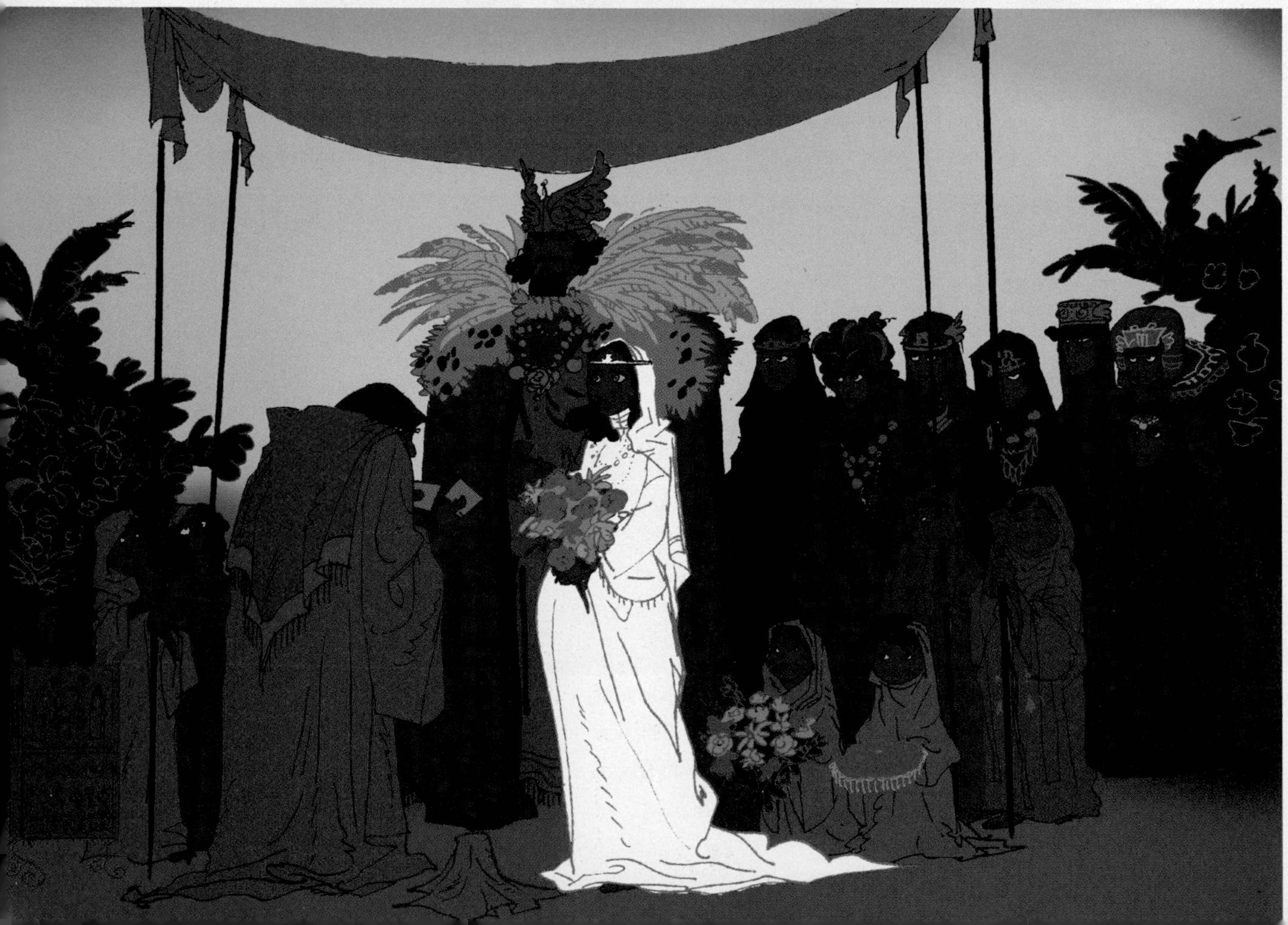

"She could have at least had a longer period of mourning," Abigail says.

" From what I hear, they don't have time," Michal whispers.

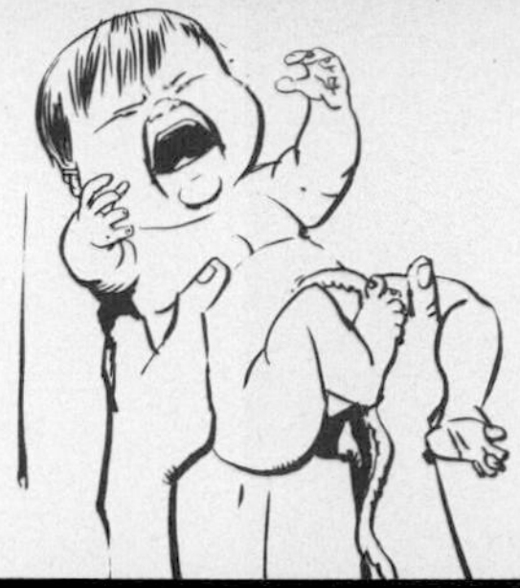

A healthy son is born to David and Bathsheba.
Some time later, David is visited by the prophet Nathan.

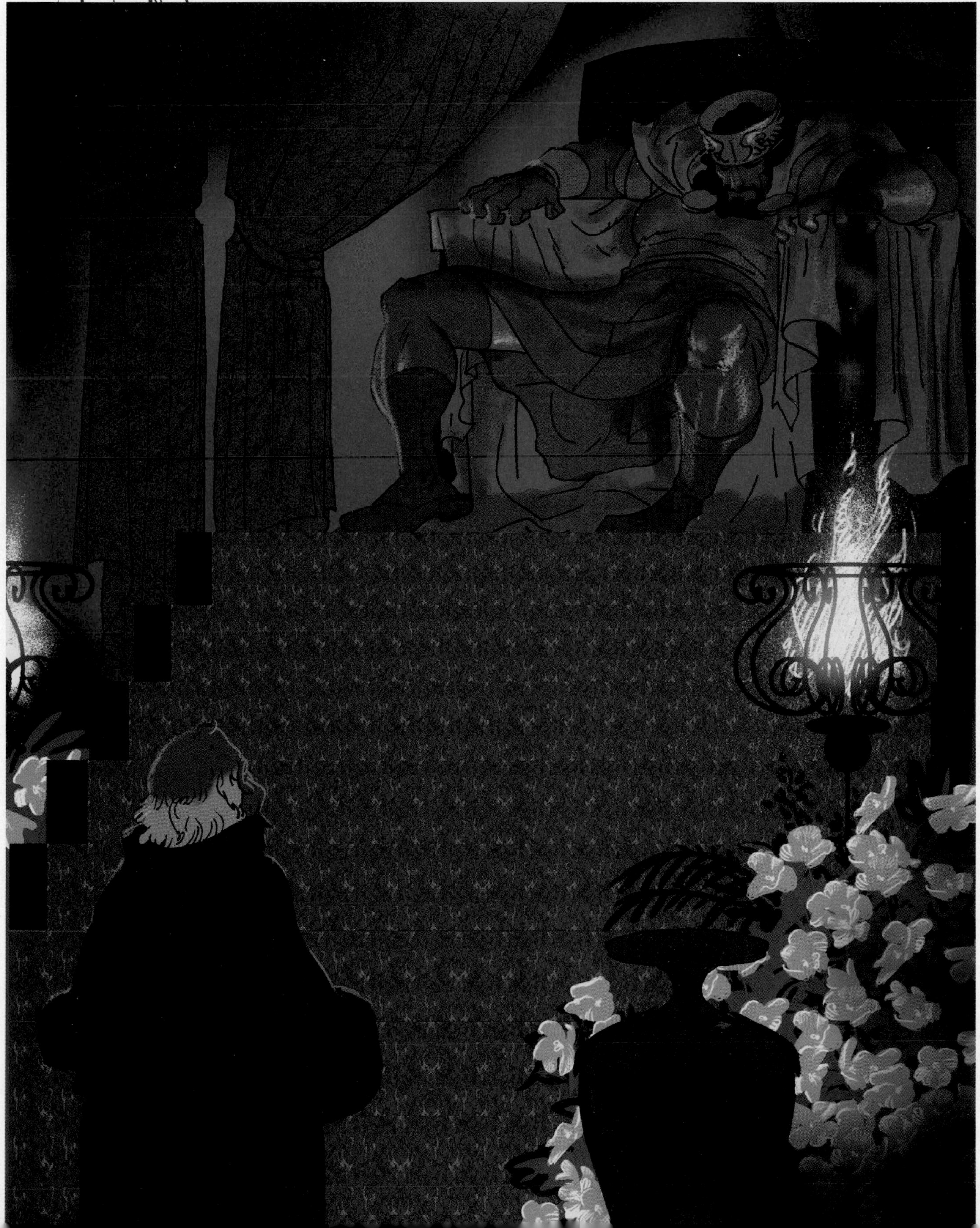

Nathan says, "There were two men in one city, the one rich, and the other poor. The rich one had flocks and very many herds. But the poor one had nothing except one little ewe lamb, which he had bought and nourished. And it grew up with him, and with his sons together, and it ate of his food, and it drank from his cup, and it lay in his bosom. And it was like a daughter to him."

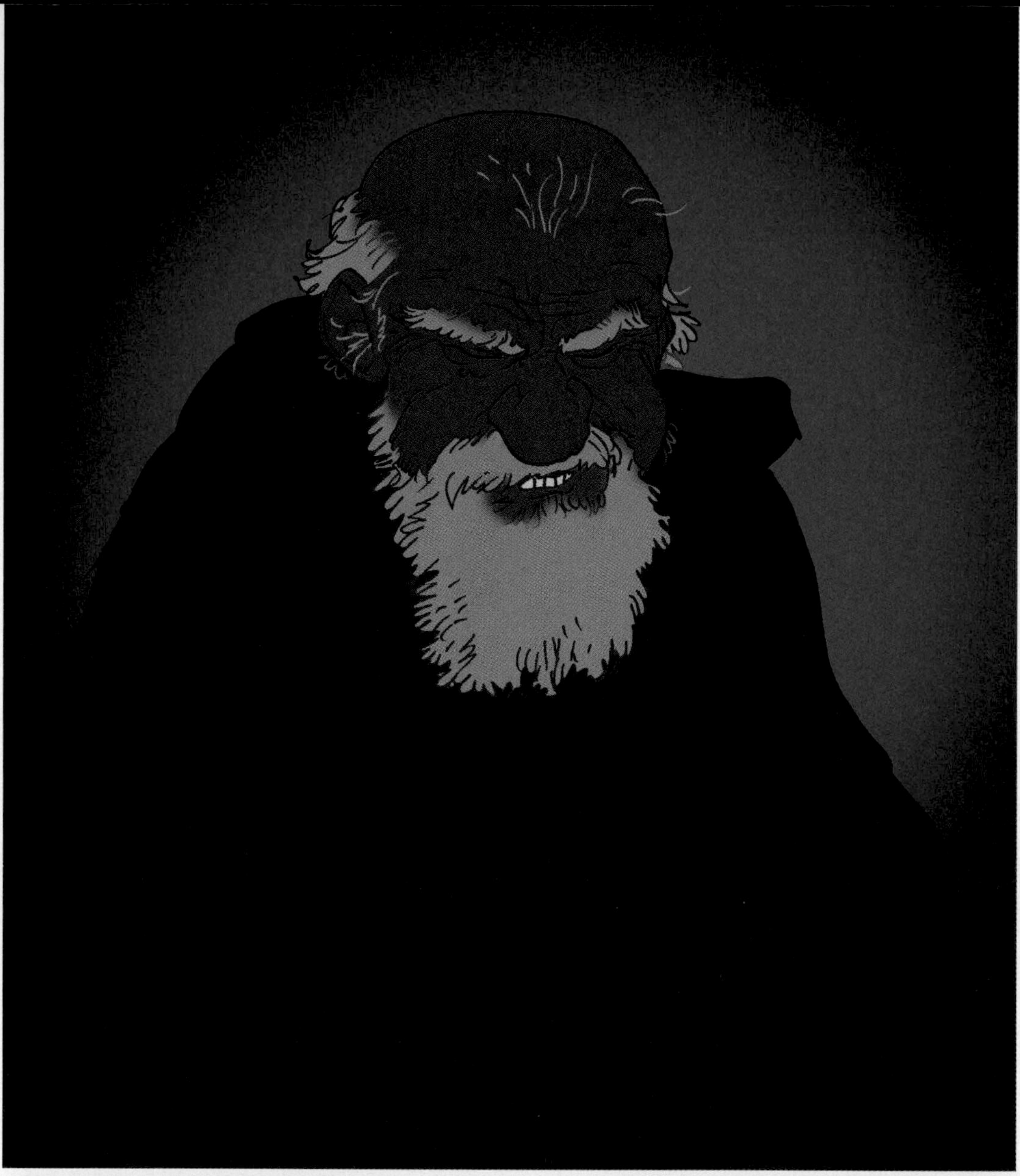

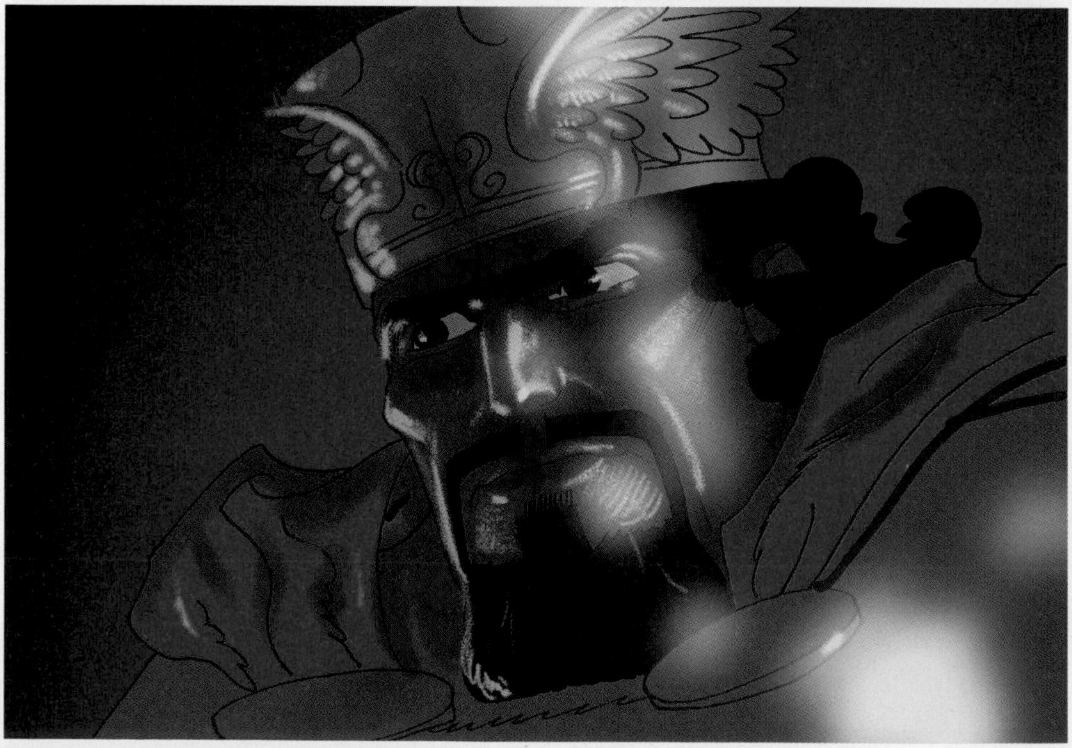

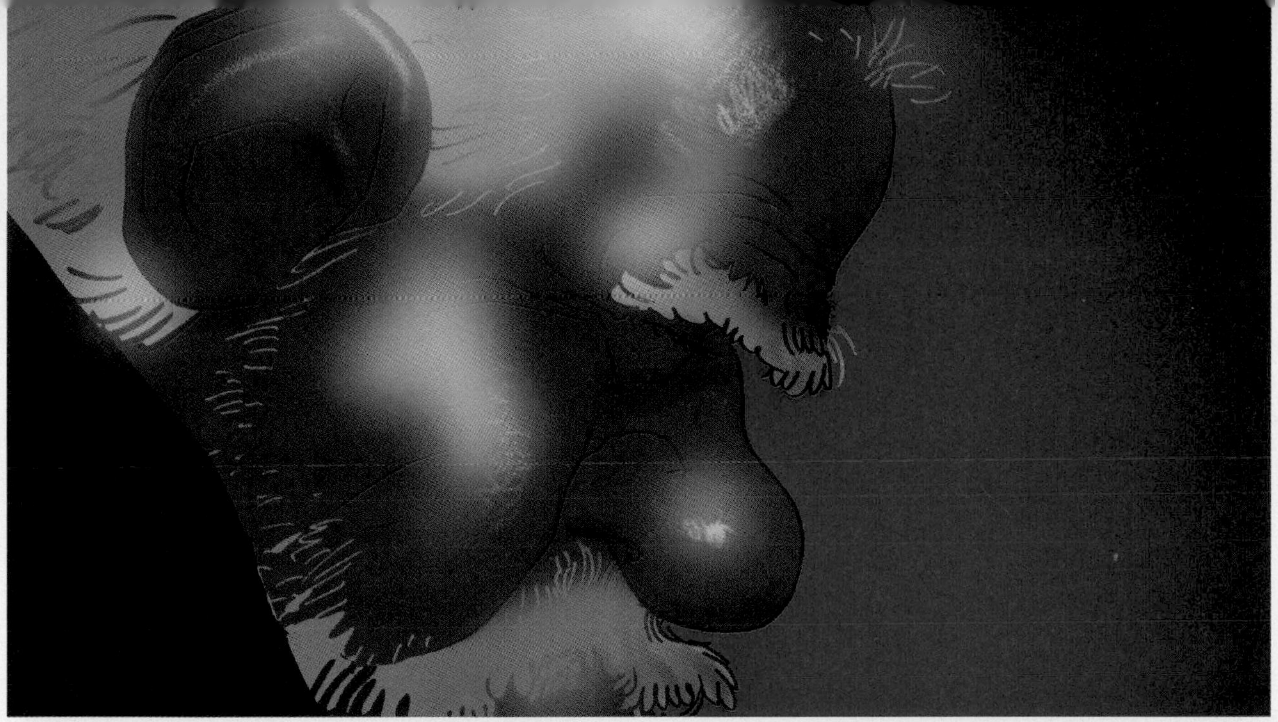

"And a traveler came to the rich one, but the rich man chose not to take one of his own flock or his own herd to prepare a meal for the traveler who had come to him. Instead, the rich man took the ewe lamb of the poor man, and prepared it for the traveler who had come to him."

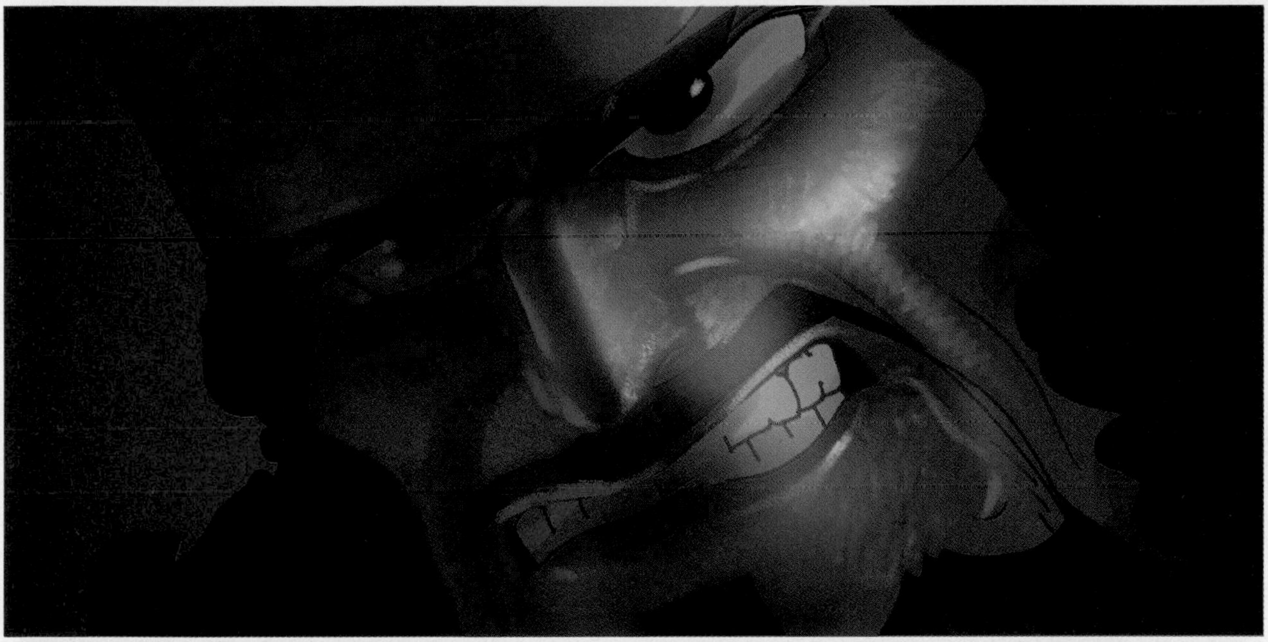

David says, ""As the LORD lives, surely the man who did this deserves to die. And he shall repay fourfold for the ewe lamb, because he has done this thing, and because he had no pity."

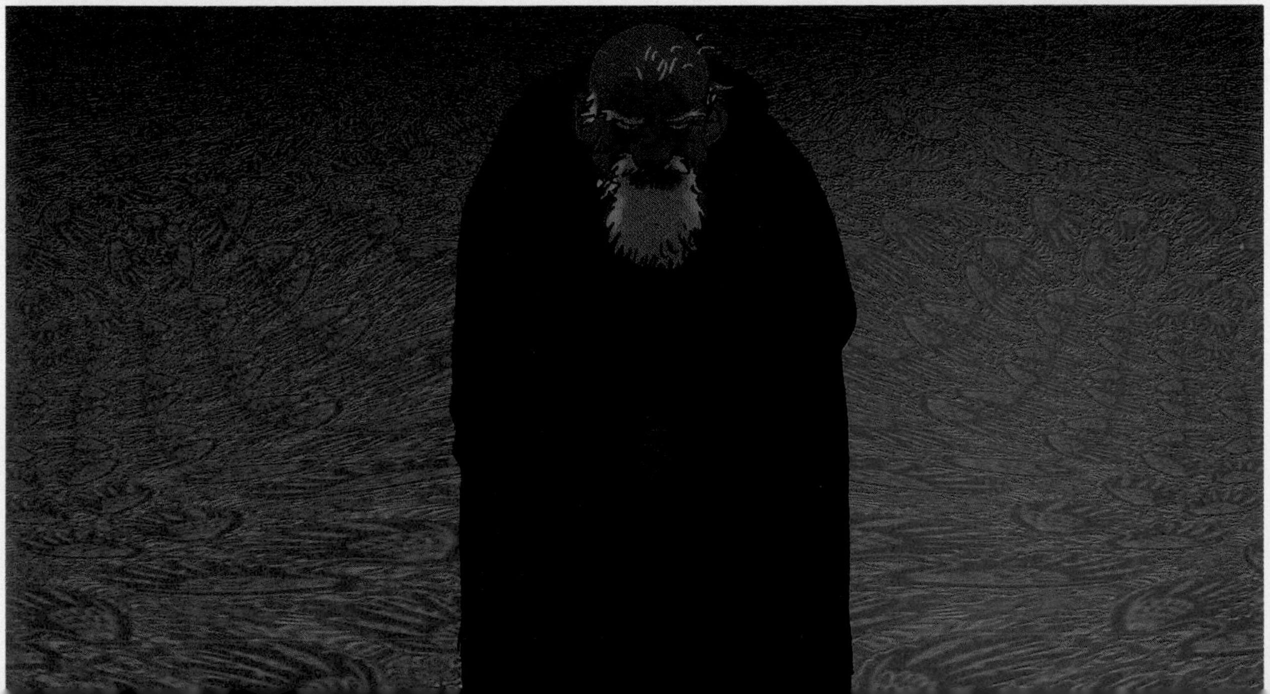

"You are that man."

"So says the God of Israel, "I anointed you as king over Israel, and I delivered you out of the hand of Saul. And I gave you the house of your master, and your master's wives into your bosom. And I gave you the house of Israel and of Judah. And if that were too little, then I would have added to you these and those things.

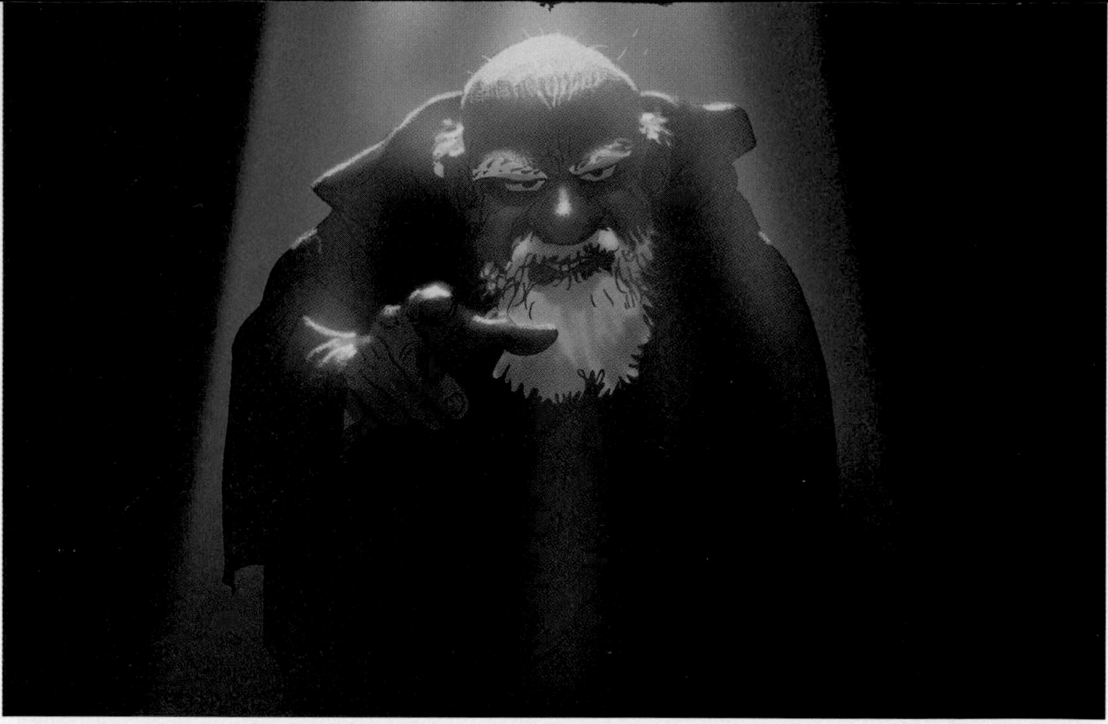

"Why have you despised the Word of Jehovah, to do the evil in His eyes? You have stricken Uriah the Hittite by the sword, and you have taken his wife to yourself for a wife. And you have killed him by the sword of the sons of Ammon.

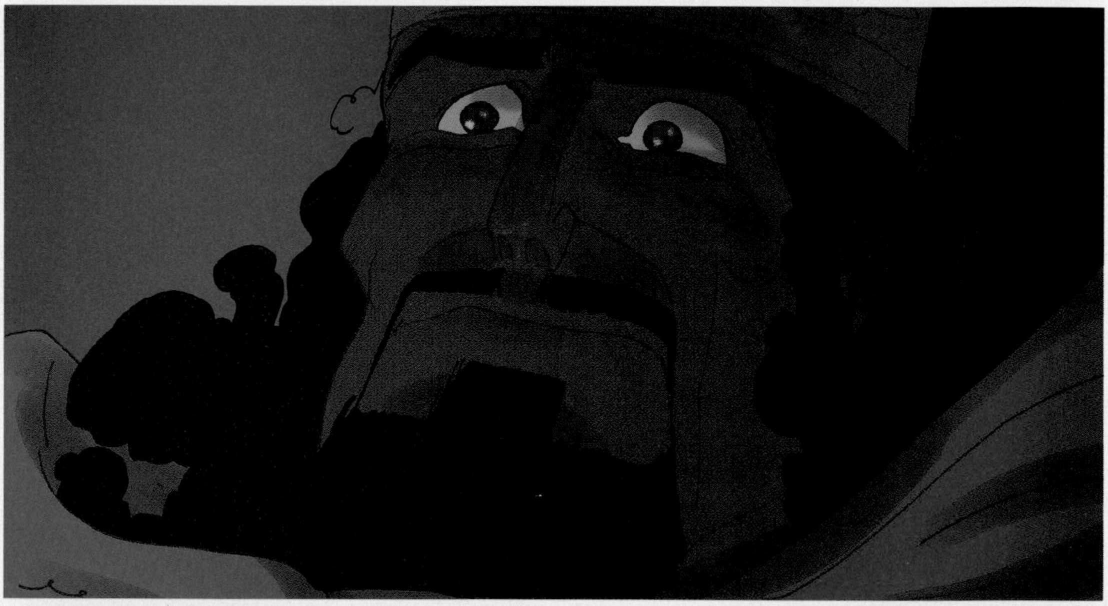

"And now the sword shall not turn aside from your house continually, because you have despised Me, and have taken the wife of Uriah the Hittite to be a wife to you.

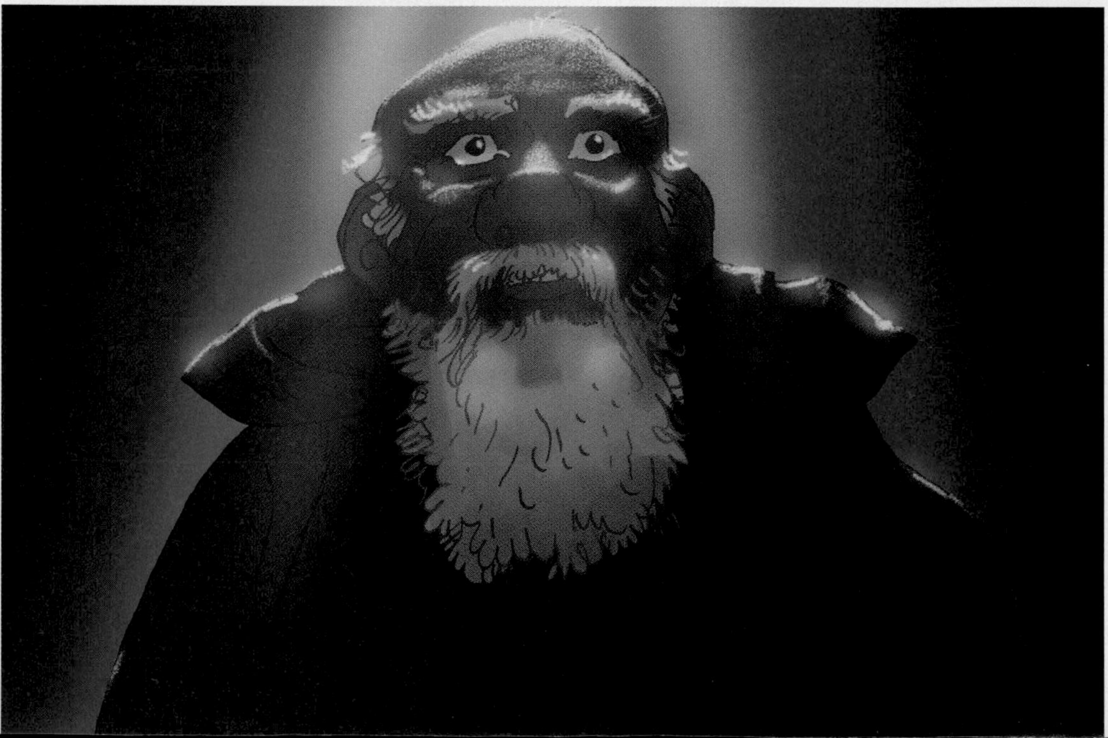

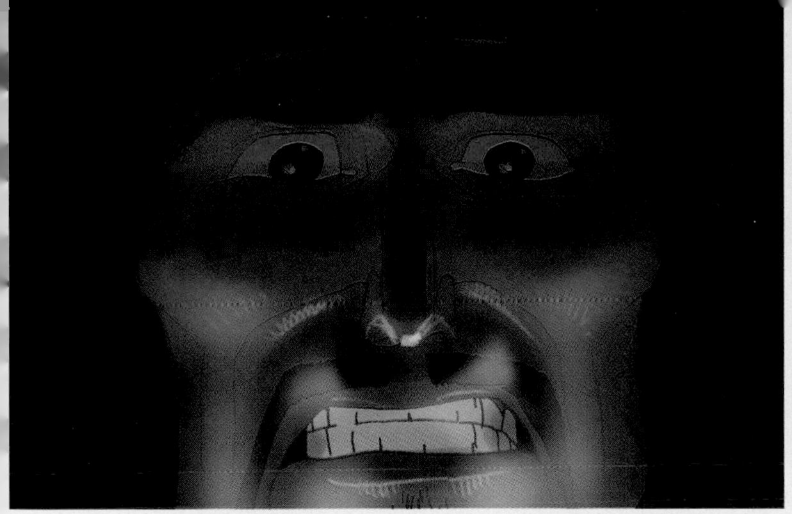

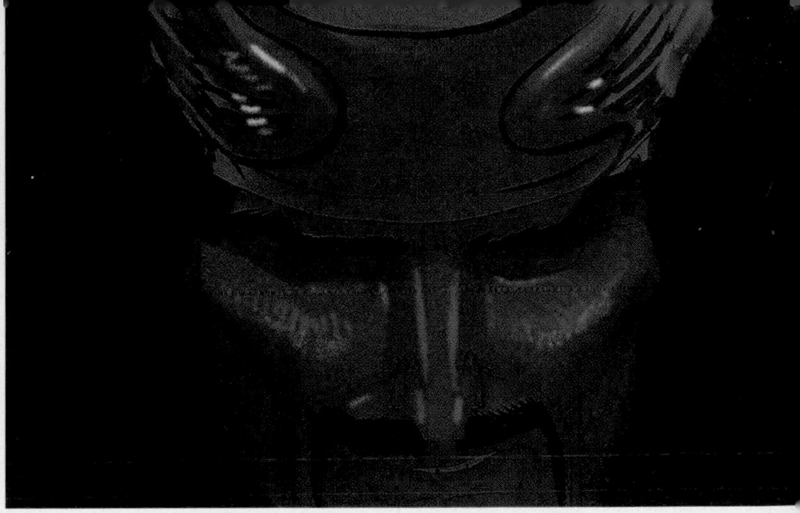

"So says the LORD, Behold, I shall raise up evil against you out of your house, and shall take your wives before your eyes and give them to your neighbor. And he shall lie with your wives in the sight of the sun. For you acted in secret, but I will do this thing before all Israel and before the sun."

"I have sinned against the LORD."

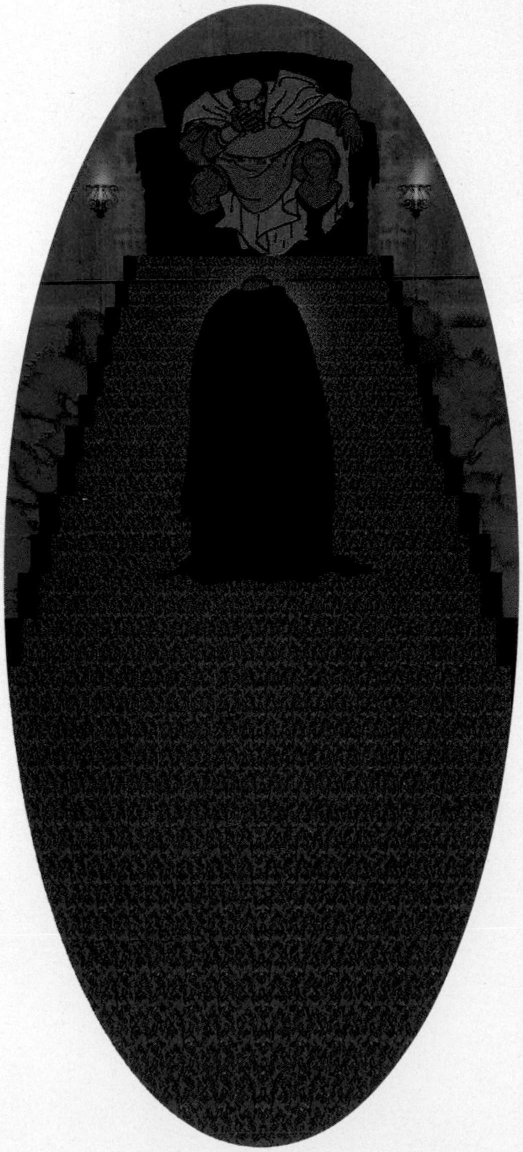

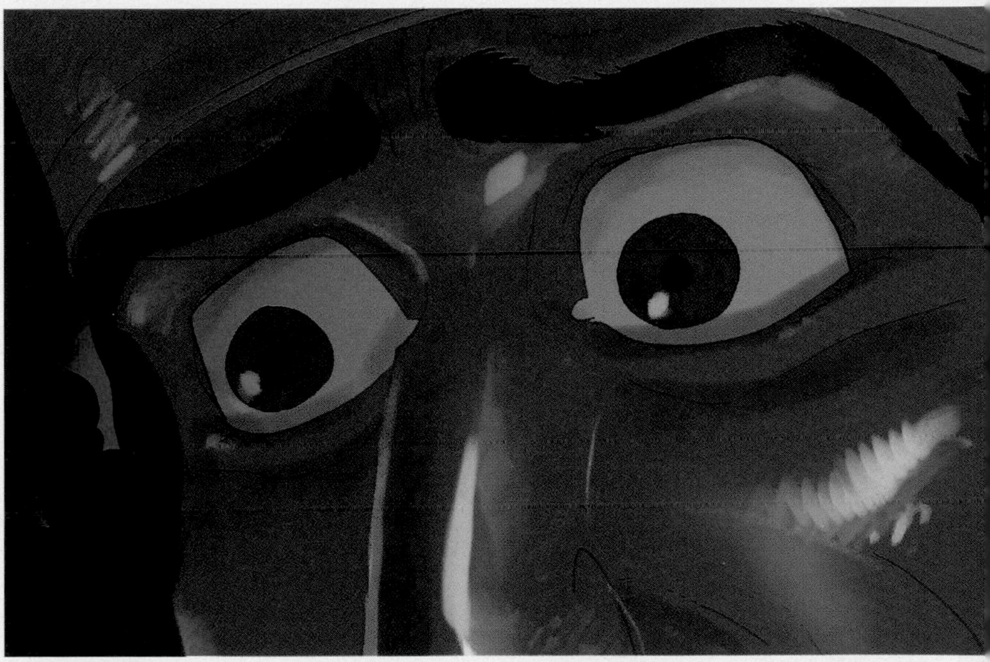

Nathan says, "The LORD also has put away your sin; you shall not die. Only, because you have made the enemies of God to scorn derisively by this thing, also the son born to you shall die.

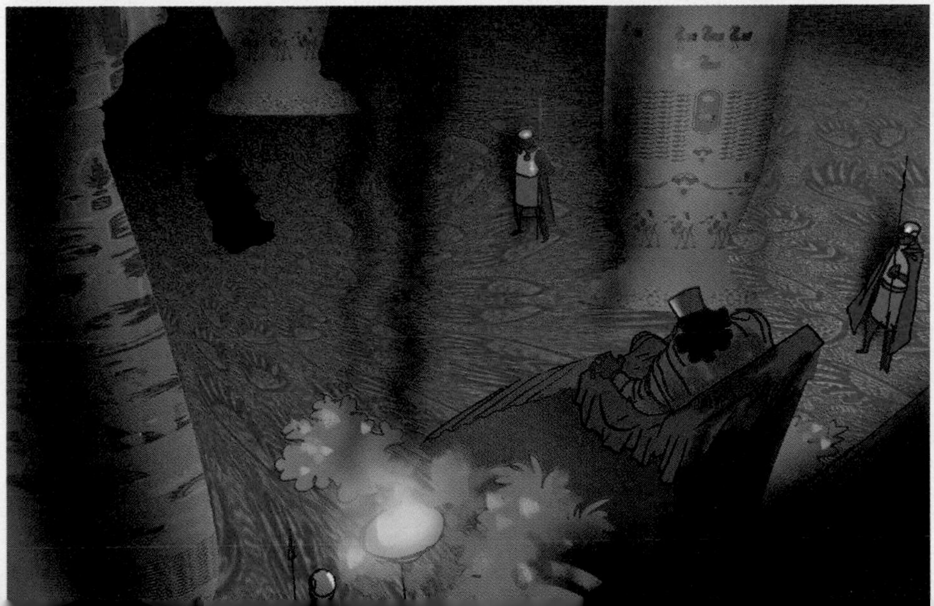

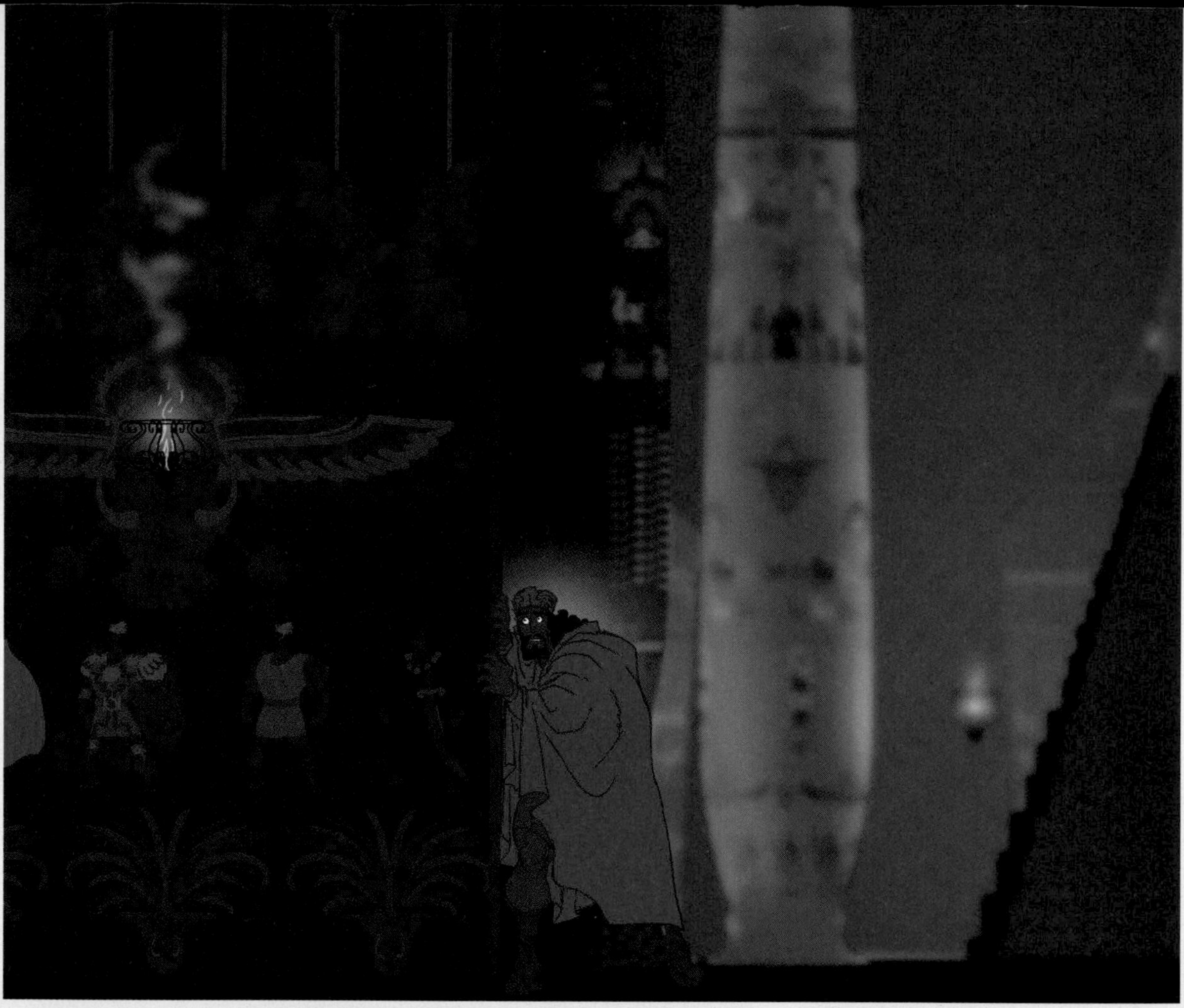
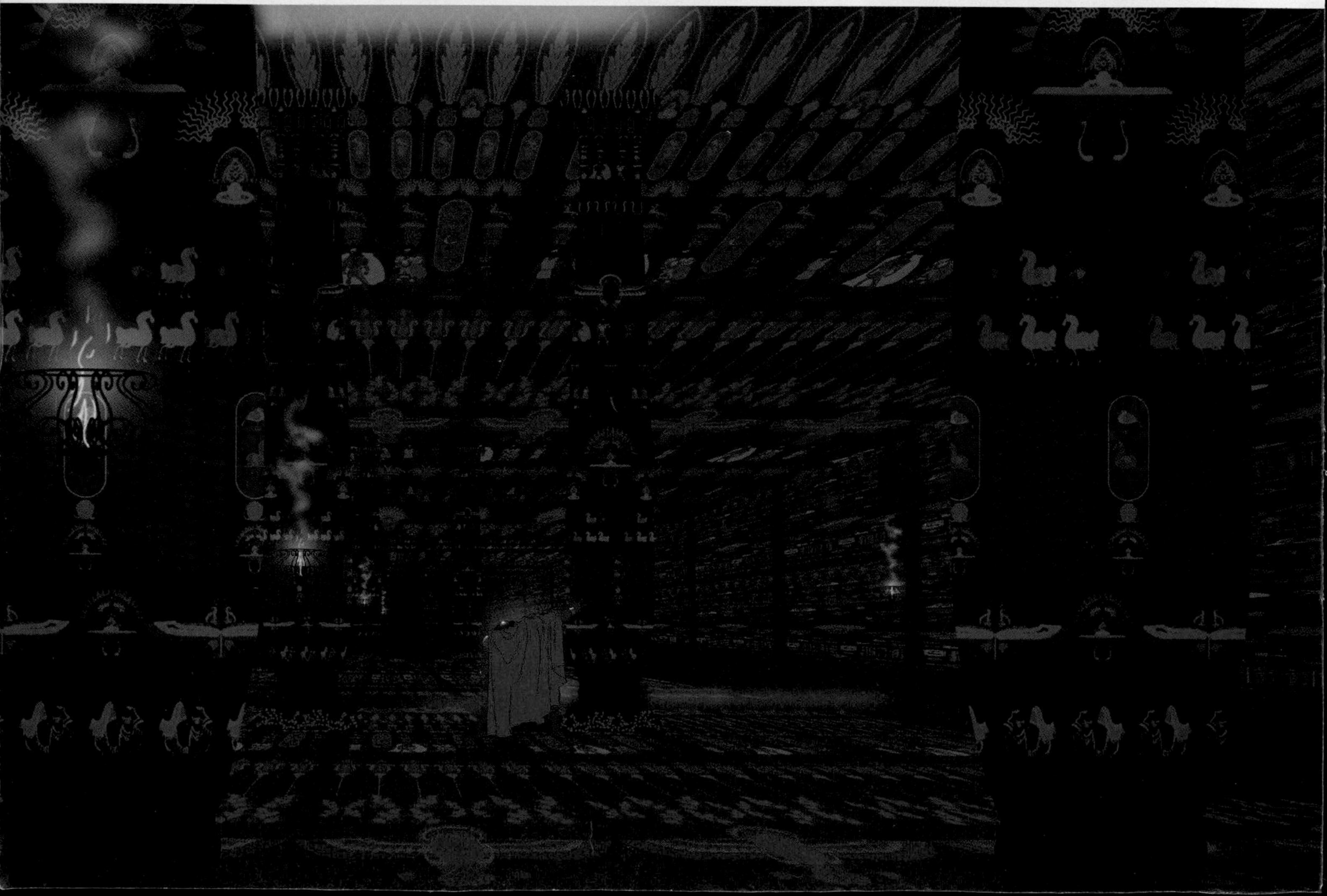

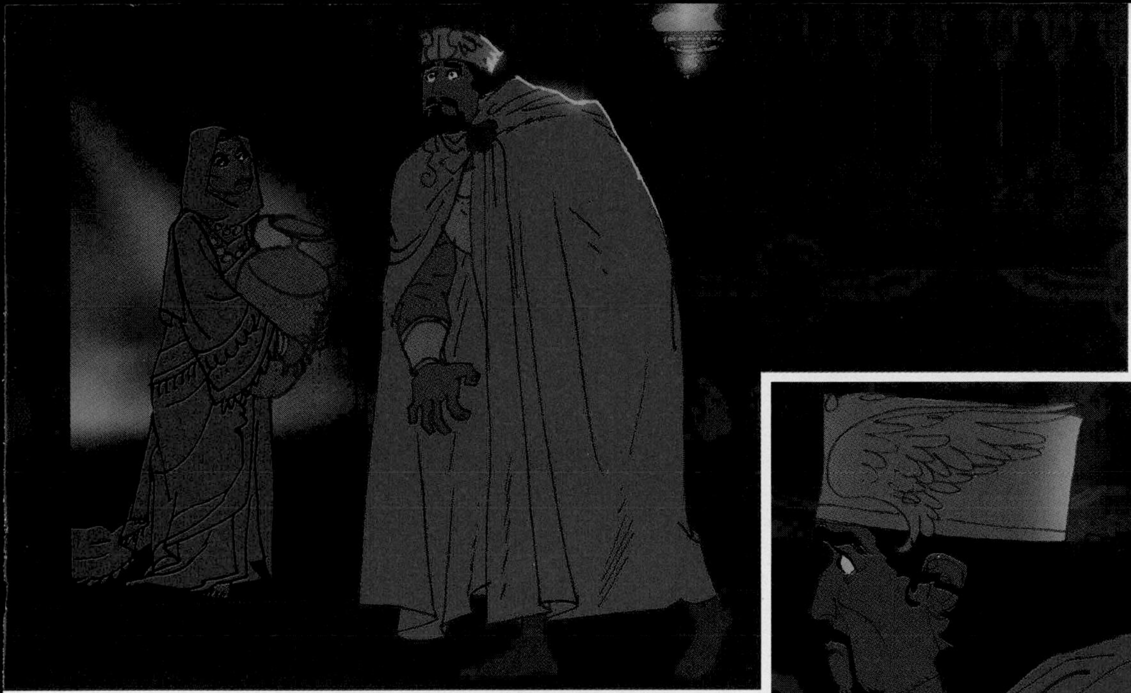

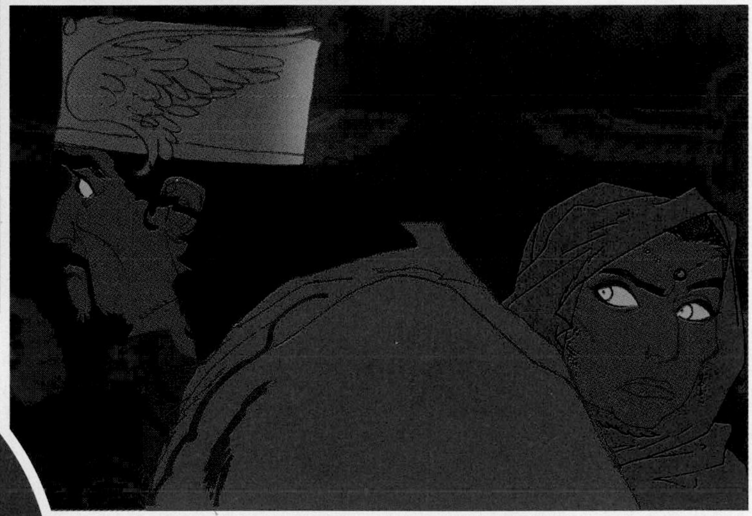

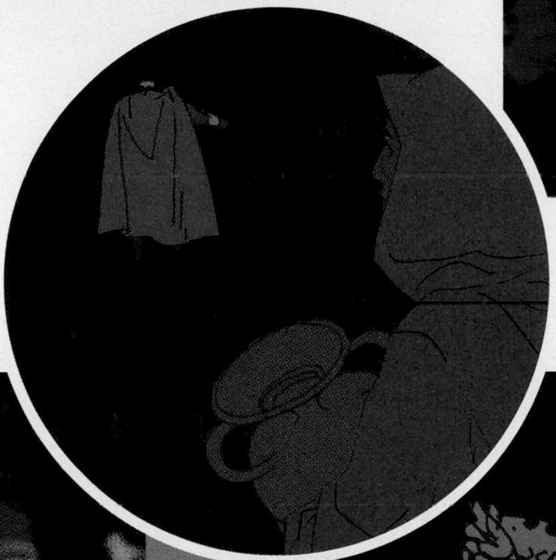

Michal wonders what's wrong.

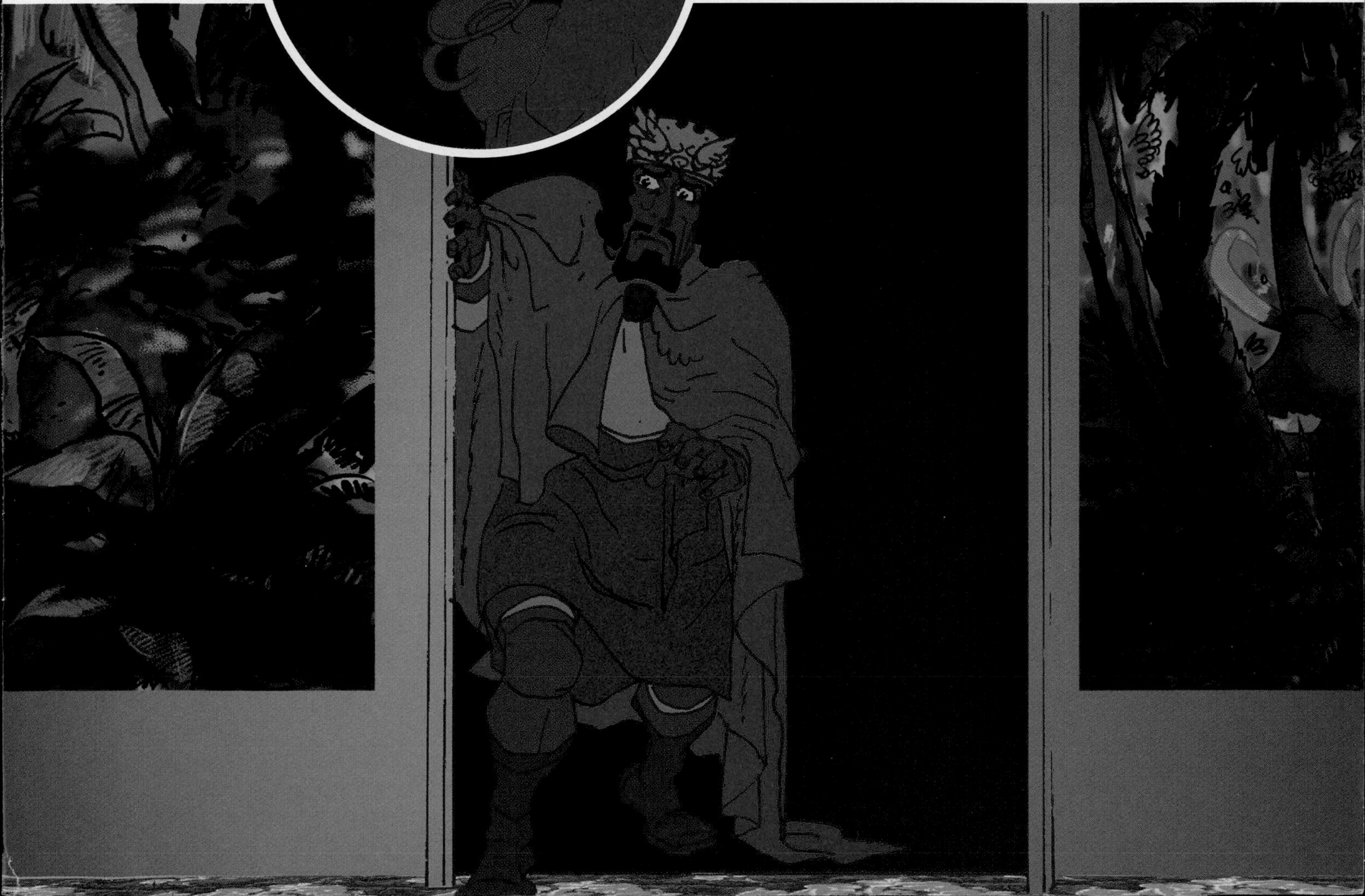

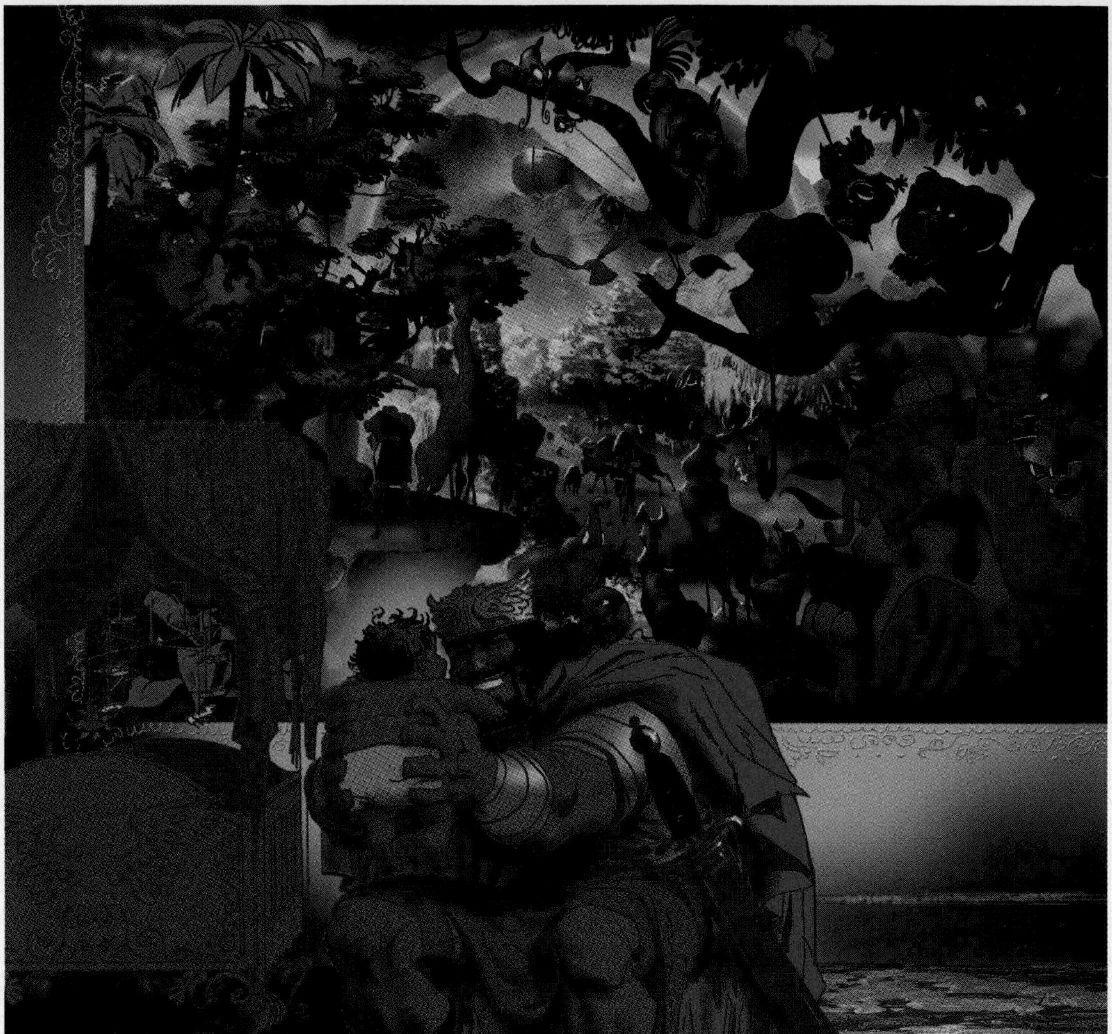

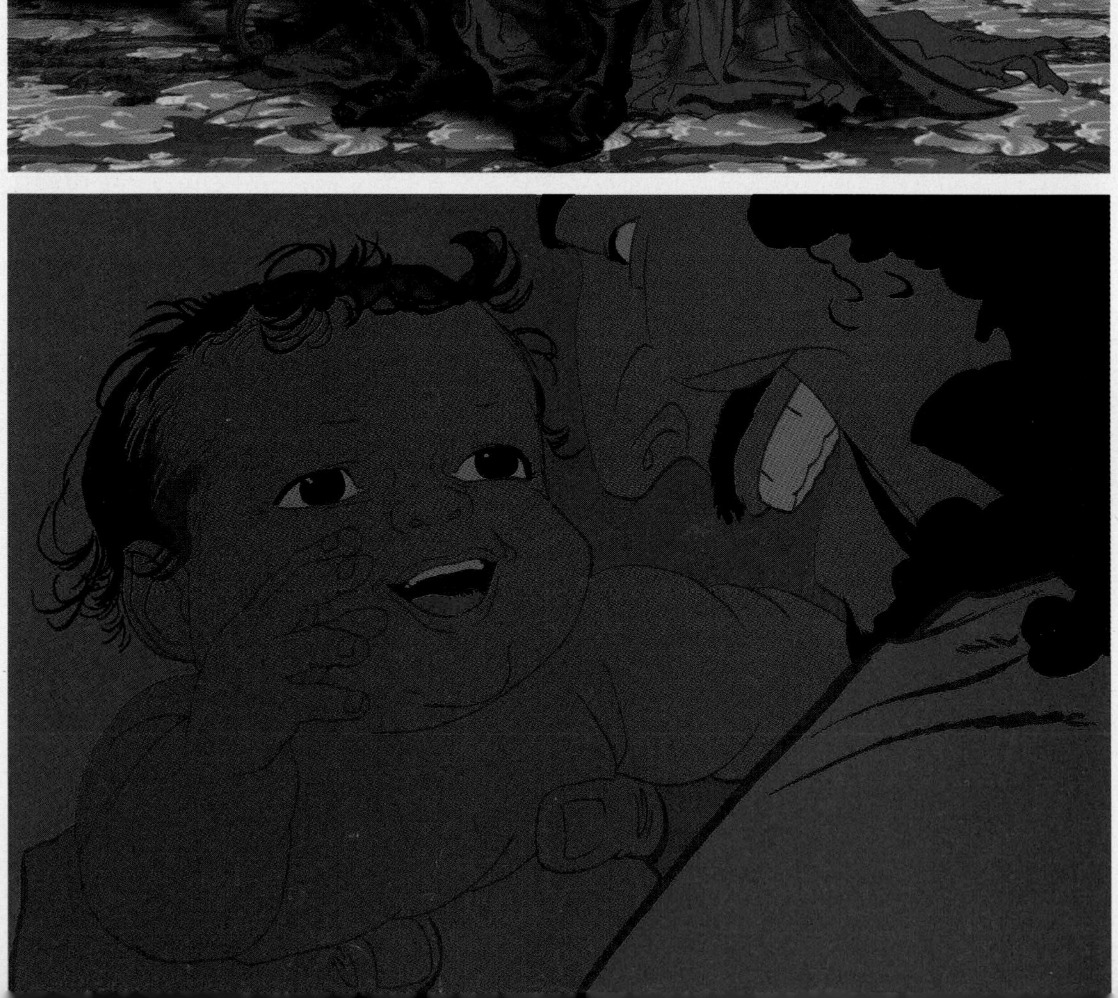

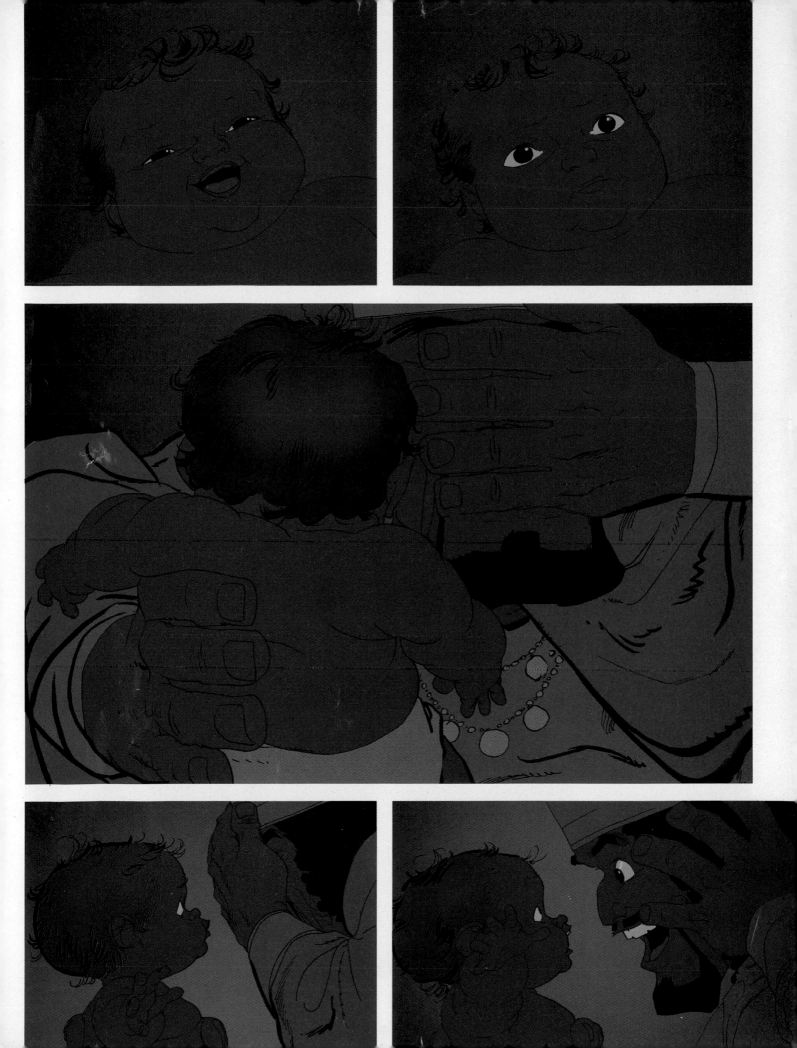

Bathsheba says, "Oh! I didn't expect to see you here."

David says nothing.

Bathsheba watches David play with their son.

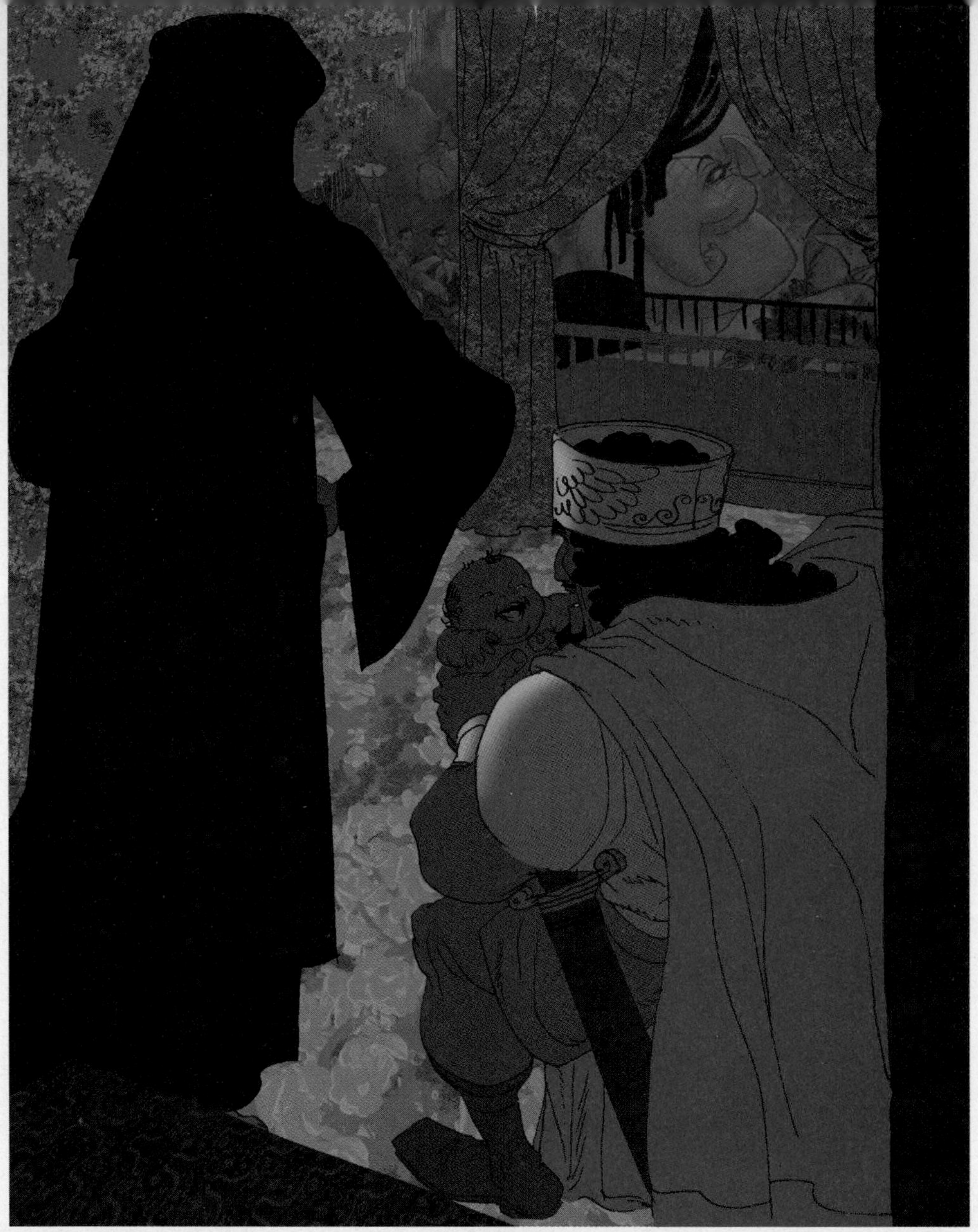

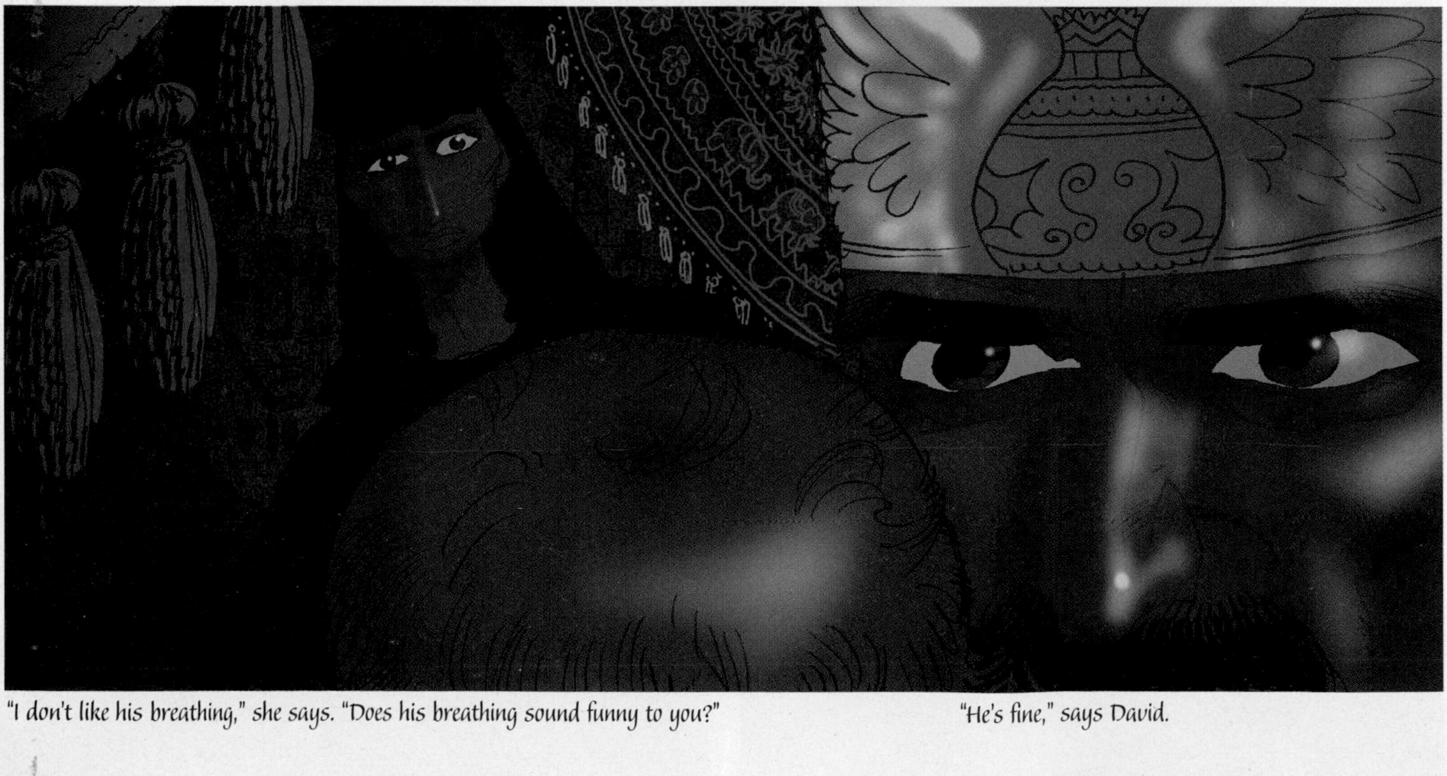

"I don't like his breathing," she says. "Does his breathing sound funny to you?"

"He's fine," says David.